~~ WEEK LOAN

SPSS 15 MADE SIMPLE

PAUL R. KINNEAR
COLIN D. GRAY

School of Psychology,
University of Aberdeen

Ψ **Psychology Press**
Taylor & Francis Group
HOVE AND NEW YORK

First published 2008 by Psychology Press
27 Church Road, Hove, East Sussex BN3 2FA

Simultaneously published in the USA and Canada
by Psychology Press 270 Madison Avenue, New York NY 10016

Psychology Press is an imprint of the Taylor & Francis Group, an Informa business

Reprinted 2008

Printed and bound in Great Britain by TJ International Ltd, Padstow, Cornwall, from pdf files
supplied by the authors. Cover design by Hybert Design.

This book is not sponsored or approved by SPSS, and any errors are in no way the responsibility
of SPSS. SPSS is a registered trademark and the other product names are trademarks of SPSS Inc.
SPSS Screen Images © SPSS Inc. SPSS UK Ltd, First Floor St Andrew's House, West Street,
Woking, Surrey, GU21 1EB, UK.

Windows is a registered trademark of Microsoft Corporation. For further information, contact:
Microsoft Corporation, One Microsoft Way, Redmond, WA 98052-6399, USA.

This publication has been produced with paper manufactured to strict environmental
standards and with pulp derived from sustainable forests.

British Library Cataloguing in Publication Data

A catalogue record for this book is available from the British Library.

Library of Congress Cataloging-in-Publication Data

Kinnear, Paul R.
  SPSS 15 made simple / Paul R. Kinnear, Colin D. Gray.
    p. cm.
  Includes bibliographical references and index.
  ISBN 978-1-84169-686-7
  1. SPSS (Computer file) 2. Social sciences--Statistical methods--Computer programs.
    I. Gray, Colin D. II. Title. III. Title: SPSS fifteen made simple

  HA32.K553 2007
  300.72'7--dc22

                        2007024118
  ISBN 978-1-84169-686-7

Contents

CHAPTER 2   Getting started with SPSS 15 *25*

CHAPTER 3   Editing and manipulating files *50*

CHAPTER 4   Exploring your data *102*

CHAPTER 5   Graphs and charts *141*

CHAPTER 6   Comparing averages and frequencies: Two-sample and one-sample tests *185*

CHAPTER 7   Introduction to ANOVA: the one-factor between subjects experiment *244*

CHAPTER 8   Between subjects factorial experiments *286*

CHAPTER 9   Within subjects experiments *315*

CHAPTER 10   Mixed factorial experiments *351*

CHAPTER 11   Measuring statistical association *381*

CHAPTER 12   Regression *428*

CHAPTER 13 Multiway frequency analysis *477*

CHAPTER 14 Discriminant analysis and logistic regression *502*

CHAPTER 15   Latent variables: exploratory factor analysis & canonical correlation *543*

Preface

SPSS 15 Made Simple, while retaining the essentially practical character of previous editions, incorporates some important changes. These changes partly reflect developments in the SPSS package itself. There have been further improvements in *Chart Builder*, which make the production and editing of a wide variety of excellent graphs and tables easier than ever before. In this edition, therefore, we have placed our major emphasis upon *Chart Builder*, rather than other graphics systems in SPSS, such as *Interactive*. The graphs available on the SPSS 14 *Graphs* menu are still available in SPSS 15 under *Legacy Dialogs*, but are much more easily produced with *Chart Builder*. We have also been responsive to the many suggestions and comments we received from readers of *SPSS 14 Made Simple*, and from our colleagues and students at Aberdeen University.

As with previous editions, we have assumed no previous knowledge of SPSS. Throughout the book, we have used annotated screen snapshots of SPSS output, windows and dialog boxes to illustrate the finer points of technique. In this edition, we have made extensive use of numbered call-outs to improve the clarity of the demonstrations and to make the correct sequence of moves clear. In response to many requests from our readers, we have expanded our chapter on regression to include partial and semi-partial correlation and the implementation of ANOVA as regression of the dependent variable upon dummy variables. We have shown how the one-way ANOVA can be accessed either on the *Compare Means* menu or the *General Linear Model* menu and the advantages of each approach. We have included a new section on reliability. There is a demonstration of the use of the odds ratio to explore the patterns in a multi-way contingency table. In the chapter on mixed ANOVA, we have included examples of more complex analyses.

As well as providing worked examples of the use of SPSS 15 to run different analyses, we have also tried to show how the results of the formal statistical tests should be presented in scientific papers and practical reports, in line with APA recommendations. Our readers continue to welcome the advice on choosing statistical tests in the first chapter.

As before, the Exercises that immediately follow most chapters contain only chapter-specific material. The six Revision Exercises at the end of the book, on the other hand, require the reader to analyse a data set without the cueing that a chapter context would provide and are intended to help the reader to develop a sense of strategy in data analysis.

Throughout the preparation of this book, we have been most fortunate in having the advice, encouragement and SPSS expertise of John Lemon, Senior Computing Adviser at Aberdeen University's Directorate of Information Technology. John kindly read the manuscript and, as always, we have found his comments invaluable. We are also very grateful to Caroline Green, Senior Teaching Fellow, for her very helpful observations on the Exercises and her reports on our students' progress with them in the practical classes. We very much appreciate the unfailing support that Martin Fraser, IT Support Officer, College of Life Sciences and Medicine, and our Chief Technician, Peter Bates, have always given us. Finally, we would like to express our gratitude to all those who, though too numerous to mention individually, have helped us in some way to produce this book.

Colin Gray and Paul Kinnear   June, 2007

CHAPTER 1

Introduction

1.1   MEASUREMENTS AND DATA

Since this book is about the analysis of data, we shall begin with a survey of the kinds of data that result from research and introduce some key terms.

1.1.1   Variables: quantitative and qualitative

A **variable** is a characteristic or property of a person, an object or a situation, comprising a set of different values or categories. Height is a variable, as are weight, blood type and gender. **Quantitative variables**, such as height, weight or age, are possessed in **degree** and so can sometimes be measured in units on an independent scale. In contrast, **qualitative** variables, such as sex, blood group or nationality, are possessed only in **kind**: they cannot be expressed in units on a scale. With qualitative variables, we can only make counts of the cases falling into the various categories, as when we might record that a theatre audience comprises 100 men and 300 women.

1.1.2   Levels of measurement: scale, ordinal and nominal data

A **data set** is a collection of numerical observations of variables. In this book, we shall use the term **measurement** to refer to the making of numerical records of any characteristic, whether quantitative or qualitative. The numbers in a data set can carry varying amounts of information about what is being recorded. Sometimes, as records of category membership,

1

they serve merely as labels; but often, as with heights or weights, they are units on an independent scale. It is useful to identify three **levels of measurement**:

1. At the highest level, **scale data** are measurements of quantity in units on an independent scale. Heights and weights are obvious examples. So also are performance scores, such as the number of times a participant hits a target, as well as IQs, responses to questionnaires and other psychometric data. In such a data set, each individual score or **datum** carries information independently of the other data.

2. At the next level, **ordinal** data are also records of quantitative variables; but these data take the form of ranks, or sequencing information. For example, if two judges rank 10 similar objects according to their perceived weight, assigning the rank 1 to the heaviest and 10 to the lightest, the data set will consist of 10 pairs of ranks, one pair for each object. If the judges cannot say which of several objects is the heaviest, and are allowed to assign the same rank to more than one object, the data set will contain **tied ranks**. Ranks are classified at a lower level of measurement than scale data, because there has been no independent measurement on a scale with units and, in that sense, a rank has no independent meaning.

3. At the lowest level, **nominal** data relate to qualitative variables or attributes, such as gender or blood group, and are merely records of category membership, rather than true measurements. Nominal data, that is, are merely **labels**: they are numbers, but these numbers do not express the degree to which any characteristic is possessed: they are arbitrary code numbers representing, say, different blood groups, genders or nationalities. Any other numbers (as long as they vary between categories) will serve the purpose just as well.

1.1.3   A grey area: ratings

Psychologists, market researchers and political pollsters frequently ask respondents to **rate** objects or people by assigning each to one of a set of ordered categories. There has been much debate about whether, from a statistical point of view, sets of ratings can be treated as scale data. Some argue that, unlike a rank, an individual rating carries information independently of the rest of the data. They do so on the grounds that raters are given reference or **anchor points** at the ends of the scale and are asked to express their judgements in relation to these. Others, however, would say that if 100 participants in a research project are asked to rate, say, 30 objects by placing each object in one of seven ordered categories, where 1 is very good and 7 is very bad, the operation will result in 100 sets of **ranks with ties**: that is, ratings are merely ordinal data and should be treated as such in the statistical analysis. In our view, the decision about which statistics to use should follow consideration of several factors, including the distribution of the data and the number of points on the rating scale.

Sometimes the term **categorical data** is used to include both purely nominal assignments and assignments to ordered categories. This term straddles our distinction between nominal and ordinal data and obscures the difference between ranks and ratings.

1.2   EXPERIMENTAL VERSUS CORRELATIONAL RESEARCH

In this section, we shall consider a distinction which has important implications for the sorts of statistics the researcher will choose to describe and summarise a data set and to confirm the findings with statistical inference.

1.2.1   True experiments

An **experiment** is the collection of comparative data under controlled conditions. In a true experiment, one variable, known as the **independent variable (IV)** is manipulated by the investigator in order to demonstrate that it has a causal effect upon another variable, which is known as the **dependent variable (DV)**. For example, a hypothesis that a drug affects performance could be tested by comparing the performance of a sample of people who have taken the drug with that of a comparison, or **control**, group who have not. (It is usual to improve the comparability of the two groups by presenting the controls with a **placebo**, that is, a neutral medium ideally identical with that in which the drug was presented in the **experimental** condition.) Here the IV is presence/absence of the drug and the DV is performance.

The IV is controlled by the investigator, and its values are determined before the experiment is carried out. This is achieved either by **random assignment** of the participants to the pre-set conditions or by testing each participant under all conditions, if that is feasible. The DV, on the other hand, is measured during the course of the investigation.

In the planning of an experiment, the researcher applies the **rule of one variable**: that is, the conditions under which participants in the different groups are tested must differ only with respect to the independent variable. In a poorly designed experiment, variables other than the independent variable may have a causal effect upon the dependent variable. In a well designed experiment, such **extraneous variables** are neutralised, or subject to **experimental control**. The rule of one variable is one of the most important principles in experimental design. Random assignment to conditions is intended to ensure that any individual differences in ability between the experimental and control groups tend to average out, so that the two groups are comparable in this regard. There are other methods of controlling extraneous variables, such as testing the same participants under all conditions, thus controlling for individual differences. In fact, good experiments are often run with only a single participant. The strategy the researcher should adopt depends on many factors, including the nature of the research question, the local situation and the resources available.

1.2.2   Correlational research

In an experiment, the IV, unlike gender, blood group, or nationality, is not an intrinsic property of the participants: the participants are assigned at random to the experimental and control groups. Such random assignment to different conditions confers upon the experiment a great advantage: should a difference be found between the groups in their performance, the researcher may draw the inference that the active experimental treatment has had a causal effect upon the dependent variable.

Suppose, however, that, with a view to understanding the extent to which a person's earning power depends upon level of education, a research gathers data on both variables. The researcher hopes to find that those with more education tend to have higher final salaries, that is, that salary is positively **correlated** with education. Such research is therefore known as **correlational research**.

In this second research scenario, as in the first, the research was motivated by the hypothesis that one variable has a causal effect upon another: in the drug example, the ingestion of Drug X improves memory; in the second, education improves earning power. There is an important difference between the two situations, however: in the second scenario, neither variable was manipulated by the experimenter: both salary and education are measured as they occur in the participants.

When interpreting the results of correlational research, we should bear in mind the dictum that **correlation does not imply causation**. The researcher may believe that income is, to at least some extent, causally determined by education. Other variables, however, such as IQ, socio-economic status and parental attitude to education, may be the true determinants of final salary. There are situations, in fact, where the direction of causality itself may itself be in doubt: violent people may watch violent television and films; but has viewing screen violence over the years made the viewers violent or are such programmes merely the preferred entertainment of those with violent disposition?

1.2.3   Quasi-experiments

Does smoking shorten one's life? Researchers have conducted many studies comparing the longevity of smokers and non-smokers. In such research, those in the smoking and non-smoking groups are matched with respect to as many possible confounding variables as possible, such as socio-economic status, education, lifestyle and so on. In this way, it is hoped to achieve a comparison between two groups of people who differ only in their smoking category. A difference in longevity between smokers and non-smokers is taken as evidence for the hypothesis that smoking shortens life.

In a quasi-experiment, as in a true experiment, the researcher attempts to control extraneous variables, so that the groups compared differ only with respect to the supposed causal variable. As in correlational research, however, the variables are properties of the participants: there is no random assignment to the smoking and non-smoking conditions. However careful the researchers have been to control the influence of extraneous variables, therefore, there remains the possibility that the groups may yet differ on some other crucial characteristic, such as personality or physical type. Arguably, the quasi-experiment is essentially a refinement of the correlational approach, where **statistical control** is used as an imperfect substitute for true **experimental control**.

1.3   SOME STATISTICAL TERMS AND CONCEPTS

This book, though not a statistics text, is concerned, nevertheless, with the analysis of data. While we must assume that the reader is already familiar with statistics to at least some extent, a review of some key terms and concepts may not go amiss at this point. At the end of the chapter, we make some recommendations for further reading.

1.3.1   Samples and populations

In many disciplines, the units of study (people, plants, coelacanths) vary with respect to what is being studied. When the units of study vary, it is dangerous to generalise about *all* people, *all* animals, *all* trees, *all* coelacanths) on the basis of knowledge about only *some* of them. This is why researchers in such disciplines must make use of the methods of statistics.

A **sample** is a selection of observations (often assumed to be random) from a reference set, or **population**, of possible observations that might be made. By analogy with a lottery, it may be helpful to think of a population as the numbers being churned around in the barrel at a lottery, and the sample as those numbers actually drawn. Selections of numbers picked at random from the same barrel show considerable variation: sampling implies **sampling variability**. It follows that a random sample is not necessarily **representative**: it may have very different characteristics (e.g. mean and standard deviation) from those of the population from which it has been drawn.

When we measure the reaction speeds of 100 participants, we invariably do so because we want to make inferences about the reaction speeds of people in general: it is the **population** that is of primary interest, not the **sample**: the 100 reaction speeds we have obtained are merely a sample from the population of reaction speeds. But to make an inductive inference about *all* people on the basis of data from just *some* people is to risk error. (In statistics, the term **error** denotes the extent to which the properties of a sample deviate from the corresponding values in the population.)

1.3.2   Parameters and statistics

Measures of the characteristics of a sample (such as its mean and standard deviation) are known as **statistics**. The corresponding characteristics in the population are known as **parameters**. Our research question is invariably about parameters, not statistics. **Statistical inference** is a set of methods for making inductive (and hence error-prone) inferences about parameters from the values of statistics.

Conventionally, sample and population characteristics are denoted by the use of Greek and Arabic letters, respectively (Table 1).

Table 1 Notation for parameters and statistics

Greek and Roman letters are used to denote the characteristics of **populations** and **samples** (i.e. parameters and statistics), respectively.

The mean and standard deviation of a **population** are denoted by the symbols μ and σ, respectively.

The mean and standard deviation of a **sample** are denoted by the symbols M and s, respectively.

1.3.3   Description or confirmation?

We turn to the discipline of statistics when:
1. We want to **describe and summarise** the data as a whole.
2. We want to **confirm** that other researchers repeating our study would obtain a similar result.

It is in connection with the second requirement that the need for formal **statistical tests** arises. The researcher may find a theoretically important pattern in a set of data; but is this merely the result of sampling variability or is it an important discovery, which would emerge again if the project were to be repeated?

1.3.4   Statistical inference

We shall consider two kinds of statistical inference:
1. **Estimation of parameters**.
2. **Hypothesis testing**, which we shall consider later.

Since statistical inference, being inductive, is subject to error, all inferences must be qualified by statements of probability or confidence. These two terms are not synonymous. A **probability** arises in the context of an experiment of chance and is a measure of likelihood ranging from 0 (for an impossible outcome) to 1 (a certainty). A **confidence** is a retrospective measure of how sure one ought to be that a parameter lies within a certain range, given that the statistics of a sample have certain values (see below).

Point estimation and interval estimation

The sample mean is said to be a **point estimate** of the population mean: e.g. M is an estimate of μ; and s is an estimate of σ. Our sample mean, however, may be wide of the mark as an estimate of the population mean. From the statistics of a sample, however, it is also possible to specify a range of values, known as a **confidence interval**, within which one can say, with a specified level of certainty, or 'confidence', that the true population mean lies. A confidence interval is an **interval estimate** of the value of a parameter.

Formal statistical tests: hypothesis testing

Data are not gathered just for the sake of it. Research is driven by the desire to test a provisional supposition about nature known as a **hypothesis**. Often, a scientific hypothesis states that there is a causal relationship between two variables: it is an assertion that one variable influences or helps to determine another.

Does a supposedly memory-preserving drug X improve the working memory capacities of those suffering from the early stages of dementia? Two comparable groups of 20 patients are selected: one group is treated with X; the other is a comparison group, which receives a neutral saline solution (a **placebo**) from which the drug is absent. After receiving either a solution containing X or a placebo, the patients attempt a test of memory consisting of 20 questions, so that each patient receives a score in the range from 0 to 20. Suppose that the means and standard deviations of the scores for the X and placebo groups are 12.3 (SD = 2.8) and 9.7 (SD = 3.1), respectively.

The scientific hypothesis is that the presence of X results in better memory performance than when X is absent. While these results appear to support the scientific hypothesis, it is necessary to make formal statistical tests to confirm that the findings are unlikely to have resulted from sampling variability.

Statistical hypotheses

A statistical hypothesis is a statement about a population or populations. The scores of the 20 participants in the Placebo condition are a sample from the population of such scores; likewise the 20 scores of the group who received X are also a sample from a population of scores.

In statistics, the **null hypothesis (H_0)** is the hypothesis of 'no effect': it is the negation of the scientific hypothesis. According to the null hypothesis, the mean performance levels of patients of this kind under drug and placebo conditions are the same. We can write this as follows:

$$H_0: \mu_1 = \mu_2$$

where μ_1 and μ_2 are the means of the populations of scores under the placebo and drug conditions, respectively. Because of sampling variability, of course, the two sample means are very unlikely to have exactly the same value.

In traditional significance testing, there was a preparedness to reject the null hypothesis, but a reluctance to accept it. This is because it was recognised that, because H_0 is unlikely to be exactly true, a test of H_0 would inevitably show significance, provided the sample was large enough (see Chapter 6, Section 6.3.1).

See Section 6.3.1

Critics of significance testing, however, pointed out that its advocates, in focusing exclusively upon the null hypothesis, failed to acknowledge that in order to specify a critical region of values that will lead to rejection of the null hypothesis, attention must be paid to the **alternative hypothesis (H_1)**, that is, the statistical equivalent of the scientific hypothesis. Otherwise, there is no basis for claiming that the critical region should lie in the tails of the distribution of the test statistic, as opposed to a narrower band of more frequently occurring values anywhere else within the range of possible values.

In the system of Neyman and Pearson, the problem of hypothesis testing was re-conceived in terms of a choice or decision between the **null hypothesis (H_0)** and the **alternative hypothesis (H_1)**, against which H_0 is tested. In their view, the null hypothesis could be accepted as well as rejected.

Returning to the drug experiment, the alternative hypothesis (H_1) states that the means of the Placebo and Drug populations are not equal. The alternative hypothesis may be written as follows:

$$H_1: \mu_1 \neq \mu_2$$

The two statistical hypotheses, H_0 and H_1, are complementary, that is, they exhaust the possibilities: in this case, for instance, either the population means are equal or they are not.

Testing the hypotheses

As statements about hypothetical populations, statistical hypotheses must be tested by using the values of sample characteristics, that is, statistics. Special statistics, known as **test statistics**, such as t, F and χ^2, are used to test statistical hypotheses. A test statistic must have a known **sampling distribution**, so that we can determine the probability of obtaining values within a specified range.

In hypothesis testing, it is not the scientific hypothesis that is tested directly, but the null hypothesis. A small, fixed probability known as a **significance level** is decided upon before the data are gathered. Conventionally, the significance level is set at .05 or (less commonly) .01.

Percentiles

The **xth percentile** is the value in a distribution below which x% of values lie. So the 50th percentile is the median, because the latter is the value below (or above) which 50% of values lie. The 97.5th percentile (Figure 1) is the value below which 97.5% of values lie; but it is also the value above which 2.5% of values lie. The 2.5th percentile is the value below which 2.5% of values lie, so 2.5 + 2.5 = 5% of values lie in the tails of a distribution, below the 2.5th percentile and above the 97.5th percentile.

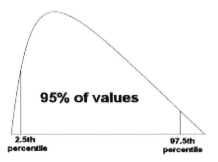

Figure 1. Distribution showing 5% of values lie in the tails of a distribution, above the 97.5th percentile and below the 2.5th percentile.

The critical region

Once the significance level has been decided upon, a **critical region** is chosen, that is, a range of atypical values for the test statistic under the null hypothesis such that the probability of a value in the range is equal to the significance level. The critical region is taken to lie in one or both **tails** of the distribution, where values of the test statistic would be least commonly found if the null hypothesis is true. If the significance level has been set at .05, and the alternative hypothesis is that the means are not equal, the critical region is divided equally between the two tails of the distribution of the test statistic: in the upper tail, the critical region will lie above the 97.5th percentile; in the lower tail, it will lie below the 2.5th percentile.

Statistical 'significance': the p-value

If the value of the test statistic falls within the critical (tail) region, the result is said to be **significant**, the null hypothesis is rejected and the alternative (scientific) hypothesis is supported.

The **p-value** of a test statistic is the probability, under the null hypothesis, of obtaining a value at least as extreme (as far out in the tails of the distribution) as the one obtained. A statistical test is said to show **significance** if the p-value is less than the significance level, which means that the value of the test statistic has fallen within the critical region.

Directional hypotheses: one-tailed and two-tailed tests

Suppose that two supposedly equivalent forms of a test, A and B, have been prepared and that 50 people take each form. A large difference between the mean scores in either direction (A > B or B > A) is evidence against the null hypothesis that in the population there is no difference between the means for A and B. If the significance level is set at .05, the critical region is therefore divided equally between the two tails of the sampling distribution of the test statistic, that is, the top .025 and bottom .025 of the distribution of the test statistic. When the critical region is distributed symmetrically in this way, we are said to be making a **two-tailed test.**

Often, however, the experimental hypothesis specifies the direction of the difference: Group A might be expected to perform better than Group B. The negation of this **directional** hypothesis is the null hypothesis that, in the population, the mean score under condition A is **not** better than the mean score under condition B, including the possibility that it may be worse. Some argue that, since only a large difference **in favour of Group A** will count as evidence against the null hypothesis, the entire region of rejection can be located in the upper tail of the distribution: that is, we can reject the null hypothesis if the value of the test statistic falls in the top .05 of the distribution, rather than the top .025. If we follow this approach, we are said to be making a **one-tailed test**. Clearly, if you obtain a difference in the expected direction, you are twice as likely to reject the null hypothesis on a one-tailed test as you are on a two-tailed test.

The difficulty with being prepared to reject the null hypothesis when you obtain a less extreme result in the expected direction is that, were the direction of the obtained difference to be opposite to that predicted, however large that difference might be, you would still have to accept the null hypothesis, which now states merely that the mean for condition A is not greater than the mean for condition B. Suppose that the value of t is below the 2.5^{th} percentile and that you decide to reject the null hypothesis. That practice would enlarge the critical region to 5% + 2.5% = 7.5% of the distribution, which is arguably too high. For this reason, some are opposed to the use of one-tailed tests. By default, SPSS gives the results of two-tailed tests of significance in the output.

Journal editors vary in their views on one-tailed and two-tailed tests. Their decision in a particular case is likely to depend partly upon non-statistical considerations, such as the cogency of the scientific hypothesis. For instance, one would hardly expect brain damage to result in an improvement in performance on cognitive tests. It makes a difference whether a specified directional difference is predicted from a coherent theory, rather than having emerged as a result of *ex post facto* data-snooping.

When reporting the results of the test, the researcher must provide:
1. Full information about the statistics.
2. p-values.
3. Whether the p-values are 2-tailed or 1-tailed.

Errors in hypothesis testing

All statistical inference, being inductive, is subject to error. Suppose that the calculated value of a test statistic falls within the critical region and the null hypothesis is rejected. Such a value however, though unlikely under H_0, is still possible. If H_0 is actually true, we shall have made an error in rejecting it. This is known as a **Type I error**.

Suppose that the value of our test statistic falls outside the critical region, so that H_0 is accepted. This is the correct decision if H_0 is really true; however, it may not be true. Suppose that H_1, a directional hypothesis, is true and states that the population mean has a value above the value stated by H_0. The test statistic has a distribution of values under H_1, and the two distributions are likely to overlap, perhaps to a considerable extent. Should the value of the test statistical fall below the 95th percentile of the distribution under H_0, the researcher will decide, wrongly, to accept H_0; whereas, actually, H_1 is true. The decision to accept H_0 when H_1 is true is known as a **Type II error**.

In summary,
1. We may reject the null hypothesis when it is true, thus making a **Type I error**.
2. We may accept the null hypothesis when it is false, thus making a **Type II error**.

The **probability of a Type I error** is denoted by the Greek symbol **alpha** α, which is the significance level (.05 or .01). The **probability of a Type II error** is denoted by the Greek symbol **beta** β. The **Power (P)** of a statistical test is the probability that the null hypothesis, if false, will be rejected. Since one must either accept or reject the null hypothesis and the two events are complementary (i.e. they exhaust the possibilities), the power of a statistical test is $1 - (\text{Type II error rate})$ i.e. $P = 1 - \beta$. The decisions made in hypothesis testing are set out in Table 2.

		Experimenter's Decision	
Table 2. Correct decisions and errors in hypothesis testing: Type I and Type II errors and power (P)			
		Accept H_0	**Accept H_1**
State of Nature	**H_0 is true**	Correct decision	**Type I error** Probability $= \alpha$
	H_1 is true	**Type II error** Probability $= \beta$	Correct decision Power $P = 1 - \beta$

Figure 2 shows the relationships among the Type I and Type II error rates and power for a one-tailed test of the null hypothesis (H_0) that the mean of a population has a specified value (μ_0)

against the alternative hypothesis (H_1) that the population mean is μ_1. The test statistic is the sample mean and the curves are the sampling distributions of the mean under H_0 and H_1. Since the test is one-tailed, the entire critical region is located in the upper tail of the sampling distribution of the mean. With a two-tailed test, values in the critical region would have a probability of α /2 under H_0.

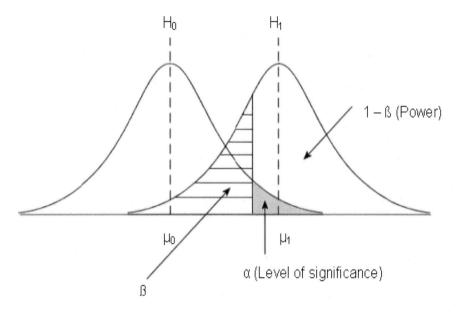

Figure 2. Relations among Type I and Type II error rates and power

1.3.5   Effect size

An important consideration when you plan to test the significance of, say, a difference between two means for significance is the size of the effect. For the simple two-group between subjects experiment, Cohen (1988) has suggested as a measure of effect size the statistic d, where

$$d = \frac{\mu_1 - \mu_2}{\sigma}$$

Cohen's measure expresses the difference between the two population means as so-many standard deviations. In practice, the parameters μ_1, μ_2 and σ would be estimated from the means of the two samples and an estimate of the supposedly homogeneous population standard deviation. Suppose, for example, that in a drug experiment, the group who had ingested the drug had a mean score of 12, whereas the controls had a mean score of 10. The average standard deviation of the scores in the two groups was 2. According to Cohen's measure, the strength of the effect is (12–10)/2 = 1.

On the basis of a study of a considerable body of published literature, Cohen (1988) has suggested a categorisation of effect size as shown in Table 3:

Table 3. Cohen's categories of effect size	
Effect size (d)	**Size of Effect**
$0.2 \leq d < 0.5$	Small
$0.5 < d < 0.8$	Medium
$d \geq 0.8$	Large

The drug experiment, therefore, found that the drug had a 'large' effect upon performance.

Cohen's measure d is much used in **meta-analysis**, that is, the combination of statistics from several independent studies with a view to integrating all the evidence into a coherent body of empirical knowledge.

Many journal editors now insist that reports of the results of statistical tests should include measures of effect size as well as the statistics, the p-value and the confidence interval.

1.4   CHOOSING A STATISTICAL TEST: SOME GUIDELINES

It is common for authors of statistical texts to offer advice on choosing statistical tests in the form of a flow chart, decision tree or similar diagram. The numerous schemes that have been proposed vary considerably, and sometimes seem to contradict one another. Almost any system of classification tends to break down when the user encounters cases that straddle category boundaries. In this area, moreover, the correct choice of statistical technique for certain types of data has been hotly disputed.

On one matter at least, there is general agreement: there is no such thing as a decision tree that will automatically lead the investigator to the correct choice of a statistical test in all circumstances.   Some of the later chapters contain illustrations of the penalties that an automated, scheme-reliant approach can incur. At best, a decision tree can serve only as a rough guideline.   Ultimately, a safe decision requires careful reflection upon one's own research aims and a thorough preliminary exploration of the data. GET TO KNOW YOUR DATA BEFORE YOU PROCEED TO MAKE ANY FORMAL STATISTICAL TESTS.

1.4.1   Considerations in choosing a statistical test

The choice of a statistical test depends upon several considerations, including:
1.   Your **research question**.
2.   The **plan**, or **design**, of your research.
3.   The **nature of the data** that you wish to analyse.

This list is by no means comprehensive; nor do we intend to imply that any fixed ordering of these three considerations is appropriate in all situations or that they are independent issues.

In general, an important consideration in deciding upon a statistical analysis is whether the research is experimental or correlational. The experimenter is usually interested in **making comparisons** between the average performance level of participants tested under different conditions.   Statistical methods such as t-tests and analysis of variance (ANOVA) were designed for the purpose of making comparisons. The correlational researcher typically seeks **statistical associations** among the variables in the study, with a view to imputing causality to theoretically important variables. Correlation and regression are suitable techniques for that purpose.

Five common research situations

We shall identify five basic research situations in which formal statistical tests can be applied (Figure 3). In this book, the techniques appropriate for various situations will be discussed more fully in the sections indicated in the figure.

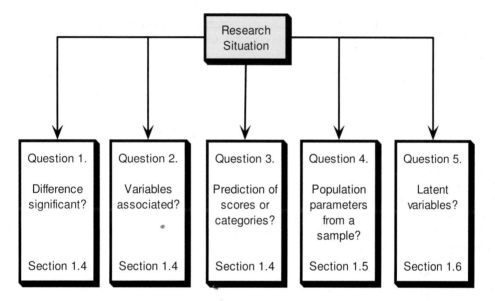

Figure 3. Five types of research situation

The questions are as follows:

1. Is a difference (between averages) significant? For example, is resting heart rate the same before and after a fitness course? (Sections 1.4.2 to 1.4.4)

2. How strongly are variables associated? For example, do tall parents tend to have tall children? (Sections 1.4.5 to 1.4.8)

3. Can scores on a target variable (or category membership, if the variable is qualitative) be predicted from data on other variables? For example, can university performance be predicted by scores on aptitude tests? (Section 1.4.9 to 1.4.13)

4. From a single sample of data, what can be said about the population? For example, if we know the vocabulary test scores of 100 children, what can we infer about the scores of the entire population of children in the same age group? (Section 1.5)

5. The user has a multivariate data set, perhaps people's scores on a battery of ability tests. Can these scores be accounted for (or classified) in terms

of a smaller number of hypothetical latent variables or **factors**? For example, can performance in a variety of intellectual pursuits be accounted for in terms of general intelligence? (Section 1.6)

1.4.2   Testing a difference between means for significance

The question of whether two or more means are significantly different is one that arises naturally in the context of experimental or quasi-experimental research, where the performance of the participants under different conditions is being compared.

Suppose that in a drug experiment, performance under two different conditions (experimental and control) has been measured and that the means have somewhat different values. This may seem to support the experimenter's hypothesis; but would a similar difference be found if the experiment were to be repeated? Could the obtained difference merely be the result of sampling variability? Here the researcher wishes to test the **statistical significance** of the difference, that is, to establish that the difference is too large to have been merely a chance occurrence.

1.4.3   The design of the experiment: independent versus related samples

Of crucial importance in the choice of an appropriate statistical test for comparing levels of performance is the question of whether the experiment would have resulted in **independent** or **related samples** of scores.

Independent samples

Suppose we select, say, 100 participants for an experiment and randomly assign half of them to an experimental condition and the rest to a control condition. With this procedure, the assignment of one person to a particular group has no effect upon the group to which another is assigned. The two **independent samples** of participants thus selected will produce two independent samples of scores, each consisting of 50 values. A useful criterion for deciding whether you have independent samples of data is that there must be **no basis for pairing the scores in one sample with those in the other**. An experiment in which independent samples of participants are tested under different conditions is known as a **between subjects experiment**.

Related samples

Suppose that each of fifty participants shoots ten times at a triangular target and ten times at a square target of the same area. For each target, each participant will have a score ranging from 0 (ten misses) to 10 (ten hits). As in the previous example, there will be two samples of 50 scores. This time, however, each score in either sample can be paired with the same participant's score with the other target. We have here two **related samples** of scores, or a set of **paired data**. The scores in two related samples are likely to be substantially correlated, because the better shots will tend to have higher scores with either target than will the poorer shots. An experiment like this, in which each participant is tested under both (or all) conditions, is known as a **within subjects experiment**. Within subjects experiments are also said to have **repeated measures** on the IV (the shape of the target).

There are other ways of obtaining paired data. Suppose that in the current example, the participants were pairs of identical or fraternal twins: each participant shoots at only one target and the twin shoots at the other. This experiment will also result in two related samples of scores, because, as in the repeated measures experiment, there is a basis for pairing the data. Different statistical tests are appropriate for use with independent and related samples of data.

1.4.4 Flow chart for selecting a suitable test for differences between means

Figure 4 outlines *some* of the considerations leading to a choice of a statistical test of the significance of differences between means (or frequencies, if one has nominal data). If there are more than two conditions or groups, an analysis of variance (ANOVA) may be applicable. In this section, we shall consider only the comparison between two groups or conditions, such as male versus female, or experimental group versus control group.

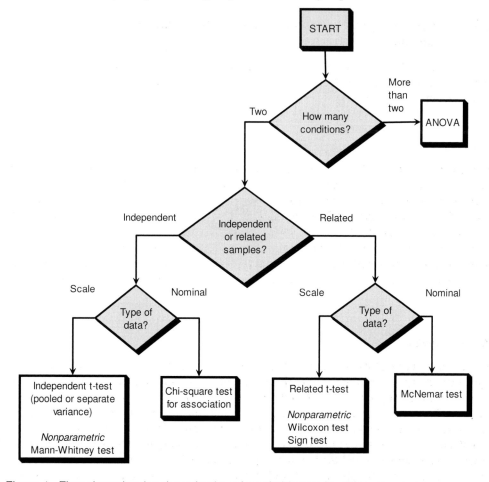

Figure 4. Flow chart showing the selection of a suitable test for differences between means

To use the chart, begin at the START box and consider how many conditions there are in the experiment. If there are two conditions, proceed down the chart to the next stage. The next questions are whether the samples are independent or related and whether the data are **scale data** or **nominal data** (see Section 1.1.2) . The appropriate test is shown in the bottom box.

The tests for comparing scores under **two** conditions (t-tests and their nonparametric equivalents) will be described in Chapter 6.

See Chap. 6

The tests for making comparisons among scores obtained under three or more conditions will be discussed in Chapters 7-10, which are concerned with analysis of variance (ANOVA).

See Chaps 7-10

1.4.5   Measuring strength of association between variables

Do tall fathers tend to have tall sons, short fathers to have short sons and fathers of medium height to have sons of medium height? This question is one of a **statistical association** between the two variables *Father's Height* and *Son's Height*. To answer the question, you would need a data set comprising the heights of a substantial sample of fathers and those of their (first) sons.

1.4.6   Flow chart for selecting a suitable test for association

Figure 5 outlines the questions one needs to answer in order to make a decision about an appropriate measure of association.

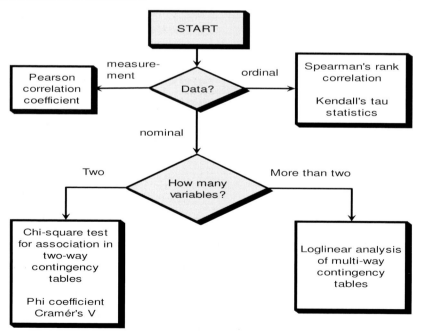

Figure 5. Flow chart showing measures of association

Begin at the START box and consider whether the data are scalar or ordinal. If the two variables are in the form of measurements, a **Pearson correlation** should be considered. However, as we shall see in Chapter 11, there are circumstances in which the Pearson correlation can be highly misleading. **It is essential to examine the data first before proceeding to obtain the Pearson correlation coefficient.**

> See
> Chap.
> 11

Measuring association in ordinal data

Now suppose we ask two judges to rank twenty paintings in order of preference. We shall have a data set consisting of twenty pairs of ranks. Do the judges agree? Again, our question is one of a statistical association. However, since the data are ordinal, a **rank correlation** is an appropriate statistic to use. The two most common kinds of rank correlation are:

> See
> Chap.
> 11

    1.   **Spearman's rank correlation**;
    2.   **Kendall tau** statistics.

Both are considered more fully in Chapter 11.

1.4.7   Measuring association in nominal data: Contingency tables

A medical researcher suspects that the incidence of an antibody may be higher in patients of tissue type X, compared with its incidence in patients of tissue types, A, B and C. Seventy-nine patients are tissue-typed and tested for the presence of the antibody. Such an exercise will result in a set of nominal data on two qualitative variables or attributes, *tissue type* (A, B, C, X) and *presence* (Yes, No). Here the scientific hypothesis is that there is an association between the two variables. Table 4 is a **contingency table**, which shows the joint classification on the two variables of the 39 patients in the study. The expected association is indeed evident in the table: there is a much higher incidence of the antibody in patients of tissue type X.

Table 4. A contingency table showing the incidence of an antibody in patients with four different types of tissue		
Tissue type	**Presence**	
	No	**Yes**
A	14	8
B	11	7
C	5	7
X	6	21

The presence of an association can be confirmed by using a **chi-square test** (see Chapter 11). Since the value of the chi-square statistic depends partly upon the sample size, however, it is unsuitable as a measure of the *strength* of the association between two qualitative variables. Figure 5 identifies two

> See
> Chap.
> 11

statistics that measure strength of association between qualitative variables: **Cramér's V** and the **phi coefficient**. Both measures are discussed in Chapter 11.

1.4.8   Multi-way contingency tables

In recent years, there have been dramatic developments in the analysis of nominal data in the form of multi-way contingency tables. Previously, tables with three or more attributes were often 'collapsed' to produce two-way tables. The usual chi-square test could then be applied. Such 'collapsing', however, is fraught with risk, and the tests may give highly misleading results. The advent of modern **loglinear analysis** has made it possible to tease out the relationships among the attributes in a way that was not possible before (see Chapter 13).

See Chap. 13

1.4.9   Predicting scores or category membership

If there is an association between variables, it is natural to ask whether this can be exploited to predict scores on one variable from knowledge of those on another. For example, in some American universities, students take aptitude tests at matriculation and received an academic grade point average (GPA) at the end of their first year of study. Can students' GPAs be predicted from their earlier scores on the aptitude tests? Such prediction is indeed possible, and the methods by which this is achieved will be briefly reviewed in this section.

There are also circumstances in which one would wish to predict not scores on a target or criterion variable, but membership of a category of a qualitative variable. For example, it is of medical and actuarial interest to be able to assign individuals to an 'at risk' category on the basis of their smoking and drinking habits. Statistical techniques have been specially devised for this purpose also.

The purpose of the methods reviewed here is to predict a target, or **criterion** variable (the term **dependent variable** is also used in this context) from scores on other variables, known variously (depending on the context) as **regressors**, **predictors**, **independent variables**, and **covariates**. The predictors need not always be quantitative variables: qualitative variables, such as gender and blood group, are often included among the predictor variables in research of this kind.

1.4.10   Flow chart for selecting the appropriate procedure for predicting a score or category membership

To use the flow chart (Figure 6) for selecting the appropriate prediction procedure, begin at the START box and consider whether the target variable is qualitative (e.g. a set of categories such as *Pass* and *Fail*) or quantitative (e.g. examination scores, which are scale data).

Begin at the START box and consider the purpose of the test. If it is to test for goodness-of-fit, move down the left-hand side of the chart. If it is to estimate the population mean or its probable range, move down the right-hand side. The next consideration is the nature of the data: different types of data require different tests. If the target variable is quantitative, a **regression** method should be considered. In **simple regression**, there is one predictor; in **multiple regression**, there are two or more (Chapter 12). If the criterion variable is qualitative, the techniques of **discriminant analysis** and **logistic regression** should be considered (Chapter 14).

See Chaps. 12 & 14

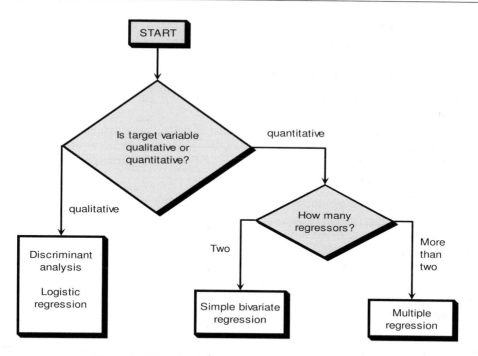

Figure 6. Flow chart showing procedures for prediction

1.4.11   Simple regression

In **simple regression**, a target or criterion variable is predicted from **one** predictor or regressor.

Suppose that, given a student's verbal aptitude score at matriculation, we want to predict the same student's grade point average a year later from the verbal aptitude score alone. This is a problem in **simple regression**, and the method is described in Chapter 12.

See Chap. 12

1.4.12   Multiple regression

A student's grade point average may be associated not only with verbal aptitude, but also with numerical ability. Can grade point average be predicted even more accurately when both verbal ability and numerical ability are taken into account? This is a problem in **multiple regression**. If grade point average is correlated with both verbal and numerical aptitude, multiple regression will produce (provided certain conditions are met) a more accurate prediction of a student's grade point average than will a simple regression upon either of the two regressors considered separately.

See Chap. 12

1.4.13   Predicting category membership: Discriminant analysis and logistic regression

Two statistical techniques designed to help the user make predictions of category membership are **discriminant analysis** and **logistic regression** (both of which are discussed in Chapter

14). In recent years, logistic regression, being a somewhat more robust technique than discriminant analysis, has become the preferred method.

See Chap. 14

1.5   ONE-SAMPLE TESTS

Much psychological research involves the collection of two or more samples of data. This is by no means always true, however: sometimes the researcher draws a **single** sample of observations in order to study just **one** population.

The situations in which one might use a one-sample test are of two main kinds:

1. One may wish to compare a sample distribution with a hypothetical distribution, such as the normal. This is a question of **goodness-of-fit**.
2. One may wish to make **inferences about the parameters of a single population** from the statistics of a sample, either for the purpose of ascertaining whether the sample is from a known population or estimating the parameters of an unknown population.

1.5.1   Flow chart for selecting the appropriate one-sample test

Figure 7 summarises the circumstances in which a researcher might make various kinds of one-sample tests. The tests reviewed in this section are more fully considered in Chapter 6.

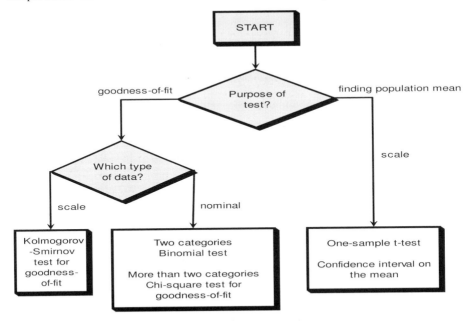

Figure 7. Flow chart of one-sample tests

Begin at the START box and consider the purpose of the test. If it is to test for goodness-of-fit, move down the left-hand side of the chart. If it is to estimate the population mean or its probable range, move down the right-hand side. The next consideration is the level of measurement: data at different levels require different tests.

1.5.2 Goodness-of-fit: scale data

A question about a single population may be one of **goodness-of-fit**: has the sample been drawn from a population with a specified distribution shape? Suppose, for example, that one has a sample of measurements and wishes to ascertain whether these have been drawn from a normal population. Figure 7 shows that the **Kolmogorov-Smirnov test** is appropriate for this purpose.

See Chap. 6

1.5.3 Goodness-of-fit: nominal data

Suppose a researcher wants to know whether 5-year-old children of a certain age show a preference for one of two toys (A or B). The choices of one hundred 5-year-olds are noted. Here the population comprises the choices (A or B) of 5-year-olds in general. Of the hundred children in the study, 60 choose toy A and 40 choose toy B. The null hypothesis states that the probability of choosing A (or B) is 0.5: more formally, it states that we have sampled 100 times from a Bernoulli distribution with $p = 0.5$. Does this theoretical distribution fit our data? Figure 7 indicates that a **binomial test** can be used to test this hypothesis.

See Chap. 6

If, in the foregoing situation, there were three or more toys to choose from, the **chi-square test for goodness-of-fit** can be used to test the null hypothesis that the children have no preference for any particular toy.

1.5.4 Inferences about the mean of a single population

Suppose we want to know whether the performance of a group of schoolchildren on a standardised test is typical of those in their age group. Figure 7 shows that a **one-sample t test** can be used to test the null hypothesis that a sample has been drawn from a population with a mean of a specified value. Often, however, as when the researcher is working with a non-standardised test, it may not be possible to specify any null hypothesis. Suppose that a lecturer wishes to ascertain the typical reaction speed of first-year university students within a certain age group. The lecturer may have data on, say, two hundred first-year students; but the research question, being about the reaction speeds of first-year students in general, concerns the population of reaction times. The sample mean is a **point estimate** of the unknown population mean. The t distribution can also be used to build a **confidence interval** on the sample mean, so that the researcher has a range of values within which the true population mean can, with a specified degree of 'confidence', be assumed to lie.

See Chap. 6

The one-sample t test can also be used to test the difference between the means of two related samples of scores. If the difference between scores under the two conditions is found for each participant, we shall have a single sample of differences. If the null hypothesis is correct, the mean difference in the population is zero, which is equivalent to stating that, in the population, the mean scores under the two conditions have equal values. The related-samples t test and the one-sample t test, in fact, are exact equivalents and will produce exactly the same result.

1.5.5 ◔ Nominal data: Testing a coin for fairness

When we toss a coin a large number of times to ascertain its fairness, we obtain a sample from the (infinite) population of such tosses. We might find that the coin turned up heads on 58 out of 100 tosses. Is the coin 'fair', that is, in the population, are the relative frequencies of heads and tails both 0.5? (Here, when we speak of the 'population', we refer to a hypothetical experiment in which the coin is tossed an infinite number of times. We should certainly not expect exactly 50 heads in every 100 tosses of the coin.)

The **binomial test** can be used to test the hypothesis that the population proportion is ½ (or, indeed, that it is any other specified proportion). A **confidence interval** can also be constructed on the sample proportion to give a range of values within which we can be confident to a required degree that the true population proportion lies.

See
Chap.
6

1.6   FINDING LATENT VARIABLES: FACTOR ANALYSIS AND CANONICAL CORRELATION

Suppose that 500 people are measured on twenty tests of ability and that the correlations between each test and every other test are arrayed in a square array known as a **correlation matrix (R-matrix)**. It is likely that, since those who are good at one thing tend also to be good at others, there will be substantial positive correlations among the tests in the battery.

Factor analysis (see Chapter 15) is a set of techniques which, on the basis of the correlations in an R-matrix, classify all the tests in a battery in terms of relatively few underlying (or **latent**) dimensions or **factors**. (The term factor has more than one meaning in statistics. In analysis of variance [ANOVA], a factor is an independent variable, that is, a set of related treatments or categories.) In **exploratory factor analysis**, the object is to find the minimum number of **factors** necessary to account for the correlations among the psychological tests. In **confirmatory factor analysis**, specified models are compared to see which of them gives the best account of the data.

See
Chap.
15

While factors are hypothetical underlying dimensions, they are estimated, essentially, by sums of participants' scores on all the tests in the battery. Thus, in addition to scores on the tests, each person also receives one or more **factor scores**, each of which represents that person's endowment with the latent variable in question.

Other statistical techniques, such as **canonical correlation**, have also been devised for the purpose of identifying latent variables (Section 15.4).

1.6.1   Multivariate statistics

Factor analysis and canonical correlation belong to a set of techniques collectively known as **multivariate statistics**. While these methods arise naturally in the context of correlational research, however, they are also applicable to certain kinds of experimental data.

In Section 1.2, in which we considered experimental research, we spoke of the dependent variable (DV), which was measured during the course of the experiment and the independent variable (IV), which was manipulated by the experimenter with a view to showing that it had the power to affect the DV.

The DV in an experiment is often, in a sense, a representative or proxy variable. In a test of maze-learning proficiency, for instance, we may use the speed at which participants draw lines through the maze. Arguably, however, another consideration, number of errors, also reflects maze-learning skill; indeed, in some situations there may be several reasonable potential dependent variables, any one of which could be taken as representative of proficiency. Statistical methods relating to a single DV are called **univariate**.

Multivariate statistics are methods designed for the analysis of data sets in which there are two or more DVs. In this context, however, the terms independent and dependent variable tend to be applied more generally to any research, whether experimental or correlational, in which some variables (the IVs) are thought to have a causal influence upon others (the DVs).

In experimental and quasi-experimental research, the t-tests and ANOVA are generalised to multivariate analysis of variance (**MANOVA**). In correlational research, factor analysis and canonical correlation are thought of as explaining associations among the observed variables (the DVs) in terms of latent 'causal' variables (i.e. factors or canonical variables), which are, essentially, sums of the observed variables.

1.7   A FINAL COMMENT

In this chapter, we have offered some advice about using formal statistical tests to support the researcher's claim that what is true of a particular data set is likely to be true in the population. At this point, however, a word of warning is appropriate.

Formal tests, statistical models and their assumptions

The making of a formal statistical test of significance always presupposes the applicability of a statistical **model**, that is, an interpretation (usually in the form of an equation) of the data set as having been generated in a specified manner. The model underlying the one-sample *t* test, for example, assumes that the data are from a normal population. To some extent, statistical tests have been shown to be **robust** to moderate violations of the assumptions of the models upon which they are based, that is, the actual error rates do not rise above acceptable levels. But there are limits to this robustness, and there are circumstances in which a result, declared by an incautious user to be significant beyond, say, the 0.05 level, may actually have been considerably more probable than that. There is no way of avoiding this pitfall other than by getting to know your data first (see Chapters 4 and 5) to ascertain their suitability for specified formal tests.

See
Chaps
4 & 5

Recommended reading

Terms and ideas in research design

There are available many excellent textbooks on research methodology. We have considered only those terms and principles that we consider to be essential for the purposes of data analysis with SPSS. (SPSS uses many of the terms we have introduced in this chapter.)

Field, A., & Hole, G. (2003). *How to design and report experiments*. London: Sage.

Chapter 1 discusses many of the methodological terms and issues touched upon in this chapter in greater depth and considers some more general issues in methodology.

Readable statistics texts

The reader with a limited mathematical background who is looking for a text on basic statistics is faced with a bewildering array of choices. We suggest the following book:

Sani, F., & Todman, J. (2006). *Experimental design and statistics for psychology: A first course*. Oxford: Blackwell.

For the reader who is more comfortable with algebraic notation, we suggest

Howell, D. C. (2007). *Statistical methods for psychology (6th ed.)*. Belmont, CA: Thomson/Wadsworth.

A useful dictionary of statistical terms

The following is a very useful reference book, with clear definitions.

Nelson, D. (2004). *The Penguin dictionary of statistics*. London: Penguin Books.

CHAPTER 2

Getting started with SPSS 15

2.1   Outline of an SPSS session

2.2   Opening SPSS

2.3   The SPSS Data Editor

2.4   A statistical analysis

2.5   Closing SPSS

2.6   Resuming work on a saved data set

2.1   OUTLINE OF AN SPSS SESSION

There are three stages in the use of SPSS:
1.   The data are entered into the **Data Editor**.
2.   Descriptive and statistical procedures are selected from the **drop-down menus**.
3.   The output is examined and edited in the **SPSS Viewer**.

2.1.1   Entering the data

There are several ways of placing data in the **Data Editor**. They can be typed in directly or read in from SPSS data files that have already been created. SPSS can also read data from files produced by other applications, such as EXCEL and STATISTICA, as well as text files.

Once the data are in the **Data Editor**, the user has available a wide variety of editorial functions. Not only can the data be amended in various ways, but also selections from the original set can be targeted for subsequent analysis.

In this chapter, we shall give considerable attention to the **Data Editor**, because it enables the user to control important features of the output (such as the labelling of variables) which can make the results of a statistical analysis easier to interpret.

The user can also access important editing functions from an array of **drop-down menus** at the top of the screen.

2.1.2 Selecting the exploratory and statistical procedures

It is also from the drop-down menus that the user selects statistical procedures. The user is advised to explore the data thoroughly before making any formal statistical tests. SPSS offers many graphical methods described in Chapters 4 and 5 of displaying a data set, which are of great assistance when you are getting to know your data.

2.1.3 Examining the output

The results of the analysis appear in the **SPSS Viewer**. In addition to the selection and trimming of items, the SPSS **Viewer** also offers facilities for more radical editing. The appearance of tables and other output can be dramatically transformed to tailor them to the purposes of the user.

From the SPSS **Viewer**, material can readily be transferred to files produced by other applications, such as Word, or printed out in hard copy.

2.1.4 A simple experiment

In this chapter, we shall illustrate the stages in a typical SPSS session by entering the results of a fictional experiment into the **Data Editor**, describing the data by choosing some statistics from the menu and examining the output. At this stage, we shall concentrate on the general procedure, leaving the details for later consideration.

Table 1 shows the results of an experiment designed to show the effects of a drug upon skilled performance.

Table 1. Results of an experiment designed to show whether a drug improves skilled performance							
Group							
Placebo				**Drug**			
Case	**Score**	**Case**	**Score**	**Case**	**Score**	**Case**	**Score**
1	6	6	3	11	8	16	8
2	5	7	2	12	6	17	6
3	5	8	4	13	6	18	7
4	1	9	5	14	7	19	5
5	2	10	1	15	6	20	10

The experiment was of simple, two-group between subjects design, in which twenty participants attempted a test of skill. Ten participants (cases) were assigned at random to one of two conditions:

1. A *Placebo* condition, in which the participant ingested a harmless saline solution;
2. A *Drug* condition, in which the participant ingested a small dose of a drug.

The dependent variable was the participant's score on the skilled task. The independent variable was the condition to which the participant was assigned: *Drug* or *Placebo*. The experimental hypothesis was that the group that had been assigned to the *Drug* condition would outperform the group assigned to the *Placebo* condition.

We shall shortly show how these data can be placed in the **SPSS Data Editor** and the results summarised with a few statistics.

2.1.5   Preparing data for SPSS

The data shown in Table 1 are not in a form that the SPSS **Data Editor** will accept. In an SPSS data set, **each row must represent only one case** (equivalent terms are **'participant'** and **'subject'**) and each column represents a variable or characteristic on which that case has been measured. In other words, **each row of an SPSS data set must contain data on just one case or participant**. The data in Table 1 do not conform to this requirement: the first row of entries contains data from four different participants.

To make them suitable for analysis with SPSS, the data in Table 1 must be rearranged in a new format. In Table 2, the data in Table 1 have been re-tabulated, so that each row now contains data on only one participant.

Table 2. The data set of Table 1, recast in a form suitable for entry into SPSS		
Participant	**Condition**	**Participant's Score**
1	1	6
2	1	5
3	1	5
4	1	1
5	1	2
6	1	3
7	1	2
8	1	4
9	1	5
10	1	1
11	2	8
12	2	6
13	2	6
14	2	7
15	2	6
16	2	8
17	2	6
18	2	7
19	2	5
20	2	10

In Table 2, the *Condition* variable identifies the group to which each participant belongs by means of an arbitrary code number, in this case *1* (for the *Placebo* condition) or *2* (for the *Drug* condition). Unlike the numbers in the *Score* column, which express level of performance, the code numbers in the *Condition* column **serve merely as category labels**: the

Condition variable is a special kind of **categorical variable** known as a **grouping variable** (see Chapter 1).

2.2   OPENING SPSS

There are several ways of beginning a session with SPSS, depending upon whether you intend to build a new file or access an old one. When SPSS is opened for the first time by clicking the SPSS icon, an introductory dialog box will appear with the title **SPSS 15.0 for Windows**.

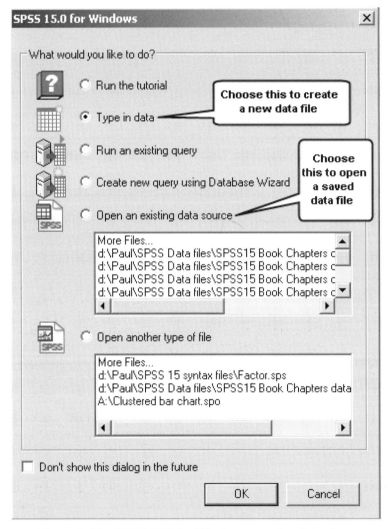

Figure 1. The **SPSS 15.0 for Windows** opening dialog box

Underneath the title is the question: *What would you like to do?* Make your choice by clicking one of the six small radio buttons and then **OK** (Figure 1). Here we shall assume that you wish to enter data for the first time, in which case click the button labelled **Type in data**. When you click **OK**, the **Data Editor** will appear on the screen.

At a later stage, you may wish to omit the introductory dialog box, in which case click the square labelled **Don't show this dialog in the future** in the bottom left corner of the dialog box.

2.3   THE SPSS DATA EDITOR

The SPSS **Data Editor** provides two alternative spreadsheet-like arrays:
1.   **Data View**, into which the user can enter new data or (if an old file has been accessed) view whatever data the file contains.
2.   **Variable View**, which contains the names and details of the variables in the data set.

When you are creating a file for the first time, it is advisable to lay the foundations in **Variable View** first, so that when you come to enter data in **Data View**, the columns in the spreadsheet will already have been labelled, reducing the risk of transcription errors.

A notational convention

In this book, we shall use *italics* to indicate variable names and values. We shall use a **bold** typeface for the names of menus, the names of dialog boxes and the items therein. Emboldening will also be used for emphasis and for technical terms.

2.3.1   Working in Variable View

When the **Data Editor** appears, you may find that you are in **Data View**. If so, click the tab labelled **Variable View** at the bottom left-hand side of the window and you will access **Variable View** (Figure 2).

When the **Data Editor** first appears, the caption in the title bar reads, '**Untitled1 [DataSet0] – SPSS Data Editor**'. Any additional data sets (SPSS 15 allows more than one data set to be available during an SPSS session) would be numbered DataSet1, DataSet 2 and so on. When you finish entering your data (or preferably during data entry as a protection against losing data should the system crash), you can supply a name for the file by selecting the **Save As...** item from the **File** drop-down menu and entering a suitable name in the **File Name** box. After you have done this, the title bar will display your new name for the file.

Recent Releases of SPSS allow more than one data file to be available on the screen though only one of them can be active and is marked with a green cross superimposed on the icon of a grid   at the left-hand end of the title bar. A file is activated by clicking anywhere within its window.

The word **Untitled** in the title bar is a warning to the user that the file has not yet been given a name and saved.

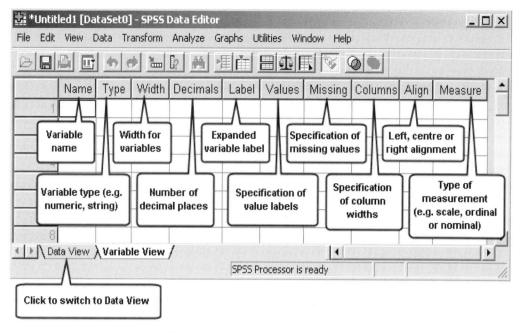

Figure 2. Variable View
(For this figure, some of the columns have been narrowed.)

Notation for selecting from a menu

We shall adopt a notation for selecting items from a drop-down menu by which the sequence of selections is shown by arrows (**➜**). For example, selection of the **Copy** item from the **Edit** drop-down menu will be written as
Edit➜Copy

*The **Name** and **Labels** columns*

Some of the column headings in **Variable View** (such as number of places of decimals) are self-explanatory. The **Name** and **Labels** columns, however, require some explanation. The **name** of a variable is a string of characters (normally letters and spaces but it can include digits) which will appear at the head of a column in **Data View**, but not in the output. In other words, a variable name is a convenient shortened name for use only within **Data View**. There is a set of rules for naming variables. This can readily be accessed by entering SPSS's **Help** menu and choosing
Help➜Topics➜Index➜Variable names

The main message is that a variable name must be a **continuous** sequence (no spaces) of up to 64 characters (though long variable names are not recommended), **the first of which must be a letter**. It can be defined with any mixture of upper and lower case characters, and case is preserved for display purposes (e.g. *TimeofDay*). Although certain punctuation marks are permitted, it is simpler merely to remember to use letters and digits only.

Making entries in Variable View

- To name the variables *Case*, *Group* and *Score*, first check that there is a thickened border around the top leftmost cell (see Figure 2). If it is not there, move the cursor there and click with the mouse.
- Type *Case* and press the ↓ cursor key to move the highlighting down to the cell below to complete the entry of *Case* in the cell above. (Entry of information into a cell is only complete when the cursor is moved away by clicking on another cell.)
- Type *Group* into the second cell with a thickened border and press the ↓ cursor key to move the highlighting down to the next row, completing the entry of *Group* in the cell above.
- Use the same procedure to enter the variable name *Score*.

SPSS will accept eight different **types** of variable, two of the most important being **numeric** (numerals with a decimal point) and **string** (e.g. names of participants, cities or other non-numerical material). Initially, some of the format specifications of a variable are set by default, and the pre-set values will be seen as soon as the variable name has been typed and control transferred from the **Name** cell. Unless you specify otherwise, **it will be assumed that the variable is of the numeric type.**

The number of places of decimals that will be displayed in **Data View** is pre-set at *2*. Since the scores in Table 2 are all integers, it would be tedious to read entries such as *46.00, 34.00* and *54.00*, as opposed to *46, 34* and *54*. It is better to suppress the display of decimals in **Data View** by clicking on the **Decimals** column to obtain the following display

By clicking twice on the downward-pointing arrow, you can replace the number *2* already in the cell with zero (see Figure 3). Note that this countermanding of the default specification will apply **only to the variable concerned**. Rather than over-riding the default specifications piecemeal in this way, you can reset the decimal display to zero for every numeric variable in the data set by choosing

    See
    Chapter
    3

Edit➜Options...➜Data
and resetting the number of decimal places to zero. See Chapter 3 for details.

The **Label**, which should be a meaningful phrase, with spaces between the words, is the description of the variable that will appear **in the output**. In order to make the output as clear as possible, therefore, it is important to devise **meaningful** labels for all the variables in the data set. The labels shown in Figure 3, *Case Number* and *Experimental Condition*, are more informative than the corresponding variable names *Case* and *Group*, respectively, which are adequate for use within the **Data Editor**.

		Name	Type	Width	Decimals	Label	Values
	1	Case	Numeric	8	0	Case Number	None
	2	Group	Numeric	8	0	Experimental Condition	None
	3	Score	Numeric	8	0	Score	None

File Edit View Data Transform Analyze Graphs Utilities Window Help

Figure 3. Part of **Variable View**, with entries specifying the names and details of the three variables

The **Values** column is for use with **grouping variables**. By clicking on **Values**, the user can supply a key to the meanings of the code numbers. In this case, the grouping variable is *Experimental Condition* and we can arbitrarily decide that *1* = *Placebo* and *2* = *Drug*. Click the first cell of the Values column to obtain the following display:

Note the grey area on the right with the three dots (…). Clicking this grey area will produce the **Values** dialog box (see Figure 4).

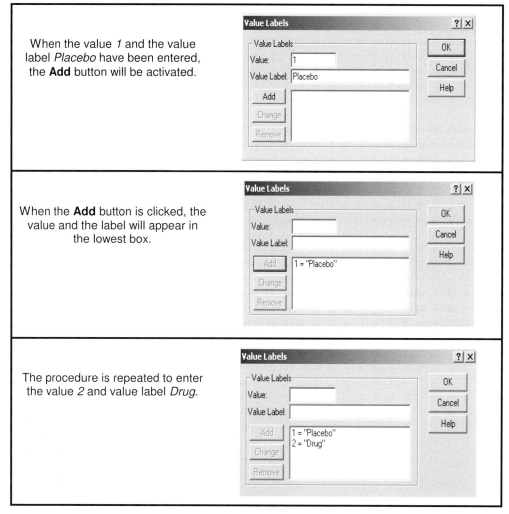

When the value *1* and the value label *Placebo* have been entered, the **Add** button will be activated.

When the **Add** button is clicked, the value and the label will appear in the lowest box.

The procedure is repeated to enter the value *2* and value label *Drug*.

Figure 4. How to enter value labels which, in the output, will replace the code numbers making up a grouping variable

Figure 4 shows how to fill in the **Values** dialog box so that, in the output, the code numbers *1* and *2* will be replaced by the more informative value labels *Placebo* and *Drug*, respectively.

In addition, as you type 1 or 2 in **Data View**, the value labels will appear provided either **Value Labels** within the **View** drop-down menu is ticked or by clicking the icon 🔳 in the toolbar.

*The **Width** column*

With string variables, the **Width** column controls the maximum length (in number of characters) of the string you will be allowed to enter when you are working in **Data View**. (The setting in Width has no effect upon the number of characters you can type in when working with a numeric variable.)

The default setting for Width is *8*, but this can be changed by choosing **Edit➔Options➔Data** and changing the **Width** setting there. For more details, see Chapter 3. If a string is too long for the set width, you will find that you can no longer type in the excess letters in **Data View**.

> See
> Chapter
> 3

*The **Columns** column*

The cells of this column display the actual widths, for all the variables in the data set, of the columns that will appear in **Data View**. Initially, the cells in **Columns** will show the same setting as the **Width** column: *8*. Were you to create a new numeric variable with a name whose length exceeded the preset width, only part of the name would be displayed in the **Name** column of **Variable View**. Moreover, in **Data View**, only part of the variable name would be visible at the head of the column for that variable.

To specify wider columns for a variable in **Data View** while working in **Variable View**, click the appropriate cell in **Columns** and adjust the setting there.

*The **Align** column*

This determines whether the data are **Left**, **Right** or **Centre** aligned. The default setting is **Right**.

*The **Measure** column*

This enables the user to declare whether the data are **Scale** (i.e. measurements), **Ordinal** or **Nominal** (see Section 1.1.2 *Levels of measurement: scale, ordinal and nominal data*). The default measure is **Scale**. It is important to declare categorical variables such as sex or blood group as **Nominal** and categorical variables such as rating scales as **Ordinal** especially if a graphic (e.g. an item from **Chart Builder**) is going to be used. For our example, *Case* and *Score* would be **Scale** and *Group* would be **Nominal**.

> See
> Section
> 1.1.2

Copying settings

Values in the cells of **Variable View** can be copied and pasted to other cells using the standard Windows methods (see Section 2.3.3). For example, having adjusted the **Columns** setting to, say, *15* characters for one variable of the data set, the new setting can be applied to other variables by copying and pasting the contents of the cell with the entry *15* into the cells for the other variables.

Modified settings can also be copied to **Columns** from the **Width** Column. Having adjusted an entry in the **Width** column to, say, *16*, the new setting can be copied and pasted into **Columns** in the usual way. The effect will be to widen the columns in **Data View** for the variables to which the new **Columns** setting has been copied.

2.3.2   Working in Data View

Once the appropriate specifications have been entered in **Variable View**, click the **Data View** tab at the bottom of the **Variable View** window to enter **Data View** (Figure 5). When **Data View** is accessed, the variable names *Case*, *Group* and *Score* will be seen at the heads of the first three columns as specified in **Variable View**. The default name *var*, which appears in the third, fourth and fifth columns, indicates that those columns have yet to be assigned to specified variables.

Running along the bottom of the **Data View** window is a horizontal band, in which various messages appear from time to time. When SPSS is accessed, the message reads: **SPSS Processor is ready**. The horizontal band is known as the **Status Bar**, because it reports not only whether SPSS is ready to begin, but also on the stage that a procedure has reached. If, for example, a large data set is being read from a file, progress is continually monitored, case by case, in the status bar.

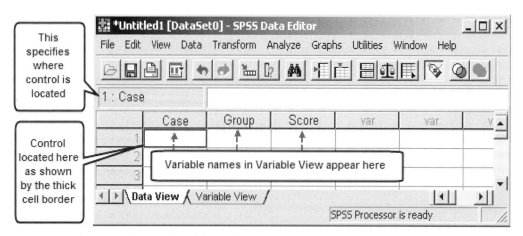

Figure 5.   Part of **Data View**, showing the variable names and active cell

2.3.3   Entering the data

Figure 6 shows a section of **Data View**, in which the data in Table 1 have been entered.

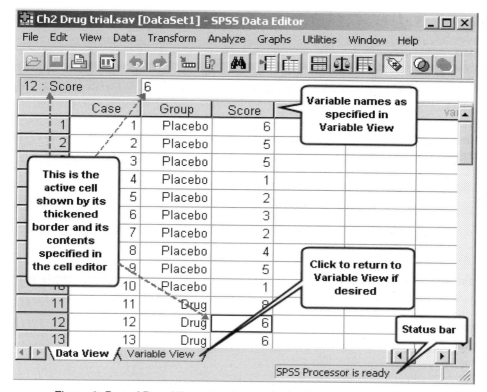

Figure 6. Part of **Data View** after the results in Table 1 have been entered

The first variable, *Case*, represents the case number of the participants. Enter the number of each participant from *1* to *20*. The second variable *Group*, identifies the condition under which each participant performed the task: *1* = *Placebo*; *2* = *Drug*. Enter ten *1*'s into the first ten rows of the *Group* variable, followed by ten *2*'s. In the first ten cells of the *Score* column, enter the scores of the ten participants who performed the task under the *Placebo* condition, followed by those of the ten participants who performed under the *Drug* condition.

Notice that in Figure 6, location of control is indicated by the thickened border of the cell in the 12th row of the second column. The value in this cell is 6. The contents of this cell are also displayed in a white area known as the **cell editor** just above the column headings. The value in the **cell editor** (and the cell itself) can be changed by clicking in the **cell editor**, selecting the present value, typing a new one and pressing ⏎. The new value will appear in the grid.

Blocking, copying and pasting

Initially, only one cell in **Data View** is highlighted. However, it is possible to highlight a whole block of cells, or even an entire row or column. This **blocking** operation (when all the cells appear in **inverse video**, with the characters printed in white against a black background) is achieved either by clicking and dragging with the mouse or proceeding as follows:

- To **highlight a whole row or column**, click the grey box containing the row number or the column heading.

- To highlight a **block of cells within a row or column**, click on the first cell and (keeping the left button of the mouse pressed down) drag the pointer to the cell at the end of the block. The same result can be obtained by clicking the first cell in the block, pressing the **Shift** key and keeping it held down while using the appropriate cursor key ($\uparrow$ or $\downarrow$) to move the highlighting along the entire block.

The blocking operation can be used to **copy the values in one column into another** or to **place them elsewhere in the same column**.

- Highlight a column of values that you wish to copy and then choose
  Edit➜Copy
- Next, highlight the cells of the target column and choose
  Edit➜Paste

The values in the source column will now appear in the target column. (Make sure that the number of highlighted target cells is equal to the number of cells copied.) For example, the successions of *1*'s and *2*'s identifying the *Placebo* and *Drug* conditions could have been entered as follows.

- Place the value *1* in the topmost cell of the *Group* column. Move the black rectangle away from the cell to complete the entry of the value and return the highlight to the cell, which will now contain the value *1*.
- Choose
  Edit➜Copy
  to store the value *1* in the clipboard.
- Highlight cells *2* to *10* and choose
  Edit➜Paste
  to place the value *1* in all the highlighted cells.

Using key combinations to copy and paste

Copying and pasting can also be carried out by using the key combinations **Ctrl + C** (that is, by holding the **Ctrl** key down while pressing C) and **Ctrl + V**, respectively.

Deletion of values

Whether you are working in **Variable View** or in **Data View**, entries can be removed by selecting the target items in the manner described above and pressing the **Delete** key.

Switching between Data View and Variable View

You can switch from one **Data Editor** display to the other at any point. While in **Data View**, for instance, you might want to return to **Variable View** to name further variables or add further details about existing ones. Just click the **Variable View** tab. When you have finished the new work in **Variable View**, click **Data View** to continue entering your data.

Creating more space for entries in Data View

While the widths of the columns in **Data View** can be controlled from **Variable View** in the manner described above, you can also control column width while working in **Data View**. To widen a column, click on the grey cell containing the variable name at the top of the column and click and drag the right-hand border to the right.

Displaying value labels in Data View

The values assigned to the numerical values of a grouping variable can be displayed in **Data View** by choosing
View➡Value Labels (See Figure 7).

Should the *Group* column in **Data View** not be sufficiently wide to show the value labels completely, create more space by placing the cursor in the grey cell at the head of the column containing the label *Group* and click and drag the right-hand border of the cell to the right.

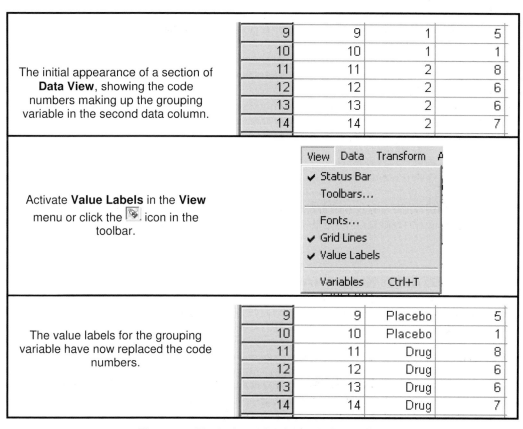

The initial appearance of a section of **Data View**, showing the code numbers making up the grouping variable in the second data column.				
	9	9	1	5
	10	10	1	1
	11	11	2	8
	12	12	2	6
	13	13	2	6
	14	14	2	7

Activate **Value Labels** in the **View** menu or click the icon in the toolbar.	View Data Transform A
	✔ Status Bar
	Toolbars...
	Fonts...
	✔ Grid Lines
	✔ Value Labels
	Variables Ctrl+T

The value labels for the grouping variable have now replaced the code numbers.				
	9	9	Placebo	5
	10	10	Placebo	1
	11	11	Drug	8
	12	12	Drug	6
	13	13	Drug	6
	14	14	Drug	7

Figure 7.   Displaying value labels in **Data View**

Using the display of values in the Data Editor as a guide when entering data

Having specified the variable type as *numeric* when in **Variable View**, you will find that **Data View** will accept, in the first instance, only numerical entries. You can arrange, however, for the first numerical entry, say *1*, to be displayed as the value label by choosing
View➔Value Label

Although you typed in *1*, you will now see the label *Placebo* in the cell. Moreover, you can copy and paste this label to the other nine cases in the *Placebo* group. When you come to the *Drug* group, however, you will need to type in *2* which, when you click another cell, will then appear as the value *Drug*. **Data View will not accept the word *Drug* typed in directly**. You can then copy and paste the second numerical label to the remaining cases in the Drug group. This procedure can be useful if, momentarily, as when your SPSS session has been interrupted, you have forgotten the number-label pairings you assigned in **Variable View**. It also helps you to avoid transcription errors when transferring your data from response sheets.

Saving the data file

When you finish entering your data (but preferably during data entry at intervals in case the system crashes), you can supply a name for the data file by choosing the **Save As...** item from the **File** drop-down menu, selecting an appropriate drive and/or folder and then entering a suitable name in the **File Name** box. After you have done this, the title bar will display your new name for the file. Note that if you do not do this, you will be prompted to supply a name for the data file when you wish to terminate your SPSS session and close down SPSS.

SPSS tutorials

For an animated step-by-step tutorial on entering data into SPSS, readers can work through the tutorial provided by SPSS. Click the **Help** drop-down menu, select **Tutorial** and then **Using the Data Editor**. The arrow buttons in the right-hand bottom corner of each page of the tutorial enable the user to navigate forward and backward through the tutorial.

2.4   A STATISTICAL ANALYSIS

2.4.1   An example: Computing means

In this section, we shall use SPSS to summarise the results of the experiment by obtaining some descriptive statistics such as the mean and standard deviation of the scores for each treatment group (Placebo and Drug).

- From the drop-down **Analyze** menu, choose
  Compare Means➔Means ....
  as shown in Figure 8.
- Click **Means...** to access the **Means** dialog box (Figure 9).

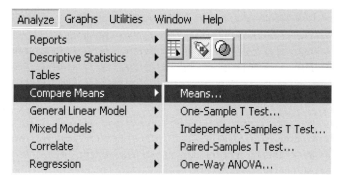

Figure 8. Finding the **Means** menu

Initially, in the left-hand panel the variable names are obscured; but you can view the entire label by touching it with the screen pointer.

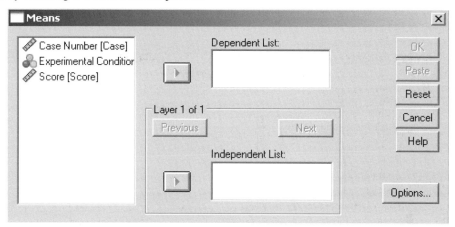

Figure 9. The **Means** dialog box showing the three variables in the data set

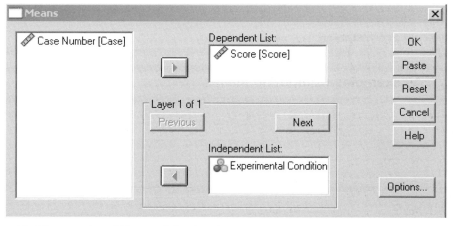

Figure 10. The completed **Means** dialog box for computing the mean scores for the two experimental conditions

- Click on *Score* to highlight it and then on the arrow pointing to the **Dependent List** box. The variable name and label will then be transferred to the Dependent List box.

- In a similar manner transfer the variable *Experimental Condition* to the **Independent List** box (see Figure 10).

- Click **OK** to run the analysis. The results will appear in a new window called the **SPSS Viewer**, a section of which is shown in Output 1.

The SPSS **Viewer** window is divided into two 'panes' by a vertical grey bar. The left pane shows the hierarchical organisation of the contents of the **Viewer**. The right pane contains the results of the statistical analysis and various other items. The contents of the **Viewer** on both sides of the bar can be edited.

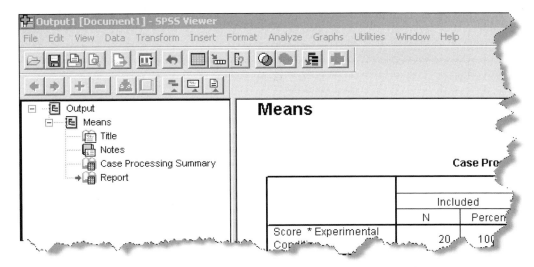

Output 1. Part of the **SPSS Viewer** window showing the list of output items in the left pane and the output tables in the right pane

For the moment, however, the main item of interest is the **Report** (Output 2), which appears in the right pane. From the **Report**, it can be seen that the mean performance of those tested under the *Drug* condition was over twice the level of those tested under the *Placebo* condition.

Report

Score

Experimental Condition	Mean	N	Std. Deviation
Placebo	3.40	10	1.838
Drug	6.90	10	1.449
Total	5.15	20	2.412

Output 2. The **Report** table showing the mean, number of scores and standard deviation in each of the two groups

It would seem, therefore, that the results of the experiment support the hypothesis. This, however, is insufficient: formal tests are necessary to confirm the appearance of the data. It should be noted, however, that before the researcher makes any formal statistical tests, the data should first be thoroughly explored. SPSS has an exploratory data analysis procedure, **Explore**, which offers a wide range of useful statistics. **Explore** can be run by choosing **Analyze➜Descriptive Statistics➜Explore…**.

We shall consider **Explore** more fully in Chapter 4.

> See
>
> Chapter 4

Editing the output in SPSS Viewer

The **SPSS Viewer** offers powerful editing facilities, some of which can radically alter the appearance of a default table such as that shown in Output 3. Many of the tables in the output are **pivot tables**, that is, tables in which the columns and rows can be transposed and to which other radical alterations can be made.

Report

Variables	Score	

Experimental Condition	Mean	N	Std. Deviation
Placebo	3.40	10	1.838
Drug	6.90	10	1.449
Total	5.15	20	2.412

Output 3. An item which has been prepared for editing. On double-clicking the item, a hatched border appears around it

Suppose, for example, like the editors of many scientific journals, you would prefer the experimental conditions *Placebo* and *Drug* to be column headings and the group means, standard deviations and *N*'s to be below them. If you double-click the **Report**, a hatched border will appear around the table (Output 3).

You will notice that, along the drop-down menus at the top of the **Viewer** window, a new menu, **Pivot**, has appeared.

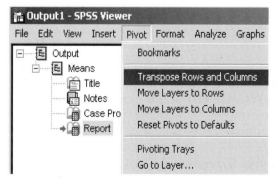

Figure 11. The **Pivot** drop-down menu with **Transpose Rows and Columns** selected

Choose
- **Pivot➔Transpose Rows and Columns** (Figure 11).

The effect (see Output 4) is dramatic! The descriptive statistics now occupy the rows and the experimental conditions the columns.

The **Pivot** menu can be used to edit complex tables with three, four or more dimensions of classification. Such manipulation can be of great assistance in bringing out the most important features of your results.

Report

Score

| | Experimental Condition | | |
	Placebo	Drug	Total
Mean	3.40	6.90	5.15
N	10	10	20
Std. Deviation	1.838	1.449	2.412

Output 4. The transposed **Report** table

2.4.2   Keeping more than one application open

One useful feature of Windows is that the user can keep several applications open simultaneously. It is therefore quite possible to be writing a document in **Word** while at the same time running **SPSS** and importing output such as the **Report** in the previous section. If more than one application is open, the user can move from one to another by clicking on the appropriate button on the **Taskbar** (usually located at the foot of the screen). Alternatively, you can hold down the **Alt** key and press the **Tab** key repeatedly to cycle control through whatever applications may be open.

2.5   CLOSING SPSS

SPSS is closed by choosing **Exit** from the **File** menu. If you have not yet saved the data or the output at any point, a default dialog box will appear with the question: **Save contents of data editor to untitled?** or **Save contents of output viewer to Output 1?**. You must then click the **Yes**, **No** or **Cancel** button. If you choose **Yes**, you will be given a final opportunity to name the file you wish to save. Beware of saving unselected output files because they can become very large in terms of computer storage, especially if they contain graphics.

2.6   RESUMING WORK ON A SAVED DATA SET

There are several ways of resuming work on a saved data set. After opening SPSS and obtaining the introductory **SPSS 15 for Windows dialog box**, you can click the radio button **Open an existing data source** (Figure 1). A list of saved files with the extension *.sav* will appear in the upper **More Files** window. Select the appropriate file and click **OK**. The data file will then appear in **Data View**. Other kinds of file, such as SPSS output files, can be retrieved from the lower **More Files** window by clicking on the radio button labelled **Open another kind of file**.

While you in the **Data Editor**, it is always possible to access files by choosing **Open** from the **File** menu. A quicker method of accessing an SPSS data file is to double-click its icon. The data will immediately appear in **Data View**.

EXERCISE 1

Some simple operations with SPSS 15

Before you start

Before you begin the first exercise, make sure you have read Sections 2.1, 2.2 and 2.3.

An experiment on role models of aggression

In a study of the effects of adult models on the development of aggression, two groups of children were assessed on aggression after they had viewed the behaviour of either an aggressive or a neutral adult.

Aggressive	10	11	20	15	2	5	16	8	18	16
Neutral	9	9	12	8	10	2	7	10	11	9

Do these results support the view that aggressive role models promote aggressive behaviour?

Opening SPSS and preparing a data file

Open SPSS as described in Section 2.2. Click the radio button labelled **Type in data** and then **OK** to open the SPSS **Data Editor** (see Section 2.3). In order to compute means and other statistics, you could create two variables called *Neutral* and *Aggressive* and enter the scores in the appropriate columns. We suggest, however, that you proceed as in Section 2.1.5 and create a grouping variable, with some informative full label such as *Adult Behaviour*, and a shorter name, such as *Condition*, for use in the **Data Editor**. The full variable label for the dependent variable might be *Aggression Score* and the shorter name for the **Data Editor** could be *Score*.

Lay the foundations in **Variable View** first before typing in the data. Change the **Decimals** setting to zero to display only whole numbers in **Data View**. Decide on two arbitrary code numbers and value labels for the two conditions, such as *1 = Neutral* and *2 = Aggressive*. Enter these in the **Values** column, as described in Section 2.3.

Click the **Data View** tab to enter **Data View**. Try entering the data by copying and pasting, as described in Section 2.3. To see the value names as you are entering the data, click on **Value Labels** in the **View** menu.

We suggest that, early in the session, you save your work to a file with an informative name using

File➔Save As...

Computing the means and standard deviations

Obtain, in the manner described in Section 2.4.1, the means and standard deviations of the aggression scores for the children exposed to the neutral and aggressive adult models.

- **Which group has the higher mean?**

- **How does the size of the difference between the means compare with the standard deviations of the scores in the two groups?**

Pivoting the output table

Pivot the output table as described in Section 2.4.1 so that the headings *Neutral*, *Aggressive* and *Total* become those of columns rather than rows.

Closing SPSS

Close SPSS as described in Section 2.5.

EXERCISE 2

Questionnaire data

Introduction

Exercises 2 to 7 in this and later chapters are concerned with the preparation and entry of data into SPSS, and with various **exploratory data analysis (EDA)** procedures such as calculating descriptive statistics, drawing graphs, transforming and selecting data and so on.   In this Exercise, the reader is asked to complete a short questionnaire and to enter the data from it into SPSS. In Exercise 3, your own data will be merged with a larger data set, consisting of the responses of *334* other people to the same questionnaire. Subsequently, the combined file will be used as the data set for the various EDA procedures described in later exercises.

A questionnaire

Please complete the questionnaire below by writing in, on the table itself, the appropriate values or circling the appropriate options. It is sufficient to enter your age as a whole number of years. Enter your weight either, in traditional British units, as so-many stones plus so-many pounds (e.g. 8 in the upper box, 7 in the lower box if your weight is 8 stones 7 pounds) or, in metric units, as so-many kilos. Similarly, if you wish to give your height in British units, fill in two values, one for feet, the other for inches (e.g., 5 feet, 3 inches); whereas in metric units enter a single value, expressed to two places of decimals (1.52 metres).

What is your age?	Years			
What is your sex?	Male	1	Female	2
What is your Faculty of study?	Arts	1	Science	2
	Medicine	3	Other	4
What is your status?	Undergraduate	1	MSc postgraduate	2
	PhD postgraduate	3	Other	4
What is your approximate weight? Use British or metric measures				
British units			Stones	
			Pounds	
Metric units			Kilograms	

What is your approximate height? Use British or metric measures		
British units	Feet	
	Inches	
Metric units	Metres (include	
	two decimal places)	
Do you smoke?	Yes 1 No 2	
If so, how many a day?		

Having filled in the questionnaire in the usual way with pen or pencil, we are now going to ask you to do the same thing electronically, that is, by creating an SPSS file and entering your own data. The file will be saved for further use.

Opening SPSS

Log in to SPSS as described in Section 2.2. Select the radio button for **Type in data** from the opening **SPSS 15** window and click **OK**. If **Data View** appears first, click the **Variable View** tab to open **Variable View**.

Entering the data into the Data Editor

Data entry has two aspects:

Within **Variable View**, naming the variables and specifying their properties.   Note that category variables such as *Sex*, *Faculty*, *Status* and *Smoker* must be specified as **Nominal** within the **Measure** column.

Within **Data View**, entering the data into the named columns representing the variables previously specified in **Variable View.**

Variable names, provided they conform to the rules for naming variables (Section 2.3.1), are normally a matter of individual preference. In this exercise, however, we have to take account of the fact that your data will later be merged with another (large) data set consisting of information from many people on the same variables.   That operation requires that the corresponding variables in both data sets must have **exactly the same variable names**. It is also essential that you use the same **values** as in the larger data set (e.g. *1* for *Male*, *2* for *Female*). For this reason we ask you to use the following variable names and values:

CaseNo	(Add a variable label *Case number* - see below)
MyName	(Specify your name as a **string variable** - see below)
Age	
Sex	(Enter the numerical values and their value labels: *1* for *Male*, *2* for *Female* - see below)
Faculty	(Add values and value labels: *1* for *Arts*, *2* for *Science*, *3* for *Medicine*, *4* for *Other* - see below)
Status	(Add values and value labels: *1* for *Undergrad*, *2* for *MSc postgrad*, *3* for *PhD postgrad*, *4* for *Other* - see below)

Stones

Pounds

Kilos

Feet

Inches

Metres

Smoker   (Add values and value labels: 1 for Yes, 2 for No - see below)

NpDay   (Add the variable label Number of Cigarettes per Day - see below)

You will have noticed that the questionnaire did not ask for your name; nor indeed are names included in the large data set we shall be dealing with presently. Nevertheless, we ask you to include your name in the file you are building in order to clarify some aspects of file merging in SPSS.

In **Variable View**, enter all the variable names in the **Name** column, using the methods described in Section 2.3.1. In the **Type** column, retain **numeric** format (the default type) for all the variables except Name for which a **string** format (**alphanumeric**, or letters and numbers) will be used. In general, we recommend using the numeric format wherever possible: e.g. we prefer to enter qualitative variables such as gender, nationality or blood group as numeric grouping variables, taking care to **assign meaningful value labels** to the code numbers.

The string option for **Type** is selected by clicking anywhere in the corresponding cell of the **Type** column and then clicking the ellipsis (…) on the right to open the **Variable Type** dialog box. Select the **String** radio button and click **OK** to return to **Variable View**. You should also expand the column labelled **Width** to, say, *25* and copy and paste that value to **Columns** to allow your name to be entered in **Data View**.

While working in **Variable View**, use the **Values** column to assign value labels to the code numbers for *Sex, Faculty, Status* and *Smoker*. It is also useful to include a fuller description of any variable in the **Label** column, especially if the variable name is opaque (e.g. *Number of Cigarettes per Day* is clearer than *NpDay*).   In the **Measures** column, all the non-string variables are **Scale** except *Sex, Faculty, Status* and *Smoker* which must be specified as **Nominal**.

The data are much easier to read if no decimals are displayed for any variable except *Metres* for which two decimal places will be required. Change the number in the **Decimals** column to *0* for all the variables except *Metres*, for which the default value *2* should be retained. Note that, for those respondents giving their weights or heights in British units, two SPSS variables will be allocated to each measure: *Stones* and *Pounds* for weight, and *Feet* and *Inches* for height. Those responding in metric units will enter their data in the *Kilos* and *Metres* variables. In Exercise 5, we shall be transforming British Units into metric units, so there is no need to worry about not knowing your metric measurements.

After specifying all the variables and their characteristics, click the **Data View** tab at the foot of **Variable View** to open **Data View** as described in Section 2.3.2. Enter your data along the first row, putting a *1* for your *Case*, typing in your name, age, a value for your sex, a value for your faculty and so on. If you do not smoke, do not enter anything in the *NpDay* column.

If you wish to enter your weight in stones plus pounds, enter values in the *Stones* and *Pounds* columns; otherwise enter a single value under *Kilos*. Similarly, if you want to enter your height in British units, enter values in the *Feet* and *Inches* columns; whereas a metric entry requires only a single value in the *Metres* column.   If you have recorded your weight in pounds only, enter a *0* in the *Stones* column. If you have recorded your height in inches only, enter a *0* in the *Feet* column.

Saving the data

Once you have entered your data and checked them for accuracy, select

File➜ Save As

to obtain the **Save Data As** dialog box.

You must now decide upon a suitable destination for your file (e.g. the computer's own hard disk C, a USB memory stick, a floppy disk in drive A, or a disk drive available on a networked system). We suggest you save your own data in a folder with a name such as *SPSS 15 Book Exercises data*, which you will have to create beforehand or by selecting the icon shown in the figure below and naming a new folder.

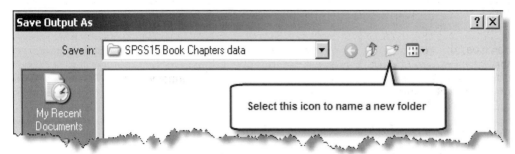

Choose **Save As** and, having made sure that *SPSS 15 Book Exercises data* is showing at the top of the dialog box, type the name *Ex2 Questionnaire Data* in the **File Name** box. Click **Save** to save your own questionnaire responses as the SPSS file *Ex2 Questionnaire Data*. You will be loading this file when you first open SPSS in the next Exercise.

Finishing the session

Close down SPSS and any other open windows before logging out of the computer.

CHAPTER 3

Editing and manipulating files

3.1   More about the SPSS Data Editor

3.2   More on the SPSS Viewer

3.3   Selecting from and manipulating data files

3.4   Importing and exporting data

3.5   Printing from SPSS

3.1   MORE ABOUT THE SPSS DATA EDITOR

3.1.1   Working in Variable View

In Section 2.2, we introduced the **Data Editor**, with its two alternative displays, **Variable View** and **Data View**. Here we describe some additional features of **Variable View** (see Section 2.3.1).

> See Section 2.3.1

Inserting new variables among those already in Variable View

An additional variable can be inserted in **Variable View** by highlighting any row (click the grey cell on the left), and choosing
Data➜Insert Variable

The new variable, with a default name such as VAR00004 (i.e. the next free name), will appear **above** the row that has been highlighted.

In **Data View,** the new variable will appear in a new column **to the left** of the variable that was highlighted in **Variable View**.

Rearranging the order of variables in Variable View

In Figure 1, is a section from **Variable View**, in which the top-to-bottom ordering of the variables determines their left-to-right order of appearance in **Data View**, which is *Case*, *Group*, then *Score*.

	Name	Type	Width	Decimals
1	Case	Numeric	8	0
2	Group	Numeric	8	0
3	Score	Numeric	8	0

Figure 1. The arrangement of the variables in **Variable View** determines their order of appearance in **Data View**

Suppose that you want to change the sequence of the variables in **Data View**: you want *Score* to appear to the left of *Group*. In **Variable View**, click the grey box to the left of the *Score* variable to highlight the whole row. Holding the left mouse button down, drag the screen pointer upwards. A red line will appear above the *Group* row. On releasing the mouse button, the variable *Score* will appear immediately under *Case* (Figure 2). In **Data View**, the variable *Score* will now appear to the left of the variable *Group*.

	Name	Type	Width	Decimals
1	Case	Numeric	8	0
2	Score	Numeric	8	0
3	Group	Numeric	8	0

Figure 2. The arrangement of variables after moving *Score* above *Group*

Large data sets: the advantages of numbering the cases

In the small data set we considered in Chapter 2, each row had a number and could be taken as representing one particular case or person. Suppose, however, that we had a much larger data set, containing thousands of cases. Suppose also that, from time to time, cases were to be removed from the data set or the data were sorted and re-sorted on different criteria. As a result, any particular row in the data set, say the 99th, may not always contain data on the same person throughout the exercise.

With a large data set like this, especially one that is continually changing, it is good practice to create, as the first variable, one with a name such as *Case*, which records each participant's original case number: 1, 2, ..., and so on. The advantage of doing this is that, even though a given person's data may occupy different rows at different points in the data-gathering exercise, the researcher always knows which data came from which person.

Should the accuracy of the transcription of a participant's data into SPSS later be called into question, that person's data can always be identified and checked throughout the entire process of data entry.

Suppose you wish to add case numbers to a data set not currently containing such a variable. This is very conveniently done, especially when the data set is large, by using the **Compute Variable** procedure as follows:

- Ensure that the data file is present in the **Data Editor**.
- In **Variable View**, click on the grey cell to the left of the first row to highlight the entire row.
- Choose
  Data➜Insert Variable
  to create a new empty row above the original first row with the default variable name *VAR00001*.
- Remove the highlighting from the row by clicking elsewhere in the grid. Click on the **Name** cell and type in the variable name *Case*.
- Adjust the **Decimals** setting to zero.
- Enter the label *Case Number* in the **Label** column.
- Choose
  Transform➜Compute…
  to open the **Compute Variable** dialog box.
- Place the cursor in the **Target Variable** slot and enter the variable name *Case*.
- Follow the instructions shown in Figure 3 and click **OK**.
- A warning box will appear with the question **Change existing variable?** Click **OK**.
- Click the **Data View** tab to confirm that a new variable named *Case* has appeared, containing the counting numbers *1, 2, … .*

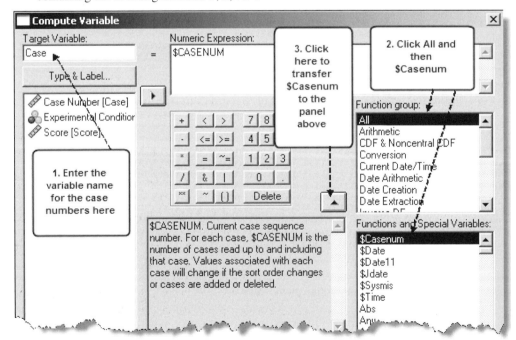

Figure 3. Part of the **Compute Variable** dialog box for generating case numbers

Note that this procedure cannot be used for creating case numbers in an empty data file. If it is desired to create case numbers before entering data, then dummy data must be entered (e.g.

entering *1* in the first row of the variable *Case* and then copying it down for as many rows as the data set will need) before using *$casenum* in the **Compute Variable** procedure. The warning box with the question **Change existing variable?** will appear as before to which the response is **OK**.

Changing the global default number of decimal places and maximum width for string variables using the Edit menu

The default settings for variable width and the number of places of decimals are *8* and *2*, respectively. If you wish to enter several new variables and display them all as whole numbers (integers), choose
Edit➔Options➔Data
and change the pre-set values. Figure 4 shows the top of the **Options** dialog box.

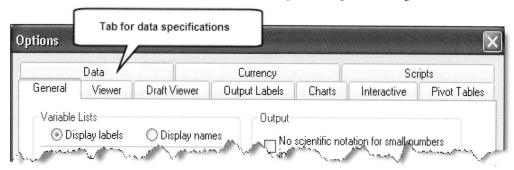

Figure 4. The top of the **Options** dialog box

- Click the tab labelled **Data**. In the new dialog box is an area headed **Display Format for New Numeric Variables** (Figure 5), in which both the width and number of decimal places can be amended.
- In the box containing the number of **Decimal Places**, click the downward arrow on the right until *0* appears. Click **OK** and the **Options** dialog box will close. The changes you have specified will apply only to any **new** numeric variables that you may create. You will find that, even after amending the default settings in **Options**, the appearance of numerical data already in **Data View** is unchanged.
- At the foot of the **Data** dialog box, is a button labelled **Apply**, which is activated when you change the settings. The purpose of the **Apply** button is to register the changes you have made **without closing the dialog box**. You can then click other tabs and make whatever changes you wish to make in those before leaving **Options** by clicking on **OK**.

If you are working on a networked computer where the software and settings are held on a central server, any changes you may make by changing the entries in **Options** may apply only for the duration of your own session: when you log off, the system will restore the original default values.

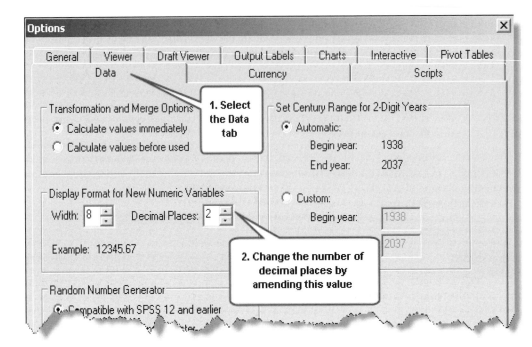

Figure 5. The **Options** dialog box showing the panel for adjusting the **Display Format for New Numeric Variables**

*Changing the type of variable (the **Type** column)*

In **Variable View**, there is a column headed **Type**. The **Type** column specifies the general form that an entry for a particular variable will take when it appears in the data set. By default, the variable type is assumed to be **numeric**, but seven other types can be specified in SPSS.

A **string** is a sequence of characters, such as a person's name, which is treated as a qualitative variable (not as a numeric variable) by the system. Had we entered, in the variable *Name*, the names of all the participants taking part in the drug experiment, *Name* would have been a **string variable**.

To create a string variable, proceed as follows:
- After typing in the name of the variable, highlight the cell in the **Type** column thus

- Click the grey area with the three dots to the right of **Numeric** to open the **Variable Type** dialog box (Figure 6).
- In the dialog box is a list of eight variable types, each with a radio button. Initially, the **Numeric** button will be marked.
- Descriptions of the different types of variable will be found by clicking the **Help** button in the dialog box.

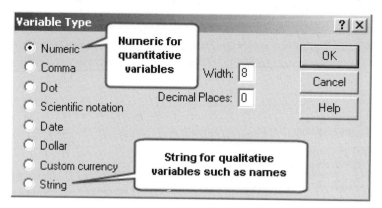

Figure 6. The **Variable Type** dialog box

- Click the **String** radio button at the foot of the list. The **Width** and **Decimal Places** boxes will immediately be replaced by a box labelled **Characters**.
- Change the default value *8* in the **Characters** box to some larger number such as *20* to accommodate the longest likely name. Do this by moving the cursor into the number box, selecting the *8* and typing in *20*.
- Click **OK**. In **Variable View**, the variable type *String* will now appear in the **Type** column and the cell for the *Name* variable in the **Width** column will now show *20*.
- Click the **Width** column and copy the specifications either by choosing **Copy** from the **Edit** menu or with the key combination **Ctrl + C**.
- Click on **Columns** and paste the new **Width** specification *(20)* there either by choosing **Paste** from the **Edit** menu or with the key combination **Ctrl + V**. The effect of this move will be to make sufficient space available in **Data View** to see the longest name in the data set. Alternatively, in **Data View**, the right-hand edge of the box containing the variable *Name* can be dragged to the right by holding down the left mouse button and dragging it as far as desired.

*Missing values (the **Missing** column)*

SPSS assumes that all data sets are complete (i.e. that the cells in every row and every column have something in them). The user, however, may not have entries for every case on every variable in the data set (e.g. a participant's age might not have been recorded). Such missing entries are marked by SPSS with what is known as a **system-missing** value, which is indicated in the **Data Editor** by a full stop. SPSS will exclude system-missing values from its calculations of means, standard deviations and other statistics.

It may be, however, that for some purposes the user wishes SPSS to treat certain responses actually present in the data set as missing data. For example, suppose that, in an examination, some candidates either walked out the moment they saw the paper or, having attempted at least some of the examination, earned only a nominal mark (say 20% or less) from the examiner. In either case, you might wish to treat the candidate's response as a missing value, but for some purposes you might want to retain information about the relative frequencies of the two responses in the output. In SPSS terminology, the user wants certain responses to be treated as **user-missing** values (as opposed to **system-missing** values).

Suppose you want SPSS to treat as missing:
1. Any marks between *0* and *20*.
2. Cases where the candidate walked out without giving any written response at all.

A walk-out could be coded as an arbitrary, but salient, number, such as -9: the negative sign helps the number to stand out as impossible mark.

To define such user-missing values:
- In **Variable View**, move the cursor to the **Missing** column and click on the appropriate cell for the variable concerned.
- Click the grey area with the ellipsis ⬚ to the right of **None** to open the **Missing Values** dialog box.
- Initially, the **No missing values** radio button is marked. The three text boxes underneath give the user the opportunity to specify up to three **Discrete Missing Values**, referred to in SPSS as *missing (1)*, *missing (2)*, and *missing (3)*. These may either be numerical, as with a grouping variable, or short string variables (up to 8 characters in length), but they must be consistent with the original variable type. In the case of a string variable, the procedure is case sensitive. The other options in the dialog box are for scale (quantitative) variables: the user may define a missing value as one falling within a specified range, or one that falls either within a specified range or within a specified category.
- Click the **Range plus one discrete missing value** button. Enter the values *0* and *20* into the **Low** and **High** boxes, respectively, and *-9* into the **Discrete value** box. The completed dialog box is shown in Figure 7.
- Click **OK** and the values will appear in the **Missing** column cell.

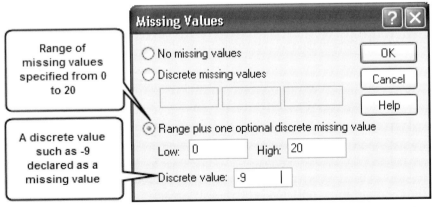

Figure 7. The completed **Missing Values** dialog box showing a range of missing values between *0* and *20* and a discrete value of -9

As with the attributes of number of decimals places and width, missing value specifications can be copied to other variables by pasting them into the appropriate cells.

*Data alignment (the **Align** column)*

In **Data View**, by default, numbers are right-aligned and strings are left-aligned. These settings can be changed by clicking on the appropriate cell in the **Align** column and choosing **Left**, **Right** or **Center**.

*Measurement level (the **Measure** column)*

The default measurement level is **Scale** for numeric variables and **Nominal** for **String** variables. Although a grouping variable refers to a set of qualitative categories, its representation in SPSS is still numeric, because it is a set of code numbers for the groups or conditions; it should be specified as **Nominal** within the **Measure** column in **Variable View**. In most chart-drawing and table-producing procedures, it is imperative that category variables are specified as **Nominal**.

3.1.2　Working in Data View

In Sections 2.3.2 and 2.3.3, the entry of data in **Data View** was briefly considered. Here we shall describe some additional features of **Data View**.

> See Sections 2.3.2 & 2.3.3

Reading in SPSS files

- When the opening SPSS window appears, select **Open an existing data source**.
- Select the appropriate file. (If you are working on a networked computer, you may have to click **More files ...** and locate the file or folder containing the file.)
- Click **OK** to load the data file into **Data View**.

Alternatively, one of the following methods can be used:

- Click the radio button of the opening SPSS window labelled **Type in data** and then **OK** to bring **Data View** to the screen. Select
  File➔Open➔Data
  to show the **Open File** dialog box. The target file can then be specified.
- If SPSS has not yet been opened, you can use the Windows **Find** menu or **My Computer** to locate the file, which should open SPSS with the data loaded in **Data View** (or the variables loaded in **Variable View**) when the file name is double-clicked. Sometimes, especially with networked computers, it may be necessary to open SPSS first. While data are being read into **Data View** from a file, the hour-glass will appear and messages will appear in the **Status Bar** at various stages in the operation. The message **SPSS Processor is ready** signals the end of the reading process.

*Entering data into **Data View** before specifying variables in **Variable View***

Although we strongly recommend that you lay the foundations in **Variable View** before actually entering the data in **Data View**, it is possible to begin immediately to enter data into **Data View**. It is also possible to copy blocks of data directly into **Data View**, which can be useful when you are importing data from another application which does not have one of the many data formats recognised by SPSS. The details of the variables can be added in **Variable View** later.

- Choose **File➔New** to create an empty SPSS data file.
- Enter **Data View** and type the value *23* into the cell in the second row of the fourth column. **Data View** will now appear as in Figure 8.

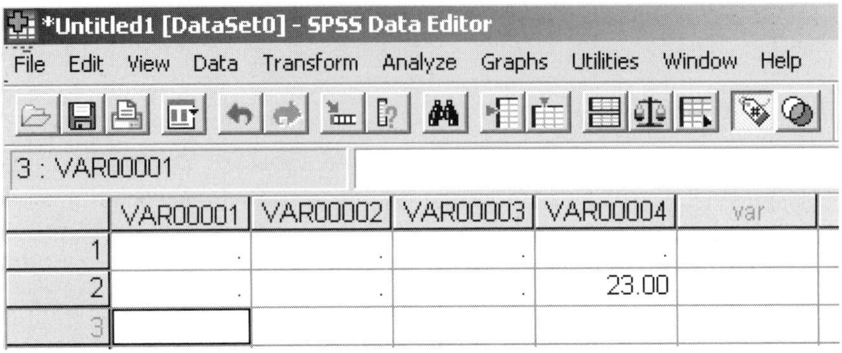

Figure 8. The appearance of **Data View** after entering a datum without previously naming variables in **Variable View**

The fourth variable has now been given the default name *VAR00004*. Notice that SPSS has assumed that we have a 2 × 4 matrix of data and filled in the blank cells with the system-missing symbol. Should you type values into cells to the right of the fourth column, more default variable names will appear as SPSS expands the supposed data matrix to include the new column and row. If you click on a cell underneath the lowest row of dots, more rows of dots will appear, the lowest of which contains the cell you have just clicked.

To assign meaningful names and labels to the default variables visible in **Data View**, switch to **Variable View** and assign the specifications there. You can either enter **Variable View** in the usual way by clicking the **Variable View** tab at the bottom of **Data View** or double-click the default heading of the variable you wish to name. Either way, when you enter **Variable View**, you will see that the default variable names have been entered there. In other words, the two display modes of the **Data Editor** are interchangeable in the order in which they are completed.

Inserting additional variables while working in Data View

To add a new variable **to the right of those already in Data View**, you have only to type a value into a cell to the right of the present matrix of data. To add a new column **between two of those within the present data set**,

- Highlight the variable **to the right of** the intended position of the new variable.
- Choose
  Data➔Insert Variable
  to create a new, empty, variable to the left of the variable you have highlighted.

Rearranging the variables in Data View

Suppose that in **Data View**, the order of the variables is *Case*, *Group* and *Score*, and you want to change the order to *Case*, *Score* and *Group*.   We recommend that you do this in **Variable View** (see Section 3.1.1), but the following procedure works in **Data View**.
* Create a new, empty variable to the left of *Group* in the manner described above.
* Click on the grey cell at the head of the *Score* column to highlight the whole column.
* Choose
  Edit➔Cut
  to remove the *Score* variable and place it in the clipboard.
* Click the grey cell at the head of the new, empty variable to highlight the whole column.
* Use **Edit** and **Paste** to move the *Score* variable including its data and definitions into its new position to the left of *Group*.

Adding new cases

Columns can be lengthened by choosing
Data➔Insert cases
which will have the effect of adding new empty rows underneath the existing columns.

There are occasions, however, when you may want to place rows for additional cases in the middle of the data set. Suppose that, in the drug experiment, you want to add data on an additional participant who has been tested under the *Placebo* condition. Proceed as follows.
* Click the grey cell on the left of the row of data **above** which you want to insert the new case. (This will be the row of data for the first participant who performed under the Drug condition.) The row will now be highlighted.
* Choose
  Data➔Insert Cases
  to create a new empty row above the one you highlighted.

You can now type in the data from the additional placebo participant.

Validation of data

When entering data into a data file, especially a large file, it is possible to mistype a value (e.g. 100 for 10) or when adding more data, to duplicate a case number. In this subsection we look at a way of checking for aberrant data and in the next subsection a way for detecting duplicate values.

SPSS provides a means of checking out the validity of data within the **Validation** item of the **Data** menu where various rules can be specified either for individual variables or across all variables. For example, suppose we wish to check that no score greater than 20 and no case number greater than 50 have been entered into our data set.
* From the drop-down **Data** menu, choose
  Validation➔Define Rules… to access the **Define Validation Rules** dialog box (Figure 9).
* Within the **Rule Definition** window, change the **Name** *SingleVarRule1* to *Range of Scores*, enter the values 1 and 20 into the **Minimum** and **Maximum** boxes respectively.

- Click **New** and then repeat the procedure but this time replacing *SingleVarRule1* with *Case Number* and enter the values 1 and 50 into the **Minimum** and **Maximum** boxes respectively. Additional rules can be added as desired. Finally click **OK**.

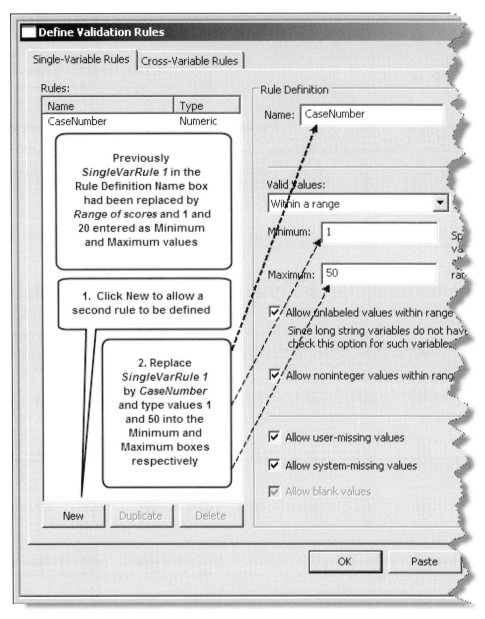

Figure 9. The Define Validation Rules dialog box with two rules defined

Having defined the rules, the next step is to validate the data by applying the rules. For illustration, imagine that three more cases have been entered in the data file, one with a case number of 21 and a score of 15, another with a case number of 22 and a score of 20 and another with a case number of 200 and a score of 8.

- From the drop-down **Data** menu, choose **Validation➜Validate Data…** to access the **Validate Data** dialog box.
- Select the variable *Score* in the **Variables** box and click ▶ to transfer it to the **Analysis Variables** box   Do likewise with *Case Number* (Figure 10) and then click the **Single-Variable Rules** tab to open the **Single-Variables Rules** dialog box (Figure 11).
- Click the variable names and the check boxes as shown in Figure 12 and then **OK**.

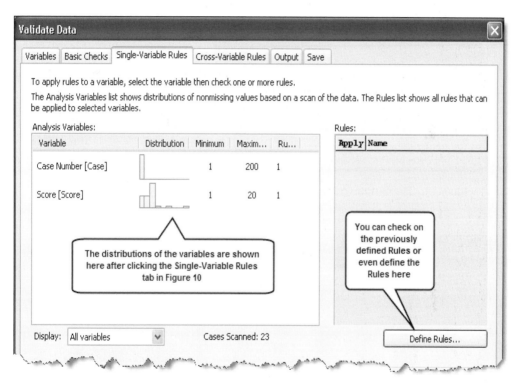

Figure 10. Part of the **Validate Data** dialog box showing the transfer of variable names

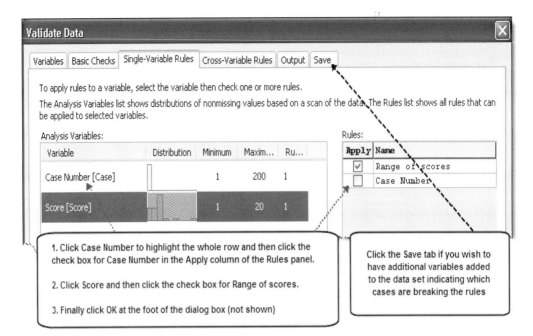

Figure 11. The **Single-Variable Rules** dialog box of the **Validate Data** procedure

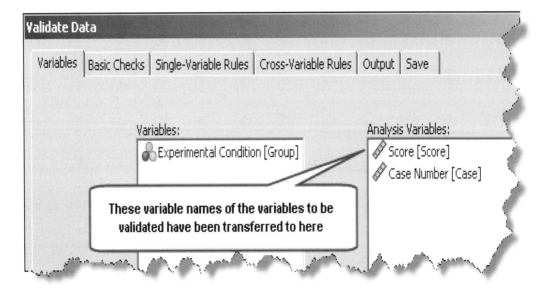

Figure 12. The **Single-Variables Rules** dialog box with the rules checked for each variable

The output of the validation starts with a table of **Rule Descriptions** (not reproduced here) followed by two tables listing the number of violations and their case numbers for each variable analysed (Output 1). One out-of-range *Case Number* and two out-of-range *Scores* have been detected.

Variable Summary

	Rule	Number of Violations
Case Number	Case Number	1
	Total	1
Score	Range of scores	2
	Total	2

Case Report

Case	Validation Rule Violations Single-Variable [a]
21	Range of scores (1)
22	Range of scores (1)
23	Case Number (1)

a. The number of variables that violated the rule follows each rule.

Output 1. Two of the tables in the output showing that one Case Number and two Scores were out-of-range, namely Cases 21, 22 and 23

Identifying duplicate cases

Sometimes, especially when incrementing a data set with fresh cases, it is useful to ensure that the same case number is not duplicated. SPSS provides a routine for checking out possible duplications in any variable.

- From the drop-down **Data** menu, choose
  Identify Duplicates Cases … to access the **Identify Duplicate Cases** dialog box (Figure 13). Click the variable name *Case Number* and transfer it to the **Define matching cases by** window.
- Assuming that later cases with the same case numbers have been incorrectly numbered, click the radio button **First case in each group is primary** to replace the default option that the **Last case in each group is primary**.
- Click **OK**.

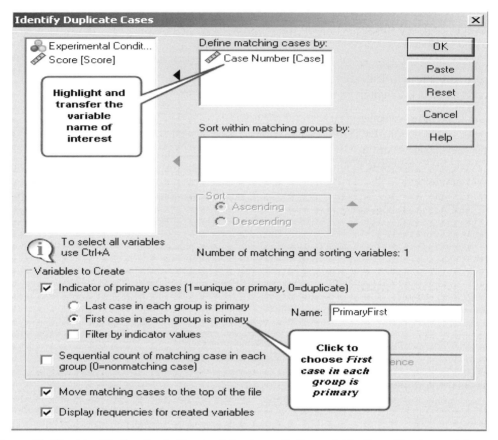

Figure 13. The **Identify Duplicate Cases** dialog box with the variable *Case Number* and the **First Case in each group is primary** option selected

For illustration, assume that another case has been added to the file with a case number of 20. After clicking **OK** in the **Identify Duplicate Cases** dialog box, the data file would appear with the duplicated cases at the top (Figure 14). The case with 1 in the *PrimaryFirst* column is the original case, the most recently added case (with 0 in the *PrimaryFirst* column) is the one with the duplicate case number. The **SPSS Viewer** also contains tables (not reproduced) showing how many duplicated cases there are.

Case	Group	Score	PrimaryFirst
20	2	10	1
20	2	7	0
1	1	6	1
2	1	5	1
3	1	5	1
4	1	1	1

Figure 14. The first few cases of the data set showing the original and the duplicated cases

3.2   MORE ON THE SPSS VIEWER

We described the **SPSS Viewer** in part of Section 2.4.1 and how the output can be edited. The **Viewer** consists of two panes (see Output 1 in Chapter 2), the widths of which can be adjusted by clicking and dragging the vertical bar separating them.   The left pane lists the items of output in order of their appearance in the right pane, each item having an icon and a title.

See
Section
2.4.1

The icon shows whether the item is visible in the right pane (open-book icon) or invisible (closed-book icon). By double-clicking the icon, the item can be made visible or invisible in the right pane, where all actual output is presented. The output can also be rearranged by moving the appropriate icons around in the left pane by clicking and dragging them. A single click on an item in the left pane will bring the item into view in the right pane. Unwanted items in the output can be deleted by highlighting them in the left pane and pressing the **Delete** key. In this book, only selections from the right pane will normally be reproduced.

Report

Score

Experimental Condition	Mean	N	Std. Deviation	Median
Placebo	3.40	10	1.838	3.50
Drug	6.90	10	1.449	6.50
Total	5.15	20	2.412	5.50

Output 2. Output from **Compare Means** procedure, with means, sample sizes, standard deviations and medians

In Section 2.4.1 we tabulated the results of the Drug experiment using the **Compare Means** procedure. Here (see Output 2) we have added a column of medians by clicking **Options...** in the **Means** dialog box and transferring **Median** from the **Statistics** panel to the **Cell Statistics** panel. (It is often a good idea, when exploring data, to compare means with medians: if they have similar values, symmetrical distributions are suggested. Here, however, the medians have been included merely to demonstrate some editing in the **Viewer**.)

3.2.1   Editing the output

In Section 2.4.1, we demonstrated that the output in the **SPSS Viewer** could be edited by showing the effect of a pivoting procedure. Here we consider some more ways of improving the appearance of the output.

To edit an item, say a table, in the **Viewer**, double-click it. The table will now be surrounded by a hatched box indicating that you are now in the **Viewer**'s editor. Once a selected item has been surrounded by a hatched box, the following changes can be made:

• To **widen or narrow columns**, move the cursor on to a vertical line in the table and click and drag the line to the left or the right.

• Items can be **deleted** by highlighting them and pressing the **Delete** key.

• **Whole columns or rows** can be **deleted** by highlighting them and pressing the **Delete** key (see below for details).

- **Text** can sometimes be altered by double-clicking an item and deleting letters or typing in new ones.
- If values are listed, it is possible to re-specify the number of decimal places shown by highlighting the numbers concerned in a block, pressing the **right-hand** mouse button, selecting **Cell Properties…** and changing the specification in the **Cell Properties** dialog box.

For example, suppose that, in the **Report** table (Output 2), we want to dispense with the third row (*Total*) containing the statistics of all twenty scores in the data set considered as a single group and also the column of **Medians**.

- Click the left cell in the bottom row.
- Press the **Ctrl** button and, keeping it pressed, click the other cells in the *Total* row and the numbers in the *Median* column. The **Report** table will now appear as in Output 3.

Report

Variables	Score			
Experimental Condition	Mean	N	Std. Deviation	Median
Placebo	3.40	10	1.838	3.50
Drug	6.90	10	1.449	6.50
Total	5.15	20	2.412	5.50

Output 3. Highlighting material to be deleted

- Press the **Delete** key to remove the bottom row and the rightmost column.
- Click outside the shaded border to leave the **Editor**. The **Report** table will now appear as in Output 4.

Report

Score

Experimental Condition	Mean	N	Std. Deviation
Placebo	3.40	10	1.838
Drug	6.90	10	1.449

Output 4. The edited **Report** table after removing the *Total* row and *Median* column

3.2.2   More advanced editing

The **Data Editor** offers even more powerful editing facilities, some of which can radically alter the appearance of a default table such as the **Report** table we have been editing. Many of the tables in the output are **pivot tables**, that is, tables in which the columns and rows can be transposed and to which other radical alterations can be made.

In Chapter 2, we showed how, by choosing **Pivot➜Transpose Rows and Columns** we could change the rows of the default **Report** table into columns and vice versa (see Section 2.4.1). Here we illustrate the manipulation of a

See Section 2.4.1

three-way table of means.

A three-way table of means

It is well known that generally females are better at recalling verbal material and males are better at recalling graphic material. An experiment was carried out recalling verbal or graphic items after either a short, medium or long period of inspection of the items. Male and female participants were each divided into six subgroups looking at verbal or graphic items for the three inspection times.

Coding variables for *Sex*, *Task*, and *Inspection Time* were named in **Variable View** along with *Score* for the number of items recalled. Corresponding **Labels** were specified as *Sex*, *Type of Task*, *Inspection Time* and *Number of Items Recalled*. The **Means...** procedure with *Number of Items Recalled* entered in the **Dependent List** and each of *Sex*, *Type of Task* and *Inspection Time* entered as layers in the **Independent List** generated Output 5 when only **Mean** was selected for the **Cell Statistics** box within **Options**. The rows for Total have been edited out of Output 5 for simplicity.

It is possible to effect a simple transposition of all the rows in Output 5 into columns and vice versa by choosing **Transposing rows and Columns** from the **Pivot** menu. There is little to be gained from this, however, because of the complexity of the table. To improve the clarity of the table, we want to select individual variables for transposition. This finer control is achieved by using the **Pivoting Trays** procedure.

- After highlighting the **Report** table (Output 5) by double-clicking anywhere within it, choose **Pivot➔Pivoting Trays** to obtain the **Pivoting Trays1** display shown in Figure 15.

Report

Mean

Sex	Type of Task	Inspection Time	Number of Items Recalled
Male	Verbal	Short	4.00
		Medium	5.00
		Long	5.00
	Graphic	Short	2.67
		Medium	3.67
		Long	4.00
Female	Verbal	Short	5.33
		Medium	5.67
		Long	6.33
	Graphic	Short	1.67
		Medium	2.33
		Long	3.33

Output 5. The output from the **Mean** procedure

The icons in the grey borders represent the dimensions of the table, the identity of which can be seen by placing the screen pointer on the icon. The best way to see how the pivoting trays work is to click and drag the icons to other grey borders in the display and observe the resulting changes in the table of means.

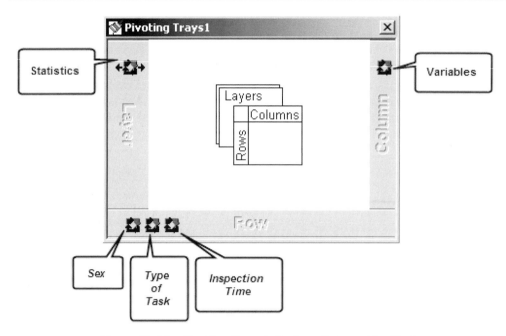

Figure 15. The **Pivoting Trays1** display with icons identified

From left to right, the three icons in the bottom **Row** border represent the variables *Sex*, *Type of Task* and *Inspection Time* respectively, which is the order in which these three dimensions appear in the table. This order can be changed by clicking and dragging the three icons to different positions. For example, if we click and drag the present rightmost icon (*Inspection Time*) to the left of the other two icons, that dimension will now appear in the leftmost position

Report

Mean

Inspection Time	Sex	Type of Task	Number of Items Recalled
Short	Male	Verbal	4.00
		Graphic	2.67
	Female	Verbal	5.33
		Graphic	1.67
Medium	Male	Verbal	5.00
		Graphic	3.67
	Female	Verbal	5.67
		Graphic	2.33
Long	Male	Verbal	5.00
		Graphic	4.00
	Female	Verbal	6.33
		Graphic	3.33

in the table (Output 6).

Output 6. The appearance of the table after the order of the icons in the **Rows** margin of the pivoting trays has been changed (compare with Output 5)

In Outputs 4 and 5, the labels of the three factors in the experiment are all in rows. Should we wish to retain the levels of *Sex* and *Type of Task* in rows, but move those of *Inspection Time* into columns, we need only click and drag the icons for *Inspection Time* from the grey margin labelled **Row** to the right-hand grey margin labelled **Column** (Figure 16).

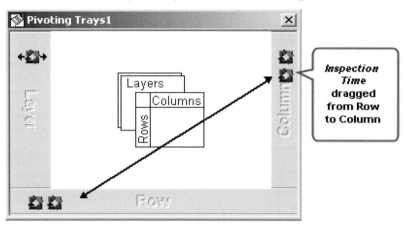

Figure 16. The *Inspection Time* icon has been dragged to the **Column** margin

The effect of this manipulation is that, whereas the two types of *Sex* and *Type of Task* will appear in rows as before, the three levels of *Inspection Time* now appear at the heads of three columns (Output 7).

Report

Mean

| Sex | Type of Task | Number of Items Recalled | | |
| | | Inspection Time | | |
		Short	Medium	Long
Male	Verbal	4.00	5.00	5.00
	Graphic	2.67	3.67	4.00
Female	Verbal	5.33	5.67	6.33
	Graphic	1.67	2.33	3.33

Output 7. Edited table in which *Inspection Time* has been transposed to columns

The left grey margin of the pivot tray is labelled **Layer**. A **layer** is a tabulation at one particular level of another factor. In the tables we have looked at so far, all the dimensions have been shown. Suppose, however, that we want to view the two-way table of means for *Type of Task* and *Inspection Time* for each level of *Sex*. Simply click and drag the *Sex* icon from the grey **Rows** margin of the pivot tray to the **Layer** margin (Figure 17). The table will now appear as in Output 8.

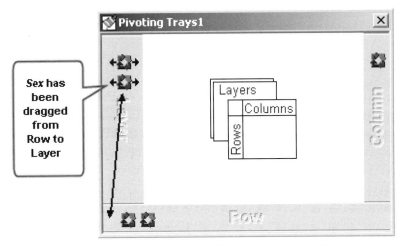

Figure 17. The *Sex* icon has been dragged from Row to Layer

We can see the means for *Type of Task* and *Inspection Time* only for the Male level of *Sex*. To see the means for Female, simply click on the arrow to the right of Male and select Female.

Report

| Statistics | Mean ▼ |
| Sex | Male ▼ |

Type of Task	Inspection Time	Number of Items Recalled
Verbal	Short	4.00
	Medium	5.00
	Long	5.00
Graphic	Short	2.67
	Medium	3.67
	Long	4.00

Output 8. A layered table, in which the means for *Type of Task* and *Inspection Time* are displayed at only one level of *Sex*. The means for Female can be seen by clicking the arrow to the right of Male and selecting Female

3.2.3 Tutorials in SPSS

The SPSS package now includes some excellent tutorials on various aspects of the system, including the use of the **Viewer** and the manipulation of pivot tables.

To access a tutorial choose:
Help➜Tutorial
and double-click to open the tutorial menu. The buttons in the right-hand bottom corner of each page of the tutorial enable the user to see the list of items (magnifier) and to navigate forward and backward through the tutorial (right and left arrows).

3.3 SELECTING FROM AND MANIPULATING DATA FILES

So far, the emphasis has been upon the construction of a complete data set, the saving of that set to a file on disk, and its retrieval from storage. There are occasions, however, on which the user will want to operate selectively on the data. It may be, for instance, that only some of the cases in a data set are of interest (those contributed by the participants in one category alone, perhaps); or the user may wish to exclude participants with outlying values on specified variables. In this section, some of these more specialised manoeuvres will be described.

Transformation and recoding of data will be discussed in Chapter 4.

3.3.1 Selecting cases

Let us assume that, in **Data View**, we have the results of the Drug experiment. In the original data set, there were two variables: *Experimental Condition* and *Score*. Suppose, however, that a *Gender* variable has been added, where *1 = Male* and *2 = Female*, and that we want to examine the data from the female participants only.

- Choose
  Data➜Select Cases...
  to obtain the **Select Cases** dialog box (see Figure 18).
- Initially, the **All cases** radio button is marked. Click the **Select Cases: If** button and complete the **Select Cases: If** dialog box as shown in Figure 19.
- Return to the **Select Cases** dialog box and click **OK** to select only the female participants for analysis.

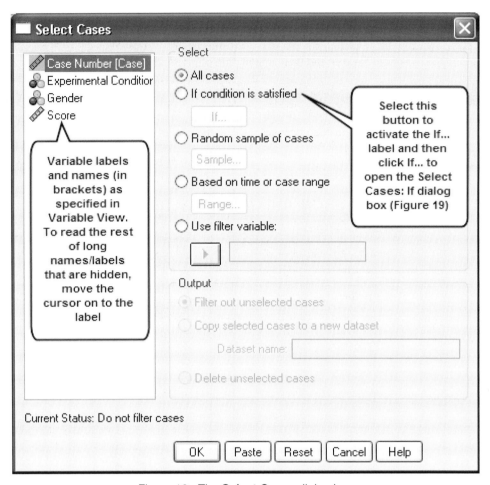

Figure 18. The **Select Cases** dialog box

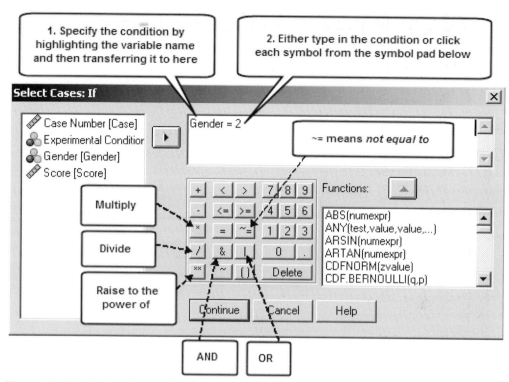

Figure 19. The **Select Cases: If** dialog box with the expression for selecting only Gender 2 (the female participants)

A section of **Data View** is shown in Figure 20. Another column, headed *filter_$*, has now appeared, containing the entries *Not Selected* and *Selected*. Note that, although the name *filter_$* will appear in subsequent dialog boxes, it should not be selected as a variable for analysis because it will only report the number of selected cases.

	Case	Group	Gender	Score	filter_$
1	1	Placebo	Male	6	Not Selected
2	2	Placebo	Female	5	Selected
3	3	Placebo	Male	5	Not Selected
4	4	Placebo	Female	1	Selected
5	5	Placebo	Male	2	Not Selected
6	6	Placebo	Female	3	Selected
7	7	Placebo	Male	2	Not Selected

Figure 20. **Data View**, showing that only the scores of the female participants will be included in the analysis. The oblique bars are deselected cases

The row numbers of the unselected cases (the males) have been marked with an oblique bar. This is a useful indicator of **case selection status.** The status bar (if enabled at the foot of **Data View**) will carry the message **Filter On**. Any further analyses of the data set will exclude cases where *Gender = 1.*

Case selection can be **cancelled** as follows:
- From the **Data menu**, choose **Select Cases** and (in the **Select Cases** dialog box) click **All cases**.
- Click **OK**.

3.3.2   Aggregating data

In a School of Business Studies, students take a selection of five courses each. (There is a degree of choice, so that different students may take somewhat different selections of courses.) On the basis of their performance, the students are marked on a percentage scale. We shall be concerned with the marks of ten of the students, whose marks on the five courses they took are contained in the SPSS data file *Students marks* and reproduced in the Appendix to this Chapter. Figure 21 is a section of **Data View**, showing some of their marks.

	Student	Course	Mark
1	Anne	Accountancy	80
2	Rebecca	Accountancy	78
3	Susan	Accountancy	87
4	Anne	Computing	49
5	Fred	Computing	55
6	Rebecca	Computing	65
7	Susan	Computing	56
8	Anne	German	40
9	Fred	German	72
10	Jim	German	73

Figure 21.   Part of the file *Students marks* in **Data View**

*Finding course averages: The **Aggregate** procedure*

Suppose we want to find the mean mark for each of the courses that were taken. SPSS's **Aggregate** procedure groups cases according to the nominal variable specified (e.g. *Course*) and then aggregates the values of the quantitative variable specified (e.g. *Mark*). Various options are available for how the aggregation is done (e.g. mean, median, percentage above a specified value). We shall use the **Aggregate** procedure to group the marks according to course and calculate the mean mark for each course.

Choose
Data➜Aggregate…
to obtain the **Aggregate Data** dialog box.

In the **Aggregate Data** dialog box, the **Break Variable** is the variable on the basis of which the marks are to be grouped (i.e. *Course*). The **Aggregated Variable** is the mark that a student received (i.e. *Mark*). In case of unintentional actions, it is wiser to create a new dataset or a new file rather than replace the active dataset. A new dataset is created by clicking the radio button **Create a new dataset containing only the aggregated variables** in the bottom left corner of the dialog box. Type in a name for the dataset such as *CourseMarks* – see Figure 22 for the completed dialog box.

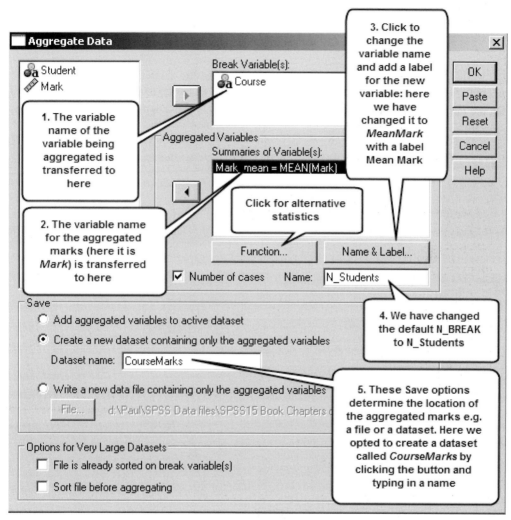

Figure 22. The completed **Aggregate Data** dialog box. The results of the aggregated marks for courses will be saved in the variable *MeanMark* within the dataset *CourseMarks* along with the count of cases in the variable *N_Students*

Notice that in the **Aggregated Variable(s)** panel is the expression Mark_mean = MEAN(Mark). Unless otherwise instructed, SPSS will calculate the mean mark for each course. You can choose another statistic (such as the Median) by clicking on the **Function...** button and changing the specification. You can also change the variable name and specify a variable label by clicking **Name & Label...** and completing the dialog box. Here the variable has been named as *MeanMark* with a label *Mean Mark*.

Since the students had a degree of choice and some courses were more popular than others, the means calculated by the **Aggregate** procedure are based on varying sample sizes. It is therefore wise to request the inclusion of sample sizes by clicking the checkbox **Number of cases** and changing the variable name from *N_Break* to a more meaningful one such as *N_Students*. Finally click **OK**.

To see the results of the aggregation, you need to open the new dataset *CourseMarks* (Figure 23) by clicking *Untitled[CourseMarks]* along the foot of the screen. The dataset shows the mean mark (*Mean*) awarded to the students taking each of the courses that were selected and the size of the sample of marks from which the mean was calculated in the column *N_Students*.

	Course	MeanMark	N_Students
1	Accountancy	81.67	3
2	Computing	56.25	4
3	German	67.50	4
4	Graphics	57.43	7
5	Law	82.88	8
6	Management	50.43	7
7	Mathematics	63.67	6
8	Politics	51.00	5
9	Spanish	57.33	3
10	Statistics	67.33	3

Figure 23. Mean mark on each of the courses together with the number of students who took each course in the new dataset *CourseMarks*

Note that if the **Add aggregated variables to active dataset** button in Figure 22 had been selected instead of the **Create a new dataset**... button, the mean marks would have appeared in a column alongside the students' actual marks thus allowing a comparison to be made.

3.3.3   Sorting data

Suppose that, in order to appraise the courses, you want to list them in order of the mean marks the students achieved.

• With the data file *CourseMarks* in the **Data Editor**, choose
    Data➔Sort Cases...

to obtain the **Sort Cases** dialog box. Figure 24 shows the completed dialog box.

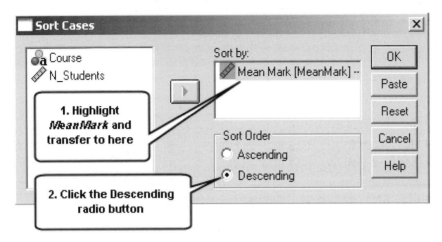

Figure 24. The completed **Sort Cases** dialog box

- Since you will probably want the marks to be arranged with the highest at the top and the lowest at the bottom, we have marked the **Descending** button in **Sort Order**. (Note, however, that in **file merging** – see below – the sort order must be the same as the file to be merged.)
- Click **OK** to see the mean marks listed in descending order of magnitude (Figure 25).

	Course	Mean	N_Students
1	Law	82.88	8
2	Accountancy	81.67	3
3	German	67.50	4
4	Statistics	67.33	3
5	Mathematics	63.67	6
6	Graphics	57.43	7
7	Spanish	57.33	3
8	Computing	56.25	4
9	Politics	51.00	5
10	Management	50.43	7

Figure 25. Results of the sorting procedure. The courses are now listed in descending order of their mean marks

3.3.4   Merging files

SPSS offers a powerful procedure known as **file merging**, which enables the user to import data into a file known as the **working file** from an **external** file. The **File Merge** procedure has two principal uses:

1. You can use it to import extra data (i.e., more cases) on **the same set of variables**.
2. You can use it to import data on **extra variables** that are not already in the working file.

*Using **Merge Files** to import more cases of the same variables from an external file*

In Chapter 2, an experiment was described in which the skilled performance of ten people who had ingested a small quantity of a supposedly performance-enhancing drug was compared with the performance of a placebo group of the same size. The scores of the twenty participants were stored in a file named *Drug Experiment*. Suppose, however, twenty more participants were to be tested under exactly the same conditions (ten under the *Placebo* condition and ten under the *Drug* condition) and the new data stored in a file named *Drug more data*.

The **Merge Files** procedure can be used to import the new data from the file *Drug more data* into the file *Drug Experiment*, so that, instead of having ten scores for each condition we shall have twenty. The success of this type of file-merging operation requires that **the specifications for the two variables must be exactly the same in both files**. Before attempting the following exercise, check both files in **Variable View** to make sure that the specifications (name, width, type, values) of the variables *Case*, *Group* and *Score* are identical.

Ensure that the file containing the original data *Drug Experiment* is in the **Data Editor**. Then
- Choose
  Data➜Merge Files➜ Add Cases ...
  to obtain the **Add Cases to [dataset name]** dialog box (Figure 26).
- Use **Browse...** to select the file *Drug more data* from wherever it is stored and click **Continue** to obtain the **Add Cases from [dataset name]** dialog box (Figure 27).
- Since both data files contain only the variables *Case*, *Group* and *Score*, the right-hand panel headed **Variables in New Active Dataset** contains *Case*, *Group* and *Score* and no variable names appear in the left-hand panel headed **Unpaired Variables**. Had the external file contained an extra variable (or variables), or a variable specification did not match between the two files, its unmatched name (or names) would have appeared in the left-hand panel.
- Click **OK** to obtain the merged file, a section of which is shown in Figure 28.
- If desired, the cases can be sorted to list all the Drug scores and then all the Placebo scores using **Sort Cases...** in the **Data** menu.

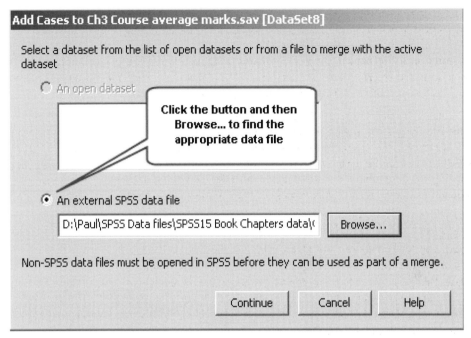

Figure 26. The **Add Cases to...** dialog box

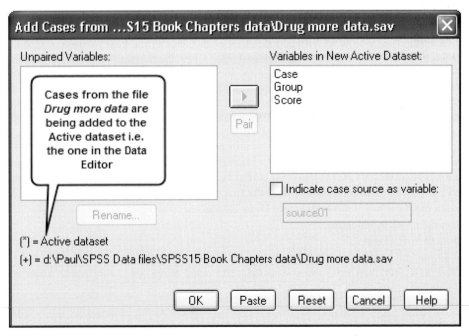

Figure 27. The **Add Cases from ...** dialog box listing the variables existing in both files

	Case	Group	Score
18	18	Drug	7
19	19	Drug	5
20	20	Drug	10
21	1	Placebo	5
22	2	Placebo	3
23	3	Placebo	6

Figure 28. A section of the merged file showing the first three cases from the file *Drug more data* added on beneath the last three cases from the file *Drug Experiment*

Using **Merge Files** *to add extra variables*

Suppose you wished to add the mean mark for the courses (using the means created by the **Aggregate** procedure in Section 3.4.2 and stored in the file *Course mean marks*) to the table of Students' Marks in the data file *Students marks* so that the students could compare their marks with the mean for their course. This can be done by the procedure **Merge Files Add Variables…**. What we are trying to do, in effect, is to look up in the *Course mean mark* file (Figure 23), the means for all the courses and assign the appropriate mean to each student taking a particular course in the original file *Students marks*. The **Merge Files** procedure uses the common variable (in this case *Course*) as a **key variable**. When matches for cases (in this example *Course*, not students) are found in the external file, the corresponding entries for the target variable *Mean* are imported into the working file.

In the terminology of SPSS, the external file *Course mean marks* is to be used as a **lookup file**, or **keyed table**. We also want **Merge Files** to use the cases of the **key variable** (i.e. *Course*) in the working file, not those in the external file, since there could be (though not in our example) courses there that were not taken by any of the students we are studying. We want matches only with those courses that are specified in the file *Students Marks*.

The success of this second kind of file-merging operation has two essential prerequisites:
1. The **specifications of the key variable** must be exactly the same in both files.
2. The cases in both files must be sorted **in ascending order of the key variable**.

In our example, *Students marks* has been sorted in alphabetic order of the *Course* name but the file of *Course mean marks* has not. Thus the first step is to do this by
• Open the file *Course mean marks* in **Data Editor**.
• Sort the cases by selecting
  Data➔Sort Cases…
  and transferring the variable name *Course* to the **Sort by** box.
• Click **OK** and then save the sorted data file using **Save As…** to *Course mean marks sorted*.

Now the **Merge Files** procedure can be started.

- Ensure that the data file *Students marks* is in the **Data Editor**.
- Choose
  Data➔Merge Files➔Add Variables...
  to obtain the **Add Variables to [dataset name]** dialog box (Figure 29).

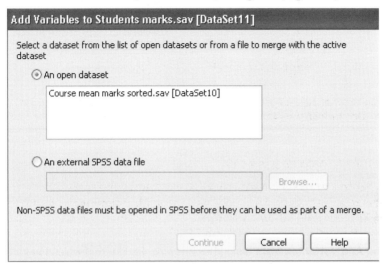

Figure 29. The **Add Variables to** dialog box for selecting the file to which the variables will be added

- Select the required file either from an open dataset (as here) by highlighting it (after which the **Continue** button will become active) or from a saved data file. Click **Continue** to obtain the **Add Variables from [dataset name]** dialog box (Figure 30).

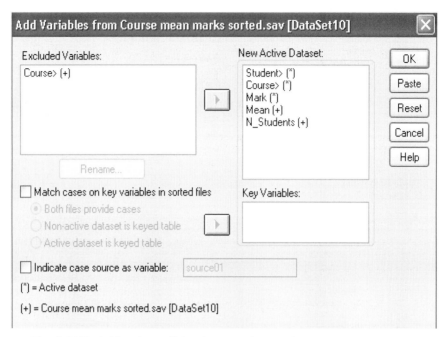

Figure 30. The **Add Variables from** dialog box showing the file from which the variables are coming and the common variables in the merged file

Notice that, for the moment, the common variable *Course* appears in the left-hand panel as an **Excluded Variable**. However, we are going to use *Course* as a **key variable** and use the non-active dataset *Course mean marks sorted* as a **look up file** or **keyed table** to import the means for each course associated with those cases of the variable *Course* that **File Merge** finds in the active data file *Students marks*. We also want to reject the variable *N_Students* from the final data file.

Proceed as follows.
- Click **Match cases on key variables in sorted files**.
- Mark the button labelled **Non-active dataset is keyed table**.
- Highlight *Course* in the **Excluded Variables** box and click on the arrow to the left of the **Key Variables** box to transfer it there.
- Click *N_Students* in the **New Active Dataset** panel to highlight it and then click on the arrow to transfer it to the **Excluded Variables** panel on the left. The completed dialog box is shown in Figure 31.
- Click **OK** to run the file merge. A section of the merged file is shown in Figure 32.

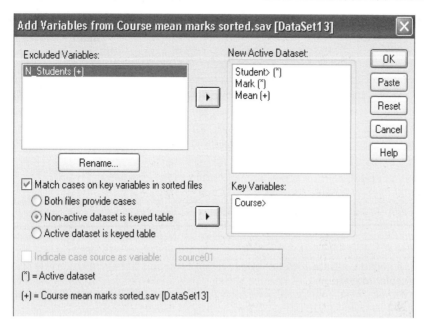

Figure 31. The completed **Add Variables from ...** dialog box showing the key variable as Course as in the non-active dataset and the exclusion of the variable N_Students

	Student	Course	Mark	Mean
1	Anne	Accountancy	80	81.67
2	Rebecca	Accountancy	78	81.67
3	Susan	Accountancy	87	81.67
4	Anne	Computing	49	56.25
5	Fred	Computing	55	56.25
6	Rebecca	Computing	65	56.25
7	Susan	Computing	56	56.25
8	Anne	German	40	67.50
9	Fred	German	72	67.50
10	Jim	German	73	67.50

Figure 32. Part of the merged file, in which the means of the courses have been 'looked up' in the non-active dataset *Course mean marks* sorted and added to the dataset *Students marks*

3.3.5   Transposing the rows and columns of a data set

In an experiment on time estimation, a researcher asks nine participants to make five verbal estimates of each of seven time intervals ranging from 10 to 40 seconds in duration. Each participant, therefore, makes a total of thirty-five judgements.

In the data set shown in Figure 33, the cases represent particular time intervals. For some purposes, such as averaging judgements across participants, we might wish to transform this data set to one in which each row represents a participant and each column represents a time interval.

	Interval	Amy	Fred	Joe	Stephen
1	10	8	120	7	8
2	10	6	10	9	7
3	10	5	20	6	10
4	10	7	5	8	9
5	10	5	10	6	11
6	15	15	25	10	13
7	15	6	8	9	12
8	15	14	12	10	12
9	15	7	8	12	12
10	15	14	10	12	15
11	20	20	60	15	18
12	20	10	18	14	15

Figure 33. A section of **Data View**, showing verbal estimates of the time intervals specified by the first variable, *Interval*

- Choose
  Data➔Transpose…
  to view the **Transpose** dialog box (Figure 34).

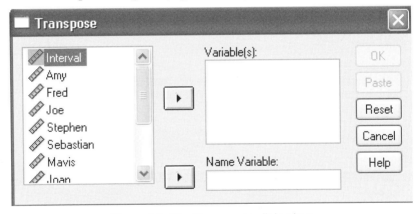

Figure 34. The **Transpose** dialog box

- Select all the variables and transfer them to the **Variable(s)** box on the right by clicking the central black arrow.
- Click **OK** to view the transposed matrix (Figure 35).

It can be seen from Figure 35 that SPSS has created a new variable *CASE_LBL* containing not only the names of the participants but also the *Interval* variable. The row containing the Interval variable should now be deleted and the default names *var001, var002, …*   replaced (in **Variable View**) with names such as *Ten1, Ten2, …, Fifteen1, Fifteen2, …*   remembering that SPSS will not allow duplication of variable names. In addition, the first variable CASE_LBL should be renamed *Name*. Part of the final transformed data set is shown in Figure 36.

1 : CASE_LBL		Interval			
	CASE LBL	var001	var002	var003	var004
1	Interval	10	10	10	10
2	Amy	8	6	5	7
3	Fred	120	10	20	5
4	Joe	7	9	6	8
5	Stephen	8	7	10	9
6	Sebastian	6	5	7	6

Figure 35. The transposed data set, in which the data from the participants are now contained in rows

	Name	Ten1	Ten2	Ten3	Ten4	Ten5	Fifteen1	Fifteen2
1	Amy	8	6	5	7	5	15	6
2	Fred	120	10	20	5	10	25	8
3	Joe	7	9	6	8	6	10	9
4	Stephen	8	7	10	9	11	13	12
5	Sebastian	6	5	7	6	5	9	9
6	Mavis	10	8	10	8	10	15	10

Figure 36. Part of the transformed data set in which the columns and rows of the original data set have been transposed

3.4   IMPORTING AND EXPORTING DATA

It is possible to import data into SPSS from other applications or platforms such as Microsoft EXCEL and SPSS for Macintosh. SPSS can also read ASCII tab-delimited or comma-delimited files, with values separated by tabulation symbols or fixed format files with variables recorded in the same column locations for each case. It is also possible to export SPSS data and output into other applications such as word processors and spreadsheets.

3.4.1   Importing data from other applications

Importing EXCEL files

When importing files from EXCEL, the following points should be observed:
1. If the first row of the EXCEL file does not contain variable/column names or data, then the material may not be read into SPSS properly. Either delete blank rows or amend the **Range** in SPSS's **Opening Excel Data Source** dialog box after selecting the EXCEL file to be read.
2. Dates must be formatted as *DD-MMM-YYYY in EXCEL.
3. It may be necessary to have a number of attempts to ensure a satisfactory import. For example, some file types may need changing (e.g. from **String** to **Numeric**) within **Variable View**.

To import the EXCEL file named *test1.xls*, which is stored in the author's folder *SPSS 15 Book Chapters data*:

*   Choose
    File➔Open➔ Data...
    to obtain the **Open File** dialog box (Figure 37).
*   Click the directory of file types in the **Files of type:** box and highlight **Excel (*.xls)**.
*   Select the appropriate **Look in** folder.
*   A list of Excel files will then appear in the white panel above. Click the appropriate file and its name will appear in the **File name:** box.

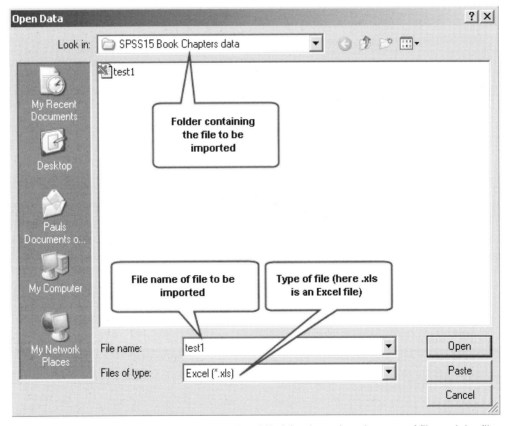

Figure 37. The **Open File** dialog box with Excel [*.xls] selected as the type of file and the file test1 selected from the folder SPSS 15 Book Chapters data

*   Click **Open** to open the **Opening File Options** dialog box (Figure 38). Activate the **Read variable names** check box to transfer the EXCEL variable names into the SPSS **Data Editor**.

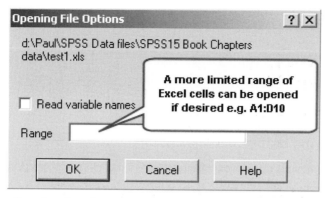

Figure 38. The **Opening File Options** dialog box with **Read variable names** selected

- If the EXCEL file has more than one worksheet, the **Opening File Options** dialog box will contain an extra panel labelled **Worksheet**
  Worksheet: Sheet1 [A1:N7893]   . Different worksheets can then be selected by clicking the directory arrow.
- If an error message appears stating that SPSS cannot load an EXCEL worksheet, it may be necessary to return to EXCEL and re-save the file in the format of a different version of EXCEL, to copy and paste columns of data directly into SPSS **Data View**, or to re-format the cells.
- Click **OK** to transfer the file into SPSS. **Variable View** will list the variable names and their types, and **Data View** will show the transferred data and variable names (Figure 39). It may be necessary to change variable types in **Variable View**. The **SPSS Viewer** will list the names, types and formats of the variables. Note that SPSS Viewer may initially obscure the data file beneath.
- The file can then be saved as an SPSS data file.

	A	B	C	D
1	**Name**	**Sex**	**Age**	**Score**
2	Brown, G	m	25	87
3	Green, F	m	18	78
4	Mason, P	f	23	100
5	Sampson, G	m	24	67
6	Winston, P	f	20	50

	name	sex	age	score
1	Brown, G	m	25.00	87.00
2	Green, F	m	18.00	78.00
3	Mason, P	f	23.00	100.00
4	Sampson, G	m	24.00	67.00
5	Winston, P	f	20.00	50.00

Figure 39. Transfer of an EXCEL file (left) to SPSS (right)

It is also possible to copy columns of data from an EXCEL file by highlighting the data (but not the column headings), selecting **Copy** from EXCEL's **Edit** menu and then within SPSS, selecting **Paste** from SPSS's **Edit** menu and pasting the data into **Data View**. (Again, do not include the cell at the head of the SPSS column in the selection.) The variables can then be named in the usual manner within **Variable View**. Should the EXCEL columns contain strings (e.g. names), make sure that, in **Variable View**, you change the **Type** of variable to **String** before pasting. Other types of file can be transferred in a similar manner.

Exporting data from SPSS to EXCEL

The **Save As** procedure allows you to save an SPSS file (or a selection of data) as an EXCEL file. The procedure is entirely straightforward.

SPSS data can also be prepared for export to another application or platform by saving it to a wide range of formats, including **SPSS portable (*.por)**. Full details of importing and exporting files are available in SPSS's **Help** facility.

3.4.2   Copying output

SPSS 15 offers a new facility for exporting output. To copy output, proceed as follows:

- Ensure that the item of output in SPSS **Viewer** has a box around it by clicking the cursor anywhere within the table or graphic. If you wish to copy more than one table, then ensure that all the desired tables are boxed by holding down the **Ctrl** key whilst clicking on each table in turn.
- Choose
  File➜Export... (Figure 40)
  to obtain the **Export Output** dialog box (Figure 41).

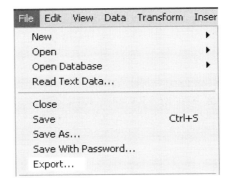

Figure 40. The location of the **Export...** item

- Complete the **Export Output** dialog box (Figure 41) by naming the file to where the output is going and its format (e.g. *.doc for a Word file; *.xls for an Excel file; *.ppt for a Powerpoint file; *.htm for a HTML file). Either type in the file name or use the **Browse...** to locate the appropriate folder (a **Save As** dialog box will appear from which the folder can be selected: insert a file name in the **File Name** panel and click **Save** to return to the **Export Output** dialog box).

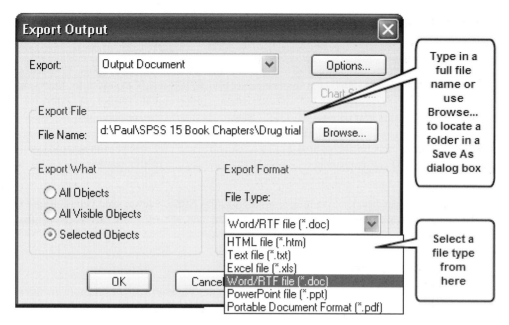

Figure 41. The **Export Output** dialog box for naming the output file and selecting its format

Alternatively, to **copy a table**, proceed as follows:
- Ensure that the table of output in SPSS **Viewer** has a box around it by clicking the cursor anywhere within the table or graphic. If you wish to copy more than one table, then ensure that all the desired tables are boxed by holding down the **Ctrl** key whilst clicking on each table in turn.
- Click **Copy** in the **Edit** menu.
- Switch to the word processor and ensure that the cursor is located at the intended insertion point.
- Select **Paste Special...** in the word processor's **Edit** menu and then **Formatted Text (RTF)** if it is desired to edit or format the table within the word processor.
- Alternatively, select **Paste Special...** in the word processor's **Edit** menu and then **Picture.** The picture can be repositioned and resized within the word processor but it cannot be edited. However the quality of the image is higher than it is when **Paste** is used.

To **copy a graphic**, proceed as follows:
- Ensure that the graphic in the SPSS **Viewer** has a box around it by clicking the cursor anywhere within it. If you wish to copy more than one graphic, ensure that all the desired graphics are boxed by holding down the **Ctrl** key whilst clicking on each chart or graph in turn.
- Click **Copy** in the **Edit** menu.
- Switch to the word processor and ensure that the cursor is located at the insertion point.
- Click **Paste Special...** and select **Bitmap.** The item can then be centred, enlarged or reduced by clicking it so that it acquires a box around it with the usual Windows tabs. To centre the box, click and drag it to the desired position. To enlarge or reduce the size of the graphic, drag one of the tabs in the appropriate direction.

3.5   PRINTING FROM SPSS

It is possible to make extensive use of SPSS without ever printing out either the contents of the **Viewer** or the data in the **Data Editor**.   Both data and output can easily be backed up electronically by saving to disk; and important SPSS output is easily exported to the document you actually want to print out.   Moreover, SPSS output can be extremely extensive and indiscriminate printing can be very wasteful.   In the worst scenario, an inept printing operation could result in dozens of sheets of paper, with a single line of print on each.   There are, nevertheless, occasions on which it is both useful and necessary to print out selected items in the **Viewer** window or even a hard copy of the raw data.   In this section, we offer some suggestions to help you control and improve printed output from SPSS.

There are differences between printing output from the **SPSS Viewer** and printing data from the **Data Editor**.   In either case, however, problems can arise if there has been insufficient editorial control.

3.5.1   Printing output from the Viewer

We shall illustrate some aspects of printing from the **Viewer** with the data from the drug experiment.   Suppose that, having entered the data into the **Data Editor**, we run the **Means** procedure, with requests for several optional extras such as medians, range statistics, measures of effect size and one-way ANOVAs to increase the extent of the output.

We strongly recommend that, before you print any output, you should make full use of the **Viewer**'s editing facilities to **remove all irrelevant material**.   When using SPSS, one invariably requests output which, at the end of the day, proves to be superfluous.   Moreover, as we have seen, radical changes in tables and other output can be made (and great economies in space) by using the **Viewer**'s powerful editing facilities.   Since some of the output tables can be very wide, unnecessary columns can be removed.   Some pivoting may help not only to make a table more readable but also more manageable for a printing operation.

For some kinds of material, it is better to use **landscape** orientation for the sheet, that is, have the shorter side vertical, rather than the more usual **portrait** orientation.   It is easy to make such a specification while working in the **Viewer** before printing anything out.   To clarify a batch of printed output, we also recommend that you add explanatory captions, such as *Output for the Drug Experiment*.   Otherwise, it is only too easy to accumulate pages of SPSS output, the purpose of which becomes increasingly unclear as time passes.   All these things can easily be done while you are working in the **Viewer**.   Often, however, even after you have edited and severely pruned the **Viewer**'s contents, you will only be interested in printing out a **selection** of the items.

*Using **Print Preview***

- To ascertain the content of each page of the output that will be printed before any selection of items has been made, choose
  File➡Print Preview…
  to view the content of the first page in the **Viewer (all visible output) box** (Figure 42).
  - The contents of the other pages can be viewed by pressing the **PgDn** key as often as you need.   Alternatively, you can click on the **Next Page** button in the row of buttons at the

top of the dialog box. You will see that, when no item has been selected, the output extends to several pages.

Selecting items for printing

To select two or more items, click the first and, pressing the **Ctrl** key and keeping it held down, click the other items that you wish to select. (You will also need to hold down the **Ctrl** key if you are clicking icons in the left pane to achieve a multiple selection.) The items need not be adjacent. If you now choose **Print Preview**, you will see that it shows only the items you have selected, and it is only those items that will actually be printed.

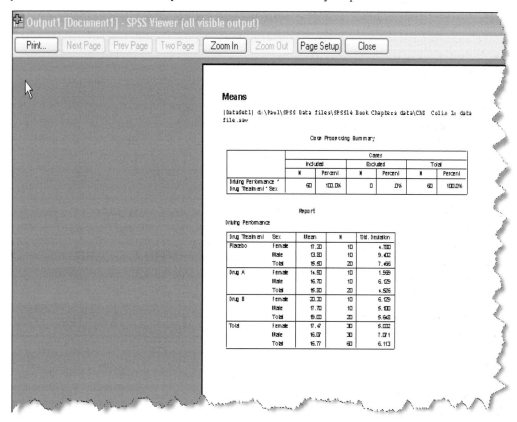

Figure 42. Part of the **Viewer (all visible output)** dialog box for viewing page content when printing from the SPSS **Viewer**

There are two ways of selecting items: you can click the item's icon in the left pane of the **Viewer**; or you can click the item itself in the right pane. Either way, a rectangle with a single continuous border will appear around the item or items concerned. It is, perhaps, easier to click on the items in the right pane directly to make it immediately clear what has been selected.

Try selecting any item in the **Viewer** and choose **Print Preview**, to see the **SPSS Viewer (selected output)** window, which will display only the item you have selected. If you return to the **Print** dialog box, you will see that the **Selection** radio button in the **Print range** panel has now been activated. Were you to click **OK** at this point, only the selected item would be printed.

Deleting items from the Viewer

Items are removed from the **Viewer** by selecting them and pressing the **Delete** button. After a multiple selection, pressing the **Delete** button will remove all the selected items.

Re-arranging the items in the Viewer

Items can be rearranged very simply by clicking and dragging them in the left-hand pane, a red arrow showing where the item will be relocated as you drag. Alternatively items in the right-hand pane can be cut and pasted in the usual manner by selecting the item, choosing **Cut** from the **Edit** menu, moving the cursor to the desired new position and choosing **Paste** from the **Edit** menu. Key combinations of **Ctrl + X** for cutting and **Ctrl + V** for pasting can also be used.

Creating page breaks

You can also exert some control over the appearance of the output in the **Viewer** by creating a **page break** between items that clearly belong to different categories.
• Click the item above which you want to create a page break.
• Choose
    Insert→ Page Break
• Return to the **Viewer** and click outside the selection rectangle to cancel the selection.

If you now return to **Print Preview**, you will see that a page break has been created and the item you selected is now at the top of a fresh page. Used in conjunction with re-ordering, page breaks can help you to sort the items in the **Viewer**. Bear in mind, however, that creating page breaks always increases the number of sheets of paper in the printed output.

Changing from portrait to landscape using Page Setup

• Click either the **Page Setup** button at the top of the **Print Preview** dialog box or **Page Setup** in the **File** menu to enter the **Page Setup** dialog box (Figure 43).
• In the **Orientation** panel, is the radio button for changing from **Portrait** to **Landscape** orientation. Sometimes, for printing purposes, the landscape orientation can accommodate particularly wide tables that will not fit in portrait orientation.
• Click **OK** to return to the **Viewer**.

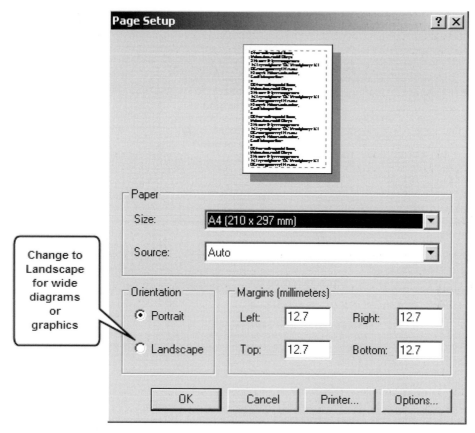

Figure 43. The **Page Setup** dialog box

*The Viewer's **Print** dialog box*

- Access the **Viewer**'s **Print** dialog box (Figure 44) by choosing **File➜Print...**.

Note the **Print Range** section in the lower left area of the box. By default, the radio button labelled **All** is active, which means that pressing **OK** will result in the **entire contents** of the **Viewer** being printed out indiscriminately. The default setting of copies is *1*, but obviously an increase in that value to *2* will double the volume of the printed output.

This **Print** dialog box differs from the dialog you will receive when you print from the **Data Editor**, in which you would be offered the choice of printing either the entire output or the pages within a specified range. It is also possible to print out only the current page. However, no page range is offered in the dialog shown in Figure 44. When you are printing from the **SPSS Viewer**, the radio button marked **Selection** will only become active when a selection from the items in the **Viewer** has been made.

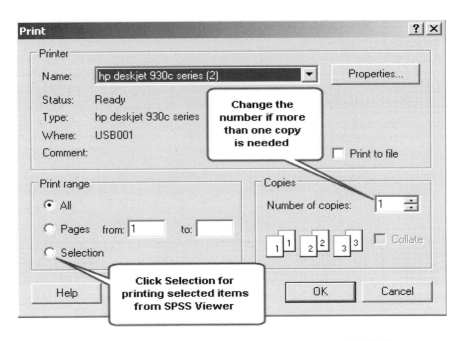

Figure 44.   The **Print** dialog box for printing output from the **SPSS Viewer**

Printing from the Data Editor

It is possible to print out data from **Data View**. There are, however, several problems with this approach. Most notably, if there are too many variables to fit on to one page of printed output and hundreds of cases, it can be difficult to keep track of the output. It sometimes helps to add dummy columns, each cell of which contains a single numerical value, but this can be quite tedious.

To print only selected parts of the data set, use the click-and-drag method to define the target sections by highlighting them to display the material in reverse video. This requires a little practice; but it will be found that when the screen pointer touches the lower border of the window, the latter will scroll down to extend the blackened area to the desired extent. If the pointer touches the right border, the window will scroll to the right across the **Data Editor**. When the **Print** dialog box (Figure 44) appears, the marker will now be on **Selection** (the lowest radio button). Click **OK** to obtain a hard copy of the selected areas.

*Transferring data to the **Viewer** for printing*

An alternative way of obtaining a hard copy of the raw data is to print the data from the **Viewer**.

• Choose
   Analyze➔Reports➔Case Summaries…

to obtain the **Summarize Cases** dialog box (Figure 45).

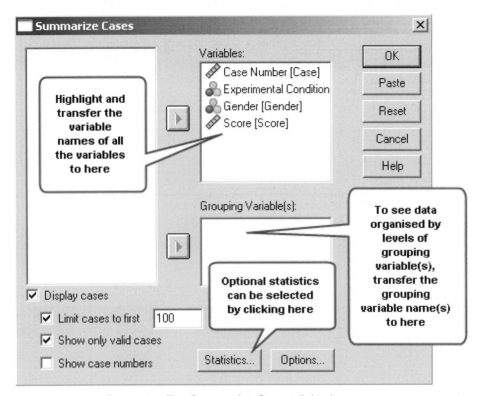

Figure 45. The **Summarize Cases** dialog box

- To see the data arranged as in **Data View**, transfer all the variable names into the **Variables** box. Alternatively, the data can be reorganised by levels of the grouping variables by transferring the grouping variable names to the **Grouping Variable(s)** box. To see all the data, click off the **Limit case to first** check box.
- The **Case Summary** table is shown in Output 9.

Case Summaries

	Case Number	Experimental Condition	Gender	Score
1	1	Placebo	Male	6
2	2	Placebo	Female	5
3	3	Placebo	Male	5
4	4	Placebo	Female	1
5	5	Placebo	Male	2
6	6	Placebo	Female	3
7	7	Placebo	Male	2
8	8	Placebo	Female	4
9	9	Placebo	Male	5
10	10	Placebo	Female	1
11	11	Drug	Male	8
12	12	Drug	Female	6
13	13	Drug	Male	6
14	14	Drug	Female	7
15	15	Drug	Male	6
16	16	Drug	Female	8
17	17	Drug	Male	6
18	18	Drug	Female	7
19	19	Drug	Male	5
20	20	Drug	Female	10
Total N	20	20	20	20

Output 9. The **Case Summaries** of the data from the drug experiment

EXERCISE 3

Merging files – Adding cases & variables

This Exercise shows you how to open a saved file and how to merge your data with other files. The relevant sections are 2.6 (resuming work on a saved data set), 3.1.2 (reading in SPSS files) and 3.3.4 (merging files).

Opening your saved file in SPSS

Log in to SPSS as described in Section 2.2. Open the file that you saved under the name *Ex2 Questionnaire Data* from the previous Exercise. Select the radio button **Open an existing data source** in the SPSS opening window and highlight the filename. It may be necessary, especially in a networked computer, to select the **More Files...** option and select another disk drive or folder. Alternatively, select the **Type in data** radio button to open **Data View**, choose **File**, click **Open**, and finally **Data** to open the **Open File** selection box. Change the **Look in:** selection to the folder and/or disk drive where the file has been stored, click the filename so that it appears in the **Filename** box, and then **Open**. Your file should appear in **Data View**, where part of your own data might appear as follows:

	CaseNo	MyName	Age	Sex	Faculty	Status	Stones	Pounds
1	1	Alan Brown	25	1	1	1	14	0

Locating the larger data set

The file containing the large data set with which you are going to merge your own data is to be found at the following WWW address:

http://www.abdn.ac.uk/psychology/materials/spss.shtml

in the file labelled *Ex3 Questionnaire data* within the section *Release 15*. If this file has not already been downloaded on to a file server or hard disk drive for easier access, enter *WWW* and save the file to a more convenient place such as your hard disk drive. (In order to see the appropriate icons for accessing WWW, reduce the size of the SPSS window.

Merging your data with the larger data set

To carry out the file merge, select
Data➜Merge Files➜Add Cases
to obtain the **Add Cases: Read File** selection box, which prompts you to specify the file (the large data set) from which you want to merge other cases with your own. Locate the file *Ex3 Questionnaire Data* and click it. You should now see the **Add Cases: Read File** dialog box, with *Ex3 Questionnaire Data* in the **File Name:** box. Click **Open**. A new dialog box labelled **Add Cases from**, together with the full name of the data file, will appear.

If you have entered the correct variable names in your own data file, the **Add Cases from** dialog box should show just one variable name *(MyName)* in the **Unpaired Variables:** box and all the other variable names should be in the **Variables in New Working Data File:** box (see Figure 1). A match will not be found for your variable *MyName*, because the large data set does not contain the names of the participants.

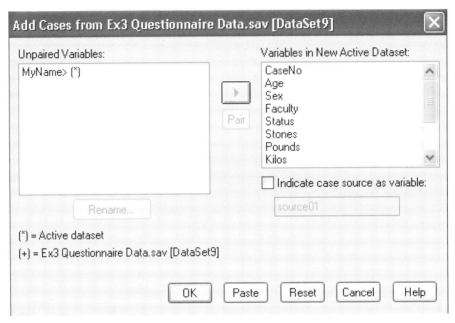

Figure 1. The **Add Cases from** dialog box showing the names of Unpaired Variables (here there is just one, *MyName*) and corresponding names from both files (Variables in New Active Dataset)

Suppose, however, there had been a mismatch between one of the variable names you had typed into **Data View** and the name of the corresponding variable in the large data set. Suppose that, when you were building *Ex2 Questionnaire Data*, you had typed *Ages* instead of *Age*. The variables *Ages* and *Age* would both have appeared in the **Unpaired Variables:** box. You would have then had to select *Ages* and click **Rename** to obtain another dialog box, allowing you to rename it as *Age*. The correct variable name *Age* would then be transferred to the list in **Variables in the New Working Data File**.

Click **OK** to merge the files. The first few variables in the first two lines of the merged data set might appear as follows (click on the labels icon to see the labels for *Sex*, *Faculty* etc.):

	CaseNo	Age	Sex	Faculty	Status	Stones	Pounds
1	1	25	1	1	1	14	0
2	1	23	1	1	1	11	0

Notice that the same case number appears in the first two rows. Since your own case is being added to the *334* cases already in the data set, change your case number to *335*.

Clearly, since yours is the 335th case, you want your own data to appear below the others in **Data View**. To rearrange the cases in ascending order of magnitude, choose **Data➜Sort Cases...**

to see the **Sort Cases** dialog box. Transfer *CaseNo* to the **Sort By** panel on the right and click **OK**.

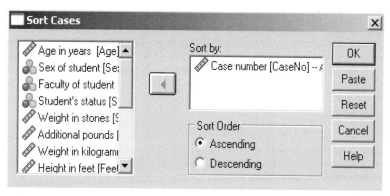

You will now find that your own data occupy the bottom row in **Data View**. Save the merged file as *Merged Questionnaire Data*.

A warning

In the large data set, the *Faculty* variable was of the numeric type, with values assigned as follows: *1 = Arts, 2 = Science, 3 = Medicine, 4 = Other*.

Suppose that you had inadvertently assigned *1* to *Science* and *2* to *Arts*, instead of the other way round, and that as a science student, you had recorded a *1* in your own data set. SPSS will not warn you of the discrepancy. Instead, it will adopt your convention throughout the merged data set and all those people who recorded *1*s in the larger original data set will now be recorded as scientists, not arts students. You can confirm this by choosing Value Labels from the View menu. All those previously recorded as science students will now be recorded as arts students and vice versa.

When two files are being merged, it is the value assignments **in the first file** that determine those for the entire merged file, even when, as in the present example, the former contains only a single case.

Another file-merging exercise: Adding extra variables to a file

In Section 3.3.2, we described the use of the **Aggregate** procedure to create a file showing the average marks of students who had taken various courses at a business school. Open the *Students marks* file from the website specified earlier or enter it from the Appendix after this Exercise. Follow the **Aggregate** procedure described in Section 3.3.2 to obtain the course averages and the numbers of students taking the courses. Save the new information to a file named *Course average marks*.

Also available from the website or from the Appendix is the *Assignment* file which contains the courses to which the lecturers at the business school were assigned. The aim of this Exercise is to add, to the file containing the course averages, the names of the lecturers who were assigned to those courses. The link between the course averages and the lecturers can be made with the **Merge Files** procedure, using *Assignment* as a lookup file to obtain the names of the lecturers who gave the courses listed in *Course average marks*.

• Open *Course average marks*.
• Choose
  Data➜Sort Cases …

- Fill in the **Sort Cases** dialog box, specifying that you are sorting by *Course*. Keep the sorting order as Ascending. Click **OK**.

Save the sorted file as *Course average marks*.

(It would normally be necessary to check that the other file being used for the merging of data also had its entries in the variable *Course* arranged alphabetically and if not, to use a **Sort Cases...** procedure to do so. In this case, the file *Assignment* already has its *Course* entries arranged alphabetically.)

Choose
- **Data➜Merge Files➜Add Variables...** (see Section 3.3.4)
- In the **Add Variables to Course average marks.sav** dialog box (see Figure 29), ensure that the radio button for **An external SPSS data file** is active, click **Browse...**, select *Assignment* and click **Continue**.
- In the **Add Variables from Assignment.sav** dialog box, click the selection box **Match cases on key variables in sorted files** and then click the **Active data set is keyed table** radio button.
- Highlight *Course* from the **Excluded Variables** box and transfer it to the **Key Variables** box.
- Click **OK**.

Look at the resulting data file and notice the new column headed *Lecturer*. This shows that the lecturer's name has been paired with each course and the average mark that those students taking the course received.

- **Which of Tom Fielding's courses has the highest average mark and what is the average mark for that course?**

Finishing the session

Close down SPSS and any other windows before logging out.

Appendix of files

Student	Course	Mark	Student	Course	Mark
Anne	Accountancy	80	Rebecca	Law	85
Rebecca	Accountancy	78	Susan	Law	91
Susan	Accountancy	87	Fred	Management	70
Anne	Computing	49	Jim	Management	57
Fred	Computing	55	Joe	Management	53
Rebecca	Computing	65	John	Management	41
Susan	Computing	56	Kevin	Management	45
Anne	German	40	Rebecca	Management	43
Fred	German	72	Sebastian	Management	44
Jim	German	73	Jim	Mathematics	66
Susan	German	85	Joe	Mathematics	60
Anne	Graphics	58	John	Mathematics	68
Fred	Graphics	54	Kevin	Mathematics	71
Jim	Graphics	65	Mary	Mathematics	56
Joe	Graphics	55	Sebastian	Mathematics	61
Kevin	Graphics	58	Joe	Politics	62
Mary	Graphics	50	John	Politics	45
Rebecca	Graphics	62	Kevin	Politics	49
Anne	Law	93	Mary	Politics	56
Fred	Law	88	Sebastian	Politics	43
Jim	Law	89	John	Spanish	62
Joe	Law	91	Mary	Spanish	57
John	Law	43	Sebastian	Spanish	53
Kevin	Law	83	Mary	Statistics	70
Rebecca	Law	85	Sebastian	Statistics	62

Lecturer	Course
EvelynBrown	Accountancy
TimRice	Book Keeping
DavidJones	Computing
EvelynBrown	German
JoanSmith	Graphics
TimRice	Investment Management
SarahAlbert	Law
TomFielding	Management
EvelynBrown	Mathematics
TomFielding	Politics
TomFielding	Spanish
TimRice	Spreadsheets
EvelynBrown	Statistics
JoanSmith	The Internet
JoanSmith	Web Management

CHAPTER 4

Exploring your data

4.1   Introduction

4.2   Some useful menus

4.3   Describing data

4.4   Manipulation of the data set

4.1   INTRODUCTION

In recent years, statisticians have devised a set of statistical methods specially designed for the purpose of examining a data set. Together, they are known as **Exploratory Data Analysis (EDA)**. (For a readable account of EDA, see Howell, 2007, Chapter 2). EDA has now found its way into all good statistical computing packages, including SPSS.

Suppose we have a set of measurements, say the heights in centimetres of a group of children. There are usually three things we want to know about such a data set:
1.   The general **level**, or **average value**, of their heights.
2.   The **dispersion** of height, i.e. the degree to which the individual scores tend to **vary** around or **deviate** from the average, as opposed to clustering closely around it.
3.   The **distribution shape**, i.e. the relative frequencies with which heights are to be found in various regions of the total range of the variable.

We assume that the reader is familiar with the most common measures of level (the **mean**, the **median** and the **mode**) and of dispersion (the **standard deviation** and **quantile range** statistics). We also assume familiarity with terms relating to the distribution of the data set, such as **skewness**, **bimodality** and so on.

Different statistics are appropriate for data of different types: there is little point in finding the mean of a set of ranks, for example, because the resulting average would depend solely upon the number of people (or objects) in the sample. Should the reader be a little rusty on such matters, we strongly recommend reading the relevant chapters of a good textbook on the topic. However before embarking on EDA, it is vital to check the integrity of the data in case there have been date entry errors (e.g. typing 100 instead of 10).

The influence of outliers and asymmetry of distribution

Statistics such as the mean and standard deviation are intended to express, in a single number, some characteristic of the data set as a whole: the former is intended to express the **average**, that is, the general level, typical value, or **central tendency**, of a set of scores; the latter is a measure of their **spread**, or **dispersion**. There are circumstances, however, in which the mean and standard deviation are poor measures of central tendency and dispersion. This can occur when the distribution is markedly skewed, or when extreme cases known as **outliers** exert undue **leverage** upon the values of these statistics.

4.2 SOME USEFUL MENUS

The most important procedures for exploring data are to be found in the **Analyze** and **Graphs** menus. A powerful and complex system such as SPSS can often offer many different approaches to a problem in data analysis. Similar graphics, for instance, can be produced by procedures on either the **Analyze** or the **Graphs** menus. Descriptive statistics are available on several different procedures.

In the **Analyze** menu are **Reports**, **Descriptive Statistics**, **Tables** and **Compare Means**. When the **Reports** or **Descriptive Statistics** are highlighted, the submenus shown in Figure 1 appear.

Reports	Descriptive Statistics
OLAP Cubes... Case Summaries... Report Summaries in Rows... Report Summaries in Columns...	Frequencies... Descriptives... Explore... Crosstabs... Ratio...

Figure 1. The submenus of **Reports** and **Descriptive Statistics**

The **Reports** submenu (left side of Figure 1) provides facilities for calculating various descriptive statistics of selected quantitative variables subdivided by categories of specified grouping variables. The **OLAP Cubes** (Online Analytical Processing) procedure initially outputs the selected statistics for selected quantitative variables summed across *all* categories of the grouping variables. The initial **OLAP Cubes** table in the output, however, is a pivot table, double-clicking on which brings the **Pivot** menu to view. You can then specify particular categories and combinations of categories by clicking tabs at the top of the table in the usual way (see Chapter 3). The desired combination will then appear as a layer of a multi-way table. As with all pivot tables, the appearance of **OLAP Cubes** can be improved by using the **Viewer**'s editing facilities.

In Chapter 3, we saw that **Case Summaries** provide very useful summaries of data sets, including the raw data themselves. This is ideal for printed records.

The output for **Row Summaries in Rows** or **Report Summaries in Columns** is not tabulated in boxes, is printed in less clear font and is rather difficult to read.

The **Descriptive Statistics** submenu (right side of Figure 1) includes **Frequencies**, **Descriptives**, **Explore**, **Crosstabs** and **Ratio**. All are highly recommended and will be described and illustrated in later sections of this Chapter.

The **Tables** submenu (left side of Figure 2) enables the user to display output in attractive tables, which can be pasted directly into reports of experiments or surveys. The **Basic Tables** and **Tables of Frequencies** procedures are particularly useful.

Tables	Compare Means	Transform
Custom Tables... Multiple Response Sets... Basic Tables... General Tables... Multiple Response Tables... Tables of Frequencies...	Means... One-Sample T Test... Independent-Samples T Test... Paired-Samples T Test... One-Way ANOVA...	Compute Variable... Count Values within Cases... Recode into Same Variables... Recode into Different Variables... Automatic Recode... Visual Binning... Optimal Binning... Rank Cases...

Figure 2.   The submenus of **Tables**, **Compare Means** and **Transform**

The **Compare Means** submenu (middle of Figure 2) contains just one item of relevance to exploring data, namely **Means**. This title is misleading because the procedure can only be used for listing the means of variables subdivided by categories of grouping variables: there must be at least one grouping variable present in your data set for the procedure to work. To obtain the means of ungrouped scores, you must turn to **Reports**, **Tables**, or to **Descriptives**, which is found in the **Descriptive Statistics** menu.

Finally, in the **Transform** menu (right of Figure 2) there are several useful procedures, some of which will be described and illustrated at the end of this Chapter.

The **Graphs** menu (not reproduced here) will form the material in Chapter 5, although we shall meet some graphics in this Chapter, since they are options in several of the other exploratory procedures.

4.3   DESCRIBING DATA

To illustrate the data-descriptive procedures, we shall make use of a medical-actuarial data set comprising *Case*, two quantitative variables, *Weight* and *Height*, and two qualitative variables, *Sex* and *Bloodtype*. Table 1 shows the data set already entered in **Data View** (*Case* has been omitted from the Table for clarity).

4.3.1   Describing nominal and ordinal data

Suppose we want to know the frequencies of cases in the categories in the two grouping variables *Sex* and *Bloodtype*. We might also want a graphical display of these frequencies, such as a **bar chart** or **pie chart**. For measurements such as heights or weights, a **histogram** is a useful graph. There are several ways of obtaining such displays.

Table 1. The Blood Group, Sex, Height and Weight data in **Data View**

	Bloodtype	Sex	Height	Weight		Bloodtype	Sex	Height	Weight
1	Group O	Male	178	75	17	Group O	Female	163	60
2	Group O	Male	196	100	18	Group O	Female	142	51
3	Group A	Male	145	60	19	Group A	Female	150	55
4	Group O	Male	170	71	20	Group O	Female	165	64
5	Group B	Male	180	80	21	Group A	Female	160	53
6	Group O	Male	175	69	22	Group O	Female	175	50
7	Group AB	Male	185	78	23	Group O	Female	182	72
8	Group A	Male	190	90	24	Group B	Female	169	65
9	Group O	Male	183	70	25	Group O	Female	162	62
10	Group B	Male	182	85	26	Group B	Female	182	80
11	Group A	Male	170	72	27	Group O	Female	165	67
12	Group O	Male	160	77	28	Group A	Female	171	50
13	Group O	Male	170	95	29	Group O	Female	146	55
14	Group AB	Male	172	68	30	Group AB	Female	151	48
15	Group B	Male	190	120	31	Group O	Female	164	59
16	Group O	Male	180	75	32	Group B	Female	176	71

General Tables or **Tables of Frequencies** (on the **Tables** menu), and **Crosstabs** (on the **Descriptive Statistics** menu) all provide a convenient two-way contingency table (e.g. rows representing blood groups and columns representing sexes) but **Crosstabs** also supplies a column of totals and statistics such as **chi-square** and various **correlation coefficients**. **Frequencies** (in **Descriptive Statistics**) gives frequency distributions for both nominal and ordinal data, as well as percentages and cumulative percentages. There are options for selecting graphics such as bar charts, pie charts and histograms.

To obtain a table of frequencies with percentages:
- Choose
    Analyze➜Tables➜Tables of Frequencies...
    to open the **Table of Frequencies** dialog box.
- Transfer the variable names as shown in Figure 3.
- Click the **Statistics** button and select **Display** in the **Percents** tick box. Click **Continue**.
- Click **OK**.

The output is shown in Output 1.

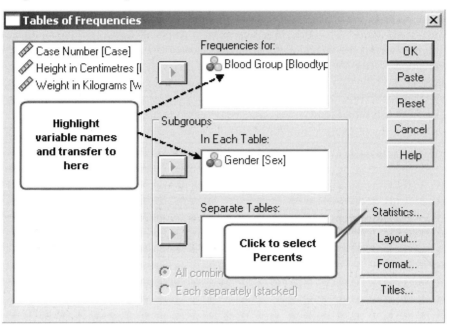

Figure 3. The **Table of Frequencies** dialog box for frequencies and percents of *Blood Group* and *Gender*

	Gender			
	Male		Female	
	Blood Group		Blood Group	
	Count	%	Count	%
Group A	3	18.8%	3	18.8%
Group B	3	18.8%	3	18.8%
Group AB	2	12.5%	1	6.3%
Group O	8	50.0%	9	56.3%

Output 1. Frequencies and percents of *Blood Group* for each gender

Tables such as that shown in Output 1 quickly show whether the data have been entered correctly by comparing the blood group counts with those in the original data set.   Checks should also be conducted on the other variables (e.g. checking the minimum and maximum heights by using the **Descriptives** procedure for *Height* as shown in Section 4.3.2). A height of over 200 cm or under 100 cm would merit a scrutiny of the data in **Data View** for a possible transcription error.

The following procedure offers not only frequencies but also charts.

- Choose
  Analyze➜Descriptive Statistics➜Frequencies…
  to open the **Frequencies** dialog box.
- Follow the steps shown in Figure 4.
- Click **Charts** to obtain the **Frequencies: Charts** dialog box (Figure 5) and select the **Bar Chart(s)** radio button. There is also the choice of frequencies or percentages for the y axis in the **Chart Values** box.
- Click **Continue** to return to **Frequencies** and then **OK** to run the procedure.

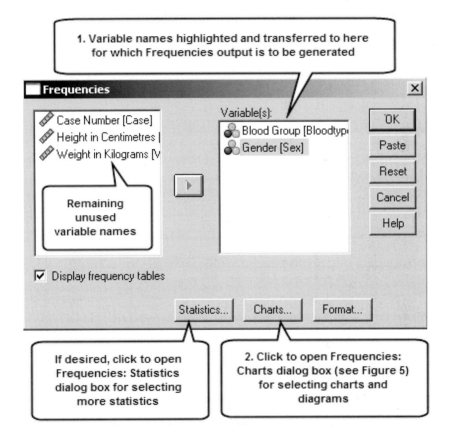

Figure 4. The **Frequencies** dialog box for *Blood Group* and *Gender*

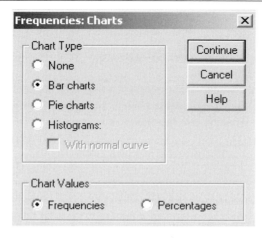

Figure 5. The **Frequencies: Charts** dialog box with **Bar charts** selected

The output consists of a couple of tables (Output 2) and the bar chart for Blood Group is shown in Output 3 (the bar chart for Gender has been omitted). Note that the bar chart can also be requested directly with the **Bar** procedure in the **Graphs** menu. It is possible to edit the bar chart to centre or change the axis labels, the title, the shading of the boxes and other aspects of the graph; more details about editing graphics will be given in the next chapter.

Blood Group

		Frequency	Percent	Valid Percent	Cumulative Percent
Valid	Group A	6	18.8	18.8	18.8
	Group B	6	18.8	18.8	37.5
	Group AB	3	9.4	9.4	46.9
	Group O	17	53.1	53.1	100.0
	Total	32	100.0	100.0	

Gender

		Frequency	Percent	Valid Percent	Cumulative Percent
Valid	Male	16	50.0	50.0	50.0
	Female	16	50.0	50.0	100.0
	Total	32	100.0	100.0	

Output 2. Frequency listings for *Blood Group* and *Gender*

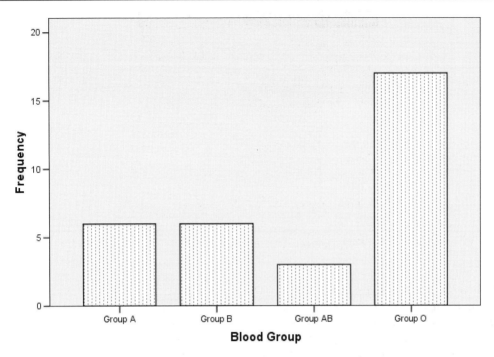

Output 3. Bar Chart for *Blood Group*

- Contingency tables can also be obtained with several procedures. **Crosstabs** generates contingency tables from nominal or ordinal data. Here we illustrate its use with *Blood Group* and *Gender*.
- Choose
  Analyze➜Descriptive Statistics➜Crosstabs…
  to open the **Crosstabs** dialog box.
- Transfer the variable names as shown in Figure 6 and click **OK**.
  If one of the variables has more than about four categories, it is better to use it for **Rows** rather than **Columns**, otherwise the output will be too wide for printing on a single page. In this example, a narrower table is produced if *Blood Group* is nominated for **Rows**.
- The output is shown in Output 4.

Crosstabs is only applicable to contingency tables. It should be requested only for nominal or ordinal data (i.e. categories or ranks) and not for measurements such as heights or scores unless they have been recoded into categories (e.g. tall; medium; short).

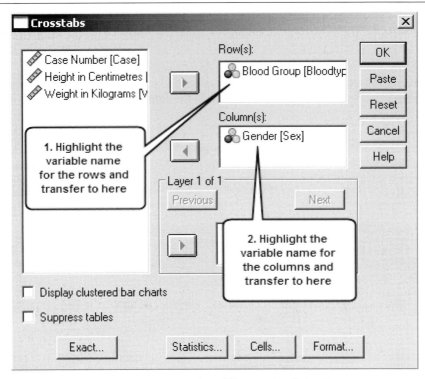

Figure 6. The completed **Crosstabs** dialog box

Blood Group * Gender Crosstabulation

Count

		Gender		Total
		Male	Female	
Blood Group	Group A	3	3	6
	Group B	3	3	6
	Group AB	2	1	3
	Group O	8	9	17
Total		16	16	32

Output 4. Contingency table from **Crosstabs** for *Gender* and *Blood Group*

4.3.2   Describing measurements

There are many procedures for describing and exploring data in the form of measurements.

Exploring variables without subdivision into categories of grouping variables

The most basic procedure is **Basic Tables** within the **Table** menu.
- Choose
  Analyze➜Tables➜Basic Tables …
  to open the **Basic Tables** dialog box.

- Transfer the desired variable names to the **Summaries** box.
- The default statistic is the mean. Others can be selected by clicking the **Statistics** button and selecting **Mean, Median** and **Standard Deviation**, for example. Click **Continue**.
- Click **OK**.

The completed dialog box is shown in Figure 7 and the output in Output 5.

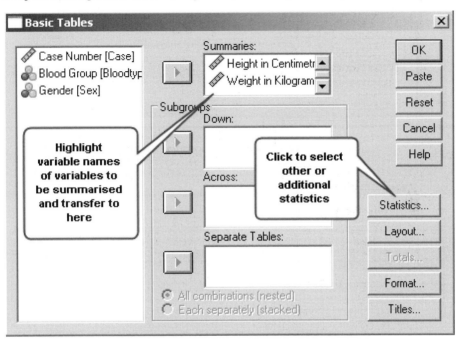

Figure 7. The **Basic Tables** dialog box with *Height* and *Weight* selected

	Mean	Median	Std Deviation
Height in Centimetres	170	171	14
Weight in Kilograms	70	70	16

Output 5. Output from **Basic Tables** showing the mean, median and standard deviation of Height and Weight

A similar output can be obtained using **Descriptives** in the **Descriptives Statistics** menu.
- Choose
  Analyze➜Descriptive Statistics➜Descriptives…
  to open the **Descriptives** dialog box.
- Transfer the variable names as shown in Figure 8 and click **OK**.

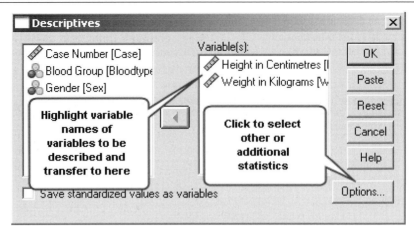

Figure 8. The completed **Descriptives** dialog box

The output is shown below in Output 6.

Descriptive Statistics

	N	Minimum	Maximum	Mean	Std. Deviation
Height in Centimetres	32	142	196	170.28	13.68
Weight in Kilograms	32	48	120	70.22	15.93
Valid N (listwise)	32				

Output 6. Descriptive statistics for *Height* and *Weight*

To obtain percentiles (e.g. quartiles), or to draw various graphics such as boxplots, stem-and-leaf tables or histograms, the appropriate procedures are **Frequencies** and **Explore**.

The next example illustrates the use of **Frequencies** to draw a histogram, compute some descriptive statistics, and display some percentile values for the variable *Height*. Proceed as follows:

- Choose
  Analyze➜Descriptive Statistics➜Frequencies…
- In the **Frequencies** dialog box (Figure 4), enter the variable name Height in Centimetres into the **Variables** box. Check that the **Display frequency tables** checkbox is not showing ✓ , otherwise a full frequency table will be listed. For a large data set, this table could be huge.
- Click **Charts** to open the **Frequencies: Charts** dialog box (Figure 5).
- In the **Chart Type** box, click the **Histograms** radio button, and mark the **With normal curve** box by clicking that also. Click **Continue**.
- Back in the **Frequencies** dialog box, click **Statistics** to open the **Frequencies: Statistics** dialog box and follow the steps shown in Figure 9.
- Click **Continue** to get back to the **Frequencies** dialog box and click **OK**.

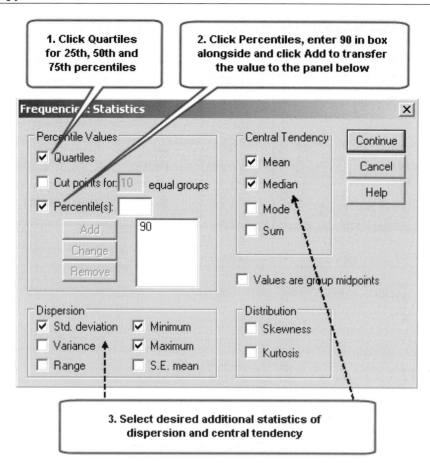

Figure 9. The **Frequencies: Statistics** dialog box with various statistics selected

The statistical output is shown in Output 7 and the edited histogram in Output 8.

Explore also produces stem-and-leaf displays and boxplots.

Statistics

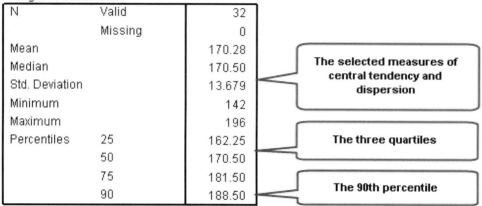

Output 7. The requested percentiles and descriptive statistics for *Height*

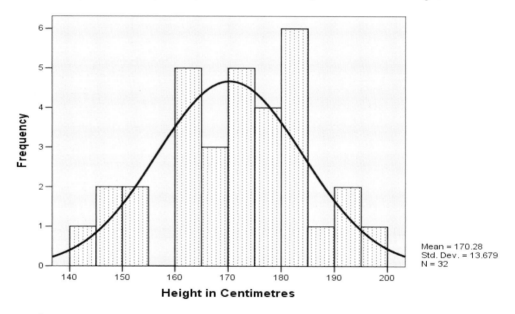

Output 8. Histogram and superimposed normal curve of the distribution of *Height*

Exploring variables with subdivision into categories of grouping variables

When the user wishes to explore quantitative variables subdivided by categories of grouping variables (e.g. the heights of men and women), several procedures are available including **Basic Tables**, **Explore** in the **Descriptive Statistics**, and **Means** in the **Compare Means** menu. There is also the option of a one-way analysis of variance. Note especially that **Means** cannot be used for variables that have not been grouped by another variable: for such variables, **Descriptives** must be used instead. **Explore** in the **Descriptive Statistics** menu contains a large variety of graphs and displays (which are also available directly from the **Graphs** drop-down menu), as well as a variety of statistics.

The first example uses the **Basic Tables** procedure (see Figure 7); but this time the variable name *Blood Group* is transferred to the **Subgroups Down** box and *Gender* to the **Subgroups Across** box. We have selected **Count**, **Mean**, and **Standard Deviation** from the Statistics option box. The output is shown in Output 9.

| | | | Gender | | | | | |
| | | | Male | | | Female | | |
			Count	Mean	Std Deviation	Count	Mean	Std Deviation
Blood Group	Group A	Height in Centimetres	3	168.3	22.5	3	160.3	10.5
		Weight in Kilograms	3	74.0	15.1	3	52.7	2.5
	Group B	Height in Centimetres	3	184.0	5.3	3	175.7	6.5
		Weight in Kilograms	3	95.0	21.8	3	72.0	7.5
	Group AB	Height in Centimetres	2	178.5	9.2	1	160.3	.
		Weight in Kilograms	2	73.0	7.1	1	160.3	.
	Group O	Height in Centimetres	8	176.5	10.7	9	162.7	12.5
		Weight in Kilograms	8	79.0	11.8	9	60.0	7.2

Output 9. Output from **Basic Tables** showing statistics for *Height* and *Weight* across *Blood Group* and *Gender*

The next example shows the use of **Means** to compute statistics such as the mean and standard deviation when one variable has been grouped by categories of another (e.g. height grouped by gender). Proceed as follows:

- Choose

    Analyze➔Compare Means➔Means...

    to open the **Means** dialog box (the completed version is shown in Figure 10).
- Follow the steps in Figure 10 and click **OK**.

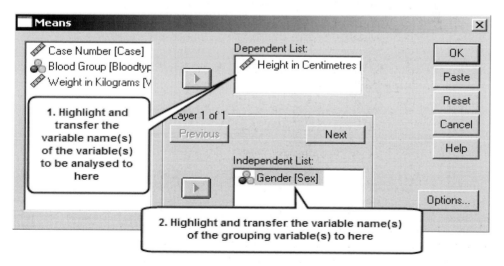

Figure 10. The **Means** dialog box for *Height* categorised by *Gender*

The output is listed in Output 10. The **Means** procedure has computed statistics such as the mean and standard deviation for the male and female participants separately.

Height in Centimetres

Gender	Mean	N	Std. Deviation
Male	176.63	16	12.46
Female	163.94	16	12.06
Total	170.28	32	13.68

Output 10. The mean *Height* for each level of *Gender* requested with **Means**

Breaking down the data with two or more classificatory variables: Layering

In Figure 10, notice the centrally located box containing two sub-dialog buttons **Previous** and **Next,** as well as the caption **Layer 1 of 1.** Here a **layer** is a qualitative variable, such as *Sex*. If you click **Next**, you can add another qualitative variable such as Blood Group [*Bloodtype*], so that the data are classified thus:

1st Layer	*Sex*	Male	Female
2nd Layer	*Bloodtype*	A AB B O	A AB B O

The output tabulates the mean *Height*, N and standard deviation for all combinations of *Gender* and *Blood Group* as shown in Output 11.

Height in Centimetres

Gender	Blood Group	Mean	N	Std. Deviation
Male	Group A	168.33	3	22.55
	Group B	184.00	3	5.29
	Group AB	178.50	2	9.19
	Group O	176.50	8	10.66
	Total	176.63	16	12.46
Female	Group A	160.33	3	10.50
	Group B	175.67	3	6.51
	Group AB	151.00	1	.
	Group O	162.67	9	12.47
	Total	163.94	16	12.06
Total	Group A	164.33	6	16.33
	Group B	179.83	6	7.00
	Group AB	169.33	3	17.16
	Group O	169.18	17	13.35
	Total	170.28	32	13.68

Output 11. The use of layering to compute the mean *Height*, N and standard deviation for all combinations of *Gender* and *Blood Group*

Note that if you had not clicked on **Next** before adding the second classificatory variable, the output would have consisted of *Height by Gender* and *Height by Blood Group* separately (i.e. only a single layer would have been used for each analysis).

Explore (in the **Descriptive Statistics** menu) can be regarded as a general exploratory data analysis (EDA) procedure. **Explore** offers many of the facilities already illustrated with other procedures, and (like **Means** and **Compare Means**) allows quantitative variables to be subdivided by the categories of a qualitative variable such as gender. If, for example, a data set contains the heights of 50 men and 50 women collected into a column headed *Height* and (in another column) code numbers making up the grouping variable *Sex*, the procedure **Explore** will produce statistical summaries, graphs and displays either for the 100 height measurements considered as a single group, or the heights of males or females (or both) considered separately.

A useful first step in the analysis of data is to obtain a picture of the data set as a whole. **Explore** offers three kinds of graphs and displays:
1. Histograms.
2. Stem-and-leaf displays.
3. Boxplots.

Readers unfamiliar with these can find, in Howell (2007), clear descriptions of histograms on pp. 19–20, of stem-and-leaf displays on pp. 21–23 and of boxplots on pp. 51-54.

The basis of all three types of graph is a table called a **frequency distribution**, which sets out either (in the case of nominal data) the categories comprising a qualitative variable and gives the frequency of observations in each category or (with measurements) divides the total range of values into arbitrary **class intervals** and gives the frequency of measurements that fall within each interval, that is, have values between the upper and lower **bounds** of the interval concerned. With data on height recorded in centimetres, for example, the total range could be divided into the class intervals (140–149, 150–159, 160–169, ….), and the frequency distribution would give the **frequencies** of heights within each of these ranges.

A **bar graph** (SPSS calls this a 'bar chart': see Output 3) is suitable for qualitative (nominal) data, such as the numbers of people in a sample belonging to the various blood groups. In a bar graph, the bars are separated to clarify the fact that the horizontal axis contains no scale of measurement; in fact, the order of the bars in Output 3 is arbitrary, since the Group AB bar could as well have followed the Group A bar. A **histogram** (see Output 8), on the other hand, is appropriate for measurements. Here the class intervals are stepped out along the horizontal axis and above each interval a bar is drawn whose height represents the number of people whose measurements fell within that interval. *In a histogram, as compared with a bar graph, the bars touch one another.*

To use the **Explore** procedure:
- Choose
  Analyze➜Descriptive Statistics➜Explore…
  to open the **Explore** dialog box.
- Follow the steps shown in Figure 11.

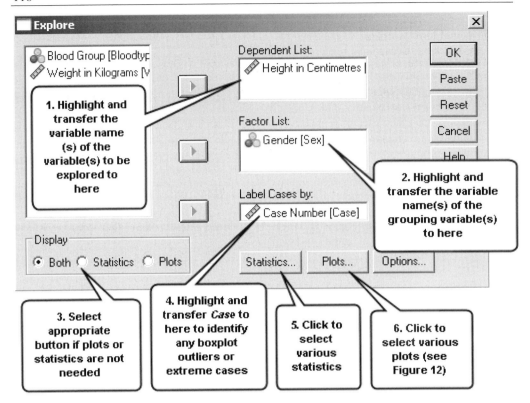

Figure 11. The **Explore** dialog box for *Height* categorised by *Gender*

- If there is a variable identifying the cases (e.g. *Case*), then click *Case* and ▶ to transfer it to the **Label Cases by** box. Outliers or extreme cases (these will be explained later) are identified in boxplots by their row numbers by default or by the identifier in the variable entered in the **Label Cases by** box.
- Click **Plots** to open the **Explore: Plots** dialog box (Figure 12). The default setting for the **Boxplots** is a side-by-side (**Factor levels together**) plot for each level of the factor (i.e. *Female* and *Male*) and **Stem-and-leaf** table. Had we not seen the histogram earlier, we might have clicked the check box for **Histogram**.
- Click **Continue** and then **OK**.

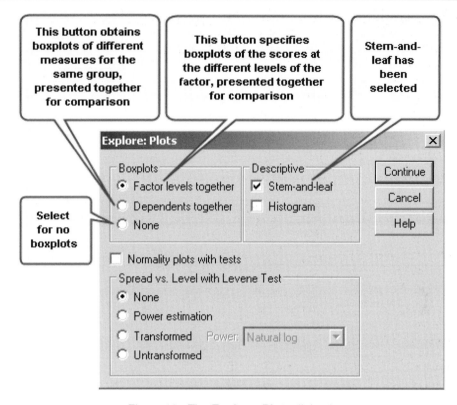

Figure 12. The **Explore: Plots** dialog box

Should you wish to have boxplots of two dependent variables side-by-side at each level of a classificatory variable (such as gender, or blood group), both dependent variables must be entered into the **Dependent List** box, and (in the **Boxplots** dialog box) the **Dependents together** radio button must be selected. In the present example, of course, it would have made no sense to plot boxplots of *Height* and *Weight* side-by-side at each level of *Sex*, since height and weight measurements have quite different scales.

The tables and the boxplots are shown in Outputs 12 and 13.

The descriptive statistics (upper table) and stem-and-leaf display (lower table) of *Height* for Males (one of the levels of *Sex*) is shown in Output 12; the output for Females is not shown. In the **stem-and-leaf display**, the central column of numbers (16, 16, 17, 17, ..., 19), which is the **stem**, represents the leading digit or digits (here they are hundreds and tens of centimetres). The numbers in the column headed **Leaf** are the final digits (centimetres). Each stem denotes the lower bound of the class interval: for example, the first number, 16, represents the lower bound of the class interval from 160 to 164, the second 16 from 165 to 169, the first 17 from 170 to 174 and so on. The column headed **Frequency** lists the number of cases on each stem. In stem 18, for example, there are four cases with heights between 180 and 184 centimetres. They are 180, 180, 182 and 183, since the leaves are listed as 0, 0, 2, 3. In addition, there is one case with a height between 185 and 189, namely 185. The display also shows extreme cases: there is one value equal to or less than 145. The stem-and-leaf display is very useful for displaying information about small data sets, but care should be taken when it is applied to larger databases as it can be ponderous: in this case a histogram is more suitable.

Descriptives

Gender				Statistic	Std. Error
Height in Centimetres	Male	Mean		176.63	3.12
		95% Confidence Interval for Mean	Lower Bound	169.98	
			Upper Bound	183.27	
		5% Trimmed Mean		177.31	
		Median		179.00	
		Variance		155.32	
		Std. Deviation		12.46	
		Minimum		145.00	
		Maximum		196.00	176.63
		Range		51.00	169.98
		Interquartile Range		14.50	183.27
		Skewness		-.95	177.31
		Kurtosis		1.64	179.00

```
Height in Centimetres Stem-and-Leaf Plot for
SEX= Male

 Frequency     Stem &  Leaf

     1.00 Extremes      (=<145)
     1.00         16 .  0
      .00         16 .
     4.00         17 .  0002
     2.00         17 .  58
     4.00         18 .  0023
     1.00         18 .  5
     2.00         19 .  00
     1.00         19 .  6

 Stem width:         10
 Each leaf:      1 case(s)
```

Output 12. Descriptive statistics, and stem-and-leaf display for *Height* categorised by *Gender* (only the output for Males shown here)

The structure of a boxplot is shown in Table 2. The box itself represents that portion of the distribution falling between the 25th and 75th percentiles, i.e. the **lower** and **upper quartiles** (in EDA terminology these are known as **hinges**). The xth percentile is the value below which x% of the distribution lies, so 50% of the heights lie between the 25th and 75th percentiles. The thick horizontal line across the interior of the box represents the median. The vertical lines outside the box, which are known as **whiskers**, connect the largest and smallest values that are not outliers or extreme cases.

Table 2. Structure of a boxplot	
✳2	**Extreme case** - more than 3 box-lengths above the box. The number is the identifier, either the row number or from the variable entered in the **Label Cases by** box.
○21	**Outlier** - more than 1.5 box lengths above the box. The number is the identifier.
Whisker ➜	Largest value which is not an outlier or an extreme score.
	Top of box: 75th percentile (upper quartile)
Box ➜	Bar: Median (50th percentile)
	Bottom of box: 25th percentile (lower quartile)
Whisker ➜	Smallest value which is not an outlier or an extreme score.
○25	**Outlier** - more than 1.5 box lengths below the box. The numbers are the identifiers.
○26	
✳27	**Extreme case** - more than 3 box-lengths below the box. The number is the identifier.

Output 13 shows one **outlier** but no **extreme cases**. An **outlier** (**o**) is defined as a value more than 1.5 box-lengths away from the box, and an **extreme case** (*) as more than 3 box-lengths away from the box. The number(s) alongside o and * are the case number(s). The case numbers are either the row numbers in **Data View** by default, or the identifiers from the variable entered in the **Label Cases by** box.

Skewness is indicated by an eccentric location of the median in the box. Notice that the distribution of heights for females is much more symmetric than that for males. The o^3 under the Male boxplot in Output 13 indicates the existence of an outlier and that it is the value for the case in row 3. This value (145cm) is well below the average height for males and its presence is also noted in the stem-and-leaf display in Output 12.

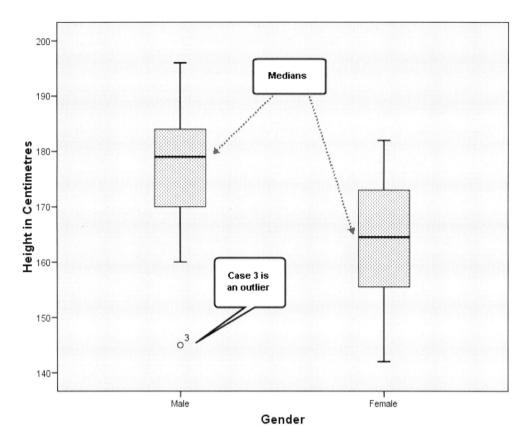

Output 13. Boxplots of *Height* categorised by *Gender*

Boxplots are particularly useful for identifying outliers and extreme cases in data sets, and can be requested directly by choosing

*   **Graphs➜Chart Builder**
    and selecting **Box** from the gallery (see Section 5.4 in the next Chapter).

See Section 5.4

4.4   MANIPULATION OF THE DATA SET

4.4.1   Reducing and transforming data

After a data set has been entered into SPSS, it may be necessary to modify it in certain ways. For example, an exploratory data analysis may have revealed that one or two extreme cases have exerted undue leverage upon the values of statistics such as the mean and standard deviation. One approach to this problem is to de-select the extreme cases and repeat the analysis with the remaining scores (cf. Tabachnick & Fidell, 2007). Any exclusions, however, should be mentioned in the experimental report. Cases can be dropped from the analysis by using the **Select Cases** command (Section 3.3.1).

Sometimes, in order to satisfy the distribution requirements for the use of a particular statistic, it may be necessary to **transform** the values of a variable. For example, a distribution of response latencies is often **positively skewed,** i.e. it has a long tail to the right; whereas the distribution of the logarithms of the raw scores is more symmetrical. Transformations are easily implemented with the **Compute** procedure (Section 4.4.2).

Finally, it is sometimes convenient to combine or alter the categories that make up a qualitative or ordinal variable. This is achieved with the **Recode** procedure, which can construct a new variable with the new category assignments (Section 4.4.3).

4.4.2 The COMPUTE procedure

Transforming the data

The **Compute** procedure was used in Chapter 3 to number the cases in a data set. **Compute** can also be used to calculate many different kinds of transformations of the original data set. New variables of transformed data can be created or the values of existing variables can be replaced by the transformed values. We do not recommend the second approach, because the original values for the variable cannot then be recovered. The **Compute** procedure also allows transformation of subsets of the original data set that have been specified by logical conditions.

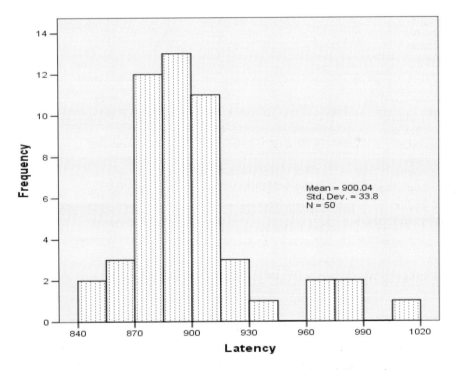

Output 14. Histogram of the response latencies of 50 people

Output 14 shows a histogram of the response latencies of fifty people. Typically, such data show a positively skewed distribution, with a long tail to the right. For the purposes of statistical testing, the investigator might want to transform the original data to make the distribution more symmetrical. Such normalisation can often be achieved by taking the logarithms, square roots, reciprocals and other functions of the original scores. These transformations, however, have different effects upon distribution shape, as the following exercise will demonstrate. We shall begin by using the **Compute** procedure to calculate the natural logarithms of the raw data

Assuming the data set is present in the **Data Editor**,

- Choose
  Transform➜Compute…
  to open the **Compute Variable** dialog box (the completed version is shown in Figure 13).
- Click in the **Target Variable** box at top left and type the name *LogLatency*.

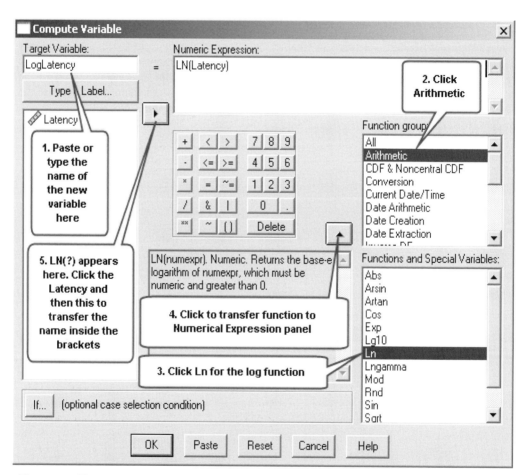

Figure 13. The completed **Compute Variable** dialog box for computing the natural logarithm of *Latency*

- Scroll down through the **Functions group:** box on the right to find the **Arithmetic** group. Click on it to open the list of arithmetic functions in the box below. Scroll down to the natural logarithm function **Ln**. Click on it and then ⬆ to paste it into the **Numeric Expression** box where it will appear as **LN[?]**.

- In the list of variables in the lower left panel, click *Latency* and ▶ to make this variable the argument of the log function (i.e. *Latency* replaces ?). The expression **LN[Latency]** will now appear in the **Numeric Expression** box (see Figure 13).
- Click **OK**.

A new column *LogLatency*, containing the natural logs of the values of *Latencies*, will appear in **Data View**. You may wish to add a label (e.g. Log of Latency) for this new variable and to change the number of decimal places – see Section 2.3.1. A setting of two decimal places works well in this example; but with a reciprocal transformation (see below), four places of decimals would be required. Output 15 shows the histogram of the logs of the original latencies. The transformation has clearly reduced the skewness of the distribution.

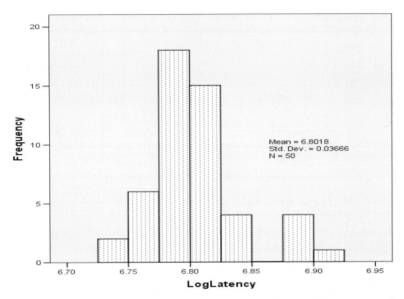

Output 15. Histogram showing the distribution of the natural logs of the response latencies. The distribution is more symmetrical than that of the untransformed values of *Latency*

Other functions produce even more striking transformations of the original data. The reciprocal transformation (1/x), for example, produces the distribution pictured in Output 16. This time, there is a tail to the left, indicating that this is an inappropriate transformation for these data.

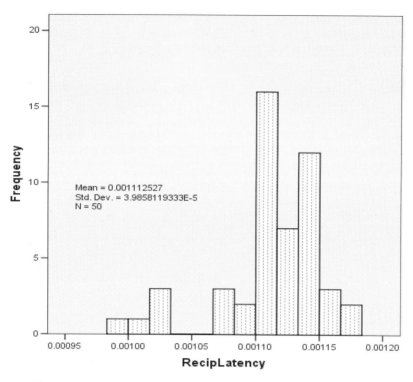

Output 16. The distribution of a reciprocal (1/x) transformation of the response latencies. This distribution is negatively skewed, with a tail to the left

Using Compute to obtain functions of several variables

Compute can also be used to combine values of variables. Suppose you have a data set comprising the marks of schoolchildren in their French, German and Spanish examinations. You might be interested in averaging each child's score over the three examinations.

One way of doing this is to write your own numerical expression in the **Numerical Expression** box of the **Compute Variable** dialog box (e.g. name the new variable *MeanMark* and enter the expression *(French + German + Spanish)/3*. Should any child not have taken all three examinations, however, the mean would not be calculated and a system-missing mark would appear in **Data View** instead.

Another way is to paste the **MEAN** function from the **Functions and Special Variables** list (Figure 13) into the **Numerical Expression** box and transfer the variable names *French*, *German* and *Spanish* into the pasted function taking care to have a comma between each name and to ensure that ? is no longer present (e.g. **MEAN**(*French, German, Spanish*)). Should a child's mark be missing, the mean of the other two marks will be calculated. The function MEAN, therefore, calculates the mean from whatever valid values may be present. Only if a child has sat none of the three examinations, will a system-missing value of the mean be recorded.

Figure 14 is a section of **Data View** comparing the results of using these two ways, *MeanbyDiv* for the first way and *MEAN* for the second way.

ChildsN	French	German	Spanish	MeanbyDiv	MEAN
Fred	67	78	23	56.00	56.00
Mary	50	50	.	.	50.00
John	.	.	.	.	.
Peter	0	50	50	33.33	33.33
Amy	0	.	.	.	.00
Jack	23	.	.	.	23.00

Figure 14.   Two ways to computing the means of three variables

It can be seen from Figure 14 that the add-then-divide way only works when there are marks on all three examinations. It fails with Mary, John, Amy and Jack. The MEAN way fails to produce a result only with John, who did not sit any of the examinations. The MEAN function also makes a clear distinction between zeros and missing values: Mary correctly receives the mean of 50 and 50 (50); whereas Peter correctly receives the mean of 0, 50 and 50 (33.33). Jack correctly receives a mean of 23 even though he sat only one examination.

Conditional computations

A medical researcher has gathered some data on the drinking and substance intake of patients. Figure 15 shows a section from **Data View**, in which *0 = No Abuse and 1 = Abuse*.

	Patient	Alcohol	Substances
1	Sarah	No Abuse	No Abuse
2	Alan	Abuse	No Abuse
3	Jim	No Abuse	Abuse
4	Joe	Abuse	Abuse

Figure 15.   A section of the data set for substance abuse in patients

The researcher wants to create a third variable, *Addict*, with values as follows:
>   0 for patients with No Abuse on both variables
>   1 for patients with Abuse on *Alcohol* but No Abuse on *Substances*
>   2 for patients with No Abuse on *Alcohol* but Abuse on *Substances*
>   3 for patients with Abuse on both variables.

The problem can be solved in several ways. We could begin by letting *Addict = Alcohol + Substances + 1*. We could then instruct the **Compute** routine to proceed as follows.   If either *(Alcohol = Substances = 0) or (Alcohol = 1 and Substances = 0)*, subtract *1* from *Addict*. This will solve the problem, because the remaining combinations would fail to meet either condition and no subtraction would take place.
- Choose
    Transform➜Compute
    to access the **Compute Variable** dialog box.
- Type *Addict* into the **Target Variable** box.

- Transfer the variable names *Alcohol* and *Substances* to the **Numeric Expression** box and create the expression *Alcohol + Substances + 1* (see Figure 16).
- Click **OK**.

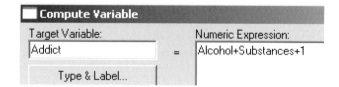

Figure 16. Part of the **Compute Variable** dialog box for computing values for the new variable
Addict

The values of *Addict* will then appear in **Data View** as shown in Figure 17.

	Patient	Alcohol	Substances	Addict
1	Sarah	No Abuse	No Abuse	1
2	Alan	Abuse	No Abuse	2
3	Jim	No Abuse	Abuse	2
4	Joe	Abuse	Abuse	3

Figure 17. **Data View** showing the newly computed variable *Addict*

These values for *Addict* are correct except for Sarah and Alan who should have a value of *0* and *1* respectively. We therefore have to modify the computation of these values of *Addict* by subtracting *1* from the total when both variables have *0*, or if *Alcohol = 1* and *Substances = 0*. This is done by constructing a conditional expression in the **Compute Variable: If Cases** dialog box.

- Return to the **Compute Variable** dialog box and change the Numeric Expression entry to *Addict – 1*.
- Click the **If...** button to open the **Compute Variable: If Cases** dialog box.
- Click the radio button labelled **Include if Case satisfies condition:**
- In the box on the right enter the expression:
  (Alcohol = 0 & Substance = 0) | (Alcohol = 1 & Substances = 0).
  The symbol **&** means **AND** and the symbol | means **OR** in this logical expression. Care must be taken with inserting brackets in the conditional expression to ensure the logical operators **AND** and **OR** operate appropriately.
- The top part of the completed dialog box will appear as in Figure 18.

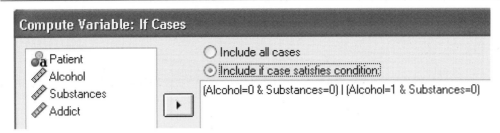

Figure 18. Top part of the **Compute Variables: If Cases** dialog box with the specially written conditional expression

- Click **Continue** to return to the **Compute Variable** dialog box.
- Click OK to compute the altered values of *Addict*.

The entries in **Data View** will now appear as shown in Figure 19.

	Patient	Alcohol	Substances	Addict
1	Sarah	No Abuse	No Abuse	0
2	Alan	Abuse	No Abuse	1
3	Jim	No Abuse	Abuse	2
4	Joe	Abuse	Abuse	3

Figure 19. The desired values for *Addict* after using a conditional expression in the **Compute Variable** dialog box

An alternative method would be to compute *Addict* = *Alcohol**10 + *Substances* and then use the **Recode** procedure (next Section) to recode the resulting set of values.

4.4.3   The RECODE and VISUAL BINNING procedures

We have seen that the **Compute** procedure operates upon one or more of the variables in the data set, so that there will be as many values in the transformed variable as there were in the original variable.   Sometimes, however, rather than wanting a transformation that will systematically change all the values of a variable, the user may want to assign relatively few code numbers to values that fall within specified ranges of the variable.

For example, suppose we have a set of 18 children's examination marks on a scale from 0 to 100 (Table 3). We shall recode these into three bins: 0-49 as Fail; 50-74 as Pass; 75-100 as Good. This can easily be done by using either of two other procedures on the **Transform** menu: the **Recode** procedure or the **Visual Binning** procedure.

| Table 3. Children's examination marks ||||||
Child	Mark	Child	Mark	Child	Mark
1	62	7	70	13	50
2	51	8	40	14	50
3	40	9	63	15	42
4	68	10	81	16	65
5	38	11	62	17	30
6	40	12	78	18	71

*Using the **Recode** procedure*

Enter the data into **Data View** in variables named *Case* and *Marks* and then:

- Choose
  Transform➔Recode into Different Variables…
  to open the **Recode into Different Variables** dialog box (Figure 20). Just as in the case of the **Compute** procedure, it is possible to change the values in the same variable to the recoded values but we recommend placing the recoded values in a new variable, perhaps *Grade*.

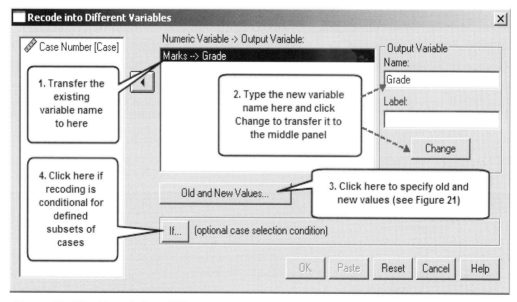

Figure 20. The **Recode into Different Variables** dialog box showing the original variable and the one to which the recoded values will be placed

- Click *Marks* and 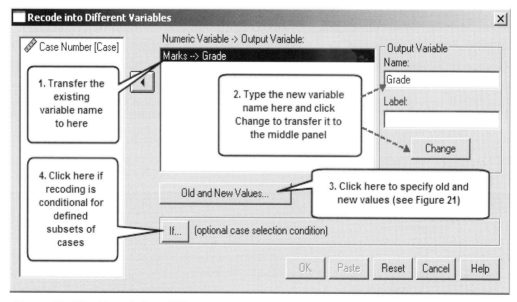 to paste the name into the **Numeric Variable→Output Variable** box.
- Type the name of the output variable *Grade* into the **Name** box and click **Change** to insert the name into the **Numeric Variable→Output Variable** box (Figure 20).

- Click the **Old and New Values** box to open the **Recode into Different Variables: Old and New Values** dialog box (the completed dialog box is shown in Figure 21).
- Follow the steps in Figure 21 for defining the old and new values. These will categorise all exam marks less than 50 as *Fail,* 50-74 as *Pass* and 75 and over as *Good.*
- Click **Continue** and **OK**.

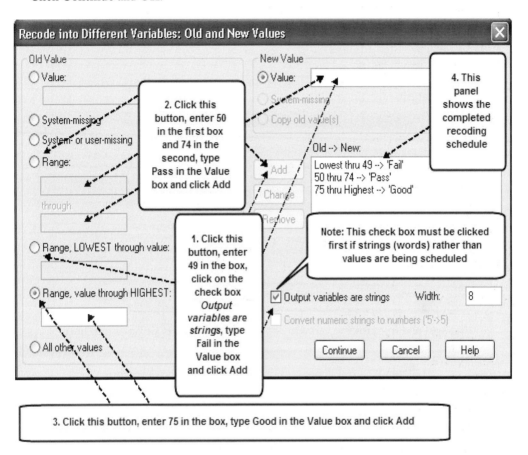

Figure 21. The **Old and New Values** dialog box with defined ranges for Pass, Fail and Good

A new string variable *Grade* containing the recoded labels *Pass, Fail* and *Good* will appear in **Data View** (Figure 22).

	Case	Marks	Grade
8	8	40	Fail
9	9	63	Pass
10	10	81	Good
11	11	62	Pass
12	12	78	Good

Figure 22. Part of **Data View** showing the new string variable *Grade* with the labels Pass, Fail and Good

*Using the **Visual Binning***

The **Visual Binning** procedure provides many different ways of categorising variables on the basis of cut-off values, equal-width intervals, equal-percentile intervals or on means and selected standard deviation intervals. We shall illustrate its use with the medical data by categorising the height data into three bins: (1) tall (greater than 180 cm); (2) intermediate (160 to 180 cm); (3) short (less than 160 cm).

- Choose
  Transform➜Visual Binning
  to open the **Visual Binning** dialog box.
- Select *Height in Centimetres* and click on arrowhead to transfer the variable name to the **Variables to Bin** box (Figure 23).

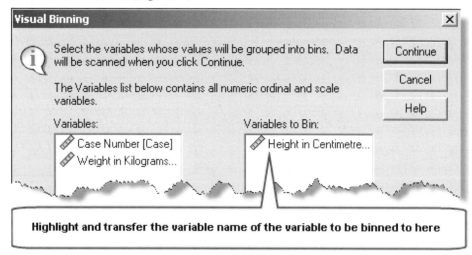

Figure 23. The upper part of the **Visual Binning** dialog box

- Click **Continue** to open the next dialog box.
- Click *Height in Centimetres* in the **Scanned Variable List** box to show the histogram of heights (Figure 24).
- Enter *160* in the first **Value** cell (it overwrites HIGH) and *Short* in the first **Label** cell. Click the lower radio button **Excluded (<)** to indicate that the category *Short* is greater than 160 cm. Had we defined the category as "160 and less", then the default radio button **Included (<=)** would apply.
- Enter *180* in the second **Value** cell and *Medium* in the second **Label** cell.
- Enter *220* (any value beyond the tallest value would suffice) in the third **Value** cell and *Tall* in the third **Label** cell.
- Enter a variable name such as observing the usual rules for naming variables (e.g. *HeightBin*) in the **Binned Variable** cell (Figure 25).
- Click **OK**.

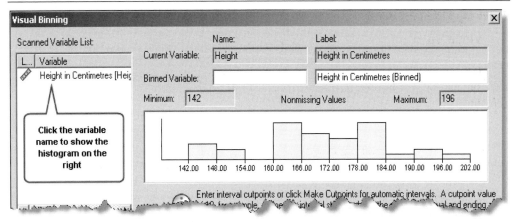

Figure 24. The histogram of *Height* is visible after clicking the variable name

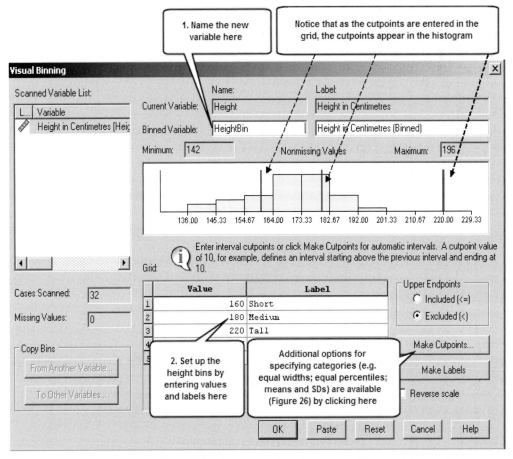

Figure 25. The completed **Visual Binning** dialog box for categorising *Height* into three bins

Notice that as each cutpoint is entered, its position is drawn into the histogram above as soon as the cursor is moved to another cell. If desired, the cursor can be positioned over one of these lines and moved left or right by clicking and dragging. The new variable *HeightBin* in the data set is shown in Figure 28.

To split the heights into equal percentiles (i.e. $<25^{th}$ percentile, 25-50th percentile, 50-75th percentile and $>75^{th}$ percentile), proceed as follows:

- Follow the steps of the previous example but instead of entering values and labels, click **Make Cutpoints** and enter *3* into the **Number of Cutpoints** (Figure 26) i.e. one less than the number of intervals. SPSS will automatically show *25* in the **Width%** box below.
- Click **Apply**, fill in suitable labels in the usual place (Figure 27).
- Enter a new variable name (e.g. *HeightPercentiles*) in the **Binned Variable** box.
- Click **OK**.

The new variable *HeightPercentiles* in the data set is shown in Figure 28.

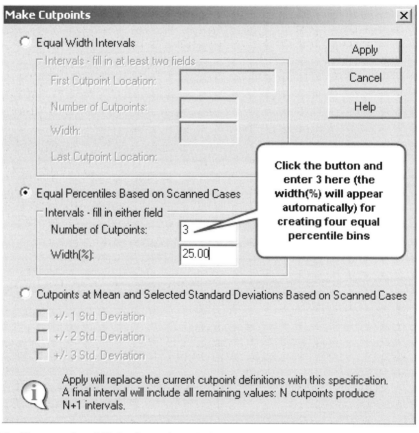

Figure 26. The completed **Make Cutpoints** dialog box for creating four equal percentile bins

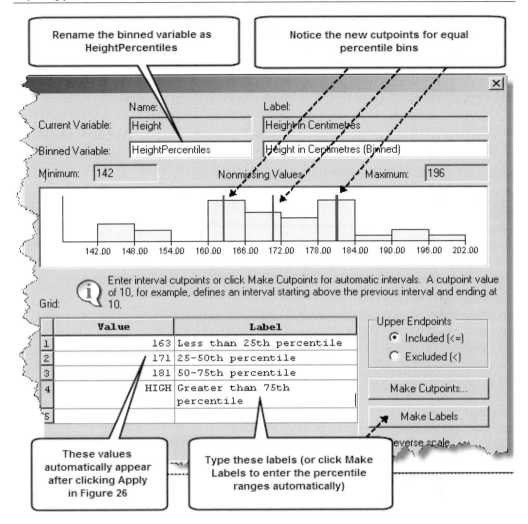

Figure 27. The **Visual Binning** dialog box with new variable name *HeightPercentiles* and labels for the percentile bins. The values were entered automatically by SPSS and are shown on the histogram above

Case	Bloodtype	Sex	Height	Weight	HeightBin	HeightPercentiles
1	Group O	Male	178	75	Medium	50th-75th percentile
2	Group O	Male	196	100	Tall	Greater than 75th percentile
3	Group A	Male	145	60	Short	Less than 25th percentile
4	Group O	Male	170	71	Medium	25th-50th percentile
5	Group B	Male	180	80	Tall	50th-75th percentile
6	Group O	Male	175	69	Medium	50th-75th percentile

Figure 28. The first six cases of the original dataset showing the new variables *HeightBin* and *HeightPercentiles* created by **Visual Binning**

EXERCISE 4

Correcting and preparing your data

This Exercise explores the data in your saved file of merged data (see Exercise 3), consisting of the responses of 335 people (including yourself) to a questionnaire.

Opening SPSS

Open SPSS in the usual way, selecting the data file *Merged Questionnaire Data* which was saved in the previous Exercise. Ensure that the value labels (e.g. Female) are visible in **Data View** (if not, choose **Value Labels** in the **View** drop-down menu or click the **Labels** icon in the toolbar).

Describing categorical data: Obtaining a frequency distribution

Use
Analyze➔Descriptive Statistics➔Frequencies... procedure described in **4.3.1** to obtain a frequency listing for the variable *Smoker*. In the **Frequencies** dialog box, click **Charts...** . In the **Frequencies: Charts** dialog box, select **Bar Chart(s)**.

Inspect the frequency table in the **SPSS Viewer**. Is the information in the table what you expected? Before taking any steps to remedy the situation, inspect the bar chart as well.

The bar chart

You will notice immediately that, although the variable *Smoker* was supposed to consist only of Yes and No responses, the horizontal axis of the bar chart also shows a bar for 3. There is obviously an error in the data set. Look at the frequency table again. It shows that the 335 cases that were processed included an entry of 3. There is also one missing value labelled *System*. In **Data View**, this will be represented by a full stop. Return to **Data View** by clicking the name of your merged file in the **Task Bar** at the foot of the screen.

In **Data View**, you will see that for the variable *Smoker*, Case 10 has a 3 and Case 14 has no value. The 3 in Case 10 should obviously be a 2, since there is no entry in *NpDay*. In Case 14, the person is recorded as smoking 5 cigarettes per day, so the missing value should be replaced by 1 (Yes). Such transcription errors are common when one is preparing large data sets, which is why it is so important to screen your data before carrying out any analysis. Sometimes it is more convenient to find suspicious values by highlighting the appropriate variable in **Data View** and selecting
Edit➔Find...

You then enter the suspect value (in this case *3*) in the **Find what** box and click **Find Next**.

To remedy the two transcription errors that you have found, click *3* for Case 10 to get ⟦ 3 ▾ ⟧ , click the arrow and select *No* from the choice of options. Do the same for Case 14, but select *Yes* from the choice of options.

Save the corrected data file, using the **Save As** item within the **File** drop-down menu, to a new file name *Questionnaire Data (corrected)* so that you do not confuse it with the uncorrected data file *Merged Questionnaire Data*.

Now re-run the **Frequencies** procedure and notice the differences in the output. Your data-screening operation has detected and rectified two errors in the original data set.

Obtaining a bar chart from the Graphs menu

You can obtain a bar chart directly, without any additional statistics, by selecting **Graphs➔Chart Builder...** and selecting the **Simple Bar** from the gallery of **Bar** to obtain the **Simple Bar** preview. Click and drag the variable name *Smoker* to the *X-Axis* box. Click **OK** to obtain the bar chart.

Editing a bar chart

Now try to edit the bar chart in the **Viewer**. (There will be more on editing graphs in Chapter 5.) Initially, bar charts (and other graphics) appear in colour on the screen. A coloured screen image, however, does not print well in black and white. To make the image suitable for black-and-white printing, some editing is necessary. Proceed as follows.

- Double-click anywhere on the bar chart to open the **Chart Editor** window. To edit any part of the figure, you must select that part of the screen figure and double-click it to open the editing dialog box. At the same time, the item(s) will show a purple colour or appear within a purple frame. So double-click one of the bars to see the **Properties** dialog box or alternatively right click to open the **Properties** dialog box.
- Click the **Fill & Border** tab at the top. Click **Fill** and select the desired colour (e.g. a light grey). If you click **Apply**, you can preview the result in the chart and change to another colour if desired. Once you are satisfied with the change, click **Close**. You can also change the fill pattern by clicking the **Pattern** box at the bottom left of the **Color** panel.

It is possible to control many other features of charts and graphs with the **Chart Editor**. For example, by double-clicking an axis, a dialog box will appear enabling you to label the axis and position the label either centrally or to right or left (use the **Justification** selection). You can also change other aspects of the screen figure, such as the spacing of bars and boxes in graphs. (Select the **Bar Options** tab in the **Properties** dialog box.)

There are many other adjustments that can be made; but the way forward is to try some more editing yourself.

When you have finished editing the graph, return to **SPSS Viewer** by clicking ☒ in the top right-hand corner. (You can also leave the Chart Editor by choosing **File** and **Close**.) To save your edited chart, ensure that it has a box around it; if not, click anywhere within the bar chart and a box will appear. Then select
File➔Save
to obtain a directory dialog box for selecting the disk drive and folder for the file.

Try printing out your chart, following the instructions in Section 3.5.

Describing categorical data: Cross-tabulation

The next part of the Exercise is to produce some contingency tables, using the **Crosstabs** procedure (Section 4.3.1). A cross-tabulation is a table showing the frequency of observations in each combination of two categorical variables. Cross-tabulate the *Sex* and *Faculty* of the cases in your merged data set as follows:

Choose **Analyze➔Descriptive Statistics➔Crosstabs...** to open the **Crosstabs** dialog box. Enter one of the variables into the **Row(s)** box by clicking its name and then on ▶. Enter the other variable into the **Column(s)** box. Click **OK**.

From an inspection of the output answer the following question:

- **How many females are in the Faculty of Medicine?**

You can re-arrange this table by using the **Pivot** procedure (see Section 3.2.2). Double-click on the table so that a hashed box surrounds it. Select the **Pivot** drop-down menu, then **Pivoting Trays**. Experiment with the data by interchanging the variables among the **Layer**, **Column** and **Row** borders. (Do this by clicking and dragging the variables between the borders in the **Pivoting Trays1** box.)

If you want to save the cross-tabulation output, click the second sub-table containing the cross-tabulation and then **Save**. Complete the dialog box.

Finishing the session

Close down SPSS and any other windows before logging out.

EXERCISE 5

Preparing your data (continued)

Opening SPSS

For this Exercise, you should have available the corrected merged data set that you corrected in the course of the previous Exercise and saved as *Questionnaire Data (corrected)*. Open SPSS with this data set in the usual way.

Describing interval data

The next part of the Exercise is to explore the *Age* variable by tabulating a range of statistics and drawing a histogram with a superimposed normal curve.

Choose
Analyze➜Descriptive Statistics➜Frequencies…
to see the **Frequencies** dialog box. Transfer *Age* to the *Variables* box.

Click **Statistics…** to see the **Frequencies: Statistics** dialog box. Choose Quartiles, Mean, Median, Std. Deviation, Range, Minimum and Maximum. Click **Continue**.

Back in the **Frequencies** dialog box, turn off **Display Frequency Tables**.

Now choose
Charts➜Histograms
and click the **With Normal Curve** option. Click **Continue** to return to the **Frequencies** dialog box.

- **Edit the histogram to make it suitable for black-and-white printing**

- **Print the histogram**.

Manipulation of the data set – transforming variables

It is sometimes useful to change the data set in some way. For instance, in the current data set, some people have entered their weight in stones and pounds, others in kilograms. Likewise, some people may have entered their height in feet and inches (or just inches), others in metres. In order to have useful data on weight and height, you must use the same units of measurement. In this Exercise we shall adopt metric units (kilograms and metres). This will necessitate converting any other measurements into metric measurements. Use the **Compute** procedure (Section 4.4.2) by selecting
Transform➜ Compute Variable...
to see the **Compute Variable** dialog box. In the **Target Variable** box, type the name of the variable (*Kilos*) which contains the kilograms data. In the **Numeric Expression** box, enter the conversion function: entering **(Stones*14 + Pounds) * 0.453** to convert pounds to kilograms. (One pound is 0.453 kilograms and stones convert to pounds by multiplying by 14.) Note that, in computing, the symbol * is used for multiplication. Do not click **OK** yet!

There remains one further problem: what about those cases whose weight is already in *Kilos* and do not have any values in the *Stones* and *Pounds* variables? If the formula above were to be immediately applied, these people would end up with no values in the *Kilos* column.

To convert only the cases with stones and pounds measurements, you must select the **If** box in the **Compute Variable** dialog box, then the **Include if case satisfies condition** box and enter the following expression **stones > 0** which tells the program to calculate the kilograms if the entry in *Stones* is nonzero. Select **Continue** and then **OK**.

You will receive a message which asks **Change existing variable?**. Select the **OK** option. Now the program will calculate all the missing *Kilos* data and enter them in the data set. Check that it has done this. Save the file using the **Save As** option, giving the amended file a new name (e.g. **Metric Data**). This ensures that you still have a copy of the old file, in case you have made any mistakes in calculation and you wish to retrieve the old data at some future time. (It is often regarded as a safer procedure to recode data into a new variable since it allows one to check that the correct recoding procedure has been requested. This has not been done here because we need to preserve the values in *kilos* already present for some cases.)

Now do a similar conversion for the height data, converting feet and inches to metres. To do this you will need to know that there are 12 inches in a foot and 1 inch is 0.0254 metres. Work out a conversion factor with this in mind. Remember to change the condition to **Feet >0**. When you have converted the height data, save the file again, this time by simply clicking **Save** rather than **Save As** since you have already nominated *Metric Data* as the new file.

Describing interval data – means of cases categorised by a grouping variable

You can obtain a table of means for one variable at different categories (or combinations) of another variable (or variables). Use the **Means** procedure described in Section 4.3.2 to obtain a two-way table of means for *Metres* by *Sex*. Then use the same procedure to obtain a three-way table of *Kilos* by *Sex* by *Faculty*. (Look carefully at Section 4.3.2 to see how to layer the variables, using **Next**, to produce the three-way table.)

- **Print the output of this exercise.**

Finishing the session

Close down SPSS and any other windows before logging out of the computer.

CHAPTER 5

Graphs and charts

5.1   INTRODUCTION

SPSS offers a wide range of graphs and charts. We shall first consider some general points about graph-drawing in SPSS. It is worth noting that the most elaborate charts do not necessarily bring out the results of an investigation in the clearest way. Three-dimensional effects, for example, though they may be aesthetically attractive, can obscure the very point that you are trying to bring out.

5.1.1   Graphs and charts on SPSS

There are several different ways of producing graphics with SPSS. There is a selection of procedures on the **Graphs** menu (Figure 1) but graphs are options in analytical procedures as well. For instance, there is a **Charts** option in the **Frequencies** procedure and a **Profile Plot** option in the ANOVA procedures. These are standard charts although they can be customised to a considerable extent. The appearance of graphs can be controlled to an even greater extent by using **Chart Builder** or **Interactive** at the top of the menu. The gallery of charts and graphs obtained by clicking on the **Chart Builder** item in the **Graphs** menu (Figure 2) is useful for selecting the type of chart or graph desired. If the gallery does not initially appear, click **Gallery** at the left of the **Chart Builder** dialog box.

Figure 1. The **Graphs** menu

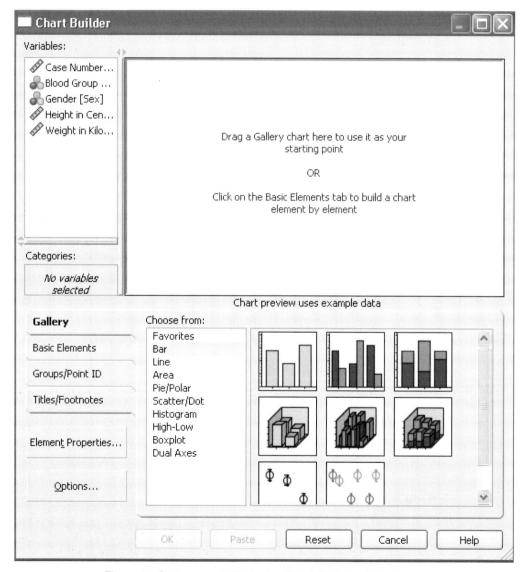

Figure 2. Options available in the **Chart Builder** dialog box

Readers who have used the graphic procedures in earlier releases of SPSS may be comforted to see that they are still available in the **Legacy Dialogs** submenu with a similar list available in the **Interactive** submenu (Figure 3). In this chapter we shall concentrate on using the **Chart Builder** as our principal means of drawing graphics.

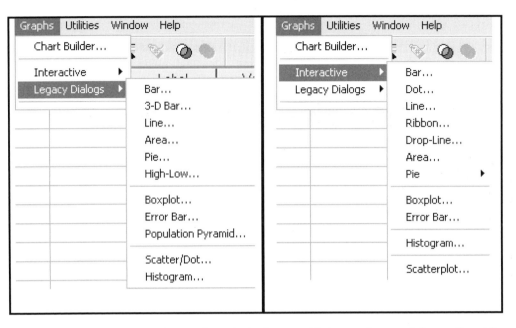

Figure 3. The list of graphical procedures in the **Legacy Dialogs** submenu (left panel) and the **Interactive** submenu (right panel)

For best results, the data set should be carefully prepared beforehand. It is easier to change variable names and labels in **Variable View** than afterwards at the editing stage of a chart.

If there are missing data, specify beforehand whether they should be included in the chart. They can be excluded from graphs by turning off the **Display groups defined by missing values** box in the **Options** dialog box. Once you are in a chart procedure, it is often easier to add a title within the **Title** option rather than at the editing stage after the chart has been produced.

When completing a dialog box for a graph, you can often leave some boxes unchecked. The acid test of whether enough information has been specified in a dialog box is whether the **OK** button is enabled: if it is not, more information is needed before the chart can be plotted.

5.1.2 Viewing a chart

A chart in **SPSS Viewer** may occasionally disappear from the screen. You can recall it by clicking its icon in the left-hand pane of SPSS Viewer. If you are working in another window, you can restore the chart by selecting it from the **Window** menu at the top of the screen.

You can make a chart narrower by clicking it and dragging the right-hand handle of the surrounding frame leftwards. If you wish to change the aspect ratio of **all** charts to make them narrower, select
Edit➔Options➔Charts

and amend the value in the **Chart Aspect Ratio** box. The default value is *1.25*, but if you change that to, say, *1,* graphs and charts will appear narrower.

Unwanted images use up memory. Bear in mind that images can always be recreated from saved data files. Save only those that you need at the moment.

Once a dialog box for a chart has been completed, the **command syntax** (see Chapter 15) can be saved to a file by clicking **Paste** from which the (unedited) graph can be generated at any time in the future. Graphs that have been edited can be stored as **chart templates** for future use. Chart templates are very useful for generating whole sets of similar graphs for analogous tables of data, such as those at different layers of a multi-way table.

5.1.3   Editing charts and saving templates

SPSS provides a special **Chart Editor** for graphic material which allows a wide range of changes to be made to a graph or chart, though proficiency takes practice. Enter the **Chart Editor** by double-clicking anywhere in the image. A single click will draw a single frame around the image. After double-clicking, the original image is shaded and a copy of it is shown in the **Chart Editor**.

The **Chart Editor** allows the user to change text, colours, type of graphic, title, axis ticks and labels, and other features. Many of these changes are made by double-clicking the item in the chart and completing dialogs.

For black-and-white printing, it is usually best to use the **Chart Editor** to remove the colours and replace them with patterns. Alternatively, the default setting for charts can be changed from cycling through colours to cycling through patterns. To do this

- Choose
  Edit➜Options...
  and select the **Charts** tab in the **Options** dialog box.
- Within the **Style Cycle Preference** selection panel, select **Cycle through patterns only**.
- Click **Fills...** and select whichever pattern you wish for **Simple Charts** and delete the empty pattern box in **Grouped Charts** by clicking the radio button for **Grouped Charts**, selecting the empty box pattern and clicking **Remove**. Click **Continue**.
- Click **Apply** and then **OK**.

This change will only apply for the current session if your computer is part of a networked system.

If it is likely that the same chart may be requested on subsequent occasions using different data, the user may wish to save the editing changes as a **Chart Template** so that the template can be applied to the later charts. Instructions about how to save and how to invoke a template will be given in Section 5.2.6.

5.2   BAR CHARTS

This section describes simple bar charts, clustered bar charts, panelled bar charts, 3-D charts, chart templates and how to edit bar charts.

5.2.1   Simple bar charts

A bar chart for comparing the means of groups of observers such as those of the drug experiment (see Table 1 in Section 2.1.4) is most easily obtained as follows:

- Choose
  Graphs➜Chart Builder…
- A warning box (Figure 4) will appear asking the user to ensure that each variable has been defined in the **Measure** column of **Variable View** either as **Scale**, **Ordinal** or **Nominal**, and that each level of categorical variables has been assigned a label. **Variable View** by default assumes variables are **Scale** so it may be necessary to change categorical variables to **Nominal** either in **Variable View** or by clicking on **Define Variable Properties…** in the warning box. Click **OK** to continue.

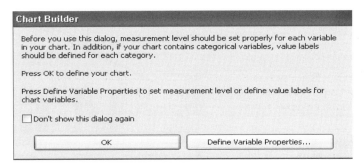

Figure 4. The warning box when **Chart Builder** is opened

- Ensure that the illustrations correspond to **Bar** by checking that **Bar** is highlighted in the **Choose from** panel (Figure 5). Click the first (top left) picture of simple bars to highlight it and then drag it to the **Chart preview** in the panel above. In addition, an **Element Properties** dialog box will also appear (Figure 6).
- Click the variable name *Score* to highlight it and then drag it to the **Y-Axis** box. Do likewise with *Experimental Condition* to the **X-Axis** box.
- To include the 95% Confidence Intervals, click the **Display error bars** box in the **Element Properties** dialog box (Figure 6) and then select the first radio button.
- To add a title, click **Titles/Footnotes** (left side of **Chart Builder** dialog box) and then click **Title 1** from the list of check-boxes which will appear in place of the gallery of graphics choices. A panel will appear in the **Element Properties** dialog box where a title such as *Means and 95% Confidence Intervals* can be typed in. Then click **Apply** followed by **Close**. Notice that **T1** appears at the top of the preview (Figure 5).
- Finally click **OK** in the **Chart Builder** dialog box to create the chart (Output 1).

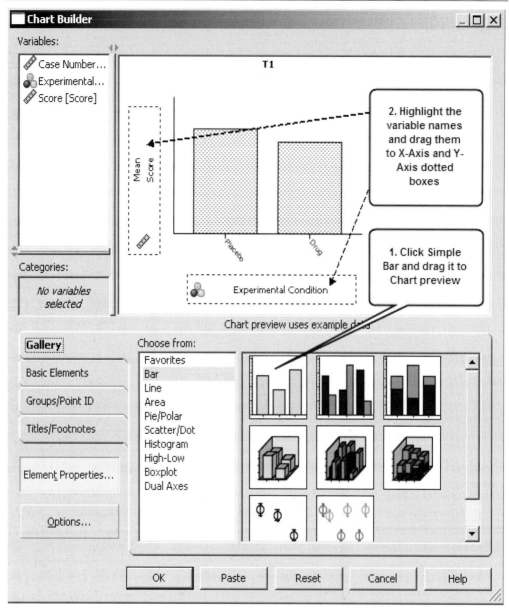

Figure 5. The **Chart Builder** dialog box showing the simple bar chart preview

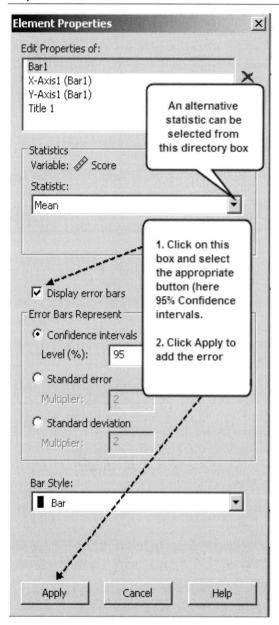

If the chart is to be printed in black and white, it is best to use the **Chart Editor** to change the colours of the graph to shades of grey. In fact, we have found it most effective to change the fill colour to white and mark the bars with distinguishing fill patterns. Alternatively changing the default **Chart** options to **Cycle through patterns only** as described in Section 5.1.3 renders editing unnecessary.

A simple bar chart shows only a single category variable, in this case the *Experimental Condition* under which the participants in the study performed. Additional category variables can be included either by using the options in **Groups/Point ID** in Figure 5 (select **Rows panel variable** or **Columns panel variable** and then transfer the appropriate variable name into the box which will appear on the right of the bar chart in the Chart preview) or by opting for **Clustered** bar charts as described in the next subsection by clicking on the second figure in the **Chart Builder** dialog box (Figure 5). The **Rows panel variable** option enables the user to plot bar charts one-above-the-other (Rows) and the **Columns panel variable** option side-by-side (Columns) when there is an additional category variable such as sex. When **Clustered** is used, the bars are clustered in a single graphic whereas the **panel** facility displays the levels of the second category variable in separate graphics. An example of panelled bar charts is shown in the **Panelled bar chart** subsection after the **Clustered bar charts** subsection.

Figure 6. The **Element Properties** dialog box for altering (if desired) the statistic to be used for the bars and for selecting (if desired) error bars

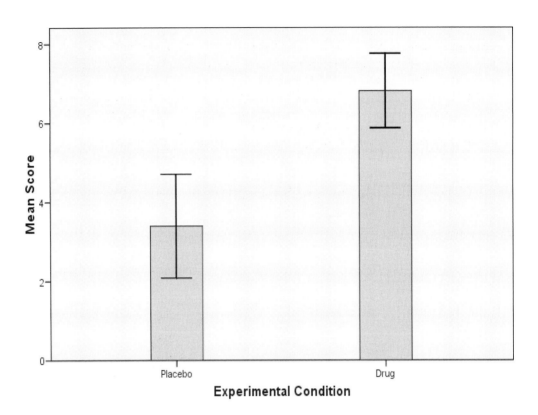

Output 1. A simple bar chart and optional 95% confidence intervals with *Experimental Condition* as the category variable

5.2.2   Clustered bar charts

A **clustered bar chart** shows two category variables in the same graphic as explained in the previous subsection. Suppose in addition to the *Experimental Condition* variable, we also knew the *Gender* of the participants. Then a clustered bar chart could be plotted with *Experimental Condition* as the first category variable subdivided according to the second category variable *Gender*. This second variable defines the **clusters**. Output 2 shows a clustered bar chart summarising the results of the drug experiment. On the horizontal axis, as before, is the independent variable *Experimental Condition*. In addition, the variable *Gender* has been used to cluster the data under the separate *Placebo* and *Drug* conditions.

To obtain such a clustered bar graph, open **Chart Builder** (see Section 5.2.1) and then:

- Ensure that the illustrations correspond to **Bar** by checking that **Bar** is highlighted in the **Choose from** panel. Click the second picture of Clustered Bar to highlight it and then drag it to the **Chart preview** in the panel above. In addition, an **Element Properties** dialog box will also appear.

- Click the variable name *Score* to highlight it and then drag it to the **Y-Axis** box. Do likewise with *Experimental Condition* to the **X-Axis** box and with *Gender* to the **Cluster: set pattern** box.
- To include the 95% Confidence Intervals, click the **Display error bars** box in the **Element Properties** dialog box (Figure 6) and then select the first radio button.
- To add a title, click **Titles/Footnotes** (left side of **Chart Builder** dialog box) and then click **Title 1** from the list of check-boxes which will appear in place of the gallery of graphics choices. A panel will appear in the **Element Properties** dialog box where a title such as *Means and 95% Confidence Intervals* can be typed in. Then click **Apply** followed by **Close**. Notice that **T1** appears at the top of the preview.
- Finally click **OK** in the **Chart Builder** dialog box to create the chart (Output 2).

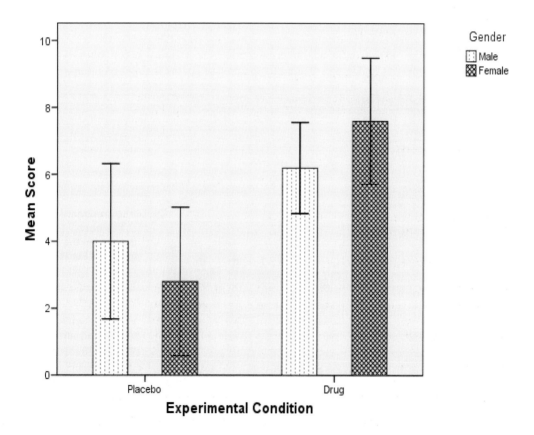

Output 2. A clustered bar chart and optional 95% confidence intervals with *Experimental Condition* as the category variable and *Gender* as the cluster variable

5.2.3   Panelled bar charts

Yet another way of including a second or third independent variable in bar charts is to panel them either by rows or by columns. For example, the data used in Chapter 8 investigating the effects upon simulated driving performance of two new anti-hay fever drugs when male and female drivers are either alert or tired could be graphically depicted as shown in Output 3. To obtain a panelled bar chart, open **Chart Builder** (see Section 5.2.1) and then:

- Ensure that the illustrations correspond to **Bar** by checking that **Bar** is highlighted in the **Choose from** panel. Click the second picture of Clustered Bar to highlight it and then drag it to the **Chart preview** in the panel above. In addition, an **Element Properties** dialog box will also appear.

- Click the variable name *Driving Performance* to highlight it and then drag it to the **Y-Axis** box. Do likewise with *Alertness* to the **X-Axis** box and with *Gender* to the **Cluster: set pattern** box.

- Click **Groups/Point ID** on the left-hand edge of the **Chart Builder** dialog box and then click the **Columns panel variable** box. This will result in another box labelled **Panel** appearing in the **Chart preview** panel. Click *Drug* to highlight it and then drag it to the **Panel** box.

- To include the 95% Confidence Intervals, click the **Display error bars** box in the **Element Properties** dialog box (Figure 6) and then select the first radio button.

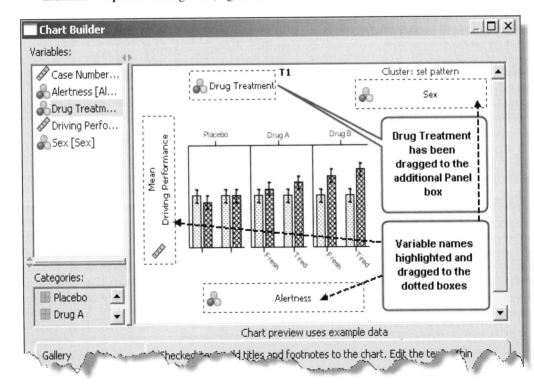

Figure 7. The **Chart preview** panel for the panelled clustered bar chart shown in Output 3

- To add a title, click **Titles/Footnotes** (left side of **Chart Builder** dialog box) and then click **Title 1**. A panel will appear in the **Element Properties** dialog box where a title such as *Means and 95% Confidence Intervals* can be typed in. Then click **Apply** followed by **Close**. Notice that **T1** appears at the top of the preview (Figure 7).
- Finally click **OK** in the **Chart Builder** dialog box to create the chart (Output 3).

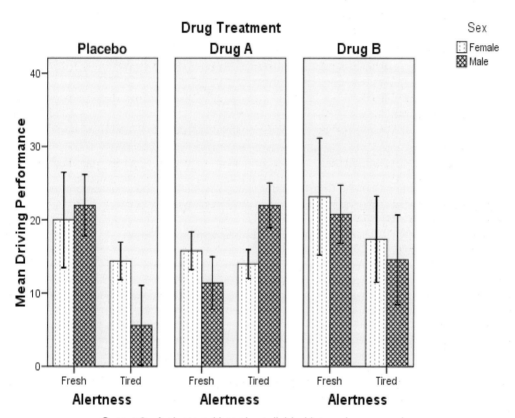

Output 3. A clustered bar chart divided into column panels

Note that simple bar charts can also be panelled so that this option could be used instead of a clustered bar chart. For example, we could have presented the data in Output 2 as simple bar charts for the *Experimental Condition* with *Males* in one row and *Females* in another row.

5.2.4   3-D charts

The **Chart Builder** can also be used to draw more exotic charts such as three-dimensional ones. As an example, a 3-D chart of *Height* against *Blood Group* and *Gender* can be drawn by selecting the image of a Simple 3-D Bar (first in second row) and filling in the variable names as shown in Figure 8. The output is shown in Output 4.

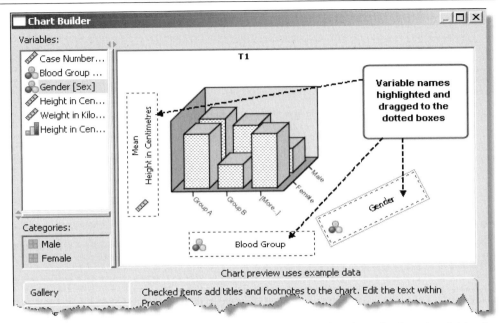

Figure 8. The upper part of the **Chart Builder** dialog box showing the selection of variables for a 3-D bar chart

Height categorised by Blood Group and Gender

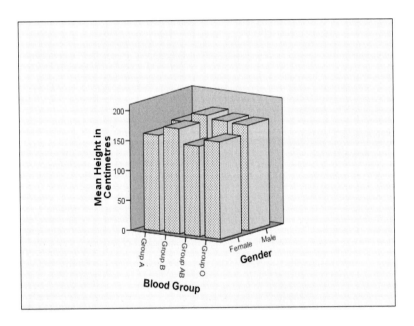

Output 4. The 3-D bar chart of *Height* categorised by *Blood Group* and *Gender*

5.2.5 Editing a bar chart

- Double-click the chart (or right click and select **SPSS Chart Object→Open**) to open the **Chart Editor** (Figure 9).
- To change, say, the bars representing *Males*, click within the *Sex* key the identification for Male. All the bars representing males will then appear with a purple frame.

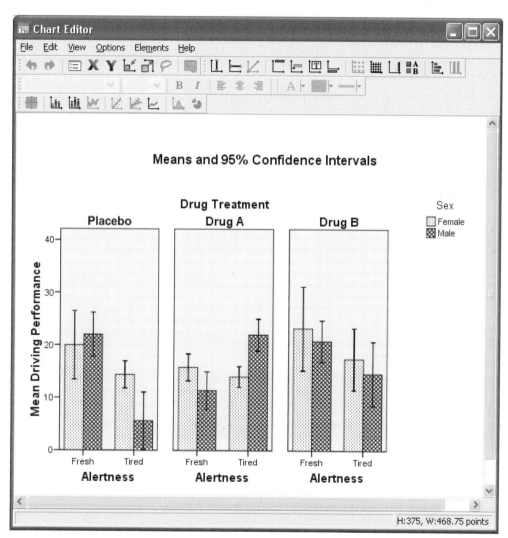

Figure 9. The **Chart Editor** window

- Double-click any of the purple-framed bars or right click to open the **Properties** dialog box (Figure 10). Note that within the **Bar Options**, it is possible to change the width of the bars and the size of the gaps between clusters by moving the sliders or changing the numbers in the % boxes.

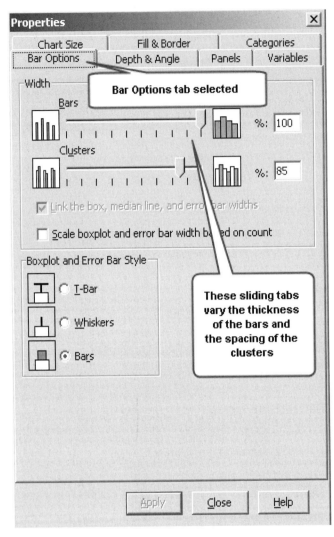

- To change the colour and fill of the bars, click the **Fill & Border** tab to open a dialog box for selecting fill colours, border colours and fill patterns.

- To change the fill colour, click the **Fill** box and then select a colour from the right-hand palette of colours, white and black.

- To change the fill pattern, click the **Pattern** box and select a fill.

- Click **Apply** to make these changes in the chart without leaving the editor.

- The variable bars can be rearranged by clicking the **Variables** tab, selecting the variable to be moved, pressing the right-hand mouse button, and then selecting the move to be made. For example, you can see what the chart would look like if the clustering was done by *Experimental Condition* rather than by *Gender*.

- Other changes can also be made, such as alterations to the axis labels and the bar identification key.

Figure 10. The **Properties** dialog box for **Bar Options** but also showing the various editing tabs for other features of a graphic

5.2.6   Chart templates

If it is desired to apply these editing changes to future bar chart requests, a lot of time can be saved by saving the final format as a **Chart Template** and then invoking this template each time a similar bar chart is requested.

- Whilst still in **Chart Editor**, select **File➔Save Chart Template…** to open the **Save Chart Template** dialog box (Figure 11).

- Click the **All settings** check box and type a description of the template in the panel at the foot of the dialog box e.g. *Panelled clustered bar chart with error bars*. Click **Continue**.

- The **Save Template** dialog box will appear. Select a suitable folder and file name (e.g. *Panelled clustered bar chart*) for the template and click **Save**. For networked computers it may be necessary to store the file on portable memory (e.g. a memory stick) in order to have it available on a later occasion.
- Close the **Chart Editor** to return the chart to **Output1 – SPSS Viewer**.

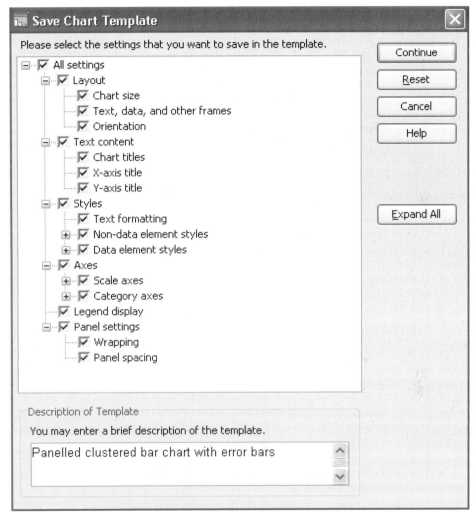

Figure 11. The **Save Chart Template** dialog box for selecting all or specific chart settings

Invoking a chart template

There are three ways of invoking a previously saved chart template. The first is to install it as the default template within the **Charts** section of the **Options** (the last item in the **Edit** drop-down menu) dialog box, the second within the **Chart Builder** dialog box, and the third within the **Chart Editor** window.

To apply our saved chart template for another panelled clustered bar chart (e.g. for a new data set), we will illustrate the second way within the **Chart Builder** dialog box. To obtain a panelled bar chart, open **Chart Builder** (see Section 5.2.1) and then:

•   Click the **Use chart specifications from** check box at the foot of the **Clustered Bar Chart** dialog box and then **File…** to open the directory box for locating where the template is saved. Change the folder as necessary and highlight the template file name.

•   Click **Open** to transfer the template name to the **Clustered Bar Chart** dialog box (Figure 12).

•   Click **OK** to draw the panelled clustered bar chart.

The new chart will appear with the changes made to the original chart incorporated in it.

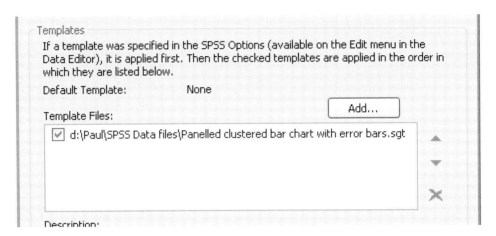

Figure 12. The **Template** section of the **Clustered Bar Chart** dialog box showing the template name

Chart 'favorites'

SPSS also has a facility of saving what SPSS calls 'favorites' in the **Chart Builder** portfolio of images. For example, if the user wants to create a number of graphics with the same style from different data sets, then the original graphic acts as a prototype (called by SPSS a 'favorite') and can be invoked from the **Favorites** panel in the **Chart Builder** dialog box.

To save a prototype, proceed as follows:

•   Whilst still in the **Chart Builder** dialog box after completing all the details such as including 95% confidence intervals and specifying a title, move the cursor to anywhere in the Chart preview panel and right click to open a small choice panel (Figure 13).

•   Select **Add to Favorites…** and then enter a file name for the template (SPSS refers to it as prototype) such as Clustered panelled bar chart and click **OK**. The template will then appear in a panel in the **Chart Builder** dialog box with **Favorites** highlighted in the **Choose from** directory.

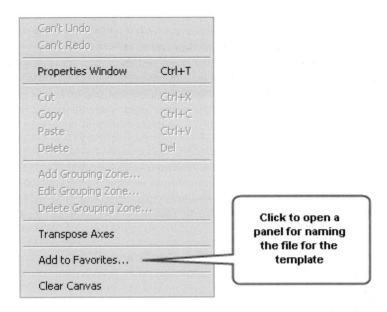

Figure 13. The choice panel for saving a chart template to **Add to Favorites...**

Using a favorite in Chart Builder as a prototype for a graphic

To apply our saved panelled clustered bar chart template to another data set, we will illustrate the use of our newly created **Favorite** in the **Chart Builder** dialog box. To do so, open **Chart Builder** (see Section 5.2.1) and then:

- Ensure that the illustrations correspond to **Favorites** by checking that **Favorites** is highlighted in the **Choose from** panel. Click the picture of the panelled clustered bar graphic and then drag it to the **Chart preview** in the panel above. In addition, an **Element Properties** dialog box will also appear.
- The various variable names must then be transferred but it is not necessary to specify either the title or the 95% confidence intervals.
- Click **OK** to draw the panelled clustered bar chart using the new data set.

The new chart will appear with the changes made to the original chart incorporated in it.

SPSS offers helpful tutorials on editing charts. You can access these by clicking
Help➜Tutorial
and then double-clicking each of
Tutorials➜Creating and Editing Charts

The usual buttons in the right-hand bottom corner of each page of the tutorial enable the user to see the index (magnifier), the table of contents (house) and to navigate forward and backward through the tutorial (right and left arrows).

5.3   ERROR BAR CHARTS

An alternative to a bar graph is an **Error Bar chart**, in which the mean of the scores in a particular category is represented by a single point and the spread (confidence interval for the mean, multiples of the standard deviation or multiples of the standard error of the mean – the user can choose between these) is represented by a vertical line (T-bar or whiskers) passing through the point. Output 5 is a clustered error bar chart summarising the results of the drug experiment.

To obtain an error bar chart, open **Chart Builder** (see Section 5.2.1) and then:

•   Ensure that the illustrations correspond to **Bar** by checking that **Bar** is highlighted in the **Choose from** panel. Click the second picture of the third row (clustered error bars shown in green and blue – see Figure 2) to highlight it and then drag it to the **Chart preview** in the panel above. In addition, an **Element Properties** dialog box will also appear.

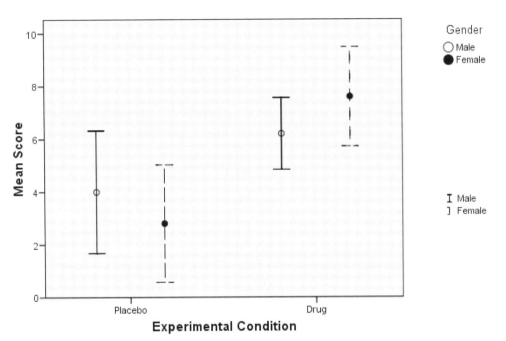

Output 5. A clustered error bar chart with *Experimental Condition* as the category variable and *Gender* as the cluster variable

•   Click the variable name *Score* to highlight it and then drag it to the **Y-Axis** box. Do likewise with *Experimental Condition* to the **X-Axis** box and with *Gender* to the **Cluster: Set symbol** box.

•   **95% Confidence Intervals** is the default setting appearing in the **Element Properties** dialog box. The percentage can be changed or the user can select Standard error or

Standard deviation (together with the desired multiplier). If a change from the default is selected, it will be necessary to click **Apply**.

- To add a title, click **Titles/Footnotes** (left side of **Chart Builder** dialog box) and then click **Title 1**. A panel will appear in the **Element Properties** dialog box where a title such as *Means and 95% Confidence Intervals* can be typed in. Then click **Apply** followed by **Close**. Notice that **T1** appears at the top of the preview.

- Finally click **OK** in the **Chart Builder** dialog box to create the chart (Output 5).

The symbols used for the means and the form of the lines used for the error bars can be changed by double-clicking anywhere within the graphic to open the **Chart Editor**. Double-clicking on the appropriate symbol or line in the *Gender* key will open the corresponding **Properties** dialog box where changes can be made.

You will notice that in Output 5, there are no lines linking the error bars. This is entirely appropriate, since the bars represent qualitatively distinct categories. In other circumstances, however, as when the categories are ordered, it may be desirable to join up the points (when there are more than two) with interpolation lines. This is easily achieved in the **Chart Editor** by clicking the means to highlight them, selecting the **Elements** drop-down menu and clicking **Interpolation line** (or alternatively clicking the ⊾ icon).

5.4   BOXPLOTS

Three types of boxplots are available in **Chart Builder**, a single boxplot (called 1-D Boxplot in the gallery), simple boxplot for plotting the boxplots across categories of a grouping variable and clustered boxplot for plotting boxplots across categories of two grouping variables. Here we shall illustrate the procedure by plotting a boxplot of *Height in Centimetres* categorised by *Gender*. The structure of a boxplot is shown in Table 2 in Chapter 4.

> See Table 2
> in Chapter 4

To obtain a clustered boxplot, open **Chart Builder** (see Section 5.2.1) and then:

- Ensure that the illustrations correspond to **Boxplot** by checking that **Boxplot** is highlighted in the **Choose from** panel of **Gallery**. Click the first picture of Simple Boxplot to highlight it and then drag it to the **Chart preview** in the panel above. In addition, an **Element Properties** dialog box will also appear.

- Click the variable name *Height in Centimetres* to highlight it and then drag it to the **Y-Axis** box. Do likewise with *Gender* to the **X-Axis** box.

- To add a title, click **Titles/Footnotes** (left side of **Chart Builder** dialog box) and then click **Title 1**. A panel will appear in the **Element Properties** dialog box where a title such as *Boxplots of Height categorised by Sex* can be typed in. Then click **Apply** followed by **Close**. Notice that **T1** appears at the top of the preview (Figure 14).

- Finally click **OK** in the **Chart Builder** dialog box to create the boxplot (Output 6).

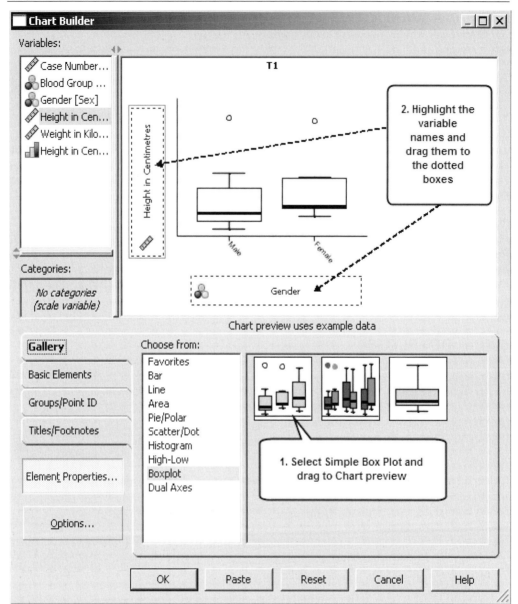

Figure 14. The completed **Chart Builder** dialog box for plotting a boxplot of *Height* for each *Sex*

Notice in the output that there is one case identified as an outlier with o. Any extreme case would have been identified with *.

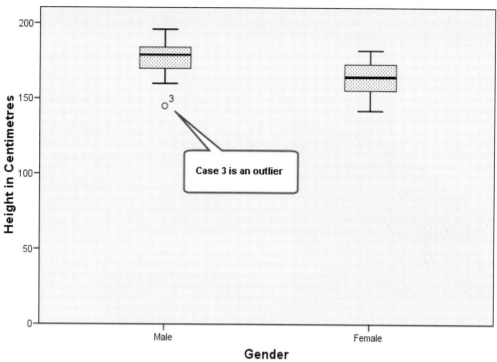

Output 6. Boxplots of *Height* categorised by *Sex*

5.5   PIE CHARTS

The **pie chart** is an alternative to a bar graph that provides a picturesque display of the frequency distribution of a qualitative variable.   It is a particularly valuable kind of graph for displaying the relative frequencies of the same set of categories over time or for bringing out the varying compositions of two things.   Pie charts can be panelled in a similar way to bar charts as previously described in Section 5.2.

> See Section 5.2

To illustrate the production of a pie chart, we shall use the data set of blood group, gender, height and weight.

To draw a pie chart of the categories within *Blood Group*, open **Chart Builder** (see Section 5.2.1) and then:

- Ensure that the illustration corresponds to **Pie/Polar** by checking that **Pie/Polar** is highlighted in the **Choose from** panel. Click the picture and drag it to the Chart preview in the panel above. In addition, an **Element Properties** dialog box will also appear.

- Click the variable name *Blood Group* to highlight it and drag it to the **Slice by?** box. The **Angle Variable?** box will then change to **Count**.

- To change **Count** to **Percentages**, click the arrow to the right of *Count* in the **Statistic** panel within **Element Properties**, select **Percentage (?)** and then click **Apply**.
- To add a title, click **Titles/Footnotes** (left side of **Chart Builder** dialog box) and then click **Title 1**. A panel will appear in the **Element Properties** dialog box where a title such as *Blood Group Percentages* can be typed in. Then click **Apply** followed by **Close**. Notice that **T1** appears at the top of the preview.
- Finally click **OK** in the **Chart Builder** dialog box to create the chart (Output 7).

Blood Group Percentages

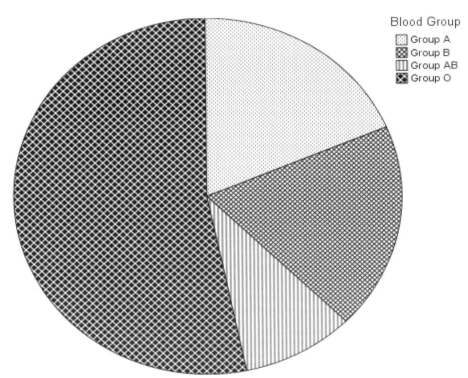

Output 7. The **Pie Chart** of the distribution of *Blood Group*

The pie chart in Output 7 can be edited (see Section 5.1.3) to change the fill patterns, to rotate the slices if it is desired to bring a particular slice to the top, to insert labels and to 'explode' a slice as shown in Output 8. If desired, the changes can be stored as a **Chart Template** and then this template can be invoked for future pie chart drawings for similar data.

See
Section
5.1.3

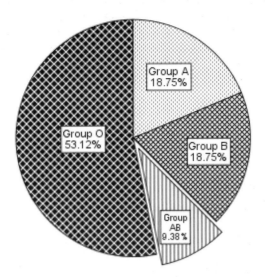

Output 8. The edited **Pie Chart** with slice labels, percentages and one slice exploded

5.6   LINE GRAPHS

Suppose that, in our analysis of the medical data, we want to produce a **line graph** of mean weight against height for both sexes. Line graphs can be drawn with just one line or more than one line in the graph; they can also be panelled as we have seen for bar and pie charts.

Along the horizontal axis, the total range of heights is divided into fixed intervals. Above the mid point of each interval is plotted for each sex the mean of the weights of people whose heights fall within the interval and adjacent points are joined by straight lines. The total range of heights of the participants is split into, say, five intervals by using the **Visual Binning** procedure (see Section 4.4.3) to create a new ordinal variable *HeightBin* consisting of the intervals <155, 156-165, 166-175, 176-185, >185. Specify the upper limits (155, 165, 175, 185, 210) in the **Value** cells and the intervals in the **Label** cells.

To plot a line graph of mean weight against height bins, open **Chart Builder** (see Section 5.2.1) and then:

- Ensure that the illustrations correspond to **Line** by checking that **Line** is highlighted in the **Choose from** panel (Figure 2). Click the second picture (Multiple Line) and drag it to the **Chart preview** in the panel above. In addition, an **Element Properties** dialog box will also appear.
- Click the variable name *Weight in kilograms* to highlight it and then drag it to the **Y-Axis** box. Do likewise with *Height in centimetres (binned)* to the **X-Axis** box and with *Gender* to the **Set pattern** box (Figure 15).

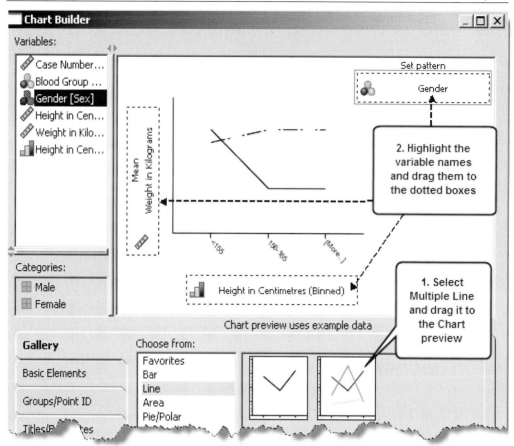

Figure 15. The upper part of the **Chart Builder** dialog box showing the transferred variable names for plotting the multiple line graph

- To add a title, click **Titles/Footnotes** (left side of **Chart Builder** dialog box) and then click **Title 1**. A panel will appear in the **Element Properties** dialog box where a title such as *Mean Weight against Height bins for each Sex* can be typed in. Then click **Apply** followed by **Close**. Notice that **T1** appears at the top of the preview (Figure 15).
- Finally click **OK** in the **Chart Builder** dialog box to create the chart (Output 9).

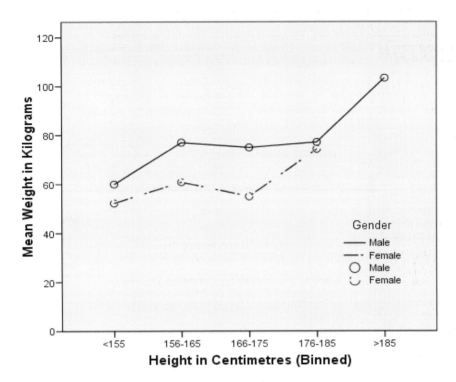

Output 9. The edited multiple line graph of mean *Weight* against *Height* category for each sex

The edited line graph is shown in Output 9. The editing operations included the following:
1. Re-setting the y-scale with a minimum of 0. This is achieved by double-clicking the graph to open the **Chart Editor**, double-clicking on the y-scale values, clicking the **Scale** tab within the **Properties** dialog box, clicking off the **Minimum** auto box, entering 0 in the **Custom** box alongside, and finally clicking **Apply**.

2. Inserting circles for the means by clicking on the **Show Line Markers** icon . Initially unfilled circles will appear: these can be made solid by clicking on them and changing **Fill** to black in the **Properties** box.

3. Moving the **Gender** legend to inside the grey panel of the graph by clicking on the legend, reducing the size of its box and dragging it to the desired position.

If preferred, the lines for males and females could have been plotted in separate line graphs side-by-side or one-above-the-other by selecting the single line graph in the **Chart Builder** dialog box, transferring the y-axis and x-axis variable names as before, clicking **Groups/Point ID**, clicking the check box for **Rows panel variable** or **Columns panel variable**, transferring *Gender* to the new box labelled **Panel** and finally clicking **OK**.

These changes can be saved as a **Chart Template** – see Section 5.2.6.

5.7   SCATTERPLOTS AND DOT PLOTS

Scatterplots

Another diagram for displaying the relationship between two variables is the **scatterplot,** in which the scales of values of the two variables (such as height and weight) are set out on the horizontal and vertical axis and each person is represented as a point whose co-ordinates are his or her particular height and weight. As with the other charts, scatterplots can also be panelled. A scatterplot should always be plotted and examined before a correlation coefficient is calculated (Chapter 11) or a regression analysis is carried out (Chapter 12).

See Chaps.
11 & 12

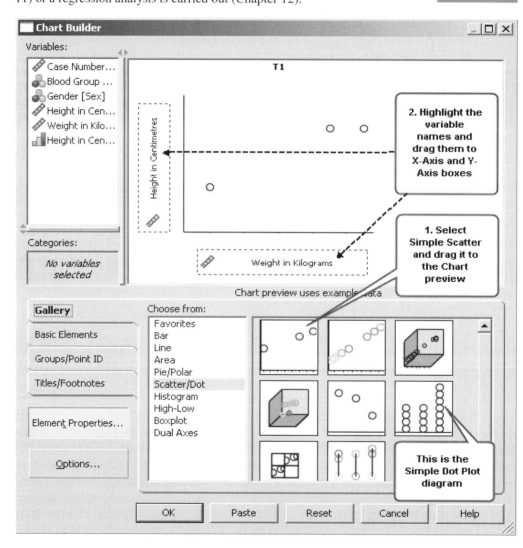

Figure 16. The **Chart Builder** dialog box with **Scatterplot/Dot** highlighted to show the various scatterplots options and with a simple scatterplot of *Height* against *Weight* prepared in the preview panel

To plot a simple scatterplot, open **Chart Builder** (see Section 5.2.1) and then:

- Ensure that the illustrations correspond to **Scatter/Dot** by checking that **Scatter/Dot** is highlighted in the **Choose from** panel (Figure 2). Click the first picture of a Simple Scatter to highlight it and then drag it to the **Chart preview** in the panel above (Figure 16). In addition, an **Element Properties** dialog box will also appear.

- Click the variable name *Height in Centimetres* to highlight it and then drag it to the **Y-Axis** box. Do likewise with *Weight in Kilograms* to the **X-Axis** box.

- To add a title, click **Titles/Footnotes** (left side of **Chart Builder** dialog box) and then click **Title 1**. A panel will appear in the **Element Properties** dialog box where a title such as *Scatterplot of Height against Weight* can be typed in. Then click **Apply** followed by **Close**. Notice that **T1** appears at the top of the preview.

- Finally click **OK** in the **Chart Builder** dialog box to create the chart (Output 10).

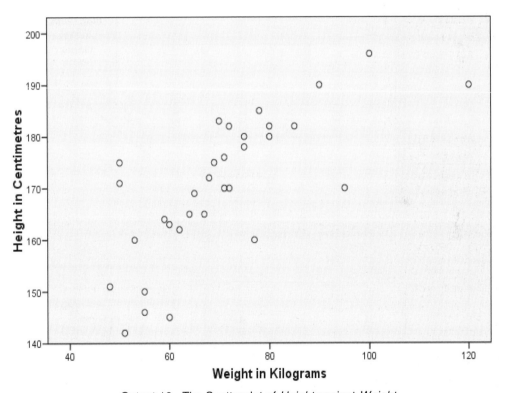

Output 10. The Scatterplot of *Height* against *Weight*

Inspection of the scatterplot shows that the line graph in Output 9, although bringing out a clear positive relationship between height and weight when average weights are considered, masks considerable individual variability. The heights of people of around 50 kg in weight range from just over 140 cm to 175 cm in height.

Dot plots

A **dot plot** plots one variable on a scale axis. The cases are represented by points that are stacked at the variable values. Thus weights for each sex could be plotted in charts side-by-side by choosing **Chart Builder** (see Section 5.2.1) and then:

- Ensure that the illustrations correspond to **Scatter/Dot** by checking that **Scatter/Dot** is highlighted in the **Choose from** panel. Click the third picture in the second row of a Simple Dot Plot to highlight it and then drag it to the **Chart preview** in the panel above (Figure 17). In addition, an **Element Properties** dialog box will also appear.

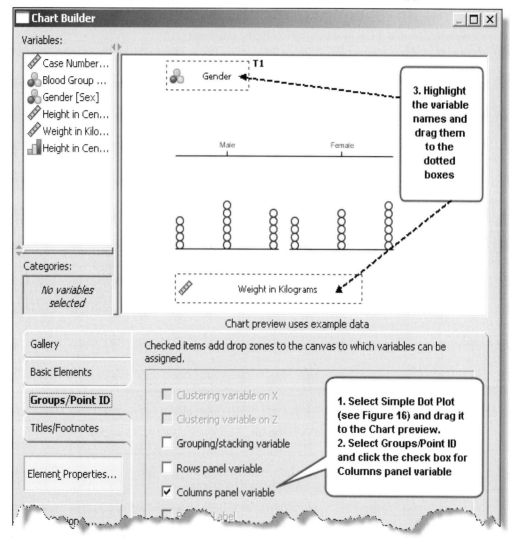

Figure 17. The upper part of the **Chart Builder** dialog box with **Groups/Point ID** highlighted to show the panel options for a simple dot plot of *Weight* for each sex prepared in the preview panel

- Click the variable name *Weight in Kilograms* to highlight it and then drag it to the **X-Axis** box.

- Click **Groups/Point ID** on the left-hand edge of the **Chart Builder** dialog box and then click the **Columns panel variable** box. This will result in another box labelled **Panel** appearing in the **Chart preview** panel. Click *Sex* to highlight it and then drag it to the **Panel** box.

- To add a title, click **Titles/Footnotes** (left side of **Chart Builder** dialog box) and then click **Title 1**. A panel will appear in the **Element Properties** dialog box where a title such as *Dot plot of Weight for each Sex* can be typed in. Then click **Apply** followed by **Close**.

- Finally click **OK** in the **Chart Builder** dialog box to create the chart (Output 11).

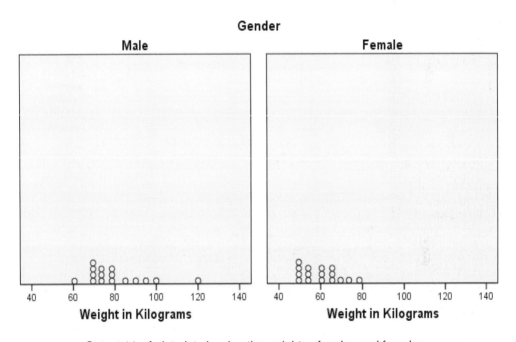

Output 11. A dot plot showing the weights of males and females

5.8   DUAL Y-AXIS GRAPHS

SPSS 15 has a facility for plotting dual y-axis charts. For example, we could plot weight and height for each sex. Here we shall illustrate the procedure using the data set from Chapter 15 to see whether competence in Latin is associated with competence in modern foreign languages such as French and German.

To plot a dual y-axis graph, open **Chart Builder** (see Section 5.2.1) and then:

- Ensure that the illustrations correspond to **Line** by checking that **Line** is highlighted in the **Choose from** panel. Click the first picture (Simple Line) to highlight it and then drag it to the **Chart preview** in the panel above. In addition, an **Element Properties** dialog box will also appear.

- Click **Basic Elements** and then click the dual y-axis picture to highlight it. Drag it to the **Chart preview** above (Figure 18).

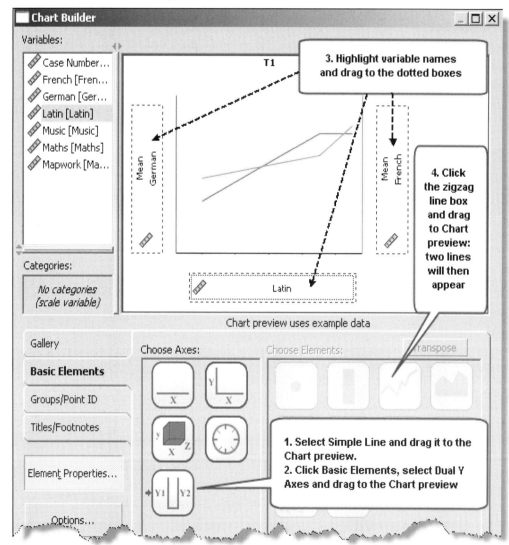

Figure 18. The **Chart Builder** dialog box for plotting two y-axis variables

- Click the variable name *German* and drag it to one of the Y-axes. Do likewise with *French* to the other Y-axis. Click and drag *Latin* to the X-Axis box.
- Click the zigzag line picture and drag it to **Chart preview**. Two lines, one green and one blue, will then appear on the graph.
- To add a title, click **Titles/Footnotes** (left side of **Chart Builder** dialog box) and then click **Title 1**. A panel will appear in the **Element Properties** dialog box where a title such

as *French and German against Latin* can be typed in. Then click **Apply** followed by **Close**. Notice that **T1** appears at the top of the preview.

- Click **OK** to plot the graph (Output 12). The line for *German* has been edited to differentiate it from the line for *French* because the colour coding is lost in a grey-scale reproduction. Annotations have also been added.

French and German against Latin

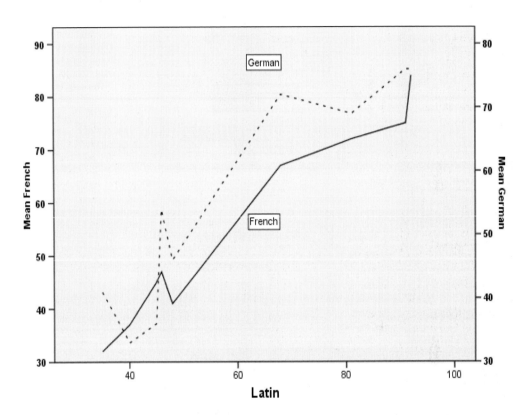

Output 12. The edited dual Y-Axis plot of *French* and *German* against *Latin*

5.9 HISTOGRAMS

Various types of histogram are easily plotted in **Chart Builder**. For example, we could plot the heights of males and females side-by-side. To plot a Population Pyramid (i.e. side-by-side histograms), open **Chart Builder** (see Section 5.2.1) and then:

- Ensure that the illustrations correspond to **Histogram** by checking that **Histogram** is highlighted in the **Choose from** panel. Click the picture in the second row to highlight it and then drag it to the **Chart preview** in the panel above. In addition, an **Element Properties** dialog box will also appear.

- Click the variable name *Height in Centimetres* to highlight it and then drag it to the Distribution Variable box and likewise *Gender* to the Split Variable box (Figure 19).

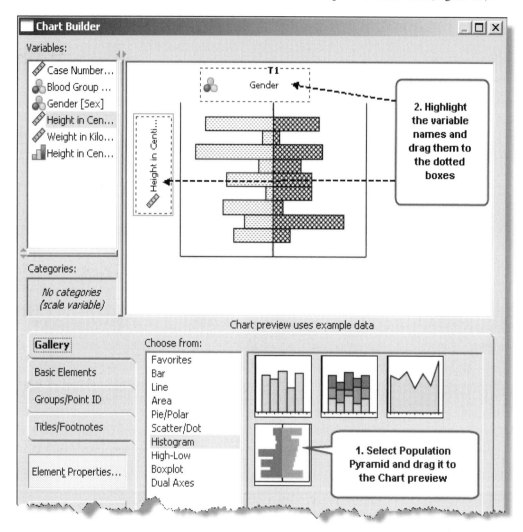

Figure 19. The upper part of the **Chart Builder** dialog box for drawing a population pyramid (side-by-side histograms) of height for each sex

- To add a title, click **Titles/Footnotes** (left side of **Chart Builder** dialog box) and then click **Title 1**. A panel will appear in the **Element Properties** dialog box where a title such as *Histograms of height for each sex* can be typed in. Then click **Apply** followed by **Close**.
- Click **OK** to plot the histograms (Output13).

Histograms of Height for each Sex

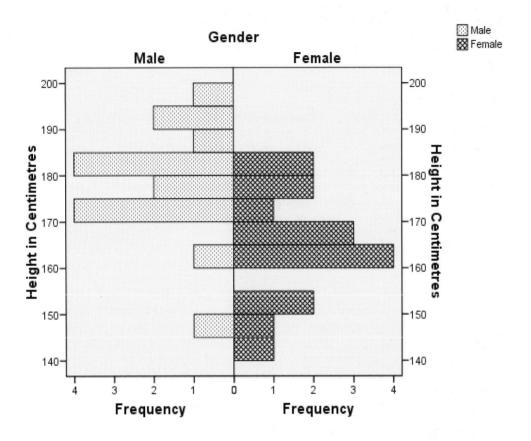

Output 13. The population pyramid of height for each sex

5.10   Receiver-Operating-Characteristic (ROC) Curve

The **ROC Curve** representation was originally developed for the detection of radio signals in the presence of noise during the Second World War. The technique has been adopted in psychophysics for detecting weak signals and in medical research for evaluating tests and drugs.

Its usefulness arises from the difficulty of determining sensory thresholds independently of how scrupulously or casually the observer is behaving. Some people will only acknowledge that they perceived (e.g. saw or heard) a signal when they are absolutely certain that they have done so whereas other people will be content to acknowledge they have done so if they felt there was the vaguest possibility that they perceived a signal. How can one determine an observer's threshold independently of their response criterion? The solution is to use an experimental paradigm in which signals are presented for some of the trials but not for all of them so that a measure of **hit rate** (saying 'yes' when there really was a signal) and of **false**

alarm rate (saying 'yes' when there was not a signal) can be determined. These rates can then be plotted on a graph of hits against false alarms.   An ideal observer would be plotted in the top left-hand corner of this graph with a hit rate of 100% and a false alarm rate of 0% whereas a completely random responder with equal rates of hits and false alarms would have a point somewhere along the diagonal from the bottom left-hand corner to the top right-hand corner.

Underlying these measures are probability distributions that a given perceptual effect will be caused by noise (i.e. all other stimuli except the signal presented by the experimenter) and by the signal superimposed on the noise (i.e. the signal occurring together with the background conditions of noise). The greater the separation between the peaks of these distributions, the greater the observer's sensitivity. This separation is called **d′** (d-prime) whose formula will be given later. In brief, therefore, the ROC provides a means of teasing out someone's perceptual threshold independently of their response criterion (i.e. whether he/she is a scrupulous or casual responder).

Here we shall look at the hypothetical development of a test for detecting pathology of the retina (retinopathy). Ideally the test should identify those with retinopathy 100% of the time and those without retinopathy 100% of the time but in the real world there are likely to be patients with retinopathy who do not fail the test and persons without retinopathy who will fail the test. Thus the aim is to establish a cut-off point on the test scale where the clinician can be about 80% certain that the person tested has the condition (hit rate) and the false alarm rate (i.e. persons without the clinical condition failing the test) is below 20%.

Table 1. The contingency table for the type of observer and passing or failing the test			
Test Result	**Type of Observer**		
	Retinopathy	**No Retinopathy**	**Total**
Fail	A ('Hit')	B ('False Alarm')	A+B
Pass	C (False passed test)	D (True passed test)	C+D
Total	A+C	B+D	A+B+C+D

We define *sensitivity* as the probability of a failed test among patients with retinopathy and *specificity* as the probability of a passed test among those without retinopathy. If we collate frequencies in a 2 x 2 table (Table 1), then *sensitivity* = probability of a hit for retinopathy i.e. A/(A+C) and *specificity* = probability of a true passed test for persons with no retinopathy i.e. D/(B+D). Ideally we want high *sensitivity* and high *specificity* (i.e. low (1 – *specificity*)).

The SPSS ROC curve is a plot of *sensitivity* (hit rate) against *1 – specificity* (false alarm rate). High discrimination is represented by a curved line almost reaching into the top left-hand corner and zero discrimination by a diagonal line at 45° to the horizontal. As an example, suppose a new computer-based test of defective colour vision has been devised and is given to twenty patients with retinopathy and twenty persons without retinopathy. The aim is to find out whether the test can be used to discriminate these two categories of observers and if so, what cut-off point of errors should be adopted. The data are given in Table 2.

Table 2. Colour vision error scores for persons with and without retinopathy							
Retinopathy				**No Retinopathy**			
40	43	36	45	34	35	31	25
35	35	33	39	36	30	36	19
34	37	45	35	32	31	29	23
34	20	50	37	28	23	29	32
25	40	30	35	24	24	32	29

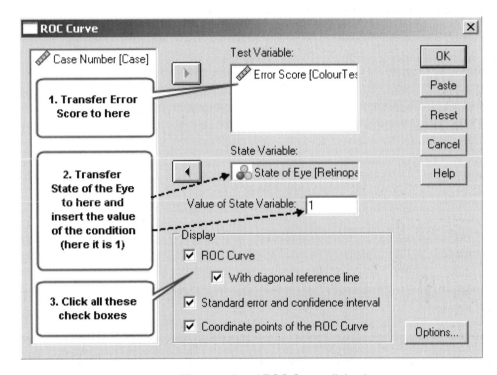

Figure 20. The completed **ROC Curve** dialog box

The data are entered into three variables in the **Data Editor**, a scale variable *Case*, a nominal variable *Retinopathy* (with variable label *State of Eye*, level 1 for Retinopathy and level 2 for No Retinopathy) and a scale variable *ColourTest* with variable label *Error Score*.

To plot the ROC Curve

- Choose **Analyze→ROC Curve…** to open the **ROC Curve** dialog box.
- Complete the dialog box as shown in Figure 20.

The first table in the output (Output 14) shows the **Case Processing Summary** – here we have 20 cases with retinopathy and 20 cases without retinopathy.

Case Processing Summary

State of Eye	Valid N (listwise)
Positive [a]	20
Negative	20

Larger values of the test result variable(s) indicate stronger evidence for a positive actual state.

a. The positive actual state is Yes.

Output 14.   The **Case Processing Summary** table

The next output item is the **ROC Curve** (Output 15).

ROC Curve

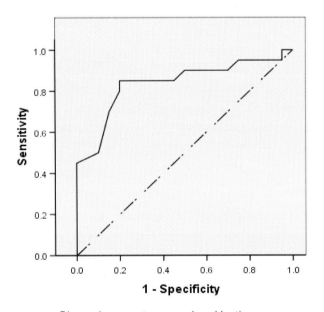

Diagonal segments are produced by ties.

Output 15. The **ROC Curve**

Output 16 is a table listing statistics relating to the area under the ROC Curve. **Area** is the probability that a randomly chosen retinopathy patient exceeds a randomly chosen person without retinopathy (here it is .838 i.e. 83.8%) and **Asymptotic Sig.** is the probability that the test is better than guessing is less than .0005, i.e. is highly significant.

Area Under the Curve

Test Result Variable(s): Error Score

Area	Std. Error[a]	Asymptotic Sig.[b]	Asymptotic 95% Confidence Interval	
			Lower Bound	Upper Bound
.838	.067	.000	.707	.968

The test result variable(s): Error Score has at least one tie between the positive actual state group and the negative actual state group. Statistics may be biased.

a. Under the nonparametric assumption

b. Null hypothesis: true area = 0.5

Output 16. Statistics relating to the area under the **ROC Curve**

Finally there is a table of co-ordinates of the curve (Output 17 on next page). Notice that a cut-off value of 33.5 in the table of co-ordinates represents a sensitivity of 0.800 (80%) and a false alarm rate (1 − Specificity) of 0.200 (20%). If it was desired to restrict the false alarm rate to 10%, it would be necessary to increase the error score to 35.5 but then the sensitivity for detecting retinopathy would be reduced to 50%.

The statistic d′ is often calculated in such applications. It is given by the formula

$$d' = \frac{\left|\mu_2 - \mu_1\right|}{\sqrt{\left(\sigma_1^{\,2} + \sigma_2^{\,2}\right)/2}}$$

and is easily computed in SPSS by entering the means and standard deviations into a new data file and then using **Compute** to calculate d′ (Figure 21). For this example, d′ = 1.24.

RetMean	RetSD	NormMean	NormSD	dPrime
36.400	6.809	29.100	4.778	1.241

Figure 21. The calculation of d′

The highest possible d′ (greatest sensitivity) is nearly 7 but typical values are up to 2.0: thus our value of 1.24 is typical.

Coordinates of the Curve

Test Result Variable(s): Error Score

Positive if Greater Than or Equal To[a]	Sensitivity	1 - Specificity
18.00	1.000	1.000
19.50	1.000	.950
21.50	.950	.950
23.50	.950	.850
24.50	.950	.750
26.50	.900	.700
28.50	.900	.650
29.50	.900	.500
30.50	.850	.450
31.50	.850	.350
32.50	.850	.200
33.50	.800	.200
34.50	.700	.150
35.50	.500	.100
36.50	.450	.000
38.00	.350	.000
39.50	.300	.000
41.50	.200	.000
44.00	.150	.000
47.50	.050	.000
51.00	.000	.000

The test result variable(s): Error Score has at least one tie between the positive actual state group and the negative actual state group.

a. The smallest cutoff value is the minimum observed test value minus 1, and the largest cutoff value is the maximum observed test value plus 1. All the other cutoff values are the averages of two consecutive ordered observed test values.

Output 17. The table of co-ordinates of the ROC Curve

EXERCISE 6

Charts and graphs

Opening SPSS

Open the data file **Metric Data** which you saved in the previous Exercise.

Charts and graphs

1) Stem-and-leaf plot and boxplot

Use the **Explore...** procedure (Section 4.3.2) to produce stem-and-leaf plots and boxplots of *Metres* categorised by *Sex*. Once you are in the **Explore** dialog box, remember to click the **Plots** radio button at the bottom left to suppress the Statistics output. Click **Plots...**, ensure that **Stem-and-leaf** has been selected (if not, click the check-box) and return to the **Explore** dialog box by clicking **Continue**. Enter the variable name *Case* into the **Label Cases by...** box.

The **stem-and-leaf plot** provides more information about the original data than does a histogram. As in a histogram, the length of each row corresponds to the number of cases that fall into a particular interval. However, the stem-and-leaf plot represents each case with a numeric value that corresponds to the actual observed value. This is done by dividing observed values into two components – the leading digit or digits, called the **stem**, and a trailing digit, called the **leaf**. For example, the value 64 would have a stem of 6 and a leaf of 4. In the case of heights in metres, the stems are the metres expressed to the first decimal place, the leaves are the second decimal place. Thus the **modal** height (i.e. the most frequent height) for males is shown with a stem of 17 (1.7 metres), the leaves being the second decimal place. If there are too many 'leaves' for one stem, the stem is repeated in further rows.

The **boxplot** is another type of display, which is more fully explained in Section 4.3.2. The central box spans 50% of the cases (those between the upper and lower quartiles) and the extensions (**whiskers**) cover the remaining cases, excluding **outliers** (shown as o's) or **extreme scores** (shown as asterisks).

- **Prepare the boxplot for printing in black-and-white, and print the Output.**

- **Within the female group, which stem contains the most leaves?**

Examine the boxplot for males and note the case numbers of the outliers so that you can check their actual heights in the data set. To locate a specific case in the data set, select **Edit➜Go to Case ...** to obtain the **Go to Case** dialog box. You then enter the required case number and click **OK**.

- **Write down the actual heights of the males identified as outliers on the box plots.**

2) Bar charts

Plot a bar chart of the mean number of cigarettes smoked (*NpDay*) categorised by *Sex* and by *Faculty*. Do this by choosing
Graphs➔Chart Builder➔Bar

and select the second chart (Clustered Bar) to highlight it (see Section 5.2.2). Drag it to the Chart preview above. Click and drag the appropriate variable names to the boxes (*NpDay* to Y-Axis; *Faculty* to X-Axis; *Sex* to Cluster: set pattern). Add a title by choosing Title/Footnotes from the Gallery, clicking the checkbox for Title 1, entering a title into the Content box within the **Element Properties** dialog box and clicking **Apply**. Finally click **OK** in the **Chart Builder** dialog box to draw the bar chart.

In the **SPSS Viewer** window you should see a bar chart arranged by sex, with each cluster consisting of three bars representing the three Faculties (apparently there are no cases in Other).

Now specify a chart with three clusters (Faculties) of two (sex) instead of two clusters (sex) of three (Faculties). This can be done by returning to the **Chart Builder** dialog box and changing *Sex* and *Faculty* around (drag one of the names back to the **Variables** list; drag the other to the vacated variable box in the Chart preview and then drag the remaining variable name to the other vacated variable box).

Try changing the colours into black-and-white **Fill Patterns**. This is a two-stage procedure involving changing each colour to white and then selecting a different fill pattern for each. Follow the steps described in Section 5.2.5.

Finally return the edited barchart to the **SPSS Viewer** by closing the **Chart Editor** (by clicking ✗ in the top right-hand corner). Try printing the edited barchart from the **SPSS Viewer**.

Pie chart

Draw a pie chart (see Section 5.5) for the *Status* variable and give the chart a title, including your **own** name in the title (e.g. Pie Chart of Status produced by Mary Smith).

To show the count in each slice (or perhaps the percentage), proceed as follows:

- Double-click near the pie chart to open the **Chart Editor** window.
- Click on one of the pie slices to highlight them with a purple frame.
- Select the icon ▟▙ on the top toolbar (bars with label boxes in them and called **Show Data Labels**) or alternatively click the **Elements** drop-down menu and select **Show Data Labels** to open the **Properties** dialog box.
- Something will now appear in each slice (it may be a count or a percentage depending on what is displayed in the Displayed panel within the **Properties** dialog box.
- To change the information displayed (e.g. percentages instead of counts), proceed as follows:
  - Return to the **Properties** dialog box (ensuring that the **Data Value Labels** tab at the top of the **Properties** dialog box is current) and delete whatever slice label is not required from the Displayed panel by highlighting it and then clicking the red X on the right.
  - To insert other slice labels, choose and highlight one or more of the labels in the Not Displayed panel and click the green arrow on the right to transfer the labels to the Displayed panel. Finally click **Apply** and **Close** to close the **Properties** dialog box.

Try the following:

- **Edit the chart to make it suitable for black-and-white printing.**

Return the edited pie chart to SPSS Viewer by closing the Chart Editor in the usual way.

- **Print the pie chart.**

Finishing the session

Close down SPSS and any other windows before logging out of the computer.

EXERCISE 7

Recoding data; selecting cases; line graph

Aim

This Exercise shows you how to recode data, select cases and draw a line graph.

Opening SPSS

Open SPSS with the data file *Metric Data* saved in an earlier Exercise.

Recoding data

Sometimes you may wish to recode values or categories within a variable (e.g. you might want to combine more than one value or category into a single new value or category). Suppose that you are not particularly interested in whether people are doing a MSc degree or a PhD degree, but just want to know whether they are postgraduates. You can change the data set to give you this information, either within the original variable, *status*, or by creating a new variable containing the recoded information.

In this session you are going to use a new variable, since this retains the original variable *status* for checking that the recoding has been done correctly. It also maintains the original values in the data set.

Use the **Recode** (Section 4.4.3) procedure to recode the status codes *MSc Postgrad* and *PhD Postgrad* (i.e. categories 2 and 3) into a new category 1 and the codes *Undergrad* and *Other* (i.e. categories 1 and 4) into a new category 2.

You will need to follow the section carefully. The **Recode** procedure creates a new variable which you are asked to name: we suggest *NewStatus*. To do this, you will have to choose the **Recode into Different Variables** option within the **Recode** procedure.

- Choose
  Transform→Recode into Different Variables... to open the **Recode into Different Variables** dialog box.
- Highlight *Status* and click [▶] to transfer it into the **Input Variable → Output Variable** box.
- Type *NewStatus* (remember no space between *New* and *Status*) in the **Name** box within the **Output Variable** box and click **Change**. The new variable name *NewStatus* will now appear alongside *Status*.
- You might also type *New Status* (a space is allowed here) into the **Output Variable Label** box as a label for the new variable *NewStatus*.
- Click **Old and New Values** and then fill in the corresponding values in the **Value** box of **Old Value** and in the **Value** box of **New Value**, clicking **Add** each time. The following should then appear in the right-hand box: $1 \rightarrow 2$, $2 \rightarrow 1$, $3 \rightarrow 1$, $4 \rightarrow 2$.
- Finally click **Continue** and **OK**.

When you have followed this procedure, check that you have the new variable at the far right of your data set. Now you should clarify the values by adding suitable labels. To do this, switch to **Variable View** and then click **None** in the cell in the **Values** column for the row of the new variable *NewStatus*.

When the grey box with three dots appears, click it to open the **Values Labels** dialog box. Complete this box in the usual way by assigning *Postgrad* to value 1 and *Others* to value 2, and finally click **OK**. To see whether this has worked, switch to **Data View** and check the data for the new variable *NewStatus*.

Save the data file again.

Now use the **Visual Binning** procedure to recode the heights of people as Tall, Medium or Short.

- Click **Visual Binning...** in the **Transform** drop-down menu, transfer the variable *Height in metres* to the **Variables to Bin** box by highlighting *Height in metres* and clicking on the arrow. Click **Continue**.

- When the **Visual Binning** dialog box re-appears, click the variable name *Height in metres* in the **Scanned Variable List** box. A histogram will now appear on the right.

- Name the new variable in the **Binned Variable** box as *HeightBin*.

- Enter the following values and labels into **Value** and **Label** cells: 1.70 Short; 1.80 Medium; 2.10 Tall. By accepting the default **Included (<=)** in **Upper Endpoints**, Short is defined as 1.70m or less, Medium as 1.71m to 1.80m, and Tall as 1.81 to 2.10m. The value of 2.10m is arbitrary; any value greater than the tallest person would suffice. Re-read the end of Section 4.4.3 for extra help.

- Click **OK** and note the information that the procedure will create 1 variable. Click **OK** within the information panel.

Check your data to make certain that they have all been classified in the manner that you planned.

Pie chart

Produce a pie chart with a title showing what percentages of the cases are tall, medium or short. Since there are a few people whose height is not known, use **Select Cases...** (Section 3.1.1) in the **Data** menu to select cases with a height, say, of more than 1 metre by clicking the radio button **If condition is satisfied** and then entering Metres > 1 in the panel. Edit the pie chart to show the percentage for each slice (see Exercise 6 if you need to refresh your memory).

- **Edit the pie chart to prepare it for black-and-white printing. Print the pie chart.**

Select cases

It is also useful to be able to select the cases you want to analyse. Suppose, for example, that you wished to consider only the data relating to females. Use **Select Cases** (Section 3.3.1) to specify that only the female cases will be analysed.

Now suppose that, since smoking is said to suppress appetite, you wanted to see whether female smokers were lighter in weight than non-smokers. Use the **Compare Means** (Section 4.3.2) procedure to do this. Remember the **Dependent** variable will be *Kilos* and the **Independent** variable *Smoker*.

- **Print the Report table produced. Note that as a result of the Select Cases procedure you have just followed, this table will apply to the female respondents only.**

- **Are there any differences between the smokers and the non-smokers? Comment briefly on any differences you find. (When you think about this, bear in mind the difference in size between the smoking and non-smoking groups.)**

Line graph

A **line graph** is suitable when there is an interval or ordinal scale for one of the variables with not more than about ten values. When the scale is nominal, a bar chart is preferable. Now that you have an ordinal scale of height with three values in the variable *HeightBin*, you can draw a line graph of *Sex* against *HeightBin*.

First, however, the selection of females in the previous section must be reversed by returning to the **Select Cases** dialog box and clicking the **All cases** radio button.

- Choose
  Graphs➔Chart Builder➔Line
  and click the Multiple Line picture to highlight it. Drag it to the **Chart preview** above.

- Insert the variable *HeightBin* into the **X-Axis** box and *Sex* into the **Set pattern** box.

- Select the **Statistic** directory in the **Element Properties**, click **Percentage (?)** and then click **Apply**.

- Click **OK** to plot the lines.

A two-line graph should then appear, one line for Male and one line for Female, with the points on the abscissa labelled Short, Medium and Tall. Click the chart to enter **Chart Editor** and delete **(Binned)** from the x-axis label by clicking on it so that it is highlighted with a purple border and then move the cursor in and delete the appropriate section. In order to differentiate the sexes clearly in the printed graph, change one of the lines to a discontinuous line by clicking on one of the lines in the Sex of Student legend box and then selecting a different **Style** from the choice in the **Lines** dialog box. You can change the colour within the same dialog box. Click **Apply** and **Close.** You may also wish to show the markers for the different categories, in which case, select the icon ⊞ from the toolbar (**Show Line Markers**). If you wish to change the style of the markers, double-click on one of them to open the **Properties** dialog box. There the type, size and colour can be altered.

Finishing the session

Close down SPSS and any other windows before logging out of the computer.

CHAPTER 6

Comparing averages and frequencies: Two-sample and one-sample tests

6.1 Overview

6.2 The *t* tests

6.3 Effect size, power and the number of participants

6.4 Other tests for comparing averages

6.5 One-sample tests

6.1 OVERVIEW

In Chapter 1, five research scenarios were described (Section 1.4.1, Figure 3). In the first, the researcher has **two samples** of scores and wants to know whether the difference between their two means is significant. As an aid to choosing an appropriate test, we offered a flow chart (Figure 4 in Chapter 1), the important proviso being that the data must meet the requirements of the statistical model upon which the test is based. The first question in the flow chart concerned the number of groups or conditions. This chapter shows how to use SPSS to carry out the tests recommended by the chart when there are two samples of scores. (We shall also consider some one-sample tests.)

> See Section 1.4.1

In Figure 1 in this chapter, we reproduce the flow chart for selecting a suitable test for differences between averages or (with nominal data) relative frequencies. The chart indicates whether a parametric test (e.g. a *t* test) or a nonparametric test (e.g. a chi-square test) is appropriate for the type of data in hand.

Table 1 identifies the appropriate SPSS menu items for the various two-sample tests. The left half of the table lists **parametric tests**, which make assumptions about population distributions and parameters. The right half of the table lists **non-parametric tests**, which make fewer assumptions. Each half of the table is subdivided according to whether the samples are independent or related. (Incidentally, in the context of the *t* test, SPSS uses the term **paired samples** rather than **related samples**.)

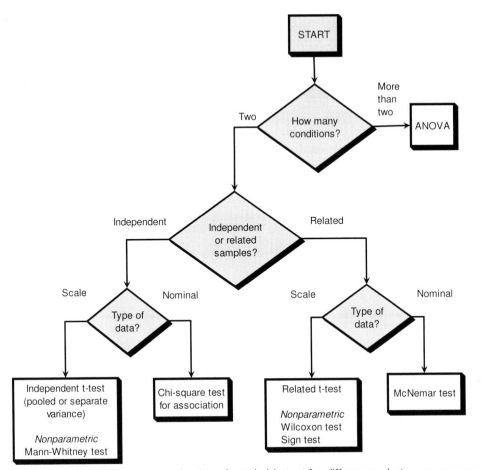

Figure 1. Flow chart showing the selection of a suitable test for differences between averages or frequencies

Table 1. Comparing the averages of two samples: The SPSS menus			
Assumptions			
Populations assumed to have normal distributions and equal variances		No specific assumptions about the population distributions	
Independent samples	Paired samples	Independent samples	Related samples
SPSS procedures			
Compare Means		**Nonparametric Tests**	
Independent-Samples T Test...	**Paired-Samples T Test...**	**2 Independent Samples...**	**2 Related Samples...**

In the fourth scenario in Section 1.4.1, the researcher has only a single sample of scores, on the basis of which he or she wishes either to make an inference about the mean of the population or to decide whether the distribution of the sample is sufficiently well fitted by a theoretical distribution. This chapter will describe the use of SPSS to make appropriate **one-sample tests** in such situations. Where there are two related samples of scores, the appropriate *t* test can be viewed as a one-sample test. One-sample tests, however, have many uses other than comparing means. We shall consider some of those applications as well.

In Figure 2, we reproduce the scheme we described in Chapter 1 for selecting a suitable one-sample test. This flow chart will indicate whether a parametric (e.g. a *t* test) or a nonparametric test (e.g. a chi-square test) is appropriate for the type of data in hand. Table 2 identifies the appropriate SPSS menu items for the various one-sample tests.

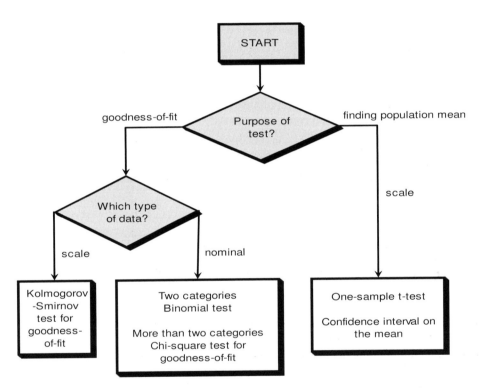

Figure 2. Flow chart showing the selection of a suitable one-sample test

Table 2. One-sample tests: Parametric and nonparametric tests in the SPSS **Analyze** and **Nonparametric Tests** procedures, respectively

Parametric tests	Nonparametric tests		
SPSS procedures			
Analyze	Nonparametric Tests		
⬇	⬇	⬇	⬇
Compare Means (One-Sample T Test...)	Chi-Square...	Binomial...	1-Sample K-S...

⬇ indicates that the item below is part of the submenu of the item above

6.2   THE T TESTS

While we assume the reader has some familiarity with statistics, this section may serve as a review of some of the terms you will come across in the SPSS output.

6.2.1   One-sample and two-sample tests

In a one-sample test, the null hypothesis (H_0) states that, in the population, the value of the mean is some specific value, k:

$$H_0 : \mu = k$$

H_0 is tested by drawing a single sample from the population and making an inference on the basis of the statistics of the sample.

In the only two-sample test that we are going to consider, the null hypothesis states that, in the populations, the means have the same value:

$$H_0: \mu_1 = \mu_2$$

H_0 is tested by drawing a sample from each of the populations and making an inference about the truth or falsity of H_0 on the basis of the statistics of the two samples.

6.2.2   Sampling distributions

In both two-sample and one-sample tests, a key notion is that of the **sampling distribution**, that is, the distribution of a statistic when samples of the same size are repeatedly drawn from the population specified by the null hypothesis. For the one-sample test, the relevant sampling distribution is the **sampling distribution of the mean** and for the two-sample test, it is the **sampling distribution of the differences between means**.

Let X be a variable with a normal distribution and M be the mean of a sample of size n. The distribution of M (the sampling distribution of the mean) is also normal, with a mean equal to the value of the population mean μ.

Let X_1 and X_2 be scores selected at random from normal populations with means μ_1 and μ_2, respectively. Let M_1 and M_2 be the means of samples of sizes n_1 and n_2 selected from these populations. The values of the means and their difference $M_1 - M_2$ are also random variables. The distribution of the difference $M_1 - M_2$ is also normal, with a mean equal to the difference $\mu_1 - \mu_2$ between the population means. In all the examples we shall consider, the null hypothesis is that $\mu_1 - \mu_2 = 0$, that is, there is no difference between the population means.

The standard error of the mean

The standard deviation of the distribution of means is known as the **standard error of the mean** σ_M, which is related to the standard deviation σ of the parent population and the size of the sample n according to

$$\sigma_M = \frac{\sigma}{\sqrt{n}} \qquad (1)$$

The square of the standard error of the mean σ_M^2 is **the sampling variance** of the mean.

The standard error of the difference between means

The standard deviation of the sample distribution of the difference between means is known as the **standard error of the difference** $\sigma_{M_1-M_2}$, which is given by

$$\sigma_{M_1-M_2} = \sqrt{\sigma_{M_1}^2 + \sigma_{M_2}^2} = \sqrt{\sigma^2 \left(\frac{1}{n_1} + \frac{1}{n_2} \right)} \qquad (2)$$

It is easy to understand this formula. If independent samples are drawn repeatedly from the two populations, the sample means M_1 and M_2 are independent (i.e. uncorrelated) random variables, each taking different values from sample to sample. The variance of the sum of independent random variables (or indeed, perhaps less obviously, their difference) is the sum of their variances, which in this case is the sum of the sampling variances of the means of the two samples. This is the **sampling variance of the difference**. The standard deviation of the difference, that is, the **standard error of the difference**, is the square root of the sampling variance, hence equation (2).

6.2.3   The *t* distribution, p-values, effect size & confidence intervals

If the parent populations are normally distributed, the sampling distributions of the means and the difference between means are also normal; in fact, provided the samples are sufficiently large, the sampling distributions will approach normality, even if the parent populations are not normal. Any normally distributed variable (X) can be converted to the standard normal variable z by subtracting the population mean (μ) and dividing by the population standard deviation (σ) thus:

$$z = \frac{X - \mu}{\sigma}$$

The standard normal variable z has a mean of zero and a standard deviation of 1. Ninety-five per cent of values in any normal distribution lie within 1.96 standard deviations on either side of the mean, that is, within the interval $[\mu - 1.96\sigma, \mu + 1.96\sigma]$. Since the standard deviation of the standard normal distribution is 1 and its mean is zero, 95% of values of the standard normal variable z lie in the interval $[-1.96, +1.96]$ (see Figure 3).

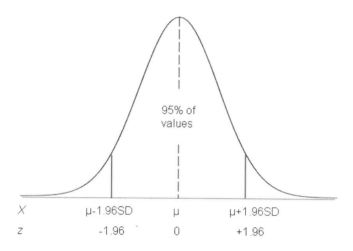

Figure 3. Interval containing 95% of the values in the normal and standard normal distributions

If we knew the population variance σ^2, we could test the null hypothesis with the standard normal variable z, and reject H_0 if z were to fall outside the range of values between the 2.5th and 97.5th percentiles, that is, either below -1.96 or above +1.96. The statistics we should use are, for the one-sample test,

$$z = \frac{M - \mu}{\sigma_M}$$

where M is the value of the sample mean and, for the two-sample test,

$$z = \frac{(M_1 - M_2) - (\mu_1 - \mu_2)}{\sigma_{M_1 - M_2}}$$

where M_1 and M_2 are the values of the sample means. When H_0 states that $\mu_1 = \mu_2$, $\mu_1 - \mu_2 = 0$ and the two-sample formula simplifies to

$$z = \frac{M_1 - M_2}{\sigma_{M_1 - M_2}}$$

When the population variance and standard deviation are unknown: the t distribution

Unfortunately, we rarely know the value of the population variance σ^2 and therefore cannot use the standard normal variable z as our test statistic unless the samples are very large. Instead, we use the test statistic t, which is analogous to the z statistics above, with the population variances replaced by estimates thus:

$$t = \frac{M - \mu}{s_M} \text{ where } s_M = \frac{s}{\sqrt{n}}$$

and

$$t = \frac{M_1 - M_2}{s_{M_1 - M_2}} \text{ where } s_{M_1 - M_2} = \sqrt{s^2 \left(\frac{1}{n_1} + \frac{1}{n_2} \right)} \quad (3)$$

Estimates of the standard error of the mean and difference between means

In the estimate of the standard error of the difference $s_{M_1 - M_2}$, s^2 is an estimate of the supposedly constant population variance σ^2.

A t distribution resembles the bell-shaped standard normal distribution, but has thicker tails: large positive and negative values are more likely than large values of z. It has a single parameter, namely, the degrees of freedom (df), which is obtained from the sizes of the samples (see below). The larger the samples, the more closely the distribution of t approximates to the standard normal distribution; with very large samples, in fact, percentiles of z can be used to make the test.

In the one-sample test, the degrees of freedom of the t statistic are $n - 1$, where n is the size of the sample: this value is the degrees of freedom of the variance estimate used to calculate the estimate the standard error of the mean. A variance estimate s^2 from n scores is made as follows:

$$s^2 = \frac{\Sigma(\text{score} - \text{mean})^2}{n - 1} = \frac{SS}{df}$$

In the two-sample test, the degrees of freedom of the t statistic are $n_1 + n_2 - 2$, that is, the sum of the degrees of freedom of the two variance estimates used to estimate the standard error of the difference: $df_1 + df_2 = (n_1 - 1) + (n_2 - 1) = n_1 + n_2 - 2$.

The independent samples t test

Table 3 summarises the results of an experiment in which half the participants were tested on shooting accuracy after ingesting a dose of caffeine; the remaining participants took a placebo and took the same test.

Table 3. Number of hits achieved by participants under caffeine and placebo conditions		
	Placebo	**Caffeine**
Mean number of hits	9.25	11.90
Standard deviation	3.16	3.28
Number of cases	20	20

An experiment of this kind must be seen as a process of sampling. We have two sets of scores from two populations of possible scores: a Caffeine population; and a Placebo population. If the null hypothesis (H_0) is true and the scores achieved by the 20 participants tested under the Caffeine condition are a sample from a population with the same mean as the population of scores for the Placebo condition, the difference $M_1 - M_2$ between the means is most likely to be close to zero: only rarely would the sampling process throw up a 'large' difference, positive or negative.

Large or not, it is still necessary to verify the difference between the Caffeine and Placebo means by testing the null hypothesis that the Caffeine and Placebo score distributions have the same mean:

$$H_0: \mu_1 = \mu_2$$

Since the alternate hypothesis (H_1) is the negation of H_0, it is written as follows:

$$H_1: \mu_1 \neq \mu_2$$

If we can assume that the Caffeine and Placebo populations have the same (unknown) variance (the homogeneity of variance assumption), the null hypothesis of equality of population means can be tested with the statistic t, which is defined as follows:

$$t = \frac{M_1 - M_2}{\sqrt{s^2 \left(\frac{1}{n_1} + \frac{1}{n_2} \right)}} \qquad (4)$$

Formula for the t statistic for testing the difference

where n_1 and n_2 are the sizes of the two independent samples (in this case $n_1 = n_2 = 20$) and s^2 is a pooled estimate of the variance of scores in either the Placebo or the Caffeine population. When the sample sizes are equal (i.e. $n_1 = n_2$) as in the present example, s^2 is calculated simply by taking the mean of the group variance estimates s_1^2 and s_2^2:

$$s^2 = \frac{s_1^2 + s_2^2}{2} = \frac{3.16^2 + 3.28^2}{2} = 10.37$$

If $n_1 \neq n_2$, the pooled estimate of the supposedly homogeneous population variance σ^2 is given by

$$s^2 = \frac{SS_1 + SS_2}{df_1 + df_2} = \frac{SS_1 + SS_2}{n_1 + n_2 - 2} \quad (5)$$

General formula for pooling the variance estimates

where SS_1 and SS_2 are the numerators of the two variance estimates and df_1 and df_2 are their respective degrees of freedom: i.e. $df_1 = n_1 - 1$ and $df_2 = n_2 - 1$. The degrees of freedom df of the pooled estimate s^2, therefore, is $df = df_1 + df_2 = n_1 + n_2 - 2$. This is also the value of the degrees of freedom of the t statistic itself. In this example, $df = 20 + 20 - 2 = 38$. We specify the t distribution on 38 degrees of freedom with the notation $t(38)$: in general, we specify a t distribution with degrees of freedom k by the term $t(k)$.

If the significance level (α) is set at .05 (i.e., at the 5% level), the null hypothesis that, in the population, the Caffeine and Placebo means are equal is rejected if t is either greater than the 97.5[th] percentile or less than the 2.5[th] percentile. Substituting in the formula for t, we have

$$t = \frac{M_1 - M_2}{\sqrt{s\left(\dfrac{1}{n_1} + \dfrac{1}{n_2}\right)}} = \frac{2.65}{\sqrt{10.37\left(\dfrac{1}{20} + \dfrac{1}{20}\right)}} = 2.60$$

The two-tailed test

In the hypothetical population of values of t, it matters not which of the Placebo and Caffeine means the symbols M_1 and M_2 refer to. Theoretically, however, the subtraction is always in the same direction (e.g. the Caffeine mean is always be subtracted from the Placebo mean, or vice versa). If H$_0$ is true and $\mu_1 = \mu_2$, there will be as many large positive values of t as large negative values. If the significance level is set at .05, we shall reject the null hypothesis if t is either greater than the 97.5[th] percentile or less than the 2.5[th] percentile of the distribution of t on 38 degrees of freedom.

In practice, it will, of course, be more convenient simply to subtract the larger mean from the smaller one: in this example, we would subtract the Placebo mean from the Caffeine mean; had the Placebo mean been larger, we should have subtracted the Caffeine mean. Alternatively, we could simply ignore the sign of t. With either practice, however, large positive values of t will be twice as probable as they would be if we were always to subtract in the same direction and take the sign into consideration. We need to bear this in mind when calculating the p-value.

The cumulative probability and the two-sided p-value

In the present example, $t = 2.60$. The **cumulative probability** of 2.60 is the probability of a value less than or equal to 2.60 and is written as $\Pr[t \leq 2.60]$. The value of the cumulative probability of a specified value of t will depend upon the degrees of freedom of the distribution. For the t distribution on 38 degrees of freedom, the cumulative probability is .9934, so the probability of a value *greater* than 2.60 is $1 - .9934 = .0066$. Since large *negative* values of t are just as likely as large positive values under H$_0$, however, we must multiply the probability of obtaining a value at least as great as +2.60 by 2 in order to obtain the p-value. The p-value is therefore $2 \times .0066 = .013$. The p-value of t is automatically included in the SPSS output.

The test of the null hypothesis (H_0) has shown a significant difference between the Placebo and Caffeine means. We write this result briefly as follows:

$$t(38) = 2.60; p = .01.$$

The p-value should be given to two places of decimals. Should the p-value be less than .01, report it as 'p < .01'. Note that in a research report, the results of a statistical test should always be accompanied by the appropriate descriptive statistics, plus some measure of effect size (see below).

Effect size

Cohen's measure of **effect size** d (see Section 1.3.5) for the difference between the two means is

| See Section 1.3.5 |

$$d = \frac{\mu_1 - \mu_2}{\sigma}$$

Assume that the sample means are the best estimates of the population means and that the population standard deviation is the square root of the pooled variance estimate s^2 in the t test formula (4): $\sqrt{10.37} = 3.22$. The effect size is thus estimated as:

$$d = \frac{11.90 - 9.25}{3.22} = 0.82$$

According to Table 3 in Chapter 1, this is a 'large' effect.

How to report the results of a statistical test

The 2001 *Publication Manual of the American Psychological Association* (APA) recommends that when reporting a statistical result, the researcher should, in general:

'...include sufficient information to allow the reader to fully understand the analysis conducted and possible alternative explanations for the results of these analyses' (p.138).

In particular, as well as the value of a statistic such as t, you should include the degrees of freedom (with other statistics such as correlation coefficients, the number of observations is given), the p-value and a statement about the statistical significance (or insignificance) of the result. The report of a statistical test should be preceded by a brief statement of the results, including relevant statistics such as the mean and standard deviation, and the effect size. Your complete report of the result of the t test would look something like this:

> The scores of the Caffeine group (M = 11.90; SD = 3.28) were significantly higher than those of the Placebo group (M = 9.25; 3.16): $t(38) = 2.60$; p = .01 (two-tailed). Cohen's $d = 0.82$, a 'large' effect.

The one-tailed test

Some would argue that, since the experiment was run in order to show that performance under the Caffeine condition is superior to that under the Placebo condition, a one-tailed test is appropriate.

Note carefully, however, that if the scientific or alternative hypothesis H_1 is that μ_2 (the Caffeine mean) is *greater than* μ_1 (the Placebo mean), the null hypothesis H_0, being the negation of H_1, is that μ_2 is *not greater* than μ_1, that is, H_0 must state that μ_2 is less than or equal to μ_1. We must write these directional hypotheses as follows:

$$H_1 : \quad \mu_2 > \mu_1$$
$$H_0 : \quad \mu_2 \leq \mu_1$$

When calculating the value of t, therefore, you must always subtract the Placebo mean from the Caffeine mean, *even if the former has the greater value,* with the result that t is *negative.* Moreover, however large the absolute value of t, a negative value forces the researcher to accept the null hypothesis. This is the problem with one-tailed tests: they cannot confirm an unexpected result.

The one-tailed p-value of $t = 2.60$ is half the two-tailed value. Thus for our obtained t value of 2.60, the one-tailed p-value is half .0132 (i.e. .0066) and so t is significant beyond the .01 level.

If you are making a one-tailed test of H_0 (which we would not recommend, except in unusually compelling circumstances), you might report the result of the test as follows:

> The scores of the Caffeine group (M = 11.90; SD = 3.28) were significantly higher than those of the Placebo group (M = 9.25; 3.16): $t(38) = 2.60$; p < .01 (one-tailed). Cohen's $d = 0.82$, a large effect.

Hypothesis testing with confidence intervals

In Section 1.3.4, a confidence interval was described as a range of values built around the value of a statistic such as the mean which is constructed in such a way that it is expected to 'cover' or 'include' the value of the parameter (such as μ) with a specified probability. The 95% **confidence interval on the mean** will include μ in 95% of samples; the 99% confidence interval on the mean will include μ in 99% of samples. Naturally, the 99% confidence interval is much wider than the 95% confidence interval. Imagine you are trying to throw a hoop over an upright peg some feet away. You will achieve a higher success rate if you use a hoop with a wider diameter.

See Section 1.3.4

One can also construct a confidence interval on the difference between means $M_1 - M_2$. The 95% **confidence interval on the difference** will include the population difference $\mu_1 - \mu_2$ in 95% of samples. If the 95% confidence interval on the difference does not include $\mu_1 - \mu_2$ (zero in our example), the null hypothesis of equality of the means is rejected. The use of a confidence interval to test the null hypothesis will produce exactly the same results as the procedures described earlier in this section: if the 95% confidence interval on the difference fails to include zero, we know that t will also show significance beyond the .05 level and vice versa.

Confidence intervals are readily available on SPSS. Some journal editors like confidence intervals to be included in reports of the results of some statistical tests. Like measures of effect size, a confidence interval provides valuable information over and above that provided by the results of a significance test alone. An illustration of this will be given later in this section.

Unequal variances: The Behrens-Fisher problem

The model underlying a *t* test assumes that the data have been derived from normal distributions with equal variance. (This is the assumption of **homogeneity of variance**.) Computer simulations, however, have shown that even with moderate violations of these assumptions, one may still safely proceed with a *t* test, provided the samples are not too small, do not contain outliers (atypical scores), and are of equal (or nearly equal) size. The *t* test is said to be **robust** to some violation of the assumptions of the underlying statistical model.

There are limits to this robustness, however. When the sample variances are very disparate, especially in company with markedly discrepant sample sizes, error rates become unacceptably high. When the two samples have very disparate variances, so that the assumption of homogeneity of variance in the population is untenable, the statistic t^* is used, where

$$t^* = \frac{M_1 - M_2}{\sqrt{\dfrac{s_1^2}{n_1} + \dfrac{s_2^2}{n_2}}} \qquad (6)$$

The separate-variance t statistic

The statistic t^* is distributed on degrees of freedom df^*, which is smaller than df. The determination of the exact degrees of freedom of t^* is known as the **Behrens-Fisher problem**. Several formula for the degrees of freedom for t^* have been proposed, most of which are based upon one suggested many years ago by Satterthwaite (see Howell, 2007, p.214). SPSS uses one of these formulae to obtain df^* but, since the formula is complex, we shall not give it here. The greater the disparity between the two sample variance estimates, the smaller will be the value of df^* and the greater t^* will have to be for the test to show significance. There are, nevertheless, situations in which t^* may be significant when t is not. There are yet other situations, however, in which neither statistic can safely be used. When the data set is small and there are marked extreme scores or outliers, the denominator of either t or t^* can be inflated to a relatively greater extent than the numerator of t (i.e., the difference between the means). The square root operation used to estimate the standard error of the difference does not entirely negate the leverage exerted by outlying scores upon the sum of squares.

The 'pooled' and 'separate-variance' t tests

In this book, we shall use the terms **pooled** *t* test and **separate-variance** *t* test to refer to the use of the statistics t and t^*, respectively: in the former, under the assumption of homogeneity of variance, the sample variances are averaged or pooled; in the latter, they are kept separate.

6.2.4   The independent-samples *t* test

The complete data set is shown in Table 4.

Prepare the data file from this data set in Table 4 as follows:
- In **Variable View**, name the variables as *Case* for the case number, *Group* for the grouping (independent) variable, and *Hits* for the dependent variable.
- In the **Label** column, add the labels *Case Number*, *Group* and *Number of Hits*.

See
Section
2.3

- In the **Values** column, define the values and their labels for the variable *Group* as follows: 1 = Placebo, 2 = Caffeine.
- In the **Measure** column, change **Scale** to **Nominal** for *Group*.
- Open **Data View** and type in the case number, the value for *Group* and number of hits for each participant.

Case	Placebo	Case	Placebo	Case	Caffeine	Case	Caffeine
1	5	11	9	21	2	31	13
2	6	12	9	22	8	32	13
3	6	13	10	23	9	33	13
4	7	14	10	24	9	34	13
5	7	15	10	25	10	35	14
6	8	16	11	26	11	36	14
7	8	17	11	27	11	37	15
8	8	18	11	28	12	38	15
9	8	19	12	29	12	39	15
10	9	20	20	30	12	40	17

Table 4. Number of hits for the Placebo and Caffeine groups

Exploring the data

Before running the *t* test, it is important to check the data for anomalies such as extreme values or skewed distributions. Such considerations are particularly important with small data sets such as this one. Since this data set contains a grouping variable, the **Explore** procedure (Chapter 4, Section 4.3.2) is appropriate.

> See Section 4.3.2

- Choose
    Analyze➔Descriptive Statistics➔Explore...
    to open the **Explore** dialog box (see Chapter 4, Figure 11).
- Transfer the dependent variable *Hits* in the left-hand box to the **Dependent List:** box. Transfer the grouping variable *Group* to the **Factor List:** box.
- Click **Plots...** to open the **Explore: Plots** dialog box, deselect the **Stem-and-leaf** check box and select the **Histogram** check box. Click **Continue** to return to the **Explore** dialog box.
- Click **OK** to run the **Explore** procedure.

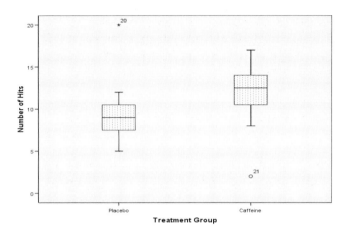

Output 1. The boxplots from the **Explore** procedure

The output is extensive. In Output 1, the *Placebo* boxplot shows an extreme value for case 20 ($*^{20}$ means, 'Case 20 is an extreme value').

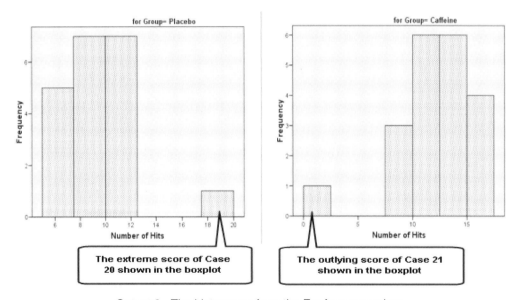

Output 2. The histograms from the **Explore** procedure

In Output 2, which shows histograms of the same distributions, the same extreme value appears as the isolated right-hand box in the *Placebo* histogram. Another score, for Case 21, appears as an outlier (o^{21} means, 'Case 21 is an outlier') in the *Caffeine* boxplot and is shown as the isolated left-hand box in the *Caffeine* histogram.

See Table 2, Chap. 4

With such a small sample, the presence of the markedly atypical scores of Cases 20 and 21 is likely to exert undue leverage on the values of the statistics summarising the data set. We shall therefore de-select Cases 20 and 21 before running the *t* test. This is easily done using the **Select Cases** procedure described in Chapter 3, Section 3.3.1.

See
Section
3.3.1

- Choose
  Data➜Select Cases…
  to open the **Select Cases** dialog box (see Chapter 3, Figure 18).
- Click the **If condition is satisfied** radio button and then **If…** to open the **Select Cases: If** dialog box.
- Transfer *Case* to the conditional statement box. Type in the expression *Case ~= 20 & Case ~= 21* to select all cases except 20 and 21. Click **Continue** to return to the **Select Cases** dialog box.
- Click **OK**.

Inspection of the data in **Data View** will show that cases 20 and 21 have been de-selected. Now we can continue with the *t* test.

Running the t test
- Choose
  Analyze➜Compare Means➜Independent-Samples T Test ...
  to open the **Independent-Samples T Test** dialog box (Figure 4).

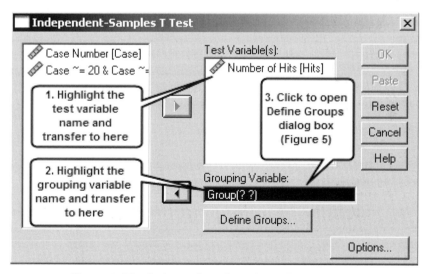

Figure 4. The **Independent-Samples T Test** dialog box

- Transfer the dependent variable *Number of Hits* to the **Test Variable(s)** box. Transfer the grouping variable *Group* to the **Grouping Variable** box. At this point the **Grouping Variable** box will appear with **Group[? ?]** as shown in Figure 4.
- Define the values of the groups by clicking **Define Groups** to obtain the **Define Groups dialog box** (Figure 5).

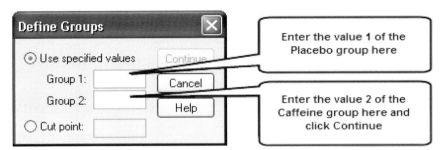

Figure 5. The **Define Groups** dialog box before defining the values of the two groups

- Type the value *1* into the **Group 1** box and the value *2* into the **Group 2** box, and click **Continue**. The values 1, 2 will then appear in brackets after *Group* in the **Grouping Variable** box:
  Grouping Variable:
  Group(1 2)

- Click **OK** to run the *t* test.

Early in the output, a table of **Group Statistics** (Output 3) will appear, listing some statistics of the two samples, including the means (8.68 and 12.42). The two means are certainly different but are they significantly different?

Group Statistics

	Treatment Group	N	Mean	Std. Deviation	Std. Error Mean
Number of Hits	Placebo	19	8.68	1.945	.446
	Caffeine	19	12.42	2.364	.542

Output 3. Summary table of group statistics

Output 4 summarises the results of the *t* tests. Notice that the first two columns of the table refer to **Levene's test**. This is not the result of the *t* test proper: Levene's test is a test of the assumption of **homogeneity of variance**. Its purpose is to help us to decide whether to make our decision about the null hypothesis on the basis of the **pooled** *t* test or the **separate variance** *t* test. Notice too that, in Levene's test, the test statistic is *F*, not *t*. For the moment, we need only look at the p-value of *F*, which is .49. Since the p-value of *F* is greater than .05, the variances can be assumed to be homogeneous and the **Equal Variances** line of values for the *t* test can be used. (This is the **pooled *t* test** discussed earlier in Section 6.2.3.)

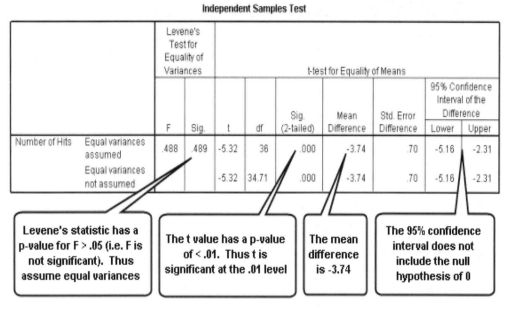

Output 4. T test output for **Independent Samples**

In summary:
- Since p > 0.05, the homogeneity of variance assumption is tenable, and the equal-variance (pooled) *t* test (**Equal variances assumed**) can be used.
- Had p been less than .05, the homogeneity of variance assumption would have been untenable and the separate variance *t* test (**Equal variances not assumed**) would have been used.

The reader will have observed that in this example, both the p-values and *t*-values for **Equal variance assumed** and **Equal variance not assumed** are identical. That would not have been the case had the variances been heterogeneous: the two *t* tests can lead to different decisions about the null hypothesis. In this example, the **Levene Test** is not significant (p > 0.05), so the *t* value calculated with the pooled variance estimate (**Equal variances assumed**) is acceptable.

Turning now to the *t* test itself, we see that *t* (*df* = 36) is 5.32 (ignore the negative sign), with a two-tailed p-value, **Sig. (2 tailed)** of <.01. (For a one-tailed test, we would halve the p-value.) The *t* test rejects the null hypothesis and so confirms the scientific hypothesis that the number of hits differs between participants taking a dose of caffeine or a placebo.

It will be noticed that the value of *t* and the p-value are different from the corresponding values we calculated using the entire data set of 40 scores. We worked with the reduced data set on the assumption that it is better to describe most of the data correctly than 100% of them badly.

Note carefully that the value in the **Sig.** column in Output 4 is the **p-value**, not the **significance level** (which is set beforehand at .05 – sometimes at .01). With a non-significant result, the p-value would be high, perhaps .6 or .7. This high value would still be reported in the **Sig.** column, even though the test has not shown significance.

The **95% Confidence Interval on the Difference** is [-5.16, -2.31], i.e. −5.16 to −2.31. Earlier, we observed that a test of significance can also be made from a confidence interval: if the interval does not include the value stated by the null hypothesis, H_0 is rejected. In this example, the confidence interval does not include zero, so H_0 is rejected. Had one of these values been positive, the interval would have included zero and the result of the t test would not have been significant.

The **effect size** (see Section 1.3.5) for a two-sample (between subjects) experiment is

$$d = \frac{\mu_1 - \mu_2}{\sigma}$$

Here we must use estimates of these values. In the numerator, we place the difference between the sample means, which Output 4 tells us is 3.74. We obtain a pooled estimate of the supposedly constant population standard deviation using

$$s = \sqrt{\frac{SS_1 + SS_2}{df_1 + df_2}} = \sqrt{\frac{(n_1 - 1) \times s_1^2 + (n_2 - 1) \times s_2^2}{n_1 + n_2 - 2}}$$

Thus

$$s = \sqrt{\frac{18 \times 1.945^2 + 18 \times 2.364^2}{36}} = 2.16$$

and so our estimate of effect strength is

$$d = \frac{3.74}{2.16} = 1.73$$

In Cohen's classification of effect size (Table 3 in Chapter 1), this is a **large** effect.

The results of the independent-samples t test would be reported as follows:

> The mean numbers of hits of the Placebo group (M = 8.68; SD = 1.945) were significantly different from those of the Caffeine group (M = 12.42; SD = 2.364): t(36) = 5.32; p = <.01 (two-tailed) after two cases were excluded from the analysis. Cohen's d = 1.73, a large effect. This confirms the hypothesis that the number of hits is affected by the ingestion of caffeine.

Demonstration of the effects of outliers and extreme scores in a small data set

Recall that the t test we have described was run on a data set with two outliers removed. You might wish to re-run the test on the complete data set (Table 4). You would find that the value of t is smaller: t(38) = 2.60; p = .01 (two-tailed), p <.01 (one-tailed). Cohen's d = .82. These are exactly the same values that we obtained from our calculations earlier in the chapter. The 95% confidence interval is (-4.71, -.59), which does not include zero.

The t value from the full data set is smaller than the value calculated from the reduced data set because the outlier and the extreme score have the effect of increasing the standard error of the difference (the denominator of t) from .70 to 1.02, thereby reducing the value of t. In small data sets such as this, the presence of outliers, even when they result in a greater difference between the means $M_1 - M_2$, can have the effect of increasing the denominator of the t statistic more than the numerator and so reduce the value of t to insignificance. (This did not happen with the full data set in the present example.) The elements of the variance (and standard deviation) are the **squares** of deviations from the mean, and large deviations thus continue to have a disproportionate influence, even after the square root operation has been carried out.

6.2.5 The related-samples t test

In an experiment on lateralisation of cortical functioning, a participant looks at a central spot on a computer screen and is told to press a key on recognition of a word that may appear on either side of the spot.

Table 5. Median reaction times for words presented in the left and right visual fields

Case	Left Field	Right Field	Difference (d)
1	323	304	19
2	512	493	19
3	502	491	11
4	385	365	20
5	453	426	27
6	343	320	23
7	543	523	20
8	440	442	-2
9	682	580	102
10	590	564	26

The experimental hypothesis is that words presented in the right visual field will be more quickly recognised than those in the left visual field, because the former are processed by the left cerebral hemisphere, which is thought to be better adapted to the processing of verbal information. For each participant, the median response time to forty words in both the right and the left visual fields is recorded, as indicated in Table 5.

Also shown in Table 5 are the differences resulting from subtracting the right field scores from the left field scores. As the researcher hoped, there is a clear tendency for the differences to be positive, that is, the right field times tend to be shorter.

Here, since each participant was tested with words in both visual hemifields, we have two related samples of scores. A **related-samples t test** is therefore appropriate.

The null hypothesis (H$_0$) we wish to test is that the 10 scores obtained under the *Left Field* and *Right Field* conditions are samples from populations with the same mean:

$$H_0: \quad \mu_1 = \mu_2$$

This would seem to be a situation calling for a two-sample test. There is, however, another way of conceiving the problem of testing the difference between the means of related samples for significance. The 10 difference scores in Table 5 can be regarded as a single sample from the population of such differences. Let X_1 and X_2 be the *same participant's* left hemifield and right hemifield scores, respectively. (The following move works only with *paired* data.) Let $d = X_1 - X_2$. If H_0 is true, the mean difference in the population μ_d is zero. We can therefore re-formulate the null hypothesis as follows:

$$H_0: \mu_d = 0$$

Re-conceived in this way, the problem of testing H_0 becomes one of making a one-sample test with the statistic t, where

$$t = \frac{M_d}{s_{M_d}} = \frac{M_d}{\left(\dfrac{s_d}{\sqrt{n}}\right)} \qquad (7)$$

The paired-samples t statistic

where M_d is the mean of $X_1 - X_2$ in the sample, s_d is the standard deviation of the differences and s_{M_d} is the estimate of the standard error of the mean (difference). Here, even though we are making a one-sample test, the denominator of t is actually an estimate of the **standard error of the difference between means** $s_{M_1 - M_2}$: that is,

$$s_{M_d} = s_{M_1 - M_2}$$

the numerator of t, of course, is the difference $M_1 - M_2$.

The **Descriptives...** procedure in SPSS's **Descriptive Statistics** menu will show us that $M_d = 26.50$ and $s_d = 27.814$. Substituting in the formula, we have

$$t = \frac{26.50}{\left(\dfrac{27.814}{\sqrt{10}}\right)} = 3.01$$

The two-tailed p-value of $t = 3.01$ is .02, so we have found a significant difference between the mean response latencies for the left and right visual fields: $t(9) = 3.01$; p = .02.

Paired-samples data file

Prepare the data file from the data set in Table 5 as follows:
* Using the techniques described in Chapter 2 (Section 2.3), open **Variable View** and name the variables *Case*, *LeftField* and *RightField*. Add fuller labels, such as *Case Number, Left Visual Field* and *Right Visual Field*.
* Now switch to **Data View** (which will show the variable names) and enter the data.

> See Section 2.3

Notice that, since in this example the same participants perform under both the *Left Visual Field* and the *Right Visual Field* conditions, there is no grouping variable.

Exploring the data

Since each participant has performed under both conditions, we can expect some consistency in level of performance across conditions: those who are quickest to recognise words in the *Left Visual Field* should also be among the quickest to recognise words in the *Right Visual Field*; those who are slowest in *Left Visual Field* recognition should also be among the slowest in *Right Visual Field* recognition. We should therefore expect a positive correlation between reaction times under *Left Visual Field* and *Right Visual Field* conditions (see Chapter 11). This positive correlation should be reflected in the appearance of the scatterplot (Output 5), in which the cloud of points should take the shape of a narrow ellipse sloping up from left to right.

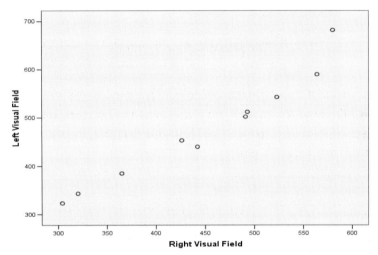

Output 5. The scatterplot of *Left Visual Field* against *Right Visual Field*

To check for anomalies in the data before running the *t* test, plot a scatterplot as described in Section 5.7. Drag *Left Visual Field* to the **Y-Axis** dotted box and *Right Visual Field* to the **X-Axis** dotted box. The scatterplot is shown in Output 5.

See Section 5.7

No outlier appears in the scatterplot. When outliers are present, the user can either consider removing them or choosing a nonparametric method such as the **Sign test** or the **Wilcoxon matched pairs test**. The former is completely immune to the influence of outliers; the latter is much more resistant than the *t* test. Should there be no contraindications against the use of the *t* test, however, the parametric *t* test is preferable to a nonparametric test, because the latter would incur the penalty of a loss of **power** (see page 10).

Running the t test

Proceed as follows:

* Choose
  Analyze➔Compare Means➔Paired-Samples T Test ... (see Figure 6) to open the
  Paired-Samples T Test dialog box (the completed version is shown in Figure 7).

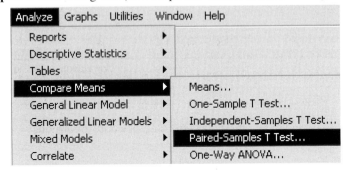

Figure 6. The **Compare Means** menu

* Transfer the variable names to the **Paired Variables** box as described in Figure 7.
* Click **OK**.

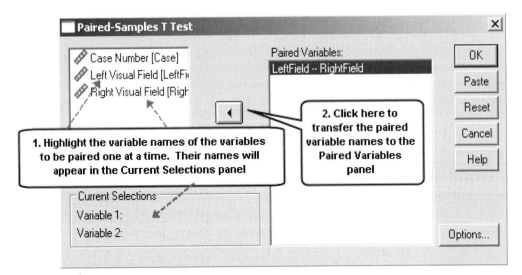

Figure 7. The **Paired-Samples T Test** dialog box for pairing *Left Visual Field* and *Right Visual Field*

Since it is possible to run *t* tests on several pairs of variables at the same time, the output specifies the pair under consideration in each sub-table. In this example, there is only one pair. The upper part of Output 6, **Paired Samples Statistics**, tabulates the statistics for each variable. The second output table (lower part of Output 6), **Paired Samples Correlations,** gives the value of the correlation coefficient, which is 0.97.

Paired Samples Statistics

		Mean	N	Std. Deviation	Std. Error Mean
Pair 1	Left Visual Field	477.30	10	112.09	35.45
	Right Visual Field	450.80	10	97.09	30.70

Paired Samples Correlations

		N	Correlation	Sig.
Pair 1	Left Visual Field & Right Visual Field	10	.97	.00

Output 6. Paired samples statistics and correlations

The final table (Output 7), **Paired Samples Test,** shows various statistics and their p-values.

Paired Samples Test

| | | Paired Differences | | | | | | | |
| | | | | | 95% Confidence Interval of the Difference | | | | |
		Mean	Std. Devia- tion	Std. Error Mean	Lower	Upper	t	df	Sig. (2-tailed)
Pair 1	Left Visual Field - Right Visual Field	26.50	27.81	8.80	6.60	46.40	3.01	9	.015

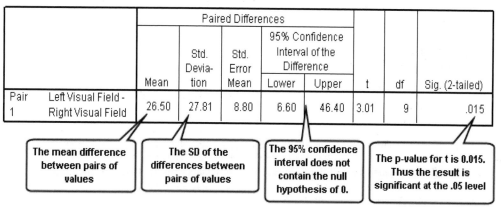

The mean difference between pairs of values

The SD of the differences between pairs of values

The 95% confidence interval does not contain the null hypothesis of 0.

The p-value for t is 0.015. Thus the result is significant at the .05 level

Output 7. T test output for paired samples

Earlier, it was explained that the related-samples t test is actually a **one-sample** test, in which the null hypothesis states that we have a single sample from a population of **differences** d, with a mean of zero. All the statistics in Output 7, therefore, refer to differences between paired raw scores $X_1 - X_2$, rather than the raw scores X_1 and X_2 themselves. Notice the entry called the 'Std. Error Mean'. Its value, 8.80, was obtained as explained in Section 6.2.2:

$$s_{M_d} = \frac{s_d}{\sqrt{n}} = \frac{27.81}{\sqrt{10}} = 8.80$$

We see that the value of t (on 9 degrees of freedom) is 3.01, and that the p-value, 'Sig. (2-tailed)', is 0.015. The result of the t test is significant beyond the .05 level.

Since t is significant beyond the .05 level, we can expect that the 95% confidence interval will not include the value 0, which was specified by the null hypothesis. Indeed, the confidence interval [6.60, 46.40] does not include zero.

The **effect size**, Cohen's d, is estimated as $\dfrac{M_d}{s_d} = \dfrac{26.50}{27.81} = 0.95$

In Cohen's classification of effect size, this is a large effect.

Reporting the results of the t test

We can report the results of the test as follows.

> The mean response latency for the Left Visual Field (M = 477.30, SD = 112.09) was greater than the mean for the Right Visual Field (M = 450.80, SD = 97.09). A related-samples t test showed significance beyond the .05 level: t(9) = 3.01; p = .02 (two-tailed). The 95% confidence interval was (6.60, 46.40), which does not include the value of zero specified by the null hypothesis. Cohen's d = .95, which is a large effect.

6.3   EFFECT SIZE, POWER AND THE NUMBER OF PARTICIPANTS

6.3.1   Problems with significance testing

'Significant' versus 'substantial'

There are problems with significance testing as we have described it. A statistical test may show significance, with a p-value much smaller than .05, and yet the result may be trivial – even misleading. Suppose a manufacturer of matches claims that the mean length of their matches is 4 cm. A quality control inspector selects a sample of 900 matches and finds that the sample mean is 3.98 cm and the standard deviation is 0.15 cm (i.e. 1.5 mm). For a one-sample t test of the null hypothesis that the population mean is 4 cm, the value of t is

$$t = \frac{3.98 - 4}{\left(\dfrac{0.15}{\sqrt{900}}\right)} = 4.0$$

Locating this value of t in the distribution of t on 899 degrees of freedom, we can easily show that the p-value is 0.0000685 (2-tailed), which is significant far beyond the .01 level.

(The SPSS **CDF.T** function, available in **Compute Variable**, in the **Transform** menu, calculates the cumulative probability of a specified value of t in a distribution on any specified degrees of freedom. To obtain the two-sided p-value, we must subtract the cumulative probability from 1 and multiply by 2. All this can be done by making the appropriate specifications in the **Compute Variable** dialog box.)

The difference of .02 between the claimed mean (4 cm) and the sample mean (3.98 cm) is very small. The standard error of the mean, however, which is given by $\sigma/\sqrt{n}$, is very small indeed with such a large n. In fact, the null hypothesis can **always** be rejected, provided the sample is large enough. This is the rationale for the dictum that you **cannot prove the null hypothesis**. The eminent statistician, Sir Ronald Fisher, who pioneered significance testing, took the view that while significance implied that the null hypothesis was false, an insignificant result did not allow the researcher to accept H_0.

The 95% confidence interval on the mean is (3.970187 cm, 3.989813 cm). This tells the true story, because even the lower limit of the confidence interval is 4 cm to one decimal place. What the manufacturer is really claiming is that the mean length of the matches is 4 cm to the nearest millimetre (0.1cm), a claim which the data have shown to be substantially correct. Statistical 'significance', therefore, does not demonstrate the existence of a **substantial** difference.

Power

In Section 1.3.4, the concept of **power** in statistical testing was introduced. Here we reproduce Figure 2 in that section (Figure 8). It is clear from Figure 8 that a factor in the power of a test is the degree of overlap between the sampling distributions under the null and alternative hypotheses: the less the overlap, the greater the power. Since the standard deviation of the sampling distribution of the mean is $\sigma/\sqrt{n}$, the degree of overlap is reduced (and the power of the test increased) by increasing the sample size.

See Section 1.3.4

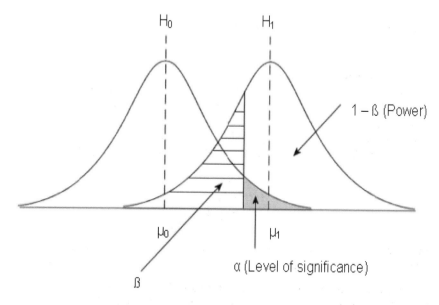

Figure 8. Relations among Type I and Type II error rates and power

Among the other factors affecting the power of a test are the type of test (parametric or nonparametric), the design of the experiment (within subjects or between subjects) and (in the latter case) the degree of discrepancy between the sizes of the samples. The reliability of the measurement is another important consideration.

Our example of the lengths of matches, which demonstrated a misleading result with a test that was too powerful, is quite unrepresentative of many areas of research, in which there is often a shortage, rather than a surplus, of data. Cohen (1962, 1988) drew attention to the low power of the tests used on the data from many of the experiments reported in the literature, a state of affairs arising from a general tendency to test too few participants. It is generally agreed that the power of a test should be at least 0.75, and in many reported studies the power is much lower than this. The issue of over-powerful tests, however, is likely to arise with modern Internet research, in which very large data sets can be gathered.

Power, however, is not the only consideration. Since P depends upon the difference between the means under the null and alternative hypotheses, we must decide upon the smallest difference that we would wish a test to show to be significant on 80% of occasions, assuming the null hypothesis to be false.

6.3.2   How many participants shall I need in my experiment?

Several authors, such as Clark-Carter (2004) have published tables giving the power that will be achieved by using different numbers of participants, given that one is hoping to reveal an effect of a minimum specified size, as measured by Cohen's statistic d and other measures of effect size. For example, suppose that you plan to carry out an experiment comparing the performance of a group of participants who have taken a supposedly performance-enhancing drug with that of a placebo group. You wish to make a t test that will reveal an effect of medium size and achieve a power of 0.8. According to Table A15.2 on p.590 of Clark-Carter's book, if you wish to achieve a power of 0.8 on a between subjects t test for an effect size of 0.5, you will need to test 60 participants in each group, that is a total of 120 participants. Clark-Carter provides a useful selection of tables giving the sample sizes necessary to achieve specified power levels in a variety of commonly used statistical tests.

6.3.3   Useful software

Some useful programs for determining the sample size necessary to achieve specified levels of power for different effect sizes are now available. One of these, G*POWER (Erdfelder, Faul & Buchner, 1996), is available on the Internet and its use is free. You can obtain information about G*POWER (and many other aspects of effect size and power analysis) by using a internet search engine such as Google. You can download G*POWER into your own computer. Keppel and Wickens used G*POWER to construct a table (Keppel & Wickens, 2004: Table 8.1, p.173) showing the sample sizes necessary for a range of combinations of power, effect size and values of estimated omega-squared $\hat{\omega}^2$ (another measure of effect size). If this table is used to estimate sample size, the values obtained will be similar to those given in Clark-Carter's tables.

6.4   OTHER TESTS FOR COMPARING AVERAGES

In this section, we shall consider some equivalent tests for comparing the average performance of two groups or the average performance of the same participants under two different conditions.

6.4.1 Nonparametric tests

The t test is an example of a **parametric test**: that is, it is assumed that the data are samples from two normally distributed populations with the same variance. Other tests, known as **nonparametric tests**, do not make specific assumptions about population distributions and are therefore also referred to as **distribution-free tests**.

There are circumstances in which a t test can give misleading results. This is especially likely to occur when the data set is small and there are some highly deviant scores, or **outliers**, which can inflate the value of the denominator of t.

Figure 1 identifies the nonparametric equivalents of the independent and related samples t tests. A nonparametric alternative to the independent-samples t test is the **Mann-Whitney U test**. Two nonparametric equivalents of the related-samples t test are the **Wilcoxon test** and the **Sign test**. These are fully described in Section 6.4.2.

There has been much controversy about the use of nonparametric tests instead of t tests with some kinds of data. While some authors (e.g. Siegel & Castellan, 1988) strongly recommend the use of nonparametric tests, others, such as Howell (2007) emphasise the robustness of the parametric t tests to violations of their assumptions and the loss of power incurred by the use of the equivalent nonparametric tests. We suggest that, provided the data show no obvious contraindications, such as the presence of outliers, marked skewness or great disparity of variance (especially if the last is coupled with a large difference in sample size), a t test should generally be used. With some kinds of data, the presence of outliers or extreme scores is almost inevitable and there may be a good case for removing them. A good example is the recording of reaction time (RT), where a momentary lack of participant readiness can result in an atypically large RT. Here, arguably, it may be permissible to remove the outliers and repeat the analysis on the reduced data set. Otherwise, a nonparametric equivalent should be considered. Ratings are a grey area, and there has been considerable debate over whether they should be analysed with parametric or nonparametric tests. If, however, the data are measurements at the ordinal level in the first place, as with sets of ranks, or nominal data, a nonparametric test is obligatory.

Planned experiments usually produce scale or continuous data. Occasionally, however, one might have a situation in which each participant attempts a task and either a pass or a fail is recorded. If so, a two-group experiment will yield two independent samples of **nominal data**. Here the research question is still one of the significance of differences, albeit differences between relative frequencies, rather than differences between means. With independent samples, a **chi-square test of association** will answer the question of whether the success rates in the two groups are significantly different (see Chapter 11).

See Chap. 11

Two correlated samples of dichotomous nominal data: the McNemar test

Suppose that, before they hear a debate on an issue, ten people are asked whether they are for or against the proposal. Afterwards, the same people are asked the same question again. This is a **within subjects experiment**, in which each participant is observed under two conditions: Before (an event) and After. On each occasion of testing, a person's response is coded either as 1 (For) or 0 (Against).

Since the same person produces two responses, we have a set of paired nominal data. The **McNemar test** is appropriate if one wishes to claim that the debate has resulted in a change of opinion. The McNemar test is described in Section 6.4.5.

6.4.2   Nonparametric equivalents of the *t* tests

SPSS offers a wide selection of nonparametric tests in the **Nonparametric Tests** submenu of **Analyze**. The **Mann-Whitney** test is an alternative to the independent samples *t* test; the **Sign** and **Wilcoxon** tests are nonparametric counterparts of the paired samples *t* test. Most nonparametric methods use statistics, such as the median, that are resistant to outliers and skewness. In the tests described here, H_0 states that, in the population, the two **medians** are equal.

'Asymptotic' p-values

With large samples, several of the most common nonparametric test statistics have sampling distributions approximating to known continuous distributions and the approximation is close enough to provide serviceable estimates of p-values. (The term **asymptotic** means that the approximation becomes ever closer as the sample size grows larger.) With small samples, however, the approximation can be poor.

Fortunately, with the usual reports of the approximate, **asymptotic** p-values, SPSS can also provide **exact** p-values. We recommend that, when the data are scarce, you should choose exact tests and report the **exact** p-values for nonparametric tests, rather than the **asymptotic** p-values.

6.4.3   Independent samples: Mann-Whitney test

Here we will use the original data set shown in Table 4, rather than the set after removal of the two outliers which we used for the *t* test. With the data in **Data View**,

- Choose
  Analyze➜Nonparametric Tests➜2 Independent Samples ...
  to obtain the **Two-Independent-Samples** dialog box (Figure 9).
- Carry out the steps shown in Figure 9.

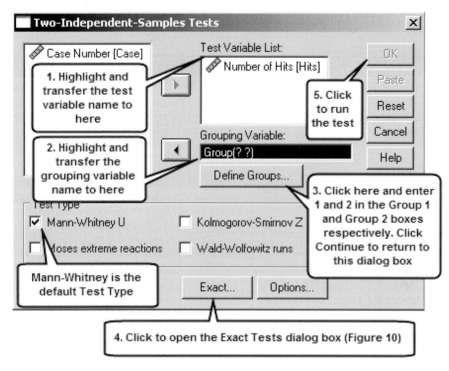

Figure 9. The **Two Independent Samples** dialog box for *Number of Hits* categorised by *Group* with the **Mann-Whitney U** test selected

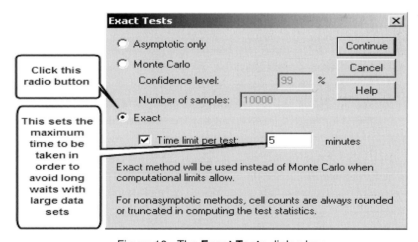

Figure 10. The **Exact Tests** dialog box

- Click the **Exact** radio button in the **Exact Tests** dialog box (Figure 10) and then **Continue** to return to the **Two-Independent-Samples Tests** dialog box.
- Click **OK** to run the test.

The first table (Output 8) in the output, **Ranks**, tabulates the mean ranks and the sums of ranks for the Placebo and Caffeine groups.

Ranks

	Treatment Group	N	Mean Rank	Sum of Ranks
Number of Hits	Placebo	20	14.50	290.00
	Caffeine	20	26.50	530.00
	Total	40		

Output 8. The table of ranks for the **Mann-Whitney test**

Test Statistics[b]

	Number of Hits
Mann-Whitney U	80.000
Wilcoxon W	290.000
Z	-3.261
Asymp. Sig. (2-tailed)	.001
Exact Sig. [2*(1-tailed Sig.)]	.001 [a]
Exact Sig. (2-tailed)	.001
Exact Sig. (1-tailed)	.000
Point Probability	.000

Take note of the exact p-values rather than the asymptotic one

a. Not corrected for ties.

b. Grouping Variable: Treatment Group

Output 9. The output for the **Mann-Whitney test**

In the process of determining the value of the test statistic U, all the scores in the data set are ranked in order of magnitude, after which the means of the ranks of the scores in each of the two groups are calculated. In Output 8, you can see that the mean rank of the scores obtained under the *Placebo* condition is less than that of the scores obtained under the *Caffeine* condition.

From Output 9, we see from the exact p-values that the **Mann-Whitney** tests shows significance on both a one-tailed or a two-tailed test. Your report of the results of the **Mann-Whitney U test** would run along the following lines.

> The mean number of hits for the Placebo group (M = 9.25, SD = 3.16) was less than the mean number of hits for the Caffeine group (M = 11.90, SD = 3.275). A Mann-Whitney U test showed this difference to be significant: U = 80.0; exact p <.01 (two-tailed).

We have already seen that with small data sets, in which there are extreme scores and outliers, parametric statistical tests such as the *t* test can produce misleading results. This is also true of nonparametric tests. Despite its greater robustness to the influence of outliers and extreme scores, the **Mann-Whitney test** is certainly not immune to the influence of disorderly data, particularly when the samples are small.

6.4.4   Related samples: Wilcoxon, Sign and McNemar tests

With the data from Table 5 in the **Data Editor**,
• Choose
Analyze➜Nonparametric Tests➜2 Related Samples ...
to obtain the **Two-Related-Samples Tests** dialog box (Figure 11).

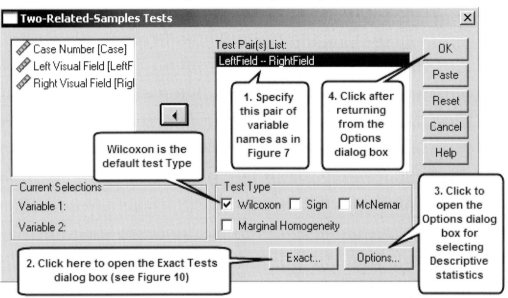

Figure 11. **Two-Related-Samples Tests** dialog box with **Wilcoxon** Test selected

• Carry out the steps described in Figure 11.

The first table in the output (Output 10) gives the means and standard deviations of the scores obtained under the *Left Visual Field* and *Right Visual Field* conditions.

Descriptive Statistics

	N	Mean	Std. Deviation	Minimum	Maximum
Left Visual Field	10	477.30	112.091	323	682
Right Visual Field	10	450.80	97.085	304	580

Output 10.   Table showing the means and standard deviations of the scores obtained under the *Left Visual Field* and *Right Visual Field* conditions

In the **Wilcoxon test**, each participant's score under the *Right Visual Field* condition is paired with the same person's score under the *Left Visual Field* condition. A set of difference scores is obtained by consistently subtracting the *Left Visual Field* score in each pair from the *Right Visual Field* score. Output 11 shows that in 9 out of 10 cases, the Left Visual Field score was greater. The differences are then ranked in order of their absolute values (that is, ignoring their signs). The test statistic W is the smaller sum of ranks of the same sign: in this case, $W = 1$.

Ranks

		N	Mean Rank	Sum of Ranks
Right Visual Field - Left Visual Field	Negative Ranks	9[a]	6.00	54.00
	Positive Ranks	1[b]	1.00	1.00
	Ties	0[c]		
	Total	10		

a. Right Visual Field < Left Visual Field

b. Right Visual Field > Left Visual Field

c. Left Visual Field = Right Visual Field

Output 11. Table of ranks for the **Wilcoxon test**. Note that W is the smaller of the two Sums of Ranks, so W = 1

Test Statistics[b]

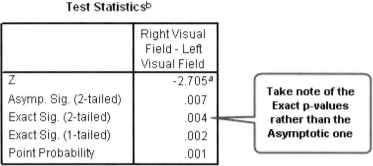

	Right Visual Field - Left Visual Field
Z	-2.705[a]
Asymp. Sig. (2-tailed)	.007
Exact Sig. (2-tailed)	.004
Exact Sig. (1-tailed)	.002
Point Probability	.001

Take note of the Exact p-values rather than the Asymptotic one

a. Based on positive ranks.

b. Wilcoxon Signed Ranks Test

Output 12. The output for the **Wilcoxon** test

The third table (Output 12), **Test Statistics**, gives the exact two-tailed and one-tailed p-values for the statistic W (for **Wilcoxon**). Clearly the test has shown significance beyond the .01 level.

In Output 12, the statistic z is the basis of the asymptotic p-value. Since we also have available the exact p-value, however, that is the value we shall report. Your report of the results of this test would run along the following lines:

A Wilcoxon matched-pairs, signed ranks test showed that the difference between the median response time for words presented in the left visual field (M = 477.30 ms, SD = 112.09 ms) and the right visual field (M = 450.80; SD = 97.09) was significant beyond the .01 level: exact p <.01 (two-tailed). The sums of ranks were 54 and 1 for the negative and positive ranks, respectively, therefore W = 1.

6.4.5   Other nonparametric alternatives to the paired *t* test

Although the **Wilcoxon test** assumes neither normality nor homogeneity of variance, it does assume that the two samples are from populations with the same distribution shape. It is therefore also vulnerable to the influences of outliers – though not to nearly the same extent as the *t* test. The **Sign test**, which is even more robust than the Wilcoxon, can be requested by clicking its check box (report its result by quoting the p-value in the **Exact Sig. (2-tailed)** row).

The **McNemar test** is applicable to paired nominal data. Suppose that 100 people attending a debate on a contentious political issue are asked before and after hearing the debate whether they support the motion. Their responses are shown in Table 6.

Table 6. Number of people supporting a political motion		
Before	**After**	**Frequency**
Yes	Yes	27
Yes	No	13
No	Yes	38
No	No	22

You will notice that in Table 6, the cases have not been entered individually: the first row summarises the responses of the 27 people who said they were in favour of the motion both before and after hearing the debate; the fourth row summarises the responses of the 22 people who were against the motion before and after hearing the debate. The other two rows summarise the responses of those who changed their response. (The McNemar test, incidentally, uses only the data from those who *changed* their responses.)

Prepare the data file by naming two nominal variables *Before* and *After* and a scale variable *Frequency*. Name values 1 and 2 as Yes and No respectively for the nominal variables and then enter the data appropriately. At this point, SPSS must be instructed to weight the rows by their frequencies of occurrence by choosing **Data➜Weight Cases...** and, in the **Weight Cases** dialog box, transfer the variable name *Frequency* into the **Frequency Variable** box.

- To run the **McNemar** test, choose **Analyze➜Nonparametric Tests➜2 Related Samples...** to open the **Two-Related-Samples Tests** dialog box.
- Follow the steps in Figure 12.

The output (not reproduced here) shows that there was indeed a tendency for those of the audience who changed their position to change it in favour of the motion. We shall return to this test later (Section 6.5.2) and also in Chapter 11, when we discuss the analysis of contingency tables.

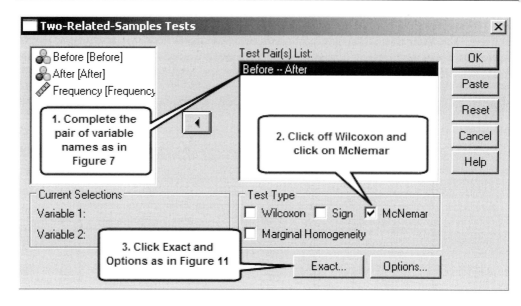

Figure 12. The **McNemar** test for paired nominal data

6.5   ONE-SAMPLE TESTS

In Section 1.5 of Chapter 1, two situations were identified in which a researcher might wish to make a one-sample test:

1.   You may wish to compare a sample distribution with a hypothetical distribution, such as the normal distribution. On this basis, you would hope to claim that your data are (approximately) normally distributed. In technical terms, this is a question of **goodness-of-fit**.

2.   You may wish to make **inferences about the parameters of a single population from the statistics of a sample**, either for the purpose of ascertaining whether the sample is from a known population or estimating the parameters of an unknown population. For example, if you have the heights of a hundred children in a certain age group, what can be said about the **typical** height of children in that age group?

Section 1.5.1 also contained a flow chart (which we reproduce here in Figure 2 in Section 6.1) for selecting the appropriate one-sample test.

The scope of goodness-of-fit tests extends far beyond ascertaining normality of distribution. With nominal data, for example, goodness-of-fit tests can be used to confirm the existence of preferences among a range of choices, or the fairness of a coin or a die.

6.5.1   Goodness-of-fit: scale or continuous data

Table 7 shows the IQs of 50 people. Have these 50 scores been drawn from a normal population? Testing for normality of distribution is one of the commonest applications of a **goodness-of-fit** test. The **Kolmogorov-Smirnov test** is appropriate for this purpose.

The **cumulative probability** P of any particular value in a distribution is the probability of obtaining a value less than or equal to that value. For example, the cumulative probability of an IQ of 100 is 0.5, because in a symmetrical distribution, the mean splits the population (and the total area under the curve) into two equal parts. For a normal distribution, the curve of P has the shape of a flattened S (Figure 13):

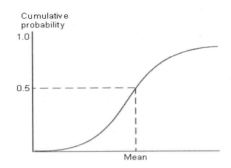

Figure 13. The cumulative probability distribution

Table 7. Fifty IQ scores sampled from a normal population with μ=100 and σ = 15									
104.6	101.1	122.5	116.5	87.7	105.9	71.7	107.4	92.4	107.3
76.4	90.5	98.6	99.3	118.5	85.7	118.5	107.1	81.8	104.3
91.4	90.7	128.7	118.7	103.7	123.0	102.7	95.3	105.0	70.7
100.3	100.0	117.1	135.1	111.0	90.8	81.8	103.1	112.1	116.8
84.4	96.4	120.6	92.1	118.3	93.7	112.3	100.9	88.7	104.5

The **Kolmogorov-Smirnov test** for goodness-of-fit compares the cumulative probabilities of values in your data set with the cumulative probabilities of the same values in a specified theoretical distribution. If the discrepancy is sufficiently great, the test indicates that your data are not well fitted by the theoretical distribution. The **Kolmogorov-Smirnov statistic D** is the greatest discrepancy in cumulative probabilities across the entire range of values. If its value exceeds a cut-off level, the null hypothesis that your sample is from the specified population is rejected. Table 7 shows some fictitious IQ data that were selected randomly by SPSS from a normal population with a mean of 100 and a standard deviation of 15, so we know the answer to our question already!

To test the distribution for goodness-of-fit to a normal distribution, use the **Kolmogorov-Smirnov test**.
- In **Variable View**, name a variable *IQ* (assign the label *Intelligence Quotient*). Enter the data in **Data View**.
- Choose
  Analyze➔Nonparametric Tests➔1-Sample K-S...

to obtain the dialog box for the **One-Sample Kolmogorov-Smirnov Test** dialog box (Figure 14).

- Follow the steps in Figure 14 and then click **OK**.

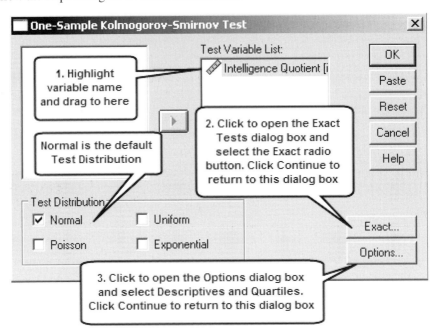

Figure 14. The **One-Sample Kolmogorov-Smirnov Test** dialog box

Output 13 shows the **Descriptive** statistics and **Quartiles** that we requested from **Options**.

Descriptive Statistics

	N	Mean	Std. Deviation	Minimum	Maximum	Percentiles		
						25th	50th (Median)	75th
Intelligence Quotient	50	102.15	14.5457	70.7	135.1	91.250	102.900	113.350

Output 13. The descriptive statistics of the fifty **IQ** scores

The 'Differences' referred to in Output 14 are the differences between the cumulative probabilities for various sample values and the corresponding cumulative probabilities assuming a normal distribution. The absolute value of the largest difference (D) is 0.078. We see that the exact p-value of D (two-tailed) is .898. The null hypothesis of normality of distribution is accepted. That is exactly what you would expect, because we know that the data have indeed been drawn from a normal population.

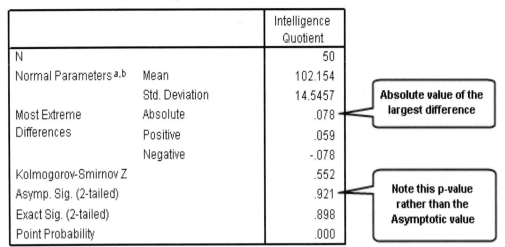

One-Sample Kolmogorov-Smirnov Test

		Intelligence Quotient
N		50
Normal Parameters [a,b]	Mean	102.154
	Std. Deviation	14.5457
Most Extreme Differences	Absolute	.078
	Positive	.059
	Negative	-.078
Kolmogorov-Smirnov Z		.552
Asymp. Sig. (2-tailed)		.921
Exact Sig. (2-tailed)		.898
Point Probability		.000

(Callout: Absolute value of the largest difference)

(Callout: Note this p-value rather than the Asymptotic value)

a. Test distribution is Normal.

b. Calculated from data.

Output 14. Results of the **Kolmogorov-Smirnov test** of goodness-of-fit

We write the result as follows:

A one-sample Kolmogorov-Smirnov test of goodness-of-fit provided no evidence against the null hypothesis that the sample has been drawn from a normal population: D = .078; exact p = .91 (two-tailed).

6.5.2   Goodness-of-fit: nominal data

Dichotomous nominal data

Suppose a researcher wants to know whether 5-year-old children of a certain age show a preference for one of two toys (A or B). The choices of one hundred 5-year-olds are noted. Of the hundred children in the study, 60 choose toy A and 40 toy B. As another example, suppose that, in order to determine whether a coin is 'fair' (that is, heads and tails are equally likely to occur), we toss a coin 100 times, and find that the coin turns up heads on 58 tosses.

In both examples, the null hypothesis states that the probability of choosing A (or B) on each trial is 0.5. The term **Bernoulli trials** is used to denote a series of events or experiments with the following properties:

1. The outcomes of every trial can be divided into the same two dichotomous categories, one of which can be regarded as a 'success', the other as a 'failure'.
2. The outcomes of the trials are independent.
3. The probability of a 'success' is the same on all trials.

Note that (1) does not imply that there are only two outcomes, only that we can divide the outcomes into two categories. Suppose that a candidate sitting a multiple-choice examination with six alternatives per question were to choose the answer by rolling a die each time. In that case, although there are six outcomes per question, they can be classified dichotomously into Pass (with a probability of 1/6) and Fail (with a probability of 5/6).

When we have Bernoulli trials, the **Binomial test** can be used to test the null hypothesis that the probability of a success on any trial has a specified value. In the case of coin-tossing, that specified probability will usually be 0.5. The binomial test, however, can be used to test the hypothesis that the population proportion has **any** specified value.

To illustrate the binomial test, we shall use our first example of the children's choices between two toys. Of the 100 five-year-olds studied, 60 chose toy A and 40 chose toy B. Proceed as follows:

- Assign code numbers to the two choices, say 1 to toy A and 2 to toy B.
- In **Variable View**, name a variable *Toy* and assign the values 1 to Toy A and 2 to Toy B. Change **Scale** to **Nominal** in the **Measure** column.
- Name a second variable *Frequency* for the number of choices.
- Enter the data in **Data View**.
- In order to ensure that the two choices will be weighted by their frequencies of occurrence, select **Weight Cases...** in the **Data** menu to obtain the **Weight Cases** dialog box, select the **Weight Cases by** radio button, transfer *Frequency* to the **Frequency Variable** box, and click **OK**.
- Select
  Analyze➜Nonparametric Tests➜Binomial ...
  to open the **Binomial Test** dialog box (Figure 15).

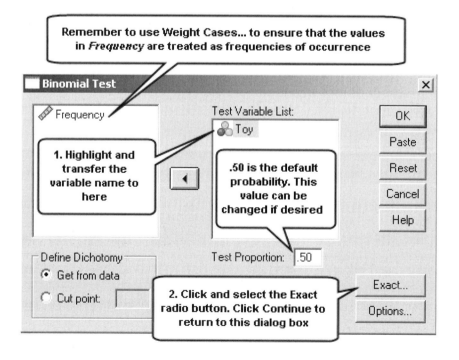

Figure 15. The **Binomial Test** dialog box with *Toy* selected for the **Test Variable List**

- Transfer *Toy* to the **Test Variable List**. Notice the small **Test Proportion** box on the right, containing the default value 0.5. This is appropriate for the present test, because if the experiment was conducted properly and the children had no preference, the probability of each choice is 0.5. In other situations, however, that would not be the case, as when a candidate is guessing the correct answers to the questions in a multiple-choice examination, in which case, if there were four choices, the **Test Proportion** would be 0.25. The **Weight Cases** procedure ensures that the two choices will be weighted by their frequencies of occurrence.
- Click **Exact…** to see the **Exact Tests** dialog box and choose **Exact**. Click **Continue** to return to the **Binomial Test** dialog box.
- Click **OK** to run the **Binomial** test.

The output is shown in Output 15.

Binomial Test

		Category	N	Observed Prop.	Test Prop.	Asymp. Sig. (2-tailed)	Exact Sig. (2-tailed)
Toy	Group 1	Toy A	60	.60	.50	.057[a]	.057
	Group 2	Toy B	40	.40			
	Total		100	1.00			

a. Based on Z Approximation.

> The exact p-value is > .05 so the choice of toys is not significant

Output 15. The output for the **Binomial Test**

The important item here is the rightmost entry, headed **Exact Sig (2-tailed)**. Since this p-value exceeds 0.05 (in fact, it is almost 0.06), the null hypothesis is accepted. The result of the test is written as follows:

> Although more children (60%) chose toy A than toy B (40%), a binomial test failed to reject the hypothesis that there is no preference: Exact $p = .06$ (two-tailed).

Small numbers of trials: omitting the Weight Cases procedure

Should we have only the outcomes of a few Bernoulli trials, as when a coin is tossed twenty times, it is easier to enter the result of each toss directly, rather than aggregate the data and use the **Weight Cases** procedure. In **Variable View**, name one variable *toss* with two values (1 is a Head, 2 a Tail), enter the data in **Data View**, and complete the **Binomial Test** dialog box by transferring the variable name *Toss* to the **Test Variable List:** box.

Goodness-of-fit test with three or more categories

If, to extend the example of toy preferences, there were three or more toys to choose from, the **Chi-square goodness-of-fit test** can be used to test the null hypothesis that all three toys are equally attractive to children.

Suppose that there were three toys, A, B and C. Of 90 children tested, the numbers choosing the three toys were 20, 41 and 29, respectively. This is the distribution of **observed frequencies (O)**. If there is no preference in the population (the null hypothesis), we should expect that 30 children would choose each of the three toys. This is the distribution of **expected frequencies (E)**.

Table 8. A nominal data set showing observed and expected frequencies			
	A	**B**	**C**
O	20	41	29
E	30	30	30

The test of the null hypothesis of no preference is made with what is known as an **approximate chi-square (χ^2) test**. The test is 'approximate' because the chi-square variable is defined in the context of a normally distributed variable (see Howell, 2007). The statistic we are about to describe is only approximately distributed as χ^2. The approximate chi-square statistic is defined as follows:

$$\chi^2 = \sum \frac{(O-E)^2}{E} \quad (\Sigma \text{ means 'sum of '})$$

A chi-square distribution has one parameter, the **degrees of freedom**. In the context of nominal data in a one-way classification, the value of the degrees of freedom (df) is one less than the number of categories in the one-way classification. In this example, $df = 3 - 1 = 2$.

How well does this theoretical **uniform distribution** fit the observed distribution? It is clear from the formula that the greater the differences between the observed and expected frequencies, the greater will be the magnitude of the χ^2 statistic. Its value is:

$$\chi^2 = \frac{(-10)^2 + 11^2 + (-1)^2}{30} = \frac{222}{30} = 7.4$$

The **Chi-square goodness-of-fit test** is run as follows:
- In **Variable View** define the variables *Preference* and *Frequency*, the former with three levels: 1 for Toy A, 2 for Toy B, 3 for Toy C. Change **Scale** to **Nominal** for *Preference*.
- Enter the data in **Data View**.
- Use **Weight Cases…** to weight the values in *Frequency*.
- Choose
  Analyze➔Nonparametric Tests➔Chi-Square…
  to open the **Chi-Square Test** dialog box (Figure 16).
- Follow the steps in Figure 16.
- Click **OK**.

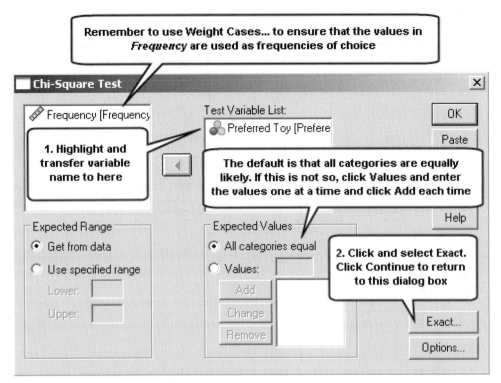

Figure 16. The **Chi-Square Test** dialog box with *Preferred Toy* transferred to the **Test Variable List** box

The first table (Output 16) in the output shows the observed and expected frequencies.

Preferred Toy

	Observed N	Expected N	Residual
Toy A	20	30.0	-10.0
Toy B	41	30.0	11.0
Toy C	29	30.0	-1.0
Total	90		

Output 16. The observed and expected frequencies

Any transcription errors will immediately be apparent here.   Notice that the expected frequencies are 30 for each choice, because if there is no preference, the three choices are equally likely, and we should have approximately equal numbers of children choosing A, B and C.

The next table (Output 17) presents the results of the Chi-square goodness-of-fit test.

Test Statistics

	Preferred Toy
Chi-Square [a]	7.400
df	2
Asymp. Sig.	.025
Exact Sig.	.026
Point Probability	.003

The value of Chi-square

The p-value is < .05. Thus the choice of toys is not equally likely at the .05 level

a. 0 cells (.0%) have expected frequencies less than 5. The minimum expected cell frequency is 30.0.

Output 17. The output for the **Chi-square goodness-of-fit test**

Output 16 showed marked discrepancies between the expected and observed frequencies, and it is not surprising that the **Exact Sig.** (i.e. the p-value) in Output 17 is small (.026). The report of the results of this test would run along the following lines. (The bracketed value with the chi-square symbol is the degrees of freedom, which is the number of categories minus one.)

> Inspection of the frequency distribution shows that twice as many children (41) chose Toy B as chose Toy A (20). Approximately the expected number (29) preferred Toy C. A chi-square test of the null hypothesis that the three toys were equally attractive to the children showed significance beyond the .05 level: $\chi^2(2) = 7.4$; exact $p = .03$.

The interpretation of the results of this test requires care. The experimenter may have had theoretical reason to expect that Toy B would be preferred to the other toys. All the chi-square test has shown, however, is that the hypothesis of no preference is untenable. We have not demonstrated that any one toy was preferred significantly more (or less) than either of the others. Had the purpose of the investigation been to show that Toy B was preferable to the other two, a better analytic strategy would have been to dichotomise a child's choice as either B or NotB. This can be done by dichotomising the data into B and NotB: 49 for *B* and 41 for NotB. A binomial test would test the null hypothesis that the number of children choosing B exceeded the expected value. In the **Binomial Test** dialog box, the **Test Proportion** would be set at 1/3 = .33. The binomial test shows significance beyond the .05 level: p = .01. This result does support the scientific hypothesis that Toy B is preferred to either of the other two toys.

The McNemar test again

In Table 9, we reproduce the data in Table 6.

Table 9. Number of people supporting a political motion		
Before	**After**	**Frequency**
Yes	Yes	27
Yes	No	13
No	Yes	38
No	No	22

We run the McNemar test by choosing:
Analyze➔Nonparametric Tests➔2 Related Samples ...
as described more fully in Section 6.4.5.

It can be seen from Table 10, that of the 100 people studied, 51 appear to have changed their minds. The rationale of the McNemar test is that, under the null hypothesis that hearing the debate has no effect, we can expect half of those who changed their minds to change in one direction; the other half should change in the other direction. We can therefore prepare the following table:

Table 10. Number of participants changing their minds		
	No➔Yes	**Yes➔No**
Observed	38	13
Expected	25.5	25.5

The original McNemar test is an approximate chi-square goodness-of-fit test. It has been argued that the approximation is poor when there are only two categories and that the **Yates correction for continuity** should be used to remedy this. Essentially, the Yates correction subtracts .5 from the absolute (sign ignored) value of each $O - E$ difference before squaring it thus:

$$\chi^2 = \sum \frac{(|O - E| - .5)^2}{E}$$

Applying this formula to the data in Table 10, we have

$$\chi^2 = \frac{(|38 - 25.5| - .5)^2 + (|12 - 25.5| - .5)^2}{25.5} = \frac{144 + 169}{25.5} = 12.27$$

There has been much discussion about whether the Yates correction is really necessary. Fortunately, we now have access to exact tests. Note that if the responses of those 51 participants who changed their opinions are viewed as 51 Bernoulli trials, the Binomial test can be used to test the null hypothesis that p = .5. There is now no need to use an approximate test.

Test Statistics[b]

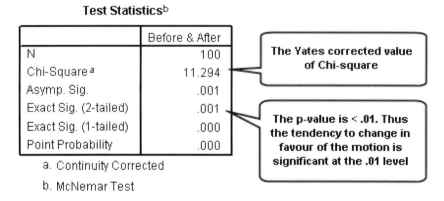

	Before & After
N	100
Chi-Square [a]	11.294
Asymp. Sig.	.001
Exact Sig. (2-tailed)	.001
Exact Sig. (1-tailed)	.000
Point Probability	.000

a. Continuity Corrected

b. McNemar Test

The Yates corrected value of Chi-square

The p-value is < .01. Thus the tendency to change in favour of the motion is significant at the .01 level

Output 18. Results of the **McNemar** test

The results of the McNemar test are shown in Output 18. The Yates-corrected value of chi-square is 11.29, in agreement with our calculated value. Since the case for a one-tailed test does not appear to us to be very strong, we suggest you should use the **Exact Sig. (2-tailed)** p-value, which is less than .01. We can report this result as follows:

> A McNemar test for the significance of changes showed a significant tendency for those who changed their responses to do so in favour of the motion: $\chi^2(1) = 11.29$; Exact p <.01.

6.5.3   Inferences about the mean of a single population

The mean and standard deviation of the 50 IQ scores in Table 7 (Section 6.5.1) are 102.15 and 14.6 respectively. (You can confirm this with **Descriptives...** in **Descriptive Statistics** submenu in the **Analyze** menu.) What can we infer about the population mean?

On the sample mean, a **95% confidence interval** can be constructed, that is, a range of values centred on the sample mean which will include the population mean in 95% of samples. Once we have found this range of values, we can say, with '95% confidence', that the population mean µ lies within this range.

If a variable is normally distributed, the sampling distribution of the mean of n scores is also normally distributed. 95% of values of M lie within the range from $\mu - 1.96\sigma_M$ to $\mu + 1.96\sigma_M$: that is,

$$\Pr\left[(\mu - 1.96\sigma_M) \le M \le (\mu + 1.96\sigma_M)\right] = 0.95$$

By manipulating this inequality, it is easy to show that the probability that μ will be included in an interval centred on M is also 0.95: that is,

$$\Pr\left[(M - 1.96\sigma_M) \le \mu \le (M + 1.96\sigma_M)\right] = 0.95$$

Since we rarely know the population standard deviation σ^2, we must estimate the value of σ_M from sample statistics and replace the values ± 1.96, which are the 2.5^{th} and 97.5^{th} percentiles of the standard normal distribution with the 2.5^{th} and 97.5^{th} percentiles of the appropriate t distribution

$$\Pr\left[(M - t_{.975} s_M) \le \mu \le (M + t_{.975} s_M)\right] = 0.95$$

where $t_{.975}$ is the 97.5^{th} percentile of the t distribution on $n - 1$ degrees of freedom and n is the size of the sample.

In this case, since $n = 50$, $df = 49$. A simple operation with SPSS's **Compute Variable...** command (Section 6.2), tells us that the critical value of t is 2.0096. (To obtain this critical value, we can use SPSS's **inverse distribution function** thus: IDF.T[.975, 49].)   Since $M = 102.154$, $s_M = 14.5546/\sqrt{50} = 2.05833$ and $t = 2.0096$, the 95% confidence interval on the mean is

$$\left[(102.154 - 2.0096 \times 2.05833),\ (102.154 + 2.0096 \times 2.05833)\right] = [98.02,\ 106.29]$$

Note that, when interpreting this confidence interval, it is incorrect to infer that the probability that μ lies between 98.02 and 106.29 is 0.95. A confidence interval is not a sample space. The die, as it were, has already been rolled: either the interval [98.02, 106.29] includes μ or it does not. The '95% confidence' that we should feel arises from the fact that this interval was generated by a process which, over many repeated samples, could be expected to cover μ on 95% of occasions.

To find this confidence interval with SPSS, proceed as follows.
- Choose
  Analyze➔Descriptive Statistics➔Explore...
  to obtain the **Explore** dialog box.
- Transfer the variable name Intelligence Quotient (*IQ*) to the **Dependent List** box.
- If you click **Statistics...** (not the **Statistics** radio button), you will obtain the **Explore: Statistics** subdialog box, in which it can be seen that the **Descriptives** check box has been selected, and a **Confidence Interval for Mean** with *95* in the % box has already been specified by default. (The user may wish to specify a higher confidence level, such as 99%.)
- Click **Continue** to return to the **Explore** dialog box.
- Click **OK**.

An edited version of the output is shown in Output 19. The output gives the sample **Mean** as *102.154* and the **95% Confidence Interval for Mean** as extending from *98.020* to *106.288*, which agrees with the calculation above.

Descriptives

			Statistic	Std. Error
Intelligence Quotient	Mean		102.154	2.0571
	95% Confidence Interval for Mean	Lower Bound	98.020	
		Upper Bound	106.288	

Output 19. The mean and the **95% Confidence Interval for Mean**

Not surprisingly, the actual population mean (100) lies within this range since, as we have seen, the data were actually generated by commanding SPSS to select 50 scores from a normal population with a mean of 100 and a standard deviation of 15. Note, incidentally, that, because of sampling error, the sample mean is not *exactly* 100: in fact, we should be very surprised indeed to find that it was.

6.5.4 Using a confidence interval to test a hypothesis about the mean of a single population

A hypothesis about the mean of a single population can be tested by constructing a confidence interval on the sample mean. If the hypothetical mean value lies outside the confidence interval, the null hypothesis can be rejected beyond the .05 level (for the 95% confidence interval) and the .01 level (for the 99% confidence interval). In the present case, the null hypothesis that the population mean IQ is 100 must be accepted, which (since we know the true parent population) is the correct decision.

6.5.5 Using a one-sample *t* test to test a hypothesis about the mean of a single population

We have claimed that the fifty IQ scores are a random sample from a normal population with a mean of 100 and a standard deviation of 15. We have seen that one way of testing this hypothesis is to construct a 95% confidence interval on the mean and reject the hypothesis if the sample mean falls outside this interval.

Another approach is to make a **one-sample *t* test** of the null hypothesis that the mean is 100.

To do so:
- Choose
  Analyze➔Compare Means➔One-Sample T Test…
  to open the **One-Sample T Test** dialog box (Figure 17).
- Follow the steps in Figure 17.
- Click **OK**.

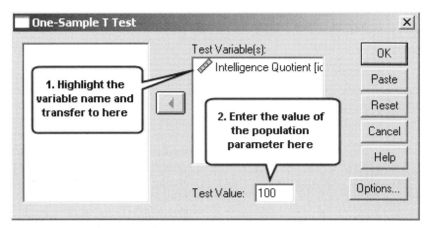

Figure 17. The **One-Sample T Test** dialog box with *IQ* transferred to the **Test Variable(s)** box and *100* entered for the **Test Value**

The first table in the output (Output 20), **One-Sample Statistics**, tabulates some descriptive statistics.

One-Sample Statistics

	N	Mean	Std. Deviation	Std. Error Mean
Intelligence Quotient	50	102.15	14.55	2.06

Output 20. The descriptive statistics table

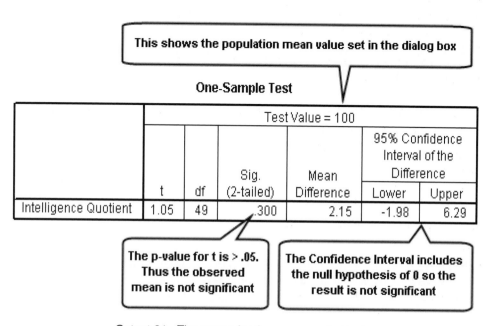

This shows the population mean value set in the dialog box

One-Sample Test

					Test Value = 100		
						95% Confidence Interval of the Difference	
	t	df	Sig. (2-tailed)	Mean Difference		Lower	Upper
Intelligence Quotient	1.05	49	.300	2.15		-1.98	6.29

The p-value for t is > .05. Thus the observed mean is not significant

The Confidence Interval includes the null hypothesis of 0 so the result is not significant

Output 21. The output for the one-sample *t* test

The second table (Output 21) includes the *t* **test** results and the **95% Confidence Interval**. It can be seen from the table that the null hypothesis must be accepted.

The **effect size** (see Section 1.3.5) here is

$$d = \frac{M - \mu_0}{s} = \frac{102.15 - 100}{14.55} = 0.15$$

In Cohen's Table, this is less than the lowest value for a **Small** effect.

This result of the one-sample *t* test is written as follows:

> The mean intelligence quotient (M = 102.15, SD = 14.55) was greater than the population value of 100. A one-sample *t* test showed that this value was not significant: $t(49) = 1.05$; p = .30 (two-tailed). The 95% confidence interval on the mean is (-1.98, 6.29), which includes the population mean difference of 0 specified by the null hypothesis. Cohen's $d = 0.15$, which is a small effect.

The related t test as a special case of the one-sample t test

Earlier we said that a related-samples *t* test was a special case of a one-sample *t* test. From a set of paired data, we can obtain a single column of differences by consistently subtracting, say the scores on the right from those on the left. The null hypothesis states that, in the population, the mean of these **difference scores** is zero. If we enter the differences as the **Test Variable** in the **One-Sample T Test** dialog box, enter 0 in the **Test Value** box and run the test, we shall obtain exactly the same result as we would have done if we had run a related-samples *t* test on the two columns in the original data set.

Recommended reading

In this chapter, we have reviewed some statistical ideas, terms and concepts that we thought you might require in order to understand the SPSS output for the various tests that we described. We realise, however, that, should you be unfamiliar with statistics, you may have found Section 2 rather indigestible. Howell (2007) provides a lucid coverage of most of the terms and formulae used in this chapter: in Chapter 6 of his book, he describes the use of the chi-square test in the analysis of nominal data; in Chapter 7, he explains the *t* tests; in Chapter 8, he discusses power and effect size.

Howell, D. C. (2007). *Statistical methods for psychology (6th ed.)*. Belmont, CA: Thomson/Wadsworth.

EXERCISE 8

Comparing the averages of two independent samples of data

Aim

The previous Exercises have used data from a questionnaire. The next few Exercises will be based on data from experiments designed to test experimental hypotheses. In real experiments, of course, a larger number of participants would have been used.

Before you start

Before proceeding with this Exercise, we suggest you read Chapter 6 carefully. In this Exercise, we shall be making an **independent samples *t* test** (Section 6.2.4). In Exercise 9, we shall be making a **paired-samples *t* test** (Section 6.2.5). Finally in Exercise 10, we shall be making **one-sample tests** (Section 6.5).

An investigation of the effects of a drug upon performance

The data we are going to explore in this Exercise might have been produced by the following project. A team of investigators has good reason to believe that a small dosage of a certain drug changes the speed with which people can make decisions. They decide to try to confirm this by carrying out an experiment in which the decision times of 14 people who have taken the drug are compared with those of a control group of 14 other people who have performed the task under a placebo condition. The experimenters expect that the average decision time of the experimental group will differ from that of the placebo group. The results are shown in Table 1.

Table 1. Decision times of the experimental and placebo groups in the drug experiment

\multicolumn{4}{DRUG GROUP}					\multicolumn{4}{PLACEBO GROUP}			
Case	Time	Case	Time	Case	Time	Case	Time
1	390	8	425	15	446	22	440
2	494	9	421	16	749	23	471
3	386	10	407	17	599	24	501
4	323	11	386	18	460	25	492
5	660	12	550	19	390	26	392
6	406	13	470	20	477	27	578
7	345	14	393	21	556	28	398

Opening SPSS

In the opening window of SPSS, select the **Type in data** radio button. If **Data View** appears first, click the tab **Variable View** to open **Variable View**.

Constructing the SPSS data set

Construct the data set as described in Section 3.1. In **Variable View**, the first variable, *Case*, will represent the participants. The second is the grouping variable (i.e. the type of treatment – drug or placebo). Call the grouping variable *Condition* and label the values: *1 = Drug; 2 = Placebo*. Label the variable *Experimental Condition*. The third variable, which can be named *Score*, contains all the participants' scores on the dependent variable. Notice that the *Score* variable includes the scores for **both** treatments. The grouping variable *Condition* is needed to enable the computer to identify the group to which a score belongs. Since there are no decimals in the data, ensure that the values in the **Decimals** column are all *0*.

Click the **Data View** tab and enter the data of Table 1 into **Data View** in the manner described in Section 3.1.2. When the data have been entered, save them to a file with a name such as *Drugs*.

Exploring the data

The first step is always to examine the data set to see whether there are any odd features.

We shall want a table of means and standard deviations, together with indicators of distribution shape such as histograms and boxplots. The statistics for the subgroups are most easily obtained with the **Means** procedure. (The plots are obtained with the **Explore** procedure.) Follow the instructions in Section 4.3.2, remembering that the dependent variable name is *Score* and the independent variable name is *Condition*.

- **Write down the values of the means and standard deviations. Do these statistics appear to support the scientific hypothesis?**

(Note that the **Means** procedure requires the presence of a grouping variable in the data set. Should the mean and standard deviation of a set of ungrouped data be required, use the **Descriptives** procedure.)

Graphical displays of the data

To draw the boxplots, proceed as described in Section 4.3.2. The dependent variable is *Score*, the factor is *Condition*, and the **Labels Cases by** is *Case*. (This choice labels any outliers or extreme scores in the boxplots with the number of the case, which is more useful than the default row number, especially if some cases have been deselected.) Remember to click the **Plots** radio button in the **Display** section of the **Explore** dialog box, thus turning off the **Both** radio button and ensuring that the descriptive statistics tables are omitted. Click **Plots**, deselect the **Stem-and-leaf** check box and select **Histogram** check box. Click **Continue** and finally **OK**.

The output in **SPSS Viewer** begins with the usual **Case Processing Summary** listing the number of valid cases in each group. Then it shows **Boxplots** and **Histograms** for the two groups. The boxplots show two outliers with the identifying numbers of the participants concerned (because you specified the participants' numbers in the **Label Cases by** box in the **Explore** dialog box).

When there is a marked discrepancy between the mean and median of a set of scores, the distribution is probably skewed or otherwise asymmetrical. Atypical scores, or **outliers** can also pull the value of the mean away from that of the median. Read Section 4.3.2 carefully for an explanation of SPSS's boxplot displays.

- **Identify any outliers by means of their identifiers, which are values in the variable *case*. State their values.**

Printing the output

If you want a hard copy of the output, follow the procedure described in Section 3.5. The precise details will depend upon your local set-up.

The independent samples *t* test

Run an independent samples *t* test on the full data set as described in Section 6.2.4 but do not remove any outliers at this stage.

Output for the independent samples *t* test

Guidance on how to interpret the output is given in Section 6.2.4. We suggest you study that section and try to answer the following questions.

- **On the basis of the Levene test p-value, which row of the *t* test results will you use?**

- **Write down the value of *t* and its tail probability. Is the p-value evidence against the null hypothesis? Remember that if the result is sufficiently unlikely (i.e. p < 0.05) under the null hypothesis, it is regarded as evidence against the null hypothesis and hence in favour of the experimental hypothesis.**

- **Write down your interpretation of the result of the test: has the *t* test confirmed the pattern shown by the means of the two groups?**

- **If the hypothesis had been one-tailed (e.g. that decision times of the experimental group will tend to be shorter than those of the control group), then the appropriate p-value would be obtained by dividing the two-tailed p-value by 2. What would be the one-tailed p-value in that case?**

- **Calculate the effect size using the formula given in Section 6.2.4. Is the effect size small, medium or large according to Cohen's table?**

A nonparametric equivalent of the independent samples *t* test: The Mann-Whitney U test

The running of the **Mann-Whitney** test on SPSS is described in Section 6.4.3. Run the procedure as described in that section.

Output for the Mann-Whitney test

The output gives the values of the statistics U and W (the W statistic belongs to a test by Wilcoxon which is the exact equivalent of the Mann-Whitney), followed by a standard normal deviate score z and a 2-tailed probability value corrected for ties. An exact 2-tailed probability value not corrected for ties concludes the table. If the p-value is less than 0.05, the null hypothesis can be rejected and the groups declared to differ significantly.

- **Write down the results of the Mann-Whitney test, including the value of U and its p-value. State whether the result is significant and whether the Mann-Whitney test confirms the result of the *t* test. In what circumstances might you expect the p-values of U and *t* to differ?**

Printing the output

To obtain a hard copy of the output, proceed as described in Section 3.5.

Re-running the tests after deselecting the two outliers

Deselect the two outliers using the **Select Cases...** procedure (see Section 3.3.1) by entering score <600 in the **Select Cases** dialog box. Then re-run the *t* test and the Mann-Whitney test.

- **Write down the new value of *t* and its p-value (assuming a two-tail test). Is the conclusion different from what it was with the complete data set?**

- **Calculate the effect size using the formula given near the end of Section 6.2.4. Is the effect size small, medium or large according to Cohen's table?**

- **Write down the results of the Mann-Whitney test (assuming a two-tail test), including the value of U and its p-value. Is the conclusion different from what it was with the complete data set?**

- **Write down your interpretation of the effects on each test of eliminating the outliers.**

Finishing the session

Close down SPSS and any other windows before logging out of the computer.

EXERCISE 9

Comparing the averages of two related samples of data

Before you start

The methods described in the previous Exercise, (the **independent samples *t* test** and the **Mann-Whitney** test), are appropriate for data from a between subjects experiment, that is, one with independent samples of participants in the two groups. Suppose, however, that the data had come from an experiment in which the same participants had been tested under both the experimental and control conditions. Such a within subjects experiment would yield a set of paired (or related) data. In this Exercise, we shall consider some methods for comparing the averages of the scores obtained under the experimental and control conditions when we have a set of paired data (SPSS calls such sets **paired samples**), rather than independent samples. Before proceeding with this exercise, the reader should review the material in Section 6.2.5.

THE PAIRED-SAMPLES T TEST

An experiment on hemispherical specialisation

In an experiment investigating the relative ease with which words presented in the left and right visual fields were recognised, participants were instructed to fixate a spot in the centre of the field. They were told that, after a short interval, a word would appear to the left or the right of the spot and they were to press a key as soon as they recognised it. In the trials that followed, each word was presented an equal number of times in each field, though the order of presentation of the words was, of course, randomised. From the results, a table of median decision times was constructed from the participants' reactions to presentations of 40 words in each of the two visual fields (Table 1).

<table>
<tr><td colspan="6">Table 1. Median decision times for words presented to the right and left visual fields</td></tr>
<tr><td>Case</td><td>Right visual field</td><td>Left visual field</td><td>Case</td><td>Right visual field</td><td>Left visual field</td></tr>
<tr><td>1</td><td>323</td><td>324</td><td>8</td><td>439</td><td>442</td></tr>
<tr><td>2</td><td>493</td><td>512</td><td>9</td><td>682</td><td>683</td></tr>
<tr><td>3</td><td>502</td><td>503</td><td>10</td><td>703</td><td>998</td></tr>
<tr><td>4</td><td>376</td><td>385</td><td>11</td><td>598</td><td>600</td></tr>
<tr><td>5</td><td>428</td><td>453</td><td>12</td><td>456</td><td>462</td></tr>
<tr><td>6</td><td>343</td><td>345</td><td>13</td><td>653</td><td>704</td></tr>
<tr><td>7</td><td>523</td><td>543</td><td>14</td><td>652</td><td>653</td></tr>
</table>

The question is whether these data support the experimental hypothesis that there is a difference between the response times for words in the left and right visual fields? Before proceeding with this Exercise, we suggest you read Section 6.2.5, which describes the procedure for a paired-samples *t* test.

Opening SPSS

In the opening window of SPSS, select the **Type in data** radio button. If **Data View** appears first, click the tab labelled **Variable View** to open **Variable View**.

Preparing the SPSS data set

In the data set for the independent samples *t* test, one of the variables must be a grouping variable, showing which participants performed under which conditions. With the paired-samples *t* test, however, there are no groups, so no coding variable is needed.

After naming a variable *Case*, name two more variables: *RVF* with the label *Right Visual Field* in the **Label** column, and *LVF* with the label *Left Visual Field* in the **Label** column. Since there are no decimals in the data, ensure that the values in the **Decimals** column are all 0.

Select **Data View** and enter the data in the usual way, as described in Section 3.1.2.

Exploring the data

As always, it is wise to explore the data, rather than automatically pressing ahead with a formal test. Select **Graphs➔Chart Builder...** (see Section 5.7) and then **Scatter/Dot...** in the gallery so that the **Simple Scatter** diagram becomes visible. Click and drag it to the **Chart preview** and then click and drag in turn the variable names to the X-Axis and Y-Axis dotted boxes. Click **OK** to plot the scatterplot.

From inspection of the scatterplot, it is quite clear that there is a glaringly obvious outlier. It is instructive to ascertain the effect of its presence upon the results of the *t* test, in comparison with the nonparametric **Wilcoxon** and **Sign** tests.

Running the paired-samples *t* test

Run the **paired-samples *t* test** by following the procedure described in Section 6.2.5.

Output for the paired-samples *t* test

From the details given in the *t* test output, it is clear that there are contraindications against the use of the paired-samples *t* test for the data in the present experiment. There is marked discrepancy between the standard deviations of the scores obtained under the *Right Visual Field* and *Left Visual Field* conditions, which arises from the presence of an outlier, which showed up dramatically in the scatterplot.

- **Write down the value of *t* and its p-value. Is *t* significant? Write down, in terms of the research hypothesis, the meaning of this result.**

- **Calculate the effect size using the formula at the end of Section 6.2.5. Is the effect size small, medium or large according to Cohen's table?**

What has happened here? You should find the *t* test result puzzling to say the least. You might find another clue by examining the distribution of differences between the scores. Use **Compute** to calculate a difference between *Left Visual Field* and *Right Visual Field*, putting the answer in a variable called *Differences*.

- What do you notice about the values in *Differences*? Is there a discernible pattern? (What about the directions of the differences?) Relate this to the scientific hypothesis.

NONPARAMETRIC ALTERNATIVES TO THE PAIRED-SAMPLES T TEST

The Wilcoxon matched pairs test

Now carry out the **Wilcoxon matched pairs** test, following the procedure described in Section 6.4.4.

- Write down the value of the statistic and its p-value. Compare the p-value with that for the *t* test. Do the results of the test support the scientific hypothesis?

The Sign test

This test is based very simply on how many positive and negative differences there are between pairs of data, assuming that the value of one variable is consistently subtracted from the value of the other. It is a straightforward application of the **binomial test** to paired data, such as the results of the visual field experiment above. To merely record the signs (rather than the magnitudes) of the differences between the times for the left and right visual fields is certainly to lose a considerable amount of information.

When paired data show no contraindications for using a parametric test, the *t* **test** is preferable to the **Sign test** because the latter would incur a needless sacrifice of statistical power. The great advantage of the **Sign test** is its robustness to the influence of outliers and no assumptions about bivariate normality in the original paired data. The procedure is very similar to that for the **Wilcoxon test** except that within the **Test Type** box, the **Wilcoxon** check box should be clicked off and the **Sign** check box clicked on. Click **OK** to run the test.

- Write down the results of the Sign test, including the p-value. Is the result significant? Compare this with the result of the paired samples *t* test and explain any discrepancy.

Eliminating the outliers

When there are contraindications for the *t* **test**, the use of a nonparametric test is not the only alternative available. Another approach is to consider the possibility of deselecting some of the data. In the present set of paired data, there is one difference between scores value in the variable *Differences* that is much larger than all the others. This may have arisen because *Case 10* had special difficulty in recognising words in the left visual field. At any rate, that participant's performance is quite atypical, and certainly calls into question the claim that he or she was drawn from the same population as the others. It is instructive to re-analyse the data after excluding the scores of *Case 10*. This is done by using the **Select Cases...** procedure (Section 3.3.1). Follow the procedure described in that section to eliminate *Case 10* from the data. (Hint: give the instruction to select cases if *case* ~= 10. The sign ~= means 'not equal to'.)

Now re-run the **paired-samples *t* test**, and run both the **Wilcoxon** and the **Sign** test on the reduced data set. Examine the new output.

- **Write down the value of *t* and its tail probability. Write down your interpretation of this new result. Similarly give the statistics and their p-values for the Sign and Wilcoxon tests. Explain your findings.**

Finishing the session

Close down SPSS and any other windows before logging out of the computer.

EXERCISE 10

One-sample tests

Before you start

Before beginning this Exercise, the reader should study Section 6.5.

The Kolmogorov-Smirnov test for goodness-of-fit

A researcher wishes to ascertain whether response latencies have been drawn from a normal population. The **Kolmogorov-Smirnov test** is an appropriate goodness-of-fit test for this purpose. Table 1 shows the decision-making response latencies of fifty young adults.

Table 1. Response latencies of fifty young adults (ms)									
910	1013	921	895	879	906	892	902	902	858
874	900	894	872	909	878	935	878	849	969
879	926	877	861	876	906	897	860	887	968
896	905	876	906	928	899	899	899	889	903
977	900	899	892	986	891	881	879	850	874

Name a variable *Latency* and enter the data. Draw a histogram of the distribution, along with a normal curve using
Analyze➜Descriptive Statistics➜Frequencies...
to open the **Frequencies** dialog box. Click **Charts...** and select **Histograms**, together with the checkbox **With normal curve**. Return to the **Frequencies** dialog box by clicking **Continue** and ensure that the tick in **Display frequency tables** has been turned off. Finally click **OK**.

- **From inspection of the histogram, would you expect the Kolmogorov-Smirnov test to accept or reject the null hypothesis of normality of distribution?**

- **If the normal curve were a good fit, where would you expect most of the area under the bars to lie?**

Run a **Kolmogorov-Smirnov** test for goodness-of-fit on the data in Table 1, as described in Section 6.5.1.

- **Write out the result of the Kolmogorov-Smirnov test.**

- **Is the result what you had expected?**

Nominal data: The binomial test

A die is rolled ten times, during which 6 sixes turn up. Have we grounds for suspecting that the die is unfair? Note that the probability of obtaining a six from the roll of a die is 1/6 (0.17). This is the null hypothesis value to enter as the **Test Proportion** in the **Binomial Test** dialog box (see Section 6.5.2).

Use the procedure described in Section 6.5.2 to enter the data but now define the grouping variable as *Die* with the values *1* for *Six* and *2* for *Not Six*. Remember to apply **Weight Cases...** to the second variable *Freq* and to change the value of **Test Proportion** in the **Binomial Test** dialog box.

- Write out the result of the binomial test.

- Do we have grounds for suspecting that the die is unfair?

Nominal data: The chi-square test for goodness-of-fit

One hundred 5-year-old children are asked which of five toys they prefer. Their choices are as in Table 2.

Table 2. Toy preference				
Toy A	Toy B	Toy C	Toy D	Toy E
40	25	15	15	5

Is there evidence that some toys are preferred to others?

The data are entered as in Section 6.5.2, but with five categories here instead of three. Remember to apply **Weight Cases...** to the second variable *Freq*.

- Write down the result of the chi-square test for goodness-of-fit.

- Referring to this result, write down your answer to the research question. What is the null hypothesis here? What does falsification of the null hypothesis imply?

The one sample *t* test

Table 3 contains the heights of fifty 18-year-old female college students, measured in the year 2000.

Table 3. Heights of female college students (cms)									
162	157	166	157	168	177	168	166	168	166
168	166	161	158	162	167	175	161	171	173
166	178	177	174	178	166	159	175	168	168
166	167	163	173	166	172	166	177	171	168
156	166	165	172	168	162	163	160	169	170

Past records, which ended in 1910, showed that over the previous decade, the mean height of women in the same college was 160 cms. No data on spread (or dispersion) are available. Do the present data suggest that women going to this college are taller (or shorter) nowadays?

The directional question of whether today's college women are taller than their predecessors can be approached by making a **One sample *t* test** (see Section 6.5.5) on the data of Table 3. Enter the data into a variable such as *Height*.

Choose
Analyze➔Compare Means➔One-Sample T Test...
to obtain the **One-Sample T Test** dialog box. For the **Test Value**, enter the value *160*. Click **OK** to run the test.

- **Write out the result of the one-sample *t* test.**

- **Does the result of the test indicate that today's college women are taller?**

Finishing the session

Close down SPSS and any other windows before logging out of the computer.

CHAPTER 7

Introduction to ANOVA: the one-factor between subjects experiment

7.1	Introduction
7.2	How the one-way ANOVA works
7.3	The one-way ANOVA with SPSS
7.4	Making comparisons the among treatment means
7.5	Trend analysis
7.6	Power
7.7	Alternatives to the one-way ANOVA

7.1   INTRODUCTION

In Chapter 6, we discussed the use of the *t* test and other techniques for comparing mean levels of performance under *two* different conditions. In this chapter, we shall also be describing techniques for comparing means, but in the context of more complex research designs with *three or more* conditions or groups.

7.1.1   An experiment with five treatment conditions

If two groups of participants perform a task under different conditions, an independent samples *t* test can be used to test the null hypothesis (H_0) of equality of the two population means:

$$H_0 : \mu_1 = \mu_2$$

If the test shows significance, we can reject H_0 and conclude that there is a difference between the two population means. The same null hypothesis, however, can also be tested by using the **analysis of variance** (**ANOVA** for short). Like the *t* test, the ANOVA was designed for the purpose of comparing means but is more versatile than the *t* test. Suppose that in an investigation of the effects of four supposedly performance-enhancing drugs upon skilled performance, five groups of subjects are tested:

1. A control group, who have received a Placebo.
2. A group who have received Drug A.
3. A group who have received Drug B.
4. A group who have received Drug C.
5. A group who have received Drug D.

Do any of the drugs affect level of performance? Our scientific hypothesis is that at least one of them does. The null hypothesis is the negation of this possibility: H_0 states, in effect, that none of them does: in the population, the mean performance score is the same under all five conditions:

$$H_0 : \mu_1 = \mu_2 = \mu_3 = \mu_4 = \mu_5$$

The **ANOVA** provides a direct test of this hypothesis.

The results of the experiment are shown in Table 1.

Table 1. The results of a one-factor, between subjects experiment, including the raw data, the group means, the grand mean (GM), and the standard deviations

	Placebo	Drug A	Drug B	Drug C	Drug D	
	10	8	12	13	11	
	9	10	14	12	20	
	7	7	9	17	15	
	9	7	7	12	6	
	11	7	15	10	11	
	5	12	12	24	12	
	7	7	14	13	15	
	6	4	14	11	16	
	8	9	11	20	12	
	8	8	12	12	12	
Mean	8.00	7.90	12.00	14.40	13.00	GM 11.06
SD	1.83	2.13	2.49	4.50	3.74	

It is apparent from Table 1 that there are considerable differences among the five sample means. Drugs B, C and D did indeed boost performance: the means for those conditions are substantially greater than the Placebo mean. Drug A, on the other hand, would seem to have been ineffective. The question is, could the null hypothesis actually be true and the differences we see in the table have come about merely through sampling error?

7.1.2 The analysis of variance (ANOVA): some basic terms

ANOVA is actually a whole set of techniques, each of which is based upon a model of how the data were generated and culminates in an appropriate test, provided that the assumptions of the model apply to the data. It is therefore important to be clear about the terms for the various ANOVA designs, so that SPSS will run the correct tests. In this book, only a few of the most common kinds of ANOVA will be described. There are many others, which can be found in standard statistics textbooks such as Winer, Brown & Michels (1991) and Keppel & Wickens (2004).

Factors, levels and measures

In ANOVA, a **factor** is a set of related conditions or categories. The conditions or categories making up a factor are known as its **levels**, even though, as in the qualitative factors of gender or blood group, there is no sense in which one category can be said to be 'higher' or 'lower' than another. The terms **factor** and **level** are the ANOVA equivalents of **independent variable (IV)** and **value**, respectively. In the ANOVA, the **dependent variable (DV)** is known as a **measure**. In our current example, the measure (or dependent variable) is *Score*.

Between subjects and within subjects factors

In Chapter 1 (Section 1.4.3), we observed that **between subjects** experiments, in which different groups of participants (subjects) are tested under the different conditions, result in independent samples of scores; whereas **within subjects** experiments, in which each participant is tested under all conditions, result in related samples of scores.

In ANOVA designs, a factor is said to be **between subjects** if each participant is either tested under only one condition or has been selected from one of a set of mutually exclusive natural categories. In our drugs experiment, *Drug Condition* (Placebo, Drug A, Drug B, Drug C, Drug D) is a between subjects factor. Between subjects factors must be distinguished from **within subjects** factors, in which the participant is tested at all levels (i.e. under all the conditions making up the factor). In ANOVA designs, an experiment with a within subjects factor is also said to have **repeated measures** on that factor: the measure or DV is taken at all levels.

Our drug experiment is a one-factor between subjects experiment. The **one-way ANOVA** is applicable here.

7.2   HOW THE ONE-WAY ANOVA WORKS

Table 2 shows the statistics from Table 1. The one-way ANOVA works by comparing the variability among the treatment means (the **between groups** variance) with the typical spread of scores **within groups** around their group means (as measured by the standard deviations and variances of scores within their treatment groups). ANOVA compares these two variance estimates by means of a statistic known as an **F ratio**. If F is small, the differences among the treatment means can be attributed to sampling error; but if F is large, this is taken as evidence for differences, in the population, among the treatment means and the null hypothesis of equality of means is rejected.

Table 2. Some statistics of the data in Table 1					

Score

	Drug Condition				
	Placebo	Drug A	Drug B	Drug C	Drug D
Mean	8.00	7.90	12.00	14.40	13.00
Std. Deviation	1.83	2.13	2.49	4.50	3.74
Variance	3.33	4.54	6.22	20.27	14.00

7.2.1 Between and within groups mean squares

In ANOVA, the numerator of a variance estimate is known as a **sum of squares** (**SS**). The denominator is known as the **degrees of freedom** (**df**). The variance estimate itself is known as a **mean square** (**MS**), so that $MS = SS/df$. The familiar formula for the variance of a sample (s^2) of n scores may therefore be re-written as follows:

$$s^2 = \frac{\displaystyle\sum_{\text{all scores}} (score - mean)^2}{n-1} = \frac{SS}{df} = MS$$

The between groups variance estimate is measured by the **between groups mean square** (MS_{between}); the within groups variance is measured by the **within groups mean square** (MS_{within}).

The between groups mean square

The between groups sum of squares MS_{between} is calculated by summing the squared deviations of the group mean about the grand mean over all participants. Since there are several participants (subjects) in each group, they all have the same between groups deviation.

$$SS_{between} = \sum_{\text{all participants}} (M_{group} - GM)^2 = \sum_{\text{groups}} n(M_{group} - GM)^2 = n \sum_{\text{groups}} (M_{group} - GM)^2$$

where M_{group} is a group mean, n is the number of observations per group and GM is the grand mean. In our example, $n = 10$ and so

$$SS_{between} = 10\left[(8.00 - 11.06)^2 + (7.90 - 11.06)^2 + ... + (13.00 - 11.06)^2\right] = 351.52$$

Degrees of freedom of MS_{between}

In Chapter 6 (Section 6.2.3), we saw that the degrees of freedom of a statistic can be obtained by taking the number of independent observations and subtracting the number of parameters that have been estimated. The value of the between groups mean square $MS_{between}$ is calculated from the values of the group means alone. There are five group means, but their variance is calculated from deviations from the grand mean GM. Since one parameter (the grand mean) has been estimated, $df_{between} = (5 - 1) = 4$. In general, if there are k groups, $df_{between} = k - 1$. The general formula for $MS_{between}$, therefore, is

$$MS_{between} = \frac{SS_{between}}{df_{between}} = \frac{SS_{between}}{(k-1)}$$

In the present example, $SS_{between} = 351.52$ and $df_{between} = 4$, so $MS_{between} = 351.52/4 = 87.88$.

Calculating the within groups mean square

In the **equal-n case**, that is, when there are equal numbers of participants in the different treatment groups, the within subjects mean square MS_{within} is simply the mean of the variance estimates from the scores in the various groups. In our current example, we have

$$MS_{within} = \frac{(3.33 + 4.54 + 6.22 + 20.27 + 14.00)}{5} = 9.67$$

Each of the five variance estimates has $n - 1 = 10 - 1 = 9$ degrees of freedom. Therefore $df_{within} = 5(9) = 45$.

7.2.2   The *F* ratio

The culmination of the one-way ANOVA is the F statistic, which compares the between groups and within groups mean squares thus:

$$F = \frac{\text{between groups variance}}{\text{within groups variance}} = \frac{MS_{between}}{MS_{within}}$$

The denominator of an F ratio is known as the **error term**, because it reflects sampling error or 'data noise'.

The value of the between groups variance estimate, however, reflects not only data noise, but also the presence and magnitude of any differences, in the population, among the treatment means. Should there be no differences, as the null hypothesis asserts, the values of $MS_{between}$ and MS_{within} should be of similar magnitude and the value of F will be close to 1; but if H_0 is false, the value of $MS_{between}$ (and therefore of F) may be large (Table 3). A high value of F, therefore, is evidence against the null hypothesis of equality of all three population means.

Table 3. What F is measuring

$$F = \frac{MS_{between}}{MS_{within}}$$

Error plus real differences

Error only

- If there are differences among the population means, the numerator will be inflated and F will increase.
- If there are no differences among the population means, F will be close to 1.

In our current example, $MS_{between} = 87.88$ and $MS_{within} = 9.67$. The value of F is, therefore,

$$F = \frac{MS_{between}}{MS_{within}} = \frac{87.88}{9.67} = 9.09$$

Since a variance, which is the sum of squared deviations, cannot have a negative value, the value of F cannot be less than zero. On the other hand, F has no upper limit and, when testing the null hypothesis, we shall only be looking at the *upper* tail of the distribution of F.

7.2.3 Finding the significance of F

The value of F that we have calculated from the data (9.09) is several times the expected value of F under the null hypothesis, which is about 1. But is our value of F large enough for us to be able to reject H_0? To answer this question, we need to know the sampling distribution of F.

Parameters of the F distribution

The F distribution has two parameters:
1. The degrees of freedom of the between groups mean square $df_{between}$;
2. The degrees of freedom of the within groups mean square df_{within}.

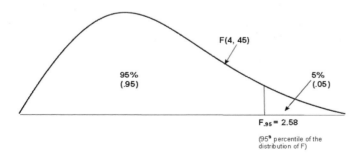

F(4, 45)

95% (.95)

5% (.05)

$F_{.95} = 2.58$

(95th percentile of the distribution of F)

Figure 1. Distribution of F with 4 and 45 degrees of freedom. The critical value of F (2.58) is the 95th percentile of this distribution

An F distribution is positively skewed, with a long tail to the right (Figure 1). For the test of the null hypothesis that, in the population, all five means have the same value, we must refer specifically to the F distribution with 4 and 45 degrees of freedom: $F(4, 45)$.

The critical value of F

It can be seen from Figure 1 that, under the null hypothesis, only 5% of values in the distribution of $F(4, 45)$ have values as great as 2.58. Our obtained value (9.09) of F greatly exceeds this critical value; in fact, fewer than 1% of values of F are as large as this.

The p-value of 9.09 (which will be included in the SPSS output) is 0.000018, which is very small indeed. The null hypothesis of equality of the treatment means is therefore rejected. The result of the F test is written as follows:

> A one-way ANOVA showed significant differences among the means in
> Table 1: $F(4, 45) = 9.09$; $p < .01$.

Note that, in accordance with APA recommendations, the p-value is reported to two decimal places only: where the p-value is very small (as in the present example), the inequality sign ($<$) is used. It is now common practice to give the p-value with the report of *any* statistical test, even when the result is statistically insignificant (e.g. $p = .56$).

When reporting the result of any statistical test, make sure that the reader has ready access to the descriptive statistics: the fact that F is significant tells the reader nothing whatsoever about either the directions or the magnitudes of differences among the group means.

7.3   THE ONE-WAY ANOVA WITH SPSS

There are several ways of running a one-way ANOVA on SPSS. The easiest method is to select an option in the **Compare Means** menu. For the experienced user, however, the **General Linear Model (GLM)** offers a wider range of techniques although the preliminary dialog and the output are more complex than in **Compare Means**. The preliminary work in **Variable View** and the entry of the data are the same for either approach.

7.3.1   Entering the data

As with the independent samples *t* test, you will need to define two variables:
1. a grouping variable with a simple name such as *Group*, which identifies the condition under which a score was achieved. (The grouping variable should also be given a more meaningful variable label such as *Drug Condition*, which will appear in the output.)
2. a variable with a name such as *Score*, which contains all the scores in the data set. This is the dependent variable.

The grouping variable will consist of five values (one for the placebo condition and one for each of the four drugs). We shall arbitrarily assign numerical values thus: 0 = Placebo; 1 = Drug A; 2 = Drug B; 3 = Drug C; 4 = Drug D.

Proceed as follows:

- Open **Variable View** first and amend the settings so that when you enter **Data View**, your variables are already labelled, the scores appear without unnecessary decimals and (when you are working in **Data View**) you will have the option of displaying the value labels of your grouping variable.
- In the **Values** column, assign clear **value labels** to the code numbers you choose for grouping variables (Figure 2). When you are typing data into **Data View**, having the value labels available can help you to avoid transcription errors.

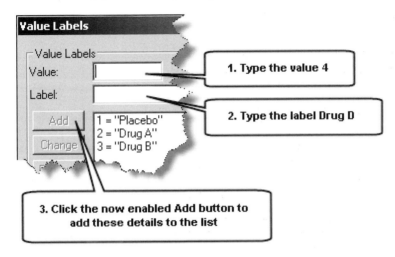

Figure 2. Assigning value labels to the code numbers making up the grouping variable

- In the **Measure** column, specify the **level of measurement** of your grouping variable, which is at the nominal level of measurement (Figure 3). (The numerical values that we have assigned were arbitrary and are merely labels for the five different treatment conditions.)

	Name	Type	Width	Decimals	Label	Values	Missing	Columns	Align	Measure
1	Group	Numeric	8	0	Drug Condition	{1, Placebo}...	None	8	Right	Nominal
2	Score	Numeric	8	0		None	None	8	Right	Scale

Figure 3. The completed Variable View window, specifying the nominal level of measurement for the grouping variable *Group*.

Having thoroughly prepared the ground in this way while in **Variable View**, you will find that when you enter **Data View**, the names of your variables appear at the heads of the first two columns. When you type in the values of the grouping variable, you can view their labels by checking the value labels option in the **View** menu or by clicking the ⬧ icon. Figure 4 shows the same part of **Data View** after the data have been entered, with and without value labels.

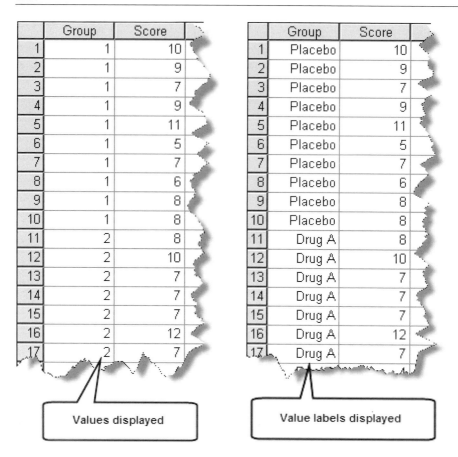

Figure 4. Two displays of the same part of **Data View** after the data have been entered: on the left, in the *Group* column, the values are shown; on the right, in the same column, the value labels are shown.

7.3.2 Running the one-way ANOVA in Compare Means

The one-way ANOVA can be found in the **Analyze** menu, under **Compare Means** (Figure 5).

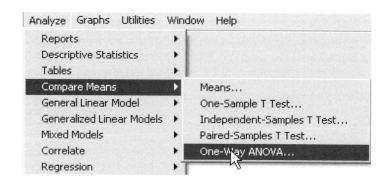

Figure 5. Choosing the **One-way ANOVA...** from the **Compare Means** menu

The **One-way ANOVA** dialog box appears as in Figure 6. The basic ANOVA can be ordered very easily as shown. Click **OK** to run the ANOVA.

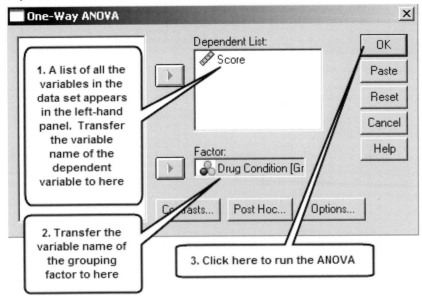

Figure 6. Completing the **One-way ANOVA** dialog box

In the ANOVA summary table (Output 1), the values of *F*, the *SS*, the *MS* and the *df* are the same as those we calculated earlier. Confirm also that the values in the *Mean Square* column are the *Between Groups* and *Within Groups* sums of squares divided by their respective degrees of freedom. The value of *F* has been obtained by dividing the *Between Groups* mean square by the *Within Groups* mean square.

ANOVA

Score

	Sum of Squares	df	Mean Square	F	Sig.
Between Groups	351.52	4	87.88	9.08	.000
Within Groups	435.30	45	9.67		
Total	786.82	49			

Notice that the Total Sum of Squares is the sum of the Between Groups and Within Groups values

The associated p-value for F is <.01 (i.e. significant at the .01 level). Write it as 'p<.01'

Output 1. The **One-way ANOVA** summary table

In the *df* column, note that the *Between Groups* degrees of freedom (4) is one less than the number of groups in the experiment. In general, in a one-way ANOVA with *k* treatment groups, the between groups mean square has $k - 1$ degrees of freedom. In our current example, there were five treatment groups, each containing 10 participants. For each group, the variance calculated from the ten scores has $n - 1 = 10 - 1 = 9$ degrees of freedom. The *Within Groups* mean square in Output 1 is the mean of the five variance estimates, so $df_{within} = 5 \times 9 = 45$.

7.3.3 Measuring effect size

Ouput 1 also gives the value of the total **sum of squares** (SS_{total}), which is the sum of the squares of the deviations of the 50 scores in the data set from the grand mean (GM):

$$SS_{total} = \sum_{all\ participants} (score - GM)^2$$

The value of SS_{total} is a measure of the total variability of the scores. It can be seen from Output 1 that

$$SS_{total} = SS_{between} + SS_{within}$$

In words, the total variability of the scores is the sum of between groups and within groups components. This important identity is known as the **partition of the total sum of squares**. In the context of ANOVA, effect size is conceived as the proportion of the total variability among the scores that can be explained by manipulation of the treatment factor: that is,

$$effect\ size = \frac{explained\ variability}{total\ variability}$$

This concept is readily understood in relation to the partition of the total sum of squares.

The oldest measure of effect size is the statistic η^2 (**eta squared**), which is also known as the **correlation ratio**. For reasons that will be explained in Chapter 12, eta squared is also known as R^2. For the one-way ANOVA, the value of η^2 (or R^2) is given by the following formula:

$$\eta^2 = \frac{SS_{between}}{SS_{total}}$$

Using the values in the ANOVA summary table (Output 1), we have

$$\eta^2 = \frac{351.520}{786.820} = 0.447$$

This is a large effect size (see Table 4 in the next Section).

The output of the **One-Way ANOVA…** procedure in **Compare Means** does not include η^2. For this and several other important measures and techniques, we must turn to SPSS's **General Linear Model (GLM)** procedure.

7.3.4 Running the one-way ANOVA in GLM

In addition to all the techniques in the **One-Way ANOVA** procedure, the **General Linear Model** (GLM) menu offers measures of effect size, as well as other important tests, such as

Analysis of covariance (ANCOVA). In this subsection, we shall describe how to run the one-way ANOVA in GLM. First, however, it will be necessary to explain some of the terms that will appear in the GLM dialog box.

Factors with fixed and random effects

The experimenter does not select experimental conditions at random: their inclusion is driven either by theory or by the need to resolve some practical issue. A factor consisting of a set of theoretically-determined conditions is said to have **fixed effects**. Most factors in experimental research are fixed effects factors.

There are occasions, however, on which the conditions making up a factor can be viewed as a random sample from a large (perhaps infinitely large) pool of possible conditions. In research on reading skills, for example, an investigator studying the effects of sentence length upon passage readability may select or prepare some passages which vary systematically in sentence length. With such a procedure, however, reading performance may reflect passage properties other than sentence length; moreover, these additional properties cannot be expected to remain the same from passage to passage. The effects of using different passages must be included as a factor in the analysis, even though the experimenter is not primarily interested in this nuisance variable. Since, arguably, additional passage characteristics are a random selection from a pool of possible conditions, the passage factor is said to have **random effects**. Factors with random effects arise more commonly in applied research and their presence has important implications for the analysis.

Covariates

Often the researcher has available information about participants other than that directly relevant to the research project. A **covariate** is a variable which, because it can be expected to correlate (i.e. 'co-vary') with the DV, is likely to add to the variability (or 'noisiness') of the data and inflate the error term with a consequent loss of power in the statistical test. An obvious example of a covariate is IQ, which can be expected to correlate substantially with any measure of cognitive or skilled performance.

The **analysis of covariance (ANCOVA)** is a technique whereby the effects of a covariate upon the DV are removed from the data, thus reducing their 'noisiness' and increasing the power of the F test. The manner in which this is achieved is described in statistical texts such as Winer, Brown & Michels (1991) and Keppel & Wickens (2004).

Univariate versus multivariate ANOVA

In all the experiments we have considered so far, there has been a single DV. In the current example, the DV is the score a participant achieves on a task. The one-way ANOVA and the *t test* are **univariate tests**, because they were designed for the analysis of data from experiments with a single DV. If, however, we had also recorded the time the participant took to complete the task, there would have been two DVs. **Multivariate tests** are techniques designed for the analysis of data from experiments with two or more DVs. An example of a multivariate technique is **Multivariate Analysis of Variance (MANOVA)**, which is a generalisation beyond the univariate ANOVA to the analysis of data from experiments with several DVs. This topic is illustrated in Chapter 10 (Section 10.5).

Running the ANOVA in GLM

The **General Linear Model** (GLM) menu is shown in Figure 7. The **Univariate** option is clearly appropriate for our example, since there is only one dependent variable.

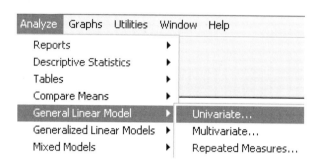

Figure 7. The **General Linear Model** menu

In this section, we shall use **GLM** to run the basic one-way ANOVA only, so that we can compare the output with the **Compare Means** One-Way ANOVA summary table.

Proceed as follows:
- Choose
  Analyze➜General Linear Model ➜Univariate...
  to open the **Univariate** dialog box (the completed box is shown in Figure 8).
- As before, the left panel of the dialog box will contain a list of all the variables in the data set. Transfer the variable names as shown in Figure 8. In our example, the *Drug Condition* factor has fixed effects, since its levels were selected systematically.
- Click **OK** to run the basic one-way ANOVA.

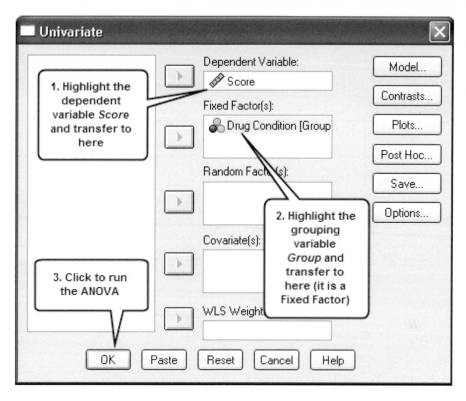

Figure 8. Completing the General Linear Model **Univariate** dialog box

The **GLM ANOVA** summary table is shown in Output 2, with the table from the **Compare Means One-Way ANOVA** procedure below it for comparison. The GLM table contains some additional terms: **Corrected Model**, **Intercept**, **Corrected Total** and **Type III Sum of Squares**. These are terms from another statistical technique called **regression**, which is discussed in Chapter 12. As we shall see in Chapter 12, it is quite possible to recast the one-way ANOVA (or, indeed, *any* ANOVA) as a problem in regression and make exactly the same test of the null hypothesis. If that is done (as in the GLM procedure), the mean squares, their degrees of freedom, the value of F and the p-value will all be exactly the same as with the ANOVA procedure. In the GLM summary table, the rows labelled as **Corrected Model**, **Group**, **Error** and **Corrected Total** contain exactly the same information that we shall find in the **Between Groups**, **Within Groups** and **Total** rows of the One-Way ANOVA table below. The values of F are also exactly the same in both tables.

Output 2 also contains another item that is missing from the table we obtained from the **One-Way** procedure in **Compare Means** (Output 1). Underneath the table is the information that **R Squared** (that is, η^2) = .447 and that **Adjusted R Squared** = .398.

Univariate Analysis of Variance

Tests of Between-Subjects Effects

Dependent Variable: Score

Source	Type III Sum of Squares	df	Mean Square	F	Sig.
Corrected Model	351.52[a]	4	87.88	9.08	.000
Intercept	6116.18	1	6116.18	632.27	.000
Group	351.52	4	87.88	9.08	.000
Error	435.30	45	9.67		
Total	6903.00	50			
Corrected Total	786.82	49			

a. R Squared = .447 (Adjusted R Squared = .398)

Oneway

> Gray areas are the same in both tables

> The values of F are the same

ANOVA

Score

	Sum of Squares	df	Mean Square	F	Sig.
Between Groups	351.52	4	87.88	9.08	.000
Within Groups	435.30	45	9.67		
Total	786.82	49			

Output 2. Comparison of the **Univariate** ANOVA summary table from the **GLM** menu (upper panel) with the **One-Way** ANOVA summary table from the **Compare Means** menu (lower panel).

Adjusted R^2

The statistic η^2 tends to overestimate the effect size in the population: it is **positively biased**. Adjusted R^2 corrects this bias. In our current example, the value of adjusted R^2 is 0.398.

Other measures of effect size in ANOVA have also been proposed, most notably, **estimated omega squared** $\hat{\omega}^2$. Since both adjusted R^2 and omega squared were designed to remove positive bias, their values are very similar.

Table 4 shows how η^2 maps on to Cohen's classification of **effect size**.

Table 4. Cohen's classification of effect size, with equivalent values of eta squared		
Effect size (d)	**Eta squared**	**Size of Effect**
$0.2 \leq d < 0.5$	$.01 \leq \eta^2 < .06$	Small
$0.5 \leq d < 0.8$	$.06 \leq \eta^2 < .14$	Medium
$d \geq 0.8$	$\eta^2 \geq .14$	Large

When using Table 4, we suggest that you enter the table in the middle column with the value of adjusted R^2, rather than the value of R^2, which has not been corrected for positive bias. Our value of adjusted R^2 (.398) is a large effect.

7.3.5 The special case of two groups: equivalence of *F* and *t*

In Chapter 6, we described the use of an independent-samples t test to compare the mean level of performance of a group of 20 participants who had ingested a dose of caffeine with that of another group of 20 participants (the Placebo group) who had ingested a neutral saline solution. An edited SPSS table (Output 3) showing the result of the pooled t test is shown below.

Independent Samples Test

		t-test for Equality of Means		
		t	df	Sig. (2-tailed)
Performance Score	Equal variances assumed	2.604	38	.013

Output 3. The independent samples *t* test output

If a one-way ANOVA is run on the same data set, the summary table appears as follows.

ANOVA

Performance Score

	Sum of Squares	df	Mean Square	F	Sig.
Between Groups	70.225	1	70.225	6.781	.013
Within Groups	393.550	38	10.357		
Total	463.775	39			

Output 4. The ANOVA output giving an *F* value and its p-value

Notice that the ANOVA p-value is exactly the same as the t test p-value. In fact, it can be shown that the F and t statistics are related according to: $F = t^2$. We can write:

$$F(1, df) = t^2(df)$$

where df is the number of degrees of freedom of MS_{within} and also the degrees of freedom of t.

In the present example, $t^2 = 2.604^2 = 6.781 = F$. Note also that the p-value of F is equal to the *two-tailed* p-value of t: thus, although the critical region of F lies in the upper tail of the distribution only, the F test is non-directional.

7.3.6   Additional items with GLM Univariate

The basic ANOVA output includes little other than the ANOVA summary table. We shall require several other statistics, which can be selected from the GLM **Univariate** dialog box (Figure 8). For clarity, we shall consider these measures separately here; but they would normally be requested with the basic ANOVA. Among the items we shall select are the **descriptive statistics** (including the means and standard deviations for the five conditions in the experiment), **homogeneity tests** (testing the assumption of homogeneity of variance among the levels of the DV), **estimates of effect size** and a **profile plot** (a line graph of the treatment means). These are obtained by making the appropriate responses in the **Univariate** dialog box.

Requesting various statistics

The first three recommended options are obtained by clicking on the **Options** button in the **Univariate** dialog box (Figure 9).

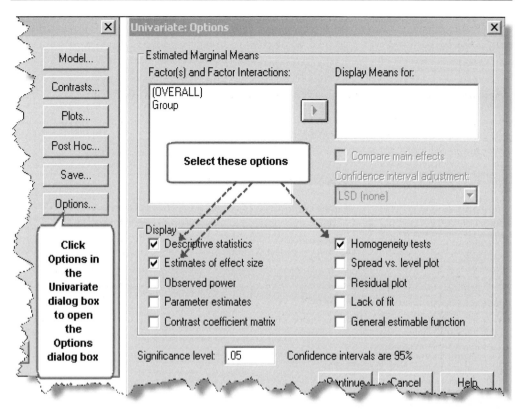

Figure 9. The **Options** dialog box with **Descriptive statistics**, **Estimates of effect size** and **Homogeneity tests** selected

When the box labelled **Estimates of effect size** is checked in **Options**, the ANOVA summary table will include **partial eta squared (η_p^2)** which, in the context of the one-way ANOVA, is identical with eta squared (R^2 in Output 2). You may wish to confirm that when the **Estimates of effect size** box is checked in Options (Figure 9), the output will give the value of partial eta squared as .447.

It is now usual to include a measure of effect size with reports of statistical tests. We suggest that your complete report of the results of the ANOVA might run along the following lines:

> The mean skill score for the placebo was (M = 8.00, SD = 1.83) and for the four drugs respectively, the means were: M = 7.90 (SD = 2.13); M = 12.00 (SD = 2.49); M = 14.40 (SD = 4.50); M = 13.00 (SD = 3.742). The one-way ANOVA showed *F* to be significant beyond the .01 level: $F(4, 45) = 9.08$; p <.01. Adjusted R Squared = .398.

Ordering profile plots

Figure 10 shows how to request a **Profile Plot** of the five treatment means from the **Univariate** dialog box.

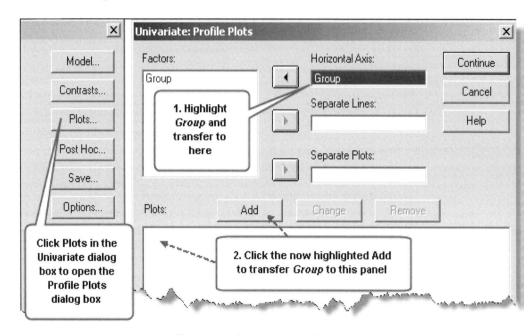

Figure 10. Ordering a profile plot

Design specifications output

In addition to the requested statistics, the GLM output includes a table of design specifications. These should be checked to make sure that you have communicated the experimental design correctly to SPSS. Output 5 shows the specifications of the independent variable *Drug Condition.*

Between-Subjects Factors

		Value Label	N
Drug	0	Placebo	10
Condition	1	Drug A	10
	2	Drug B	10
	3	Drug C	10
	4	Drug D	10

Output 5. Design specifications: the values and value labels of the grouping variable

Check this table to make sure that SPSS agrees that the factor has five levels, that 10 participants are tested at each level and that the code numbers are correctly paired with the five conditions. Mis-specifications in **Variable View** can emerge at this point. Transcription errors in **Data View** could result in incorrect entries in the N column.

Descriptive statistics output

Output 6 tabulates the requested **Descriptive statistics**.

Descriptive Statistics

Dependent Variable: Score

Drug Condition	Mean	Std. Deviation	N
Placebo	8.00	1.826	10
Drug A	7.90	2.132	10
Drug B	12.00	2.494	10
Drug C	14.40	4.502	10
Drug D	13.00	3.742	10
Total	11.06	4.007	50

Output 6. The Descriptive Statistics output: means and standard deviations for the five groups.

The Levene test output

Output 7 shows the result of Levene's test for homogeneity of variance.

Levene's Test of Equality of Error Variances[a]

Dependent Variable: Performance Score

F	df1	df2	Sig.
2.529	4	45	.054

Tests the null hypothesis that the error variance of the dependent variable is equal across groups.

a. Design: Intercept+Group

> Despite considerable differences among the sample variances, the test does not reject the null hypothesis of homogeneity of variance

Output 7. Levene's test for homogeneity of variance

The non-significance of the **Levene F Statistic** for the test of equality of error variances (homogeneity of variances) indicates that the assumption of homogeneity of variance is tenable; however, considerable differences among the variances are apparent from inspection.

The profile plot of means output

The requested profile plot of the means is shown in Output 8. Note carefully that the zero point of the vertical scale does not appear on the axis. This is something that still happens in default profile plots on SPSS. Always be suspicious of such a graph, because it can give the appearance of a strong effect when actually there is very little happening. The difficulty can easily be remedied by double-clicking on the graph to bring it into the **Chart Editor**, double-clicking on the vertical axis and specifying zero as the minimum point on the vertical scale (Output 9). The effect can sometimes be quite dramatic: with some data sets, an exciting-looking range of peaks suddenly becomes a boring plain! In this case, however, it is clear that even when the zero point is shown on the vertical axis, there really is something happening in this data set.

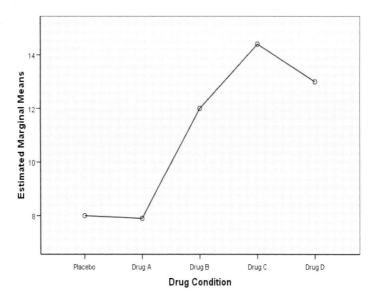

Output 8. The plot of the means as originally shown in SPSS output

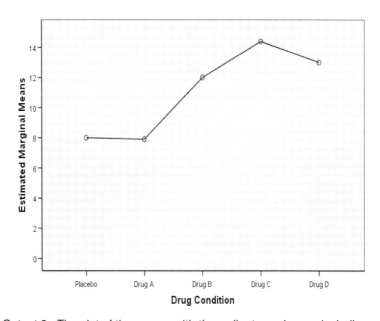

Output 9. The plot of the means with the ordinate scale now including zero

7.4   MAKING COMPARISONS AMONG TREATMENT MEANS

We have found evidence against the null hypothesis (H_0: all five means in the population have the same value) but what can we conclude from this? If H_0 states that all the means are equal, the alternative hypothesis is simply that they are not all equal. The falsity of H_0, however, does not imply that the difference between any and every pair of group means is significant. If the ANOVA *F* test is significant, we can conclude there is at least one difference *somewhere* among the means; but we cannot claim that the mean for any particular group is significantly different from the mean of any other group. Further analysis is necessary to confirm whatever differences there may be among the individual treatment means. We shall consider some techniques for making comparisons among means in Section 7.4.2.

Planned and unplanned comparisons

Before running a drug experiment in the current example, the experimenter may have some very specific questions in mind. It might be expected, for example (perhaps on theoretical grounds), that the mean score of every group who have ingested one of the drugs will be greater than the mean score of the Placebo group. This expectation would be tested by comparing each drug group with the Placebo group. Perhaps, on the other hand, the experimenter has theoretical reasons to suspect that Drugs A and B should enhance performance, but Drugs C and D should not. That hypothesis would be tested by comparing the Placebo mean with the average score for groups A and B combined and with the average score for groups B and C combined. These are examples of **planned comparisons**.

Often, however, the experimenter, perhaps because the field has been little explored, has only a sketchy idea of how the results will turn out. There may be good reason to expect that *some* of the drugs will enhance performance; but it may not be possible, *a priori*, to be more specific. Unplanned, *a posteriori* or **post hoc**, comparisons are part of the 'data-snooping' that inevitably follows the gathering of a data set.

The per comparison and familywise Type I error rates

We have seen that when we use the *t* test to compare two means, the significance level α is the probability of a Type I error, that is, the rejection of the null hypothesis when it is actually true. When, however, we intend to make several comparisons among a group of means, we must distinguish between the individual comparison and the whole set, or **family**, of the comparisons that we intend to make. It can be shown that if we make a set of comparisons, the probability, under the null hypothesis, of at least one of them being significant, may be considerably greater than α. We must, therefore, distinguish between the Type I error rate *per comparison* (**α**) and the Type I error rate *familywise* (**α**$_{family}$). If we intend to make *c* comparisons, the *familywise* Type I error rate can be shown to be approximately *c*α

$$\alpha_{family} \approx c\alpha \quad (1)$$

Equation (1) shows that when the researcher is making many comparisons among the treatment means of data from complex experiments, the probability of at least one test showing significance can be very high. It is therefore essential to control the *familywise* Type I error rate by making data-snooping tests more conservative. Several procedures for doing this have been proposed.

The Bonferroni method

Equation (1) is the basis of the *Bonferroni method* of controlling the *familywise* Type I error rate. If c is the number of comparisons in the family, the p-value for each test is multiplied by c. This procedure obviously makes the test of a comparison more conservative. For example, suppose that, having decided to make 4 comparisons, we were to make an ordinary t test of one comparison and find that the p-value is .04. In the Bonferroni procedure, we must must now multiply this p-value by 4, obtaining .16, a value well above the desired *familywise* error rate of .05. We must, therefore, accept the null hypothesis (or, at any rate, not conclude that we have evidence to reject it).

It is common practice, following the running of an experiment with several different conditions, to make unplanned or **post hoc** multiple pairwise comparisons among the treatment means. Here, the Bonferroni method can result in extremely conservative tests, because in this situation c (the size of the comparison family) is arguably the number of different pairs that can be drawn from the array of k treatment means; otherwise we risk capitalising upon chance and making false claims of differences among the population means.

The great problem with the Bonferroni correction is that when the array of means is large, the criterion for significance becomes so exacting that the method finds too few significant differences. In other words, the Bonferroni tests are conservative to the point that they may have very little power to reject the null hypothesis. The **Tukey** tests and the **Newman-Keuls** test are less conservative, the Tukey (or variant) being generally preferred for post hoc tests of pairwise differences following the one-way ANOVA. For more complex comparisons, such as the comparison of one mean with the mean of several others, the **Scheffé test** is highly regarded; but it is thought to be over-conservative when used for pairwise comparisons.

The situation may arise in which the researcher wishes to compare performance under each of several active conditions with that of a baseline control group. The **Dunnett test**, described in Howell (2007; p.374), is regarded as the most powerful test available for this purpose.

These tests (and many others) are available within SPSS.

7.4.1. Unplanned or post hoc multiple comparisons with SPSS

Figure 11 shows the boxes that must be checked to order the **Bonferroni**, **Tukey** and **Dunnett** tests.

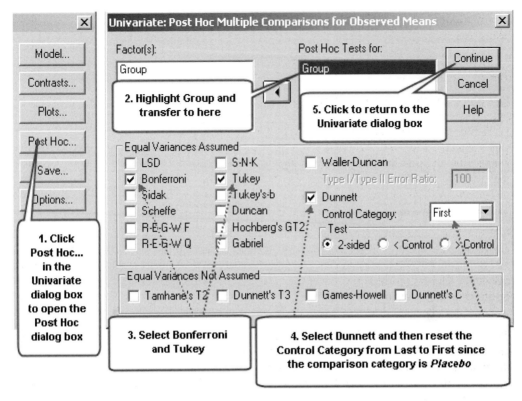

Figure 11. Selecting **Post Hoc** tests

Output 10 is only part of an extensive table of the results of multiple pairwise comparisons with the **Tukey**, **Bonferroni** and **Dunnett** tests. The most conservative test of the three, the **Bonferroni,** has the widest confidence intervals and the largest p-values; the least conservative test, the **Dunnett** test, has the smallest p-values and the narrowest confidence intervals.

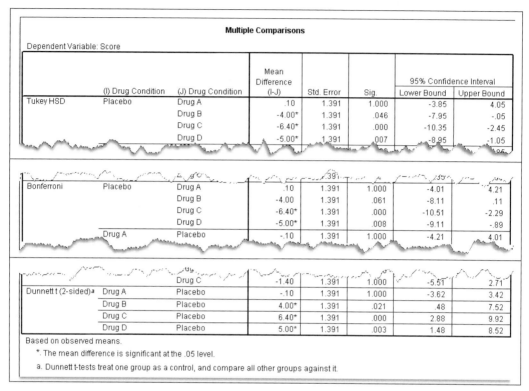

Multiple Comparisons

Dependent Variable: Score

	(I) Drug Condition	(J) Drug Condition	Mean Difference (I-J)	Std. Error	Sig.	95% Confidence Interval Lower Bound	Upper Bound
Tukey HSD	Placebo	Drug A	.10	1.391	1.000	-3.85	4.05
		Drug B	-4.00*	1.391	.046	-7.95	-.05
		Drug C	-6.40*	1.391	.000	-10.35	-2.45
		Drug D	-5.00*	1.391	.007	-8.95	-1.05
Bonferroni	Placebo	Drug A	.10	1.391	1.000	-4.01	4.21
		Drug B	-4.00	1.391	.061	-8.11	.11
		Drug C	-6.40*	1.391	.000	-10.51	-2.29
		Drug D	-5.00*	1.391	.008	-9.11	-.89
	Drug A	Placebo	-.10	1.391	1.000	-4.21	4.01
		Drug C	-1.40	1.391	1.000	-5.51	2.71
Dunnett t (2-sided)a	Drug A	Placebo	-.10	1.391	1.000	-3.62	3.42
	Drug B	Placebo	4.00*	1.391	.021	.48	7.52
	Drug C	Placebo	6.40*	1.391	.000	2.88	9.92
	Drug D	Placebo	5.00*	1.391	.003	1.48	8.52

Based on observed means.

*. The mean difference is significant at the .05 level.

a. Dunnett t-tests treat one group as a control, and compare all other groups against it.

Output 10. Comparison of the outputs for the **Tukey**, **Bonferroni** and **Dunnett** tests.

Output 11 shows a second part of the output for the Tukey test.   The output shows that there are two subgroups of tests. Within each subgroup there are no significant pairwise differences; on the other hand, any member of either subgroup is significantly different from any member of the other subgroup. For example, there are no differences among Drugs B, C and D; but each of those is significantly different from both the Placebo and Drug A. In a word, of the four drugs tested, the only one not to produce an improvement over the Placebo was Drug A.

Homogeneous Subsets

Performance Score

	Drug Condition	N	Subset 1	Subset 2
Tukey HSD [a,b]	Drug A	10	7.90	
	Placebo	10	8.00	
	Drug B	10		12.00
	Drug D	10		13.00
	Drug C	10		14.40
	Sig.		1.000	.429

1. There are no significant differences among the means in either group.

2. Any member of either group is significantly different from a member of the other group.

Means for groups in homogeneous subsets are displayed.
Based on Type III Sum of Squares
The error term is Mean Square(Error) = 9.673.

a. Uses Harmonic Mean Sample Size = 10.000.

b. Alpha = .05.

Output 11. The two subgroups of treatment means identified by the **Tukey** multiple comparisons test

7.4.2 Linear contrasts

We have data from a one-factor between subject experiment with five treatment groups, the mean levels of performance of which are M_1, M_2, M_3, M_4 and M_5.

A comparison between two of an array of k treatment means (or combinations of the means) can be expressed as a **linear contrast**, that is, a linear sum of the five treatment means, with the constraint that the coefficients (weights) add up to zero. We have 5 treatment means and we want to compare M_1 with M_2. The difference $M_1 - M_2$ can be expressed as the linear contrast ψ_1, where

$$\psi_1 = (1)M_1 + (-1)M_2 + (0)M_3 + (0)M_4 + (0)M_5$$

This expression may seem highly artificial; but we need to develop a notation for a whole set of contrasts that might be made among a given set of treatment means. We must have the same number of terms in all contrasts, even if we have to have coefficients of zero for the irrelevant terms.

Similarly, if we wish to compare M_3 with the mean of M_1 and M_2, the difference

$M_3 - \dfrac{(M_1 + M_2)}{2}$ can be expressed as the linear contrast ψ_2, where

$$\psi_2 = (-0.5)M_1 + (-0.5)M_2 + (1)M_3 + (0)M_4 + (0)M_5$$

In general, for a set of k treatment means M_j, any contrast Ψ can be represented as

$$\psi = \sum_{j}^{k} c_j M_j$$

where c_j is the coefficient of the treatment mean M_j and $\Sigma c_j = 0$.

Sums of squares for contrasts

Associated with a particular contrast ψ is a sum of squares SS_ψ, the formula for which is

$$SS_\psi = \frac{n\psi^2}{\Sigma c_j^2} = \frac{n\left[\sum_j c_j M_j\right]^2}{\Sigma c_j^2}$$

This sum of squares can be thought of as the variability of the scores that can be attributed to the difference between the means that are being compared. The term $\sum_j c_j^2$ in the denominator acts as a scaling factor, ensuring that the sum of squares attributable to a particular contrast can be compared with the ANOVA between groups mean square $SS_{between}$.

Table 5 interprets this formula for the first contrast that we considered (ψ_1).

	Placebo	Drug A	Drug B	Drug C	Drug D	Total
Mean	8.00	7.90	12.00	14.40	13.00	
c_j	1	−1	0	0	0	$\Sigma c_j^2 = 2$
$c_j M_j$	8.00	-7.90	0	0	0	$\Sigma c_j M_j = 0.10$

Table 5. Steps in calculating a contrast sum of squares

It can be seen from Table 5 that

$$\psi_1 = (1)M_1 + (-1)M_2 + (0)M_3 + (0)M_4 + (0)M_5 = 8.00 - 7.90 = 0.10$$

$$SS_{\psi_1} = \frac{n\psi_1^2}{\Sigma c_j^2} = \frac{10(0.10)^2}{2} = 0.05$$

This sum of squares has one degree of freedom because, essentially, we are comparing two means.

Testing a contrast for significance

A contrast can be tested for significance by making either an *F* test or a *t* test. (We have seen that when there are only two groups, the two tests are exactly equivalent.) Since a contrast sum of squares has only one degree of freedom, the F statistic is

$$F_{\psi_1}(1,\ df_{within}) = t(df_{within})^2 = \frac{MS_{\psi_1}}{MS_{within}} = \frac{SS_{\psi_1}}{MS_{within}} = \frac{0.05}{9.673} = 0.005$$

or

$$t(df_{within}) = t(45) = 0.07$$

Testing contrasts in the One-Way ANOVA procedure

The GLM menu offers several entire sets of contrasts, each set serving a different purpose. To make a test of a few specified contrasts, however, we shall turn to the **One-Way ANOVA** procedure in the **Compare Means** menu. In the **One-Way ANOVA** dialog box, click on the **Contrasts ...** button at the foot of the dialog box and proceed as shown in Figure 12.

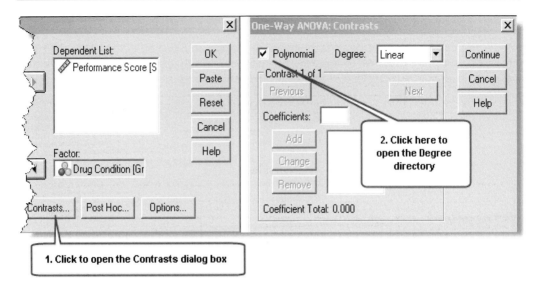

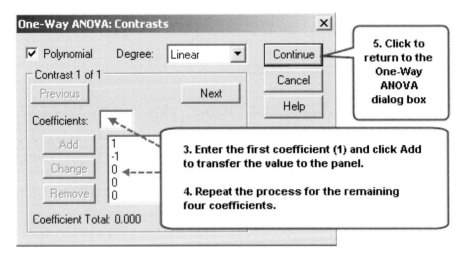

Figure 12. Specifying a specific contrast in the **One-Way ANOVA: Contrasts** dialog box

Output 12 shows the result of the t test of the contrast ψ_1.

Contrast Coefficients

Contrast	Drug Condition				
	Placebo	Drug A	Drug B	Drug C	Drug D
1	1	-1	0	0	0

Contrast Tests

		Contrast	Value of Contrast	Std. Error	t	df	Sig. (2-tailed)
Score	Assume equal variances	1	.10	1.391	.072	45	.943
	Does not assume equal	1	.10	.888	.113	17.584	.912

Output 12. Result of the test of the contrast ψ_1

The t-value (0.07) agrees with the result of our previous calculation. In the upper panel of Output 12, the coefficients of the contrast ψ_1 are listed.

Running contrasts in the GLM procedure

Table 6 shows the different types of contrasts that can be ordered from the GLM dialog box.

Table 6. The types of contrast sets available on GLM	
Type	**Description**
Simple	A pre-specified reference or control mean is compared with each of the other means.
Helmert	Starting from the leftmost mean in the array, each mean is compared with the mean of the remaining means.
Difference (Reverse Helmert)	Starting from the leftmost mean in the array, each mean is compared with the mean of the means that preceded it.
Repeated	First with second, second with third, third with fourth, ...
Deviation	Each mean is compared with the grand mean.

We shall illustrate the procedure by ordering a set of simple contrasts. The upper panel of Figure 13 shows the GLM **Univariate: Contrasts** dialog box, which is accessed by clicking on the **Contrasts ...** button in the GLM **Univariate** dialog box.

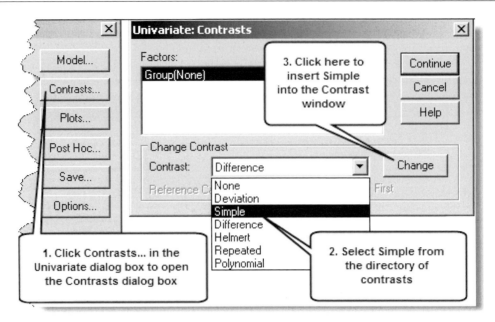

Figure 13. Accessing the **Contrasts** menu in the **Univariate** dialog box

Figure 13 shows how to obtain the directory of contrasts. Move the highlight to **Simple** and click the **Change** button. The **Contrasts** dialog box will now appear as in Figure 14, upper panel. To specify the *Placebo* category as the Reference Category, you will need to click the appropriate radio button at the foot of the dialog box and click change to complete the specification (Figure 14, lower panel).

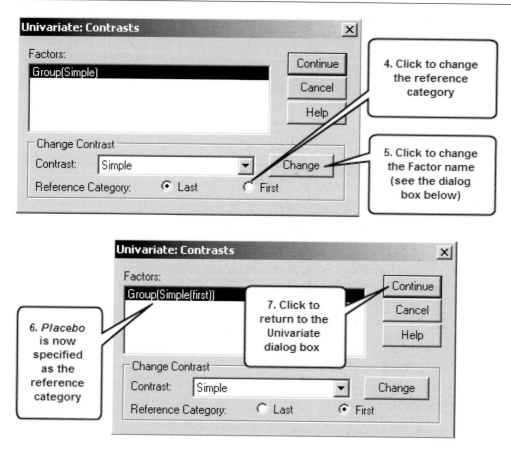

Figure 14. Completing the specifications of simple contrasts with *Placebo* as the reference category.

Output 13 shows part of the table of results of the set of simple contrasts. No *t*-values are given; but if the 95% confidence interval fails to include zero, the contrast is significant. The first test reported in Output 13 is the one we made by specifying the same contrast in the **One-Way ANOVA** procedure. To obtain the value of *t*, we need only divide the 'Contrast Estimate' by the 'Std. Error':

$$t(35) = \frac{-0.10}{1.391} = -0.07 \quad \text{(as before)}$$

Custom Hypothesis Tests

Contrast Results (K Matrix)

		Dependent Variable
		Performance Score
Drug Condition Simple Contrast[a]		
Level 2 vs. Level 1	Contrast Estimate	-.100
	Hypothesized Value	0
	Difference (Estimate - Hypothesized)	-.100
	Std. Error	1.391
	Sig.	.943
	95% Confidence Interval for Difference Lower Bound	-2.901
	Upper Bound	2.701
Level 3 vs. Level 1	Contrast Estimate	4.000
	Hypothesized Value	0
	Difference (Estimate - Hypothesized)	4.000
	Std. Error	1.391
	Sig.	.006
	95% Confidence Interval for Difference Lower Bound	1.199
	Upper Bound	6.801
Level 4 vs. Level 1	Contrast Estimate	6.400

Not significant since p-value > .05

Significant since p-value < .05

Output 13. Part of the simple contrasts output with *Placebo* as the reference category

7.5   TREND ANALYSIS

In the data sets that we have been considering so far, the sets of categories or conditions making up the factor differ only qualitatively, so that the order in which the data for the various levels are entered into the SPSS **Data Editor** is entirely arbitrary. If, however, the levels making up a factor are equally-spaced points on a single quantitative dimension, the question arises as to the nature of the functional relationship between the factor (the independent variable) and the measure (the dependent variable).

Suppose that, in a drug experiment of similar design to our running example, the groups vary, in steps of 10 units, in the size of the dosage of a single drug that they have ingested: the Placebo, Drug10, Drug20, Drug30 and Drug40 groups, receive dosages of 0, 10, 20, 30 and 40, respectively. The profile plot shows a strong positive linear pattern, so we shall run a trend analysis to confirm the existence of this pattern in the population.

The linear trend in the data would be reflected in the linear contrast ψ, where, as usual, $\psi = \sum c_j M_j$, and the coefficients are -2 -1 0 +1 +2

These coefficients are increasing values of a linear function, which means that, associated with this contrast is a sum of squares which represents the variability among the treatment means that can be accounted for in terms of the linear component in the function relationship between performance and speed. This sum of squares can be tested for significance, thus confirming the existence of the trend in the population.

It is quite common for more than one trend to be evident in a set of data. That possibility can be investigated by choosing a set of orthogonal contrasts, each capturing one particular kind of functional relationship (linear, quadratic, cubic and so on). The manner in which this is achieved is described with admirable lucidity by Howell (2007) and Keppel & Wickens (2004).

SPSS offers powerful facilities for the running of trend analyses.

7.5.1 Running a trend analysis in GLM

A trend analysis can be run by choosing the **Polynomial** option in the **Univariate:Contrasts** menu (see Figure 13).

Output 14 shows the results of the trend analysis.

Custom Hypothesis Tests

Contrast Results (K Matrix)

Drug Condition Polynomial Contrast[a]			Dependent Variable Performance Score
Linear	Contrast Estimate		5.218
	Hypothesized Value		0
	Difference (Estimate - Hypothesized)		5.218
	Std. Error	Significant since the p-value < .05	.984
	Sig.		.000
	95% Confidence Interval for Difference	Lower Bound	3.237
		Upper Bound	7.199
Quadratic	Contrast Estimate		-1.149
	Hypothesized Value		0
	Difference (Estimate - Hypothesized)		-1.149
	Std. Error	Not significant since the p-value > .05	.984
	Sig.		.249
	95% Confidence Interval for Difference	Lower Bound	-3.130
		Upper Bound	.832
Cubic	Contrast Estimate		-2.530

Output 14. Section of the output for the trend analysis for polynomial contrasts including linear and quadratic trends

In Output 14, the p-value for the test of linear trend is less than .01, confirming the trend. For the quadratic and remaining trends, the p-values are all very high, indicating that the trend in the data is largely (or wholly) linear.

7.6   POWER

The **power** of a statistical test is determined by several factors, including the size of the samples, the variance of the scores and the sizes of any real differences there may be among the population means. When you are planning an investigation, you will naturally want to have sufficient numbers of participants to ensure that your statistical tests have adequate power to reject the null hypothesis. There is general agreement that a statistical test should have a power of at least .75.

To determine how many participants you will need to achieve a power of .75, you must specify the minimum effect size that you consider to be sufficiently substantial to make the research worthwhile.

The two principal questions about power are as follows:
1.   Given that we wish to achieve a power of 0.75 to detect an effect of medium size, how many participants shall we need in each condition? This is known as the *a priori* power question.
2.   Given a set of data from an experiment, what level of power was actually achieved by the test? This is the *a posteriori* power question.

Clark-Carter (2004) provides a series of tables for use with ANOVA designs, each table giving the sample sizes necessary to achieve specified power levels for a range of effect sizes. Each table is applicable to the ANOVA appropriate for one particular experimental design. Table 15.5.b (p.604) is appropriate for the one-way ANOVA of data from a between subjects experiment with three groups: the table is headed, 'Treatment df = 2'. Entering the table at the column headed $\eta^2 = .059$ (the nearest value to .06 for a medium-sized effect) and choosing the row with the nearest value of power to .75 (namely .74), we find that n = 45 for that row. We shall therefore need a total of 135 participants for the three conditions in the experiment.

An alternative approach to answering *a priori* power questions is to use the **G*Power** software, which is available free on the Internet. By typing the phrase 'Power and effect size' into the Google search window, you can obtain, not only a free copy of G*Power, but also an excellent manual.

Power estimates can also be calculated retrospectively from the data. *A posteriori* estimates of power from the statistics of the data are included in the SPSS output as options.

7.7   ALTERNATIVES TO THE ONE-WAY ANOVA

Monte Carlo studies have shown that the one-way ANOVA is, to some extent, robust to small to moderate violations of the assumptions of the model, such as homogeneity of variance and normality of distribution. It would seem that, if the sample sizes are similar in the various groups, variances can differ by a factor of four without the Type I or Type II error rates rising unacceptably (see Howell, 2007; pp316-7). The risk of error, however, is much increased in data sets with very unequal sample sizes in the groups. Occasionally, a data set, even when 'cleaned up' to the greatest possible extent by the removal of obviously aberrant extreme scores, may still show contraindications against the use of the usual one-way ANOVA. Nonparametric equivalents to ANOVA are available. Since, however, these involve an initial process of converting a scalar data set to ranks (a process which we might term 'ordinalisation'), we do not think they should be used as a matter of course.

The techniques described by Welch (1951) and Brown & Forsythe (1974) were specially designed for use with data sets showing marked heterogeneity of variance. They are reported to keep the error rates within acceptable limits. Both are available within SPSS.

There is one kind of data, however, that has been the focus of dispute more than almost any other, namely, ratings. From a psychological point of view, the use of anchor points seems to impart ratings with a quality that a set of ranks would lack. Many journal editors, however, when presented with the ANOVA of data in the form of ratings, are uneasy about the unquestionable fact that with ratings, means and variances tend to be associated; indeed the variance is artificially constrained by the nature of the measure being used. They would prefer the researcher to use a nonparametric equivalent of ANOVA, such as the **Kruskal-Wallis** test (see the next section). When the data are at the ordinal or nominal level of measurement in the first place, the researcher has no choice but to use a nonparametric technique.

7.7.1   The Kruskal-Wallis k-sample test

This nonparametric equivalent of ANOVA was designed for use with scalar data from a one-factor, between subjects experiment. In such a test, the data are converted to ranks and the distribution of the ranks among the various groups determines the value of the test statistic.

Proceed as follows:

- **Choose➜Analyze➜Nonparametric Tests➜K Independent Samples...** (Figure 15) to open the **Tests for Several Independent Samples** dialog box (the completed version is shown in Figure 16).

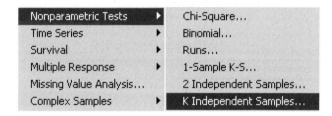

Figure 15. Part of the **Analyze** menu showing **Nonparametric Tests** and its submenu with **K Independent Samples** selected

- Transfer the variable names and define the range of the grouping variable as shown in Figure 16.
- Since the **Exact** tests can take some time, we shall content ourselves with the **asymptotic** p-value.
- Click **OK**.

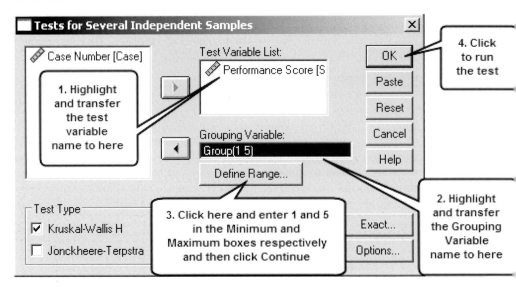

Figure 16. The **Tests for Several Independent Samples** dialog box

The test results are shown in Output 15.

Kruskal-Wallis Test

Ranks

	Drug Condition	N	Mean Rank
Score	Placebo	10	12.95
	Drug A	10	13.10
	Drug B	10	31.50
	Drug C	10	36.60
	Drug D	10	33.35
	Total	50	

Test Statistics[a,b]

	Performance Score
Chi-Square	25.376
df	4
Asymp. Sig.	.000

With a p-value < .01, the result is significant at the .01 level

a. Kruskal Wallis Test

b. Grouping Variable: Drug Condition

Output 15. The **Kruskal-Wallis One-Way ANOVA** output

The first subtable, **Ranks**, tabulates the mean rank for each group. The second subtable, **Test Statistics**, lists the value of Chi-Square, its *df* and its p-value (**Asymp. Sig.**). Since the p-value is much smaller than 0.01, the Kruskal-Wallis test agrees with the parametric test that the five groups do not perform equally well. We can report this result as follow:

> The mean rank under the Placebo is 12.95 and for Drugs A to D is respectively 13.10, 31.50, 36.60 and 33.35. The Kruskal-Wallis chi-square test is significant beyond the .01 level: $\chi^2(4) = 25.38$; $p < .01$.

7.7.2 Dichotomous nominal data: the chi-square test

Suppose that participants in an experiment are divided randomly into three equally-sized groups: two experimental groups (Group A and Group B) and a Control group (Group C). Each participant is tested with a criterion problem, a 1 being recorded if they pass, and a 0 if they fail.

See Chap. 11

This experiment would result in a nominal data set. With such data, a **chi-square test** for association can be used to test the null hypothesis that, in the population, there is no tendency for the criterion problem to be solved more often in some conditions than in others (see Chapter 11).

Recommended reading

There are available several excellent and readable textbooks on analysis of variance. Two excellent examples are:

Howell, D. C. (2007). *Statistical methods for psychology (6th ed.)*. Belmont, CA: Thomson/Wadsworth.

Keppel, G., & Wickens, T. D. (2004). *Design and analysis: A researcher's handbook (4th ed.)*. Upper Saddle River, NJ: Pearson Prentice Hall.

Both books also present ANOVA in the context of the **general linear model** (GLM).

EXERCISE 11

One-factor between subjects ANOVA

Before you start

We suggest that you review the material in Chapter 7 before working through this practical Exercise.

The purpose of a one-factor between subjects ANOVA

In one-factor between subjects ANOVA, the **F ratio** compares the spread among the treatment means with the (supposedly uniform) spread of the scores within groups about their group means. The purpose of this Exercise is to help clarify the rationale of the F ratio by showing how its value is affected by various manipulations of some (or all) of the data. Before proceeding with this Exercise, we ask you to suppose that a one-factor ANOVA has been carried out upon a set of data and yields an F value of, say, 7.23. Now suppose we were to multiply every score in the experimental results by a constant, say 10. What would happen to the value of F: would it still be 7.23? Or would it increase? Or decrease?

We also invite you to speculate upon the effect that adding a constant (say 10) to all the scores in just one of the groups would have upon F: suppose, for example, we were to add 10 to all the scores in the group with the largest mean. Would F stay the same, increase or decrease in value? Would the effect be the same if the constant were added to the scores of the group with the smallest mean?

As a first approach to answering these questions, we shall carry out a **one-factor ANOVA** on a set of data. Then we shall see what happens to the value of F when the data are transformed as described in the previous paragraphs.

Some data

Suppose a researcher is interested in how well non-Chinese-speaking students can learn Chinese characters using different kinds of mnemonic. Independent groups of participants are tested under three conditions: No Mnemonic, Mnemonic 1 and Mnemonic 2. The dependent variable is the number of Chinese characters that are correctly recalled. The data are shown in Table 1.

Table 1. Results of a completely randomised experiment on the effects of different mnemonic systems upon recall of logographic characters										
No Mnemonic (10 control subjects)	4	6	4	3	5	7	10	4	9	11
Mnemonic 1 (10 subjects trained in Mnemonic 1)	11	9	16	10	12	17	18	16	8	11
Mnemonic 2 (10 subjects trained in Mnemonic 2)	21	16	15	16	18	11	9	12	19	20

Opening SPSS

Open SPSS and select the **Type in data** radio button in the opening window.   If **Data View** appears first, click the **Variable View** tab to open **Variable View**.

Construction of the SPSS data set

Rearrange the data of Table 1 into a form suitable for analysis by SPSS by following the procedure described in Sections 2.1.5 and 7.3.1. In **Variable View**, name the variables *Case*, *Group*, *Score*, remembering to change the value in the **Decimals** column to 0 each time. The variable *Group* will need appropriate values and value labels specified in the **Values** column. It is also recommended that variable labels should be entered in the **Label** column e.g. *Case Number, Training Condition*.

Switch to **Data View** and enter the data. The easiest way of entering the case numbers is to wait until all the other data have been entered. Then access **Compute** and enter *Case* as the **Target Variable** and *$casenum* as the **Numeric Expression**. All the case numbers will automatically appear in the *Case* column of **Data View**.

Save the data set to a file such as *Ex11 Mnemonics*.

Exploring the data

As always, we recommend a preliminary exploration of the data set before any formal testing is carried out, in case there have been any data entry errors or contraindications for using ANOVA. As in Exercise 8, use the **Means** procedure for descriptive statistics and **Explore** for checks on the distributions of the scores within the groups. (Remember to click the **Plots** radio button to suppress the **Statistics** output. This will save you from being swamped with superfluous statistics.)

The output for **Means** begins with a **Case Processing Summary** table, followed by a table labelled **Report** listing the means, number of cases (N) and standard deviations for the three groups.

- **Examine the output for the Means procedure. Do the means appear to differ? Are the standard deviations similar in value?**

The output for **Explore** begins with a **Case Processing Summary** table, followed by the stem-and-leaf displays for the three groups. The final item shows the side-by-side boxplots.

- Do the boxplots suggest any anomalies in the distributions of the data in any of the three groups? Write a statement assessing the suitability of the data for ANOVA.

Procedure for the one-way ANOVA in GLM

The procedure for the one-way ANOVA is described in detail in Section 7.3.4. Remember to click the **Post Hoc...** button, select **Tukey** and click **Continue** to return to the **Univariate** dialog box. This is because if the ANOVA F-ratio is significant, you will want to know which pairs of means differ significantly.

Click **OK** to run the ANOVA and the multiple comparisons procedure.

Output for the one-way ANOVA

Examine the ANOVA Summary Table.

- Write down the value of *F* and its associated p-value. Is *F* significant? What are the implications of this result for the experimental hypothesis? What was the null hypothesis? What does the falsity of the null hypothesis imply?

Look at the table of **Multiple Comparisons**.

- Note which pairs of levels are significantly different and which are not.

RE-ANALYSIS OF TRANSFORMED DATA SETS

In this section, we return to the question of the effects of transforming the data upon the ANOVA statistics.

1)   Multiplying every score by a constant

We recommend that whenever you have occasion to transform the values of a variable in an original SPSS data set, you should construct a new target variable, rather than change (perhaps irreversibly) the original data. Use the **Compute** procedure (Section 4.4.2) to multiply each value in the data set by a factor of 10. Follow the instructions in that section, choosing, for the target variable, a mnemonic name such as *AllByTen*. Now change the **One-way ANOVA** dialog box so that the dependent variable is *AllByTen* instead of *Score* and click **OK** to run the analysis.

- Write down the value of *F* and its associated p-value. Is *F* significant? What are the implications of this result for the experimental hypothesis?

In the output, you will see that both the between groups and within groups variance estimates have increased by a factor of 100. It is easy to show algebraically that when each of a set of scores is multiplied by a constant, the new variance is the old variance times the square of the constant. Since, however, the factors of 100 in the numerator and denominator of the *F* ratio cancel out, the value of the *F* ratio remains unchanged.

2)   Adding a constant to the scores in only one group

This time, we want a dependent variable that contains, for two of the three groups, the original scores. In the third (Mnemonic 2) group, however, every score must be increased by 10. To preserve the original scores of the third group safely as well, we shall use two computing operations: (1) we shall copy all the scores to a new variable; (2) we shall add a constant of 10 to the scores of the third group only. First use **Compute** to copy the values in *Score* to a new target variable *NewScore*. Use **Compute** again to add *10* to the numbers in this new variable **only when the grouping variable has the value** *3*. To do this, type *NewScore* into the **Target Variable** box and *NewScore +10* in the **Numeric Expression** box. Click **If** to open the **Compute Variable: If Cases** dialog box. Transfer the grouping variable name *Group* into the box and add the expression *=3*. Click **Continue** and **OK** to run the procedure. In **Data View**, check that the values in *NewScore* for the third group have changed but the rest have their original values. Now re-run the **one-way ANOVA**, using *NewScore* as the dependent variable.

- **Write down the value of *F* and its associated p-value. Is *F* significant? What are the implications of this result for the experimental hypothesis?**

You will see that the effect of adding a constant of *10* to all scores in the *Mnemonic 2* group has no effect at all upon the within groups variance estimate. Adding the same constant to all the scores in a set has no effect upon the spread of the scores – it merely shifts the mean. The between groups mean square, however, computed from the values of the treatment means alone, has increased considerably. The within groups mean square, on the other hand, is the average of the variance estimates of the scores within groups and is quite independent of the spread among the group means. Consequently, it is quite possible to change the value of the former without affecting that of the latter and vice versa. The effect of increasing the mean of the third group is to increase the spread of the three treatment means. This increases the value of $MS_{between}$ while leaving MS_{within} unaltered. The result is an increase in *F*.

Finishing the session

Close down SPSS and any other windows before logging out of the network.

CHAPTER 8

Between subjects factorial experiments

8.1   INTRODUCTION

Experiments with two or more factors are known as **factorial** experiments. In the simplest case, there is a different sample of participants for each possible combination of conditions. This arrangement is known as a **between subjects** (or **completely randomised**) factorial experiment.

8.1.1   An experiment with two treatment factors

Suppose that a researcher has been commissioned to investigate the effects upon simulated driving performance of two new anti-hay fever drugs, A and B. It is suspected that at least one of the drugs may have different effects upon fresh and tired drivers, and the firm developing the drugs needs to ensure that neither has an adverse effect upon driving performance.

The researcher decides to carry out a two-factor factorial experiment, in which the factors are:
1. **Drug Treatment**, with levels **Placebo, Drug A** and **Drug B**;
2. **Alertness**, with levels **Fresh** and **Tired.**

All participants are asked to take a flavoured drink which contains either (in the **Drug A** and **Drug B** conditions) a small quantity of the drug or (in the control or **Placebo** condition) no drug. Half the participants are tested immediately on rising; the others are tested after twenty hours of sleep deprivation. A different sample of ten participants is tested under each of the six treatment combinations: (Fresh, Placebo); (Fresh, Drug A); (Fresh, Drug B); (Tired, Placebo); (Tired, Drug A); (Tired, Drug B).

Notice that in this experiment, each level of either factor is to be found in combination with every level of the other. The two factors are said to **cross**. There are experiments in which the factors do not cross: that is, not all combinations of conditions (or groups) are present, but they will not be considered in this book. The two-factor between subjects factorial experiment can be represented as a table in which each row or column represents a particular level of one of the treatment factors, and a **cell** of the table (i.e. a single rectangle in the grid) represents one particular treatment **combination** (Table 1). In Table 1, the cell on the bottom right represents the combination (Tired, Drug B). The ten participants in Group 6 were tested under that particular treatment combination.

Table 1. A completely randomised, two-factor factorial experiment on the effects of two factors upon simulated driving performance

	Levels of the Drug Treatment factor:		
Levels of the Alertness factor:	Placebo	Drug A	Drug B
Fresh	Group 1	Group 2	Group 3
Tired	Group 4	Group 5	Group 6

The mean scores of the participants are shown in Table 2. The row and column means are known as **marginal means**. They are the mean scores at each level of either factor considered separately, ignoring the other factor in the classification: for example, the mean score of all the participants tested after ingesting Drug A, disregarding whether they were fresh or tired, is 15.0; the mean performance of the Tired participants, disregarding which of the three drug conditions to which they had been assigned, is 14.7.

Table 2. Mean scores achieved by the participants in the drugs experiment

	Placebo	Drug A	Drug B	Means
Fresh	21.0	12.0	22.0	18.3
Tired	10.0	18.0	16.0	14.7
Means	15.5	15.0	19.0	16.5

8.1.2 Main effects and interactions

Main effects

In a two-factor experiment, two kinds of treatment effects are possible:
1. **Main effects**;
2. An **interaction**.

Should at least one of the differences among the means for the three levels of the Drug Treatment factor be sufficiently great as to indicate a difference in the population, the Drug

Treatment factor is said to have a **main effect**. Similarly, a large difference between the two row means would indicate that the Alertness factor also has a main effect. Since Table 2 shows that there are indeed marked differences among both row and column marginal means, it looks as if both factors have main effects. Not surprisingly the fresh participants, on average, outperformed the tired participants. In the participants as a whole, Drug A did not produce a higher overall level of performance in comparison with the mean score of those participants who received a placebo. Drug B, on the other hand, did produce a higher overall level of performance.

Simple main effects

Turning now to the cell means in Table 2, another striking feature of the results emerges. Drug A improved the performance of the tired participants in comparison with the tired participants in the Placebo condition. If we look at the fresh participants only, however, we see a sharp dip in performance with Drug A: that is, a dose of this drug actually had an *adverse* effect upon the performance of the fresh participants. Drug B, on the other hand, had no such adverse effect on another sample of fresh participants: the mean performance of the participants under that condition is much the same as that of the placebo group. The corresponding means for the tired participants show a different pattern. Under Drug A, their performance was almost as good as that of the fresh placebo group. Drug B also appears to have improved the performance of the tired participants. It would appear, therefore, that the researcher's suspicions were well founded: Drug A may improve the performance of tired drivers; but it seems to have an adverse effect upon fresh drivers.

The effect of one treatment factor (such as Alertness) at one particular level of another factor (e.g. on the Drug A participants only) is known as a **simple main effect**. From inspection of Table 2, it would appear that the Alertness factor has different simple main effects at different levels of the Drug Treatment factor: its effect is diminished with Drug B and actually reversed with Drug A.

Interactions

When the simple main effects of one treatment factor are not homogeneous at all levels of another, the two factors are said to **interact**. An interaction between two factors, such as Drug Treatment and Alertness, is indicated by a multiplication sign thus: Drug Treatment × Alertness. The results of the experiment, therefore, suggest the presence of a Drug Treatment × Alertness interaction.

8.1.3   Profile plots

The interaction pattern that we have just described can be pictured graphically, as plots of the cell means for the Fresh and the Tired participants against Drug Treatment (see Figure 1). Such graphs are called **profile plots**. In the present example, the Fresh participants' performance profile is V-shaped, plunging under the Drug A condition. The Tired participants' profile, on the other hand, rises to higher levels under both the Drug A and Drug B conditions. The presence of an interaction is indicated by **profile heterogeneity** across the levels of one of the factors, that is, by **non-parallel profiles.** This is certainly the case with the profiles across the three Drug Treatment conditions of the Fresh and Tired participants in the present experiment.

Main effects and interactions are independent: it is quite possible to obtain significant main effects without any significant interaction between the factors; it is also possible to have significant interactions without any significant main effects. The appearance of the profiles in Figure 1, however, is affected partly by the presence of main effects, as well as any interaction that might be present. It is convergence or divergence of the profiles, rather than their separation or slope, that indicates the presence of an interaction. When profiles are parallel, there is no interaction – even if they both slope sharply upwards or downwards or are widely separated on the vertical axis of the graph.

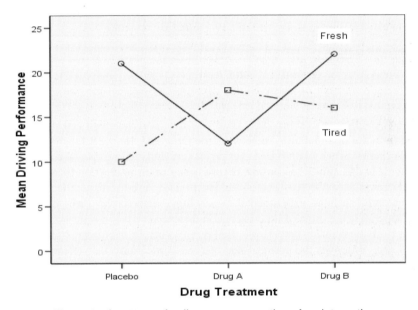

Figure 1. A pattern of cell means suggestive of an interaction

8.2   FACTORIAL ANALYSIS OF VARIANCE

8.2.1   ANOVA summary table

The ANOVA of data from a two-factor completely randomised factorial experiment is an analogical extension of the one-way ANOVA. Table 3 shows the ANOVA summary table for the data summarised in Table 2.

Compared with the one-way ANOVA summary table, the two-way table has some new features. In the first place there are three F statistics: one for each factor considered separately; the third for the interaction. Consistent with our inspection of Table 2, all three tests show significance beyond the .05 level; and the *Alertness* factor and the interaction are significant beyond the .01 level.

Table 3. ANOVA summary table						
Source	**df**	**SS**	**MS**	**F**	**p**	**Partial eta squared**
Main effects						
Alertness (A)	1	201.67	201.67	8.71	<.01	.14
Drug (D)	2	190.00	95.00	4.10	.02	.13
Interaction						
Interaction (A×D)	2	763.33	381.67	16.49	<.01	.38
Within groups (Error)	54	1250.00	23.15			
Total	59	2405.0				

The two-way ANOVA, therefore, has confirmed the most interesting feature of the data, namely, the presence of an interaction between the *Drug* and *Alertness* factors: while the *Drug* improved the performance of the tired participants, it impeded the performance of the fresh participants. It is this ability to confirm the existence of an interaction that accounts for the fact that the factorial ANOVA is one of the most widely used statistical techniques in some fields of research, such as experimental psychology; indeed, the main effects of factors considered separately are often of little interest in themselves. It is not surprising, for example, to learn that fresh participants outperform tired participants. It is of interest, however, to learn that while a drug improves the performance of tired participants, that effect is reversed with fresh participants.

8.2.2   Reporting the results of the two-way ANOVA

The results of the three F tests shown in Table 3 should be reported by specifying the name of the factor, followed by the value of the F ratio (with the df of the numerator and denominator separated by a comma in brackets) and the p-value as follows:

For the Alertness factor: $F(1, 54) = 8.71$; $p < .01$; partial eta squared = .14.
For the Drug factor: $F(2, 54) = 4.10$; $p = .02$; partial eta squared = .13.
For the interaction: $F(2, 54) = 16.49$; $p < .01$; partial eta squared = .38.

The general form of a report on an F test is as follows:

$$F(df_{source}, df_{error}) = \langle value\ of\ F \rangle;\ p = \langle probability \rangle;\ partial\ eta\ squared = \langle value \rangle$$

As always, however, the reader should never be confronted with the result of a statistical test without further information. The values of the descriptive statistics must also be immediately available, either in a written commentary or in a nearby table. Additional statistics, such as measures of effect size (see below), should also be given. The following report embodies these requirements. Note that p-values are given to two places of decimals only; with probabilities less than .01, the inequality sign < is used thus: $p < .01$.

The mean Driving Performance scores for the Fresh and Tired conditions of the Alertness factor (see Table 3) differed significantly beyond the .01 level: $F(1, 54) = 8.71; p < .01$. Partial eta squared = .14 representing a large effect. The mean Driving Performance scores for the two Drug conditions and the Placebo condition (Drug Treatment factor) differed significantly at the 5% level: $F(2, 54) = 4.10; p = .02$. Partial eta squared = .13 representing a large effect. The mean Driving Performance scores for the interaction of Alertness and Drug differed significantly beyond the .01 level: $F(2, 54) = 16.49; p < .01$. Partial eta squared = .38, representing a large effect.

The precise manner in which the quantities in Table 2 are calculated is lucidly described in many excellent textbooks, such as Howell (2007) and Keppel & Wickens (2004). Here, we merely draw your attention to one or two further additional features of the ANOVA summary table.

8.2.3 The partition of the total sum of squares

We have seen that, in the context of a single data set, the total sum of squares can be viewed as representing the total variability in the scores. In the one-way ANOVA, SS_{total} is **partitioned**, so that it is seen as the sum of between groups and within groups components, namely, $SS_{between}$ and SS_{within}:

$$SS_{total} = SS_{between} + SS_{within}$$

In the two-way ANOVA, the between groups sum of squares is further partitioned into three components, one for each main effect and the third for the interaction:

$$SS_{between} = SS_{Alertness} + SS_{Drug} + SS_{Alertness \times Drug}$$

8.2.4 Degrees of freedom of the three treatment sources of variance

Recall that in the one-way ANOVA of data from an experiment with k treatment groups, the degrees of freedom (df) of the between groups mean square is the number of treatment groups minus one: $df = k - 1$. In a similar way, in a two-way ANOVA, the degrees of freedom of each of the source mean squares for main effects is the number of levels making up the source, minus one: thus for the *Alertness* factor (Fresh, Tired), df = 1; for the *Drug* factor (Placebo, Drug A, Drug B), df = 2.

Turning now to the degrees of freedom of the interaction, the rule is as follows: the degrees of freedom of an interaction mean square is the product of the degrees of freedom of the factors involved. Since $df_{Alertness} = 1$ and $df_{Drug} = 2$, $df_{interaction} = 1 \times 2 = 2$, which is the value in the two-way ANOVA summary table.

In general, let Factor A and Factor B have a and b levels, respectively. The degrees of freedom of their interaction $(df_{interaction}) = (a - 1)(b - 1)$.

In Chapter 7, we noted an isomorphism between the sums of squares and the degrees of freedom, so that the identities that hold for sums of squares hold also for the degrees of freedom. This is true in the two-way ANOVA also. Notice that in Table 3, the total degrees of freedom is the sum of the degrees of freedom for all the sources of variance:

$$df_{total} = df_{Alertness} + df_{Drug} + df_{Alertness \times Drug}$$

8.2.5   The three *F* ratios

In ANOVA, an *F* ratio always has the general form:

$$F = \frac{MS_{source}}{MS_{error}}$$

In the two-way ANOVA, the numerator can be any of the three source mean squares MS_{Drug}, $MS_{Alertness}$ or $MS_{interaction}$.

In the two-way ANOVA, the error term is MS_{within} which, as in the one-way ANOVA, is the mean of the variance estimates from all the samples in the experiment. In the one-way ANOVA for a one-factor experiment with *k* treatment groups, there is a variance estimate for every condition or group. In the equal-n case (i.e., there are equal numbers of participants in all treatment conditions), there will be *k* variance estimates, each with n – 1 df. The df of MS_{within} is therefore k(n – 1) = N – k, where N is the total number of observations in the experiment and *n* is the number of observations at each level of the single treatment factor.

In the two-way ANOVA, MS_{within} is the average of the variance estimates from the data in all cells, that is, the variances of the scores achieved by the participants who were tested at different combinations of levels of the two factors. If A and B are the factors in the experiment, comprising *a* and *b* conditions or groups, respectively, there will be a × b cells altogether. In the equal-n case, there will be a variance estimate for each of these cells, each estimate having n – 1 df. The df of MS_{within}, therefore, is ab(n – 1) = abdn – ab = N – ab. Returning to Table 3, we note that since there are six possible treatment combinations, df_{within} = 60 – 6 = 54, which is the value given in the table.

In the two-way ANOVA, the three *F* ratios all have the same denominator or error term, namely, the pooled **within cell** estimate MS_{within}:

$$F_{Alertness} = \frac{MS_{Alertness}}{MS_{within}} ; \ F_{Drug} = \frac{MS_{Drug}}{MS_{within}} ; \ F_{interaction} = \frac{MS_{interaction}}{MS_{within}}$$

You can check that in Table 3, all three *F* ratios have the same divisor.

8.3   FURTHER ANALYSIS

In Chapter 7, we observed that the ANOVA itself is usually merely the first stage in the analysis of a set of data from a complex experiment: inevitably, further analysis will be required to clarify the results of the initial ANOVA tests. In the first place, the researcher will wish to establish the strength of the effects the experiment has demonstrated. It will also be necessary to pinpoint and confirm differences among the treatment or group means.

8.3.1   Measuring effect size in the two-way ANOVA

In Chapter 7, we introduced the measure of effect size known as **eta-squared** (η^2) which is the proportion of variance in the dependent variable accounted for by differences in the levels of the independent variable. In the case of the one-way ANOVA, η^2 is defined as follows:

> See
> Section
> 7.3.3

$$\eta^2 = \frac{SS_{\text{treatment}}}{SS_{\text{total}}} = \frac{SS_{\text{between}}}{SS_{\text{total}}}$$

Complete eta squared

Let Factor 1 and Factor 2 be the factors in a two-way ANOVA. We have seen that in the two-way ANOVA, there are three between groups sources of variance: two main effect sources and the interaction. For Factor 1, the **complete η^2** is defined as follows:

$$\eta^2 = \frac{SS_{\text{F1}}}{SS_{\text{total}}} = \frac{SS_{\text{F1}}}{SS_{\text{F1}} + SS_{\text{F2}} + SS_{\text{F1}\times\text{F2}} + SS_{\text{within}}}$$

Partial eta squared

Some authors prefer an alternative form of η^2, called **partial η^2** or **η_p^2** in which the variance of the sums of squares for a particular effect is expressed as a proportion, not of the total sum of squares, but of the sum of squares of that effect plus the error sum of squares:

$$\eta_p^2 = \frac{SS_{\text{treatment}}}{SS_{\text{treatment}} + SS_{\text{error}}}$$

SPSS provides this statistic (**Estimates of effect size**) as an option within the **Options...** dialog box. The choice between the **complete η^2** and **partial η^2** statistics will depend upon the experiment and purpose of the investigation (see Keppel & Wickens, 2004; p. 235).

Omega squared

The eta squared measures of effect size are purely descriptive: they do not allow for the **shrinkage** that results with repeated sampling. In other words, as a point estimate of effect size in the population, eta squared is positively biased. The **omega squared** statistics allow for shrinkage through sampling error and remove the positive bias in eta squared.

The omega squared statistics corresponding to eta squared and partial eta squared are, respectively, **complete omega squared (ω^2)** and **partial omega squared (ω_p^2)** – see Keppel & Wickens, 2004; pp. 232 – 233. Here we reproduce the table from Chapter 7 comparing Cohen's measure of effect size with eta squared.

Table 4. Cohen's classification of effect size, with equivalent values of eta squared. (Table reproduced from Chapter 7)		
Effect size (d)	**Eta squared**	**Size of Effect**
$0.2 \le d < 0.5$	$.01 \le \eta^2 < .06$	Small
$0.5 \le d < 0.8$	$.06 \le \eta^2 < .14$	Medium
$d \ge 0.8$	$\eta^2 \ge .14$	Large

8.3.2 How many participants shall I need for my two-factor experiment?

For simplicity, we usually work with miniature data sets, specially prepared to illustrate certain patterns and make transparent the way in which statistics are calculated. In a real research situation, the data would show much more spread, and we should have to test many more participants to achieve tests of sufficient power. But how many people would we need to test in order to achieve, say, a power of .8?

Clark-Carter (2004) provides a series of tables for use with ANOVA experiments, each table giving the value of 'n' necessary to achieve specified power levels for a range of effect sizes, where (for one-factor experiments) n is the number of participants required for each combination of conditions. These tables can also be used for factorial experiments: each table is applicable to an ANOVA source with a fixed number of degrees of freedom, irrespective of whether the source is a main effect or an interaction. With one-factor experiments, the 'n' in the table is simply the sample size. Where an experiment has two or more factors, however, the value of 'n' given in the table is not the sample size you will need to achieve a test of a specified power. Hereafter, in the context of a factorial experiment only, we shall refer to 'n' in the table as n(tabled). The quantity n(tabled) and the one we want (n) are related as follows:

$$n(tabled) = \frac{df_{error}}{df_{treatment} + 1} + 1 \qquad (1)$$

Since our target sample size n is a term in the error degrees of freedom, the value of n can easily be obtained from n(tabled) by using the following formula:

$$n = \frac{(df_{treatment} + 1)(n(tabled) - 1)}{\text{number of treatment combinations}} + 1 \qquad (2)$$

Returning to our planned two-factor factorial experiment on Drugs and Driving, what is the sample size n that would be needed to achieve a power of .80 to reject the null hypothesis in the presence of an effect of 'medium' size ($\eta^2 = .06$)? Considering the Drug Treatment factor, $df = 2$. Consulting Table A15.5 in Clark-Carter's book (2004; p.603), we find that n(tabled) = 50.

Substituting in formula (2), we have $n = \dfrac{3 \times 49}{6} + 1 = 25.5$ (i.e. 26) which means that we shall require a total of $6 \times 26 = 156$ participants for the experiment.

8.3.3 Making multiple comparisons among the treatment means

We now enter an area of controversy. A data set from a complex experiment with two or more treatment factors is likely to show some interesting patterns: the more complex the experiment, the more likely you are to find something interesting in the results. You will naturally wish to confirm that an interesting finding has not merely been turned up by sampling variability and will therefore want to make several (perhaps many) tests of significance over and above the original ANOVA F tests. The problem is that the more significance tests you make, the more significant results you will obtain – even if the null hypothesis is true!

By making many tests of significance without taking certain precautions, the researcher is 'capitalising upon chance'. In order to avoid such capitalisation, the researcher must make conservative tests. Unfortunately, there has been much dispute about which of several possible strategies one should follow. Here, we can touch upon only a few of the most common approaches.

8.3.4 The further analysis of interactions

When the ANOVA F test has shown that an interaction is significant, the researcher often has follow-up questions. In Figure 2, we have re-plotted the means from the drug experiment, so that the profiles are now *Drug* conditions and on the horizontal axis are the levels of the *Alertness* factor.

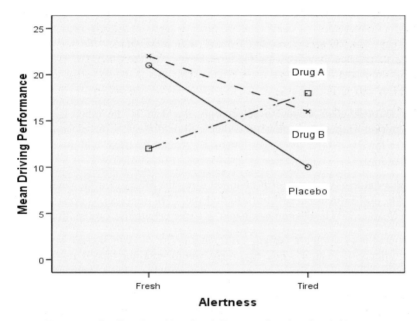

Figure 2. Profile plot of levels of *Drug* against levels of *Alertness*

From the graph it seems that, in the Fresh participants, performance is considerably better under the Placebo and Drug B conditions than it was under Drug A; whereas in the Tired participants, performance with both drugs seems superior to performance under the Placebo condition. Are these differences significant?

One approach to the problem of making conservative multiple comparisons among the individual means is to inform SPSS that this is really a one-factor experiment with six groups and request a **Tukey** test. The problem with that approach is that, even with an array of six means, the number of possible comparisons is quite large and this is reflected in a large critical value for the **studentized range statistic q**. In the next subsection, we shall describe another strategy, which has the advantage of providing a justification for defining a smaller comparison 'family' and avoiding a test that is so conservative that nothing turns out to be significant.

8.3.5   Testing for simple main effects

We have seen that in a factorial experiment, a **simple main effect** is the effect of a factor at one particular level of another.   In our drug experiment, for example, there is a simple main effect of the *Drug* factor at each of the two levels of the *Alertness* factor.

In general, let A and B be the factors in a two-factor between subjects factorial experiment, with levels (A1, A2, ...) and (B1, B2, ...), respectively. We are concerned with the simple effects of A at B1, B2, and so on, and with the simple main effects of B at A1, A2, and so on.

In the present example, one way of testing for simple main effects of the *Drug* factor at the Fresh and Tired levels of the *Alertness* factor would be to proceed as follows:
Select **Data➔Select Cases** to select data at the target level only of the *Alertness* factor.

Carry out a one-way ANOVA on the data at that level of *Alertness* only.   If there is homogeneity of variance, however, use the term MS_{within} for the whole two-way data set as the error term for the *F* test for a simple main effect. This use of the full error term will improve the power of the test.

Then select **Data➔Select Cases** to select only the data at the other target level of the *Alertness* factor and repeat the entire procedure. Should there be heterogeneity of variance, the error term for the data at the target level only should be used, with a substantial loss in degrees of freedom.

To obtain the p-value of the value of *F* obtained using the MS_{within} for the whole experiment as the error term, use **Transform➔Compute** and the **CDF** function to obtain the p-value, as described in Chapter 7. The desired p-value is 1 – (the cumulative probability of F).

If the experiment is of complex design, with many levels of A or B, and we were to test for simple main effects of A at B1, B2, etc., there would be a heightened risk that at least one comparison would show significance, even if the null hypothesis were actually true.   To control the Type 1 error rate, the **Bonferroni** procedure can be used: simply set the *per comparison* significance level at .05 divided by the number of levels in the locating factor for the simple effect.

If the presence of a simple main effect has been confirmed in this way, the **Tukey** test (or an equivalent test, such as the Bonferroni) can be used to make comparisons among the cell means at that particular level of the locating factor.   The user need only calculate the **Studentized Range statistic** and enter the table of critical values for *q* as if the cell means in the simple main effect were the only ones in the analysis. The simple effects analysis has provided justification for reducing the size of the comparison family and permitted a somewhat more powerful test.

8.4   THE TWO-WAY ANOVA WITH SPSS

Table 5 shows the raw data from the two-factor factorial **Drug × Alertness** experiment.

Levels of the Alertness factor:	Levels of the Drug Treatment factor:		
	Placebo	**A**	**B**
Fresh	24 25 13 22 16	18 8 9 14 16	27 14 19 29 27
	23 18 19 24 26	15 6 9 8 17	23 19 17 20 25
Tired	13 12 14 16 17	21 24 22 23 20	21 11 14 22 19
	13 4 3 2 6	13 11 17 13 16	9 14 11 21 18

Table 5. Results of the Drug Treatment × Alertness factorial experiment

8.4.1   Preparing the data for the factorial ANOVA

Since there are two factors, two **grouping variables** will be required to specify the treatment combination under which each score was achieved. If the grouping variables are *Alertness* and *Drug*, and performance in the driving simulator is *DrivePerf*, the data file will consist of a column for case numbers, two for the grouping variables, and a fourth for *DrivePerf*.

Proceed as follows:

- In **Variable View**, use the **Name** column to create the four named variables, as described in Chapter 2, Section 2.3.
- In the **Decimals** column, change the values to *0* to display whole numbers.
- In the **Label** column, enter informative variable labels, such as *Case Number, Alertness, Drug Treatment,* and *Driving Performance*.
- In the **Values** column, add values and labels for the grouping variables, such as *1* and *2* (with labels *Fresh* and *Tired*, respectively) for the variable *Alertness* and *1, 2,* and *3* (with labels *Placebo, Drug A,* and *Drug B*, respectively) for the variable *Drug*.
- Enter **Data View**. To display the labels for the values entered for the grouping variables, check the View menu to make sure that **Value Labels** is ticked.

See Section 2.3

Part of the completed data set is shown in Figure 3.

Case	Alertness	Drug	DrivingPerf
27	Fresh	Drug B	19
28	Fresh	Drug B	17
29	Fresh	Drug B	20
30	Fresh	Drug B	25
31	Tired	Placebo	13
32	Tired	Placebo	12
33	Tired	Placebo	14
34	Tired	Placebo	16

Figure 3. Part of **Data View** showing some of the data from Table 5

Note that the values for the grouping variables *Alertness* and *Drug Treatment* have been replaced by their corresponding labels. For example, in case 28, the value *1* has been replaced by *Fresh* and *2* has been replaced by *Drug B*. Likewise, in case 31, the value *2* has been replaced by *Tired* and *1* by *Placebo*.

8.4.2   Exploring the data: Obtaining boxplots

Before running the ANOVA, it is important to explore the data to check for any problems with the distributions.

To obtain the boxplots under each of the six treatment combinations, proceed as follows:
- Choose
  Graphs➔Chart Builder... and select **Boxplot** from the gallery.
- Drag the **Clustered Boxplot** image to the **Chart preview** and fill in the variable names with *Driving Performance* in the **Y-Axis** box, *Drug Treatment* in the **X-Axis** box and *Alertness* in the **Cluster: set pattern** box.
- Complete the details as in Section 5.4 to obtain the boxplot (Output1).

These boxplots show no extreme cases, which would have been flagged with an asterisk. (See Chapter 4, Table 2, for details of the structure of a boxplot.) None of the distributions is markedly skewed. There is therefore no need to remove any cases or apply a transformation to make the distribution more symmetrical. We can safely proceed with the ANOVA.

> See Table 2 in Chap. 4

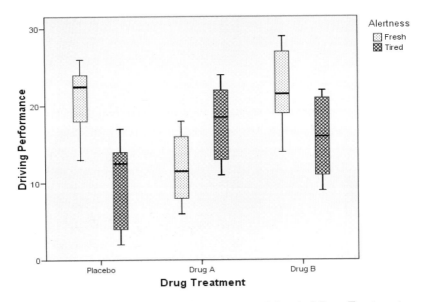

Output 1. Boxplots clustered for *Alertness* at each level of *Drug Treatment*

8.4.3   Choosing a factorial ANOVA

In SPSS, a factorial ANOVA is run by choosing from the **General Linear Model (GLM)** menu (see Figure 7 in Chapter 7).

For a between subjects factorial ANOVA, we must choose the **Univariate** option, bearing in mind that, although there are two independent variables (factors), namely, *Drug Treatment* and

Alertness, there is only one dependent variable, *Driving Performance*. See Figure 8 in Chapter 7 for details.

WLS Weight

The **WLS Weight** box in Chapter 8, Figure 7, is used for identifying a variable containing weights for weighted least-squares analysis. We do not consider this type of analysis in this book.

Factors with Fixed and Random effects

The box labelled **Random Factor(s)** in Chapter 8, Figure 7 is used only if the levels of a factor are a random sample of possible levels (Section 7.1). In practice, this is rare, and most treatment factors have **fixed effects**. In the present example, *Alertness* and *Drug Treatment* are fixed effects factors.

Analysis of covariance

We have seen (Chapter 7) that there are techniques known as **Analysis of Covariance (ANCOVA)** that essentially remove the effects of covariates upon the scores and re-run the ANOVA on a 'purified' data set. The advantage of ANCOVA is often a reduction of 'data noise' and a resulting increase in the power of the ANOVA tests. To run an ANCOVA, transfer the name(s) of the covariate(s) into the covariate box.

Profile plots

To obtain a profile plot of the means, click **Plots…** in the **Univariate** dialog box (Chapter 7, Figure 8) to open the **Univariate: Profile Plots** dialog box and follow the steps in Figure 4.

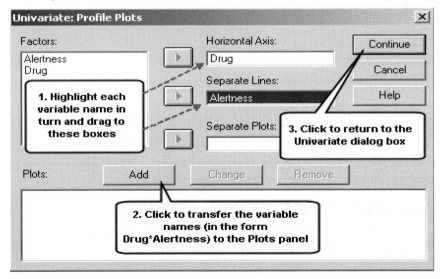

Figure 4. The **Profile Plots** dialog box for plotting *Drug*Alertness* i.e. plotting *Drug* along the horizontal axis with the separate lines representing the levels of *Alertness*

8.4.4   Output for a factorial ANOVA

The results are shown in Output Listings 2-5. The table in Output 2, **Between-Subjects Factors**, summarises the factor names and level labels, together with the number of cases at each level.

Between-Subjects Factors

		Value Label	N
Alertness	1	Fresh	30
	2	Tired	30
Drug Treatment	1	Placebo	20
	2	Drug A	20
	3	Drug B	20

Output 2. The table of **Between-Subjects Factors**

Output 3 is the table of descriptive statistics requested from **Options...** .

Descriptive Statistics

Dependent Variable: Driving Performance

Alertness	Drug Treatment	Mean	Std. Deviation	N
Fresh	Placebo	21.00	4.29	10
	Drug A	12.00	4.42	10
	Drug B	22.00	4.94	10
	Total	18.33	6.35	30
Tired	Placebo	10.00	5.66	10
	Drug A	18.00	4.64	10
	Drug B	16.00	4.78	10
	Total	14.67	5.97	30
Total	Placebo	15.50	7.47	20
	Drug A	15.00	5.38	20
	Drug B	19.00	5.65	20
	Total	16.50	6.38	60

Output 3. The table of **Descriptive Statistics**

The table in Output 4, **Tests of Between-Subjects Effects**, is the ANOVA summary table, which tabulates the sources of variation, their **Sums of Squares**, degrees of freedom (**df**), mean squares, **F** ratios and p-values (**Sig.**).   Note that, in the between subjects factorial ANOVA, each F ratio is the Mean Square for the source divided by the Error Mean Square (23.15). The final column **Partial Eta Squared** is the estimate of effect size (explained in Section 8.3).

This table was edited in **SPSS Viewer** to reduce three decimal places to two. This was done by double-clicking the whole table so that it showed a hashed border, highlighting the five columns of numbers so that they were shown in inverse video, clicking the right-hand mouse button to show a menu, selecting the item **Cell Properties…**, selecting in the **Format** box the item **#.#**, changing the number of decimals shown in the **Decimals** box to *2*, and finally clicking **OK**.

| Ignore these rows | Of interest for ANOVA is the value of *F* and its associated p-value | Values of η_p^2 are about 14% and 40% |

Tests of Between-Subjects Effects

Dependent Variable: Driving Performance

Source	Type III Sum of Squares	df	Mean Square	F	Sig.	Partial Eta Squared
Corrected Model	1155.00[a]	5	231.00	9.98	.000	.480
Intercept	16335.00	1	16335.0	705.67	.000	.929
Alertness	201.67	1	201.67	8.71	.005	.139
Drug	190.00	2	95.00	4.10	.022	.132
Alertness * Drug	763.33	2	381.67	16.48	.000	.379
Error	1250.00	54	23.15			
Total	18740.00	60				
Corrected Total	2405.00	59				

a. R Squared = .480 (Adjusted R Squared = .432)

| *Alertness* and the interaction *Alertness*Drug* have p-values < .01 (i.e. they are significant at the .01 level) | The F value for Drug has a p-value of .022 (significant at the .05 level) |

Output 4. The **ANOVA** summary table

The terms **Corrected Model** and **Intercept** refer to the regression method used to carry out the ANOVA and can be ignored. The three rows **Alertness, Drug** and **Alertness*Drug** are of most interest, since these report tests for the two main effects and the interaction. Note the **Sig.** (i.e. p-value, or tail probability) for each F ratio. There are significant main effects for both the *Alertness* and *Drug* factors: the former is significant beyond the 0.01 level, the latter beyond the 0.05 level, but not beyond the 0.01 level. In addition to main effects of both treatment factors, there is a significant interaction. The p-value is given as *.000*, which means that it is less than *0.0005*. Write 'p < .01', not 'p = .000'. Clearly, the *Drug* factor has different effects upon Fresh and Tired participants. To ascertain the nature of these effects, however, we shall need to examine the pattern of the treatment means more closely.

Optional post hoc test

The optional **Tukey** Post Hoc test results for the factor Drug Treatment are shown in Output 5. It can be seen that Drugs A and B differ significantly from one another, but neither differs significantly from Placebo.

Multiple Comparisons

Dependent Variable: Driving Performance

Tukey HSD

(I) Drug Treatment	(J) Drug Treatment	Mean Difference (I-J)	Std. Error	Sig.
Placebo	Drug A	.50	1.52	.942
	Drug B	-3.50	1.52	.064
Drug A	Placebo	-.50	1.52	.942
	Drug B	-4.00*	1.52	.029
Drug B	Placebo	3.50	1.52	.064
	Drug A	4.00*	1.52	.029

Based on observed means.

*. The mean difference is significant at the .05 level.

> The only difference with a p-value < .05 is *Drug A* and *Drug B*.
> Note these rows are highlighted with *

Output 5. Multiple Comparisons with the **Tukey Post Hoc** test for the *Drug Treatment* factor

The optional profile plot is shown in Output 6 (this is a repeat of Figure 1). It has been edited in **SPSS Viewer** to change coloured lines to black, to change one of the lines into dashes, and to represent the means as black discs.

Often, having made a preliminary graphical exploration of the cell means, the user will wish to make some unplanned pairwise comparisons among selected cell means to confirm the patterns evident in the graph. For example, Output 6 suggests that the simple fact of tiredness led to a deterioration in performance. That would be confirmed should a comparison between the means for the combination (Placebo, Fresh) and (Placebo, Tired) prove significant. To confirm that Drug A actually has deleterious effect upon the performance of Fresh participants, we should need to find a significant difference between the means for the (Fresh, Placebo) and (Fresh, Drug A) conditions. It is possible, too, that the apparent enhancement by Drug B of the performance of Fresh participants may not be significant. That would be confirmed by a non-significant difference between the means for conditions (Placebo, Fresh) and (Drug B, Fresh).

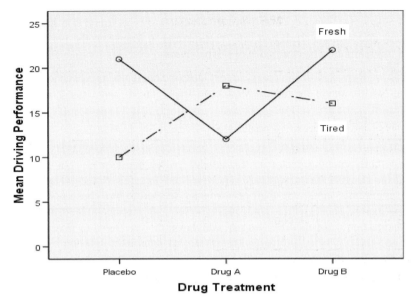

Output 6. Profile plots of *Alertness* across the levels of the *Drug Treatment* factor

Since the Alertness factor comprises only two conditions, the answer to the question of whether tiredness alone produces a significant decrement in performance under any of the three Drug conditions is answered by a test for a **simple main effect** of Alertness at the Placebo level of the Drug Treatment factor: no further comparisons need to be made. Tests for simple main effects are available using SPSS, but the user must know the syntax of the SPSS control language. Another approach is to perform an ANOVA only upon the data at the level of the qualifying factor concerned. If we go back to **Data View**, select the data only from the Placebo condition using the **Select Cases** procedure in the **Data** menu and request a one-way ANOVA with Alertness as the single factor, we shall find that

$$F(1, 18) = 23.99; \ p < .01.$$

This confirms the simple main effect of Alertness at the Placebo level of the Drug Treatment factor and hence that the difference between the means for the (Placebo, Fresh) and (Placebo, Tired) conditions is indeed significant.

Some of the other questions mentioned can only be answered by directly making pairwise comparisons between specified treatment means. Since many such comparisons are possible, it is necessary to protect against inflation of the *per family* type I error rate by using a conservative method such as the **Tukey** test.

8.5 MORE COMPLEX EXPERIMENTS

SPSS can readily be used to analyse data from more complex factorial experiments, with three or more treatment factors. In Section 8.2, we described the two-way ANOVA, with reference to an investigation of the effects of two new anti-hay fever drugs, A and B, upon simulated driving performance. It was suspected that at least one of the drugs might have different effects upon fresh and tired drivers, and the firm developing the drugs needed to ensure that neither had an adverse effect upon driving performance. It was found that Drug A did indeed have different effects upon fresh and tired participants: it improved the performance of tired drivers; but it impaired the performance of fresh drivers.

The two factor drugs-and-driving experiment demonstrated the presence of an **interaction** between the two treatment factors of Alertness (Fresh, Tired) and Drug Condition (Placebo, Drug A, Drug B). An interaction between two factors is said to occur when the **simple main effects** of one factor are not homogeneous at all levels of the other.

Now let us suppose that an investigator has good reason to suspect that, in this situation, another important potential factor is the gender of the participant. In pilot work, male participants on Drug A had frequently reported that they felt elated while performing the simulated driving task; moreover, their performance seemed to have been genuinely enhanced. Female participants, on the other hand, reported no such elation; indeed, their performance seemed to have been dampened by Drug A, whether they were fresh or tired. On the basis of pilot work and the published literature, the researcher decides to test the hypothesis that the interaction between the Alertness and Drug factors might vary between genders. The prediction was that in the male participants, Drug A would produce an improvement in the performance of tired participants, but impair the performance of fresh participants. In female participants, on the other hand, Drug A was expected to be less performance-enhancing.

The researcher decides to carry out a **three-factor between subjects factorial experiment**, in which the factors are:
1. **Drug Treatment**, with levels *Placebo, Drug A and Drug B*.
2. **Alertness**, with levels *Fresh* and *Tired*.
3. **Gender**, with levels *Female* and *Male*.

A between subjects experiment with three factors allows the investigation of more complex hypotheses than does a two factor experiment. The corresponding three-way ANOVA permits the testing not only of two-way interactions, but also a **three-way interaction** among all three treatment factors.

8.5.1 Three-way interactions

Simple interactions

A **simple interaction** is said to occur between two factors when their two-way interaction is not the same at all levels of a third factor.

The experimenter's hypothesis is about the simple interaction between the *Drug* and *Alertness* factors at different levels of the *Gender* factor: the pattern should be more evident in males than it is in females.

Three-way interactions

A **three-way interaction** is said to occur when the simple interaction between two factors is not the same at all levels of a third factor. This is exactly what is implied by the investigator's hypothesis: we can expect a three-way interaction among the factors of *Alertness*, *Drug* and *Gender*.

Figure 5 depicts the two-way interactions between the *Alertness* and *Drug* factors in female and male participants. It is quite clear from the graph that the two-way interaction between the

Alertness and *Drug* factors is different in the female and the male participants: indeed, the simple interaction between *Alertness* and *Drug* is scarcely evident at all in the females; whereas it is very evident in the males. It appears that the experimenter's hypothesis is supported and we can hope that the three-way ANOVA will confirm it by finding a significant three-way interaction.

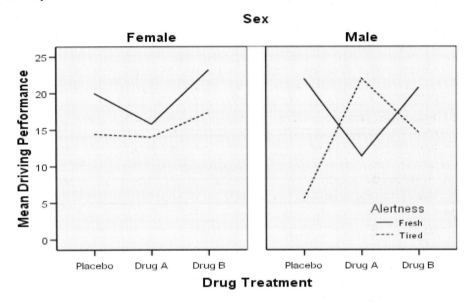

Figure 5. The two-way graphs for the female and male participants, illustrating a three-way interaction among the factors of *Alertness*, *Drug* and *Gender*. The two-way interaction between *Drug* and *Alertness* is clearly heterogeneous across the genders.

8.5.2   The three-way ANOVA

The results of the experiment are shown in Table 6.

Table 6. Results of a three-way factorial experiment				
Levels of the Alertness factor:	**Levels of the Sex factor:**	**Levels of the Drug Treatment factor:**		
		Placebo	**A**	**B**
Fresh	**Male**	23 18 19 24 26	11 16 11 8 11	23 19 17 20 25
	Female	24 25 13 22 16	14 18 15 18 14	27 14 19 29 27
Tired	**Male**	13 4 3 2 6	21 19 25 21 24	9 14 11 21 18
	Female	13 12 14 16 17	13 16 14 15 12	21 11 14 22 19

The three-way ANOVA table

The three-way ANOVA of this data set is shown in Table 7.

Table 7. Three-way ANOVA table for the data in Table 6.					
Source	**df**	**SS**	**MS**	**F**	**p**
Main effects					
Alertness (A)	1	264.60	264.60	17.49	<.01
Drug (D)	2	150.53	75.27	4.97	.01
Sex (S)	1	29.40	29.40	1.94	.17
Two-way interactions					
A × D	2	617.20	308.60	20.39	<.01
A × S	1	.60	.60	.04	.84
D × S	2	78.40	39.20	2.59	.09
Three-way interaction					
A × D × S	2	337.60	168.80	11.15	<.01
Within groups (Error)	48	726.40	15.13		
Total	59	2204.73			

It is worth examining Table 7 carefully and comparing it with the two-way table. In the three-way ANOVA, there are three possible two-way interactions, each of which is tested with an F statistic. The new feature is the test for a three-way interaction. There are, therefore, seven F tests reported in the table: three for main effects; three for two-way interactions; one for the three-way interaction.

The table brings few surprises; but it does confirm the trends that were evident from our inspection of the graphs. There are significant main effects of the *Drug* and *Alertness* factors; but none for *Sex*. There is a significant two-way interaction between *Alertness* and *Drug*. Most important of all, there is a significant three-way interaction, confirming the experimenter's hypothesis.

The results of the *F* tests are reported in the manner described for the two-way ANOVA. The result for the three-way interaction is as follows:

$$F(2, 48) = 11.15; p < .01$$

Once again, we suggest that, rather than present the reader of your report with a long list of the results of various *F* tests, you should 'talk the reader through' the patterns of means in a graph or a table, presenting each significant result in meaningful context.

Partition of the between groups sum of squares

In the one-way ANOVA, the total sum of squares is broken down or partitioned into a between groups and a within groups sum of squares:

$$SS_{total} = SS_{between} + SS_{within}$$

In the two-way ANOVA, the between groups sum of squares does not appear explicity in the ANOVA summary table: it has been further partitioned into main effect sums of squares and an interaction sum of squares:

$$SS_{between} = SS_{Alertness} + SS_{Drug} + SS_{Alertness \times Drug}$$

In the thee-way ANOVA, the between groups sums of squares is partitioned into 3 main effects sums of squares, 3 two-way interaction sums of squares and the three-way interaction sum of squares.

$$SS_{between} = SS_{Alertness} + SS_{Drug} + SS_{Sex} + SS_{A \times D} + SS_{A \times S} + SS_{D \times S} + SS_{A \times D \times S}$$

The mean squares

The mean squares are obtained by dividing the sums of squares by their degrees of freedom. The degrees of freedom are obtained in a manner analogous to the one-way ANOVA. For main effects, df is the number of conditions or groups minus 1.

$$df_A = (a-1); \quad df_B = (b-1); \quad df_C = (c-1)$$

For two-way interactions, the df is the product of the degrees of freedom of the sources considered separately.

$$df_{A \times B} = (a-1)(b-1); \quad df_{A \times C} = (a-1)(c-1); \quad df_{A \times C} = (a-1)(c-1)$$

The degrees of freedom of the three-way interaction is the product of the degrees of freedom of the three component sources.

$$df_{A \times B \times C} = (a-1)(b-1)(c-1)$$

In our current example, if A, B and C are the Alertness, Drug and Sex factors, respectively, a = 1, b = 2, c = 1 and

$$df_{A \times B \times C} = (a-1)(b-1)(c-1) = (2-1)(3-1)(2-1) = 2$$

The F ratios

As in the two-way ANOVA, all the *F* tests in the three-way ANOVA have the same denominator, namely, MS_{within}. As in the one-way and two-way ANOVA, the within groups mean square is the average of the variance estimates calculated from each sample of participants.

In general, if the three factors A, B and C have a, b & c levels, respectively, n is the number of participants in each combination of conditions and N is the total number of observations, there will be $a \times b \times c = abc$ combinations of treatments, that is, cells in the design. In our example, abc = 2 × 3 × 2 = 12. If n is the sample size (in our fictitious example, n = 5), the total number of observations is N = abcn. In our example, N = 2 × 3 × 2 × 5 = 60.

As in the one-way and two-way ANOVAs, the error term in the three-way ANOVA is a pooled estimate of the supposedly uniform population variance σ^2. In general, since there are abc cells in the design, there will be abc variance estimates, each with $(n - 1)$ degrees of freedom. The degrees of freedom of the within groups mean square MS_{within} is therefore given by

$$df_{within} = abc(n-1) = N - abc$$

In our current example,

$$df_{within} = abc(n-1) = N - abc = 60 - 12 = 48$$

which is the value given in Table 7.

8.5.3   Three-way ANOVA with SPSS

The data set in **Data View** would now have to include three grouping variables (*Alertness*, *Sex*, and *Drug*), as well as a column for the dependent variable *DrivingPerf*. Figure 6 shows a section of **Data View** with the new grouping variable *Sex* added.

	Case	Alertness	Drug	DrivingP	Sex
1	1	Fresh	Placebo	24	Female
2	2	Fresh	Placebo	25	Female
3	3	Fresh	Placebo	13	Female
4	4	Fresh	Placebo	22	Female
5	5	Fresh	Placebo	16	Female
6	6	Fresh	Placebo	23	Male
7	7	Fresh	Placebo	18	Male
8	8	Fresh	Placebo	19	Male
9	9	Fresh	Placebo	24	Male
10	10	Fresh	Placebo	26	Male

Figure 6. Part of **Data View** showing some of the data in Table 6

To run the three-factor ANOVA, proceed as follows:

- Open the **General Linear Model - Univariate** dialog box and complete it as in Chapter 7, Figure 8, with *Driving Performance* in the **Dependent Variable** box and the three grouping factors *Alertness*, *Drug Treatment* and *Sex* in the **Fixed Factors** box.
- Select the optional **Descriptive statistics** and **Estimates of effect size** check boxes from **Options...** and the **Tukey Post Hoc** test for *Drug* from **Post Hoc...**, clicking **Continue** each time to return to the **Univariate** dialog box.
- To obtain a profile plot of the means, click **Plots...** to open the **Univariate: Profile Plots** dialog box. Select *Drug* for the **Horizontal Axis** box, *Alertness* for the **Separate Lines** box and *Sex* for the **Separate Plots** box. Click **Add** to add the plot to the **Plots** list and then **Continue** to return to the **Univariate** dialog box.
- Click **OK**.

The first table in the output lists the number of cases for each level of the variables (Output 7).

Between-Subjects Factors

		Value Label	N
Alertness	1	Fresh	30
	2	Tired	30
Drug Treatment	1	Placebo	20
	2	Drug A	20
	3	Drug B	20
Sex	1	Male	30
	2	Female	30

Output 7. The table of **Between-Subjects Factors**

The next table in the output (not reproduced here) shows the descriptive statistics requested in the **Options...** dialog box.

Ignore these rows	Of interest for ANOVA is the value of *F* and its associated p-value	The values of η_p^2 are all $\geq 10\%$ except for *Sex* and for *Alertness*Sex*

Tests of Between-Subjects Effects

Dependent Variable: Driving Performance

Source	Type III Sum of Squares	df	Mean Square	F	Sig.	Partial Eta Squared
Corrected Model	1478.33[a]	11	134.39	8.88	.000	.671
Intercept	16867.27	1	16867	1114.58	.000	.959
Alertness	264.60	1	264.60	17.48	.000	.267
Drug	150.53	2	75.27	4.97	.011	.172
Sex	29.40	1	29.40	1.94	.170	.039
Alertness * Drug	617.20	2	308.60	20.39	.000	.459
Alertness * Sex	.60	1	.60	.04	.843	.001
Drug * Sex	78.40	2	39.20	2.59	.085	.097
Alertness * Drug * Sex	337.60	2	168.80	11.15	.000	.317
Error	726.40	48	15.13			
Total	19073.00	60				
Corrected Total	2204.73	59				

a. R Squared = .671 (Adjusted R Squared = .595)

Alertness, the interaction *Alertness*Drug* and the triple interaction have p-values < .01 (i.e. significant at the .01 level)	*Drug* has a p-value between .05 and .01 (i.e. significant at the .05 level) but *Sex* and its interactions have p-values > .05 (i.e. not significant)

Output 8. The three-way factorial **ANOVA** summary table

With three factors, the ANOVA summary table (Output 8) is considerably longer than in the two-factor case. As before, there are main effects. This time, however, there are three different main effects, one for each of the three factors in the experiment. In the two-factor experiment, there can be only one two-way interaction; but in the three-factor experiment, there are three and here all are significant except *Drug*Sex*.

Moreover, in the three-factor table a new interaction appears, *Alertness * Drug * Sex*. This is known as a **three-way**, or **three-factor interaction**. A three-factor interaction is said to occur when there is heterogeneity of the interaction between two factors across the levels of a third. These results are reported as follows:

> The mean Driving Performance scores for the Fresh and Tired conditions (Alertness factor) differed significantly beyond the .01 level: $F(1, 48) = 17.49$; $p < .01$. Partial eta squared = .27 representing a large effect.

> The mean Driving Performance scores for the two Drug conditions and the Placebo condition (Drug Treatment factor) differed significantly at the 5% level: $F(2, 48) = 4.97$; $p = .01$. Partial eta squared = .17 representing a large effect.

> The mean Driving Performance scores for Males and Females (Sex factor) did not differ significantly: $F(1, 48) = 1.94$; $p > .05$.

> The mean Driving Performance scores for the interaction of Alertness and Drug differed significantly beyond the .01 level: $F(2, 48) = 20.39$; $p < .01$. Partial eta squared = .46 representing a large effect.

> The mean Driving Performance scores for the interaction of Alertness and Sex did not differ significantly: $F(1, 48) = .04$; $p > .05$.

> The mean Driving Performance scores did not differ significantly for the interaction of Drug and Sex: $F(2, 48) = 2.59$; $p > .05$.

> The mean Driving Performance scores for the interaction of Alertness, Drug and Sex differed significantly beyond the .01 level: $F(2, 48) = 11.15$; $p < .01$. Partial eta squared = .32 representing a large effect.

In conclusion, in addition to the two significant main effects and one significant double interaction, there is also a significant triple interaction.

Finally there are tables in **SPSS Viewer** for the **Post Hoc Tests** and the **Profile Plots** (one for Males and one for Females) which are not reproduced here.

8.6   A FINAL WORD

We strongly recommend you to avoid factorial designs with more than three factors. While we agree that many variables may affect scores in a situation, it is usually possible to arrange that theoretically unimportant considerations, such as positional and sequential contingencies, can be made to balance by careful experimental design and need not emerge as factors in the analysis.

There are several good reasons for avoiding complex factorial designs with four or more factors. Four-way interactions are often exceedingly difficult to interpret. Moreover, although the follow-up methods we have described can, in principle, be extended to the analysis of more complex experiments, there remains the potential problem of over-analysis and hence capitalising on chance. If a comparison is of such vital theoretical importance, there is much to be said for designing a new, simpler experiment to confirm the pattern.

Recommended Reading

In this chapter, we could do no more than touch upon the analysis of data from complex factorial experiments. Howell (2007; Chapter 13) gives a lucid treatment of the analysis of interactions.

Howell, D. C. (2007). *Statistical methods for psychology (6th ed.).* Belmont, CA: Thomson/Wadsworth.

EXERCISE 12

Between subjects factorial ANOVA (two-way ANOVA)

Before you start

Before proceeding with this practical, please read Chapter 8. The following Exercise assumes a knowledge of the standard **factorial ANOVA** terminology.

An experiment on the memories of chess players

'Must have a marvellous memory!' This is something often said of a good chess player; but do good chess players necessarily have better short-term memories than those who are mediocre? To find out, a psychologist tested chess players at three levels of proficiency on their ability to reconstruct board positions they had just been shown. Some of the positions used were from real games selected from tournaments; but others were merely random placings of the same pieces. The psychologist predicted that whereas the better players would show superior reconstructions of real board positions, this superiority would disappear when they tried to reproduce random placements. The dependent variable in this experiment was a participant's *score* on reconstruction. There were two independent variables (factors):

Competence (Novice, Average, Good).

Position   (Real, Random).

An important feature of the design of this experiment was that a different sample of participants performed under each of the six treatment combinations: that is, each group of players at a given level was subdivided into those reconstructing Real positions and those reconstructing Random positions.

What the psychologist is predicting is that, when performance is averaged over Random and Real positions, the better players will achieve higher performance means; but this will turn out to be because of their superior recall of Real board positions only, and the beginners will be just as good at reconstructing Random positions. The **two-factor ANOVA**, therefore, should show a significant interaction between the factors of Competence and Position, as well as (possibly) a main effect of Competence. The latter might be expected to arise because the better players' much superior performance in reconstructing real board positions pulls up the mean value of their performance over both Real and Random positions, even though they may not outperform beginners on the Random task.

The results of the experiment are shown in Table 1.

Table 1. Results of the experiment on the reconstruction of positions by chess players

Posit-ion	Competence														
	Novice					Average					Good				
Real	38	39	42	40	40	65	58	70	61	62	88	95	86	89	89
	42	37	38	40	38	58	63	66	62	65	88	90	85	92	86
Rand-	50	53	40	41	36	50	40	43	37	38	41	40	50	42	41
om	42	44	46	44	45	42	44	38	37	43	43	46	41	44	45

Opening SPSS

Open SPSS and select the **Type in data** radio button in the opening window. If **Data View** opens first, click the **Variable View** tab to open **Variable View**.

Preparing the SPSS data set

Recast the data of Table 1 into a form suitable for entry into SPSS along the lines of the description in Section 8.4.1. You will need a variable for cases (there are 60 participants) as well as two grouping variables, *Competence* and *Position*, with appropriate values and value labels specified in the **Values** column, and one dependent variable, *Score*. Ensure that the values in the **Decimals** column have been reduced to 0.   We also recommend you to use the **Label** column to assign fuller labels to the variables: e.g. Case Number, Competence, Position of Pieces. Switch to **Data View** and enter the data, leaving the values for *case* until last, when you can use **Compute** to enter them automatically, making *case* the **Target Variable** and *$casenum* the **Numeric Expression**.

As always, save the data set with a suitable name.

Exploring the data

Before proceeding with the ANOVA, it is important to explore the data. Look at the boxplots (see Section 8.4.2) using **Graphs➔Chart Builder...** and select **Boxplot** from the gallery. Drag the **Clustered Boxplot** image to the **Chart preview** and fill in the variable names with *Score* in the **Y-Axis** box, *Competence* in the **X-Axis** box and *Position* in the **Cluster: set pattern** box. Click **OK** to plot the clustered boxplots.

- **What do you notice about the distribution of data among the three levels of *Competence* and between the two levels of *Position*?**

Although means can be requested in the dialog box for the ANOVA, it is recommended to include the calculation of the means at the exploration of data stage. Do this using the **Means command** (see Section 4.3.2) and layering the two classificatory variables *Position* and *Competence*.

- **What do you notice about the values of the means for the two levels of *Position* across the three levels of *Competence*?**

Procedure for the two-way ANOVA

Choose
Analyze➔General Linear Model➔Univariate...
to open the **Univariate** dialog box. Then complete the dialog box as described in Section
8.4.3, specifying a plot of the means using the **Plots...** dialog box, selecting **Descriptive
statistics** and **Estimates of effect size** using the **Options...** dialog box, and a **Tukey** Post
Hoc test for *Competence* (ignore *Position* since it has only two levels) using the **Post Hoc...**
dialog box.

Output for the two-way ANOVA

Tables listing the levels of the factors and descriptive statistics will appear first. The ANOVA
summary table gives F ratios for the main effects of *Competence* and *Position* and also for the
interaction between the two factors.

- Write down the values of *F* (and the associated p-values) and the
  values of Partial Eta Squared (the measure of effect size) for the main
  effect and interaction tests. Do these results confirm your predictions
  from inspection of the output from the Means procedure? Relate these
  results to the experimental hypothesis about the short-term memory of
  chess players. Are the effect sizes large, medium or small?

Post hoc comparisons among the levels of competence

Inspect the output for the post hoc comparisons of the levels of competence.

- Construct your own table showing clearly which pairs of levels are
  significantly different and which (if any) are not.

Graph of cell means

Inspect the graph.

- What do you conclude from the plot?

Finishing the session

Close down SPSS and any other windows before logging out of the computer.

Within subjects experiments

9.1   INTRODUCTION

9.1.1   Rationale of a within subjects experiment

A potential problem with between subjects experiments (Chapters 7 & 8) is that if there are large individual differences in performance, searching for a meaningful pattern in the data can be like trying to listen to a radio programme against a loud background crackle of interference. For example, in a Drug experiment such as the one described in Chapter 7, some of the scores obtained by participants in the Placebo condition may well be higher than those of participants tested under any of the drug conditions.   There are some people who can bring a natural dexterity and flair to almost any test of skill; others, on the other hand, must work much harder to learn a new activity. Since, in a between subjects experiment, a different sample of participants performs under each condition, variation in natural aptitude is likely to introduce considerable **noise** into the data and inflate the error terms of the *F* statistics.

Another drawback with the between subjects experiment is that it is wasteful of participants: if the experimental procedure is a short one, a participant may spend more time travelling to and from the place of testing than actually performing the experiment. We shall now consider another experimental strategy which allows the researcher to make fuller use of the participant's time and trouble.

A researcher wishes to investigate the effects upon shooting accuracy of the shape of the target. Each participant is asked to shoot twenty times at each of four differently-shaped targets. Since each participant is tested under all the conditions making up the factor of target shape, this experiment is said to be of **within subjects** design, or to have **repeated measures** on target shape. Table 1 compares this one-factor, within subjects experiment with a one-factor between subjects experiment similar to the drug experiment in Chapter 7.

Table 1. Between subjects and within subjects experiments in which there is one treatment factor with four levels

(a)   A one-factor between subjects experiment

	Levels of the Drug factor			
	Control	Drug A	Drug B	Drug C
Participants	Group 1	Group 2	Group 3	Group 4

(b)   A one-factor within subjects experiment

	Levels of the Shape factor			
	Circle	Square	Triangle	Diamond
Participants	The same participants perform with all four shapes. The order of presentation of the four conditions is varied, or **counterbalanced**, so that each condition occurs with equal frequency in each of the four ordinal positions across all the participants in the study.			

The variance in the scores from the Shape experiment will certainly reflect individual differences every bit as marked as they are likely to be in the Drug experiment. There is, however, an important difference between the two experiments. In being tested under every condition, each participant is effectively serving as his or her own control. That person's average performance over all conditions will provide a baseline against which performance under the different conditions can be evaluated.

9.1.2   The within subjects ANOVA

The advantage of the within subjects strategy is apparent from inspection of the ANOVA tables for the two experiments, which are shown in Table 2.

Table 2. The ANOVA summary tables for the one-factor between subjects (the one-way ANOVA) and within subjects experiments

Source	df	SS	MS	F		Source	df	SS	MS	F
Drug	3			$\dfrac{MS_{drug}}{MS_{within}}$		Shape	3			$\dfrac{MS_{shape}}{MS_{residual}}$
Within	36					Subjects	9			
						Residual	27			
Total	39					Total	39			

The entries for degrees of freedom in the two tables assume that in the Drug experiment, there were 10 participants in each group, making a total of 40 participants in the experiment; whereas in the Shape experiment, there were only 10 participants but, since each was tested under all four conditions, 40 scores were generated, as in the Drug experiment. The total degrees of freedom therefore has the same value in both experiments, namely, $40 - 1 = 39$.

No actual values need be entered in Table 2 because, as we have seen, the degrees of freedom tell the same story as the sums of squares. In the within subjects Shape experiment, the degrees of freedom of the Subjects and Residual sources add up to 36, the degrees of freedom of the within groups sums of squares in the Drug experiment. Since what is true of the degrees of freedom is true of the sums of squares also, we can see that

$$SS_{within} = SS_{subjects} + SS_{residual}$$

Since each participant (subject) has performed under all conditions, that person's mean performance can be calculated. A variance estimate can then be calculated from the mean performance level of each of the ten participants in the within subjects Shape experiment. This partialling out of the variance in levels of competence among the participants leaves a smaller residual sum of squares, which is the basis of the error term in the within subjects ANOVA.

In general, let n be the sample size: that is, n is the group size in the between subjects experiment and the number of participants in the within subjects experiment. In the within subjects experiment $df_{subjects} = n - 1$. In the between subjects experiment, $df_{within} = k(n - 1)$, where k is the number of conditions in the treatment factor. Subtracting $df_{subjects}$ from df_{within}, we find that

$$df_{residual} = k(n-1) - (n-1) = (k-1)(n-1)$$

This has the form of an interaction degrees of freedom – and that is exactly what it is. Since each participant performs under all conditions, the Subjects source becomes a 'factor', albeit a non-treatment factor: what we have in the one-factor within subjects experiment is essentially a two factor design with one observation per cell. For this reason, the one-factor, within subjects experiment is often referred to as a **Subjects × Treatments** design.

If Subjects is a 'factor', it is one with **random effects**: that is, the participants in the experiment are assumed to be a random sample from a large pool of possible participants. This is why the residual (Subjects × Treatments) mean square is suitable as the error term for the F test. (Howell, 2007, gives a lucid discussion of the theory of the F tests in ANOVA, including the within subjects ANOVA.)

Since the degrees of freedom of the residual sum of squares is less than the df of MS_{within}, the critical value for F is larger. In practice, however, the partialling out of a major part of the variance arising from individual differences results in an increase in power, so that the power efficiency (that is, power in relation to the number of participants) of the within subjects experiment exceeds that of the between subjects experiment.

In summary, therefore, the within subjects experiment has two advantages over the between subjects experiment:

1. It cuts down data noise, resulting in a test of greater power in relation to the number of participants in the experiment.
2. It makes more efficient use of time and resources.

The within subjects experiment, however, also has disadvantages, which in some circumstances can outweigh considerations of convenience and the maximisation of the signal-to-noise ratio. One such disadvantage is discussed in Section 9.1.4.

See Section 9.1.4

9.1.3 A within subjects experiment on the effect of target shape on shooting accuracy

Table 3 shows the results of an experiment on the effects of target shape on shooting accuracy. (In this experiment, there were only three target shapes.) The order of presentation of the three targets was counterbalanced in an attempt to neutralise any order effects.

	Table 3. Results of a one-factor within subjects experiment		
Participant (Subject)	**Target**		
	Circle	Square	Triangle
1	10	12	14
2	18	10	16
3	20	15	16
4	12	10	12
5	19	20	21
6	25	22	20
7	18	16	17
8	22	18	18
9	17	14	12
10	23	20	18

The ANOVA summary table is shown in Table 4.

Table 4. The ANOVA summary table.					
Source	**df**	**SS**	**MS**	**F**	**p**
Shape	2	39.267	19.633	4.86	.02
Subjects	9	370.170	40.608		
Residual (Shape × Subjects)	18	72.730	4.04		
Total	29	482.167			

We can report the result of the F test as follows:

The factor of Target Shape had a significant main effect: $F(2, 18) = 4.86$; $p = .02$.

9.1.4   Order effects: counterbalancing

A potential problem with repeated measures is that a participant's performance on one task may well be affected by the experience of having performed another task, particularly when the two tasks are attempted in close succession. Such an effect upon performance is an example of a **carry-over** (or **order**) **effect**. Sometimes, of course, carry-over effects are of great interest, as in memory research, where the researcher might wish to demonstrate the proactive interference of learning one list of words with the recall of the words in another list learned subsequently. More usually, however, carry-over effects in within subjects experiments are potential **confounds**, whose influence can be difficult to disentangle from that of the treatment factor itself.

If participants are tested on not one but several tasks, their performance on the later tasks may improve through a **practice effect**. Practice effects, however, are only one type of carry-over effect. Not all carry-over effects are positive: proactive and retroactive interference in memory are negative effects. In within subjects experiments, carry-over effects are potential **extraneous variables**, whose effects may be confounded with those of the treatment factor.

The possibility of carry-over effects confounding the effects of the treatment factor is reduced by the procedure known as **counterbalancing**, in which the order of the conditions making up a within subjects factor is varied from participant to participant, in the hope that carry-over effects will balance out across conditions. Counterbalancing is not always effective, however, because order effects can be quite asymmetrical. There are also situations in which a within subjects strategy would be quite inappropriate: the drug experiment in Chapter 7 is a good example.

9.1.5   The variance-covariance matrix

The covariance

Since the same participants shoot at all three targets, we can expect strong statistical **associations** or **correlations** between the scores that the participants achieved under any two of the conditions: high scores with one target are likely to be paired with high scores on the other; and low scores on one target are likely to be accompanied by low scores on the other. (We shall consider the topic of correlation more closely in Chapter 11.)

Figure 1 is the scatterplot of *Square Target* against *Triangular Target*. This plot does indeed show evidence of a positive association or correlation between the scores the participants achieved under these two conditions. (For the meaning of positive correlation, see Chapter 11.)

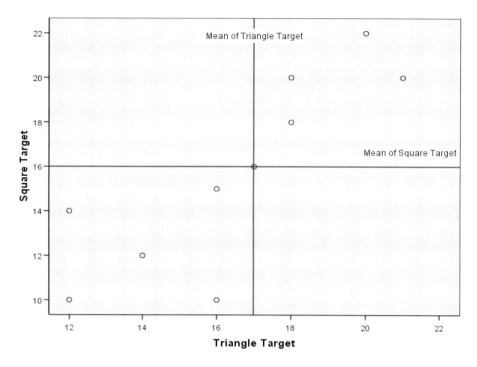

Figure 1. Scatterplot of *Square target* against *Triangle target* scores showing a high positive correlation between them

The **covariance** is a measure of the strength of the association between two variables. Its formula is analogous to the formula for the variance:

Variance of X   Variance of Y   Covariance of X & Y

$$s_X^2 = \frac{\Sigma(X - M_X)^2}{n - 1} \qquad s_Y^2 = \frac{\Sigma(Y - M_Y)^2}{n - 1} \qquad COV_{XY} = \frac{\Sigma(X - M_X)(Y - M_Y)}{n - 1}$$

The covariance of a variable with itself is simply its variance: the sum of products SP becomes a sum of squares SS.

In the formulae for the variance and covariance, it is often more convenient to write the sum of squares and sum of products (the numerators of the variance and covariance, respectively) as SS and SP, respectively:

$$S_X^2 = \frac{SS_X}{n - 1} \quad S_Y^2 = \frac{SS_Y}{n - 1} \quad COV_{XY} = \frac{SP}{n - 1}$$

In the formulae, SS and SP represent squared deviations and products of deviations, respectively. In Figure 1, scores above the horizontal line (representing the mean score for the square target) will have positive deviations; scores below will have negative deviations. Similarly scores to the right of the vertical reference line (representing the mean score for the triangular target) will have positive deviations; scores to the left will have negative deviations.

The scatterplot shows that most of the points (the participants) are in the lower left and upper right quadrants. Scores in either quadrant will have positive sums of products, so we can expect the covariance to have a substantial positive value. Had the scores been located largely in the upper left and lower right quadrants, where deviations are negative, the sum of products would have had a substantial negative value. Had the points been equally distributed among the four quadrants, the positive and negative sums of products would have tended to cancel out and the covariance would have been close to zero, indicating an absence of any association between the two variables.

Suppose that X and Y are standardised, that is, converted to z_X and z_Y, where

$$z_X = \frac{X - M_X}{s_X} \ and \ z_Y = \frac{Y - M_Y}{s_Y}$$

The covariance between z_X and z_Y is the **Pearson correlation**:

$$COV_{z_X z_Y} = \frac{\sum z_X z_Y}{n - 1} = r_{XY}$$

The simplicity of this particular formula for the Pearson correlation (several others are given in Chapter 11) derives from two properties of z-scores that they have:
1. A mean of zero;
2. A standard deviation of 1.

The covariance has no upper limit. The Pearson correlation, however, can vary only within the range from -1 to $+1$, inclusive. This property makes the Pearson correlation a more generally useful descriptive measure of association than is the covariance.

The variance-covariance matrix

In Table 5, calculated from the data in Table 3, is shown the **variance-covariance matrix**. The italicised values along the diagonal (21.60; 18.23; 9.38) are the variances (each is the covariance of a variable with itself); the off-diagonal elements are covariances.

Table 5. Variance-covariance matrix for the scores in Table 3.			
	Circle	**Square**	**Triangle**
Circle	*21.60*	15.91	10.38
Square	15.91	*18.23*	10.80
Triangle	10.38	10.80	*9.38*

Notice the symmetry of the variance-covariance matrix: the covariance of X with Y is identical with the covariance of Y with X.

9.1.6   Assumptions underlying the within subjects ANOVA

We have said that a given participant, when tested on several different tasks in the same experiment, is likely to score at similar percentiles on all tasks; on the other hand, participants' mean levels of performance over all conditions is likely to vary considerably.

A statistical test always assumes that the data have been generated in a manner described by a statistical **model**, and so must have certain properties. For example, the ANOVA for between subjects experiments (Chapters 7 and 8) requires that there must be homogeneity of variance from group to group.   The model for the within subjects ANOVA makes additional assumptions, over and above those made by the between groups models. The most important of these is **homogeneity of covariance**. If this assumption is violated, the Type I error rate (i.e. the probability of rejecting H_0 when it is true) may be inflated. Tests for homogeneity of covariance are made on the variance-covariance matrix.

SPSS tests for homogeneity of covariance with the **Mauchly sphericity test**. Should the data fail the sphericity test (i.e. p-value < 0.05), the ANOVA F test must be modified to make it more *conservative* (less likely to reject the null hypothesis). SPSS offers three such tests, varying in their degree of conservativeness: the **Greenhouse-Geisser**, the **Huynh-Feldt**, and the **Lower-bound**. All three tests reduce the degrees of freedom of the numerator and the denominator of the F ratio (by multiplying them by a factor termed **epsilon**), thus increasing the value of F required for significance.

9.1.7   Effect size and power in within subjects ANOVA

As with the between subjects ANOVA, SPSS provides, as a measure of the size of the effect of an independent variable, the statistic known as **partial eta-squared $\eta_p{}^2$**, where

$$\eta_p{}^2 = \frac{SS_{treatment}}{SS_{treatment} + SS_{error}}.$$

The usual benchmarks for classifying the value of eta squared are presented in Table 6.

Table 6. Cohen's classification of effect size, with equivalent values of eta squared. (Table reproduced from Chapter 7)		
Effect size (d)	**Eta squared**	**Size of Effect**
$0.2 \le d < 0.5$	$.01 \le \eta^2 < .06$	Small
$0.5 \le d < 0.8$	$.06 \le \eta^2 < .14$	Medium
$d \ge 0.8$	$\eta^2 \ge .14$	Large

For a given number of data points, a within subjects ANOVA can (provided the assumptions of the underlying model are met) make tests of greater power than those of a between subjects ANOVA with the same numbers of factors and levels. Clark-Carter (2004) suggests that approximate guidelines on sample size and power for within subjects experiments can be obtained by using the procedures he describes for between subjects ANOVAs.

9.2   A ONE-FACTOR WITHIN SUBJECTS ANOVA WITH SPSS

9.2.1   Entering the data

Since the participants have not been divided into groups, no grouping variable is required for entry of these data into the **SPSS Data Editor**. In **Variable View**, using the procedures described in Section 2.3, define the variables *Case*, *Circle*, *Square* and *Triangle*. Using the **Label** column, expand the variable names to *Case Number*, *Circle Target*, *Square Target* and *Triangle Target*. Set the number of decimal places displayed to zero. In **Data View**, enter the data from Table 3 into the first four (pre-labelled) columns.

> See
> Section
> 2.3

9.2.2   Exploring the data: Boxplots for within subjects factors

*   To draw boxplots of the data at the various levels of a within subjects factor, select
    Analyze➔Descriptive Statistics➔Explore...
    to open the **Explore** dialog box (Figure 2).
*   Follow the steps shown in Figure 2.
*   In the **Explore: Plots** dialog box (Figure 3), click on the **Dependents together** button and click off the **Stem-and-leaf** check box. Click **Continue** and then **OK**.

The boxplots (Output 1) reveal no extreme cases (which would have been flagged by * - see Table 2 in Section 4.3.2 for details of the structure of a boxplot). None of the distributions is markedly skewed. There is therefore no need to remove any cases or apply any transformation to symmetrise the distribution. We can carry on with the ANOVA.

> See Table 2 in
> Section 4.3.2

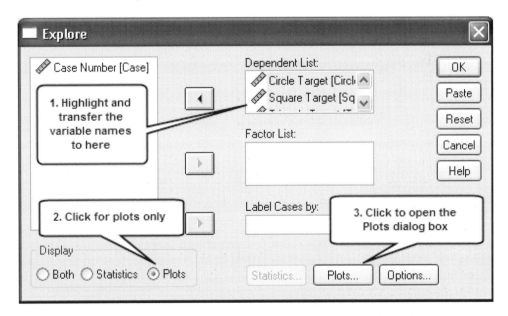

Figure 2. The **Explore** dialog box with the dependent variable names transferred to the **Dependent List** panel and the **Plots** button checked.

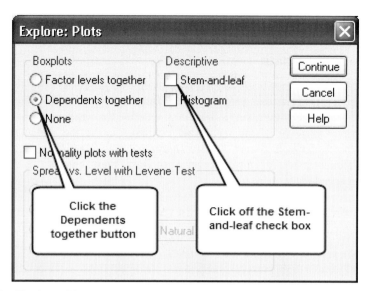

Figure 3. The **Explore: Plots** dialog box with **Dependents together** selected and **Stem-and-leaf** deselected

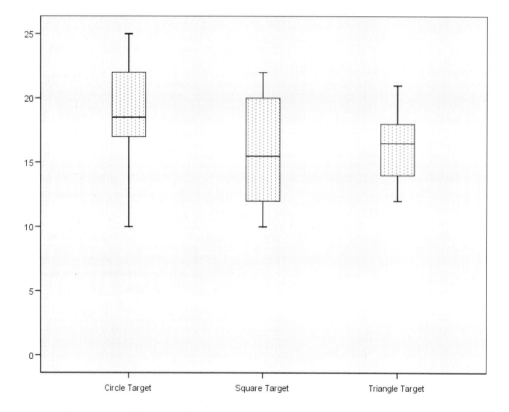

Output 1. Boxplots of the data for the three shapes

9.2.3   Running the within subjects ANOVA

The within subjects ANOVA is selected as follows:
*   Select
    Analyze➜General Linear Model➜Repeated Measures... (Figure 4) to
open the **Repeated Measures Define Factors** dialog box (Figure 5).

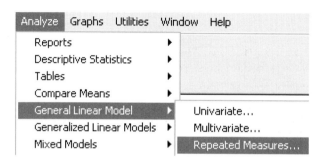

Figure 4. The **General Linear Model** menu

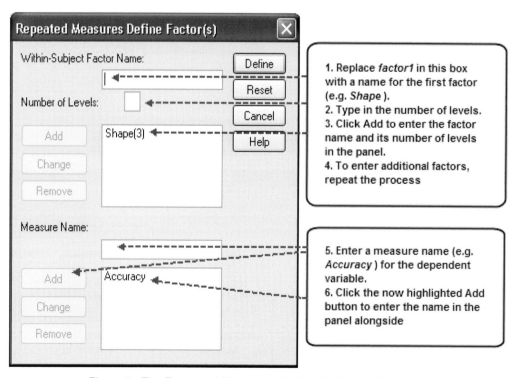

Figure 5. The **Repeated Measures Define Factor(s)** dialog box

*   Follow the steps described in Figure 5 to obtain the situation in Figure 6.
*   Click **Define** to return to the **Repeated Measures ANOVA** dialog box (the upper half of
    which is shown in Figure 6).

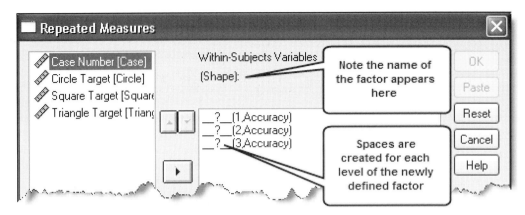

Figure 6. The upper half of the **Repeated Measures** dialog box after defining the **Within-Subjects Variables** factor as *Shape* with three levels and naming the measure as *Accuracy*

• Highlight the variables *Circle, Square* and *Triangle* (Figure 7) by clicking-and-dragging the cursor down over them and clicking ▶ to transfer all three into the **Within Subjects Variables [Shape]** box. The question marks will be replaced by the variable names as shown in Figure 7.

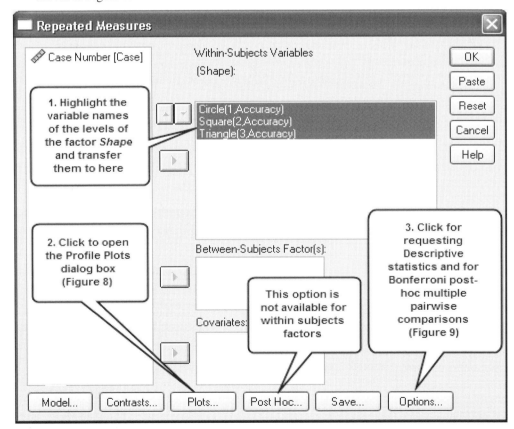

Figure 7. The completed **Repeated Measures** dialog box

- There are some useful options with a repeated measures ANOVA. For example, you can obtain a profile plot of the levels of the within subjects factor by clicking **Plots...** and following the steps shown in Figure 8. Click **Continue** to return to the original dialog box.

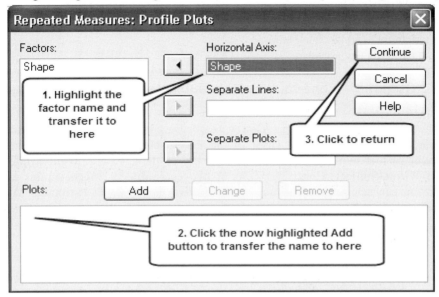

Figure 8. The **Profile Plots** dialog box for a plot at each level of a factor

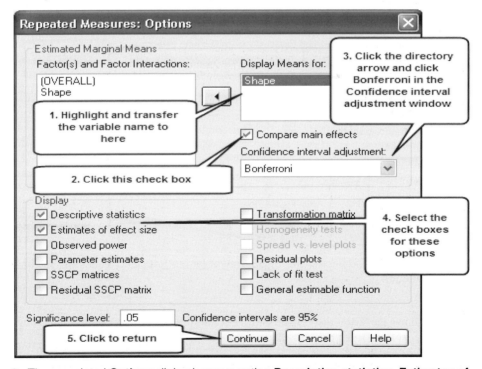

Figure 9. The completed **Options** dialog box requesting **Descriptive statistics**, **Estimates of effect size** and **Bonferroni** comparisons

- A table of **Descriptive statistics, Estimates of effect size** and a table of **Bonferroni adjusted pairwise comparisons** among the levels of the within subjects factor are requested by clicking **Options...** in the **Repeated Measures** dialog box and following the steps shown in Figure 9. See Section 9.2.5 regarding the choice of the Bonferroni test. Click **Continue** to return to the original dialog box.

See
Section
9.2.5

- Click **OK** to run the procedure.

9.2.4   Output for a one-factor within subjects ANOVA

The output is extensive, but not all of it is required for a within subjects ANOVA. Output 2 shows the left-hand pane of the **SPSS Viewer**, in which are itemised the various subtables that appear in the right-hand pane. Three of the tables should be deleted immediately by highlighting each in turn and pressing the **Delete** key on the keyboard: **Multivariate Tests**; **Tests of Within-Subjects Contrasts**; **Tests of Between-Subjects Effects** (in this example, there are no between subjects factors). The **Multivariate Tests** in **Estimated Marginal Means** can also be deleted.

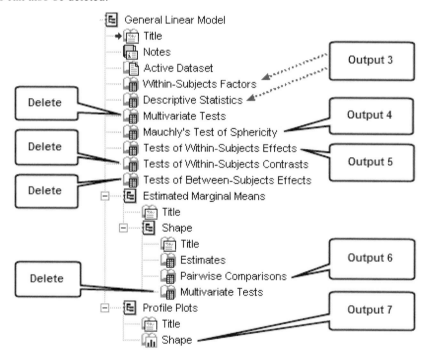

Output 2. The left-hand pane of the **SPSS Viewer** for the Repeated Measures (within subjects) analysis

Output 3 shows the **Title**, the **Within-Subjects Factors** list for the measure *accuracy* and the specially requested **Descriptive Statistics** table.

Within-Subjects Factors

Measure: Accuracy

Shape	Dependent Variable
1	Circle
2	Square
3	Triangle

Descriptive Statistics

	Mean	Std. Deviation	N
Circle Target	18.40	4.648	10
Square Target	15.70	4.270	10
Triangle Target	16.40	3.062	10

Output 3.   The **Within-Subjects Factors** list and **Descriptive Statistics** table

Output 4 reports the result of the **Mauchly's Test of Sphericity**, a test for homogeneity of covariance (see Section 9.1). There are two possible results. If the p-value (**Sig.**) is greater than .05, the null hypothesis of homogeneity of covariance (sphericity) is accepted. If the p-value is less than .05, the null hypothesis of homogeneity of covariance is rejected. The result of Mauchly's Test indicates how we should read the final ANOVA summary table.

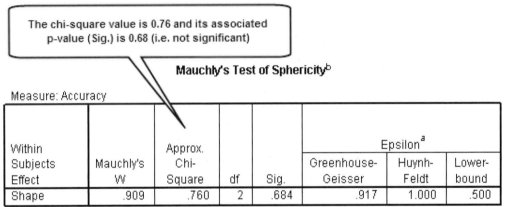

The chi-square value is 0.76 and its associated p-value (Sig.) is 0.68 (i.e. not significant)

Mauchly's Test of Sphericity[b]

Measure: Accuracy

Within Subjects Effect	Mauchly's W	Approx. Chi-Square	df	Sig.	Epsilon[a] Greenhouse-Geisser	Huynh-Feldt	Lower-bound
Shape	.909	.760	2	.684	.917	1.000	.500

Tests the null hypothesis that the error covariance matrix of the orthonormalized transformed dependent variables is proportional to an identity matrix.

   a. May be used to adjust the degrees of freedom for the averaged tests of significance. Corrected tests are displayed in the Tests of Within-Subjects Effects table.

   b.
      Design: Intercept
      Within Subjects Design: Shape

Output 4. **Mauchly's Test of Sphericity** and values of epsilon for conservative **ANOVA F** tests

The ANOVA summary table (Output 5) shows the results of four F tests of the null hypothesis that, in the population, shooting accuracy for all three shapes is the same.

The results of the tests are given in separated rows, labelled **Sphericity Assumed**, **Greenhouse-Geisser**, **Huynh-Feldt** and **Lower-Bound**. In the lower part of the table, the same row labels are used for the error terms of the four F statistics reported in the top half of the table. Each F ratio was obtained by dividing the treatment mean square in its row by the error mean square in the row of the same name in the lower half of the table. If Mauchly's Test does not show significance, we can read, in the ANOVA summary table, only the rows labelled **Sphericity Assumed**. If Mauchly's Test does show significance, we suggest that, in the ANOVA summary table, you read the rows labelled **Greenhouse-Geisser**.

The conservative test only makes a difference when:
1.   There is heterogeneity of covariance (i.e. Mauchly's Test is significant).
2.   The F with unadjusted degrees of freedom (i.e. the values shown in the **Sphericity Assumed** rows) is barely significant beyond the 0.05 level.

Should F have a low tail probability (say p<0.01), the null hypothesis can be safely rejected without making a conservative test. In the present case, Mauchly's Test gives a p-value of 0.68, so there is no evidence of heterogeneity of covariance. The usual ANOVA F test can therefore be used.

Tests of Within-Subjects Effects

Measure: Accuracy

Source		Type III Sum of Squares	df	Mean Square	F	Sig.	Partial Eta Squared
Shape	Sphericity Assumed	39.27	2.00	19.63	4.86	.021	.351
	Greenhouse-Geisser	39.27	1.83	21.41	4.86	.024	.351
	Huynh-Feldt	39.27	2.00	19.63	4.86	.021	.351
	Lower-bound	39.27	1.00	39.27	4.86	.055	.351
Error(Shape)	Sphericity Assumed	72.73	18.00	4.04			
	Greenhouse-Geisser	72.73	16.50	4.41			
	Huynh-Feldt	72.73	18.00	4.04			
	Lower-bound	72.73	9.00	8.08			

Since the Mauchly result was not significant, the Sphericity Assumed rows apply. The other rows could be deleted	For F = 4.86 with a p-value of 0.02, the factor *Shape* is significant	The value of η_p^2 is 35% (i.e. a large effect size)

Output 5. The **ANOVA** summary table for the **Within-Subjects Effects**

The main result in Output 5 is the value of F and its associated p-value (**Sig.**) for the within subjects factor *Shape*. This table has been edited to reduce the number of decimal places to two in some of the columns and to narrow some of the columns.

In the case of the factor *Shape*, note that the p-value for F in the **Sphericity Assumed** row is *0.021*: that is, the obtained value of F is significant beyond the five per cent (.05) level, but not beyond the 0.01 level. We can therefore conclude that the shape used does affect shooting accuracy. We can write this result as:

The mean scores for the three shapes of target differed significantly at the 5% level: $F(2, 18) = 4.86$; $p = .02$ Partial eta squared $= .35$, which is a large effect.

The value of 18 for the error *df* can be seen in the row labelled **Error (Shape) Sphericity Assumed**. In the present case, there was no need to make a conservative *F* test because Mauchly's Test was not significant. It is apparent from the **Sig.** column that *in this particular example* the conservative tests make no difference to the result of the ANOVA *F* test.

The next table (Output 6) shows the pairwise comparisons adjusted according to the **Bonferroni** method.

Pairwise Comparisons

Measure: Accuracy

(I) Shape	(J) Shape	Mean Difference (I-J)	Std. Error	Sig.[a]	95% Confidence Interval for Difference[a]	
					Lower Bound	Upper Bound
1	2	2.70*	.90	.044	.075	5.325
	3	2.00	1.01	.238	-.966	4.966
2	1	-2.70*	.90	.044	-5.325	-.075
	3	-.70	.78	1.000	-2.974	1.574
3	1	-2.00	1.01	.238	-4.966	.966
	2	.70	.78	1.000	-1.574	2.974

Based on estimated marginal means

*. The mean difference is significant at the .05 level.

a. Adjustment for multiple comparisons: Bonferroni.

> Only one comparison has a p-value (Sig.) < .05

Output 6. The Bonferroni adjusted **Pairwise Comparisons** among the levels of the within subjects factor *Shape* for the measure *Accuracy*

The requested profile plot is shown in Output 7, which is an edited version of the default plot, adjusted to include zero on the vertical scale. The default plot, with only a small section of the scale on the vertical axis, makes the differences among the means look enormous.

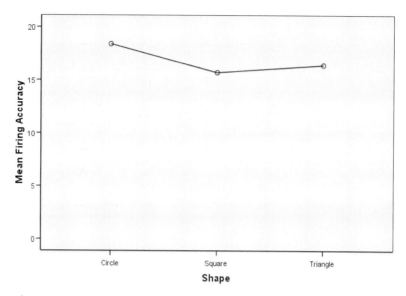

Output 7. The plot of the mean shooting accuracy for the three shapes

9.2.5 Unplanned multiple comparisons

There is some doubt as to whether, following significant main effects of within subjects factors, the **Tukey test** affords sufficient protection against inflation of the *per family* type I error rate. It is thought that the **Bonferroni** correction affords better protection.

9.3 NONPARAMETRIC EQUIVALENTS OF THE WITHIN SUBJECTS ANOVA

As with the one-factor completely randomised experiment, nonparametric methods are available for the analysis of ordinal and nominal data.

9.3.1 The Friedman test for ordinal data

Suppose that six people rank five objects in order of 'pleasingness'. Their decisions might appear as in Table 7.

If we assume that the highest rank is given to the most pleasing object, it would appear, from inspection of Table 7, that Object 3 is more pleasing to most of the raters than is Object 1. Since, however, the numbers in Table 7 are not independent measurements but ranks, the one-factor within subjects ANOVA cannot be used here. The Friedman test is suitable for such ordinal data. In **Variable View**, name the variables *Object1, Object2, ... Object5* (with no spaces before the digits). In **Data View**, enter the data in the usual way.

Table 7. Six people's ranks of five objects in order of 'pleasingness'					
	Object 1	Object 2	Object 3	Object 4	Object 5
Person 1	2	1	5	4	3
Person 2	1	2	5	4	3
Person 3	1	3	4	2	5
Person 4	2	1	3	5	4
Person 5	2	1	5	4	3
Person 6	1	2	5	3	4

To run the Friedman test:

• Choose
  Analyze➔Nonparametric Tests➔K Related Samples…
  to obtain the **Tests for Several Related Samples** dialog box (Figure 10).

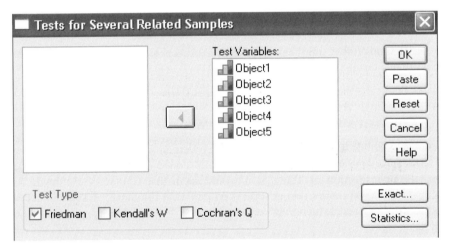

Figure 10. The **Tests for Several Related Samples** dialog box with the **Friedman** Test selected

• In the panel on the left, will appear a list of the variables. This list should include the items *Object1*, *Object2*, …, *Object5*, which will contain the numbers shown in Table 7. Simply transfer these names to the **Test Variables:** box in the usual way. Make sure the **Friedman** check box has been ticked.

• Click the **Exact…** button to see the **Exact Tests** dialog box and activate the **Exact** radio button. Click **Continue** and then **OK**.

The **Friedman Test** results are shown in Output 8.

Friedman Test

Ranks

	Mean Rank
OBJECT1	1.50
OBJECT2	1.67
OBJECT3	4.50
OBJECT4	3.67
OBJECT5	3.67

Test Statistics[a]

N	6
Chi-Square	17.200
df	4
Asymp. Sig.	.002
Exact Sig.	.000
Point Probability	.000

a. Friedman Test

The chi-square value 17.2 has a p-value (Exact Sig.) of < .0005 (significant at 0.01 level)

Output 8. **Friedman** test results

Clearly the rankings differ significantly across the objects since the p-value is less than 0.01. We can write this result as:

$$\chi^2 (4) = 17.2; p < 0.01.$$

9.3.2   Cochran's Q test for nominal data

Suppose that six children are asked to imagine they were in five different situations and had to choose between Course of Action *A* (coded *0*) and *B* (coded *1*). The results might appear as in Table 8. From inspection of Table 8, it would seem that Course of Action B (i.e. cells containing *1*) is chosen more often in some scenarios than in others. A suitable confirmatory test is **Cochran's Q** test, which was designed for use with related samples of dichotomous nominal data.

Table 8. Courses of action chosen by six children in five scenarios

	Scene 1	Scene 2	Scene 3	Scene 4	Scene 5
Child 1	0	0	1	1	1
Child 2	0	1	0	1	1
Child 3	1	1	1	1	1
Child 4	0	0	0	1	0
Child 5	0	0	0	0	0
Child 6	0	0	0	1	1

To run Cochran's Q test:

- Bring the **Tests for Several Related Samples** dialog box to the screen (see previous section and Figure 10), click off the **Friedman** check box and click the **Cochran** check box.
- Click the **Exact...** button to see the **Exact Tests** dialog box and activate the **Exact** radio button. Click **Continue** and then **OK**.

The results are shown in Output 9.

Cochran Test

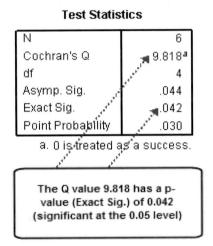

Frequencies

	Value	
	0	1
SCENE1	5	1
SCENE2	4	2
SCENE3	4	2
SCENE4	1	5
SCENE5	2	4

Test Statistics

N	6
Cochran's Q	9.818[a]
df	4
Asymp. Sig.	.044
Exact Sig.	.042
Point Probability	.030

a. 0 is treated as a success.

The Q value 9.818 has a p-value (Exact Sig.) of 0.042 (significant at the 0.05 level)

Output 9. **Cochran** test results

It is clear that the same course of action is not taken in all five scenarios:

Cochran Q = 9.82; df = 4; p = .04.

Note that, as always, we must be cautious in our statement of the implications of statistical significance. We can reject the null hypothesis that there is, in the population, no difference among the five scenarios, confirming the variation among the scenarios apparent in Table 8. We cannot, however, conclude from this that the difference between any two particular scenarios is also significant. Further pairwise post hoc comparisons could be made by using the **Sign Test**, controlling the **Type I error rate** with the **Bonferroni** procedure previously described.

9.4   THE TWO-FACTOR WITHIN SUBJECTS ANOVA

An experiment is designed to investigate the detection of certain theoretically important patterns presented on a screen. The patterns vary in shape and solidity. The dependent variable (DV) is the Number of Errors made in responding to the pattern, and the two factors Shape (Circle, Square, or Triangle) and Solidity (Outline or Solid) are the independent variables (IVs). The experimenter suspects that a shape's solidity affects whether it is perceived more readily than another shape. The same sample of participants is used for all the possible treatment combinations: that is, there are two within subjects (repeated measures) factors in the experiment. The results are shown in Table 9.

SHAPE:-	Circle		Square		Triangle	
SOLIDITY:-	Solid	Outline	Solid	Outline	Solid	Outline
Participant						
1	4	2	2	8	7	5
2	3	6	2	6	8	9
3	2	10	2	5	5	3
4	1	8	5	5	2	9
5	4	6	4	5	5	10
6	3	6	4	6	9	12
7	7	12	2	6	4	8
8	6	10	9	5	0	10
9	4	5	7	6	8	12
10	2	12	12	8	10	12

Table 9. Results of a two-factor within subjects experiment

The ANOVA summary table for the data of Table 9 is shown in Table 10 below.

Table 10. Summary table for the ANOVA of the data in Table 9

Source	Degrees of freedom	Sum of squares	Mean square	F	p
Subjects	9				
Shape	2	46.03	23.02	2.98	.08
Error (Shape)	18	138.97	7.72		
Solidity	1	117.60	117.60	54.56	<.01
Error (Solidity)	9	19.40	2.16		
Shape × Solidity	2	23.70	11.85	1.41	.27
Error (Shape × Solidity)	18	151.30	8.41		

There are three treatment sources of variance in this ANOVA: the two main effect sources Shape and Solidity; and the Shape × Solidity interaction. Each of these sources has its own error term. The error term is always the interaction between the source (i.e. Shape, Solidity or Shape × Solidity) and Subjects. So the error term for Shape is the Shape × Subjects interaction, with $2 \times 9 = 18$ degrees of freedom; the error term for Solidity is the Solidity × Subjects interaction, with $1 \times 9 = 9$ degrees of freedom; the error term for Shape × Solidity is Shape × Solidity × Subjects, with $2 \times 1 \times 9 = 18$ degrees of freedom.

The explanation of this rule for finding the correct error term lies beyond the scope of this book. Simplistically, the Subjects source can be regarded as a factor with random effects, so that the various combinations of Subjects and treatments do not cancel out across the experiment as a whole. (For more on this, see a statistical textbook such as Howell, 2007.)

9.4.1   Preparing the data set

The first four rows of data in **Data View** appear as in Figure 11.

Case	CircleSolid	CircleOutline	SquareSolid	SquareOutline	TriangleSolid	TriangleOutline
1	4	2	2	8	7	5
2	3	6	2	6	8	9
3	2	10	2	5	5	3
4	1	8	5	5	2	9

Figure 11. Part of **Data View** for the two-factor within subjects ANOVA

Extra care is needed when entering data from experiments with two or more within subjects factors. It is essential to ensure that SPSS understands which data were obtained under which combination of factors. In the present example, there are six data for each participant, each datum being a score achieved under a different combination of the two factors. We can name the data variables as *CircleSolid, CircleOutline, SquareSolid, SquareOutline, TriangleSolid* and *TriangleOutline*, representing all possible combinations of the shape and solidity factors. Such systematic, left-to-right naming not only helps to avoid transcription errors at the data entry stage, but also prevents incorrect responses when you are in the **Repeated-Measures Define Variable(s)** dialog box and are naming the within subjects factors.

Note that the left-to-right ordering of the variable names is exactly the order in which they appeared in the original table of results (Table 9).

9.4.2   Running the two-factor within subjects ANOVA

- Select
  Analyze➜General Linear Model➜Repeated Measures...
  and complete the various dialog boxes by analogy with the one-factor example, defining a second within subjects (repeated measures) factor and the dependent measure as *Errors*.
- The completed **Repeated Measures Define Factor(s)** dialog box, with the two within subjects factor names *Shape* and *Solidity*, is shown in Figure 12, together with a measure name *Errors*. (This is the name of the dependent variable in the study.)
- After **Define** has been clicked, the **Repeated Measures** dialog box appears with the six variables listed in alphabetical order on the left. (The top half is reproduced in Figure 13.)

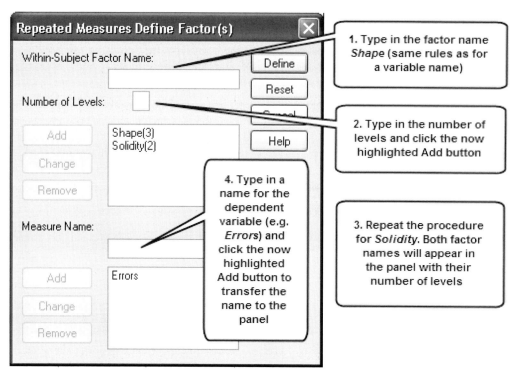

Figure 12. The **Repeated Measures Define Factor(s)** dialog box with two factors and their numbers of levels defined as well as a name for the dependent variable

On the right (Figure 13), in the box labelled **Within-Subjects Variables [Shape, Solidity]**, appears a list of the various combinations of the code numbers representing the levels of each of the two treatment factors. It will be noticed that, as one reads down the list, the first number in each pair changes more slowly than the second. When there is more than one within subjects factor, it is inadvisable immediately to transfer the variable names in a block from the left-hand box to the **Within-Subjects Variables** box by a click-and-drag operation, as in the one-factor situation. Check that the downward order of the variable names in the left-hand panel matches the order of the names in **Variable View** (or **Data View**).

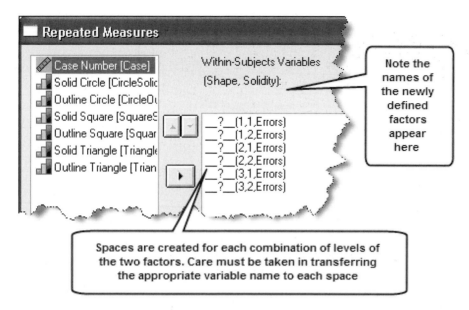

Figure 13. The top half of the **Repeated Measures** dialog box for two factors *Shape* and *Solidity* before transferring the variable names

Should your experiment be more complex, with more levels in the factors, it is safer to transfer the variables to the **Within-Subjects Variables** slots one at a time, noting the numbers in the square brackets and referring to the names of the newly defined within subjects factors (in this case *Shape* and *Solidity*) inside the square brackets in the caption above the **Within-Subjects Variables** box.

A table such as Table 11 clarifies the numbering of the levels of within subjects factors. Thus the variable *CircleSolid* is [Shape 1, Solidity 1] i.e. [1,1], *CircleOutline* is [1,2] and so on.

Table 11. Numbering of levels in within subjects variables					
Shape Factor	**Shape 1** (Circle)		**Shape 2** (Square)		**Shape 3** (Triangle)
Solidity Factor	Solidity 1 (Solid)	Solidity 2 (Outline)	Solidity 1 (Solid)	Solidity 2 (Outline)	Solidity 1 (Solid)	Solidity 2 (Outline)
Variable name	*Circle Solid*	*Circle Outline*	*Square Solid*	*Square Outline*	*Triangle Solid*	*Triangle Outline*

- The top half of the completed **Repeated Measures ANOVA** dialog box is shown in Figure 14.

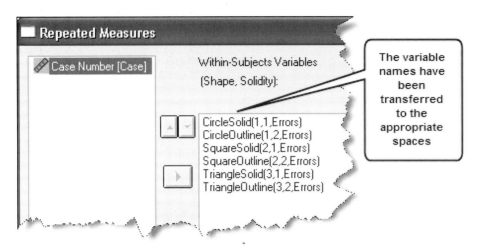

Figure 14. The **Within-Subjects Variables** section of the **Repeated Measures** dialog box after transferring the variable names

- There are some useful options associated with a repeated measures ANOVA. Request a profile plot of the levels of one of the factors across the levels of the other factor by clicking **Plots…** and following the steps shown in Figure 15. Click **Continue** to return to the original dialog box.

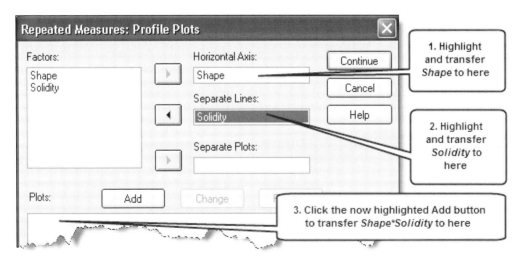

Figure 15. Part of the **Profile Plots** dialog box for requesting a profile plot *Shape*Solidity*

- A table of **descriptive statistics, estimates of effect sizes** and a table of post hoc **Bonferroni pairwise comparisons** among the levels of within subjects factors with more than two levels are requested by clicking the **Options…** button in the **Repeated Measures** dialog box and following the steps shown in Figure 16. Click **Continue** to return to the original dialog box and then **OK**.

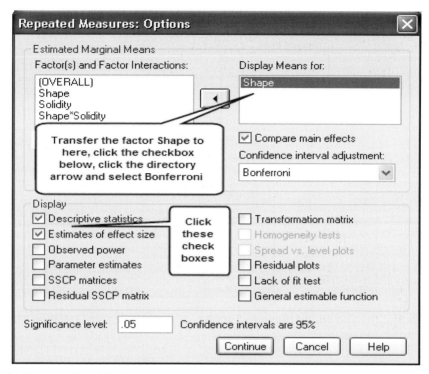

Figure 16. The completed **Options** dialog box for requesting **Descriptive statistics**, **Estimates of effect size** and **Bonferroni** comparisons among the levels of *Shape*

9.4.3 Output for a two-factor within subjects ANOVA

As in the case of the one-factor within subjects ANOVA, the output is extensive, and not all of it is required. You can make life easier by pruning some items and removing others altogether. Three of the subtables in the left-hand pane of the **SPSS Viewer** can be immediately deleted by highlighting each in turn and then pressing the **Delete** key on the keyboard: **Multivariate Tests**; **Tests of Within-Subjects Contrasts**; **Tests of Between-Subjects Effects** (in this example, there are no between subjects factors).

> See Output 2 in Section 9.2.4

Output 10 shows the **Title**, **Within-Subjects Factors** list and the specially requested **Descriptive Statistics** table.

Within-Subjects Factors

Measure: Errors

Shape	Solidity	Dependent Variable
1	1	CircleSolid
	2	CircleOutline
2	1	SquareSolid
	2	SquareOutline
3	1	TriangleSolid
	2	TriangleOutline

Descriptive Statistics

	Mean	Std. Deviation	N
Solid Circle	3.60	1.838	10
Outline Circle	7.70	3.268	10
Solid Square	4.90	3.446	10
Outline Square	6.00	1.155	10
Solid Triangle	5.80	3.190	10
Outline Triangle	9.00	3.018	10

Output 10. The **Within-Subjects Factors** list and **Descriptive Statistics** table

The next table (Output 11) reports the result of the **Mauchly's Test of Sphericity** for homogeneity of covariance (see Section 9.3).

The table is more extensive than that in Output 4, because there are two factors. Notice that the test is not applied when a factor has only two levels, as in the case of *Solidity*. The test is not significant (i.e. there is no evidence of heterogeneity of covariance) for either *Shape* or the interaction of *Shape* and *Solidity*, so the significance levels in the rows labelled **Sphericity Assumed** can be accepted. You should now remove from the ANOVA table the rows giving the results of the various conservative *F* tests.

The edited ANOVA summary table (minus the rows with the conservative tests and the words Sphericity Assumed) for the within subjects factors *Shape* and *Solidity*, and their interaction is shown in Output 12. Notice that, in contrast with a two-factor between subjects ANOVA, there are three error terms, one for each main effect and one for the interaction.

The chi-square values and their associated p-values (Sig.) show that none is significant. Note the test does not apply to factors with only two levels (e.g. *Solidity*)

Mauchly's Test of Sphericity[b]

Measure: Errors

Within Subjects Effect	Mauchly's W	Approx. Chi-Square	df	Sig.	Greenhouse -Geisser	Huynh-Feldt	Lower-bound
					Epsilon[a]		
Shape	.67	3.25	2	.197	.750	.866	.500
Solidity	1.00	.00	0	.	1.000	1.000	1.000
Shape * Solidity	.90	.82	2	.663	.911	1.000	.500

Tests the null hypothesis that the error covariance matrix of the orthonormalized transformed dependent variables is proportional to an identity matrix.

a. May be used to adjust the degrees of freedom for the averaged tests of significance. Corrected tests are displayed in the Tests of Within-Subjects Effects table.

b.
Design: Intercept
Within Subjects Design: Shape+Solidity+Shape*Solidity

Output 11. **Mauchly's Test of Sphericity** and more conservative statistics for *Shape* and for the interaction of *Shape* and *Solidity*

Tests of Within-Subjects Effects

Measure: Errors

Source	Type III Sum of Squares	df	Mean Square	F	Sig.	Partial Eta Squared
Shape	46.03	2	23.02	2.981	.076	.249
Error(Shape)	138.97	18	7.72			
Solidity	117.60	1	117.60	54.6	.000	.858
Error(Solidity)	19.40	9	2.16			
Shape * Solidity	23.70	2	11.85	1.410	.270	.135
Error(Shape*Solidity)	151.30	18	8.41			

The factor *Shape* has F = 2.98 with a p-value (Sig.) > .05 (i.e. not significant)	The factor Solidity has F = 54.6 with a p-value (Sig.) < .0005 (i.e. significant at 0.01 level)	The interaction *Shape*Solidity* has F = 1.41 with a p-value (Sig.) > .05 (i.e. not significant)	The values of η_p^2 vary from 13.5% to 86%

Output 12. The edited **ANOVA** summary table for the **Within-Subjects Effects**

Output 12 shows that the factor *Shape* has no significant main effect, since the p-value for *F* in the column headed **Sig.** is greater than 0.05. We can write this result as follows:

There was no significant effect of the *Shape* factor: F(2, 18) = 2.98; p = .08.

The factor *Solidity* is significant, since its p-value is less than 0.01 (the output value 0.000 means that the p-value is less than .0005). We can write this result as:

The *Solidity* factor had a main effect that was significant beyond the 1% level: F(1, 9) = 54.6; p = <.01. Partial eta squared = .86. This is a large effect.

Finally, there was no significant *Shape*Solidity* interaction: F(2, 18) = 1.41; p = .27.

Since the factor *Shape* is not significant, the **Bonferroni pairwise comparisons** table should be ignored.

The edited profile plot is shown in Output 13. An interaction is indicated when the profiles cross one another, diverge or converge. Obviously the slight difference in profile here is insufficient for a statistically significant interaction.

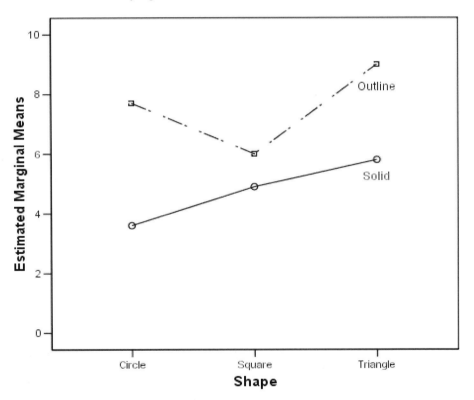

Output 13. The profile plots of the two levels of *Solidity* across the three shapes

In conclusion, Output 12 shows that only the *Solidity* factor has a significant effect: the other factor, *Shape* and its interaction with *Solidity*, are not significant.

9.4.4   Unplanned comparisons following a factorial within subjects experiment

In the example we have just considered, the question of unplanned multiple comparisons does not arise, because
1. There is no interaction.
2. The sole significant main effect involves a factor (*Solidity*) with only two levels, implying that the two means must be significantly different.

Had there been a significant interaction, however, the approach already described in the context of the one-factor within subjects experiment would also have been applicable here.

The problem with the **Bonferroni test** is that even with only six cells, it is very difficult to get a difference sufficiently large to be significant. With six cells, $c = 15$ and each t-test has to have a p-value of 0.003 or smaller to be deemed significant. There is, therefore, a case to be made for testing initially for **simple main effects** of the principal experimental factor of interest at various levels of the other factor. A significant simple main effect may justify defining the comparison family more narrowly and improves the chances of finding significant differences. As in a between subjects factorial experiment, a simple main effect of a factor can be computed by carrying out a one-way ANOVA upon the data at only one level of the other factor and applying the **Bonferroni** criterion by setting the significance level for each simple effect test at 0.05 divided by the number of tests (for simple main effects) that will be made.

9.5   A FINAL WORD

In this chapter, we have described one approach to the analysis of data from a within subjects experiment, that is, one in which each participant performs at all levels of the treatment factor. This approach is termed the **univariate** approach, because a single dependent variable (measure) was identified and the various conditions were designated as levels of the treatment factor concerned.

The univariate approach is appealing, because it maps readily on to the terminology of experimental design: we run experiments to try to demonstrate that the independent variable has a causal effect upon the dependent variable and the univariate path offered by SPSS and other computing packages marries with that very nicely. The univariate approach is satisfyingly transparent.

There is, however, another approach, which is termed the **multivariate** approach. Rather than viewing the columns of data in SPSS as representing different levels of a single independent variable or factor with k levels, they can be viewed as k dependent variables. There is a whole set of techniques, known collectively as **multivariate statistics**, which have been designed for the analysis of data regarded as comprising two or more dependent variables. Many would advocate the use of such methods in preference to the univariate approach described in this chapter. To those trained in disciplines such as psychology or biology, however, the multivariate approach often seems inaccessible and difficult to relate to their substantive research questions. Fortunately, there are now available several lucid texts on the topic, such as Tabachnick & Fidell (2007), who concentrate on the practicalities of applying multivariate methods to research problems and assume only a minimum of mathematical knowledge.

Recommended reading

There are available several readable textbooks with clear yet comprehensive accounts of within subjects ANOVA. The treatments of ANOVA in the following books are very accessible.

Field, A. (2005). *Discovering statistics using SPSS (2nd ed.)*. London: Sage.

Howell, D. C. (2007). *Statistical methods for psychology (6th ed.)*.   Belmont, CA: Thomson/Wadsworth.

Keppel, G., & Wickens, T. D. (2004).   *Design and analysis: A researcher's handbook (4th ed.)*. Upper Saddle River, NJ: Pearson Prentice Hall.

Tabachnick, B.G., & Fidell, L.S. (2007). *Using multivariate Statistics (5th ed.)*. Boston: Allyn & Bacon (Pearson International Edition).

EXERCISE 13

One-factor within subjects (repeated measures) ANOVA

Before you start

Before proceeding with this Exercise, we suggest that you study Chapter 9.

A comparison of the efficacy of statistical packages

Table 1 shows the results of an experiment in which the dependent variable was the time taken for ten participants to perform a statistical analysis using three statistical computer packages Pack1, Pack2 and Pack3. During the course of the experiment, each participant used every package and the order of use was counterbalanced across participants. Did the packages differ in their efficacy?

Table 1. Times taken by participants to carry out an analysis with different computing packages							
Case	Pack1	Pack2	Pack3	Case	Pack1	Pack2	Pack3
1	12	15	18	6	10	12	14
2	18	21	19	7	18	17	21
3	15	16	15	8	18	17	21
4	21	26	32	9	23	27	30
5	19	23	22	10	17	25	21

Opening SPSS

Open SPSS and select the **Type in data** radio button in the opening window. If **Data View** appears first, click the **Variable View** tab to open **Variable View**.

Preparing the SPSS data set

Prepare the SPSS data set as described in Section 9.2.1. Since there is just one group of participants, there is no grouping variable. Add suitable variable labels in the **Label** column such as Case Number, Package 1, Package 2, Package 3. Remember to save the data set as a data file with a suitable filename.

Exploring the data

Use the methods described in Section 9.2.2 to check for any distribution problems. Remember that outliers represented by O are not as problematic as extreme values represented by *.

Procedure for the within subjects (repeated measures) ANOVA

The within subjects ANOVA (SPSS refers to it as Repeated Measures) is selected by choosing:
Analyze➔General Linear Model➔Repeated Measures...
to open the **Repeated Measures Define Factor(s)** dialog box. Follow the procedure described in Section 9.2.3, naming the **Within-subject Factor Name** as *Package* and the **Measure Name** as *Time*. Name the **Measure Name** as *Time*. Remember to click **Plots...** and complete the **Repeated Measures: Profile Plots** dialog box by transferring *Package* to the **Horizontal Axis:** box, clicking **Add** and then **Continue** to return to the original dialog box. Remember, too, to select **Options...** and click **Bonferroni** as the measure for comparisons and to click the check boxes for **Descriptive statistics** and for **Estimates of effect size**.

Output for the within subjects (repeated measures) ANOVA

Section 9.2.4 offers some guidelines for the interpretation of the output. First, there is a **Table of Within-Subjects Factors**, which lists the levels of the *Package* factor. Then there is a table of **Multivariate Tests**, which can be deleted by clicking its icon in the left-hand pane of the **SPSS Viewer** and pressing the **Delete** key. Next comes **Mauchly's Test of Sphericity**. Check that the result does not show significance. If not, you need only read the row labelled **Sphericity Assumed** in the **Table of Within-Subjects Effects** below, in which case you should delete the other rows by double-clicking anywhere in the table, highlighting the material to be deleted and pressing the **Delete** key. The remaining two tables can be ignored.

- **What is the value of the *F* ratio and its associated p-value (tail probability) for the *Package* factor? Is *F* significant? What are the implications for the experimental hypothesis?**
- **Edit the Tests of Within-Subjects Effects table to remove the extra rows of statistics which are not needed in the light of the Mauchly test result.**
- **What is the value of Partial Eta Squared? Is this a small, medium or large effect?**

Inspect the **Profile Plots** showing the means of the three packages.
- **Is the appearance of the plot consistent with the finding from the ANOVA that there is a significant main effect?**

Finally with reference to Section 9.2.4, inspect the **Pairwise Comparisons** table to ascertain which pairs of statistical packages are significantly different.
- **List which packages differ significantly.**

Finishing the session

Close down SPSS and any other windows before logging out of the computer.

EXERCISE 14

Two-factor within subjects ANOVA

Before you start

We suggest that you read Section 9.4 before proceeding. In this Exercise, we consider the ANOVA of within subjects factorial experiments, that is, experiments with repeated measures on all factors.

A two-factor within subjects experiment

An experiment is carried out to investigate the effects of two factors upon the recognition of symbols briefly presented on a screen, as measured by the number of correct identifications over a fixed number of trials. The factors are Symbol (with levels Digit, Lower Case, and Upper Case) and Font (with levels Gothic and Roman). Each of the six participants in the experiment is tested under all six combinations of the two treatment factors. The results are shown in Table 1.

	Digit		Lower Case		Upper Case	
Case	Gothic	Roman	Gothic	Roman	Gothic	Roman
1	2	6	18	3	20	5
2	4	9	20	6	18	2
3	3	10	15	2	21	3
4	1	12	10	9	25	10
5	5	8	13	8	20	8
6	6	10	14	10	16	6

Table 1. Results of a two-factor within subjects experiment

Opening SPSS

Open SPSS and select the **Type in data** radio button in the opening window. If **Data View** appears first, click the **Variable View** tab to open **Variable View**.

Preparing the SPSS data set

In **Variable View**, define the variables as described in Section 9.4, assigning the variable names systematically, as in DigitGothic, DigitRoman, LowerGothic, LowerRoman, UpperGothic, UpperRoman. For clarity, it is recommended that self-explanatory labels such as Gothic digits, Roman digits, Gothic lowercase, and so on, be assigned by making appropriate entries in the **Label** column of **Variable View**. Enter the data into **Data View**, under the appropriate pre-headed columns. Ensure that the values in the **Decimals** column are all *0*.

Exploring the data

Obtain boxplots to check the distributions.

Running the two-factor within subjects ANOVA

To run the ANOVA, select
Analyze➔General Linear Model➔Repeated Measures...
and complete the various dialog boxes following the procedure described in Section 9.4.2. Name the factors as *Symbol* and *Font*. Name the **Measure Name** as *Recognition*. Remember to click **Plots...** and complete the **Repeated Measures: Profile Plots** dialog box by transferring *Symbol* to the **Horizontal Axis:** box and *Font* to the **Separate Lines:** box, clicking **Add** and finally **Continue**, to return to the **Repeated Measures** dialog box. Remember to click **Plots...** and complete the **Repeated Measures: Profile Plots** dialog box by transferring *Package* to the **Horizontal Axis:** box, clicking **Add** and then **Continue** to return to the original dialog box. Remember, too, to select **Options...** and click *Symbol* and then **Bonferroni** as the measure for comparisons and to click the check boxes for **Descriptive statistics** and for **Estimates of effect size** as described in Section 9.4.2.

Output for the two-factor within subjects experiment

The output for the two-factor repeated measures ANOVA is explained in Section 9.4.3. Remove the unnecessary tables at the beginning.

Next comes a table of **Mauchly's Test of Sphericity**. Check carefully to see whether there is evidence of non-sphericity. The main table of interest is the **Tests of Within-Subjects Effects**. For each factor and interaction, read the row **Sphericity Assumed** if the relevant Mauchly test is not significant; otherwise read the **Greenhouse-Geisser** row. If none of the Sphericity tests is significant, you should delete the conservative tests rows by double-clicking anywhere in the table, highlighting the material to be deleted and pressing the **Delete** key. The remaining two tables can be ignored.
- **Give the *F* ratio and p-value for each factor and the interaction. Interpret these results in terms of the aims of the study.**
- **What is the value of Partial Eta Squared for each factor? Describe each value as either a small, medium or large effect?**

Look at the table of **Pairwise Comparisons**.
- **Which symbols differ significantly?**

Finally inspect the **Profile Plots**.
- **Describe the plot and comment on whether it confirms the various ANOVA results.**

Finishing the session

Close down SPSS and any other windows before logging out of the computer.

Mixed factorial experiments

10.1   Introduction

10.2   The two-factor mixed factorial ANOVA

10.3   The three-factor mixed ANOVA

10.4   Further analysis: Simple effects and multiple comparisons

10.5   Multivariate analysis of variance (MANOVA)

10.1   INTRODUCTION

10.1.1   Rationale of a mixed factorial experiment

A researcher designs an experiment to explore the hypothesis that engineering students, because of their training in two-dimensional representation of three-dimensional structures, have a more strongly developed sense of shape discrimination than do psychology students. This, he reasons, should enable the engineers to make more accurate drawings of projections in the fronto-parallel plane of the gable-ends of buildings photographed from varying angles. The investigator creates a set of solid building-like structures with triangular, square and rectangular 'gable-ends' and the participant is required to judge which of a set of comparison shapes actually corresponds to the shape of the 'gable-end' of the object.

After a building has been viewed, the participant is required to select the correct gable-end projection from a set of figures presented on a monitor screen. The dependent variable (or measure), which we shall call *Naming*, is the number of shapes correctly identified. The results of the experiment are shown in Table 1.

It can be seen from Table 1 that there were two factors in this experiment:
   1.   Student Category, with levels Psychology and Engineering.
   2.   Shape, with levels Triangle, Square and Rectangle.

Since each participant was tested with all three shapes, *Shape* is a within subjects factor; Student Category is, of course, a between subjects factor. It is very common for factorial designs to have within subjects (repeated measures) factors on *some* (but not *all*) of their treatment factors. Since such experiments have a mixture of between subjects and within subjects factors, they are often said to be of **mixed** design. A common alternative term for this kind of design is **split-plot**, which reflects the agronomic purposes for which this type of experiment was originally designed.

Table 1. Results of a two-factor mixed factorial experiment with one within subjects factor and one between subjects factor

Group	Case	Shape		
		Triangle	Square	Rectangle
Psychology	1	2	12	7
	2	8	10	9
	3	4	15	3
	4	6	9	7
	5	9	13	8
	6	7	14	8
Engineering	7	13	3	35
	8	21	4	30
	9	26	10	35
	10	22	8	30
	11	20	9	28
	12	19	8	27

The design of this experiment is shown schematically in Table 2.

Table 2. Schematic diagram of a two-factor mixed factorial experiment

Group	Task 1	Task 2	Task 3
Group 1	Group 1 perform all 3 tasks		
Group 2	Group 2 perform all 3 tasks		

The design of this experiment is a combination of those experimental designs or plans we have been considering so far. If we were to ignore the Shape factor and calculate the mean performance of each participant across the three shapes, we should have data suitable for a one-way ANOVA; for either group, we have the results of a one-factor within subjects experiment.

Were we to run the one-way ANOVA on the mean performance of the participants across the three shapes, we should obtain the following results (Table 3).

Table 3. The ANOVA summary table					
ANOVA					
Mean					
	Sum of Squares	df	Mean Square	F	Sig.
Between Groups	359.343	1	359.343	98.952	.000
Within Groups	36.315	10	3.631		
Total	395.657	11			

Within each of the two samples of participants, however, we have, essentially, a one-factor within subjects (or Subjects × Treatments) experiment, because within each group, the Subjects factor crosses with Shape. We could run a one-factor within subjects ANOVA on the data from each group. The hybrid nature of the experimental design is demonstrated in Table 4.

Table 4. The component design elements of the mixed factorial design					
Psychologists	**Engineers**		**Triangle**	**Square**	**Circle**
Mean scores of six psychologists	Mean scores of six engineers		Psychologists		
			Triangle	**Square**	**Circle**
			Engineers		

The ANOVA summary table is shown in Table 5.

Notice that there are two error terms:
1. The between groups error term for the between subjects sources.
2. Another error term called Error (Shape) for the within subjects sources.

The term Error (Shape) is simply a pooled estimate from the error terms from the Shape × Subjects experiments in the two groups. You can see this from the degrees of freedom. Since there are six participants (subjects) within each group, the error term for either one-factor within subjects experiment is $(3 - 1)(6 - 1) = 10$. Pooling across both groups, however, doubles this value, producing the tabled df value of 20.

Table 5. ANOVA summary table for the data in Table 1					
Source	**df**	**SS**	**MS**	**F**	**p**
Between subjects sources					
Group	1	1078.03	1078.83	98.95	<.01
Error: Within Groups	10	108.94	10.89		
Within subjects sources					
Shape	2	533.56	266.78	32.62	<.01
Shape × Group	2	1308.22	654.11	79.99	<.01
Error (Shape): Pooled Shape × Subjects	20	163.56	8.18		

10.2   THE TWO-FACTOR MIXED FACTORIAL ANOVA

In Chapter 9, we saw that the within subjects ANOVA is available in **Repeated Measures** in the **General Linear Model** menu.   The mixed ANOVA also is run with the **Repeated Measures** procedure.

See Chap. 9

10.2.1   Preparing the SPSS data set

In Table 1, we chose to represent the experimental design with the levels of the within subjects factor arrayed horizontally and those of the between subjects factor stacked vertically, with Engineering under Psychology. We did so because this arrangement corresponds to the way in which the results must appear in **Data View**.

As always, the first column of **Data View** will contain the case numbers. The second column will contain a single grouping variable *Category* representing the Psychologists (1) and the Engineers (2). The third, fourth and fifth columns will contain the results at the three levels of the *Shape* factor (i.e. Triangle, Square, and Rectangle).

Using the techniques described in Chapter 2, Section 2.3, enter **Variable View** and name five variables: *Case*, *Category* (the grouping variable), *Triangle*, *Square*, and *Rectangle*.   Use the **Label** column to assign more meaningful variable names (Case Number, Category of Student) and the **Values** column to assign labels to the numerical values of the grouping variable *Category* (1 = Psychology Student, 2 = Engineering Student). Ensure that the **Decimals** column is set at 0 for each variable.

See Section 2.3

Click the **Data View** tab and enter the data into **Data View** (Figure 1). If values rather than labels appear in the variable Category, enter the **View** menu and click **Value Labels**.

Case	Category	Triangle	Square	Rectangle
1	Psychology Student	2	12	7
2	Psychology Student	8	10	9
3	Psychology Student	4	15	3
4	Psychology Student	6	9	7
5	Psychology Student	9	13	8
6	Psychology Student	7	14	8
7	Engineering Student	13	3	35
8	Engineering Student	21	4	30
9	Engineering Student	26	10	35
10	Engineering Student	22	8	30
11	Engineering Student	20	9	28
12	Engineering Student	19	8	27

Figure 1. The data from Table 1 in **Data View**

10.2.2 Exploring the results: Boxplots

As usual, the first step is to explore the data set. The boxplot was described in Section 4.3.2. Here, however, the **clustered boxplot** (which clusters the levels of the within subjects factor at different levels of the between subjects variable) is appropriate.

To obtain a clustered boxplot, proceed as follows:
- Click
  Analyze➔Descriptive Statistics➔Explore…
  to open the **Explore** dialog box.
- Complete the details as in Section 9.2.2 but with the addition of the variable name *Category of Student* transferred to the **Factor List** panel.
- Click **OK**.

The edited boxplot is shown in Output 1.

Notice the extreme score (case 3) for the number of rectangles identified by a Psychology student and the outlier (case 7) for the number of triangles identified by an Engineering student. In a real research situation, it might have been worth eliminating the two deviant scores, but here we shall work with the entire data set. Sometimes extreme scores are errors (i.e. values have been entered into the data file incorrectly) but they can also be genuine, though atypical, data.

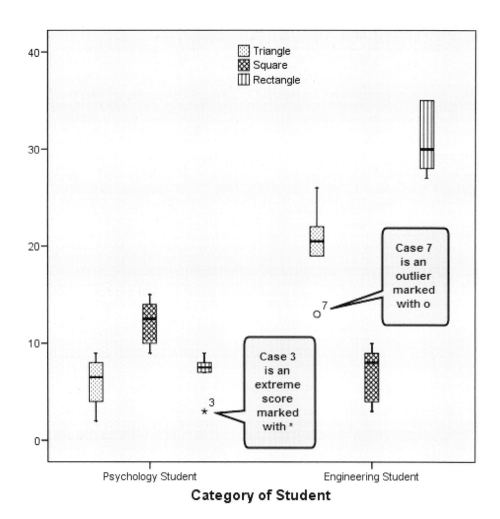

Output 1. Edited boxplots of the three shapes for each student category

10.2.3 Running the ANOVA

- Select
  Analyze➜General Linear Model➜Repeated Measures...
  to open the **Repeated Measures Define Factor(s)** dialog box. (The completed version is shown in Figure 2.)

- In the **Within-Subject Factor Name** box, delete *factor1* and type a generic name (such as *Shape*) for the repeated measures factor. This name must not be that of any of the three levels making up the factor and must also conform to the rules governing the assignment of variable names. In the **Number of Levels** box, type the number of levels (3) making up the repeated measures factor. Click **Add** and, in the middle box in Figure 2, the entry *Shape(3)* will appear. As the **Measure Name**, enter *Naming*, which is the name of the dependent variable.

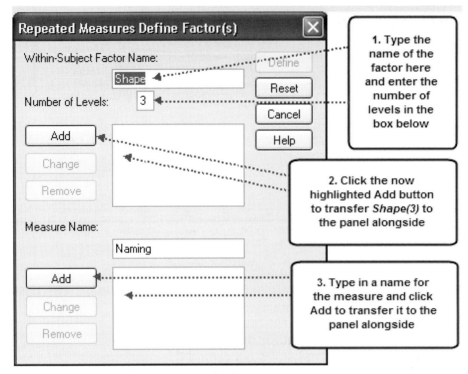

Figure 2. The **Repeated Measures Define Factor(s)** for three levels of *Shape*

- Click **Define** to open the **Repeated Measures ANOVA** dialog box.
- Transfer the variable names *Rectangle, Square, Triangle* to the **Within-Subjects Variables** box as shown in Figure 3.
- The new element is the presence of the between subjects factor *Category of Student.* Transfer its name to the **Between-Subjects Factor(s)** box as shown in Figure 3.
- You should also request a number of useful additional options. A profile plot of the levels of the within subjects factor *Shape* for each level of the between subjects variable *Category* is requested by clicking **Plots...** and following the steps shown in Figure 15 in Chapter 9. Click **Continue** to return to the **Repeated Measures** dialog box.
- A table of **descriptive statistics**, **estimates of effect size** and a table of **Bonferroni adjusted pairwise comparisons** among the levels of the within subjects factor *Shape* are requested by clicking **Options...** and following the steps shown in Figure 16 in Chapter 9. Click **Continue** to return to the **Repeated Measures** dialog box.

  See Section 9.4.2

- Had there been more than two levels in the between subjects variable *Category*, a Tukey post-hoc test could have been requested by clicking **Post Hoc...**, transferring the variable name *Category* to the **Post Hoc Tests for** box, and clicking the **Tukey** check box. Click **Continue** to return to the original dialog box.
- Click **OK** to run the ANOVA.

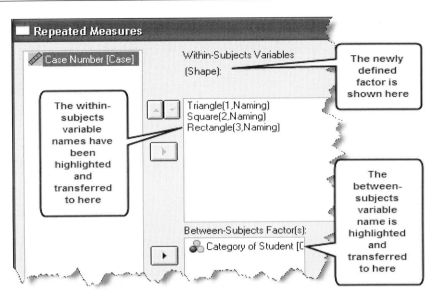

Figure 3. Part of the **Repeated Measures** dialog box showing the three levels of the within subjects factor *Shape* and the between subjects factor *Category*

10.2.4   Output for the two-factor mixed ANOVA

Output 2 shows the left-hand pane of the **SPSS Viewer**, in which the various items appearing in the right-hand pane are listed.

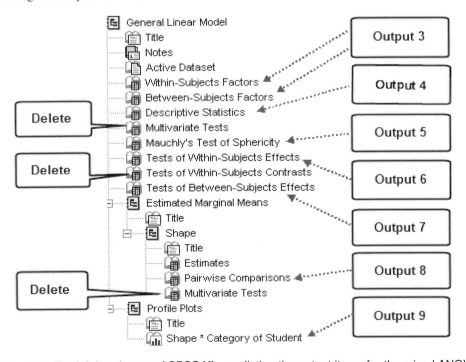

Output 2. The left-hand pane of **SPSS Viewer** listing the output items for the mixed ANOVA

Two items, **Multivariate Tests** and **Tests of Within-Subjects Contrasts**, can be deleted immediately by highlighting each in turn and pressing the **Delete** key on the keyboard. In the **Estimated Marginal Means** section, the **Multivariate Tests** table can also be deleted.

Output 3 shows the two SPSS tables identifying the levels of the Within-Subjects factors and the levels of the Between-Subjects factors.

Within-Subjects Factors

Measure: Naming

Shape	Dependent Variable
1	Triangle
2	Square
3	Rectangle

Between-Subjects Factors

		Value Label	N
Category of Student	1	Psychology Student	6
	2	Engineering Student	6

Output 3. The **Within-Subjects Factors** list of levels and the **Between-Subjects Factors** list of levels

Output 4 shows the table of descriptive statistics requested in **Options**. Inspection of the means shows different profiles across the factor *Shape* for the two student categories.

Descriptive Statistics

	Category of Student	Mean	Std. Deviation	N
Triangle	Psychology Student	6.00	2.61	6
	Engineering Student	20.17	4.26	6
	Total	13.08	8.13	12
Square	Psychology Student	12.17	2.32	6
	Engineering Student	7.00	2.83	6
	Total	9.58	3.65	12
Rectangle	Psychology Student	7.00	2.10	6
	Engineering Student	30.83	3.43	6
	Total	18.92	12.74	12

Output 4. The optional table of **Descriptive Statistics**

The next table, in Output 5, reports the result of the **Mauchly's Test of Sphericity** for homogeneity of covariance. (Section 9.2.4 describes the correct procedure when the Mauchly statistic is significant.)

See Section 9.2.4

In the present case, the **Mauchly** statistic has a p-value of 0.63, so there is no evidence of heterogeneity of covariance. The usual (**Sphericity Assumed**) F test can therefore be used. You should simplify that ANOVA table (below) accordingly by removing the information about the conservative F tests.

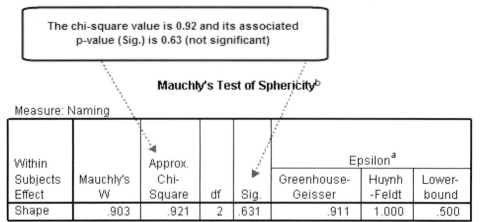

The chi-square value is 0.92 and its associated
p-value (Sig.) is 0.63 (not significant)

Mauchly's Test of Sphericity[b]

Measure: Naming

Within Subjects Effect	Mauchly's W	Approx. Chi-Square	df	Sig.	Epsilon[a]		
					Greenhouse-Geisser	Huynh-Feldt	Lower-bound
Shape	.903	.921	2	.631	.911	1.000	.500

Tests the null hypothesis that the error covariance matrix of the orthonormalized
transformed dependent variables is proportional to an identity matrix.

    a. May be used to adjust the degrees of freedom for the averaged tests of
       significance. Corrected tests are displayed in the Tests of Within-Subjects
       Effects table.

    b.
       Design: Intercept+Category
       Within Subjects Design: Shape

Output 5. **Mauchly's Test of Sphericity** and values of **Epsilon** for more conservative tests

Tests for within subjects and interaction effects

Tests of Within-Subjects Effects

Measure: Naming

Source	Type III Sum of Squares	df	Mean Square	F	Sig.	Partial Eta Squared
Shape	533.56	2	266.78	32.62	.000	.765
Shape * Category	1308.22	2	654.11	79.99	.000	.889
Error(Shape)	163.56	20	8.18			

Both the *F* values for the factor *Shape* and the
interaction *Shape*Category* have associated p-
values (Sig.) < .01 (significant at the .01 level)

The values of h_p^2 are
77% (medium) and 89%
(large) respectively

Output 6. The edited ANOVA summary table for the within-subjects factor *Shape* and its
interaction with the between-subjects factor *Category*

Note that in Output 6, the factor *Shape* is significant beyond the 1 per cent level: the p-value (**Sig.**) 0.000 is computerese for 'less than 0.0005'. Write $p < .01$, not .000. This result would be reported as:

> The mean scores for the three shapes differed significantly beyond the .01 level: $F(2, 20) = 32.62$; $p < 0.01$. Partial eta squared = .765, representing a large effect.

The *Category* × *Shape* interaction is also significant beyond the 1% level: the p-value is less than 0.0005. This result would be reported as:

> There was a significant interaction between *Category* and *Shape*: $F(2, 20) = 79.99$; $p < 0.01$. Partial eta squared = .889 which is a large effect.

Test for between subjects effects

Output 7 shows the ANOVA summary table for the between subjects factor *Category*.

Tests of Between-Subjects Effects

Measure: Naming
Transformed Variable: Average

Source	Type III Sum of Squares	df	Mean Square	F	Sig.	Partial Eta Squared
Intercept	6916.69	1	6916.69	634.9	.000	.984
Category	1078.03	1	1078.03	98.95	.000	.908
Error	108.94	10	10.89			

> Ignore the *Intercept* row. The *F* value for the factor *Category* is 98.95 with an associated p-value < .01 (significant at the .01 level)

> The value of h_{p^2} is 91% (large effect)

Output 7. The ANOVA summary table for the between-subjects factor *Category*

Ignore the terms **Intercept** and **Type III**: these refer to the regression method that was used to perform the analysis. With a p-value (**Sig.**) of less than 0.0005, there is clearly a significant difference in performance between the two groups of students. This result would be reported as:

> The mean scores for the categories of student differed significantly at the 1% level: $F(1,10) = 98.95$; $p < 0.01$. Partial eta squared = .91 which is a large effect.

The ANOVA strongly confirms the patterns discernible in Table 2: the *Shape* and *Category* factors both have significant main effects; the interaction between the factors is also significant. You will notice that that although the value given for *F* is exactly the same as in the one-way ANOVA of the mean scores of the participants over all three shapes, the mean squares for the *Category* and *Error* sources are three times the values in the one-way table. For each of the six means for each group, there were three times that number of raw scores: three scores for each mean.

Bonferroni Pairwise Comparisons for the within subjects factor

Output 8 shows the pairwise comparisons requested in **Options**.

Pairwise Comparisons

Measure: Naming

(I) Shape	(J) Shape	Mean Difference (I-J)	Std. Error	Sig.[a]	95% Confidence Interval for Difference[a]	
					Lower Bound	Upper Bound
1	2	3.50*	.97	.015	.71	6.29
	3	-5.83*	1.22	.002	-9.34	-2.32
2	1	-3.50*	.97	.015	-6.29	-.71
	3	-9.33*	1.28	.000	-13.02	-5.65
3	1	5.83*	1.22	.002	2.32	9.34
	2	9.33*	1.28	.000	5.65	13.02

Based on estimated marginal means

*. The mean difference is significant at the .05 level.

a. Adjustment for multiple comparisons: Bonferroni.

Differences significant at .01 level	Differences significant at .05 level

Output 8. The **Bonferroni pairwise comparisons** for the factor *Shape*

Profile plot

The requested profile plot is shown (edited) in Output 9. The plot confirms the pattern of the boxplots in Output 1. With squares, the Psychology students improved, while the Engineering students slumped.

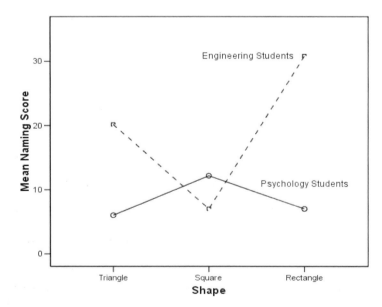

Output 9. The factor *Shape* performance profiles for each student category

10.3   THE THREE-FACTOR MIXED ANOVA

The procedures described in Section 10.2 can readily be extended to the analysis of data from mixed factorial experiments with three treatment factors. There are two possible mixed three-factor factorial experiments:

1.   Two within subjects factors and one between subjects factor (A× (B × C))
2.   One within subjects factor and two between subjects factors (A × B × (C)).

In Table 6, are shown the most common mixed ANOVA designs, all of which can be seen as elaborations of the one-factor between subjects experiment, which we shall term the 'Type A' design. In Table 6, the within subject factors are bracketed.

Table 6. The 'mixed' or 'split-plot' experimental designs, as elaborations of the simple, two-group between subjects experiment

(a) Type A design	Women		Men	
	Group 1		Group 2	

(b) Type A × (B) design	Gender	Task 1	Task 2	Task 3	Task
	Women		Group 1		
	Men		Group 2		

(c) Type A × (B×C) design	Gender	Task 1		Task 2		Task 3		Task
		L	R	L	R	L	R	Hand
	Women			Group 1				
	Men			Group 2				

(d) Type A × B × (C) Design	Gender	Hand	Task 1	Task 2	Task 3	Task
	F	R		Group 1		
		L		Group 2		
	M	R		Group 3		
		L		Group 4		

10.3.1   Two within subjects factors and one between subjects factor

Suppose that to the experiment described in Section 10.2, we were to add an additional within subjects factor, such as *Solidity* (of the shape), with two levels, Solid or Outline. The participants (either Psychology or Engineering students) now have to try to recognise both Solid and Outline Triangles, Squares, and Rectangles. Since there are six combinations of the *Shape* and *Solidity* factors, we shall need to have six variables in **Data View** to contain all the scores. Prepare the named columns systematically in **Variable View** by taking the first level of one factor (say, *Shape*) and combining it in turn with each of the levels of the second factor (*Solidity*), and then doing the same with the second and third levels of the first factor. The top part of **Data View** might appear as in Figure 4, in which it is clear that the levels of the *Shape* factor 'change more slowly' as we move from left to right across the table.

Case	Category	Triangle Solid	Triangle Outline	Square Solid	Square Outline	Rectangle Solid	Rectangle Outline
1	Psychology Student	13	15	12	23	12	14

Figure 4. The variable names for a three-factor mixed factorial experiment with two within subjects factors

Care must be taken when transferring variable names from the left to the right **Within-Subjects Variables** panel in the **Repeated Measures** dialog box. The danger is that the names in **Data View** (and hence in the list in the left-hand box) may not be moved in the required sequence. (The order of the defined factors, from which we can deduce the correct sequence of variable names in the right-hand panel, is shown in square brackets.) It may be necessary to transfer the variable names one at a time to the **Within-Subjects Variables** box to ensure that the variable names are correctly placed in the slots provided. The upper part of the completed dialog box is shown in Figure 5.

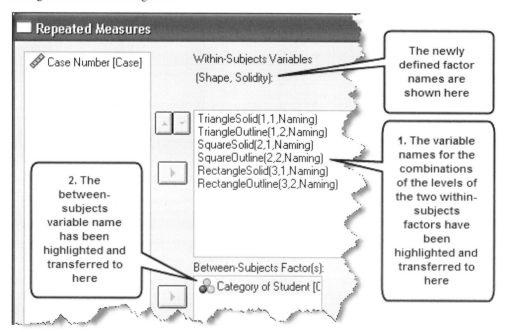

Figure 5. The upper part of the **Repeated Measures** dialog box for a three-factor mixed factorial experiment, with two within subjects factors and one between subjects factor

The output includes Output 10, which shows the within subjects factors and their various interactions with each other and with the between subjects factor, and Output 11, which shows the between subjects factor.

Tests of Within-Subjects Effects

Measure: MEASURE_1

Source	Type III Sum of Squares	df	Mean Square	F	Sig.	Partial Eta Squared
Shape	166.17	2	83.08	7.11	.017	.640
Shape * Category	109.06	2	54.53	4.67	.045	.539
Error(Shape)	93.44	8	11.68			
Solidity	25.00	1	25.00	11.25	.028	.738
Solidity * Category	28.44	1	28.44	12.80	.023	.762
Error(Solidity)	8.89	4	2.22			
Shape * Solidity	15.17	2	7.58	2.74	.124	.407
Shape * Solidity * Category	193.39	2	96.69	34.98	.000	.897
Error(Shape*Solidity)	22.11	8	2.76			

Output 10. The edited **Within-Subjects Effects** table showing the **F ratio** and **Partial Eta Squared** for the within subjects factors *Shape* and *Solidity* and their various double and triple interactions with each other and with the between subjects factor *Category*

Tests of Between-Subjects Effects

Measure: MEASURE_1

Transformed Variable: Average

Source	Type III Sum of Squares	df	Mean Square	F	Sig.	Partial Eta Squared
Category	18.78	1	18.78	.54	.504	.119
Error	139.56	4	34.89			

Output 11. The edited **Between-Subjects Effects** table showing the **F ratio** and **Partial Eta Squared** for the between subjects factor *Category*

It can be seen from the output that both factors *Shape* and *Solidity* are significant at the 5% level, that the interactions of *Shape* × *Category* and *Solidity* × *Category* are significant at the 5% level and that the triple interaction of *Shape* × *Solidity* × *Category* is significant beyond the 1% level. The interaction of *Shape* × *Solidity* is not significant. The between subjects factor *Category* is not significant.

These results are shown more clearly in the profile plots (Output 12). There are differences between the profiles of *Shape* and *Solidity* for the two categories of student and between *Shape, Solidity* and *Category*. The lack of a significant interaction between *Shape* and *Solidity* is shown in Output 13 where there is neither a crossing-over nor a large divergence between the lines for the two levels of *Solidity* across the levels of *Shape*.

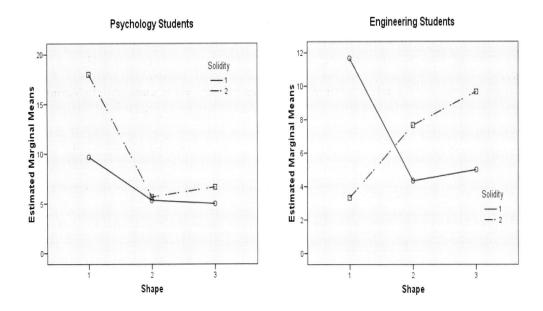

Output 12. The profile plots showing the interactions among the variables

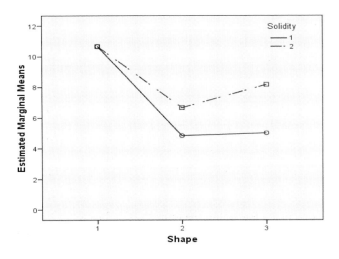

Output 13. The profile plot showing the lack of a significant interaction between Shape and Solidity

10.3.2   One within subjects factor and two between subjects factors

Suppose the experiment described in Section 10.3.1 were to have an additional between subjects factor, such as *Sex* (Male, Female) but just one within subjects factor *Shape*. The participants (either Psychology or Engineering Students, and either Male or Female) have to try to recognise different shapes of targets (Triangles, Squares and Rectangles). In **Variable View**, it will now be necessary to add a second grouping variable *Sex* (Figure 6).

Case	Category	Sex	Triangle	Square	Rectangle
1	Psychology Student	Male	2	12	7

Figure 6. The variable names for a three-factor mixed factorial experiment with one within subjects and two between subjects factors

The completed **Repeated Measures ANOVA** dialog box would then appear as in Figure 7.

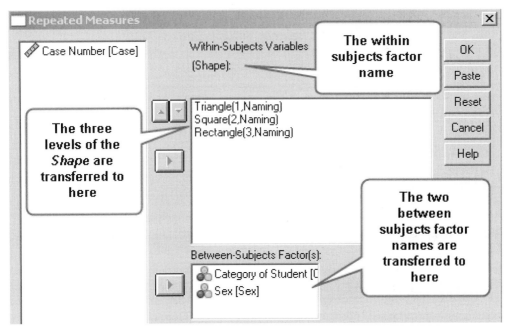

Figure 7. The upper part of the **Repeated Measures** dialog box for a three-factor mixed factorial experiment with one within subjects factor and two between subjects factors

The output includes the following tables. Output 14 shows the within subjects factor *Shape* and its various interactions with the two between subjects factors and Output 15 shows the between subjects factors *Category* and *Sex*. The results in Output 14 show that the factor *Shape* and the interaction of *Shape* and *Category* are significant at the 1% level but the interaction of *Shape* and *Sex* and the triple interaction are not significant. The results in Output 15 show that the factor *Category* is significant at the 1% level but the factor *Sex* and the interaction of *Sex* and *Category* are not significant.

The profile plot in Output 16 shows the crossing-over of the lines for the significant interaction of *Shape* and *Category*.

Tests of Within-Subjects Effects

Measure: Naming

Source	Type III Sum of Squares	df	Mean Square	F	Sig.	Partial Eta Squared
Shape	519.62	2	259.81	29.39	.000	.786
Shape * Category	1277.74	2	638.87	72.27	.000	.900
Shape * Sex	14.92	2	7.46	.84	.448	.095
Shape * Category * Sex	7.86	2	3.93	.44	.649	.053
Error(Shape)	141.44	16	8.84			

Output 14. The edited **Within-Subjects Effects** table showing the **F ratio** and **Partial Eta Squared** for the within subjects factor *Shape* and its interactions with the two between subjects factors *Category* and *Sex*

Tests of Between-Subjects Effects

Measure: Naming
Transformed Variable: Average

Source	Type III Sum of Squares	df	Mean Square	F	Sig.	Partial Eta Squared
Category	1093.34	1	1093.34	107.69	.000	.931
Sex	22.75	1	22.75	2.24	.173	.219
Category * Sex	6.28	1	6.28	.62	.454	.072
Error	81.22	8	10.15			

Output 15. The edited **Between-Subjects Effects** table showing the **F ratio** and **Partial Eta Squared** for the two between subjects factors *Category* and *Sex* together with their interaction

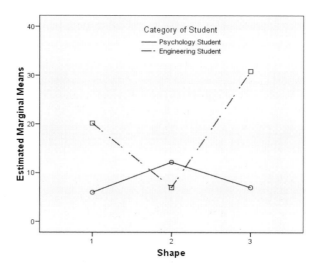

Output 16. The profile plot showing the significant interaction of *Shape* and *Category*

10.4 FURTHER ANALYSIS: SIMPLE EFFECTS AND MULTIPLE COMPARISONS

The analysis of variance is a large topic in statistics, and there are available many more techniques than we can mention in this book. For example, when an interaction is significant, it is often useful to follow up the initial ANOVA with additional tests of the effects of one factor at specific levels of another. Such analysis of **simple effects** can be combined with both planned and unplanned multiple comparisons. We urge the reader who is unfamiliar with such methods to read the relevant chapters in a statistics textbook such as Howell (2007).

At this point, it may be worth reminding the reader that the dangers of committing a **Type I error** in unplanned multiple comparisons increase enormously with the complexity of the experiment. Accordingly, the user must take precautions to control the *per family* **Type I error** rate (the probability of at least one **Type I error**). The use of simple effects tests may justify the specification of a smaller subgroup of treatment means as the 'family', increasing the power of each test.

In a three-factor experiment, for example, the significance of the three-way interaction implies that the interactions between two of the factors are not homogeneous across all levels of the third factor. Should there be a significant two-factor interaction at one particular level of the third factor (i.e. a significant **simple interaction**), one might define the comparison 'family' as the performance means at that level only. The user could then proceed to make pairwise multiple comparisons among this smaller set of means.

10.5 MULTIVARIATE ANALYSIS OF VARIANCE (MANOVA)

10.5.1 Meaning and rationale of MANOVA

All the ANOVA models we have discussed so far have involved only one DV; but there could be two or more DVs in an experiment. We have seen that ANOVA tests whether differences among group means on a *single DV* might have occurred by chance; MANOVA is an extension of ANOVA which was designed to test whether mean differences on a *combination of DVs* might have occurred by chance.

Suppose we wished to analyse the data from an experiment with more than one DV (e.g. the effects of drugs on various measures of skill). It would be possible to analyse the data on each measure of skill separately with a univariate ANOVA, but there is a danger of increasing the familywise error rate, that is, the probability of making a **Type I error**. Such a series of analyses also overlooks the possibility of finding characteristic performance profiles across measures for different drugs.

MANOVA finds orthogonal linear combinations of the DVs known as **discriminant functions** which maximise inter-group differences. (Traditionally, in fact, the one-way MANOVA was known as **discriminant analysis**.) While these discriminant functions can each be analysed with a univariate, one-way ANOVA, additional techniques are available enabling the researcher to ascertain the relative contributions of the discriminant functions to the between groups variance and of the DVs to each discriminant function. It is also possible, from the discriminant functions, to predict group membership, a process known as **classification**. For these various purposes, SPSS computes a variety of statistics, one of the most useful of which is **Wilks' Lambda**, which enables the researcher to ascertain not only the significance of the discriminants, but also their contributions to the total variance (Tabachnick and Fidell, 2007).

While MANOVA might appear to be the ideal technique for the analysis of data from experiments with two or more DVs, some cautions and caveats are in order. The highly technical terms in which the output abounds can be a formidable obstacle to the user. As with other statistical methods, MANOVA is based upon a statistical model and when the assumptions of the model are violated, the p-values of the test statistics cannot be relied upon.

10.5.2   Assumptions of MANOVA

In univariate ANOVA, the data should be normally distributed. In MANOVA, the distributions of the DVs should be **multivariate normal**: if there are k DVs, then for any set of fixed values of $k - 1$ of them, the distribution of the remaining variable must be normal. The assumption of multivariate normality is the counterpart, in multivariate statistics, of the assumption of normality of distribution in univariate ANOVA.

In univariate ANOVA, the data should meet the requirement of homogeneity of variance. In MANOVA, the counterpart of this assumption is **homogeneity of covariance**, which can be tested by analysing the variance-covariance matrix. To some extent, MANOVA is robust to some violation of the assumptions of multivariate normality and homogeneity of covariance. The greatest threat to the accuracy of the p-values of the test statistics comes from a combination of unequal sample sizes and heterogeneity of variance and covariance.

The presence of strong associations among the variables is known as **multicollinearity**. In the extreme case of a perfect correlation between two of the DVs, the variance-covariance matrix is **singular**, that is, the determinant does not exist and the key statistics cannot be calculated. If the data show multicollinearity, one or more of the dependent variables must be removed before MANOVA can run successfully.

10.5.3   Relation of MANOVA to within subjects ANOVA

The reader will recall that in Section 10.2.4, the output for the within subjects ANOVA included a table of **Multivariate tests** (see Output 2) which at that stage was ignored. Here we can note that if we consider the levels of the within subjects factor (the IV) in an ANOVA as a set of DVs, then we have an experimental design suitable for analysis with MANOVA.

10.5.4   Application of MANOVA to the recognition of shapes example

Suppose we re-analyze the data set in Section 10.1.1 with MANOVA, treating the three levels of the Shape factor as three DVs (*Triangles*; *Squares*; *Rectangles*), rather than different levels of a within subjects factor. The IV, as before, is the group factor *Category*. Thus we now have an experiment with one IV and three DVs. The previous within subjects ANOVA discussed in Section 10.3 found that the within subjects factor *Shape* and the between subjects group factor *Category* both had significant main effects and their interaction was also significant. The recasting of the data, however, makes it possible to compare the performance profiles of the two groups of students more thoroughly (and, from the testing point of view, more safely) than is possible with the univariate approach. (See Tabachnick & Fidell, 2007, Chapter 8, for a full discussion.)

- Select **Analyze➔General Linear Model➔Multivariate...** to open the **Multivariate** dialog box (Figure 8).
- Transfer the DVs to the **Dependent Variables** box.
- Click **Options** and select **Descriptive statistics**, **Estimates of effect size**, and **Homogeneity tests** for checking the assumption of homogeneity of the variance-covariance matrix (Figure 9).   Click **Continue** to return to the **MANOVA** dialog box.
- Click **OK** to run the MANOVA.

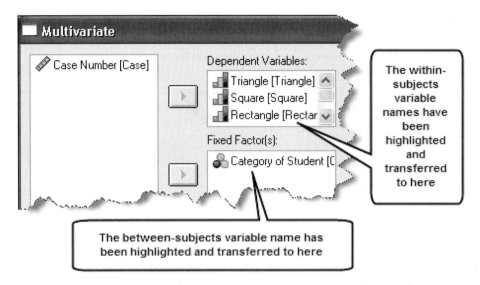

Figure 8. The **Multivariate** dialog box with the DVs transferred to the **Dependent Variables** box and the IV to the **Fixed Factor(s)** box

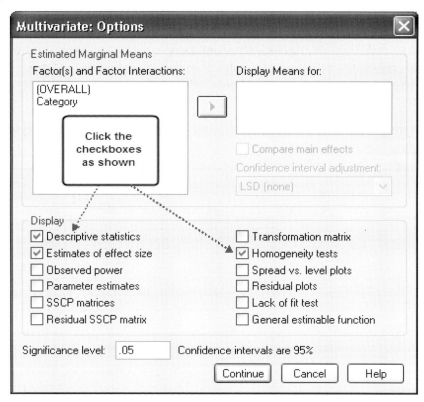

Figure 9. The **Multivariate: Options** dialog box with **Descriptive statistics**, **Estimates of effect size** and **Homogeneity tests** selected

10.5.5 Output for MANOVA

After tables of the Between Subjects Factors and Descriptive Statistics (not reproduced here), there is the **Box's Test of Equality of Covariance Matrices** (Output 17). With a p-value greater than 0.05, there is clearly no problem with lack of homogeneity.

Box's Test of Equality of Covariance Matrices[a]

Box's M	6.539
F	.727
df1	6
df2	724.528
Sig.	.628

With a p-value (Sig.) > .05, there is no problem with a lack of homogeneity

Tests the null hypothesis that the observed covariance matrices of the dependent variables are equal across groups.

a. Design: Intercept+Category

Output 17. The **Box's Test of Equality of Covariance Matrices** table

The next table (Output 18) tabulates the values of the four algorithms used by SPSS to compute the best linear combination of DVs to maximise the mean differences between the levels of the IV in the row labelled *Category* (the group factor). The table also shows the associated *F* values and their p-values (Sig.) as well as the requested estimates of effect size (partial eta squared). With only two levels of the IV, the F values are all the same.

Multivariate Tests[b]

Effect		Value	F	Hypothesis df	Error df	Sig.	Partial Eta Squared
Intercept	Pillai's Trace	.99	271.18[a]	3	8	.000	.990
	Wilks' Lambda	.01	271.18[a]	3	8	.000	.990
	Hotelling's Trace	101.69	271.18[a]	3	8	.000	.990
	Roy's Largest Root	101.69	271.18[a]	3	8	.000	.990
Category	Pillai's Trace	.96	63.47[a]	3	8	.000	.960
	Wilks' Lambda	.04	63.47[a]	3	8	.000	.960
	Hotelling's Trace	23.80	63.47[a]	3	8	.000	.960
	Roy's Largest Root	23.80	63.47[a]	3	8	.000	.960

a. Exact statistic

b. Design: Intercept+Category

> The p-value (Sig.) for the factor *Category* associated with all the multivariate statistics is <.01 (significant at the .01 level)

Output 18. The **Multivariate Tests** table

Just as in the case of ANOVA, this table shows a highly significant difference for *Group*. The effect size (.96) is larger than the ANOVA value (.91). The next table (not reproduced here) is **Levene's Test of Equality of Error Variances** which tests the null hypothesis that the error variance of the dependent variable is equal across groups.

The final edited table (Output 19) lists the univariate tests on each of the DVs for the IV in the row labelled *Group* (the three groups).

Tests of Between-Subjects Effects

Source	Dependent Variable	Type III Sum of Squares	df	Mean Square	F	Sig.	Partial Eta Squared
Category	Triangle	602.08	1	602.08	48.23	.000	.828
	Square	80.08	1	80.08	11.98	.006	.545
	Rectangle	1704.08	1	1704.08	210.81	.000	.955
Error	Triangle	124.83	10	12.48			
	Square	66.83	10	6.68			
	Rectangle	80.83	10	8.08			
Total	Triangle	2781.00	12				
	Square	1249.00	12				
	Rectangle	6079.00	12				

The relative magnitudes of *F* show that the two categories of students differ most greatly in recognising rectangles followed by triangles and finally squares

Output 19. The univariate tests for each DV

This shows that recognising squares is less different than the other shapes between the two categories of students (as also reflected in the value of its partial eta squared), a finding similarly apparent in the ANOVA Bonferroni comparisons tabulated in Output 8.

There are several ways of proceeding when a MANOVA main effect or an interaction is significant but details of these are beyond the scope of this book. SPSS provides a step-by-step tutorial - click the **Help** button in the **MANOVA** dialog box and then click **Show me** at the foot of the resulting text box. Books such as Tabachnick & Fidell (2007) and Field (2005) suggest further procedures such as Roy-Bargmann Stepdown Analysis and Discriminant Analysis.

10.5.6   Final comment

We have taken only a very brief look at MANOVA using a simple example. MANOVA designs can have many more factors and DVs as well as covariates, and can include contrast analyses to tease out the combination(s) of DVs. To learn more about these techniques, you should consult textbooks such as those already cited before embarking on a MANOVA.

Recommended reading

There are many readable textbooks on ANOVA, which provide extensive coverage of within subjects ANOVA. These include:

Howell, D. C. (2007). *Statistical methods for psychology (6th ed.)*. Belmont, CA: Thomson/Wadsworth.
Keppel, G., & Wickens, T. D. (2004). *Design & Analysis (4th ed.)*. New Jersey: Pearson Education.

There are now several excellent textbooks on multivariate statistics, including MANOVA. These include:

Field, A. (2005). *Discovering Statistics Using SPSS (2nd ed.)*. London: Sage.

Tabachnick, B. G., & Fidell, L. S. (2007). *Using multivariate statistics (5th ed.)*. Boston: Allyn & Bacon (Pearson International Edition).

Todman, J., & Dugard, P. (2006). *Approaching multivariate statistics: An introduction for psychology*. Hove: Psychology Press. This is a remarkably lucid and readable book.

EXERCISE 15

Mixed ANOVA: two-factor experiment

Before you start

Readers should study Chapter 10 carefully before proceeding with this Exercise.

Effects of ambient hue and sound on vigilance

In an experiment investigating the effect of the colour of the ambient light upon the performance of a vigilance task, participants were asked to press a button when they thought they could discern a signal against a background of random noise. The experimenter expected that the detection of different kinds of sound would differ depending on the ambient colour. Three types of signal were used: a horn, a whistle and a bell. Each signal was presented 30 times in the course of a one-hour monitoring session, during which the participant sat in a cubicle lit by either red or blue light. The dependent variable was the number of correct presses of the button. For theoretical purposes, it was necessary to use different participants for the different colour conditions. It was considered that there would be advantages in testing each individual with all three kinds of signal. In this experiment, therefore, the factor of Colour was between subjects; whereas the other factor, Signal, was within subjects.

The results are shown in Table 1.

Table 1. The results of a two-factor mixed factorial experiment

Colour	Participant	Signal		
		Horn	Whistle	Bell
Red	1	25	18	22
	2	22	16	21
	3	26	19	26
	4	23	21	20
	5	19	18	19
	6	27	23	27
Blue	7	19	12	23
	8	21	15	19
	9	23	14	24
	10	20	16	21
	11	17	16	20
	12	21	17	19

Preparing the SPSS data set

Rearrange the data of Table 1 into a form suitable for entry into SPSS. In **Variable View**, after naming a variable *Case*, you will need to have a grouping variable *Colour* and three variables for the scores: *Horn*, *Whistle*, and *Bell*. The last three variables will be the three levels of the within-subjects factor *Signal*, which is not defined until the ANOVA command is actually being run. Follow the procedure described in Section 10.2.1. Save the data with a suitable file name.

Exploring the data set

Draw boxplots as described in Section 10.2.2.

- **What do the plots tell us about the distributions? (Comment on the position of the median bar in the box.)**

- **Are there any markedly deviant scores, as shown by * or 0?**

Running the two-factor mixed ANOVA

Run the ANOVA as described in Section 10.2.3, remembering to request **Descriptive Statistics**, a **Profile Plot** and **Bonferroni Pairwise Comparisons** for the factor *Signal* (see Chapter 9, Figure 16 for details of how to request **Bonferroni pairwise comparisons**). Name the **Measure Name** as *Recognition* in the **Define Factors** dialog box. Click the check boxes for **Descriptive statistics** and for **Estimates of effect size** in the **Options** dialog box.

Output for the two-factor mixed ANOVA

The main features of the output are explained in Section 10.2.4. After tables listing the **Within-Subjects Factors** and **Between-Subjects Factors**, look at the table of **Descriptive Statistics** and the **Profile Plot**.

- **Can you discern any pattern in the means for each level of colour across the three signals?**

The next table, **Multivariate Tests**, can be deleted by highlighting its icon in the left-hand pane of **SPSS Viewer** and pressing the **Delete** key. Next, comes the table showing the results of **Mauchly's Test of Sphericity**, followed by the **Tests of Within-Subjects Effects**. If the Mauchly's Test is not significant, read the rows labelled **Sphericity Assumed** and delete the conservative test rows by double-clicking anywhere in the table, highlighting the material to be deleted and then pressing the **Delete** key. Delete the **Tests of Within-Subjects Contrasts** table.

- **For the Signal factor, write down the value of *F* and its associated p-value. Do the same with the interaction between Signal and Colour. What is the value of Partial Eta Squared and can it be described as a small, medium or large effect?**

- **Next there is a table of Tests of Between-Subjects Effects. For the Colour factor, write down the value of *F* and its associated p-value. What is the value of Partial Eta Squared and can it be described as a small, medium or large effect?**

- **Does the profile plot show a pattern consistent with the results of the ANOVA?**

- **Has the experimenter's hypothesis been confirmed?**

Finishing the session

Close down SPSS and any other windows before logging out.

EXERCISE 16

Mixed ANOVA: three-factor experiment

Before you start

Before proceeding with this Exercise, you should study Section 10.3. From the procedural point of view, the analysis of mixed experiments with three factors is a fairly simple extension of the command for two-factor mixed experiments. In general, however, the interpretation of data from factorial experiments becomes increasingly problematic as more factors are added. In particular, where there is a complex experiment with repeated measures on some factors but not on others, the naming of the factors must be carried out with special care.

A three-factor mixed factorial experiment with two within subjects factors and one between subjects factor

Imagine an experiment investigating the recognition of shapes under sub-optimal conditions on a monitor screen. The experimenter is interested in whether the different shapes are more readily recognised if they are filled rather than merely outlines, and whether Engineering students are more adept at recognising shapes than Psychology students. There are three shapes (Shape1, Shape2, Shape3), each of which can be either Open (merely an outline) or Filled. Each participant in the experiment is tested under all six combinations of these two treatment factors, which can be labelled *Shape* and *Shade*. The between subjects factor *Category* is the observer group: one group consists of Psychology students, the other of Engineering students. The dependent variable is the number of correct identifications over a fixed series of trials. The results are shown in Table 1.

Table 1. Three-factor mixed factorial experiment with two within subjects treatment factors

Particip-ant	Shape:- Shade:- Category	Shape 1 Open	Shape 1 Filled	Shape 2 Open	Shape 2 Filled	Shape 3 Open	Shape 3 Filled
1	Psychology	2	12	3	1	4	5
2	Psychology	13	22	5	9	6	8
3	Psychology	14	20	8	7	5	7
4	Engineering	12	1	3	9	6	10
5	Engineering	11	2	8	10	5	9
6	Engineering	12	7	2	4	4	10

Preparing the SPSS data set

In **Variable View,** in addition to a case variable, it will be necessary to name one grouping variable *Category* and six other variables (one for each combination of the *Shape* and *Shade* factors) to contain the results. We suggest that you name the variables in the systematic fashion described in Section 10.3.1.

The ANOVA

The command for running the **Repeated Measures ANOVA** is outlined in Section 10.3.1. The procedure is a straightforward extension of the routine for the two-factor mixed experiment. Name and specify the numbers of levels of two within subjects factors (*Shape* and *Shade*). Name the **Measure Name** as *Recognition*. Transfer the between subjects variable *Category* to the **Between-Subjects Factor(s):** box. To request the profile plots, click the **Plots...** button to open the **Repeated Measures: Profile Plots** dialog box. Enter *Shape* in the **Horizontal Axis:** box, *Shade* in the **Separate Lines:** box and *Category* in the **Separate Plots:** box. Click **Add** and then **Continue**, to return to the original dialog box. Select **Options...** to request **Descriptive Statistics, Estimates of Effect Size** and **Bonferroni Pairwise Comparisons** for the factor *Shape*. Click **Continue** and **OK** to run the analysis.

The output

Check the **Within-Subjects Factors** table and **Between-Subjects Factors** table for accuracy. Inspect the table of **Descriptive Statistics** to see if you can discern a pattern of means. Delete the table of **Multivariate Tests**. The **Mauchly** tests will appear in the table **Mauchly's Test of Sphericity**. The Mauchly test only arises with factors that have more than two levels. In this case, there will be Mauchly tests for the *Shape* factor and the *Shape* × *Shade* interaction. Check that the p-values are greater than 0.05.

The within subjects tests are given in the table **Tests of Within-Subjects Effects**. If the relevant Mauchly test is not significant, you need study only the rows in the ANOVA table labelled **Sphericity Assumed** and you can delete the rows for the conservative tests. Delete the **Tests of Within-Subjects Contrasts** table. The next table is **Tests of Between-Subjects Effects** for the factor *Category*.

- Write down the F ratios (and p-values) for the three factors, their two-way interactions and the three-way interaction. Do the values of F confirm the patterns among the treatment means you have observed in the table of Descriptive Statistics and the Profile Plots?

- Write down the corresponding Partial Eta Squared values along with whether the effect sizes are small, medium or large.

Look at the table of **Pairwise Comparisons**.

- Are any of the pairs significantly different? If not, why not, considering that the factor Shape is significant in the ANOVA?

Finally inspect the **Profile Plots** again. Compare the pattern of lines in both plots.

- Does the ANOVA confirm the appearance of the graphs? Why was the triple interaction significant?

- Has the experimenter's hypothesis been confirmed? In your answer, refer to the relevant features of the results.

Finishing the session

Close down SPSS and any other windows before logging out.

CHAPTER 11

Measuring statistical association

11.1   INTRODUCTION

So far, this book has been concerned with statistical methods devised for the purpose of comparing averages among samples of data that might be expected to differ in their typical magnitude: for example, a drug group might be compared with a placebo group; right-handed people might be compared with left-handed people; the trained might be compared with the untrained; males might be compared with females.

11.1.1 A correlational study

Suppose that a researcher believes that exposure to screen violence promotes actual violence in children. Ethical and practical considerations rule out an experiment in which the independent variable of amount of exposure to screen violence is manipulated to determine its effects upon the incidence of violent behaviour. The investigator, therefore, decides upon a correlational strategy. Twenty-seven children are measured on two variables:
1. Their exposure to screen violence (*Exposure*).
2. Their actual violence (*Actual*).

The researcher measures these variables in the expectation that they will show a positive association: there should be a tendency for those with high *Exposure* also to score highly on *Actual* violence; those who score low on *Exposure* should show *Actual* violence; and those with average *Exposure* should fall within the normal range on *Actual* violence. This strategy will not yield the strong evidence for causation that a true experiment would yield; however, an association would at least be consistent with the researcher's view that exposure to screen violence encourages actual violence in children.

Correlational research like this results in a **bivariate** data set, which can be depicted in a **scatterplot**. The scatterplot of the children's actual violence against their exposure to screen violence is shown in Figure 1. In the scatterplot, each person is represented as a point, the coordinates of which are the person's scores on the *Exposure* and *Actual* scales, which are marked out on the vertical and horizontal axes, respectively.

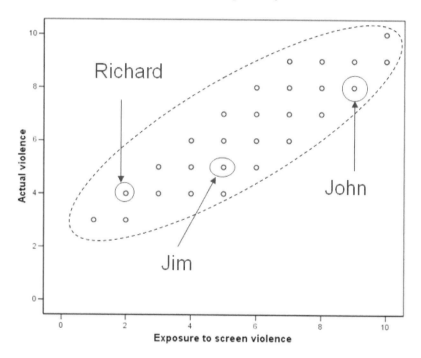

Figure 1. Scatterplot of *Actual Violence* against *Exposure to Screen Violence*

It is evident from the scatterplot that there is indeed an association between *Exposure* and *Actual* violence: John was highest on *Exposure* and he was also the most violent of the three children identified in the figure; Richard, with least *Exposure*, was also the least violent; Jim had intermediate scores on both variables. On the other hand, the association is imperfect: four children, including Jim, scored 5 on *Exposure*; but their *Actual* violence scores ranged from 4 to 7.

11.1.2 Linear relationships

One variable is said to be a **linear function** of another if the graph of the first upon the second is a straight line. Temperature in degrees Fahrenheit is a linear function of temperature in degrees Celsius, as shown in Figure 2.

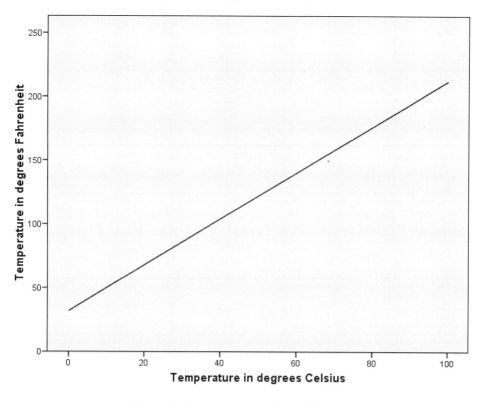

Figure 2. A linear (straight line) relationship

Errors of measurement

In many empirical disciplines, including medicine, biology and psychology, measurements have associated with them a considerable random, or **error** component. This means that, even if two variables do have a linear relationship, the points in their scatterplot will never lie on a straight line, as in Figure 2. Provided, however, that the scatterplot has an elliptical shape as in Figure 1, the relationship between the variables is *basically* linear in nature, subject to random errors of measurement.

If the slope of the longer axis of the ellipse is positive, the variables are said to be **positively correlated**; if it is negative, they are **negatively correlated**. The thinner the ellipse, the stronger the degree of linear relationship; the fatter the ellipse, the weaker the relationship.

If two variables are dissociated or independent, their scatterplot will be a circular cloud of points. Suppose two coins are each tossed 100 times and the number of heads recorded for each. The experiment is repeated, so that there are 1000 pairs of scores. We should not expect any association between the values for the first and second coins. The scatterplot will appear as in Figure 3.

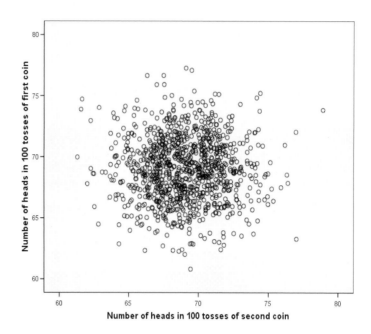

Figure 3. Scatterplot showing absence of association between two variables

11.2   THE PEARSON CORRELATION

The Pearson correlation is a measure of a supposed linear relationship between two variables. There are several different formulae for the Pearson correlation, two of the most common of which are as follows:

$$r_{XY} = \frac{\Sigma(X - M_X)(Y - M_Y)}{\sqrt{\Sigma(X - M_X)^2 \, \Sigma(Y - M_Y)^2}} = \frac{SP}{\sqrt{SS_X \, SS_Y}} \qquad (1) \; \textbf{The Pearson correlation}$$

In the SS/SP version of the formula, SS stands for 'Sum of Squares' (i.e. the sum of the squared deviations from the mean) and SP stands for 'Sum of Products' (i.e. the sum of the products of the deviations from M_X and M_Y over all the participants in the study).

The range of values of the Pearson correlation

By definition, the value of r can vary only within the range from -1 to $+1$, inclusive.

$$-1 \le r \le +1 \qquad (2) \; \textbf{Range of possible values of } r$$

This property confers upon the Pearson correlation a great advantage over another measure of association known as the **covariance**, which was described in Chapter 9. Unlike the covariance, the correlation coefficient is 'unit-free', in that it can be used to compare the degrees of association between pairs of variables measured in different units. A correlation between the heights and weights of fifty people measured in centimetres and grams respectively has the same value as the correlation between their heights and weights measured in inches and pounds.

The sign of a correlation

The sign of a correlation may reflect the natures of the variables being measured: one would not expect height to correlate negatively with weight. Often, however, the sign of a correlation is merely a matter of definition and scaling and therefore arbitrary. There exist measures of Decisiveness and Indecisiveness, which show a strong association. The strong negative correlation between the two measures, however, merely reflects the fact that the numerical scales progress in opposite directions. The two scales are, to a large extent, measuring the same dimension.

The important thing about a correlation is often its *absolute* value, i.e., its value with the sign ignored. Figure 4 shows two scatterplots: the first is the scatterplot of *Actual* violence upon *Exposure* to violence; the second is a scatterplot with the direction of the *Exposure* scale reversed (by multiplying the original *Exposure* scores by −1). In either case, the absolute value of the Pearson correlation is 0.90. A negative correlation of −.0.90 represents the same (strong) degree of linear association as a positive correlation of + 0.90.

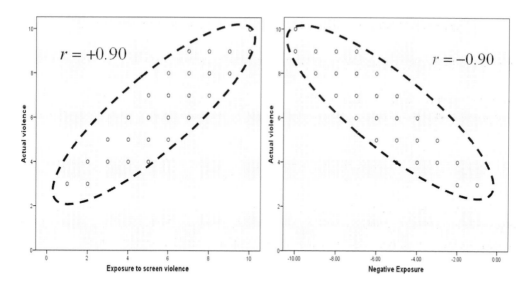

Figure 4. Scatterplots of data sets showing the same degree of association, but with correlations of opposite sign

A perfect linear association, with all the points in the scatterplot lying along the same straight line, would be reflected either in a correlation of +1 or a correlation of −1: either value would represent a perfect linear relationship.

Testing an obtained value of r for significance

The test for the significance of a correlation coefficient presupposes that the data have the property of **bivariate normality**, that is, at any particular value of either variable, the other variable has a normal distribution. If that requirement is met, the test of the null hypothesis that, in the bivariate normal population, the correlation is zero is made with the statistic *t*, where

$$ t = \frac{r\sqrt{(n-2)}}{\sqrt{(1-r^2)}} \qquad \text{with } (n-2) \text{ degrees of freedom.} $$

A word of warning

It is quite possible, from inspection of a scatterplot, to do two useful things:
1.   See whether there is indeed a linear relationship between the variables, in which case the Pearson correlation would be a meaningful statistic to use;
2.   Guess fairly accurately what the value of the Pearson correlation would be if calculated.

In other words, from inspection of the scatterplot alone, one can discern the most important features of the true relationship (if any) between two variables. So if we reason from the scatterplot to the statistics, we shall never go seriously wrong.

The converse, however, is not true: *given only the value of a Pearson correlation, one can say nothing whatsoever about the relationship between two variables.* Many years ago, in a famous paper, the statistician Anscombe (1973) presented some bivariate data sets which illustrate how misleading the value of the Pearson correlation can be. In one set, for instance, the correlation was high, yet the scatterplot showed no association whatsoever; in another, the correlation was zero, but the scatterplot showed a perfect, but nonlinear, association. The moral of this cautionary tale is clear: when studying the association between two variables, always construct a scatterplot, and interpret (or disregard) the Pearson correlation accordingly.

In the same paper, Anscombe gave us a useful rule for deciding whether there really is a robust linear relationship between two variables: should the shape of the scatterplot be unaltered by the removal of a few observations at random, the plot is an accurate depiction of the true relationship between the variables.

To sum up, the Pearson correlation is a measure of a *supposed* linear relationship between two variables; but the supposition of linearity must always be confirmed by inspection of the scatterplot.

11.2.1   Effect size

Unlike *t*, *F* or chi-square, the value of a correlation is, in itself, a measure of 'effect' size, bearing in mind that correlation does not imply causation. However, for the purposes of comparison with other measures of effect size, the **square** of the correlation r^2, which is known as the **coefficient of determination**, is often used instead. The reason for this will be explained in Chapter 12, where we shall see that the square of the Pearson correlation is the proportion of the variance of the scores on the target or criterion variable that is accounted for by regression upon another variable.

The Pearson correlation between the *Actual* and *Exposure* scores is .89. The value of the coefficient of determination (CD) is therefore $.89^2 = .80$. This means that 80% of the variance of *Actual* scores is accounted for by regression.

It may be helpful to think of the coefficient of determination as the proportion of the variance of either variable that is shared with the other variable. This sharing of variance can be depicted by two overlapping circles, where the overlapping area represents the proportion of the variance of either variable that is shared (Figure 5).

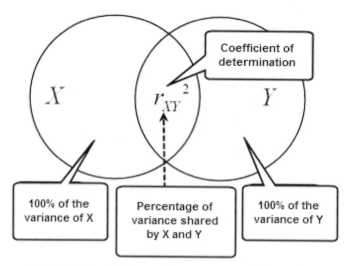

Figure 5. The coefficient of determination as the percentage of the variance of either variable that is shared with the other

In the coefficient of determination (r^2), we have a measure of effect size which is comparable to those we have met in the context of *t* tests and ANOVA. The ANOVA eta squared η^2 and adjusted R^2 statistics are actually coefficients of determination: they represent the proportion of the variance of the scores on the dependent variable that can be predicted from knowledge of the treatment categories; or, alternatively, as the proportion of shared variance. Effect size, therefore, might be classified as follows:

Effect size (r^2)	Size of Effect
<0.01 (<1%)	Small
0.01 to 0.10 (1-10%)	Medium
>0.10 (>10%)	Large

11.3   CORRELATION WITH SPSS

Table 1 shows the raw data that were pictured in the scatterplot in Figure 1.

	Exposure	Violence			Exposure	Violence
1	1	3	15	5	7
2	2	3	16	6	7
3	2	4	17	7	7
4	3	4	18	8	7
5	4	4	19	6	8
6	5	4	20	7	8
7	3	5	21	8	8
8	4	5	22	9	8
9	5	5	23	7	9
10	6	5	24	8	9
11	4	6	25	9	9
12	5	6	26	10	9
13	6	6	27	10	10
14	7	6			

Table 1. The raw data from the violence study.

Preparing the SPSS data set

As usual, begin in **Variable View**. Name the variables *Actual* and *Exposure* and assign full variable labels, such as *Actual Violence* and *Exposure to Screen Violence*. Set the **Decimals** specification to zero in order to avoid unnecessary clutter in **Data View**. Switch to **Data View** and enter the data. Save the data set.

11.3.1   Obtaining a scatterplot

The procedure for plotting a scatterplot using **Chart Builder** is described in Section 5.7. Here we want a scatterplot of *Actual* against *Exposure*.

The default scatterplot will not show the zero point on the vertical scale. If it is desired to do so, then this can be done by either editing the scatterplot *after* it has been plotted or, more simply, editing the **Element Properties** dialog box *before* plotting. Follow the steps in Figure 6 to plot the scatterplot starting at zero on the **Y-Axis**.

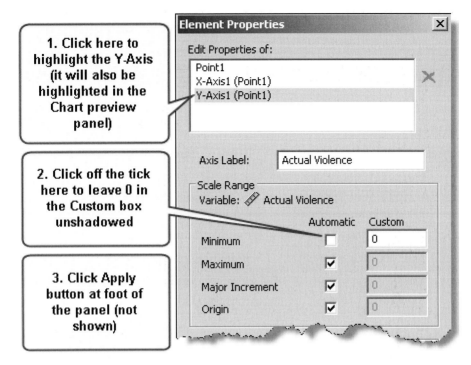

Figure 6. Editing the **Element Properties** dialog box to obtain a scatterplot showing the entire Y-Axis scale starting at zero

11.3.2 Obtaining the Pearson correlation

Choose

- **Analyze→Correlate→Bivariate...** (Figure 7) to open the **Bivariate Correlations** dialog box (Figure 8).
- Complete the dialog as in Figure 8.

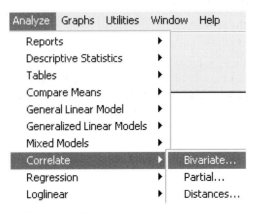

Figure 7. The **Correlate** submenu

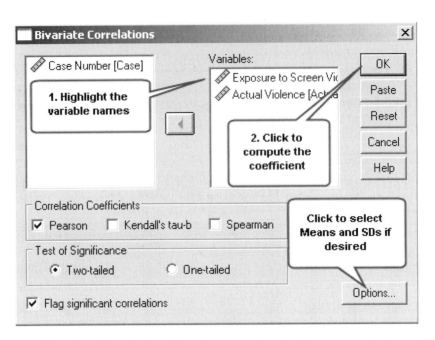

Figure 8. The **Bivariate Correlations** dialog for computing the Pearson correlation coefficient

11.3.3   Output for the Pearson correlation

Output 1 tabulates the Pearson correlation, with its p-value.

Correlations

		Exposure to Screen Violence	Actual Violence
Exposure to Screen Violence	Pearson Correlation	1	.892**
	Sig. (2-tailed)		.000
	N	27	27
Actual Violence	Pearson Correlation	.892**	1
	Sig. (2-tailed)	.000	
	N	27	27

**. Correlation is significant at the 0.01 level (2-tailed).

> r = 0.892 and is significant at .01 level

> There are 27 pairs of values

> Since the correlation of Exposure with Actual is the same as the correlation of Actual with Exposure, the second row is a repeat of the first row

Output 1. The Pearson **Correlations** table

The value for r is 0.892, which is significant beyond the 0.01 level. This is written as:

$$r(27) = 0.892; \; p < .01. \; r^2 = 0.80$$

Since 80% of the variance is shared, the association is obviously a strong one.

Notice that in Output 1, the information we need in the upper right cell of the table (the value of r, the number of pairs of data and the p-value) is duplicated in the lower left cell of the table. This is because the correlation of A with B is the same as the correlation of B with A.

Were we to have more than two variables, the results would have appeared in the form of a square matrix with entries above the principal diagonal (from top left to bottom right) being duplicated in the cells below it. When there are more than two variables, SPSS can be commanded to construct this **correlation matrix** (or **R-matrix**) by simply entering as many variable names as required into the **Variables** box (Figure 8).

11.4   OTHER MEASURES OF ASSOCIATION

The Pearson correlation is suitable only for data on continuous or scale variables. With ordinal or nominal data, other statistics must be used.

11.4.1   Spearman's rank correlation

The term **ordinal data** includes both ranks and assignments to ordered categories. When the same objects are ranked independently by two judges, the question arises as to the extent to which the two sets of ranks agree. This is a question about the strength of association between two variables which, although quantitative, are measured at the ordinal level. Suppose that the ranks assigned to ten paintings by two judges are as in Table 2.

Table 2. Ranks assigned by two judges to each of ten paintings										
Painting	**A**	**B**	**C**	**D**	**E**	**F**	**G**	**H**	**I**	**J**
First Judge	1	2	3	4	5	6	7	8	9	10
Second Judge	1	3	2	4	6	5	8	7	10	9

It is obvious that the judges generally agree closely in their rankings: at most, their assignments differ by a single rank. One way of measuring the level of agreement between the two judges is by calculating the Pearson correlation between the two sets of ranks. This correlation is known as the **Spearman rank correlation** r_s or as **Spearman's rho** ρ. Like eta squared, Spearman's rho is a *statistic*, not a parameter, and is thus an exception to the general rule about reserving Greek and Roman letters for parameters and statistics, respectively. While the defining formula for the Spearman rank correlation looks very different from that for the Pearson correlation, the two formulae are actually equivalent, provided that no ties are allowed.

The use of the Spearman rank correlation is not confined to ordinal data. Suppose the scatterplot of the bivariate distribution of two continuous variables shows that they are in a **monotonic** (increasing or decreasing together) but non-linear relationship, rendering the Pearson correlation an unsuitable measure of degree of association. The scores on both variables can be converted to ranks and the Spearman rank correlation calculated instead.

11.4.2   Kendall's tau statistics

The **Kendall's tau** (τ) statistics offer an alternative to the Spearman rank correlation as measures of agreement between rankings, or assignments to ordered categories. The basic idea is that one set of ranks can be converted into another by a succession of reversals of pairs of ranks in one set: the fewer the reversals needed to achieve the conversion (in relation to the total number of possible reversals), the larger the value of tau. The numerator of Kendall's tau is the difference between the number of pairs of objects whose ranks are concordant (i.e. they go in the same direction) and the number of discordant pairs. If the former predominate, the sign of tau is positive; if the latter predominate, tau is negative.

There are three different versions of Kendall's tau: **tau-a**, **tau-b** and **tau-c**. All three measures have the same numerator, the difference between the numbers of concordant and discordant pairs. It is in their denominators that they differ, the differences being in the way they handle tied observations.

The denominator of the correlation **tau-a** is simply the total number of pairs. The problem with tau-a is that when there are ties, its range quickly becomes restricted, to the point where it becomes difficult to interpret.

The correlation **tau-b** has terms in the denominator that consider, in either variable, pairs that are tied on one variable but not on the other. (When there are no ties, the values of tau-a and tau-b are identical.)

The correlation **tau-c** was designed for situations where one wishes to measure agreement between assignments to unequal-sized sets of ordered categories. Provided the data meet certain requirements, the appropriate tau correlation can vary throughout the complete range from -1 to $+1$.

Note that the calculation of Kendall's statistics with ordinal data, in the form of assignments of target objects to ordered categories, is best handled by the **Crosstabs** procedure (see next section); indeed, **tau-c** (which is appropriate when the two variables have different numbers of categories) can only be obtained in **Crosstabs**.

11.4.3   Rank correlations with SPSS

In **Variable View**, name two variables, *Judge1* and *Judge2*. Click the **Data View** tab to switch to **Data View** and, from Table 2, enter the ranks assigned by the first judge into the *Judge1* column and those assigned by the second judge into the *Judge2* column.
- Choose
  Analyze➜Correlate➜Bivariate...
  to obtain the **Bivariate Correlations** dialog box (the completed version of which is shown in Figure 9). By default, the **Pearson** check box will be marked. Click off the **Pearson** check box and click the **Kendall's tau-b** and the **Spearman** check boxes.
- Transfer the variable names *Judge1* and *Judge2* to the **Variables:** box.

- Click **OK** to obtain the correlations shown in Output 2.

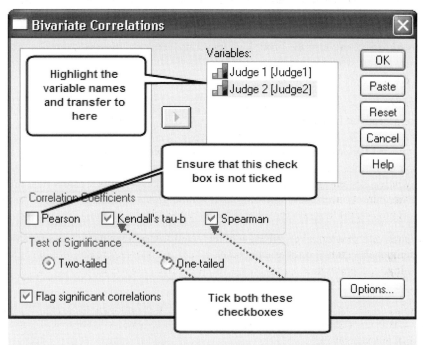

Figure 9. The completed **Bivariate Correlations** dialog for **Kendall's tau-b** and Spearman's rho

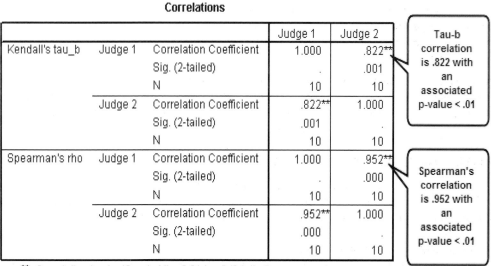

Correlations

			Judge 1	Judge 2
Kendall's tau_b	Judge 1	Correlation Coefficient	1.000	.822**
		Sig. (2-tailed)	.	.001
		N	10	10
	Judge 2	Correlation Coefficient	.822**	1.000
		Sig. (2-tailed)	.001	.
		N	10	10
Spearman's rho	Judge 1	Correlation Coefficient	1.000	.952**
		Sig. (2-tailed)	.	.000
		N	10	10
	Judge 2	Correlation Coefficient	.952**	1.000
		Sig. (2-tailed)	.000	.
		N	10	10

**. Correlation is significant at the 0.01 level (2-tailed).

Output 2. **Kendall** and **Spearman**'s rank correlations

Output 2 shows that the **Kendall correlation** is 0.82 and the **Spearman correlation** is 0.95. These values differ, but there is nothing untoward in this. The two statistics are based on quite different theoretical foundations and often take noticeably different values when calculated from the same data set. Incidentally, the Pearson option would have given the same value as the Spearman (0.95), because the procedure first transforms the raw data to ranks. The results of the Spearman test would be written as follows:

$$rho\ (10) = 0.95; p = < .01.$$

$$rho^2\ = 0.91, \text{a large effect.}$$

11.5   TESTING FOR ASSOCIATION IN NOMINAL DATA

A **nominal** data set consists of assignments of individuals to the categories making up qualitative attributes or variables, such as gender, blood group or nationality.

In Chapter 6, we discussed the use of the approximate **chi-square statistic** χ^2 to test the goodness-of-fit of a theoretical distribution of expected frequencies E to the distribution of the observed frequencies O over a set of categories.

If the attribute has k categories, the value of chi-square for the goodness-of-fit test is given by

$$\chi^2 = \sum_{all\ categories} \frac{(O - E)^2}{E} \qquad \text{with } df = k \text{ - } 1$$

The value of df is needed to specify the sampling distribution of χ^2 so that the null hypothesis (that the theoretical distribution accounts for the data) can be tested.

We have also seen that when people's membership of two sets of mutually exclusive and exhaustive categories (such as sex or blood group) is recorded, it is possible to construct a **crosstabulation**, or **contingency table** (see Chapter 4, Section 4.3.1). In the analysis of **categorical data** (that is nominal assignments or assignments to ordered categories), the crosstabulation is the equivalent of the scatterplot. Like the scatterplot, the contingency table provides an excellent means of inspecting a bivariate distribution in order to ascertain the presence of an association between the variables concerned.

See Section 4.3.1

11.5.1   The chi-square test for association

A researcher has reason to believe that there should be a higher incidence of a potentially harmful antibody in patients whose tissue is of a certain 'critical' type. In a study of 79 patients, the incidence of the antibody in patients of four different tissue types, including the 'critical' category, are recorded. The results are presented in the following contingency table (Output 3):

Tissue Type * Presence Crosstabulation

Count

		Presence		
		No	Yes	Total
Tissue Type	Critical	6	21	27
	Type C	5	7	12
	Type B	11	7	18
	Type A	14	8	22
Total		36	43	79

Output 3. Contingency table with a pattern of observed frequencies suggesting an association between *Tissue Type* and *Presence* of an antibody

The pattern of the frequencies appears to confirm the research hypothesis: there is a noticeably higher incidence of the antibody in the Critical group.

The researcher's hypothesis is that there is an association between the variables of *Group* (the type of tissue) and the *Presence* (Yes or No) of the antibody. The null hypothesis H_0 is the negation of this: there is no association between the two attributes. While it would appear from Output 3 that the null hypothesis is false, a formal statistical test is required.

The null hypothesis that there is no association between the *Group* and *Presence* variables can be tested with the **chi-square test for association**. For each cell of the contingency table, the expected frequency E is calculated on the assumption that the attributes of *Group* and *Presence* are independent, and the values of E are compared with the corresponding observed frequencies O by means of the statistic χ^2, where

$$\chi^2 = \sum_{all\ cells} \frac{(O-E)^2}{E}$$

In general, if the attributes A and B consist of a and b categories, respectively, the value of the degrees of freedom of this chi-square statistic is given by

$$df = (a-1)(b-1)$$

In the present example, $df = (4 - 1)(2 - 1) = 3$. In a 4×2 table with fixed marginal totals, the assignment of frequencies to only 3 cells completely determines the values of the frequencies in the remaining 5 cells.

The expected frequencies are calculated using estimates of probability derived from the marginal totals and the total frequency N in the following way. If R and C are the marginal totals of the row and the column that locate the cell in the contingency table, the expected frequency E_{RC} is given by

$$E_{RC} = \frac{R \times C}{N}$$

For example, for the top left cell in the contingency table, E = (27×36)/79 = 12.30. The expected frequencies in all 8 cells of the table are shown in Output 4.

Tissue Type * Presence Crosstabulation

			Presence		
			No	Yes	Total
Tissue Type	Critical	Count	6	21	27
		Expected Count	12.3	14.7	27.0
	Type C	Count	5	7	12
		Expected Count	5.5	6.5	12.0
	Type B	Count	11	7	18
		Expected Count	8.2	9.8	18.0
	Type A	Count	14	8	22
		Expected Count	10.0	12.0	22.0
Total		Count	36	43	79
		Expected Count	36.0	43.0	79.0

Output 4. The observed and expected frequencies of observations in the cells of the contingency table in Output 3.

The value of chi-square is

$$\chi^2 = \sum_{cells} \frac{(O-E)^2}{E} = \frac{(6-12.3)^2}{12.3} + \frac{(21-14.7)^2}{14.7} + ... + \frac{(14-10.0)^2}{10.0} + \frac{(8-12.0)^2}{12.0} = 10.66$$

The p-value of the chi-square value 10.66 on $df = 3$ is $< .05$. The null hypothesis is therefore rejected and we report this result as follows:

$$\chi^2(3) = 10.66; \ p < .05$$

11.5.2   Measures of strength of association for nominal data

The rejection of the null hypothesis establishes the presence of an association between the two attributes. The chi-square statistic itself, however, is not a satisfactory measure of association strength, because its magnitude is affected by the total frequency of observations in the contingency table. From the chi-square statistic itself, however, several statistics designed to measure strength of association have been devised.

An ideal measure of association should mimic the correlation coefficient by having a maximum absolute value of 1 for a perfect association, and a value of 0 for dissociation or independence. The choice of the appropriate statistic depends on whether the contingency table is 2×2 (each variable has two categories) or larger.

Several measures of strength of association for nominal data have been proposed. For two-way 2×2 contingency tables, the **phi coefficient** φ is applicable. The phi coefficient is defined as follows:

$$\varphi = \sqrt{\frac{\chi^2}{N}}$$

For two-way contingency tables involving variables with more than two categories, another statistic, known as **Cramér's V**, is preferred. Cramér's measure, unlike the phi coefficient, can still, as in the 2×2 case, achieve its maximum value of unity.

Other measures of association, such as **Goodman & Kruskal's lambda**, measure the proportional reduction in error achieved when membership of a category on one attribute is used to predict category membership on the other.

More information on the various measures of association can be found by clicking the SPSS **Help** box in the **Crosstabs: Statistics** dialog box.

11.5.3   Analysis of contingency tables with SPSS

In the usual research situation, the data on the participants would be entered on an individual basis. **Data View** would then contain as many rows of data as there were participants in the study. From these raw data, SPSS would produce the contingency table shown in Output 3. Here, for convenience, rather than having 79 rows of data in **Data View**, we shall enter the frequencies of individuals in the four combinations of the two qualitative variables *Group* and *Presence*. Normally, of course, these frequencies would not be available and we would rely upon SPSS to calculate them for us.

When the data have already been grouped in this way, the SPSS data set for a contingency table must include two grouping variables to identify the various cell counts, one representing the rows (*Group*), the other the columns (*Presence*) of the contingency table in Output 3. In this example, since the data are counts, not individual records of presence or absence, a third variable (*Count*) is needed for the cell frequencies.

- In **Variable View**, name the variables *Group*, *Presence*, and *Count*.
- In the **Values** column, define the numerical values and their labels for the two grouping variables. For the *Group* variable, assign the code numbers 1, 2, 3 and 4 to tissue types A, B, C and Critical, respectively. For the *Presence* variable, assign the numbers 1 and 2 to No and Yes, respectively.
- When you have finished working in Variable View, Click the **Data View** tab to switch to **Data View** and enter the data into the three columns, as shown in Figure 10.

	Group	Presence	Count
1	Type A	No	14
2	Type A	Yes	8
3	Type B	No	11
4	Type B	Yes	7
5	Type C	No	5
6	Type C	Yes	7
7	Critical	No	6
8	Critical	Yes	21

Figure 10. **Data View** showing the two grouping variables and the counts of presence or absence of the antibody

When you have grouped data as in this example, the next step is essential. Since the data in the *Count* column represent cell frequencies of a variable (not values), SPSS must be informed of this by means of the **Weight Cases** procedure in the **Data** menu. The procedure for weighting cases is illustrated in Figure 11.

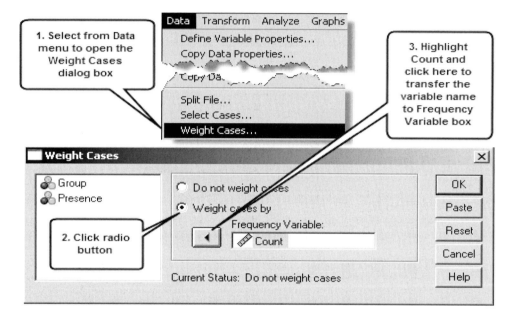

Figure 11. The **Weight Cases** procedure

Had the data been recorded case by case in the data file (i.e. not collated), there would have been no need to use the **Weight Cases** procedure because the **Crosstabs** procedure would have counted up the cases automatically.

Find the **Crosstabs** procedure in the **Descriptives** menu as shown in Figure 12.

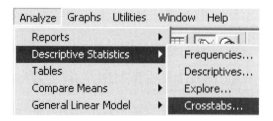

Figure 12. Finding **Crosstabs** in the **Analyze** menu

To obtain the contingency table and make the chi-square test, proceed as shown in Figures 13 and 14. Complete the **Statistics...**, **Cells...**, and **Format...** dialog boxes as shown in Figure 14. The **Format...** dialog controls the order in which rows for the values of the grouping variable appear in the contingency table. The default setting is **Ascending**, meaning that the top row of entries in the table will be the data for the value 1 and the bottom row will be the data for the value 4 (the Critical group). By changing the setting to **Descending**, this order will be reversed: the row with the value 4 (the Critical group) will now appear at the top and the row with the value 1 will appear at the bottom.

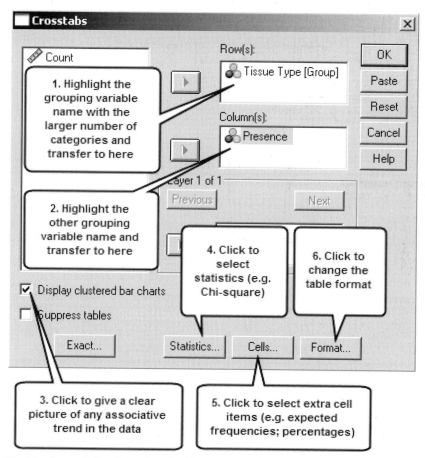

Figure 13. The **Crosstabs** dialog box for *Tissue Type* in the rows and *Presence* in the columns

The option of **Expected** cell frequencies in **Counts** enables the user to check that the prescribed minimum requirements for the valid use of chi-square have been fulfilled. Although there has been much debate about these, some leading authorities have proscribed the use of chi-square when:

1. In 2×2 tables, any of the expected frequencies is less than 5;
2. In larger tables, any of the expected frequencies is less than 1 or more than 20% are less than 5.

Output 5 shows the contingency table in Output 4, to which have been added the row percentages. In the Critical group, 77.8% of cases had the antibody; whereas the highest percentage in any of the other groups was 58.3%.

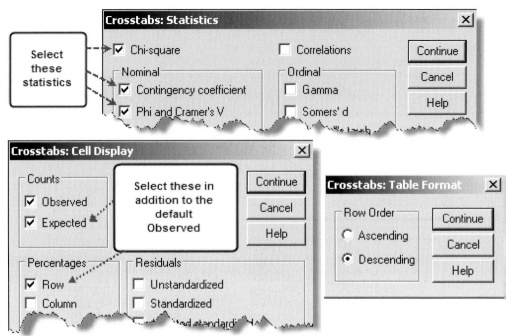

Figure 14. Appropriate choices for the **Cell Display**, **Statistics** and **Table Format** dialog boxes

Tissue Type * Presence Crosstabulation

| | | | Presence | | |
			No	Yes	Total
Tissue Type	Critical	Count	6	21	27
		Expected Count	12.3	14.7	27.0
		% within Tissue Type	22.2%	77.8%	100.0%
	Type C	Count	5	7	12
		Expected Count	5.5	6.5	12.0
		% within Tissue Type	41.7%	58.3%	100.0%
	Type B	Count	11	7	18
		Expected Count	8.2	9.8	18.0
		% within Tissue Type	61.1%	38.9%	100.0%
	Type A	Count	14	8	22
		Expected Count	10.0	12.0	22.0
		% within Tissue Type	63.6%	36.4%	100.0%
Total		Count	36	43	79
		Expected Count	36.0	43.0	79.0
		% within Tissue Type	45.6%	54.4%	100.0%

Output 5. The contingency table, to which have been added the row percentages

Output 6 shows the (edited) clustered bar chart, in which the colours in the original chart have been replaced by black and white patterns. The chart provides a striking demonstration of the predominance of the antibody in the Critical tissue group.

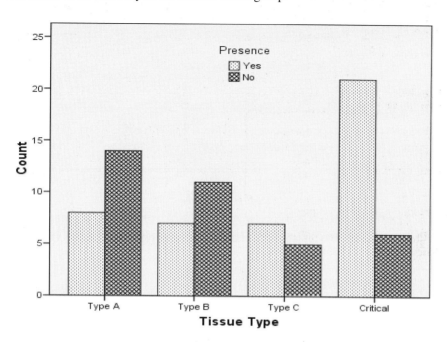

Output 6. Clustered bar chart showing the relatively high incidence of the antibody in the Critical tissue group.

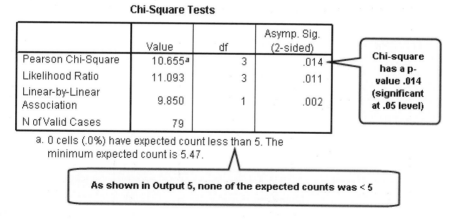

Chi-Square Tests

	Value	df	Asymp. Sig. (2-sided)
Pearson Chi-Square	10.655a	3	.014
Likelihood Ratio	11.093	3	.011
Linear-by-Linear Association	9.850	1	.002
N of Valid Cases	79		

Chi-square has a p-value .014 (significant at .05 level)

a. 0 cells (.0%) have expected count less than 5. The minimum expected count is 5.47.

As shown in Output 5, none of the expected counts was < 5

Output 7. Result of the chi-square test

Output 7 shows the results of the chi-square test. The chi-square value 10.66 is significant beyond the 0.05 level:

$$\chi^2(3) = 10.66; \quad p < .05$$

Note the remark under the table in Output 7 about expected cell frequencies, which assures the user that the data are sufficiently plentiful to permit the usual chi-square test. Output 8 gives the values of the tests of strength of association. In this particular example, where one of the attributes is a dichotomy, the values of phi and Cramer's V are the same. That would not necessarily be so in more complex tables.

Symmetric Measures

		Value	Approx. Sig.
Nominal by Nominal	Phi	.367	.014
	Cramer's V	.367	.014
	Contingency Coefficient	.345	.014
N of Valid Cases		79	

a. Not assuming the null hypothesis.

b. Using the asymptotic standard error assuming the null hypothesis.

Output 8. Statistics measuring the strength of the association between *Tissue Type* and *Presence* of the antibody

11.5.4   Getting help with the output

Should any item in the SPSS output be unfamiliar, you can find an explanation by double-clicking on the item to highlight it and right-clicking with the mouse (Figure 15).

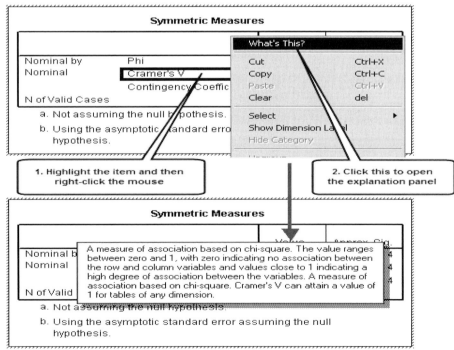

Figure 15. Getting help with unfamiliar terms in the output

11.5.5   Some cautions and caveats

Low expected frequencies

A word of warning about the misuse of chi-square should be given here. In the first place, it is important to bear in mind that, as we pointed out in Chapter 6, the 'chi-square' statistic is only **approximately** distributed as the theoretical chi-square distribution: the higher the expected frequencies, the better the approximation, hence the rule about minimum expected frequencies. When the expected frequencies fall below the recommended levels, the traditional chi-square test can produce misleading p-values. SPSS, however, provides **exact p-values**, which should be requested when the data are scarce.

Here is an example of what can go wrong if the expected frequencies fall below the acceptable limits. Returning to our example of the presence of the antibody in patients of a certain tissue type, suppose that the study has involved only 19 patients. The contingency table (Output 9) shows the same pattern as before: there is a clear predominance of the antibody in the Critical tissue group.

Tissue Type * Presence Crosstabulation

Count

		Presence		Total
		No	Yes	
Tissue Type	Critical	2	7	9
	Type C	1	0	1
	Type B	3	0	3
	Type A	4	2	6
Total		10	9	19

Output 9. A contingency table summarising a small data set

When completing the **Crosstabs** dialog, the researcher, realising that the data are less plentiful than one would wish, clicks the **Exact ...** button at the foot of the dialog box, enters the **Exact Tests** dialog box, and activates the **Exact** radio button (Figure 16).

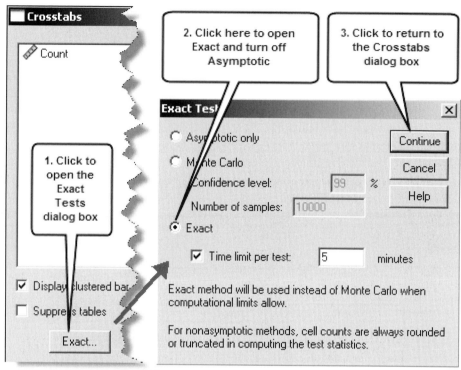

Figure 16. Choosing an exact test

Chi-Square Tests

	Value	df	Asymp. Sig. (2-sided)	Exact Sig. (2-sided)	Exact Sig. (1-sided)	Point Probability
Pearson Chi-Square	7.412[a]	3	.060	.035		
Likelihood Ratio	9.114	3	.028	.035		
Fisher's Exact Test	6.795			.035		
Linear-by-Linear Association	3.803[b]	1	.051	.065	.039	.023
N of Valid Cases	19					

a. 8 cells (100.0%) have expected count less than 5. The minimum expected count is .47.

b. The standardized statistic is -1.950.

Note the warning about cells with expected counts < 5

Output 10. Results of the exact tests

The results of both the approximate (Asymptotic) chi-square test and the exact test are shown in Output 10. The exact tests do not agree with the asymptotic tests: on the exact tests, the result is significant beyond the .05 level.

Non-independent observations

The use of the chi-square statistic requires that **each individual studied contributes to the count in only one cell in the crosstabulation**. Returning to a situation we described in Chapter 6, suppose that 100 people were asked whether they supported a motion before and after hearing a debate. The people were identified, so that it could be seen whether or not members of the audience had changed their opinions and, if so, in which direction. From this information, Table 3 was constructed.

We saw that the correct procedure here was to analyse only the responses of those who *changed* their opinion and run a goodness-of-fit test of the null hypothesis that there was no systematic tendency for those who changed their views as a result of hearing the debate to do so in one particular direction. The **McNemar** test uses the Yates-corrected chi-square approximation; but the **binomial test** with p set at .5 would serve equally well. Since 38 participants changed from No to Yes, whereas only 13 changed from Yes to No, we were not surprised when the McNemar test showed significance.

Table 3. Responses of an audience before and after hearing a debate

Agreed with motion after debate? * Agreed with motion before debate? Crosstabulation

Count

		Agreed with motion before debate?		Total
		Yes	No	
Agreed with motion after debate?	Yes	27	38	65
	No	13	22	35
Total		40	60	100

Now suppose that the researcher had merely asked people to respond before and after hearing the debate, but didn't bother to identify the people on either occasion or even, after the debate, to ask them whether they had changed their views and, if so, in which direction. That would have produced the data in Table 4.

Table 4. Table showing the frequencies of positive and negative responses of an audience before and after hearing a debate. A chi-square test is inadmissible here

Before or after the debate * Response to proposed legislation Crosstabulation

Count

		Response to proposed legislation		Total
		Yes	No	
Before or after the debate	Before	40	60	100
	After	65	35	100
Total		105	95	200

He then decides that, since he wants to see whether there was an association between the time at which an opinion was sought (Before, After) and the response to the proposed legislation (Yes, No), he will run a chi-square. The result is positive and the researcher concludes that hearing the debate influenced the opinions of the audience.

The display in Table 4 breaks the important rule that, in contingency tables, each person must contribute to the tally in one cell only. In Table 4, each person makes two contributions and, as a result, although 100 people participated in the investigation, there are 200 responses! When the assumptions underlying a statistical test are so seriously violated, no reliance can be placed upon the p-value.

The information that we need, it is worth noting, cannot be recovered from Table 4: in a contingency table, the cell totals cannot be deduced from the marginal totals alone.

There are several other potential problems with the making of chi-square tests that the user should be aware of. A lucid account of the rationale and assumptions of the chi-square test is given by Howell (2007).

11.6   DO DOCTORS AGREE? COHEN'S KAPPA

Suppose that two psychiatrists assign each of 50 patients to one of a set of five diagnostic categories, A, B, C, D and E. Their assignments are shown in Table 5.

Table 5. Assignments of patients to categories A to E					
Doctor1	Doctor2	Count	Doctor1	Doctor2	Count
A	A	4	C	D	1
A	B	1	C	E	1
A	C	1	D	A	1
A	D	1	D	B	1
A	E	1	D	C	2
B	A	1	D	D	8
B	B	4	D	E	2
B	C	0	E	A	1
B	D	4	E	B	0
B	E	2	E	C	1
C	A	2	E	D	3
C	B	0	E	E	2
C	C	6			

When these assignments are cast into a contingency table, the data appear as in Table 6.

Table 6. Contingency table showing the diagnoses of 50 patients by two doctors

(The observed frequencies are given in the rows labelled O; the expected frequencies are given in the rows labelled E.)

Second Doctor * First Doctor Crosstabulation

			First Doctor					Total
			A	B	C	D	E	
Second	A	O	4	1	2	1	1	9
Doctor		E	1.4	2.0	1.8	2.5	1.3	9.0
	B	O	1	4	0	1	0	6
		E	1.0	1.3	1.2	1.7	.8	6.0
	C	O	1	0	6	2	1	10
		E	1.6	2.2	2.0	2.8	1.4	10.0
	D	O	1	4	1	8	3	17
		E	2.7	3.7	3.4	4.8	2.4	17.0
	E	O	1	2	1	2	2	8
		E	1.3	1.8	1.6	2.2	1.1	8.0
Total		O	8	11	10	14	7	50
		E	8.0	11.0	10.0	14.0	7.0	50.0

The marked diagonal cells in Table 6 contain the numbers of patients who were assigned to the same diagnostic category by the two doctors. Intuitively, it might seem reasonable to divide the sum of the judgements on the marked diagonal by the total number of judgements and argue that the percentage of agreement is 24/50 = 48%. As with the analysis of any contingency table, however, we must take into consideration the different numbers of patients with different kinds of problem, as indicated by the varying row and column frequencies. Such discrepancies may merely reflect a tendency to make more use of some diagnostic categories than others, rather than reliable diagnosis. Accordingly, we need to obtain the **expected frequencies (E)** for the cells along the marked diagonal, given the values of the marginal row and column totals. We obtain the value of E for each cell by multiplying the marginal totals in the row and column and dividing by the total frequency (50). For example, 4 patients were assigned to diagnostic category B by both doctors. Since the row and column totals for the assignments by the first and second doctor are 6 and 11, respectively, E = 66/50 = 1.32.

Cohen (1960) offered the statistic **kappa (κ)** as a measure of agreement between the doctors. Kappa is defined as

$$\kappa = \frac{\sum_{diagonal} O - \sum_{diagonal} E}{N - \sum_{diagonal} E}$$

where O and E are, respectively, the observed and expected frequencies *for the diagonal cells only in Table 6* and N is the *total* number of patients. (For the *entire* contingency table, the totals for O and E would have the same value.) Substituting in the formula, we have

$$\sum_{diagonal} O = 4+4+6+8+2 = 24;$$

$$\sum_{diagonal} E = 1.44+1.32+2.00+4.76+1.12 = 10.64;$$

$$\kappa = \frac{\sum_{diagonal} O - \sum_{diagonal} E}{N - \sum_{diagonal} E} = \frac{24-10.64}{50-10.64} = 0.34$$

The value 0.34 is even lower than the 48% agreement we arrived at using the intuitive measure.

Cohen's kappa statistic is available in SPSS.

- In **Variable View**, set up the variables *Doctor1* and *Doctor2* as string variables and *Count* as a numeric variable. Enter all the data for each combination of doctors (Table 5).
- Follow the path **Data➔Weight Cases...** to weight the cases by *Count*.
- Choose **Analyze➔Descriptive Statistics➔Crosstabs...** to open the **Crosstabs** dialog box.
- Highlight and transfer the grouping variable names to the **Row(s)** and **Column(s)** boxes respectively
- Click the **Statistics...** button and select the **Kappa** check box. Click **Continue** to return to the **Crosstabs** dialog box and then click **OK**.

The output starts with a **Case Processing Summary** table and then the **Doctor1*Doctor2 Crosstabulation** table. The value of κ is shown in the next table (Output 11).

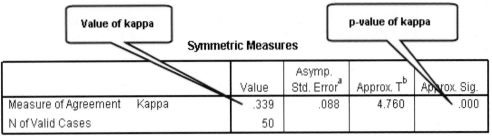

Symmetric Measures

		Value	Asymp. Std. Error[a]	Approx. T[b]	Approx. Sig.
Measure of Agreement	Kappa	.339	.088	4.760	.000
N of Valid Cases		50			

a. Not assuming the null hypothesis.

b. Using the asymptotic standard error assuming the null hypothesis.

Output 11. The kappa statistics

The value of kappa is given as .34, as calculated previously. The output also contains a test of the significance of kappa which is of little importance, because a value such as .34, while significant beyond the .01 level, is much too low for a reliability: a minimum value of .75 would be expected with a reliable diagnostic system.

The result should be reported as follows:

> Cohen's kappa statistic was used as a measure of diagnostic agreement between the two doctors: κ = .34; p < .01.

11.7 PARTIAL CORRELATION

Correlation does not imply causation

In experimental (as opposed to correlational) research, provided there are adequate controls, the independent variable (IV) can be shown to have a causal effect upon the dependent variable (DV). In correlational research, however, in which variables are measured as they occur in participants, it can be difficult or impossible to demonstrate unequivocally that one variable in any sense 'causes' another. In some situations, in fact, even when two variables are substantially correlated, *neither* variable causes the other: both are at least partly determined by a third variable. In this sense, although the correlation between the two variables may be both statistically significant and substantial, it is a 'spurious' correlation, in the sense that it suggests the presence of a direct causal link between the two variables when actually there is none.

Suppose, for example, we have a bivariate data set showing a strong positive correlation (r = +0.89) between the amount of screen violence that children witness and an independent measure of the extent to which they are actually violent. Let us call these variables *Exposure* and *Actual*. The supposition that *Exposure* increases *Actual* violence was what motivated the researcher to measure these variables in the first place: that is, the researcher wishes to sustain the following model of causation:

Model 1

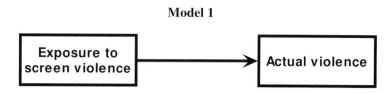

The existence of a positive correlation, however, is equally compatible with the view that the amount of screen violence a child watches is a reflection of his or her own violent tendencies:

Model 2

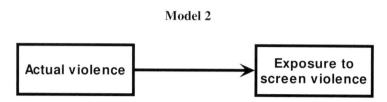

There is, however, still another possibility. Neither *Exposure* nor *Actual* causes the other: they are both determined by a third variable, parental aggression (*Parental*):

Model 3

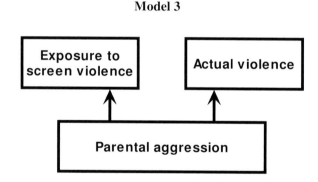

It is often impossible to determine unequivocally which of these three causal models is the correct interpretation of a correlation coefficient, unless additional data are available or theoretical considerations compel the acceptance of one particular model.

Partial correlation

A **partial correlation** is what remains of the correlation between two variables when their correlations with a third variable have been taken into consideration. If r_{AB} and r_{AC} are, respectively, the correlations of variables A and B with a third variable C, the partial correlation between A and B with C 'partialled out' ($r_{AB.C}$) is given by the following formula:

$$r_{AB.C} = \frac{r_{AB} - r_{AC} r_{BC}}{\sqrt{\left(1 - r_{AC}^2\right)\left(1 - r_{BC}^2\right)}} \qquad \textbf{Partial correlation}$$

If the two variables correlate substantially with the third variable, the partial correlation between them may be much smaller than the original correlation; indeed, it may be statistically insignificant. In that case, it may be reasonable to interpret the original correlation as having been driven by the third variable, as in the third causal model shown above. Let us suppose that, in our current example, we have data on the *Parental* variable.

To run a partial correlation within SPSS, proceed as follows:

- Select **Analyze➜Correlate➜Partial...** to enter the **Partial Correlations** dialog box.
- Complete the dialog box as shown in Figure 17.
- By clicking the **Options** button and checking the **Zero-order correlations** box in the **Options** dialog, you can obtain the original Pearson correlation between *Exposure* and *Actual* violence for comparison.

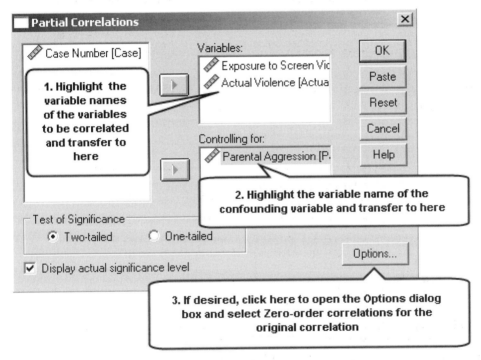

Figure 17. The **Partial Correlations** dialog box

The upper part of the edited output (Output 12) gives the Pearson correlations among the three variables. The second row gives the partial correlation between *Actual Violence* and *Exposure to Screen Violence*, after the potential confounding variable of *Parental Aggression* has been controlled or **partialled out**. The original value of .89 has been reduced to .33: rather little of the original correlation remains when the correlations of *Exposure to Screen Violence* and *Actual Violence* with the *Parental Aggression* variable have been taken into consideration. It would appear that the original correlation was driven largely by the *Parental* variable.

Correlations

Control Variables			Actual Violence	Parental Aggression
-none-a	Exposure to Screen Violence	Correlation	.892	.915
		Significance (2-tailed)	.000	.000
		df	25	25
Parental Aggression	Exposure to Screen Violence	Correlation	.328	
		Significance (2-tailed)	.102	
		df	24	

a. Cells contain zero-order (Pearson) correlations.

The Zero-order correlation between Exposure and Actual Violence is .892 and between Exposure and Parental Aggression is .915. With p-values < .01, they are both significant at the .01 level

The correlation between Exposure and Actual Violence with Parental Aggression partialled out is .328. With a p-value of .102, the correlation is not significant

Output 12. Edited table of correlations showing the partial correlation in the second row

Report this result as follows:

The partial correlation between *Actual* violence and *Exposure* with *Parental Aggression* partialled out is insignificant: $r_{partial}(27) = .33$; $p = .10$.

11.8 CORRELATION IN MENTAL TESTING: RELIABILITY

A psychological test must have two attributes:
1. It must be **reliable**;
2. It must be **valid**.

A **reliable** test gives *consistent* results: a person, if tested with the instrument on different occasions by different testers, should score at similar percentile levels. Implicit in this definition is that scores on the test must have an appropriate distribution, so that the variance reflects natural individual differences in the property concerned. Ceiling and floor effects, whereby everyone either achieves perfection or fails, vitiate reliability. A **valid** test is one that measures what it is supposed to measure. The brevity of that definition belies the complexity of the problems involved in the establishment of the validity of a test: in his Dictionary of Psychology, Reber (1985) gives more than twenty definitions of validity. In this Section, however, we shall be concerned with reliability only. Reliability is a necessary – but not a sufficient – condition for validity (in any of its conceptions). An unreliable measuring instrument would be like an elastic tape measure or a rubber ruler: even when used to measure a property of the same object, it would never give the same result twice. In particular, we shall be concerned with how the reliability of a composite test consisting of a set of items increases with the number of items.

There are several approaches to the measurement of reliability, all of which utilise the Pearson correlation. Three of these are:

1. Test-retest;
2. Parallel forms;
3. Split-half.

In the first two methods, each participant is tested twice, either (as in 1) with the same test or (as in 2) with parallel (or equivalent) forms of the same test. A Pearson correlation is then used to measure the association between the participants' scores on the two occasions of testing and thus determine the reliability of the test. It is generally accepted that the reliability of a test should be at least 0.80 for the test to be useful. In the **split-half** approach, the component items must be divisible into two equal-sized equivalent subgroups, perhaps the odd-numbered and even-numbered items. Each participant receives two subtotal scores: one for the even items, the other for the odd. The split-half reliability is the Pearson correlation between the odd totals and the even totals. In the split-half approach, the participant is tested only once. Split-half reliability can be viewed as a special case of the general problem of establishing the reliability of the total score on any composite test yielding an aggregate total in relation to that of its component items.

In psychometric theory, a score x on a test is regarded as the sum of two components:

1. A **true** component t, which is that part of x that truly expresses the property;
2. An **error** component e.

Thus

$$x = t + e$$

On the basis of some reasonable assumptions, such as the independence of the true and error components, it can be shown that

$$\sigma_{total}{}^2 = \sigma_{true}{}^2 + \sigma_{error}{}^2$$

In words, the total variance of a score is the sum of the variances of the true component and random error, remembering that different participants will be in possession of the property to varying degrees.

Earlier in this chapter, we observed that the square of the Pearson correlation could be interpreted as the proportion of the variance of a variable that was shared with another variable. In the special context of reliability, however, the *unsquared* reliability coefficient itself can be interpreted as the ratio of the variances of the true and the total scores:

$$reliability = \frac{\sigma_{true}{}^2}{\sigma_{total}{}^2} \quad \text{(1) \textbf{Reliability as a ratio of variances}}$$

The notion of a reliability as a ratio of true to total variance extends to scores that are aggregates of scores on individual items.

Reliability and number of items: coefficient alpha

Psychometric theory shows that the reliability of a test increases with the number of items it contains, according to the following formula:

$$alpha = \frac{i}{i-1}\left(\frac{\sigma_Y^2 - \sum\limits_{items}\sigma_{item}^2}{\sigma_Y^2}\right) \qquad \text{(2) Coefficient alpha}$$

where i is the number of items in the test and σ_Y^2 is the variance of the complete test.

Formula (2) brings out the intimate connection between variance and reliability. The relationship between number of items and reliability obtains because the items in a test constitute a sample from a domain of possible items and, other things being equal, the statistics of large samples are less subject to variability than are those of small samples.

There are several equivalent versions of the formula for **coefficient alpha**, one of which is the **Spearman-Brown formula**, which expresses the reliability of a test in terms of the mean of the correlations between every possible pair of items:

$$reliability = \frac{i\bar{r}}{1+(i-1)\bar{r}} \qquad \text{(3) Spearman-Brown formula}$$

where i is the number of items in the test and $\bar{r}$ is the mean of the correlations between all pairs of items. It is clear from (3) that even if the average inter-item correlation is low, the total score on a test with many items can achieve a very high level of reliability.

Suppose that a test contains four items, all of which are intended to measure the same property. Table 7 shows the scores of 6 people on the test. (These data have been borrowed from Winer, 1970, p127.)

Table 7. The scores of six participants on a four-item test					
Participant	Item 1	Item 2	Item 3	Item 4	Sum
1	2	4	3	3	12
2	5	7	5	6	23
3	1	3	1	2	7
4	7	9	9	8	33
5	2	4	6	1	13
6	6	8	8	4	26

From the **Spearman-Brown** formula, we can expect the reliability of the sum of the four test items to be greater than that of any of the individual items.

Table 8 shows the intercorrelations among the four items. The mean inter-item correlation is 0.84.

Table 8. Intercorrelations among the four items in the test

Inter-Item Correlation Matrix

	Item 1	Item 2	Item 3	Item 4
Item 1	1.000	1.000	.865	.865
Item 2	1.000	1.000	.865	.865
Item 3	.865	.865	1.000	.586
Item 4	.865	.865	.586	1.000

Applying the Spearman-Brown formula, we find that the estimate of the reliability for the aggregate test score is

$$reliability = \frac{i\bar{r}}{1+(i-1)\bar{r}} = \frac{4(0.84)}{1+3(0.84)} = 0.95$$

There were only four items in this test; but the reliability of a test with many items can be expected to be very high indeed – even if the mean inter-item correlation is low.

Measuring agreement among judges: the intraclass correlation

So far, we have been considering the question of the consistency of a test when used repeatedly on the same individuals. A related problem is the measurement of the level of agreement among *different* measuring instruments when used on the same set of objects or people. A particular instance is the measurement of the extent to which judges agree when, for example, rating the performance of musicians or skaters on a 10-point scale. Table 9 shows the marks assigned by four judges to six performers.

Table 9. Marks assigned by four judges to six performers

Performer	Judge1	Judge2	Judge3	Judge4	MeanRating
1	2	4	3	3	3.00
2	5	7	5	6	5.75
3	1	3	1	2	1.75
4	7	9	9	8	8.25
5	2	4	6	1	3.25
6	6	8	8	4	6.50

The four marks given to each performer can be regarded as belonging to a category or **class**: they all refer to the same person and should tend to be more similar to one another than they are to the marks assigned to the other performers. The total variance of the ratings σ_{total}^2 is made up of two components:

1. The variance of the true extent to which people possess the property, which we shall term σ_{people}^2 ;

2. The error variance $\sigma_{within\,people}^2$, which depends partly upon differences among the judges. The larger the first component of the total variance in relation to the second, the closer the agreement among the judges.

In summary, we can break down the total variance of the ratings as follows:

$$\sigma_{total}^2 = \sigma_{between\,people}^2 + \sigma_{within\,people}^2$$

Conceptually, the **intraclass correlation (ICC)** is defined as follows:

$$ICC = \frac{\sigma_{between\,people}^2}{\sigma_{between\,people}^2 + \sigma_{within\,people}^2} \qquad (4)\ \textbf{Intraclass correlation}$$

Comparison of (4) with (1) shows that the *ICC* is actually the ratio of hypothetical true scores to total scores and is therefore a reliability. This is why (4) is called a 'correlation'. In fact, measuring agreement among the judges and assessing the reliability of an aggregate score are actually one and the same problem. In our second example, the judges are the equivalent of separate test items measuring one and the same property in the person being tested.   The *ICC* is, at the same time, both a measure of agreement among judges and a measure of the reliability of their average ratings of the performers. In fact, the *ICC* is a form of coefficient alpha.

Reliability analysis with SPSS

We shall illustrate SPSS's computation of reliability using the scores of six people on four items (Table 7).

- Select **Analyze➜Scale➜Reliability Analysis...** (Figure 18) to open the **Reliability Analysis** dialog box (Figure 19).

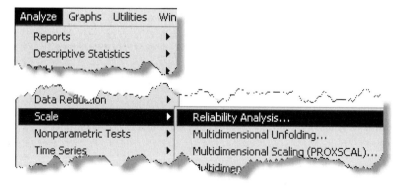

Figure 18. The menu for **Reliability Analysis**

- Complete the **Reliability Analysis** dialog box as shown in Figure 19.

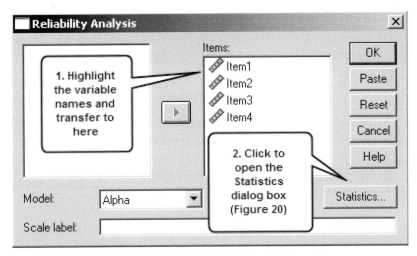

Figure 19.　The completed **Reliability Analysis** dialog box

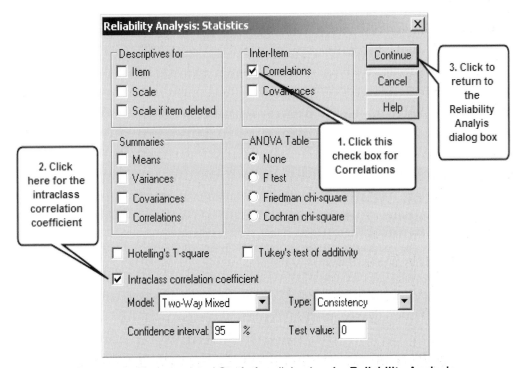

Figure 20.　The completed **Statistics** dialog box for **Reliability Analysis**

In choosing the default **Two-Way Mixed** model from the **Statistics** menu, we have assumed that four judges are the only ones of interest, whereas the performers are a random sample from a large pool of potential performers.

It can be seen in Output 13 that both **Cronbach's Alpha** and the **Intraclass Correlation Coefficient** (*ICC*) for **Average Measures** is 0.95, as calculated previously from the Spearman-Brown formula. As we should expect, the value of *ICC* for individual items (.825) is lower than it is for the whole test (.950).

The value of Alpha

Reliability Statistics

Cronbach's Alpha	Cronbach's Alpha Based on Standardized Items	N of Items
.950	.955	4

Intraclass Correlation Coefficient

	Intraclass Correlation[a]	F Test with True Value 0			
		Value	df1	df2	Sig
Single Measures	.825[b]	19.865	5.0	15	.000
Average Measures	.950[c]	19.865	5.0	15	.000

Two-way mixed effects model where people effects are random and measures effects are fixed.

a. Type C intraclass correlation coefficients using a consistency definition–the between-measure variance is excluded from the denominator variance.

b. The estimator is the same, whether the interaction effect is present or not.

c. This estimate is computed assuming the interaction effect is absent, because it is not estimable otherwise.

The value of *ICC* and its significance (p < .01)

Output 13. The values of **Alpha** and **ICC** and its significance for the aggregate and single items

11.9   A FINAL WORD

In this chapter, we turned from statistics that were designed to compare means (or other averages such as the median) to those designed to measure association. In particular, we discussed two of the most used (and misused) of all statistics, namely, the Pearson correlation and the chi-square statistic. A correlation should never be taken at its face value without first examining the scatterplot; and the user of the approximate chi-square test for association should make sure that the contingency table conforms to the requirements of minimum expected frequencies and independence of responses.

Recommended reading

Howell (2007) has an excellent chapter on correlation (Chapters 9) and on the analysis of contingency tables (Chapter 6).

Howell, D. C. (2007). *Statistical methods for psychology (6th ed.)*. Belmont, CA: Thomson/Wadsworth.

EXERCISE 17

The Pearson correlation

Before you start

Before starting to work through this practical Exercise, we recommend that you read Chapter 11. The **Pearson correlation r** is one of the most widely used (and abused) of statistics. Despite its apparent simplicity and versatility, it is only too easy to misinterpret a correlation. The purpose of the present Exercise is not only to show you how to use SPSS to obtain correlations, but also to illustrate how a given value for *r* can sometimes be misleading.

A famous data set

This exercise involves the analysis of four sets of paired data, which were constructed many years ago by Anscombe (1973), in order to make some important points about correlations.

Table 1. Anscombe's four data sets						
Participant	X1	Y1	Y2	Y3	X2	Y4
1	10.0	8.04	9.14	7.46	8.0	6.58
2	8.0	6.95	8.14	6.77	8.0	5.76
3	13.0	7.58	8.74	12.74	8.0	7.71
4	9.0	8.81	8.77	7.11	8.0	8.84
5	11.0	8.33	9.26	7.81	8.0	8.47
6	14.0	9.96	8.10	8.84	8.0	7.04
7	6.0	7.24	6.13	6.08	8.0	5.25
8	4.0	4.26	3.10	5.39	19.0	12.50
9	12.0	10.84	9.13	8.15	8.0	5.56
10	7.0	4.82	7.26	6.42	8.0	7.91
11	5.0	5.68	4.74	5.73	8.0	6.89

Each set yields exactly the same value for the **Pearson correlation**. The scatterplots, however, will show that in only one case are the data suitable for a Pearson correlation; in the others, the Pearson correlation gives a highly misleading impression of the relationship between the two variables. Ideally a scatterplot should indicate a **linear relationship** between the variables i.e. that all the points on the scatterplot should lie along or near to a diagonal straight line as shown in Chapter 11, Figure 1. Vertical or horizontal lines are not examples of linear relationships; moreover, the Pearson correlation is not defined when a data set comprises only one value of one variable in combination with various values of another.

The data are presented in Table 1. The four sets we shall examine are variable *X1* with each of the variables *Y1*, *Y2*, and *Y3*, and finally variable *X2* with variable *Y4*.

Preparing the SPSS data set

After naming the first variable in **Variable View** as *Case*, name the remaining variables as shown in the data table above. Ensure that the value in the **Decimals** column is *2*. Switch to

Data View, enter the data and save the set to a file called *Anscombe*. (This file will be used again in Exercise 20.)

Exploring the data

Obtain scatterplots of the four data sets, as described in Section 5.7. Ensure that all the variables are of the type *Scale* in the **Measure** column of **Variable View**. These plots can be produced either one at a time by choosing **Simple Scatter** within the **Gallery** of **Chart Builder** and dragging it to the Chart Preview or, more dramatically, by choosing **Scatterplot Matrix** (bottom left) within the **Gallery** and dragging it to the Chart Preview, which obtains a grid of scatterplots made up of all pairwise combinations of several variables. In the present Exercise, however, we only want the plots of variables *Y1*, *Y2* and *Y3* against variable *X1,* and of variable *Y4* against variable *X2.* Thus it is better to use **Scatterplot Matrix** for the plots with *X1* and **Simple Scatter** for the plot of *Y4* against X2.

If the matrix scatterplot is selected, transfer variables *Y1*, *Y2, Y3* and *X1* one at a time to the **Scattermatrix** dotted box (as each variable is dragged into the box, it will show a coloured outline) and click **OK**. A large matrix of scatterplots will then appear: look for the column with *X1* at the foot and ignore the other columns.

- **What do you notice about the scatterplots in this column? Which one is (in its present state) suitable for a subsequent calculation of a Pearson correlation? Describe what is wrong with each of the others.**

Return to **Chart Builder**, click Reset and run **Simple Scatter** variables *Y4* against variable *X2.*

- **Is the plot suitable for a Pearson correlation?**

The plot of *Y1* against *X1* shows a substantial linear relationship between the variables. The thinness of the imaginary ellipse of points indicates that the **Pearson correlation** is likely to be high. This is the kind of data set for which the Pearson correlation gives an informative and accurate statement of the strength of the linear association between two variables. The other plots, however, are very different: that of *Y2* against *X1* shows a perfect, but clearly non-linear, relationship; *Y3* against *X1* shows a basically linear relationship, which is marred by a glaring outlier; *Y4* against *X2* shows a column of points with a single outlier up in the top right corner.

Pearson correlations for the four scatterplots

Using the procedure described in Section 11.3.2, obtain the correlations between *X* and *Y* for the four sets of paired data. This is most easily done by entering the variables *X1, Y1, Y2, Y3* in the first run of the procedure so as to get a correlation matrix, and then *X2* and *Y4* in the second run.

- **What do you notice about the value of *r* for each of the correlations?**

Anscombe's data strikingly illustrate the need to inspect the data carefully to ascertain the suitability of statistics such as the Pearson correlation.

Removing the outliers

It is instructive to recalculate the **Pearson correlation** for the data set (*X1*, *Y3*) when the values for Participant 3 have been removed. The outlier is the value *12.74* on the variable *Y3*. Use the **Select Cases...** procedure to select all participants except Participant 3.

Return to the **Scatterplot** and **Bivariate Correlations** dialog boxes for *X1* and *Y3* (ignore the other variables) to re-run these procedures using the selected cases. Check that in the listing, only 10 rather than 11 cases have been used. You should find that the Pearson correlation for *X1* and *Y3* is now +1, which is what we would expect from the appearance of the scatterplot.

Conclusion

This Exercise has demonstrated the value of exploring the data first before calculating statistics such as the **Pearson correlation**. While it is true that Anscombe's data were specially constructed to give his message greater force, there have been many misuses of the Pearson correlation with real data sets, where the problems created by the presence of outliers and by basically non-linear relationships are quite common.

Finishing the session

Close down SPSS and any other windows before logging out.

EXERCISE 18

Other measures of association

Before you start

Please read Section 11.4 before proceeding with this Exercise. The **Pearson correlation** was devised to measure a supposed linear association between quantitative variables. There are other kinds of data (ordinal and nominal), to which the Pearson correlation is inapplicable. Moreover, even with data in the form of measurements, there may be considerations which render the use of the Pearson correlation inappropriate. Fortunately, other statistical measures of strength of association have been devised and in this Exercise, we shall consider some statistics that are applicable to ordinal and nominal data.

ORDINAL DATA

The Spearman rank correlation

Suppose that two judges each rank ten paintings, A, B, ..., J. Their decisions are shown in Table 1.

Table 1. The ranks assigned to the same ten objects by two judges										
	Best									Worst
First Judge	C	E	F	G	H	J	I	B	D	A
Second Judge	C	E	G	F	J	H	I	A	D	B

It is obvious from this table that the judges generally agree closely in their rankings: at most, the ranks they assign to a painting differ by two ranks. But how can their level of agreement be measured?

Table 2. A numerical representation of the orderings by the two judges in Table 1										
Painting	C	E	F	G	H	J	I	B	D	A
First Judge	1	2	3	4	5	6	7	8	9	10
Second Judge	1	2	4	3	6	5	7	10	9	8

The information in this table can be expressed in terms of numerical ranks by assigning the counting numbers from 1 to 10 to the paintings in their order of ranking by one judge, and pairing each of these ranks with the rank that the same painting received from the other judge, as shown in Table 2.

This is not the only way of representing the judgements numerically. It is also possible to list the objects (in any order) and pair the ranks assigned by the two judges to each object, entering two sets of ranks as before. Where the measurement of agreement is concerned, however, the two methods give exactly the same result.

Preparing the SPSS data set

In **Variable View**, name two variables, *Judge1* and *Judge2* (remembering not to put a space before the digit), and set the value in the **Decimals** column to *0*. Switch to **Data View** and enter the ranks assigned by the judges into the two columns. Save the data, because they will be used again later.

Obtaining the Spearman correlation coefficient

Draw the scatterplot using **Scatter/Dot...** in the **Graphs** menu.

- **Does the scatterplot suggest good agreement between the judges?**

Select **Correlate** and then **Bivariate...** from the **Analyze** menu to open the **Bivariate Correlations** dialog box. Transfer the variables to the **Variables** box and select the **Spearman** check box (leave the default **Pearson** check box active). Click **OK** to obtain the **Pearson correlation** and the **Spearman correlation.**

- **How closely do the judges agree (state the value of the Spearman correlation coefficient)?**

- **What do you notice about the values of the two coefficients? Explain.**

Use of the Spearman rank correlation where there is a monotonic, but non-linear, relationship

Table 3 shows a set of paired interval data. On inspecting the scatterplot, we see that there is a **monotonic relationship** between the two variables: that is, as *X* increases, so does *Y*. On the other hand, the relationship between *X* and *Y* is clearly non-linear (in fact, $Y = \log_2 X$), and the **Pearson correlation** would belie that perfect association between the two variables.

Table 3. A set of paired interval data showing a monotonic, but non-linear, relationship						
Y	1.00	1.58	2.00	2.32	2.58	2.81	3.00
X	2.00	3.00	4.00	5.00	6.00	7.00	8.00

Save the data from Table 2 (they will be needed later). To prepare a new data set (from Table 3) in a fresh file, enter the **File** drop-down menu, select **New** and then **Data** from the rightmost menu. Name the new variables in **Variable View** and enter the values into **Data View**. Obtain the **scatterplot** and compute the **Pearson** and **Spearman** correlation coefficients.

- **Describe the shape of the scatterplot and write down the values of the two correlation coefficients. Since there is a perfect (but non-linear) relationship between *X* and *Y*, the degree of association is understated by the Pearson correlation coefficient.**

- **Which value of *r* is the truer expression of the strength of the relationship between *X* and *Y*? Explain.**

Kendall's correlation coefficients

The association between variables in paired ordinal data sets (or in paired measurements) can also be investigated by using one of **Kendall's correlation** coefficients, **tau-a**, **tau-b** or **tau-c** (see Section 11.4.2). (When there are no tied observations, **tau-a** and **tau-b** have the same value.) With large data sets, **Kendall's** and **Pearson's** coefficients give rather similar values and tail probabilities. With a given data set, however, their two values will not be identical. This is because the two statistics have quite different rationales and different sampling distributions. Their p-values, however, will usually be very similar. When the data are scarce, however, Kendall's statistics are better behaved, especially when there are tied observations, and more reliance can be placed upon the Kendall tail probability. Kendall's correlations really come into their own when the data are assignments to predetermined ordered categories (rating scales and so on).

There are two ways of obtaining **Kendall's correlations** in SPSS:

1. In the **Bivariate Correlations** dialog box, mark the **Kendall's tau-b** checkbox.

2. Use the **Crosstabs** procedure (see Section 11.5.3).

Use the **Bivariate Correlations** procedure to obtain **Kendall's tau-b** (there are no ties) for the data in Table 3. Now do the same with the data set saved from Table 2.

- **Write down the values of tau-b and compare them with your previously obtained coefficient values.**

With the restored Table 2 data set, use the **Crosstabs** procedure to obtain Kendall's correlations. Note that in this application, there is no variable such as *Count* and hence no need for **Weight Cases…**. Enter *Judge1* in **Row(s):** and *Judge2* in **Column(s):**. Click the **Statistics…** button to open the **Crosstabs: Statistics** dialog box and select the checkboxes for **Correlations**, **Kendall's tau-b** and **Kendall's tau-c**. Click **Continue** and **OK** to run the correlations procedure.

- **Write down the values of all the coefficients in the output and comment on any similarities and differences.**

Finishing the session

Close down SPSS and any other windows before logging out of the computer.

EXERCISE 19

The analysis of nominal data

Before you start

Before proceeding with this practical, we strongly recommend you to read Section 11.5 (measures of association strength for nominal data) in Chapter 11.

THE CHI-SQUARE TEST OF GOODNESS-OF-FIT

Some nominal data on one qualitative variable

Suppose that a researcher, interested in children's preferences, expects a spatial response bias towards the right-hand side. Thirty children enter a room containing three identically-marked doors: one to the right; another to the left; and a third straight ahead. They are told they can go through any of the three doors. Their choices are shown in Table 1.

Table 1. The choices of one of three exit doors by thirty children		
	Door	
Left	Centre	Right
5	8	17

It looks as if there is indeed a preference for the rightmost door, at least among the children sampled. Had the children been choosing at random, we should have expected about 10 in each category: that is, the theoretical, or expected distribution (E), of the tallies is **uniform**. The observed frequencies (O), on the other hand, have a distribution which is far from uniform.

Pearson's chi-square test can be used to test the goodness-of-fit of the expected to the observed distribution. Its rationale is lucidly discussed in any good statistics textbook (e.g. Howell, 2007). Here, we shall merely describe the SPSS procedure.

Preparing the data set

In **Variable View**, name the grouping variable *Position* for the three positional categories and a second variable *Count* for the numbers of children in the different categories. To the three categories, assign the values *1*, *2*, and *3* and in the **Values** column, enter the respective labels *Left*, *Centre,* and *Right*. Check that the values in the **Decimals** column are *0*. Click the **Data View** tab and enter the data.

Weight cases

To ensure that SPSS treats the entries in *Count* as frequencies rather than scores, follow the procedure described in Section 11.5.3.

Run the Chi-square test

To obtain the correct dialog box, select
Analyze➜Nonparametric Tests➜Chi-Square...
to open the **Chi-Square Test** dialog box. Click *Position* (not on *Count*) and then ▶ to transfer
Position to the **Test Variable List:** box. Click **OK** to run the procedure.

- Write down the value of the chi-square statistic and its p-value. Is chi-square significant?

- Write down the implications for the experimenter's research hypothesis. When considering the implications, be clear about the precise null hypothesis being tested. Is the experimental hypothesis the simple negation of the null hypothesis? Can you suggest any further tests that might be useful here?

Running the goodness-of-fit test on a set of raw data

When the researcher carried out the experiment, the door that each child chose was noted at the time. In terms of the code numbers, their choices might have been recorded as:

$$1, 1, 3, 2, 1, 1, 3, 3, 3 ,\ ...,\ \text{and so on.}$$

If the user defines the variable *Position*, and enters the 30 (coded) choices that the children made, the chi-square test is then run directly: there is no need to use the **Weight Cases** procedure since there is no variable for count or frequency.

THE CHI-SQUARE TEST OF ASSOCIATION BETWEEN TWO QUALITATIVE VARIABLES

An experiment on children's choices

Suppose that a researcher, having watched a number of children enter a room and recorded each child's choice between two objects, wants to know whether there is a tendency for boys and girls to choose different objects. This question concerns two variables: *Sex* and *Choice*. In statistical terms, the researcher is asking whether they are associated: do more girls than boys choose one of the objects and more boys than girls choose the other object? Suppose that the children's choices are as in Table 2.

Table 2. Choices by 50 children of one of two objects		
Object	Boys	Girls
A	20	5
B	6	19

Procedure for the chi-square test of association between two variables

Prepare a new data set from Table 2. In **Variable View**, create the variables *Object* and *Sex*, assigning code numbers and explanatory labels in the usual way. Create a third variable *Count*. The use of the **Crosstabs** procedure is fully described in Section 11.5.3. Click **Statistics...**, select **Chi-square** within the **Crosstabs: Statistics** dialog box and click **Continue**. We recommend the inclusion of expected frequencies so that you can check for the presence of cells with unacceptably low expected frequencies. Click **Cells...**, select **Expected** within the **Crosstabs: Cell Display** dialog box and click **Continue**.

Output for the chi-square test of association

The output is discussed in Section 11.5.3. Three tables are presented: the first is a **Case Processing Summary** table showing how many valid cases have been processed; the second is a **Crosstabulation** table with the observed and expected frequencies in each cell, along with row and column totals; and the third is a table (headed **Chi-square Tests**) listing various statistics, together with their associated significance levels.

- **Write down the value of the Pearson chi-square and its associated tail probability (p-value). Is it significant?**

- **In terms of the experimental hypothesis, what has this test shown?**

MEASURES OF ASSOCIATION STRENGTH FOR NOMINAL DATA

So far we have considered the use of the **chi-square statistic** to test for the presence of an association between two qualitative variables. Recall that, provided that the data are suitable, the **Pearson correlation** measures the strength of a linear association between two interval variables. In that case, therefore, the same statistic serves both as a test for the presence of an association and as a measure of associative strength. It might be thought that, with nominal data, the chi-square statistic would serve the same dual function. The chi-square statistic, however, cannot serve as a satisfactory measure of associative strength, because its value depends partly upon the total frequency.

To illustrate the calculation of measures of association for two-way contingency tables, we shall use again the data of choice of objects by children. Run the **Crosstabs** procedure again but this time deselect **Chi-square** and ensure that **Phi and Cramér's V** are selected within the **Nominal** box of the **Crosstabs: Statistics** dialog box.

The output consists of three tables: the first is a **Case Processing Summary** table, the second is a **Crosstabulation** table, and the third is a table called **Symmetric Measures** listing the values of **Phi** and **Cramér's V** together with their associated significance levels.

- **Write down the value of Phi for the strength of the association between the qualitative variables of Gender and Object. Has a strong association been demonstrated?**

Finishing the session

Close down SPSS and any other windows before logging out of the computer.

Regression

12.1   INTRODUCTION

The associative coin has two sides. On the one hand, a single number, a correlation coefficient, can be calculated which expresses the *strength* of the association between two variables. On the other, however, there is a set of techniques, known as **regression**, which utilise the presence of an association between two variables to predict the values of one variable (the **dependent**, **target** or **criterion** variable) from those of another (the **independent variable**, or **regressor**). In **simple** regression, there is just one regressor or DV; in **complex** regression there are two or more DVs. It is with this predictive aspect of association that the present chapter is concerned.

12.1.1   Simple, two-variable regression

Returning to the study of the association between *Actual* Violence and *Exposure* to Screen Violence (Chapter 11), Figure 1 shows the **regression line** drawn through the points in the scatterplot. The equation of this line is

$$Y' = 2.09 + 0.74X$$

where Y' is the point on the line above X. (It is important to distinguish carefully between the observed values Y and the corresponding points on the line Y' for the same values of X.)

The general form of this **linear equation** is

$$Y' = b_0 + b_1 X \quad \text{(1) \textbf{The regression line}}$$

where b_0 is the **intercept** of the line and b_1 is its **slope**. The intercept is the distance from the origin to the point at which the line cuts the y-axis. At this point, $X = 0$: that is, $Y' = b_0$ (Figure 1). In SPSS output, the intercept b_0 is referred as the **constant**.

The slope of the regression line b_1 is known as the **regression coefficient**. The regression coefficient measures the estimated average change in the criterion variable Y that results from increasing the value of the regressor X by one unit. In our example, $b_1 = .74$, so an increase of one unit in *Exposure* results in an estimated average increase of .74 units in the *Actual* violence score.

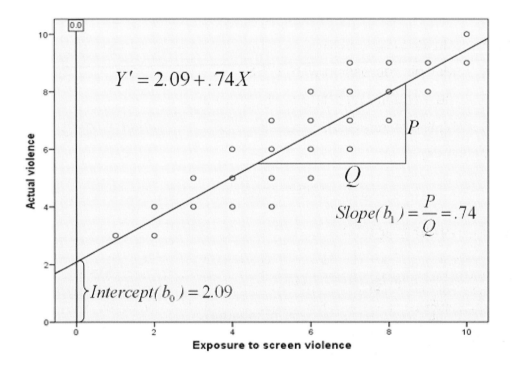

Figure 1. The regression line of Actual violence upon Exposure to screened violence

Suppose that all the points in the scatterplot were to be removed and we knew only that the mean score on *Actual* violence is 6.37. We are told that John has an *Exposure* score of 9. Without further information, our best guess of John's *Actual* violence score would be the mean *Actual* score M_Y, that is, 6.37. In the absence of further information, we should be obliged to make this guess whatever the value of John's *Exposure* score. We could do much better, however, if we knew the equation of the regression line and were to take as our guess of John's *Actual* score the point on the line above $X = 9$. From Equation (1), we see that John's predicted *Actual* score (the point on the regression line above *Exposure* = 9) is

$$Y' = 2.091 + 0.7359 \times 9 = 8.714$$

This value is much closer to John's real score Y on *Actual* violence, which is 8 (Figure 2).

12.1.2 Residuals

Although we can predict the participants' real scores on *Actual* violence more accurately when we use the regression line, we shall still make errors. The error or **residual** (*e*) is the real score on *Actual* violence minus the prediction from regression:

$$e = Y - Y' \qquad (2) \text{ The residual}$$

In John's case, since $Y = 8$ and $Y' = 8.714$, $e = 8 - 8.714 = -0.714$. John's residual score is shown in Figure 2.

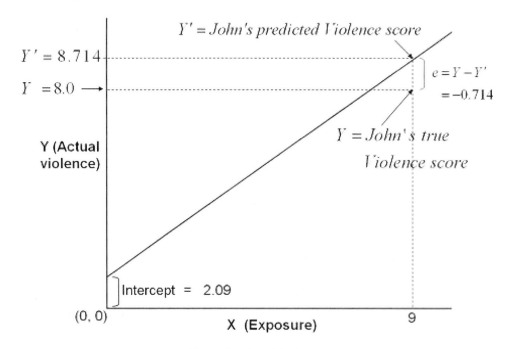

Figure 2.   A residual score

In regression, the study of the residuals is of great importance, because they form the basis for measures of the accuracy of the estimates and of the extent to which the **regression model** (see below) gives a good account of the data in question. (See Tabachnick & Fidell, 2007, for advice on **regression diagnostics**, which are based largely upon residuals and their transformations.)

12.1.3 The least squares criterion

The regression line shown in Figure 1 is the line that 'fits' the data best according to what is known as the **least squares criterion**, whereby the values of b_0 and b_1 must be such that that the sum of squares of the residuals Σe^2 is a minimum. There is a unique solution to this problem. The values of b_0 and b_1 that meet the criterion are given by the following formulae:

$$b_1 = \frac{SP}{SS_X}$$

(3) **Slope and intercept of the regression line**

$$b_0 = M_Y - b_1 M_X$$

where SS and SP are, respectively, the sum of squares and cross-products, as in the formula for the Pearson correlation (Chapter 11):

$$SS_X = \Sigma(X - M_X)^2 \qquad SP = \Sigma(X - M_X)(Y - M_Y)$$

The technique we have been describing is known as **ordinary least squares (OLS)** regression. There are other kinds of regression (such as logistic regression) which do not work in this way. It is not our intention here to present a comprehensive account of regression, simple or complex. There are, however, certain features that are common to all types of regression and therefore particularly deserving of attention.

12.1.4 Partition of the sum of squares in regression

In Chapter 7, we showed that in the one-way ANOVA, the total sum of squares can be partitioned into between subjects and within subjects components:

$$SS_{total} = SS_{between} + SS_{within}$$

(4) **Partition of the total sum of squares in ANOVA**

The larger the value of $SS_{between}$ in comparison with that of SS_{within}, the greater the proportion of the total variance accounted for by differences among the treatment means, as opposed to random error.

There is a similar relationship in regression. The basis of the total variance of the scores Y on the target or criterion variable is a set of deviations $(Y - M_Y)$: $SS_Y = \Sigma(Y - M_Y)^2$. Associated with the regression line is the regression sum of squares $SS_{regression}$, the formula for which is $SS_{regression} = \Sigma(Y' - M_Y)^2$. With measured variables, even if they are in a basically linear relationship, the regression sum of squares cannot account for all the variance in the target variable. From the residuals, can be calculated the **residual sum of squares**, $SS_{residual}$, the formula for which is $SS_{residual} = \Sigma(Y - Y')^2$. The residual sum of squares is calculated from the residuals as shown in Figure 3.

It can be shown that the total sum of squares of the target variable can be partitioned into regression and residual components according to

$$SS_Y = SS_{regression} + SS_{residual}$$

(5) **Partition of the total sum of squares in regression**

Equation (5), of course, is strongly reminiscent of the partition of the total sum of squares in ANOVA. This is no coincidence: as we shall see later, the partition of the total sum of squares in ANOVA can be viewed as a special case of (5).

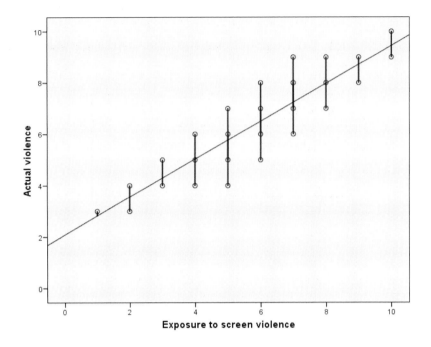

Figure 3. The residuals forming the basis of the residual sum of squares

12.1.5 Effect size in regression

Recall that in the one-way ANOVA, one measure of effect size is **eta squared** η^2, where

$$\eta^2 = \frac{SS_{between}}{SS_{total}} \quad (6) \textbf{ Eta squared in ANOVA}$$

It can be shown that, in regression, the proportion of the variance of the target variable accounted for by regression is given by the square of the Pearson correlation r^2, a statistic known as the **coefficient of determination (CD)**:

$$CD = r^2 = \frac{SS_{regression}}{SS_Y} \quad (7) \textbf{ Coefficient of determination}$$

The Pearson correlation between the *Actual* and *Exposure* scores is .89. The value of the coefficient of determination is therefore $.89^2 = .80$. This means that 80% of the variance of *Actual* scores is accounted for by regression of *Actual* violence upon *Exposure* to violent programmes.

We have already encountered the coefficient of determination in Chapter 11. There, we suggested that it is helpful to think of the *CD* as the proportion of the total variance of either variable that is shared with the other. Here, however, we see that the *CD* is the proportion of the variance of the criterion or target variable that is accounted for by the linear regression of the criterion variable on the regressor or IV.

It can be shown that the ANOVA statistic η^2 is a special case of CD. We shall return to this topic when we consider the re-interpretation of ANOVA as regression in a later section.

Here we reproduce the table from Chapter 11, which offers a rough guide to the classification of effect size in regression.

Effect size (r^2)	Size of Effect
<0.01 (<1%)	Small
0.01 to 0.10 (1-10%)	Medium
>0.10 (>10%)	Large

Picturing effect size in simple regression

In Chapter 11, it was observed that the CD can be represented diagrammatically, as the proportion of overlap between two circles, the total area of each circle representing 100% of the variance of one of the variables (Figure 4). In the context of regression, as opposed to correlation, we think of the degree of overlap as the proportion of the DV that is accounted for by regression upon the IV.

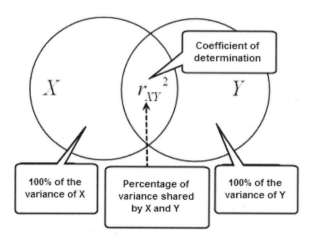

Figure 4. Diagrammatic representation of the coefficient of determination (CD)

12.1.6 Shrinkage

So far, all the statistics we have described refer to a single sample of scores. The purpose of the exercise, however, is ultimately to generalise beyond our data to the bivariate population or joint distribution of *Actual* violence and *Exposure*, which can be visualised as a scatterplot with an infinite number of points. The statistics of our sample, including the coefficient of determination, will tend to overstate the predictive power of regression in the population, the loss in predictive power with re-sampling being known as **shrinkage**. The CD, as calculated from a set of data, is positively biased as an estimate of the corresponding parameter (population value). In practice, where we are attempting to generalise beyond our own data to the population, we need to use the degrees of freedom of the relevant statistics to adjust the value of r^2 downwards to remove its positive bias. This is the reason for the 'adjustment' referred to in the SPSS output for various regression-related routines; in fact, **adjusted R^2** is referred to by some authors as '**shrunken R^2**'.

12.1.7 Regression models

The violence study was motivated by the desire to show that *Actual* violence is a linear function of *Exposure* to violence: that is, an observed score Y is made up according to the following equation:

$$Y = \beta_0 + \beta_1 + e \quad \text{(8)} \quad \textbf{A linear regression model of violence in children}$$

where β_0 and β_1 are the parameters corresponding to the intercept and slope, respectively, of the sample regression line that we have been discussing and e is a random component corresponding to the residual score.

In regression theory and tests for significance of estimates of the parameters of the regression equation, important assumptions are made about the random component e, including normality of distribution and independence of e across different values of X. The purpose of regression diagnostics (referred to earlier) is to ascertain whether these assumptions have been met.

12.1.8   Beta-weights

Rather confusingly, the term 'beta-weight' is also used to denote, not population parameters, but regression statistics that have been calculated from standardised scores z_X and z_Y, where

$$z_Y = \frac{Y - M_Y}{s_Y} \quad \text{and} \quad z_X = \frac{X - M_X}{s_X}.$$

It follows immediately from (3) that since the mean and variance of a set of standardised scores are 0 and 1, respectively, the intercept in the regression equation of z_Y upon z_X is zero. The slope can easily be shown to be r, the Pearson correlation.

$$z_Y' = \beta_1 z_X = r z_X \quad \text{(9)} \quad \textbf{Standardised form of the regression equation}$$

where z_Y', a point on the regression line, is the estimate of the observed standard score z_Y for a particular value of z_X. The advantage of beta-weights over raw regression coefficients is that they represent the estimated average change in Y, measured in standard deviations, that would result from an increase of one standard deviation in X. In this sense, beta-weights provide a 'unit-free' measure of the effects of regression.

12.1.9   Significance testing in simple regression

In Chapter 11, we saw that, provided the data have a bivariate normal distribution, the null hypothesis of independence (which states that in the population, the correlation is zero) can be tested with the statistic t with $n - 2$ degrees of freedom, where

$$t = \frac{r\sqrt{(n-2)}}{\sqrt{(1-r^2)}} \qquad \text{(10) } \textbf{The } \textit{t} \textbf{ test for correlation}$$

The Pearson correlation r is closely related to the regression coefficient b_1, so that the value of one fully determines that of the other:

$$r = b_1 \left(\frac{s_Y}{s_X} \right)$$

A test of the significance of the sample correlation r, therefore, is also a test of the significance of the regression coefficient b_1.

The testing of a regression coefficient for significance can be thought of in two equivalent ways:

1. The making of a point estimate of the population value and dividing that by an estimate of the standard error of the regression coefficient to produce a t statistic.
2. The testing of an estimate of the variance accounted for by regression (the coefficient of determination). This is achieved by an analysis of variance, in which the test statistic is F which, in the present context, is the square of t.

In the t-test approach, the test statistic is

$$t(n-2) = \frac{b_1}{s_{b_1}} \qquad (11)$$

where the standard error estimate in the denominator is given by

$$s_{b_1} = \sqrt{\frac{SS_{residual}/(n-2)}{SS_X}} \qquad (12)$$

In the ANOVA approach, the test statistic is

$$F(1, df_{residual}) = \frac{MS_{regression}}{MS_{residual}} = \frac{SS_{regression}/1}{SS_{residual}/(n-2)} = \frac{SS_{regression}(n-2)}{SS_{residual}} \qquad (13)$$

Since $SS_{regression} = r^2 SS_Y$ and $SS_{residual} = (1-r^2)SS_Y$, we see that

$$F(1, df_{residual}) = \frac{r^2 SS_Y (n-2)}{(1-r^2)SS_Y} = \frac{r^2(n-2)}{(1-r^2)} \qquad (14)$$

Notice that (14) is t^2 (see formula 10). In words, the value of t fully determines that of F, and vice versa, because $F = t^2$. The two tests are exact equivalents.

Note also that in (13), the regression mean square is equal to the regression sum of squares, because, since the value of the regression coefficient fully determines those of all the points on the line, $SS_{regression}$ has one degree of freedom. It is also easy to see that the residual sum of squares has $(n-2)$ degrees of freedom because, although there are n data points, we must subtract a degree of freedom for each of the two parameters estimated, namely, the intercept and the slope of the regression line.

12.2   SIMPLE REGRESSION WITH SPSS

As always, we recommend that you should obtain a picture of your data before making any formal statistical tests. In this example, we shall want to see the scatterplot and regression line first.

12.2.1   Drawing scatterplots with regression lines

Our starting point is the scatterplot of *Actual* violence upon *Exposure*. To add a regression line to this scatterplot, double-click on the plot to enter the **Chart Editor**, then click on the icon marked by the white cursor in Figure 5 labelled **Add Fit Line at Total**.

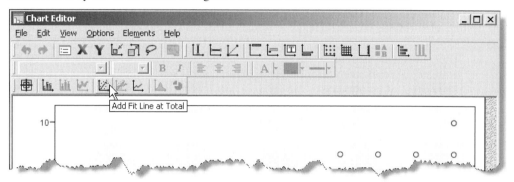

Figure 5. Choosing **Fit Line at Total** to draw the regression line

Clicking on **Fit Line at Total** will access the **Properties** dialog box, in which the **Linear** radio button is checked as the default setting. Close the **Properties** dialog box to see the complete regression line (Figure 6).

Figure 6. The regression line

In Figure 6, the vertical axis has been displaced slightly to the left, with the result that the intercept appears to be nearer the origin that the correct value of 2.09. To rectify this, enter the **Chart Editor** again and click the icon labelled **Add a reference line to the X axis** (Figure 7).

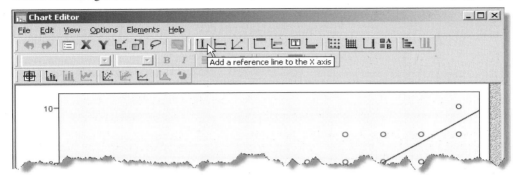

Figure 7. Adding a vertical reference line to the X axis

Clicking this icon will access the **Properties** dialog box (Figure 8).

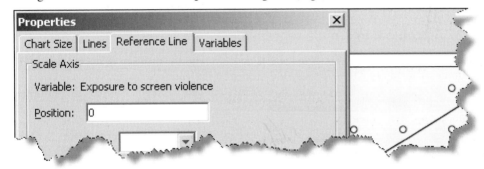

Figure 8. The **Properties** dialog box for drawing a vertical reference line on the X axis

Set the **Position** to zero and click the **Apply** button at the foot of the dialog box. The graph will now appear as in Figure 9. The regression line intercepts the vertical reference line 2.09 units above zero on the vertical axis. The value 2.09, as we know, is the correct value of the intercept.

Figure 9. Scatterplot with regression line and vertical reference line above the zero point on the X axis

12.2.2   A problem in simple regression

In some North American universities, there is concern with the efficacy of the methods used to select students for entry. How closely are scores on the entrance tests and final exam results associated? If there is an association, how accurately can we predict university performance from students' marks on the entrance tests?

Given that we have each student's final exam mark and entrance test mark, a Pearson correlation can be used to measure the degree of statistical association between these two variables. Simple regression can be used to predict final exam performance from marks on the entrance test.

12.2.3   Procedure for simple regression

In Table 1, the score *Fin* is a student's mark in the Final University Exam, and *Ent* is the same student's mark in the Entrance Exam.

Table 1. Table of the Final University Exam (Fin) and the Entrance Exam (Ent) scores											
Case	Fin	Ent	Case	Fin	Ent	Case	Fin	Ent	Case	Fin	Ent
1	38	44	10	81	53	19	105	43	28	142	56
2	49	40	11	86	47	20	106	55	29	145	60
3	61	43	12	91	45	21	107	48	30	150	55
4	65	42	13	94	41	22	112	49	31	152	54
5	69	44	14	95	39	23	114	46	32	164	58
6	73	46	15	98	40	24	114	41	33	169	62
7	74	34	16	100	37	25	117	49	34	195	49
8	76	37	17	100	48	26	125	63			
9	78	41	18	103	48	27	140	52			

The table contains the marks of 34 students: Student 1 (whose data are in the first row of the first two columns from the left) got 44 in the Entrance Exam and 38 in the Final University Exam. Student 34, on the other hand, (whose data are shown in the seventh row of the last two columns on the right), got 49 in the Entrance Exam and 195 in the Final University Exam.

Preparing the SPSS data set

Using the techniques described in Chapter 2, Section 2.3, enter **Variable View** and name the variables *Case, FinalExam* and *EntranceExam*. In the **Label** column, add more informative variable labels such as *Case Number, Final University Exam* and *Entrance Exam*. In **Data View**, enter the data in the pre-labelled columns.

See Section 2.3

Exploring the data

Usually the user would explore the data to check for incorrect enries and examine the scatterplot to detect any outliers. Here, in the interests of brevity, we shall proceed directly with the regression analysis and rely upon the regression procedure itself to find any problem cases.

Running simple regression

- Choose **Analyze➜Regression** (see Figure 10) and click **Linear...** to open the **Linear Regression** dialog box (the completed dialog is shown in Figure 11).

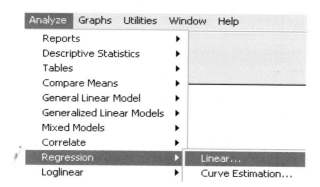

Figure 10. Finding the **Linear Regression** procedure

- Transfer the variable names as shown in Figure 11, taking care to select the appropriate variable names for the dependent variable (target) and the independent variable (regressor).
- Request additional descriptive statistics and a residuals analysis by clicking the **Statistics...** button to open the **Linear Regression: Statistics** dialog box (Figure 12) and activating the **Descriptives** checkbox. Analysis of the residuals gives a measure of how good the prediction is and whether there are any cases that are so discrepant as to be considered outliers and perhaps dropped from the analysis. Click the **Casewise**

diagnostics checkbox to include a listing of any exceptionally large residuals in the output. Click **Continue** to return to the **Linear Regression** dialog box.

- Since systematic patterns between the predicted values and the residuals can indicate violations of the assumption of linearity, we also recommend that a plot of the standardised residuals (*ZRESID*) against the standardised predicted values (*ZPRED*) be requested. Click **Plots...** to open the **Linear Regression: Plots** dialog box (Figure 13) and transfer *ZRESID* to the **Y:** box and *ZPRED* to the **X:** box. Click **Continue** to return to the **Linear Regression** dialog box.

- Back in the **Linear Regression** dialog box, predicted values and residuals can be saved to **Data View** by clicking the **Save...** button. Click **OK** to run the regression.

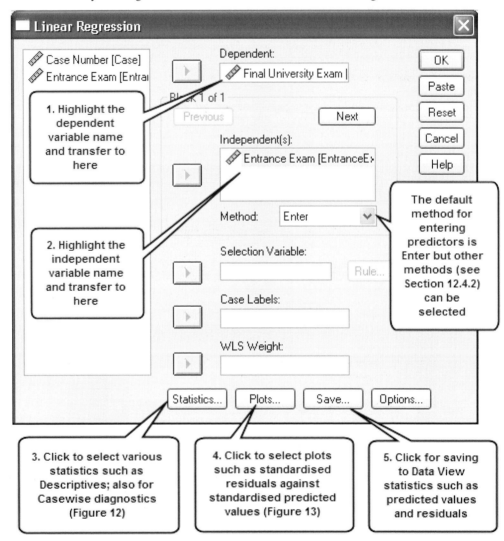

Figure 11. The **Linear Regression** dialog box

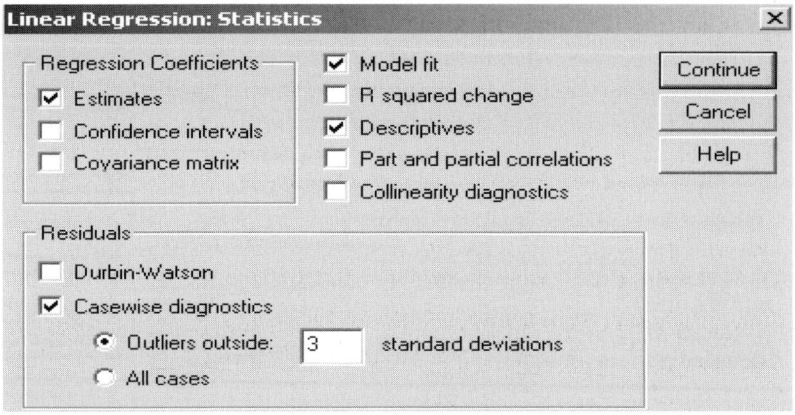

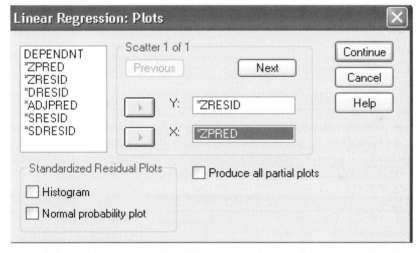

Figure 12. The **Statistics** dialog box with extra options **Descriptives** and **Casewise diagnostics** selected

Figure 13. The **Plots** dialog box with ***ZRESID** (standardised residuals) and ***ZPRED** (standardised predicted scores) selected for the axes of the plot

12.2.4   Output for simple regression

The various tables and charts in the output are listed in the left-hand pane of **SPSS Viewer**, as shown in Output 1. After the requested descriptive statistics and correlations (plus several other tables), the first table to scrutinise is **Casewise Diagnostics**. The information it contains may indicate that the regression analysis should be terminated and re-run after outliers have been removed from the data set. The table can be selected directly by moving the cursor to **Casewise Diagnostics** in the left-hand pane and clicking the left-hand mouse button.

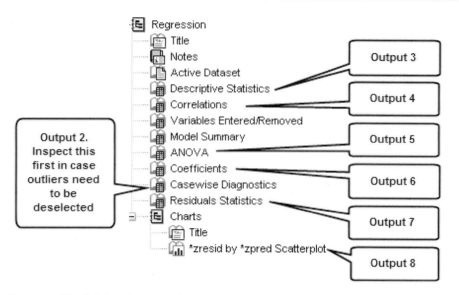

Output 1. The left-hand pane listing the tables and charts in the right-hand pane

Indication of residual outliers

The table of cases (**Casewise Diagnostics**) in Output 2 shows only one outlier with an absolute standardised residual greater than 3. This is Case 34, with a score of *195* for *Final University Exam*. From past experience, this is a suspiciously high mark and is almost certainly a typo; moreover, the candidate concerned got only 49 in the entrance exam, which is not an outstanding mark. The next section describes how to eliminate this outlier and re-run the regression analysis.

Casewise Diagnostics [a]

Case Number	Std. Residual	Final University Exam	Predicted Value	Residual
34	3.12	195	110.95	84.05

a. Dependent Variable: Final University Exam

Output 2. A list of cases with residuals greater than ± 3 standard deviations

Elimination of outliers

A more reliable regression analysis can be obtained by eliminating suspicious outliers. Use the **Select Cases** procedure described in Section 3.3.1.

See Section 3.3.1

- Choose
  Data➔Select Cases...
  to open the **Select Cases** dialog box.
- Click the **If condition is satisfied** radio button and define the condition as *Case ~=34* (the symbol ~= means 'not equal to').
- Click **Continue** and then **OK** to deselect this case.

If there are several suspicious outliers (obvious typographical errors, perhaps), it might be simpler to deselect them all by using a cut-off value for one of the variables (e.g. defining the condition with an inequality operator, as in the specification: *FinalExam* > 190). Sometimes, in order to see what value to use in the inequality, it is convenient to arrange scores in order of value by entering the **Data** menu and choosing **Sort Cases...** .

Output for simple regression after elimination of the outliers

When the regression analysis is re-run after deleting the original output, there will be no table of **Casewise Diagnostics**, since no cases will now have outlying residuals. We can therefore begin with the various tables and plots in the output. In Output 3, are the tables of descriptive statistics and the correlation coefficient for the 33 cases remaining in the data set.

Descriptive Statistics

	Mean	Std. Deviation	N
Final University Exam	102.82	32.633	33
Entrance Exam	47.27	7.539	33

Correlations

		Final University Exam	Entrance Exam
Pearson Correlation	Final University Exam	1.00	.73
	Entrance Exam	.73	1.00
Sig. (1-tailed)	Final University Exam	.	.00
	Entrance Exam	.00	.
N	Final University Exam	33	33
	Entrance Exam	33	33

Output 3. The **Descriptive Statistics** and **Correlations** tables for the data set without the outlier

Output 4 gives the value of **Multiple R**, where *R* is the **multiple correlation coefficient**. We shall have more to say about *R* when we discuss multiple regression.

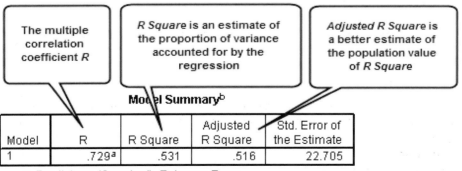

The multiple correlation coefficient *R*

R Square is an estimate of the proportion of variance accounted for by the regression

Adjusted R Square is a better estimate of the population value of *R Square*

Model Summary[b]

Model	R	R Square	Adjusted R Square	Std. Error of the Estimate
1	.729[a]	.531	.516	22.705

a. Predictors: (Constant), Entrance Exam

b. Dependent Variable: Final University Exam

Output 4. The values of the multiple correlation coefficient *R* and other statistics

When, as in the present example, there is only one regressor, however, R is simply the absolute value of the Pearson correlation between the criterion or DV and the regressor (IV). Had r been negative, say $-.729$, R would have had the same value, minus the sign: .729. In other words, R cannot have a negative value, even when r is negative. Whether, as in this example, there is only one IV or (as in a later example) there are several IVs, the multiple correlation coefficient R is the Pearson correlation between the observed scores Y and the estimates Y' from the regression equation. The least squares fitting of the regression line ensures that the slope of the regression line can never have a sign opposite to that of the Pearson correlation.

The other statistics listed in Output 4 are **R Square** (a positively biased estimate of the proportion of the variance of the dependent variable accounted for by regression), **Adjusted R Square** (which corrects this bias and therefore has a lower value), and the **Standard Error of the Estimate** (the standard deviation of the residuals). The **effect size**, as estimated by adjusted R^2 is 0.516 (52%). This, following Cohen's classification, is a 'large' effect.

Output 5 shows the regression ANOVA, which tests for a linear relationship between the variables. The F statistic is the ratio of the mean square for regression to the residual mean square. In this example, the value of F in the ANOVA Table is significant beyond the .01 level. *It should be noted, however, that only an examination of their scatterplot can confirm that the relationship between two variables is genuinely linear.*

The value of F and its associated p-value (significant at the .01 level)

ANOVA[b]

Model		Sum of Squares	df	Mean Square	F	Sig.
1	Regression	18096.33	1	18096.3	35.10	.000[a]
	Residual	15980.58	31	515.50		
	Total	34076.91	32			

a. Predictors: (Constant), Entrance Exam

b. Dependent Variable: Final University Exam

Output 5. The **ANOVA** for the regression

Output 6 presents the kernel of the regression analysis, the regression equation. The values of the **regression coefficient** and **constant** are given in column **B** of the table. Two further features of Output 6 are worthy of note. In the column headed 'Standardized Coefficients', there is no entry in the row labelled 'Constant'. This is because, as we have seen, the intercept of the regression equation disappears when the scores are standardised. In the same column, the regression coefficient is given as .73, which is the value of the Pearson correlation r because, as we have seen, the slope of the regression line of one standardised variable upon another is the Pearson correlation.

Coefficients[a]

Model		Unstandardized Coefficients		Standardized Coefficients		
		B	Std. Error	Beta	t	Sig.
1	(Constant)	-46.30	25.48		-1.82	.079
	Entrance Exam	3.15	.53	.73	5.92	.000

a. Dependent Variable: Final University Exam

The regression equation includes this constant and coefficient	Beta is the regression coefficient whan all the variables are expressed in standardised form	This tests the null hypothesis that there is no linear relationship between the variables (i.e. H₀ states that the regression coefficient is 0)

Output 6. The regression equation and associated statistics

From the values for the intercept and slope given in Output 6, the regression equation is

$$(Final\ University\ Exam)' = -46.30 + 3.15 \times (Entrance\ Exam)$$

where *(Final University Exam)'* is the predicted value of the actual *Final University Exam* mark. Thus a person scoring 60 in the *Entrance Exam* would have a predicted *Final* mark of

$$-46.30 + 3.15 \times 60 = 142.7 \quad (i.e.\ 143).$$

Notice that in Table 1, the person who scored 60 on the *Entrance Exam* actually scored 145 on the *Final University Exam*. So $Y' = 143$ and $Y = 145$. The residual $e = (Y - Y')$ is

$$145 - 143 = +2.$$

Other statistics are also listed in Output 6. The **Std. Error** is the standard error of the regression coefficient, **B**. **Beta** is the beta coefficient, which is the estimated average change in the dependent variable (expressed in standard deviation units) that would be produced by a positive increment of one standard deviation in the independent variable. The t statistic tests the regression coefficient for significance, and **Sig.** is the p-value of t. (Here .00 means <0.01, i.e. t is significant beyond the 0.01 level for the variable *Entrance Exam*. Write this p-value as '<.01', not as '.00'.)

Output 7 is a table of the statistics of the residuals. The row labelled **Predicted Value** summarises the unstandardised predicted values. The row labelled **Residual** summarises the unstandardised residuals. The row labelled **Std. Predicted Value** (identified as *ZPRED* in the **Plots** dialog box in Figure 13) summarises the standardised predicted values (i.e. *Predicted Value* transformed to a scale with mean 0 and SD 1). You can see that the calculated value for the SD (.98) is approximately 1. The row labelled **Std. Residual** (identified as *ZRESID* in the **Plots** dialog box in Figure 13) summarises the standardised residuals (with mean 0 and SD 1).

Residuals Statistics ^a

	Minimum	Maximum	Mean	Std. Deviation	N
Predicted Value	60.95	152.43	102.82	23.780	33
Residual	-54.49	30.97	.00	22.35	33
Std. Predicted Value	-1.76	2.09	.00	1.00	33
Std. Residual	-2.40	1.36	.00	.98	33

a. Dependent Variable: Final University Exam

Output 7. Table of statistics relating to the residuals

Output 8 is the scatterplot of the standardised residuals (*ZRESID*) against the standardised predicted values (*ZPRED*). The plot shows an essentially rectangular pattern, thereby confirming that the assumptions of linearity and homogeneity of variance are tenable. A crescent-shape or a 'funnel' would have indicated that a linear regression model was not a convincing interpretation of the data.

Other diagnostic plots could have been selected from within the **Standardized Residual Plots** box in Figure 13: for example, we could obtained a histogram of the standardised residuals (see Output 8) and a cumulative normal probability plot (in which, ideally, the points should lie along or adjacent to the diagonal).

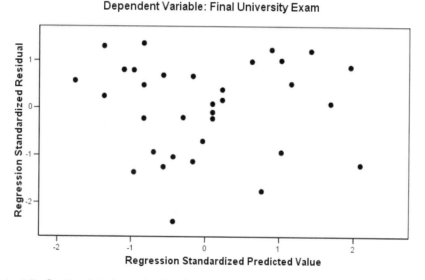

Dependent Variable: Final University Exam

Output 8. Scatterplot of standardised residuals against standardised predicted scores

12.3 MULTIPLE REGRESSION

In **multiple regression**, the values of one variable (the target, criterion or dependent variable Y) are estimated from those of two or more (in the general case, p) independent variables or regressors $(X_1, X_2, ..., Xp)$. This is achieved by the construction of a linear **multiple regression equation** of the general form

$$Y' = b_0 + b_1 X_1 + b_2 X_2 + ... + b_p X_p \qquad (15)$$

where the parameters b_1, b_2, ..., b_p are the **partial regression coefficients** and the intercept b_0 is the **regression constant**. This equation is known as the **multiple linear regression equation of Y upon X_1, X_2, ... X_p.**

A **partial regression coefficient** is the average increase in the criterion variable that would be produced by a positive increase of one unit in the IV (or regressor), with the effects of the other IVs upon either variable being held constant. Consider the partial regression coefficient b_1. Suppose we were to fix the values of all variables except regressor X_1, regress the criterion Y upon X_1 and calculate the regression coefficient. We could do this for every possible combination of fixed values for the other regressors and average the regression coefficients. This average is the partial regression coefficient b_1.

12.3.1   The multiple correlation coefficient *R*

One simple measure of the efficacy of regression for the prediction of Y is the Pearson correlation between the true values of the target variable Y and the estimates Y' obtained by substituting the corresponding values of X_1, X_2, ..., Xp into the regression equation. The correlation between Y and Y' is known as the **multiple correlation coefficient *R***. Notice that the upper case is used for the multiple correlation coefficient, to distinguish it from the correlation between the target variable and any one independent variable considered separately. It can be shown algebraically that the multiple correlation coefficient cannot have a negative value, even if there is only one regressor correlating negatively with the criterion, in which case **R** has the absolute value of the Pearson correlation **r**. The multiple correlation coefficient can only take values within the range from 0 to +1, inclusive: $0 \le R \le 1$.

An estimate of **effect size** is the coefficient of determination $\mathbf{R^2}$ which, by analogy with bivariate regression (and η^2 in ANOVA), is the proportion of variance in the dependent variable that can be accounted for by regression upon the independent variables or regressors. The positive bias in $\mathbf{R^2}$ is partially corrected in the statistic known as **adjusted R^2.**

12.3.2   Significance testing in multiple regression

Statistical testing is more complex in multiple regression than it is in simple regression. As in simple regression, an overall F test can be made of the null hypothesis of complete independence. In multiple correlation, however, the significance of F does not imply that any of the partial regression coefficients is significant. As in simple regression, there are measures of the proportion of the variance of the DV that is accounted for by multiple regression. When the IVs are correlated, however, as they nearly always are in some areas of research, it is difficult to attribute variance in the DV unequivocally to any one IV, without the help of additional collateral evidence or a well-conceived and empirically supported causal model.

If we assume that there are p independent variables, the null hypothesis of no regression at all is, by analogy with (14), tested with the statistic

$$F(p, df_{residual}) = \frac{MS_{regression}}{MS_{residual}} = \frac{SS_{regression} / p}{SS_{residual} / (n-1-p)} = \frac{R^2(n-1-p)}{(1-R^2)p} \qquad (16)$$

Associated with the independent variable X_k is the regression coefficient b_k. The null hypothesis that, in the population, this regression coefficient is zero is tested with the statistic

$$t_k = \frac{b_k}{s_{b_i}} \quad \text{where} \quad s_{b_i} = \sqrt{\frac{SS_{residual}/(n-1-p)}{\sum X_k^{\,2}(1-R^2)}} \quad (17)$$

Provided various assumptions are met, this statistic is distributed as t on $(n - 1 - p)$ degrees of freedom. Formula (16) is an obvious generalisation of (14) from the case with one IV to the case with p IVs.

12.3.3 Partial and semipartial correlation

Partial correlation

We made the acquaintance of partial correlation in Chapter 11. The **partial correlation** between two variables is what remains of the association between them when their associations with a third variable have been taken into account. Consider the multiple regression of Y (the DV) upon X_1 and X_2 (the IVs). Let e_Y and e_1 be the residuals of Y and X_1 when both variables are regressed upon independent variable X_2. The correlation between the residuals e_Y and e_1 is the partial correlation between Y and X_1. In Chapter 11, we saw that this correlation is readily obtained from the values of the correlations among the three variables.

In this chapter, we shall denote the partial correlation between Y and X_1 by using subscript notation thus $r_{Y1.2}$. In the subscript, the variable on the right of the point has been removed or 'partialled out' of the variables on the left of the point: X_2 has been removed from both Y and X_1.

We gave a formula for the partial correlation in Chapter 11. Amending the notation to apply to the present (regression) situation, the partial correlation $r_{Y1.2}$ is given by

$$r_{Y1.2} = \frac{r_{Y1} - r_{Y2}.r_{12}}{\sqrt{(1-r_{Y2}^{\,2})(1-r_{12}^{\,2})}} \quad (18)$$

The partial correlation is tested for significance with

$$t = \frac{r\sqrt{(n-3)}}{\sqrt{(1-r^2)}}$$

on $(n - 3)$ degrees of freedom. A degree of freedom has been lost from the residual variance because an additional regression coefficient has been estimated.

Semipartial (or part) correlation

Since in multiple regression we are trying to account for the variance of the DV in terms of regression upon two or more IVs, interest centres upon the proportion of the *total* variance of the DV that is accounted for, rather than the residual variance. To determine this proportion, we need to know the correlation between Y and the residual variance of X_1 after the influence of X_2 has been removed from X_1 only. The **semipartial** (or **part**) **correlation** between Y and the residuals of X_1 after the influence of X_2 has been removed is written as $r_{Y(1.2)}$. In the subscript $Y(1.2)$, the brackets indicate that X_2 has been partialled out of X_1, but not Y.

The semipartial correlation $r_{Y(1.2)}$ is given by

$$r_{Y(1.2)} = \frac{r_{Y1} - r_{Y2} \cdot r_{12}}{\sqrt{(1 - r_{12}^2)}} \qquad (19)$$

The formulae for the partial and semipartial correlations are very similar. The only difference is the additional factor in the denominator of the partial correlation, which ensures that its value is always at least as great as that of the semipartial correlation. Generally, the value of the partial correlation will be greater: it is highly unlikely that either Y or X_1 will show a correlation of exactly zero with X_2, in which case the partial and semipartial correlations would have the same value. The semipartial correlation can be tested for significance in the same way as the partial correlation. If, however, the semipartial correlation is significant, then the partial correlation must also be significant.

Variance interpretation of partial and semipartial correlations

Figure 14 depicts the relationships among the three variables when Y is regressed upon two independent variables X_1 and X_2.

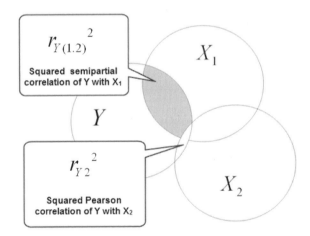

Figure 14. Variance interpretation of the semipartial correlation

Figure 14 shows that the square of the *semipartial* correlation $r_{Y(1.2)}^2$ (the grey area) is the additional proportion of the *total* variance of Y that is accounted for when the independent variable X_1 is added to the regression equation. The square of the *partial* correlation $r_{Y1.2}^2$, on the other hand, is the proportion of the *unexplained* variance of Y (the residuals when Y is regressed upon X_2) that is accounted for when X_1 is added to the regression equation. In the figure, the partial correlation is the grey area divided, not by 100% (the area of the whole circle), but by the area of the circle from which the white area of overlap has been subtracted. (The denominator of the partial correlation is thus smaller, making its value greater than that of the semipartial correlation.)

The foregoing notation for the semipartial correlation generalises to any number of independent variables. Suppose there are, not two but four independent variables X_1, X_2, X_3, X_4 and that we regress X_1 upon the other independent variables X_2, X_3, X_4. The semipartial correlation of Y with X_1 is the correlation between Y and the residuals of X_1 when X_2, X_3 and X_4 have been removed by multiple regression. This semipartial correlation is written as $r_{Y(1.234)}$, the subscripts 234 to the right of the point and the brackets signifying that the effects of X_2, X_3, X_4 have been removed from X_1 but not from Y.

Semipartial correlation and multiple correlation

If we regress Y upon two independent variables X_1 and X_2, the Pearson correlation between Y and the estimates from regression Y' is the multiple correlation coefficient, which we shall write as $R_{Y.12}$. In this expression, the subscript $Y.12$ indicates that Y is being correlated with a function of X_1, X_2 (the linear regression function). As we have seen, the square of the multiple correlation $R_{Y.12}^2$ is the proportion of the total variance of the dependent variable Y that is accounted for by regression upon the independent variables X_1 and X_2 and is known as the **coefficient of determination**.

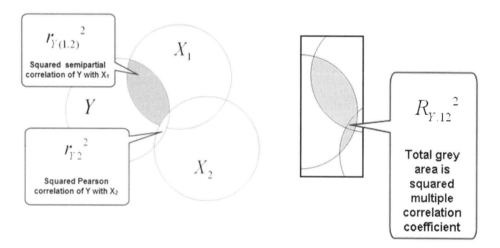

Figure 15. Relation between total proportion of variance accounted for by regression (R^2) and the squared semipartial correlation

In Figure 15, the total grey area in the right part of the figure is the coefficient of determination, that is, the total proportion of the variance of Y that is accounted for by multiple regression upon the two independent variables. The coefficient of determination can clearly be partitioned into two components:

1. The square of the Pearson correlation between Y and X_2;
2. The squared semipartial correlation between Y and the residuals of X_1 after regression of X_1 upon X_2. We can therefore write

$$R_{Y.12}^2 = r_{Y2}^2 + r_{Y(1.2)}^2 \quad (20)$$

We can also partition the coefficient of determination $R_{Y.12}{}^2$ as follows:

$$R_{Y.12}{}^2 = r_{Y1}{}^2 + r_{Y(2.1)}{}^2 \quad (21)$$

where $r_{Y(2.1)}{}^2$ is the squared semipartial correlation between Y and the residuals of X_2 after regression upon X_1.

Obtaining semipartial correlations from multiple correlations: ΔR^2

We now consider a more complex example, in which there are four independent variables X_1, X_2, X_3, X_4. In this case, we denote the multiple correlation coefficient by $R_{Y.1234}$ to indicate that the dependent variable Y is being correlated with a linear function of X_1, X_2, X_3, X_4.

We can partition the squared multiple correlation $R_{Y.1234}{}^2$ as follows:

$$R_{Y.1234}{}^2 = r_{Y4}{}^2 + r_{Y(3.4)}{}^2 + r_{Y(2.34)}{}^2 + r_{Y(1.234)}{}^2 \quad (22)$$

The first three terms on the right of equation (22), however, are a partition of the squared multiple correlation when Y is regressed upon the three independent variables X_2, X_3, X_4:

$$r_{Y4}{}^2 + r_{Y(3.4)}{}^2 + r_{Y(2.34)}{}^2 = R_{Y.234}{}^2$$

We may therefore express the squared semipartial correlation of Y with X_1 as the difference between the two squared multiple correlation coefficients thus

$$r_{Y(1.234)}{}^2 = R_{Y.1234}{}^2 - R_{Y.234}{}^2 \quad (23)$$

From (23), we see that the squared semipartial correlation is the increase in R^2 that results from adding that particular independent variable to the regression equation. For this reason, the squared semipartial correlation is referred to by some authors as ΔR^2 (**delta R^2**).

Uncorrelated independent variables

If, in the example of four independent variables, those variables were to be uncorrelated, we could represent the situation as in Figure 16. In Figure 16, none of the independent variables overlaps with any of the others, reflecting the total lack of correlation among them. In this case, the coefficient of determination (or the total proportion of the variance of the dependent variable that is accounted for by regression is given by

$$R_{Y.1234}{}^2 = r_{Y1}{}^2 + r_{Y2}{}^2 + r_{Y3}{}^2 + r_{Y4}{}^2 \quad (24)$$

The partition in (24) permits an unequivocal attribution of a portion of the variance of Y accounted for by regression to a particular independent variable. It is clear from Figure 16 that independent variable X_1 is the most important in accounting for the variance in Y.

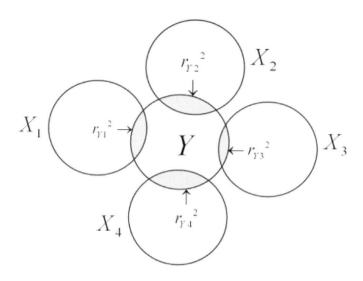

Figure 16.   Regression with uncorrelated independent variables

Variance interpretation of the test of the partial regression coefficient

The situation depicted in Figure 16 is, in practice, never encountered when the independent variables *X* are measured in the units of study, because such measurements are always subject to error.   More typically, the IVs are correlated, as in Figure 15.   There, the squared semipartial correlation between *Y* and either dependent variable is less than the square of the simple Pearson correlation between *Y* and that independent variable alone.   The squared semipartial correlation effectively places an independent variable 'at the end of the queue', as far as the attribution of variance in *Y* to each IV is concerned.

It can be shown that the test for the significance of a regression coefficient, that is,

$$t_k = \frac{b_k}{s_{b_i}}$$

is equivalent to the test of the significance of the squared semipartial correlation, or ΔR_i^2:

$$F(1, n-1-p) = \frac{\Delta R_i^2}{SS_{residual} / (n-1-p)} \quad (25)$$

where ΔR_i^2 is the squared semipartial correlation been *Y* and X_i.

'Importance' of the independent variable considered separately

The sharing of variance among the independent variables in multiple regression makes it impossible to assign variance in *Y* unequivocally to any of the independent variables. There is, therefore, a large literature on the question of which of the variables in a multiple regression is the 'most important' in explaining the variance of the dependent variable. The paper and textbook by Darlington (1968, 1990) provide a lucid discussion of the problems with the various measures of 'importance' that have been proposed.

We have already seen that the unstandardised regression coefficient is unsuitable as a measure of 'importance'. It might be thought that the simple Pearson correlation between an independent variable and the criterion would be an appropriate measure; but there are situations in which the largest squared semipartial correlation ΔR^2 does not belong to the variable showing the highest Pearson correlation with the criterion.

Suppressors

Some independent variables in a regression analysis are 'important', not in the sense that they predict the dependent variable, but because when their effects are removed from other independent variables with which they correlate substantially, those other variables predict the criterion with greater accuracy, even through the suppressor variable may itself show a negligible correlation with the criterion.

12.4 MULTIPLE REGRESSION WITH SPSS

One potential problem with multiple regression is that if we have measured several variables, some of which are highly correlated, the multiple regression package the researcher is using may not work at all. This is known as the problem of **multicollinearity**. A key notion here is that of the **tolerance** of a regressor, that is, one minus the square of the multiple correlation between the regressor and estimates of its values from its regression upon all the other regressors. If the tolerance is too low, the multiple regression will fail to run.

Even if multiple regression is feasible, there remains the problem of ascertaining which of the many variables in a study are crucial. In a situation where everything correlates with everything else, it is impossible to attribute variance in the target, criterion or dependent variable unequivocally to any one regressor or independent variable. Should the researcher be armed with a well-developed causal model of the focal health variables, this can drive both the selection of regressors and establish their relative importance. Often, however, especially in the early stages of research in an area, the researcher has no such model; indeed, the motivation for the research may be little more than the suspicion that certain variables might be important.

In Table 2, three extra variables, the subject's *Age*, the score obtained on a relevant academic *Project*, and *IQ* have been added to the original variables in Table 1. The outlier that was detected in the preliminary regression analysis, however, has been removed.

In the following discussion, we shall be concerned with two main questions:
1. Does the addition of more independent variables improve the accuracy of predictions of the value of *Final University Exam*?
2. Of these new variables, are some more useful than others for prediction of the dependent variable?

We shall see that the answer to the first question is 'Yes, up to a point'. It can be shown, in fact, that (providing the tolerance is sufficient) adding more regressors will result in a value for R which is at least as high as the previous value. On the other hand, this does not mean that more regressors should necessarily be added as a matter of course because, in some circumstances, that can result in highly unstable estimates. More is not necessarily better.

Case	Fin	Ent	Age	Pro	IQ	Case	Fin	Ent	Age	Pro	IQ
1	38	44	21.9	50	110	18	103	48	22.3	53	134
2	49	40	22.6	75	120	19	105	43	21.8	72	140
3	61	43	21.8	54	119	20	106	55	21.4	69	127
4	65	42	22.5	60	125	21	107	48	21.6	50	135
5	69	44	21.9	82	121	22	112	49	22.8	68	132
6	73	46	21.8	65	140	23	114	46	22.1	72	135
7	74	34	22.2	61	122	24	114	41	21.9	60	135
8	76	37	22.5	68	123	25	117	49	22.5	74	129
9	78	41	21.5	60	133	26	125	63	21.9	70	140
10	81	53	22.4	69	100	27	140	52	22.2	77	134
11	86	47	21.9	64	120	28	142	56	21.4	79	134
12	91	45	22.0	78	115	29	145	60	21.6	84	132
13	94	41	22.2	68	124	30	150	55	22.1	60	135
14	95	39	21.7	70	135	31	152	54	21.9	76	135
15	98	40	22.2	65	132	32	164	58	23.0	84	149
16	100	37	39.3	75	130	33	169	62	21.2	65	135
17	100	48	21.0	65	128						

Table 2. An extension of Table 1, with data on three additional independent variables

The second question, concerning the relative importance of the various regressors, is particularly problematic, and none of the available approaches to it is entirely satisfactory (see, for example, Howell, 2007).

In this section, we shall consider two general approaches to multiple regression. In **simultaneous** multiple regression, all the relevant regressors are entered in the equation directly, so that the tests for each regression coefficient effectively put it 'at the end of the queue' and test ΔR^2 in the presence of all the other variables. In **stepwise** multiple regression, the more controversial of the two techniques, the independent variables are added to (or taken away from) the equation one at a time, the order of entry (or removal) being determined by preset statistical criteria. Many would say, however, that no statistical model can justify such 'queue-jumping': a substantive causal model is also essential.

In this section, we shall begin with an example of the use of simultaneous regression. After that, for the sake of completeness (and with considerable reservations), we shall turn to stepwise regression. In fact, despite the theoretical problems with stepwise regression, we have found that the method often yields sensible results that are very similar to those from a simultaneous regression on the same data.

Constructing the SPSS data set

Restore the original data set (minus the outlier) to **Data View**. In **Variable View**, name the three new variables (e.g. *Age*, *Project* and *IQ*). Use the **Label** column to assign a variable label such as *Project Mark*. Now enter the scores in **Data View**. The first three cases are shown in Figure 17.

Case	FinalExam	EntranceExam	Age	Project	IQ
1	38	44	21.9	50	110
2	49	40	22.6	75	120
3	61	43	21.8	54	119

Figure 17. The first three cases in **Data View**

12.4.1   Simultaneous multiple regression

- In the **Linear Regression** dialog box, transfer the variable name *Final University Exam* into the **Dependent Variable:** and *Entrance Exam, Age, Project Mark* and *IQ* into the **Independent Variables:** box.
- Select the other optional items as in Section 12.2.3, then click **OK**.

Output for simultaneous multiple regression

The first table in the output is a table of the requested descriptive statistics for each variable (Output 9).

Descriptive Statistics

	Mean	Std. Deviation	N
University Exam	102.82	32.63	33
Entrance Exam	47.27	7.54	33
Age	22.518	3.046	33
Project Mark	67.94	9.14	33
IQ	129.03	9.66	33

Output 9. The Descriptive Statistics table

The next item is an edited table of correlations (Output 10) showing that the target variable *Final University Exam* correlates significantly with three of the regresssors but not with the fourth (*Age*).

Correlations

		University Exam
Pearson Correlation	University Exam	1.00
	Entrance Exam	.73
	Age	-.03
	Project Mark	.40
	IQ	.65
Sig. (1-tailed)	University Exam	.
	Entrance Exam	.00
	Age	.43
	Project Mark	.01
	IQ	.00

Output 10. Edited table of Correlations

Output 11 lists the variables entered in the model.

Variables Entered/Removed [b]

Model	Variables Entered	Variables Removed	Method
1	IQ, Age, Project Mark, Entrance Exam [a]	.	Enter

a. All requested variables entered.

b. Dependent Variable: Final University Exam

Output 11. List of variables entered, the dependent variable and the method of analysis

Output 12 shows that the multiple correlation coefficient R is 0.87 and the **Adjusted R Square** is 0.73. The effect size represented by adjusted R^2 is 73% i.e. a **large** effect.

Model Summary [b]

Model	R	R Square	Adjusted R Square	Std. Error of the Estimate
1	.87[a]	.76	.73	16.92

a. Predictors: (Constant), IQ, Age, Project Mark, Entrance Exam

b. Dependent Variable: Final University Exam

Output 12. Value of **R** and other statistics

Recall that when one regressor (*Entrance Exam*) was used to predict *Final University Exam*, the value of **R** was 0.73 and **Adjusted R Square** (the estimate of the proportion of variance accounted for by regression) was 0.52 (52%). With **R** now at 0.87 and **Adjusted R Square** up from 52% to 73%, we see that the answer to the question of whether adding more independent variables improves the predictive power of the regression equation is definitely 'Yes'. There remains, however, the question of which of the new variables is responsible for the improvement.

Not surprisingly, the ANOVA (Output 13) shows that the regression is significant beyond the .01 level.

ANOVA [b]

Model		Sum of Squares	df	Mean Square	F	Sig.
1	Regression	26059.63	4	6514.91	22.75	.000[a]
	Residual	8017.28	28	286.33		
	Total	34076.91	32			

a. Predictors: (Constant), IQ, Age, Project Mark, Entrance Exam

b. Dependent Variable: Final University Exam

Output 13. The **ANOVA** for regression

Output 14 tables the values of the regression coefficients.   From column **B**, we see that the multiple regression equation of *Final University Exam* upon *Entrance Exam, Age, Project Mark* and *IQ* is:

$$Final' = -272.13 + 2.49 \times Entrance + 1.24 \times Age + 0.50 \times Project + 1.51 \times IQ$$

where *Final'* is the predicted *Final University Exam* mark.

A person with *Age 21.6* and scoring *60* on the *Entrance Exam*, *84* on the *Project* and having an *IQ* of *132* would have an estimated score of

$$-272.13 + 2.49 \times (60) + 1.24 \times (21.6) + 0.50 \times (84) + 1.51 \times (132) = 145.37$$

Notice that case 29, who meets these specifications, actually scored 145 in the *Final University Exam*. However, not all cases have estimates so close to the actual values: for case 6, the estimate is 113.34, but the actual value is 73.

But what about the second question? Do all the new variables contribute substantially to the predictive power of the regression equation, or is one or more a passenger in the equation? We can learn little about the relative importance of the variables from the sizes of their regression coefficients B, because *the values of the partial regression coefficients reflect the original units in which the variables were measured.* For this reason, although the coefficient for *Age* is larger than that for *Project*, we cannot thereby conclude that *Age* is the more important predictor.

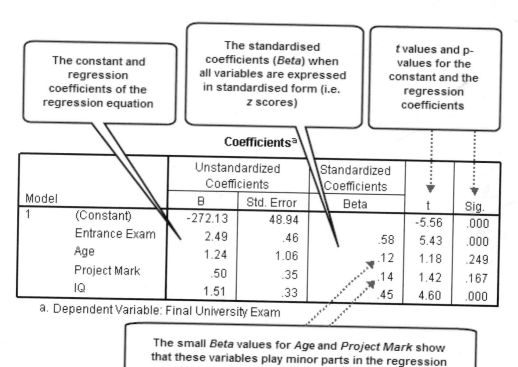

The constant and regression coefficients of the regression equation

The standardised coefficients (*Beta*) when all variables are expressed in standardised form (i.e. z scores)

t values and p-values for the constant and the regression coefficients

Coefficients[a]

Model		Unstandardized Coefficients		Standardized Coefficients		
		B	Std. Error	Beta	t	Sig.
1	(Constant)	-272.13	48.94		-5.56	.000
	Entrance Exam	2.49	.46	.58	5.43	.000
	Age	1.24	1.06	.12	1.18	.249
	Project Mark	.50	.35	.14	1.42	.167
	IQ	1.51	.33	.45	4.60	.000

a. Dependent Variable: Final University Exam

The small *Beta* values for *Age* and *Project Mark* show that these variables play minor parts in the regression

Output 14. The regression equation and associated statistics

The **beta coefficients** (in the column headed **Beta**) tell us rather more, because each gives the estimate of the average number of standard deviations change in the criterion that will be produced by a change of one standard deviation in the regressor concerned. On this count, *Entrance Exam* still makes by far the greatest contribution, because a change of one standard deviation on that variable produces a change of 0.58 standard deviations on *Final University Exam*. Next is *IQ* with a change of 0.45, but *Project Mark* produces a change in *Final University Exam* of only 0.14 standard deviations and *Age* a change of 0.12 SDs. This ordering of the standardised beta coefficients is supported by consideration of the correlations between the criterion and each of the three regressors (Output 10). If **R square change** (ΔR^2) had been selected in Figure 12, the output would have shown that the regressor with the largest beta coefficient also has the largest value of R square change.

The remaining items of output (the table of **Residual Statistics** and the scatterplot of standardised predicted values against standardised residuals) are not shown here. There were no residual outliers. Residuals are the basis of **regression diagnostics**, that is, set of procedures for identifying rogue scores that can distort the values of multiple regression statistics. The raw residuals *e* are themselves valuable measures of **distance**. But distances exert more **leverage** on the regression statistics if they are far from the mean of the IV concerned than if they are near. Leverage is captured by the statistic known as h_i, where *h* stands for 'hat'. To have influence, however, a score must have both distance and leverage. The statistic known as **Cook's D** is a respected measure of influence. (See Howell, 2007, pages 515-520, for an introduction to regression diagnostics.)

12.4.2   Stepwise multiple regression

If, in the **Linear Regression** dialog box, the choice of **Method** is changed to **Stepwise**, rather than **Enter**, a stepwise regression will be run, whereby predictors are added to (or subtracted from) the equation one at a time. In **Forward selection**, predictors are added one a time, provided they meet an entry criterion: we could decide, for example, that a variable makes a robust contribution if the increase in the variance it explains is significant beyond the 0.05 level. In **Backward deletion**, the predictors are all present initially and are removed one at a time if they do not meet a retention criterion: we could decided, for example, that a variable will be removed if the resulting reduction in the value of R^2 has an associated p-value of greater than 0.10. The SPSS **Stepwise regression** routine is a combination of these two processes: a variable, having been added at an early stage, may subsequently be removed. Selected portions of the results of a **Stepwise regression** analysis are shown in Outputs 15-19.

Variables Entered/Removed[a]

Model	Variables Entered	Variables Removed	Method
1	Entrance Exam		Stepwise (Criteria: Probability-of-F-to-enter <= .050, Probability-of-F-to-remove >= .100).
2	IQ		Stepwise (Criteria: Probability-of-F-to-enter <= .050, Probability-of-F-to-remove >= .100).

a. Dependent Variable: Final University Exam

First variable entered in Model 1	No variables were removed	Second variable added to the first in Model 2. No other variables were entered so there are no more Models

Output 15. List of variables entered (only two achieved entry in the stepwise regression)

The value of R for Model 2 is smaller than the value (0.87) given for simultaneous regression of *Final University Exam* upon *Entrance Exam*, *Project Mark*, *Age* and *IQ* but only slightly so. This shows the lack of predictive value of the two excluded variables (*Age* and *Project Mark*). The values of adjusted R^2 for Model 1 and Model 2 are large (52% & 71%, respectively) so the **effect sizes** are large.

Model Summary[c]

	Model	R	R Square	Adjusted R Square	Std. Error of the Estimate
Note the increase in the value of R (and R²) after the addition of a second variable	1	.73[a]	.53	.52	22.70
	2	.85[b]	.73	.71	17.62

a. Predictors: (Constant), Entrance Exam

b. Predictors: (Constant), Entrance Exam, IQ

c. Dependent Variable: Final University Exam

Output 16. Value of ***R*** and associated statistics for each Model

The ANOVA (Output 17) for each regression Model is significant.

ANOVA[c]

Model		Sum of Squares	df	Mean Square	F	Sig.
1	Regression	18096.33	1	18096.33	35.10	.000[a]
	Residual	15980.58	31	515.50		
	Total	34076.91	32			
2	Regression	24757.87	2	12378.93	39.85	.000[b]
	Residual	9319.04	30	310.63		
	Total	34076.91	32			

a. Predictors: (Constant), Entrance Exam

b. Predictors: (Constant), Entrance Exam, IQ

c. Dependent Variable: Final University Exam

Output 17. The **ANOVA** for each regression Model

The decision of the SPSS stepwise procedure is that, since the increment in R with the inclusion of either of the remaining variables (*Project Mark* and *Age*) does not reach the necessary statistical criterion, these variables are excluded from the final equation (Output 18).

From column **B** in Output 18, we see that the multiple regression equation of *Final University Exam* upon *Entrance Exam* and *IQ* is

$$(Final\ University\ Exam)' = -219.07 + 2.51 \times (Entrance\ Exam) + 1.58 \times IQ$$

where (*Final University Exam*)′ is the predicted value of the *Final University Exam* mark.

Thus the estimated score of a person with *Age 21.6* scoring *60* on the *Entrance Exam* and having an *IQ* of *132* is

$$-219.07 + 2.51 \times (60) + 1.58 \times (132) = 140.09$$

Notice that case 29, who meets these specifications, scored 145 in the *Final University Exam*. In this case the 'simultaneous' regression equation provides a better estimate than the stepwise regression equation; but there are other cases in which the opposite is true.

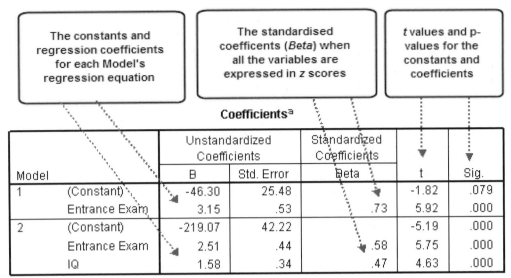

		Unstandardized Coefficients		Standardized Coefficients		
Model		B	Std. Error	Beta	t	Sig.
1	(Constant)	-46.30	25.48		-1.82	.079
	Entrance Exam	3.15	.53	.73	5.92	.000
2	(Constant)	-219.07	42.22		-5.19	.000
	Entrance Exam	2.51	.44	.58	5.75	.000
	IQ	1.58	.34	.47	4.63	.000

The boxes above the table read:
- The constants and regression coefficients for each Model's regression equation
- The standardised coefficents (*Beta*) when all the variables are expressed in z scores
- *t* values and p-values for the constants and coefficients

Coefficients[a]

a. Dependent Variable: Final University Exam

Output 18. The regression coefficients tables for the single variable (Model 1) and the two variables (Model 2) remaining in the stepwise regression analysis

Output 19 lists the statistics for the excluded variables. Note the low values of t and their correspondingly high (i.e. > 0.05) p-values.

Excluded Variables [c]

Model		Beta In	t	Sig.	Partial Correlation	Collinearity Statistics Tolerance
1	Age	.18[a]	1.42	.167	.25	.93
	Project Mark	.21[a]	1.69	.102	.29	.92
	IQ	.47[a]	4.63	.000	.65	.90
2	Age	.15[b]	1.56	.129	.28	.92
	Project Mark	.17[b]	1.77	.088	.31	.91

a. Predictors in the Model: (Constant), Entrance Exam

b. Predictors in the Model: (Constant), Entrance Exam, IQ

c. Dependent Variable: Final University Exam

Output 19. The variables excluded from the stepwise regression analysis

In the table in Output 19, **Beta In** is the standardised regression coefficient that would result if the variable were entered into the equation at the next step. The *t* test is the usual test of significance of the regression coefficient. Partial correlation is the correlation that remains between two variables after removing the correlation that is due to their mutual association with the other variables. As we have seen, **multicollinearity** is the undesirable situation where the correlations among the regressors are high. Multicollinearity can be detected by the **Tolerance** statistic, which is the proportion of a variable's variance not accounted for by other independent variables in the equation. A variable with very low tolerance contributes little information to a model, and can cause computational problems.

In conclusion, the **stepwise regression** confirms the conclusion from the beta coefficients in the simultaneous regression that only the variables *Entrance Exam* and *IQ* are useful for predicting *Final University Exam* marks. The other two variables can be dropped from the analysis.

12.5   REGRESSION AND ANALYSIS OF VARIANCE

In this section, we shall show that the similarities between the regression output and that of ANOVA are by no means coincidental; in fact, ANOVA can be viewed as a special case of regression.

12.5.1   The point-biserial correlation

In Chapter 6, we used an independent samples *t* test to compare the mean performance score of 20 participants who had ingested caffeine with the mean performance of a comparison or placebo group. It was found that the Caffeine group ($M = 11.90$; $SD = 3.28$) outperformed the Placebo group ($M = 9.25$; $SD = 3.16$). The *t* test showed the difference to be significant: $t(38) = 2.60$; p = .01.

To run a *t* test on the caffeine data, group membership is indicated by a **grouping variable**, that is, a set of code numbers, each number serving as a label for one group or condition. For the purposes of the *t* test, it doesn't matter what the code numbers are, as long as they are different. If, however, we let the value 0 denote the Placebo group and 1 denote the Caffeine group, we shall be using what is known as **dummy coding**. In some applications of regression, the choice of numbers for grouping variables is very important and different codes are appropriate for different purposes. Dummy coding highlights the equivalence of the regression and ANOVA statistics.

When we introduced the Pearson correlation *r* in Chapter 11, we emphasised that *r* was a measure of linear association suitable for continuous or scale data. There is, however, a special application of the Pearson correlation which breaks this rule. A **point-biserial** correlation is the Pearson correlation between a continuous variable and a dichotomous grouping variable. In the caffeine example, we would calculate the correlation between the column of scores in Data View and the grouping variable consisting of the code numbers for the different groups.

When, from the caffeine data set, we calculate the point-biserial correlation between the scores and the grouping variable, we obtain $r(40) = .389$. In Chapter 11, we said that, provided a bivariate data set consisting of n pairs of scores was bivariate-normal, we could test the significance of r with the statistic *t*, where

$$t = \frac{r\sqrt{n-2}}{\sqrt{1-r^2}}$$

on (n – 2) degrees of freedom.

When we apply this formula to the correlation between the dummy-coded grouping variable and the scores in the caffeine data, we find that

$$t = \frac{.38913\sqrt{38}}{\sqrt{1-.38913^2}} = 2.604$$

which is exactly the value for t that we obtained when using the independent t test to compare the means of the Caffeine and Placebo groups.

This is, of course, no coincidence. There is, as we shall see, an intimate link between using techniques such as t and F to compare group means and the regression of scores upon grouping variables. The point-biserial correlation forms an important conceptual bridge between the statistics of comparison and those of association.

12.5.2 Regression and the one-way ANOVA for two groups

In Chapter 7, we saw that if the one-way ANOVA were to be applied to the data from the two-group Caffeine experiment, the ANOVA F-test would result in exactly the same decision about the null hypothesis of equality of the population means as would the independent-samples t test. In general, F and t are related according to

$$F_{1,2(n-1)} = t_{2(n-1)}^2$$

where n is the size of a sample (equal-n case).

In this particular example,

$$F_{1,38} = 6.781 = 2.604^2 = t_{38}^2$$

In Table 3, is shown the summary table for the one-way ANOVA for comparison with the output table for regression of the scores in the Caffeine experiment upon the dummy variable.

You will notice immediately that the regression sum of squares $SS_{regression}$ has exactly the same value as the one-way ANOVA between groups sum of squares $SS_{between}$. Moreover, the regression residual sum of squares $SS_{residual}$ has the same value as the within groups sum of squares SS_{within} in the one-way ANOVA.

We have also seen that, in regression, the coefficient of determination (CD or r^2) is the proportion of the variance of the criterion or DV that is accounted for by regression. When we square the point-biserial correlation between the scores in the Caffeine experiment and the grouping variable, we obtain the coefficient of determination (r^2):

$$r^2 = .38913^2 = .1514$$

When the CD is multiplied by the total regression sum of squares SS_{total}, we obtain

$$r^2(SS_{total}) = .1514 \times 463.775 = 70.22$$

which is not only the value of the regression sum of squares, but also the value of $SS_{between}$ in the one-way ANOVA.

Table 3. Comparison between the one-way ANOVA summary table (upper panel) with the ANOVA table in the output for the regression of the scores in the Caffeine experiment upon the grouping variable (lower panel)

ANOVA

Performance Score

	Sum of Squares	df	Mean Square	F	Sig.
Between Groups	70.225	1	70.225	6.781	.013
Within Groups	393.550	38	10.357		
Total	463.775	39			

ANOVA[b]

Model		Sum of Squares	df	Mean Square	F	Sig.
1	Regression	70.225	1	70.225	6.781	.013[a]
	Residual	393.550	38	10.357		
	Total	463.775	39			

a. Predictors: (Constant), Treatment Group

b. Dependent Variable: Performance Score

We can therefore interpret the between groups sum of squares in the one-way ANOVA as a regression sum of squares. We can also interpret the square of the point-biserial correlation as the proportion of the one-way ANOVA total sum of squares that is accounted for by the difference between the means of the two groups.

This is the meaning of the **eta squared** statistic as a measure of **effect size**:

$$\eta^2 = \frac{SS_{regression}}{SS_Y} = \frac{SS_{between}}{SS_{total}}$$

Essentially, η^2 is the coefficient of determination (the square of the point-biserial correlation) when the group means are regressed upon a coding variable.

We have been considering the two-group case; but we know that the equivalence of F and t breaks down with three or more groups. The equivalence of regression and ANOVA generalises, however, to any number of groups.

12.5.3 Regression and dummy coding: the two-group case

In the previous section, we remarked upon the identity of the regression with the ANOVA statistics. In this session, we shall explain why the two sets of statistics are identical.

Equivalence of the t test and regression with a dummy variable

Figure 18 shows the scatterplot of performance scores against the values of the dummy variable X. Ordinary least squares regression will specify the line that passes through the group means. (This is because the sum of the squared deviations about the mean is a minimum: that is, its value is less than the sum of the squared deviations about any other value.)

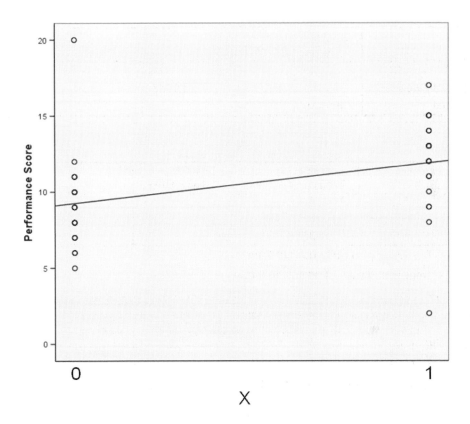

Figure 18. Scatterplot of Performance against the dummy variable X with the regression line passing through the group means

Let Y_0' and Y_1' be the points on the regression line when X has the values 0 and 1, respectively.

Applying the regression equation $Y' = b_0 + b_1 X$, we find that

$$Y_0' = M_{Placebo} = b_0 \qquad Y_1' = M_{Caffeine} = M_{Placebo} + b_1 \qquad b_1 = M_{Caffeine} - M_{Placebo}$$

In words, with dummy coding, the intercept of the regression line is the mean score of the control group and the slope of the line is the difference between the mean scores under the two conditions. As a consequence, a test of the null hypothesis that the regression coefficient is zero is also a test of the null hypothesis that, in the population, the difference between the

Caffeine and Placebo means is zero. This is why the regression on a dummy variable and the two-group ANOVA are equivalent: the regression predicts the group means exactly.

The lower part of Table 4 shows that the intercept (constant) is 9.25, the value of the Placebo mean. The slope of the line is 2.65, which is $11.90 - 9.25$, the difference between the means for the Caffeine and Placebo groups. Finally, $t(38) = 2.604$; $p = .013$. This is exactly the result we obtained from the independent samples t test.

Table 4. The intercept and regression coefficient from regression on the dummy variable. Notice that the value of F in the upper part of the table is the square of the value of t in the lower part

ANOVA[b]

Model		Sum of Squares	df	Mean Square	F	Sig.
1	Regression	70.225	1	70.225	6.781	.013[a]
	Residual	393.550	38	10.357		
	Total	463.775	39			

a. Predictors: (Constant), Treatment Group

b. Dependent Variable: Performance Score

Coefficients[a]

Model		Unstandardized Coefficients		Standardized Coefficients		
		B	Std. Error	Beta	t	Sig.
1	(Constant)	9.250	.720		12.854	.000
	Treatment Group	2.650	1.018	.389	2.604	.013

a. Dependent Variable: Performance Score

12.5.4   Regression and the one-way ANOVA

In a one-factor experiment with k treatment groups, the between groups (or treatment) sum of squares has $k - 1$ degrees of freedom, because there are only $k - 1$ deviations about the grand mean. We can carry group membership in $k - 1$ dummy variables. If we regress the scores on the $k - 1$ dummy variables, the multiple regression equation will predict the group means exactly, because the regression follows the least squares criterion, whereby the sum of squared deviations about the mean is a minimum. The regression sum of squares will have $k - 1$ degrees of freedom – one degree for each dummy variable.   In the one-way ANOVA of Chapter 7, there were 5 treatment groups. If, therefore, we regress the scores upon 4 dummy variables, we shall predict the treatment means exactly and the regression sum of squares will be equal to the between groups mean square from the one-way ANOVA.

The four dummy variables are shown in Table 5. Every member of each of the five treatment groups will be assigned the same row of values of the four dummy variables.

Table 5. Four dummy variables specifying the conditions in the drug experiment under which the scores were obtained

Group	X_1	X_2	X_3	X_4
Placebo	0	0	0	0
Drug A	1	0	0	0
Drug B	0	1	0	0
Drug C	0	0	1	0
Drug D	0	0	0	1

In Table 6, a section of **Data View** is shown, with the scores in the Placebo and Drug A groups alongside the four dummy variables.

Table 6. Section of **Data View** showing the scores of the Placebo and Drug A groups, together with the four dummy variables

	Group	Score	X1	X2	X3	X4
1	0	10	0	0	0	0
2	0	9	0	0	0	0
3	0	7	0	0	0	0
4	0	9	0	0	0	0
5	0	11	0	0	0	0
6	0	5	0	0	0	0
7	0	7	0	0	0	0
8	0	6	0	0	0	0
9	0	8	0	0	0	0
10	0	8	0	0	0	0
11	1	8	1	0	0	0
12	1	10	1	0	0	0
13	1	7	1	0	0	0
14	1	7	1	0	0	0
15	1	7	1	0	0	0
16	1	12	1	0	0	0
17	1	7	1	0	0	0
18	1	4	1	0	0	0
19	1	9	1	0	0	0
20	1	8	1	0	0	0
21	2	12	0	1	0	0
22	2	14	0	1	0	0
23	2	9	0	1	0	0

As in the case of two groups, the results of the one-way ANOVA and the regression are identical. (See Output 20.)

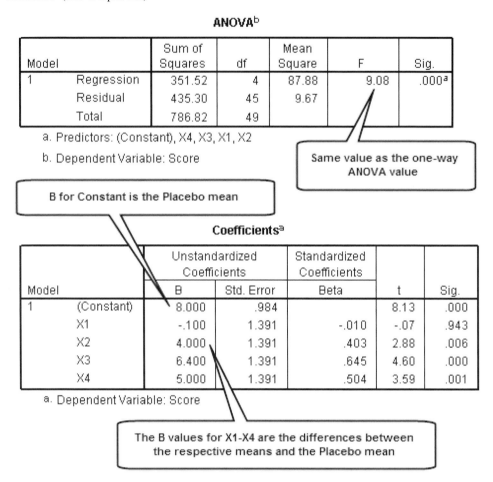

ANOVA[b]

Model		Sum of Squares	df	Mean Square	F	Sig.
1	Regression	351.52	4	87.88	9.08	.000[a]
	Residual	435.30	45	9.67		
	Total	786.82	49			

a. Predictors: (Constant), X4, X3, X1, X2

b. Dependent Variable: Score

Same value as the one-way ANOVA value

B for Constant is the Placebo mean

Coefficients[a]

Model		Unstandardized Coefficients		Standardized Coefficients	t	Sig.
		B	Std. Error	Beta		
1	(Constant)	8.000	.984		8.13	.000
	X1	-.100	1.391	-.010	-.07	.943
	X2	4.000	1.391	.403	2.88	.006
	X3	6.400	1.391	.645	4.60	.000
	X4	5.000	1.391	.504	3.59	.001

a. Dependent Variable: Score

The B values for X1-X4 are the differences between the respective means and the Placebo mean

Output 20. Output from regression of the scores in the 5-group drug experiment in Chapter 7 upon four dummy variables.

The Constant (intercept) is the mean for the Placebo group. The regression coefficients are the differences between the group means and the Placebo mean. The regression sum of squares is equal to $MS_{between}$ in the one-way ANOVA; so also are the results of the F tests in the two analyses.

12.6   MULTILEVEL REGRESSION MODELS

Underlying all the methods described so far in this chapter has been a very important assumption, namely, that the observations are independent. Suppose, for example, that we are interested in the factors that lead to school success and that we have data on the exam results of a large number of children, together with their scores on a reading test, as well as information about their school's gender policy and other variables.

If we are interested in the effect of the children's reading levels on their exam success at school, it might seem natural to regress their school exam scores on their reading scores in the manner described earlier in this chapter. We could easily enter the data into SPSS and apply the methods of least squares regression to estimate the regression coefficient and test it for significance. The difficulty with this approach is that the assumption of independence of observations is manifestly false: it is well known that schools vary considerably in the stringency of their selection processes, their policy with regard to the issue of segregation of boys and girls and so on.

Data of this kind are not a simple random sample from a pool of possible observations, as required by ordinary least squares regression models: on the contrary, they are clustered in a hierarchical fashion: students are nested within schools; schools are nested within districts and so on. It is likely that the data of children within a particular school will be more similar than the data of children from different schools. The same applies to districts. Research in many areas of study (e.g. education and health psychology) typically yield data that are hierarchically clustered in this way.

If the hierarchical dependencies in such a data set are ignored, the consequences can be serious. OLS regression will produce underestimates of the standard errors of the test statistics and the researcher may be led to conclude that there is strong evidence for non-existent effects. Rasbash et al. (2004) provide some striking examples of the consequences of inappropriate use of OLS regression with clustered data and the different conclusions the researcher would come to using multilevel modelling.

There is now available some excellent software for multilevel or hierarchical modelling, including the SPSS MIXED procedure. Jon Rasbash and his associates (Rasbash et al., 2004) have developed MLwiN, a dedicated package which provides excellent graphical feedback and an interactive learning environment for the user, backed up by an excellent manual and other documentation.

12.7   A FINAL WORD

Multiple regression is a highly complex topic and we can only touch upon it in a book of this kind. The following is a small selection from the wide choice of excellent books available.

Recommended reading

Ordinary least squares regression

Many years ago Jacob Cohen co-authored a book on multiple regression which, perhaps more than any other, made this difficult topic accessible to those other than professional statisticians. The book has continued to be updated and the latest edition has kept fully abreast with recent developments. It is strongly recommended to anyone wishing to make progress in multiple regression.

Cohen, J., Cohen, P., West, S. G., & Aiken, L. S. (2003). *Applied multiple regression/correlation analysis for the behavioral sciences (3rd ed.)*. Mahwah, NJ: Lawrence Erlbaum Associates.

Todman and Dugard have written a readable practical guide to multivariate analysis, including multiple regression:

Todman, J., & Dugard, P. (2006). *Approaching multivariate analysis: An introduction for psychology*. London: Psychology Press.

A more comprehensive, in-depth treatment of multiple regression will be found in

Tabachnick, B. G., & Fidell, L. S. (2007). *Using multivariate statistics (5th ed.)* Boston: Allyn & Bacon (Pearson International Edition).

The article and book by Darlington are well worth reading:

Darlington, R. B. (1968). Multiple regression in psychological research and practice. *Psychological Bulletin,* 69, 161 – 182.

Darlington, R. B. (1990). *Regression and linear models*. New York: McGraw-Hill.

Multilevel modelling

The topic of multilevel modelling is introduced in Tabachnick & Fidell (2007), Chapter 15. The manual by Jon Rasbash and his associates would be an excellent follow-up:

Rasbash, J., Steele, F., Browne, W., & Prosser, B. (2004). *A User's Guide to MLwiN Version 2.0*. London: Centre for Multilevel Modelling, University of London.

EXERCISE 20

Simple, two-variable regression

Before you start

Before proceeding with this Exercise, please read Chapter 12.

Purpose of the project

In this Exercise, we shall look at some of the pitfalls that await the unwary user of regression techniques; in fact, as we shall see, all the cautions and caveats about the **Pearson correlation** apply with equal force to regression.

In Exercise 17, Anscombe's specially devised data set (whose columns were named X1, X2, Y1, Y2, Y3, Y4) was saved in a file named **Anscombe**. Scatterplots and correlation coefficients were obtained for the pairings (X1, Y1), (X1, Y2), (X1, Y3) and (X2, Y4). All sets yielded exactly the same value for the Pearson correlation. When the scatterplots were inspected, however, it was seen that the Pearson correlation was appropriate for only one data set: in the other sets, it would give the unwary user a highly misleading impression of a strong linear association between X and Y. One problem with the Pearson correlation is that it is very vulnerable to the leverage exerted by atypical data points, or **outliers** as they are termed. The Pearson correlation can also have large values with monotonic but non-linear relationships. All this is equally true of the parameters of the regression equation. In this Exercise, we return to Anscombe's data to investigate the statistics of the regression lines for the four sets of paired data.

Opening SPSS

Open SPSS and select the data file **Anscombe** from the opening window. This was the file saved from Exercise 17.

Running the simple regression procedure

Following the procedure described in Section 12.2.3, obtain the regression statistics of Y1, Y2 and Y3 upon X1 and of Y4 upon X2. Remember that the dependent variable is Y, and the independent variable is X. For present purposes, the plotting of the scatterplot of *ZRESID (**y-axis** box) against *ZPRED (**x-axis** box) should provide illuminating tests of the credibility of the assumption that the data are linear. Full details of preparing the **Linear Regression** dialog box are given in Section 12.2.3.

Since we want to carry out regression upon all four (X, Y) data sets, it will be necessary to prepare the **Regression** dialog box for the first pair to include a scatterplot of *ZRESID against *ZPRED, and then change the variable names on subsequent runs for the remaining three pairs. To return to the **Regression** dialog box after inspecting the scatterplot, click the **Analyze** drop-down menu at the top of the **SPSS Viewer** window and select **Regression** and **Linear** again. Change Y1 to Y2 in the **Dependent** box and click **OK**. Follow this procedure for each pair of variables (i.e. Y3 upon X1 and then Y4 upon X2 – here you need to substitute X2 for X1 in the **Independent(s)** box. After each run, you should record the value of **R Squared** and the regression equation, and note the appearance of the scatterplot.

Output for the simple regression analyses

The main features of the Output of a simple regression analysis are fully explained in Chapte 12.
- **Compare the regression statistics and scatterplots for all four bivariate data sets. What do you notice about the values of R Squared and the appearances of the scatterplots? What is the 'take-home' message here?**

Another example

A researcher interested in the relationship between blood alcohol level and road accidents examined the accident rates for various levels of blood alcohol from 5 to 35 mg/100 ml. The data are shown in Table 1:

Table 1. Blood alcohol level and number of accidents							
Alcohol level	5	10	15	20	25	30	35
No of accidents ($\times 10^3$)	10	17	26	30	32	38	42

Find the regression of the number of accidents upon blood alcohol level and predict the number of accidents for a blood alcohol level of 40mg/100ml. Draw the scatterplot with SPSS and fit the regression line.

Preparing the data set

Prepare the data set in the usual manner with two variables.

Running the regression and inspecting the output

Run the regression command as described in Section 12.2.3, but omit the optional extras Descriptives, Casewise diagnostics, and the plot.
- **Write down the regression equation.**

Use either a calculator or SPSS to calculate the number of predicted accidents for an alcoho level of 40 mg/100 ml using the regression equation. In SPSS, insert the value of 40 in the *blood* column of **Data View** and then complete a **Compute** command by entering the appropriate coefficients and variable name to calculate predicted values for a new variable with a name such as *Predicted*.
- **What is the predicted number of accidents for a blood alcohol level of 40 mg/100 ml?**

Drawing the regression line

Use the procedure described in Section 12.2.1 to draw the scatterplot and insert the regression line. To answer the next question, you should edit the scatterplot and extend the abscissa (x axis) to 40 in order to see the position of the regression line for that value. Do this by double-clicking on the scatterplot to open the **Chart Editor** and then click on one of the axis numbers to open the **Properties** dialog box. Select the **Scale** tab at the top, click off the tick in the check box for **Maximum**, enter 40 into the **Custom** box alongside, and click on the **Apply** box. The scatterplot and regression line should then extend to include an Alcohol Level value of 40. Grid lines can be added while the scatterplot is still in the **Chart Editor** by clicking **Options➜Show Grid Lines**. Close the **Properties** dialog box and click off the **Chart Editor** to return the scatterplot to the **Viewer**.

- **Does your calculated value for 40 mg/100 ml correspond with what you can see in the scatterplot with its fitted regression line?**

Calculating residuals (difference between actual and predicted values)

To calculate the values of residuals, we need to know the predicted value of the number of accidents and then subtract it from the actual number of accidents. This could be done by using a calculator and the regression equation but it is more simply done by using SPSS. Return to the **Linear Regression** dialog box, select the **Save...** button and click on the check boxes for **Unstandardized** in the **Predicted Value** choices and on **Unstandardized** in the **Residuals** choices. After re-running the analysis, the **Data Editor** (not the **SPSS Viewer**) will show the predicted value and residual for each alcohol level.

- **What is the value of the largest residual?**

Finishing the session

Close down SPSS and any other windows before logging out of the computer.

EXERCISE 21

Multiple regression

Before you start

The reader should study Section 12.4 before proceeding with this Exercise.

A problem in reading research

Reading comprises many different component skills. A reading researcher hypothesises that certain specific kinds of pre-reading abilities and behaviour can predict later progress in reading, as measured by performance on reading tests taken some years after the child's first formal lessons. Let us, therefore, label the dependent variable (DV) in this study *Progress*. While they are still very young indeed, many children show a considerable grasp of English syntax in their speech. Our researcher devises a measure of their syntactic knowledge, *Syntax*, based upon the average length of their uttered sentences. Some researchers, however, argue that an infant's prelinguistic babbling (which we shall label *Vocal*) also plays a key role in their later reading performance. At the pre-reading stage, some very young children can acquire a sight vocabulary of several hundreds of words. The ability to pronounce these words on seeing them written down is known as logographic reading; but many authorities do not accept that this is true reading. Our researcher, who views the logographic strategy as important, includes a measure of this skill, *Logo*, in the study.

Preparing the data set

Fifty children are studied over a period beginning in infancy and extending through their school years. Their scores on the four measures, the DV *Progress* (*P*), and the three IVs *Logo* (*L*), *Vocal* (*V*) and *Syntax* (*S*), are listed in the appendix to this Exercise. Since it would be very laborious for you to type in all the data during the exercise, we must hope that you already have them available in an accessible file, with a name such as **Reading**. The data are also available on the Internet as **Ex21 Reading data for multiple regression** at:

http://www.abdn.ac.uk/psychology/materials/spss.shtml

Exploring the data

The distributions of the variables are most easily explored by using the **Boxplot** option in the **Graphs** drop-down menu. Select **Boxplot**, click the **Summaries of separate variables** button, and then click **Define**. Transfer the variable names to the **Boxes Represent** box and click **OK**. This will plot four boxes side-by-side for easy comparison.

Regression is most effective when each IV is strongly correlated with the DV but uncorrelated with the other IVs. Although the correlation matrix can be listed from within the regression procedure, it is often more useful to scrutinise the matrix before proceeding with a regression analysis in order to make judgements about which variables might be retained and which dropped from the analysis. For example, it might be advisable to make a choice between two variables that are highly correlated with one another.

Use the **Bivariate Correlations** procedure to compute the correlation matrix. The same procedure is also useful for tabulating the means and standard deviations, which are available as an option. After transferring the variable names to the **Variables** box, click **Options** and (within the **Statistics** choice box) select **Means and standard deviations**. Click **Continue** and **OK**. Notice that the DV *Progress* shows substantial correlations with both *Logo* and *Syntax*. On the other hand, there is no appreciable correlation between *Logo* and *Syntax*. The remaining variable (*Vocal*) shows little association with any of the other variables, although there is a hint of a negative correlation with *logo*.

Running the multiple regression analysis

Run the multiple regression of *Progress* upon the three predictors, by following the procedure in Section 12.4. Remember that the **Dependent** variable is what you are predicting (*Progress*) and the **Independent** variables are the predictors (*Logo, Vocal, Syntax*). On the first run, use the **Method *Enter*** (this enters all the variables simultaneously) and on the second run the **Method *Stepwise*** (this is a forward stepwise selection procedure). One outlier is identified in **Casewise Diagnostics** – run both *Enter* and *Stepwise* again with that case deselected to see whether the results differ very much.

Output for the multiple regression

The main features of a multiple regression output, both for the simultaneous and stepwise methods, are explained in Section 12.4.

- **Do the decisions of the multiple regression procedure about which variables are important agree with your informal observations during the exploratory phase of the data analysis?**
- **Compare the values of R Square for the analyses with and without the outlier.**
- **Write out the regression equation that you would use to predict progress from a participant's scores on Logo, Vocal and Syntax for the analysis without the outlier and using the Stepwise method. Use this equation to predict a Progress score for a child scoring 50 on each of the predictor variables.**
- **You can check your calculated result by requesting the computer to do the calculation for you. Within Data Editor, enter 51 into the empty 51st row Case cell and 50 into each of the Logo, Vocal and Syntax cells. Leave the Progress cell empty. Within the Linear Regression dialog box, click Save... and click the checkbox for Unstandardized followed by Continue. Run the analysis and then inspect the data file where a new variable PRE_1 will have appeared with predicted values for Progress. Does the value for the 51st row match your calculated value?**

Finishing the session

Close down SPSS and any other windows before logging out of the computer.

Appendix to Exercise 21 – The data

P	L	V	S	P	L	V	S	P	L	V	S	P	L	V	S
65	75	34	48	46	55	75	32	65	50	75	68	34	32	42	27
58	29	18	67	51	31	50	66	71	65	23	64	54	64	55	32
42	40	43	38	61	69	59	46	60	56	52	44	81	82	60	69
55	55	9	48	45	19	71	59	17	10	64	20	77	66	50	79
68	81	41	54	53	48	44	45	55	41	41	55	57	30	20	54
59	28	72	68	46	45	29	45	69	51	14	62	80	82	65	58
50	39	31	42	25	28	58	28	47	49	46	59	89	51	52	48
50	26	78	56	71	70	51	54	53	14	53	77	50	34	45	60
71	84	46	50	30	55	42	25	50	40	51	31	69	49	72	72
65	71	30	52	62	53	52	57	80	45	59	90	71	69	57	60
34	30	30	20	47	20	78	69	51	18	22	61	39	25	81	49
44	71	79	22	60	46	80	67	79	58	13	82				
47	62	26	30	70	66	40	61	51	43	31	50				

Multiway frequency analysis

13.1   Introduction

13.2   Two examples of loglinear analyses

13.3   A final word

13.1   INTRODUCTION

The starting point for the analysis of nominal data on two or more attributes is a **contingency table**, each cell of which is the frequency of occurrence of individuals in various combinations of categories. In an earlier chapter (Chapter 11), we described the use of the chi-square test to test for the presence of an association between qualitative variables in a two-way contingency table.

In a contingency table, the presence (or absence) of an association between the attributes is often apparent from inspection alone: with a 2 × 2 contingency table, for example, a predominance of tallies in the diagonal cells of the table suggests an association between the variables; on the other hand, an even distribution of frequencies across diagonal and off-diagonal cells suggests the absence of an association. The formal chi-square test often merely confirms what is evident from the table. In more complex contingency tables, however, in which individuals are classified with respect to three or more qualitative variables, patterns can be difficult to discern; moreover, it is only too easy to misinterpret frequency patterns in such a multi-way table.

The familiar Pearson chi-square statistic used with two-way tables can easily be adapted for use with multi-way contingency tables, from which the expected frequencies on the basis of total independence can be found from the marginal and total frequencies in a manner analogous to two-way contingency tables. All that this chi-square test will tell you, however, is that there is an unspecified dependency among the variables *somewhere*. In itself, however, this information is of limited usefulness. The Pearson chi-square test is still sometimes used with multi-way contingency tables in which the number of dimensions has been reduced to two by **collapsing** across the other dimensions. That approach, however, is decidedly risky; moreover, the researcher may have questions that require a test for the presence of a three-way interaction.

Recent years have seen great advances in the analysis of multi-way contingency tables, and these new methods, collectively known as **loglinear analysis**, are now available in computing packages such as SPSS. Loglinear analysis allows the user to do much more than merely reject the total independence model, which is often very unlikely to be true anyway. With loglinear analysis, the precise loci of any associations can be pinpointed and incorporated into a precise model of the data.

13.1.1   Comparison of loglinear analysis with ANOVA

To understand how loglinear analysis works, it may be helpful to recall some aspects of the completely randomised factorial analysis of variance, because there are some striking parallels between the two sets of techniques. In the factorial ANOVA, it is possible to test for **main effects** and for **interactions**. Loglinear analysis also offers tests of main effects and interactions.

There are other similarities between loglinear analysis and the between subjects factorial ANOVA. The models upon which the two techniques are based both interpret the data as the sum of main effect and interaction terms. The ANOVA model, therefore, is **hierarchical**, in the sense that together with each interaction term, the model also contains the main effects of its component factors. In hierarchical loglinear analysis, which we shall consider in this chapter, a model containing an interaction must also contain terms for the main effects; and models with higher-order interaction terms must also contain terms for lower order interactions involving their component factors.

There are, however, important differences between loglinear analysis and ANOVA. In ANOVA, the focus of interest is the cell *mean*, the average of several measurements on an independent scale with units. In loglinear analysis, since the data are nominal assignments to categories, the focus is on cell *frequencies*. Often, the marginal cell frequencies are of no interest at all in themselves, merely reflecting the vagaries of sampling. If we want to know whether there is a gender difference in agreement (yes or no) to legitimised violence, for example, neither the numbers of men and women in the study nor the numbers of individuals saying yes and no (the analogues of ANOVA main effects) are of any theoretical interest in their own right. In this situation, it is the *Gender × Agreement* interaction that is focal. The main effects, however, must be included in a loglinear model containing the interaction term.

A loglinear model that contains all the possible effect terms is known as a **saturated model**. It can be shown that a saturated model will always predict the cell frequencies (actually, the natural logs of the cell frequencies) perfectly. The purpose of a loglinear analysis is to see whether the cell frequencies can be adequately approximated by a model that contains **fewer** than the full set of possible treatment effects, subject to the hierarchical constraint that if a model includes an interaction, it must also include terms for the main effects of its component factors.

13.1.2   Building a loglinear model

When we carry out a traditional Pearson chi-square test on a two-way contingency table (or, indeed, a multi-way contingency table), we are testing the null hypothesis of complete independence between (or among) the dimensions of the table. A large value of chi-square means that the null hypothesis of independence gives a poor account of the data: that is, there are substantial differences from the frequencies expected (E) on the basis of no association and the observed (O) frequencies. Since the null hypothesis of no association is rejected by the test, we conclude that there is evidence for an association (the alternative or scientific hypothesis). With the traditional chi-square test, therefore, as far as the researcher is concerned, the larger the value of chi-square, the better.

The process of building a loglinear model of the frequencies in a contingency table works rather differently. In the **backward hierarchical** approach to model-building, for example, we begin with a saturated model containing all possible effects, which we know in advance will predict the cell frequencies perfectly. Next, we remove the most complex interaction term from the model. The effect of this removal will be to increase the value of chi-square from zero, because the reduced model will no longer predict the cell frequencies exactly. This increment in chi-square can be tested, to see if it 'makes a significant difference'. If not, we remove the term from the model. While the reduced model will now no longer predict the cell frequencies perfectly, the differences (O-E) between the observed frequencies (O) and the expected frequencies (E) on the basis of the reduced model may still be much smaller than they would be with a traditional chi-square test of total independence. The reduced model, that is, shows closer goodness-of-fit to the data. We continue the process of removing terms and testing the resulting increments in chi-square for significance until the removal of a term results in a significant increment in chi-square, in which case, we retain that term in the model. (If the term is an interaction, we must also retain any lower order interactions and the main effects of all the factors involved.) Here we see an obvious difference between traditional hypothesis-testing with chi-square and loglinear model-building: in the former, we look for a large value of chi-square to confirm our scientific hypothesis; in the latter, we want to continue to find small, insignificant increments in chi-square as we remove term after term from the saturated model.

In the foregoing account, we have spoken of the 'chi-square' statistic. Rather than the **Pearson chi-square** statistic, however, the testing of a loglinear model employs what is known as a **'maximum likelihood chi-square'**, which SPSS terms **L.R. (Likelihood Ratio) Chisq**. The L.R. chi-square has the **additive property**: its total value can be apportioned among the different terms being tested, enabling us to see whether the removal of any term from the model makes a significant difference to the total value of chi-square.

As in regression analysis, it is also advisable to examine the distribution of **residuals** (the differences between the observed and expected frequencies) or, more conveniently, the **standardised residuals** (residuals expressed in standardised form). Such regression diagnostics can cast further light on the model's goodness-of-fit for the data.

13.1.3   Odds, log odds and odds ratio

Odds

An **experiment of chance** is a procedure with an uncertain outcome, such as rolling a die or tossing a coin. In an experiment of chance, the **odds** in favour of an outcome is the number of ways it could occur, divided by the number of ways in which it could fail to occur. If a die is rolled once, there is one way of getting a six and there are five ways of not getting a six. The odds in favour of a six, therefore, are 1 to 5 or 1/5. Suppose we know that out of 100 people, 44 have an antibody in their blood. We can estimate the odds in favour of a person having the antibody at 44 to 56, or 44/56.

The odds ratio (OR)

Table 1 is a contingency table showing the results of an experiment in which male and female interviewers asked male and female participants whether, in a hypothetical situation, they would offer help.

Table 1. Results of an experiment on helpfulness

Sex of Interviewee * Would you help? * Sex of Interviewer Crosstabulation

Count

Sex of Interviewer			Would you help? No	Would you help? Yes	Total
Male	Sex of Interviewee	Male	20	5	25
		Female	8	17	25
	Total		28	22	50
Female	Sex of Interviewee	Male	14	11	25
		Female	14	11	25
	Total		28	22	50

What is the effect of the sex of the interviewer on whether male participants will help or not? When the interviewer is male (first and second rows in the table), the odds in favour of males helping can be estimated at 5/20. When the interviewer is female, the odds are 11/14.

So male participants are more likely to say that they would help when the interviewer is female. This pattern is captured by a statistic known as the **odds ratio (OR)**. The *OR* compares the odds in favour of helping in one group with the odds in another group simply by dividing the two odds estimates:

$$OR = \frac{odds\ in\ favour\ of\ males\ helping\ with\ male\ interviewer}{odds\ in\ favour\ of\ males\ helping\ with\ female\ interviewer}$$

In this example,

$$OR = \frac{5/20}{11/14} = \frac{5 \times 14}{11 \times 20} = 0.32$$

The odds ratio is a very useful tool for exploring a contingency table prior to making any formal tests. In a 2×2 contingency table, for example, an odds ratio close to 1 corresponds to the situation where there is no association between the two attributes.

The log odds and OR

It would have made just as much sense to divide the odds in favour of helping with a female interviewer with those for a male interviewer. Were we to do so, however, we should find that

OR = 3.14.   The same comparison apparently produces quite different values.   The problem with the raw odds and *OR* is asymmetry of range: if the smaller value is on top, either statistic can vary only within the range from zero to 1, inclusive; whereas if the larger value is on top, there is no limit to how large their values can be.

For this reason, for some purposes, it is easier to work with the logarithms (logs) of the odds and *OR*, rather than their raw values.   The natural logarithm (represented by ln in SPSS) to the base e is used, rather than the log to the base 10.   The logs are symmetrical in their range: the log of the odds (known as the **logit**) has the value zero when the odds in favour equal those against; it is positive when the odds in favour are greater; it is negative when the odds in favour are less.   For a given comparison, however, their absolute values are the same.   In the present example, with male odds in the numerator, ln(*OR*) = −1.145; but with the female odds in the numerator, ln(*OR*) = +1.145.

13.2   TWO EXAMPLES OF LOGLINEAR ANALYSES

13.2.1   First example: exam success

A Director of Teaching at a School of Psychology is interested in which factors determine whether a student can pass a Psychology statistics examination.   In particular, interest centres on whether a formal mathematical background is helpful; or whether extra specific training in data processing is a more important consideration. Researchers have collected a body of information on 176 students, including whether they had taken an advanced mathematics course at school and whether they had taken a data-processing examination in their first year at University.   On each student's record, it was also noted whether he or she had passed the second year Psychology statistics examination. The data are presented in Table 2, which is a **three-way contingency table**.

Table 2. A three-way contingency table showing the levels of success (Pass or Fail) in the *Psychology Statistics Exam* and the first year *Data Processing Exam*, and whether students had taken an *Advanced Maths* at school.

Advanced Maths Course	Data Processing Exam	Psychology Statistics Exam		
		Pass	Fail	Total
Yes	Pass	47	10	57
Yes	Fail	4	10	14
No	Pass	58	17	75
No	Fail	10	20	30

The predominance of frequencies in the diagonal cells of Table 2 (47 and 10; 58 and 20) suggests an association between success in the Data Processing Exam and success in the Psychology Statistics Exam, whether or not the participants had taken the Advanced Maths course at school.   For those who have taken an Advanced Maths course (upper two rows of entries in the table), the odds ratio is 11.75; for those who have not, the odds ratio is 6.82. Both these values are considerably greater than 1, indicating an association. There is thus little sign of a three-way interaction. For those who passed Data Processing, there is little evidence of an association between success in the Psychology Statistics Exam and whether an Advanced Maths course had been taken at school: the odds ratio is 1.38; and for those who failed Data Processing, the odds ratio is .8. Both these values are close to 1, indicating little or no association.

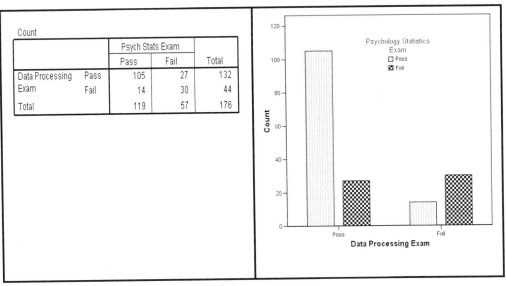

Output 1. Two-way *Psych Stats* × *Data Processing* contingency table and bar graph

Output 1 shows the two-way (*Data Processing* × *Psych Stats*) contingency table, in which it is evident that students who had passed the Data Processing Exam were much more likely to pass the Psychology Statistics Exam. This pattern is even more evident in the bar chart alongside the table. The pattern is statistically significant beyond the .01 level: Fisher's Exact p < .01.

13.2.2 Running a loglinear analysis for the exam success data

Proceed as follows:

*   In **Variable View**, name three grouping variables: *Maths, DataProc* and *PsychStats*. In the **Label** column, add suitable expanded names such as *Advanced Maths Course, Data Processing Exam* and *Psychology Statistics Exam*. In the **Values** column, label the code values: for *Maths*, 1 is Yes, 2 is No; for *DataProc* and *PsychStats*, 1 is Pass, 2 is Fail. Name a fourth variable *Count* with a label *Count of Cases* for the cell frequencies. Click the **Data View** tab and enter the data. Finally, save the data set to a file in the usual way. The complete SPSS data set is shown in Figure 1.

Maths	DataProc	PsychStats	Count
Yes	Pass	Pass	47
Yes	Pass	Fail	10
Yes	Fail	Pass	4
Yes	Fail	Fail	10
No	Pass	Pass	58
No	Pass	Fail	17
No	Fail	Pass	10
No	Fail	Fail	20

Figure 1. **Data View** showing the data set

- It is now necessary for this example to inform SPSS that the variable *Count* contains frequencies and not simply scores. Note that this step would have been omitted had the data consisted of individual cases. Choose
  Data➔Weight Cases...
  to open the **Weight Cases** dialog box and transfer the variable *Count* to the **Frequency Variable** box. Click **OK**.

The next stage is to confirm (by using the **Crosstabs** command in Chapter 11, Section 11.5.3) that the expected frequencies are sufficiently large. Just as in the case of the traditional chi-square test, loglinear analysis requires the **expected** cell frequencies (E) to meet certain requirements. Tabachnick and Fidell (2007) recommend examining the expected cell frequencies for all **two-way associations** to ensure that all **expected frequencies** are greater than 1 and that no more than 20% are less than 5.

See
Section
11.5.3

- Choose
  Analyze➔Summarize➔Crosstabs...
  and then complete the **Crosstabs** dialog box (Figure 2) by transferring *DataProc* to the **Row(s)** box, *PsychStats* to the **Column(s)** box, and *Maths* to the lowest (Layer) box.
- Click **Cells...** to bring to access the **Cell Display** dialog box (See Chapter 11, Figure 14). Within the **Counts** box, tick the **Expected** check box, click **Continue** and then **OK**.

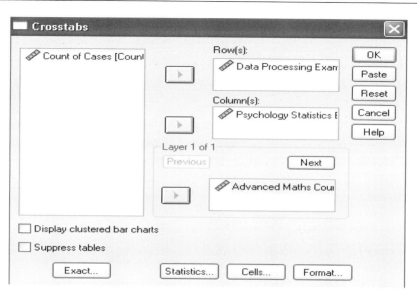

Figure 2. The completed **Crosstabs** dialog box

The **Crosstabs** command presents two-way contingency tables for each layer of *Advanced Maths Course*, because that was chosen as the layering variable.

Data Processing Exam * Psychology Statistics Exam * Advanced Maths Course Crosstabulation

Advanced Maths Course				Psychology Statistics Exam		
				Pass	Fail	Total
Yes	Data Processing Exam	Pass	Count	47	10	57
			Expected Count	40.9	16.1	57.0
		Fail	Count	4	10	14
			Expected Count	10.1	3.9	14.0
	Total		Count	51	20	71
			Expected Count	51.0	20.0	71.0
No	Data Processing Exam	Pass	Count	58	17	75
			Expected Count	48.6	26.4	75.0
		Fail	Count	10	20	30
			Expected Count	19.4	10.6	30.0
	Total		Count	68	37	105
			Expected Count	68.0	37.0	105.0

The only expected frequency less than 5

Output 2. Observed and expected frequencies for a three-way contingency table

The table (Output 2) shows that no cell has an expected frequency of less than 1 and only one cell has one of less than 5. There is no problem with low expected frequencies.

The **Loglinear** submenu (Figure 3) within the **Analyze** menu shows three items. The first (**General...**) estimates maximum likelihood parameters of hierarchical and non-hierarchical loglinear models. The second (**Logit...**) estimates parameters of a logit loglinear model expressing one qualitative attribute as a function of the other variables. For our example, the appropriate item is **Model Selection...** which analyses multiway contingency tables, fitting loglinear models using either a single step (all variables entered at once) or backward elimination procedures (variables entered or excluded one at a time).

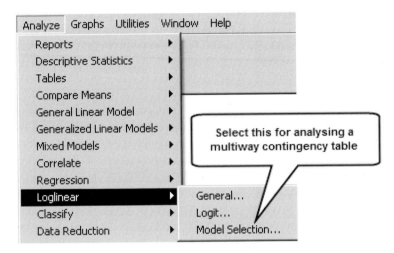

Figure 3. The loglinear menu

The model selection backward elimination loglinear command is run as follows:
- Select
  Analyze➔Loglinear ➔Model Selection...
  to open the **Model Selection Loglinear Analysis** dialog box (the completed version is shown in Figure 4).
- Transfer the three grouping variable names *Maths*, *DataProc* and *PsychStats* to the **Factor(s)** box.
- Click **Define Range** and ensuring that all three variable names are highlighted, enter *1* into the **Minimum** box and *2* into the **Maximum** box. Click **Continue** and the names will appear with [1 2] after each of them. If some of the variables had different numbers of categories, it would have been necessary to enter the ranges separately for each variable.
- The default model is **backward elimination**. Makes sure its radio button is on.
- Click **OK**.

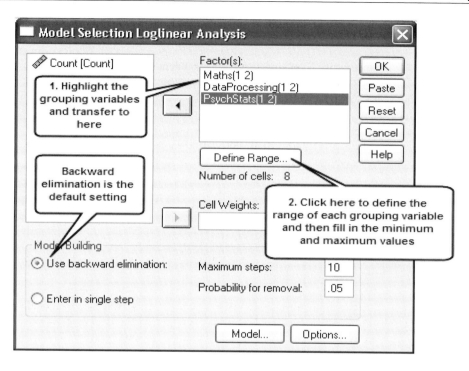

Figure 4. The completed **Model Selection Loglinear Analysis** dialog box for three factors

13.2.3 Output for the exam success loglinear analysis

The various tables and charts in the output are listed in the left-hand pane of **SPSS Viewer**, as shown in Output 3. Output 4 contains information about the data and the category names (factors).

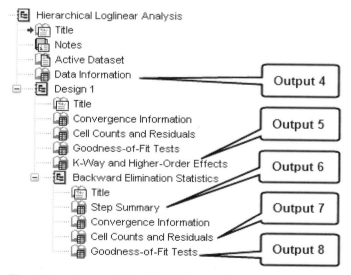

Output 3. The left-hand pane of the **SPSS Viewer** showing the contents of the output

Data Information

		N
Cases	Valid	8
	Out of Range[a]	0
	Missing	0
	Weighted Valid	176
Categories	Maths	2
	DataProc	2
	PsychStats	2

a. Cases rejected because of out of range factor values.

Output 4. Information about the number of cases and the category names (factors)

Output 4 is followed by a table (not shown here) listing the Observed and Expected counts along with a Goodness-of-Fit Test assuming **a saturated model** for the combinations of the three factors. The table is useful for checking the accuracy of the data transcription.

Output 5 shows the results of the statistical tests.

K-Way and Higher-Order Effects

	K	df	Likelihood Ratio Chi-Square	Sig.	Pearson Chi-Square	Sig.	Number of Iterations
K-way and Higher Order Effects[a]	1	7	110.28	.000	123.00	.000	0
	2	4	35.31	.000	37.08	.000	2
	3	1	.43	.512	.43	.514	4
K-way Effects[b]	1	3	74.97	.000	85.92	.000	0
	2	3	34.88	.000	36.65	.000	0
	3	1	.4	.512	.43	.514	0

a. Tests that k-way and higher order effects are zero.
b. Tests that k-way effects are zero.

> The p-value for chi-square for 3-way is > .05 but for 2-way plus 3-way effects p< .05. Thus only effects at the third level fail to reach significance

> Considering the three effect levels individually, the p-values of chi-square for 1-way and 2-way effects are < .05 but for the 3-way effect p> .05

Output 5. Tests of effects

The upper part of Output 5 shows the chi-squares and p-values for effects at a specified level **K-way and above**. The lower part **K-way Effects** gives the chi-squares and p-values of effects **at specified levels only**. That is why the chi-squares for K = 1 and K = 2 are smaller in the lower table. We can see that there are significant effects at levels 1 and 2, but not at level 3 (K = 3). The fact that there are significant effects at level 2, however, does not imply that **all** two-way interactions are significant.

Elimination of the 3-way interaction results in a non-significant change as shown by this chi-square change and p-value of 0.512. Thus this interaction can be removed and the three 2-way interactions are tested in Step 1

Step Summary

Step[b]	Effects	Chi-Square[a]	df	Sig.	Number of Iterations
0	Generating Class [c]				
	DataProc*PsychStats*Maths	.000	0	.	
	Deleted Effect 1	DataProc*PsychStats*Maths	.431	1	.512	3
1	Generating Class [c]	DataProc*PsychStats, DataProc*Maths, PsychStats*Maths	.431	1	.512	
	Deleted Effect 1	DataProc*PsychStats	32.098	1	.000	2
	2	DataProc*Maths	1.029	1	.310	2
	3	PsychStats*Maths	.198	1	.656	2
2	Generating Class [c]	DataProc*PsychStats, DataProc*Maths	.629	2	.730	
	Deleted Effect 1	DataProc*PsychStats	32.875	1	.000	2
	2	DataProc*Maths	1.806	1	.179	2
3	Generating Class [c]	DataProc*PsychStats, Maths	2.435	3	.487	
	Deleted Effect 1	DataProc*PsychStats	32.875		.000	2
	2	Maths	6.610	1	.010	2
4	Generating Class [c]	DataProc*PsychStats, Maths	2.435	3	.487	

a. For 'Deleted Effect', this is the change in the Chi-Square after the effect is deleted from the model.

b. At each step, the effect with the largest significance level for the Likelihood Ratio Change is deleted, provided the significance level is larger than .050.

c. Statistics are displayed for the best model at each step after step 0.

The 2-way interaction with the least effect (i.e. smallest chi-square change and largest p-value) is eliminated

The next 2-way interaction to be eliminated since its change in chi-square has a p-value > .05

Maths is the only remaining main effect variable not included in the remaining 2-way interaction

Output 6. Edited table showing each step of the backward elimination of factors

The purpose of the analysis was to find the unsaturated model that gives the best fit to the observed data. This is achieved by checking that the model currently being tested does not give a significantly worse fit than the one a step up from it in the hierarchy of complexity. Recall that hierarchical backward elimination begins with the most complex model (which in the present case contains all three factors, together with all their possible interactions). Testing progresses down the hierarchy of complexity, eliminating each statistically insignificant effect in turn from the model by determining which decrement in accuracy is less than the **least-significant change in the chi-square value.** At each step, such an effect is eliminated, leaving the remaining effects for inclusion, as specified by the heading:

'Generating Class'

The procedure continues until no elimination produces a decrement with a probability greater than 0.05: that is, the removal of any of the remaining effects results in a significant increase in chi-square. The model containing the remaining effects is then adopted as the final model. In this example, the final model has been reached after four steps.

These steps are shown in Output 6.

At Step 3, *DataProc*Maths* is eliminated, because it has the larger probability (which is greater than the criterion level of 0.05). The remaining interaction, *DataProc*PsychStats* cannot be eliminated, because the p-value is less than 0.05. All the interactions now having been processed, it remains for any main effect that is *not part of the remaining 2-way interaction* to be tested for inclusion. In this case, only *Maths* qualifies.

At Step 4, neither of these effects (the *DataProc*PsychStats* nor *Maths*) can be eliminated, because both probabilities are less than 0.05. Both effects, therefore, must be included in the final model. Thus the final model includes the interaction between the variables representing the Data Processing Exam and the Psychology Statistics Exam, plus a main effect of *Maths*. Note that there are no interactions involving the Maths variable. Thus the most interesting finding is the interaction between the two examinations.

Finally, the computer lists the table **Cell Counts and Residuals** showing the observed and expected frequencies, residuals and standardised residuals as estimated by the final model (Output 7). The **Goodness-of-Fit Tests** table (Output 8) shows that these expected frequencies do not differ significantly from the observed frequencies (the p-value for chi-square is not significant since it is much greater than 0.05).

Cell Counts and Residuals

DataProc	PsychStats	Maths	Observed Count	Observed %	Expected Count	Expected %	Residuals	Std. Residuals
Pass	Pass	Yes	47	26.7%	42.36	24.1%	4.64	.71
		No	58	33.0%	62.64	35.6%	-4.64	-.59
	Fail	Yes	10	5.7%	10.89	6.2%	-.89	-.27
		No	17	9.7%	16.11	9.2%	.89	.22
Fail	Pass	Yes	4	2.3%	5.65	3.2%	-1.65	-.69
		No	10	5.7%	8.35	4.7%	1.65	.57
	Fail	Yes	10	5.7%	12.10	6.9%	-2.10	-.60
		No	20	11.4%	17.90	10.2%	2.10	.50

Output 7. The observed and expected frequencies based on the final model

Goodness-of-Fit Tests

	Chi-Square	df	Sig.
Likelihood Ratio	2.435	3	.487
Pearson	2.393	3	.495

Chi-square is 2.393 with an associated p-value of .495 (not significant). There is a good fit because because the expected and observed frequencies do not differ significantly

Output 8. The goodness-of-fit test for the final model showing a very good fit

Thus the final model based on the interaction of the *Data Processing Exam* and the *Psychology Statistics Exam*, together with the main effect of the *Advanced Maths Course*, provides an excellent fit to the data. The analysis has shown that whereas the results of the *Data Processing Exam* and the *Psychology Statistics Exam* are associated, it makes no difference whether the *Advanced Maths Course* has been taken or not. Formal statistical testing, therefore, confirms the results of our preliminary exploration of the contingency table with odds ratios.

13.2.4   Reporting the results of a loglinear analysis

Reports of loglinear analyses in the literature have yet to follow a standard format. For example, once a model has been fitted, it would be possible to write out the loglinear analytic equivalent of the OLS regression equation (as explained in Howell, 2007) and report the tests for each of the terms in the equation. Many journal editors, however, would take the view that such a mathematical presentation would serve only to obscure the findings of the research; others, on the other hand, might welcome such an approach.

One of the many excellent features of the book by Tabachnick & Fidell (2007) is their inclusion of sample write-ups of the results of the multivariate procedures they describe, including a report of a loglinear analysis on pages 906-908. In their report they (quite rightly, in our view) omit any formal equations. They do, however, include the following:

1.   Details of the data that were used in the analysis, including information about the incidence of cells with low expected frequencies and the presence of outliers. It is essential to establish that there are no contraindications against the use of loglinear analysis.
2.   The maximum likelihood chi square and p-value for the final model.
3.   A table showing the results of the significance tests of the various effects on an individual basis. The entries in the table are chi-square tests of partial association on one degree of freedom.
4.   A larger table showing the parameter estimates and the ratios of the estimates to their standard errors. This table, however, is very extensive, so the researcher submitting an article might omit it from the first draft (or include it as an appendix): the table can always be included in the body of the text in a revision of the article should the editor require this.

13.2.5   Comparison with the total independence model

The reader might wish to use the loglinear command to confirm the expected frequencies that are predicted by the total independence model. This is done by specifying a model which has no interaction terms, which means that the expected cell frequencies E will be calculated from the marginal totals, in much the same way as they are found in two-way contingency tables.

- After inserting the factor names and values in the **Factor(s)** box as before, click the **Model** box to open the **Model** dialog box.
- In the **Specify Model** box, select the **Custom** radio button. Enter the three factor names into the **Generating Class** box by highlighting each name and clicking on the arrow under **Build Term(s)**. Within the **Build Term(s)** box, click **Interaction** and select **All 3-way**. Part of the completed dialog box is shown in Figure 5.
- Click **Continue** to return to the **Model Selection Loglinear Analysis** dialog box.
- Within the **Model Building** box, click the **Enter in single step** radio button.
- Click **OK**.

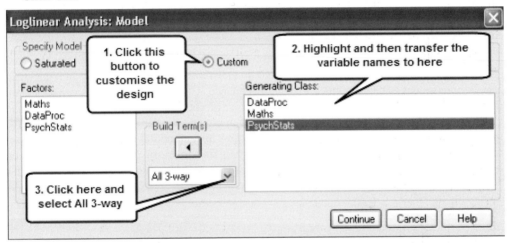

Figure 5. Part of the completed dialog box for determining the expected frequencies from the total independence model (i.e. All 3-way)

The **Cell Counts and Residuals** table (Output 9) shows the discrepancies between the observed and expected frequencies and the **Goodness-of-Fit** table (not reproduced here) lists a p-value for chi-square smaller than 0.01.

Cell Counts and Residuals

Maths	DataProc	PsychStats	Observed Count	Observed %	Expected Count	Expected %	Residuals	Std. Residuals
Yes	Pass	Pass	47	26.7%	36.0	20.5%	11.0	1.8
		Fail	10	5.7%	17.2	9.8%	-7.2	-1.7
	Fail	Pass	4	2.3%	12.0	6.8%	-8.0	-2.3
		Fail	10	5.7%	36.0	3.3%	4.3	1.8
No	Pass	Pass	58	33.0%	53.2	30.3%	4.8	.7
		Fail	17	9.7%	25.5	14.5%	-8.5	-1.7
	Fail	Pass	10	5.7%	17.7	10.1%	-7.7	-1.8
		Fail	20	11.4%	8.5	4.8%	11.5	3.9

Output 9. The table of cell counts and residuals for the total independence model

Table 3 contrasts the discrepancies between the observed cell frequencies (O) and the expected cell frequencies (E) under the best loglinear model (with interaction terms) and the main effects only model, which assumes total independence. Clearly, the (O-E) discrepancies are much smaller with the interaction model. There is, of course, no contradiction between the traditional Pearsonian approach and the loglinear approach: the former is trying to *reject* the independence model; the latter is trying to *confirm* an interaction model lying somewhere between total independence and the saturated model. The superiority of the loglinear approach lies in its ability to pinpoint the crucial associations in a complex data set.

Table 3. Observed frequencies and expected frequencies under the final loglinear model Exp(final) and the total independence model Exp(independent)							
Advanced Maths	Yes				No		
Data Processing	Pass		Fail		Pass		Fail	
Psychology Statistics	Pass	Fail	Pass	Fail	Pass	Fail	Pass	Fail
Cell Freq: Observed	47	10	4	10	58	17	10	20
Exp(final)	42.4	10.9	5.6	12.1	62.6	16.1	8.4	17.9
Exp(independent)	36.0	17.2	12.0	5.7	53.2	25.5	17.7	8.5

13.2.6   Second example: gender and professed helpfulness

As our second example, we take up once again the experiment on helpfulness that we used at the beginning of Section 13.1.3 to illustrate the use of the odds ratio to explore the patterns of frequencies in a contingency table.

In a study of gender and helpfulness, a researcher arranges for fifty men and fifty women to be presented with a scenario in which the observer has the opportunity to help a protagonist in a predicament.   Half the interviews are taken by male interviewers, the others are taken by female interviewers. At each interview, the participant is asked whether he or she would help the protagonist. The purpose of the investigation is to determine whether the incidence of reported helping is affected by whether the interviewer and interviewee are of the same or of opposite sexes. Table 4 presents the results in a three-way contingency table.

Table 4. Three-way contingency table showing the results of the gender and professed helpfulness experiment				
		Would you help?		
Sex of Interviewer	**Sex of Participant**	**Yes**	**No**	**Total**
Male	Male	4	21	25
Male	Female	16	9	25
Female	Male	11	14	25
Female	Female	11	14	25
	Total	42	68	100

In Section 13.1.3, the odds ratio was used to reveal some of the associations in these data. It is also instructive to use the **Crosstabs** procedure (see Section 11.5.3). Output 10 shows the incidence of helping in male and in female participants and Output 11 the incidence of helping with male and female interviewers.

See
Section
11.5.3

Helpfulness in male and female participants: p = .025

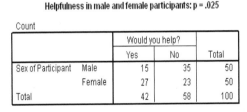

Count		Would you help?		
		Yes	No	Total
Sex of Participant	Male	15	35	50
	Female	27	23	50
Total		42	58	100

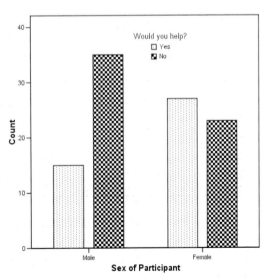

Output 10. Levels of helpfulness in male and female participants

Helpfulness with male and female interviewers: p = .840

Count

| | | Would you help? | | |
		Yes	No	Total
Sex of Interviewer	Male	20	30	50
	Female	22	28	50
Total		42	58	100

Output 11. Levels of helpfulness in male and female interviewers

It is clear from these outputs (and especially from the bar charts alongside) that the female participants were more inclined to help (Fisher's Exact two-tailed probability = .03); on the other hand, the incidence of helping was comparable with male and female interviewers (Fisher's Exact two-tailed probability = .84).

Neither of the foregoing observations, however, bears directly upon the experimenter's hypothesis, which predicted a higher incidence of helping when the participants and the interviewers were of opposite sex. This hypothesis implies an **interaction** between the factors of *Sex of Participant* and *Sex of Interviewer*; whereas, so far, we have been considering only the equivalent of main effects. (In the context of contingency tables, a 'main effect' is, from the researcher's point of view, an association between the Yes/No incidence variable and one of the attributes in the classification; but in terms of loglinear models, this is a two-way interaction. The interaction of central interest here is, in terms of loglinear modelling, a three-way interaction.)

Output 12 shows clearly that the difference between the incidence of helping in male and female participants is markedly less when the interviewer is female. Moreover, superimposed upon the general tendency for female participants to be more helpful, is an evident tendency for females to be more helpful when the interviewer is a male; on the other hand, there is no obvious tendency for the male participants to be more helpful when the interviewer is female. It does appear, however, that there may be at least some support for the researcher's opposite-sex dyadic hypothesis.

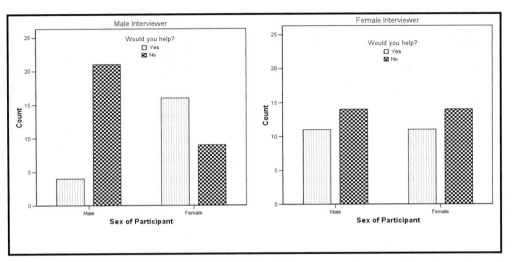

Output 12. Bar charts of the helpfulness of male and female participants with male and female interviewers showing an interaction pattern

3.2.7 Running a loglinear analysis for the professed helpfulness data

Proceed as follows:

- In **Variable View**, create three grouping variables: *Participant (Sex of Participant)*, *Interviewer (Sex of Interviewer)*, *Help (Would you help?)* and a fourth variable, *Frequency*, for the cell counts. Use the **Values** column to assign values to the code numbers, such as, for the *Help* variable, 1 = Yes, 2 = No. The complete SPSS data set is shown in Figure 6.

	Participant	Interviewer	Help	Frequency
1	Male	Male	Yes	4
2	Male	Male	No	21
3	Male	Female	Yes	11
4	Male	Female	No	14
5	Female	Male	Yes	16
6	Female	Male	No	9
7	Female	Female	Yes	11
8	Female	Female	No	14

Figure 6. **Data View** showing the Gender data set

- It is now necessary for this example to inform SPSS that the variable *Count* contains frequencies and not simply scores. Note that this step is not needed if the data set consists of individual cases. Choose
  Data➔Weight Cases…
  to open the **Weight Cases** dialog box and transfer the variable *Frequency* to the **Frequency Variable** box. Click **OK**.
- The next stage is to confirm that the expected frequencies are sufficiently large using the **Crosstabs** procedure as in Section 13.2.2. The output table (which we have omitted)

shows that no cell has an expected frequency of less than 1, so there is no problem with low expected frequencies.

See
Section
13.2.2

• Select
Analyze➔Loglinear➔Model Selection…
to open the **Model Selection Loglinear Analysis** dialog box (the completed version is shown in Figure 7).

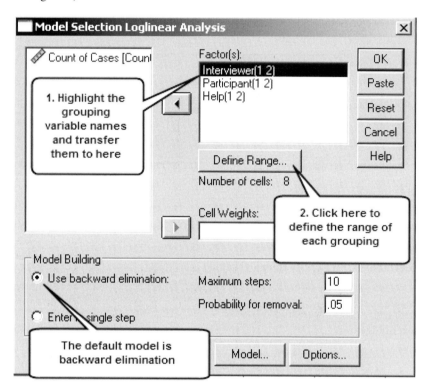

Figure 7.   The completed **Model Selection Loglinear Analysis** dialog box for three factors

• Transfer the three grouping variable names *Sex of Participant, Sex of Interviewer* and *Would you help?* to the **Factor(s)** box (see Figure 7).
• Click **Define Range** and enter *1* into the **Minimum** box and *2* into the **Maximum** box. Click **Continue** and the names will appear with [1 2] after each of them. If some of the variables had different numbers of categories, it would have been necessary to enter the ranges separately for each variable.
• The default model is **backward elimination**. Makes sure its radio button is on.
• Click **OK**.

13.2.8 Output for the professed helpfulness loglinear analysis

The first table in the output (Output 13) lists the number of cases and the names of the variables (factors) in the analysis. Check that the information is consistent with the design of the experiment as we have described it: in this example, there should be three factors, each having two levels.

Data Information

		N
Cases	Valid	8
	Out of Range [a]	0
	Missing	0
	Weighted Valid	100
Categories	Help	2
	Interviewer	2
	Participant	2

a. Cases rejected because of out of range factor values.

Output 13. Information about the number of cases and the category names (factors)

The next item is a table (not shown here) listing the observed and expected counts for the combinations of the three factors. At this stage, SPSS is fitting a **saturated model**, *Sex of Interviewer* × *Sex of Participant* × *Would you help?* to the cell frequencies. This is why, in this section of the output, the observed and expected frequencies have the same values. The table, however, is useful for checking the accuracy of the data transcription: there should be no (O − E) discrepancies at all at this stage.

K-Way and Higher-Order Effects

	K	df	Likelihood Ratio Chi-Square	Sig.	Pearson Chi-Square	Sig.	Number of Iterations
K-way and Higher Order Effects[a]	1	7	15.38	.031	14.24	.047	0
	2	4	12.81	.012	11.99	.017	2
	3	1	6.66	.010	6.52	.011	2
K-way Effects[b]	1	3	2.57	.463	2.25	.522	0
	2	3	6.15	.104	5.47	.141	0
	3	1	6.66	.010	6.52	.011	0

a. Tests that k-way and higher order effects are zero.

b. Tests that k-way effects are zero.

Note that the interactions are significant up to 3-way

Only the 3-way effect is significant

Output 14. Tests of effects

The third item (see Output 14) lists the results of the statistical tests for the various effects. The upper part shows the chi-squares and p-values for effects at a specified level **K-Way and above**. Here we see that, as the pattern of frequencies graphed in Outputs 10, 11 and 12 indicate, there is indeed a significant three-way (*Sex of Interviewer* × *Sex of Participant* × *Would you help?*) interaction in the row labelled 3 in the K column:

L.R. Chi-Square (1) = 6.66; p = .01.

The lower part **K-Way Effects** gives the chi-squares and p-values of effects **at specified levels only**. That is why the chi-squares for K = 1 and K = 2 are smaller in the lower table. Loglinear analysis, therefore, has given us something that the traditional approach of collapsing the three-way table cannot offer: a direct test for a three-way interaction.

The lower part of the output lists the changes in **L.R. Chi-Square** (and **Pearson Chi-Square**) for effects at each level considered separately. Here, in addition to the fact that the three-way interaction term is significant, we learn that no other effect (e.g. in rows labelled 1 and 2 in column K) makes a significant contribution to the total **L.R. Chi-Square**.

The fourth part of the SPSS output (Output 15) concludes that the saturated model (i.e. the three-way interaction) after just one step is the best one for the data, because removal of the interaction term would result in a significant increase in **Chi-square**. This is therefore adopted as the final model.

Step Summary

Step[b]	Effects	Chi-Square[a]	df	Sig.	Number of Iterations
0	Generating Class [c]	Help*Interviewer*Participant	.000	0	.	
	Deleted Effect 1	Help*Interviewer*Participant	6.659	1	.010	2
1	Generating Class [c]	Help*Interviewer*Participant	.000	0	.	

a. For 'Deleted Effect', this is the change in the Chi-Square after the effect is deleted from the model.
b. At each step, the effect with the largest significance level for the Likelihood Ratio Change is deleted, provided the significance level is larger than .050.
c. Statistics are displayed for the best model at each step after step 0.

> Since deletion of the 3-way interaction results in a significant increase in chi-square, it is adopted as the final model

Output 15. The final model for the *Gender* and professed helpfulness data

The loglinear analysis has confirmed the impression given by the contingency table that the difference between the incidence of helping in male and female participants is markedly less when the interviewer is female and that there is a tendency for both males and females to be more helpful when the interviewer is of the opposite sex. The loglinear analysis has shown that the results of this experiment support the opposite-sex dyadic helpfulness hypothesis.

13.3   A FINAL WORD

In this chapter, we have tried to demonstrate the power of loglinear analyis to test specific alternative hypotheses to the total independence model in a way that was impossible with the traditional Pearsonian test of the null hypothesis.

Underlying the procedures we have described are statistical models that we have made no attempt to explain in this chapter. Why 'loglinear', for instance? We suggest that once you have worked through the examples, the next step is to read a lucid introduction to the theory of loglinear analysis, which will explain why, with some kinds of data, it is useful to work with the logarithms of the data rather than the raw scores. You may remember that the logarithm of a product is the sum of the logarithms of the factors. While raw scores require complex *multiplicative* models, their logarithms can be accounted for in terms of simpler *additive* or **linear** models.

Recommended reading

Howell (2007) has an introductory chapter on the theory of loglinear analysis. Tabachnick & Fidell (2007) have an extensive chapter on loglinear analysis with various computing packages, including SPSS. Todman and Dugard (2006) take a more hands-on practical approach.

Howell, D. C. (2007). *Statistical methods for psychology (6th ed.)*. Belmont, CA: Thomson/Wadsworth.

Tabachnik, B. G., & Fidell, L. S. (2007). *Using multivariate statistics (5th ed.)*. Boston: Allyn & Bacon.

Todman, J., & Dugard, P. (2006). *Approaching multivariate analysis: An introduction for psychology*. London: Psychology Press.

EXERCISE 22

Loglinear analysis

Before you start

Before you proceed with this practical, please read Chapter 13.

Helping behaviour: The opposite-sex dyadic hypothesis

In the literature on helping behaviour by (and towards) men and women, there is much interest in three questions:
1. Are women more likely to receive help?
2. Are women more likely to give help?
3. Are people more likely to help members of the opposite sex?
   (This is known as the **opposite-sex dyadic hypothesis**.)

A male or female confederate of the experimenter approached male and female students who were entering a university library and asked them to participate in a survey. Table 1 shows the incidence of helping in relation to the sex of the confederate and that of the participant.

Table 1. Results of an experiment to test the opposite-sex dyadic hypothesis			
Sex of Confederate	Sex of Participant	Help	
		Yes	No
Male	Male	52	35
	Female	21	43
Female	Male	39	40
	Female	23	75

Preparing the SPSS data set

Prepare the data set as in Section 13.2.2 with three coding variables Confederate's Sex (*ConfedSex*), Participant's Sex (*ParticSex*), and Participant's Response (*Help*), complete with appropriately defined value labels. There will be a fourth variable (*Count*) for the cell frequencies. Remember to use the **Weight Cases** command for the cell frequency variable *count*.

Exploring the data

Before carrying out any formal analysis, a brief inspection of the contingency table (Table 1) may prove informative. First of all, we notice that, on the whole, help was more likely to be refused than given; moreover, the females helped less than did the males. In view of the generally lower rate of helping in the female participants, therefore, there seems to be little support for the hypothesis that females help more. Finally, turning to the third question, although the male participants did help the male confederate more often, the female participants tended to be more helpful towards the male confederate. This provides some support for the opposite-sex dyadic hypothesis.

Procedure for a loglinear analysis

To answer the three research questions, we shall use a **hierarchical loglinear analysis** (following the **backward elimination** strategy), with a view to fitting the most parsimonious **unsaturated model**. Run the loglinear command (ignoring the preliminary Crosstabs operation) as described in Section 13.2.2 by selecting
Analyze➜Loglinear➜Model Selection...
to open the **Model Selection Loglinear Analysis** dialog box.

Enter the coding variables in the **Factor(s)** box and the **Range** values for each factor. In the **Model Building** box, select **Use backward elimination** (the default radio button). Click **OK**.

Output for the loglinear analysis

The main features of the output for a hierarchical loglinear analysis are described in Section 13.2.3.

Look at the table of Tests that K-way and higher order effects are zero.
- **Up to what level of complexity are the effects significant?**

Now look for the effects retained in the **final model**.
- **List the effects in the final model. Does the highest order of complexity correspond with what you noted in the previous bullet point question?**

Finally look at the table of **Observed, Expected Frequencies and Residuals**. Compare the magnitudes of the observed (OBS) count and the expected (EXP) count assuming the final model.
- **Write down the value of chi-square for the Goodness-of-fit test and its associated p-value. Does this p-value suggest a good or a bad fit?**

Finally, test the hypothesis of total independence of all three variables, using the procedure described in Section 13.2.5.
- **Write down the value of chi-square for the Goodness-of-fit test and its associated p-value. Does this p-value suggest a good or a bad fit?**

Conclusion

It should be quite clear from the foregoing comparisons that the final loglinear model is a very considerable improvement upon mere dismissal of the model of total independence after a traditional chi-square test. Loglinear models provide a powerful tool for teasing out the relationships among the variables in multi-way contingency tables.

CHAPTER 14

Discriminant analysis and logistic regression

14.1   INTRODUCTION

In Chapter 12, it was shown how the methods of regression could be used to predict scores on one dependent or **criterion** variable from knowledge of scores on dependent variables or **regressors**. In the situations we discussed, both the dependent variable and the independent variables were always scale or continuous data. There are circumstances, however, in which one might wish to predict, not scores on a quantitative dependent variable, but category membership: that is, the DV is qualitative, rather than quantitative.

Suppose that a premorbid blood condition has been discovered, which is suspected to arise in middle age partly because of smoking and drinking. A hundred people are tested for the presence of the condition and a record made of their smoking and alcohol consumption. Can people's levels of smoking and drinking be used to predict whether they have the blood condition?

Here, although the independent variables (smoking and alcohol consumption) are continuous variables, the dependent variable is qualitative, consisting merely of the categories Yes (condition present) and No (condition absent). Could we assign arbitrary code numbers to the categories (dummy coding: 0 = No; 1= Yes) and carry out a regression in the usual way? There are many problems with that approach, and it is not recommended.

In this Chapter, we shall discuss two regression techniques that have been specially designed to predict category membership:
1.   Discriminant analysis.
2.   Logistic regression.

4.1.1 Discriminant analysis

Discriminant analysis

In **discriminant analysis**, all the IVs are combined into a new variable known as a **discriminant function** *D* which, like the estimate of the DV in multiple regression, is a linear function of the IVs.

Let *Y* be the dependent variable (group membership: 1 = Condition Present; 0 = Condition Absent), and $X_1, X_2, ..., X_p$ be *p* independent variables. The purpose of discriminant analysis is to find a linear function *D* of the independent variables, that is, a function of the form

$$D = b_0 + b_1 X_1 + b_2 X_2 + ... + b_p X_p$$

where the values of the coefficients and intercept of the discriminant function are chosen so that to the greatest possible extent, the group means on *D* (which are known as the **group centroids**) are as far apart as possible.

If the discriminant function D separates the group means, we can imagine two overlapping, bell-shaped distributions (normality is an assumption in discriminant analysis) centred on the values of the group centroids.

It will be possible to use *D* to classify the individuals in the study by assigning them to the Condition Present group (Y = 1) if their score on D exceeds a criterion cut-off value and to the Condition Absent group (Y = 0) if their score fails to reach the cut-off. If the group centroids (means on *D*) are sufficiently different, the number of correct assignments will exceed chance.

Given that a discriminant function can be constructed, tests are available to ascertain which of the independent variables are significant contributors to the function.

Multivariate analysis of variance (MANOVA)

In the foregoing situation, we have been concerned with finding discriminant functions *D* that will predict category membership to the greatest possible extent. Such a situation is likely to arise in medical or other contexts in which the researcher must follow an essentially correlational, rather than experimental strategy. Discriminant analysis is, then, like a multiple regression, except that the DV is qualitative, rather than continuous.

Suppose, however, that in an experiment on the effects of five different drug conditions on performance, there were, not one DV as in Chapter 7, but three DVs, such as a performance score, an error score, and a speed score. Multivariate analysis of variance (MANOVA) is a set of techniques designed to compare the different treatment groups, not on the mean scores on any one DV, but the group means on discriminant functions D of the DVs, where the term discriminant has exactly the same meaning as in the context of discriminant analysis. In fact, in terms of underlying statistical theory, the one-way MANOVA and discriminant analysis are identical.

In statistics, the term **univariate statistics** has traditionally been used to denote those techniques, such as *t* tests and ANOVA, that have been designed for the purpose of making comparisons among means on one DV. Multiple regression, in which there is one DV is thus regarded as a univariate method, even though several continuous variables are measured

during the course of the investigation. In contradistinction, MANOVA, which was designe
for use in situations in which there are two or more DVs, is a **multivariate** method.

As an alternative to MANOVA, univariate F tests can be (and frequently have been) used t
test differences among the group mean values on each DV for significance. The problem wit
that approach, however, is that since the IVs are likely to be correlated, it is difficult t
determine which are playing the most important roles. Moreover, the use of univariate F test
with the correlated DVs is also likely to result in more Type I errors.

The difference between discriminant analysis and MANOVA is one of supposed direction o
causation. In the medical, correlational context, the assumption is that the categorical variable
i.e. the presence or absence of the antibody, is caused or influenced by the continuou
variables. In the experimental context, in contrast, it is assumed that group membership (th
treatment factor) causes or influences the continuous variables, which in MANOVA are thu
seen as DVs, not IVs.

Although discriminant analysis and MANOVA have identical theoretical bases, the differer
contexts in which they are used create different emphases. There is a common core of ke
statistics and tests. In discriminant analysis, however, the researcher is interested in th
accuracy with which the technique can assign participants to the categories of the DV; wherea
in MANOVA, the researcher is interested in testing differences among the group means on th
discriminant functions of the continuous DVs. Accordingly, in the output of computin
procedures for discriminant analysis, as well as tests of the null hypothesis of no difference
between the groups, there are classification tables and statistics of the accuracy o
classification.

In this chapter, since the emphasis is upon prediction of category membership rather tha
testing differences among means for significance, the continuous variables will be regarded a
IVs, not DVs, as in MANOVA.

Statistical testing in discriminant analysis and MANOVA

In discriminant analysis (and in MANOVA), a key statistic is **Wilks' lambda (Λ)**. Recall tha
in univariate one-way ANOVA, a measure of effect size is eta squared (η^2), where

$$\eta^2 = \frac{SS_{between}}{SS_{total}}$$

For simplicity, Wilks' lambda can be thought of as the proportion of the total variance that i
within groups, rather than *between* groups, as in eta squared. In the context of one-wa
ANOVA (where there is just one DV), therefore, lambda is 1 minus eta squared:

$$\Lambda = 1 - \eta^2$$

This idea extends to the situation where, rather than one DV, we have a discriminant functio
of several DVs. In the multivariate situation, however, the within subjects and total sums o
squares are replaced with matrix algebraic equivalents. The value of Λ, like that of et
squared, can range in value from 0 to 1. Since, however, lambda is measuring *within* group
rather than *between* groups variability, a value of Λ close to zero indicates a *large* separatio
among the means; whereas a value close to unity indicates a *small* separation. An approxima

chi-square test is used to test a value of Λ for significance. A value of Λ can also be tested with a statistic that is distributed approximately as F on degrees of freedom. The formulae are complex and will not be given here. (See Tabachnick & Fidell, 2007; p. 259.)

The **canonical correlation** and the **eigenvalue** are two of the statistics that serve as measures of the power of discriminant functions to discriminate among the groups. The canonical correlation is the correlation between scores on a discriminant function and scores on coding variables defining group membership. The eigenvalue is another measure of the separation achieved by a discriminant function: it is more informative when converted to a proportional measure by dividing the eigenvalue by the sum of the eigenvalues of all the discriminants.

As in multiple regression, techniques are available to help the researcher to identify those independent variables that make the greatest contributions to the prediction of the dependent variable. There are many other parallels between multiple regression and discriminant analysis.

14.1.2   Types of discriminant analysis

There are three types of discriminant analysis (DA): **direct, hierarchical**, and **stepwise**, where these terms have exactly the same meaning as they do in multiple regression. **Direct DA** is the equivalent of simultaneous multiple regression: all the variables are entered into the regression equation at once. In **hierarchical DA**, they are entered according to a schedule set by the researcher, presumably on the basis of theory or collateral evidence; and in **stepwise DA**, statistical criteria alone determine the order of entry. Since in most analyses, the researcher has no reason for giving some predictors higher priority than others, the third (**stepwise**) method is the most generally used. On the other hand, the same uncertainties arise with stepwise discriminant analysis as with the use of stepwise methods in multiple regression.

14.1.3   Stepwise discriminant analysis

The statistical procedure for stepwise discriminant analysis is similar to multiple regression, in that the effect of the addition or removal of an IV is monitored by a statistical test and the result is used as a basis for the inclusion of that IV in the final analysis. When there are only two groups, there is just one discriminant function. With more than two groups, however, there can be several functions (one fewer than the number of groups), although it is unusual for more than the first two or three discriminant functions to be statistically robust.

Variables are added or removed from the analysis by using **Wilks' Lambda (Λ)**. The significance of the change in Λ when a variable is entered or removed is obtained from an F test. At each step of adding a variable to the analysis, the variable with the largest F (**F to Enter**) is included. This process is repeated until there are no further variables with an F value greater than the critical minimum threshold value. Sometimes a variable, having been included at one point, is removed later when its F value (**F to Remove**) falls below a critical level. (This can happen with the stepwise multiple regression procedure as well – see Section 12.4.2.)

Eventually, the process of adding and subtracting variables is completed, and a summary table is shown indicating which variables were added or subtracted at each step. The variables remaining in the analysis are those used in the discriminant function(s). The next table shows which functions are statistically reliable. The first function provides the best means of predicting group membership. Later functions may or may not contribute reliably to the prediction process. Additional tables displaying the functions and their success rates for correct prediction can be requested. Plots can also be specified.

14.1.4 Restrictive assumptions of discriminant analysis

While it is assumed that the independent variables will usually be quantitative, it is also possible to include some qualitative independent variables (e.g. sex, marital status) just as it is in multiple regression.

The use of discriminant analysis, however, carries several restrictive assumptions. It is assumed, for example, that the data are **multivariate normal** (i.e. for any fixed value of one variable, all the other variables have normal distributions). The procedure is sufficiently robust to cope with some skewness, provided the samples are not too small. The problem of outliers, however, is more serious. It is best to remove extreme values if that can be justified. In addition, there is the usual assumption of **homogeneity of variance-covariance matrices**. It is also important to avoid **multicollinearity** (high correlations among the independent variables). In particular, no variable must be an exact linear function of any of the others, a condition known as **singularity**.

14.2   DISCRIMINANT ANALYSIS WITH SPSS

A school's vocational guidance officer would like to be able to help senior pupils to choose which subjects to study at university. Fortunately, some data are available from a project on the background interests and school-leaving examination results of architectural, engineering and psychology students. The students also filled in a questionnaire about their extra-curricular interests, including outdoor pursuits, drawing, painting, computing, and kit construction. The problem is this: can knowledge of the pupils' scores on a number of variables be used to predict their subject category at university? In this study, subject category at university (psychologists, architects or engineers) is the dependent variable, and all the others are independent variables.

14.2.1   Preparing the data set

Since the data for this example are the scores of 118 participants on ten variables, it would be extremely tedious for readers to type the data into **Data View**. The data are available on WWW at:

http://www.abdn.ac.uk/psychology/materials/spss.shtml

Select *Ch14 Vocational guidance data* and save it to the hard disk (or your stick) for easier access.

A section of the data set in **Data View** is shown in Figure 1.

Case	StudySubject	Sex	ConKit	ModelKit	Drawing	Painting	Outdoor	Computing	VisModel	Quals
32	Architect	Male	4	2	7	4	2	2	4	9
33	Architect	Female	4	10	7	3	5	1	6	7
34	Psychologist	Male	2	2	0	0	1	1	2	9
35	Psychologist	Female	2	4	3	1	1	1	6	9

Figure 1. Some cases in the Vocational Guidance data set

14.2.2 Exploring the data

Before embarking on the discriminant analysis, the user should probe the data for possible violations of the underlying assumptions. A full treatment of this topic is beyond the scope of this book, but the interested reader should consult a statistical text such as Tabachnick & Fidell (2007) for more details.

Here we suggest you check for extreme scores and outliers by using the **Explore** command (see Chapter 4, Section 4.3.2) to examine the distributions of the variables within the different categories of the grouping factor (*Study Subject*).

See Section 4.3.2

- In the **Explore** dialog box, click the **Plots** radio button in the **Display** options, and transfer the variable names of all the predictors except *Sex* into the **Dependent List** box. Transfer the variable name *Study Subject* into the **Factor List** box, and the variable name *Case Number* into the **Label Cases by** box.
- Click **OK** to plot all the boxplots and stem-and-leaf displays.

Interest in Painting

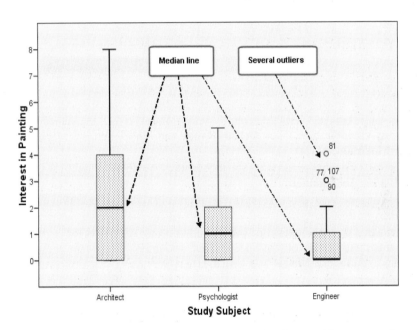

Output 1. The boxplots of *Interest in Painting* for the three subject categories

Most of the **boxplots** are satisfactory except for *Interest in Painting* (see Output 1). Here one box is much larger than the others; moreover, in the Engineers' box, the median line is positioned close to the lower side of the box, rather than centrally. There are also some outliers. (See Table 2 in Section 4.3.2 for a reminder of the layout of a boxplot.) The corresponding **stem-and-leaf** displays also show discrepancies among the distributions. Should the first run of the discriminant procedure indicate that there are problems with the data, it might be advisable to omit the independent variable *Interest in Painting*.

See Section 4.3.2

14.2.3 Running discriminant analysis

- Choose
  Analyze➜Classify (see Figure 2)➜**Discriminant...**
  to open the **Discriminant Analysis** dialog box, the completed version of which is shown in
  Figure 3.

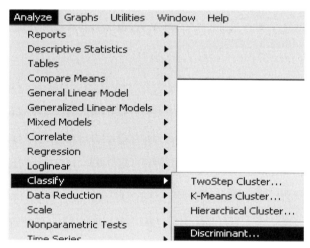

Figure 2. Finding the **Discriminant** procedure

- Transfer the dependent variable name (here it is *StudySubject*, the subject of study) to the
  Grouping Variable box. Click **Define Range** and type 1 into the **Minimum** box and 3
  into the **Maximum** box.
- Drag the cursor down the names of the independent variables to highlight them and transfer
  them all to the **Independents** box.
- Since a stepwise analysis is going to be used, click the radio button for **Use stepwise
  method**.
- Recommended options include the means and one-way ANOVAs for each of the variables
  across the three levels of the independent variable. To obtain these options, click
  Statistics... and select **Means** and **Univariate ANOVAs**. Click **Continue** to return to the
  original dialog box.
- Another recommended option is a final summary table showing the success or failure of the
  analysis. Click **Classify...** and select **Summary table**. Click **Continue** to return to the
  original dialog box.

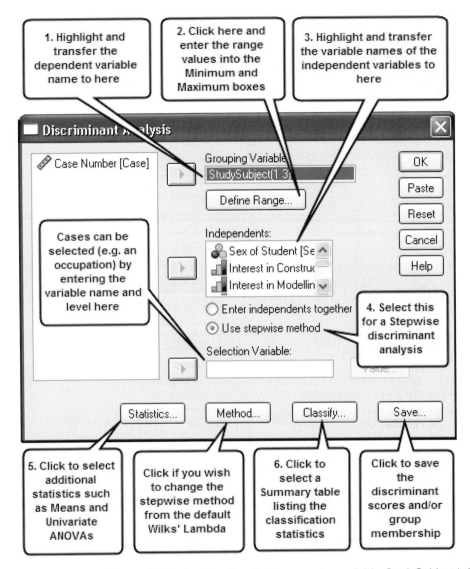

Figure 3. The **Discriminant Analysis** dialog box for the grouping variable *StudySubject* (with three levels) and several independent variables, using the **stepwise method**

- In some analyses there may be a grouping variable of which just one level is of interest. For example, we could have excluded *Sex* from the list of **Independents** and then carried out the analysis on males only by entering the variable name *Sex* in the **Selection Variable** box and then 1 for males in the **Value** box which would have appeared as soon as *Sex* was entered.
- Click **OK** to run the **Discriminant Analysis**.

14.2.4 Output for discriminant analysis

The output, as listed in the left-hand pane of the **SPSS Viewer** (Output 2), is rather daunting. Fortunately, as with the regression output, not all of it is required.

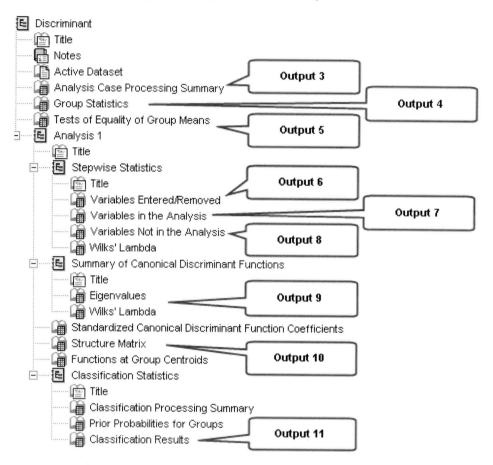

Output 2. The left-hand pane of the **SPSS Viewer**

Information about the data and the number of cases in each category of the grouping variable

Output 3 shows how many valid cases were used in the analysis. Ten cases, which were missing a score on one or more of the independent variables, have been excluded.

Analysis Case Processing Summary

Unweighted Cases		N	Percent
Valid		108	91.5
Excluded	Missing or out-of-range group codes	0	.0
	At least one missing discriminating variable	10	8.5
	Both missing or out-of-range group codes and at least one missing discriminating variable	0	.0
	Total	10	8.5
Total		118	100.0

Output 3. Information about the number of valid cases

Statistics

The next table (Output 4) is part of the **Group Statistics** table, which shows the optional statistics and the number of cases for each independent variable at each level of the grouping variable and all of them together (here only those for *Architect* are shown).

Group Statistics

Study Subject		Mean	Std. Deviation	Valid N (listwise) Unweighted
Architect	Sex of Student	1.27	.45	30
	Interest in Construction Kits	3.33	1.58	30
	Interest in Modelling Kits	3.97	2.68	30
	Interest in Drawing	5.10	2.29	30
	Interest in Painting	2.50	2.18	30
	Interest in Outdoor Pursuits	2.30	2.07	30
	Interest in Computing	1.77	1.45	30
	Ability to Visualise Model	5.53	1.25	30
	School Qualifications	6.63	2.86	30

Output 4. An edited table showing part of the optional statistics and the number of cases for each independent variable at each level of the grouping variable Study Subject

The **Univariate ANOVAs** (Output 5) show whether there is a statistically significant difference among the three grouping variable (*Study Subject*) means for each independent variable. All these differences are significant (as shown in the column **Sig.**), except for the variables *Interest in Computing* and *Interest in Modelling Kits*.

Tests of Equality of Group Means

	Wilks' Lambda	F	df1	df2	Sig.
Sex of Student	.77	15.99	2	105	.00
Interest in Construction Kits	.84	9.71	2	105	.00
Interest in Modelling Kits	.96	2.11	2	105	.13
Interest in Drawing	.90	6.09	2	105	.00
Interest in Painting	.83	10.41	2	105	.00
Interest in Outdoor Pursuits	.94	3.24	2	105	.04
Interest in Computing	1.00	.00	2	105	1.00
Ability to Visualise Model	.84	9.74	2	105	.00
School Qualifications	.88	7.38	2	105	.00

All ANOVAs are significant except those with p-value > 0.05

Output 5. Univariate **ANOVA**s

The summary table

The **Stepwise Statistics** section begins with a summary table (Output 6) showing which variables were entered and removed (though in this analysis none was removed), along with values of **Wilks' Lambda** and the associated probability levels. Notice the values of **F to Enter** and **F to Remove** in footnotes b and c. These are the default criteria, which can be changed in the **Stepwise Method** dialog box.

Variables Entered/Removed [a,b,c,d]

		Wilks' Lambda				Exact F			
Step	Entered	Statistic	df1	df2	df3	Statistic	df1	df2	Sig.
1	Sex of Student	.77	1	2	105	16.0	2	105	.00
2	Interest in Painting	.64	2	2	105	16.0	4	208	.00
3	School Qualifications	.54	3	2	105	12.4	6	206	.00
4	Ability to Visualise Model	.48	4	2	105	11.3	8	204	.00
5	Interest in Outdoor Pursuits	.44	5	2	105	10.3	10	202	.00
6	Interest in Construction Kits	.40	6	2	105	9.59	12	200	.00
7	Interest in Computing	.37	7	2	105	8.99	14	198	.00

At each step, the variable that minimizes the overall Wilks' Lambda is entered.

a. Maximum number of steps is 18.

b. Minimum partial F to enter is 3.84.

c. Maximum partial F to remove is 2.71.

d. F level, tolerance, or VIN insufficient for further computation.

Output 6. Summary table of variables entered and removed

Entering and removing variables step by step

The next table, **Variables in the Analysis**, lists the variables in the analysis at each step. Output 7 shows only Steps 1-3 and the final stage, Step 7.

Variables in the Analysis

Step		Toler-ance	F to Remove	Wilks' Lambda
1	Sex of Student	1.00	15.99	
2	Sex of Student	.88	15.71	.83
	Interest in Painting	.88	10.19	.77
3	Sex of Student	.88	15.26	.70
	Interest in Painting	.85	12.34	.67
	School Qualifications	.95	9.78	.64
7	Sex of Student	.59	7.47	.43
	Interest in Painting	.73	10.92	.46
	School Qualifications	.91	10.83	.46
	Ability to Visualise Model	.90	7.96	.43
	Interest in Outdoor Pursuits	.84	3.96	.40
	Interest in Construction Kits	.80	4.33	.41
	Interest in Computing	.70	3.85	.40

Output 7. Variables in the analysis at Steps 1 to 3, and finally at Step 7

In Output 7, the column labelled **Tolerance** lists the tolerance for a variable not yet selected and is one minus the square of the multiple correlation coefficient between that variable and all the other variables already entered. Very small values suggest that a variable can contribute little to the analysis. The column **F to Remove** tests the significance of the decrease in discrimination should that variable be removed. But since no F-ratio is less than the criterion of 2.71, none of the variables entered has been removed.

The table **Variables not in the Analysis** tabulates the variables not in the analysis at the start and at each step thereafter until the final step (Output 8 shows only Steps 0 & 1, then Step 7). It can be seen that *Sex of Student* had the highest **F to Enter** value initially (and the lowest **Wilks' Lambda**) and is, therefore, selected as the first variable to enter at Step 1 (Output 7).

At Step 1, the variable with the next highest **F to Enter** value is *Interest in Painting*, which is then entered at Step 2 as shown in Output 7. Finally at Step 7, the variables *Interest in Modelling Kits* and *Interest in Drawing* are never entered because their **F to Enter** values are smaller than the criterion of 3.84.

Variables Not in the Analysis

Step		Toler-ance	Min. Toler-ance	F to Enter	Wilks' Lambda	
0	Sex of Student	1.00	1.00	15.99	.77	This variable is entered at Step 1 (Output 7) with the largest F to Enter value
	Interest in Construction Kits	1.00	1.00	9.71	.84	
	Interest in Modelling Kits	1.00	1.00	2.11	.96	
	Interest in Drawing	1.00	1.00	6.09	.90	
	Interest in Painting	1.00	1.00	10.41	.83	
	Interest in Outdoor Pursuits	1.00	1.00	3.24	.94	
	Interest in Computing	1.00	1.00	.00	1.00	
	Ability to Visualise Model	1.00	1.00	9.74	.84	
	School Qualifications	1.00	1.00	7.38	.88	
1	Interest in Construction Kits	.93	.93	3.43	.72	This variable is entered at Step 2 (Output 7) with the largest F to Enter value
	Interest in Modelling Kits	.94	.94	2.20	.74	
	Interest in Drawing	1.00	1.00	6.04	.69	
	Interest in Painting	.88	.88	10.19	.61	
	Interest in Outdoor Pursuits	.98	.98	1.49	.75	
	Interest in Computing	.75	.75	4.20	.71	
	Ability to Visualise Model	1.00	1.00	8.83	.66	
	School Qualifications	.98	.98	7.69	.67	
7	Interest in Modelling Kits	.72	.57	.36	.37	
	Interest in Drawing	.63	.52	.91	.37	

These variables at Step 7 are excluded because their F to Enter values are <3.34

Output 8. Part of the table of variables not in the analysis at Steps 0, 1 and 7

The next table in the output, **Wilks' Lambda**, is a repeat of the table given in Output 5 and is not reproduced.

Statistics of the discriminant functions

Output 9 shows the percentage (**% of Variance**) of the variance accounted for by each discriminant function and how many of them (if any) are significant (see the **Sig.** column in the **Wilks' Lambda** table). Here we see that both functions are highly significant. The **Canonical Correlation** for a discriminant function is the square root of the ratio of the between-groups sum of squares to the total sum of squares. Squared, it is the proportion of the total variability explained by differences between groups.

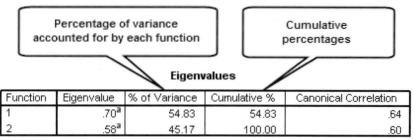

Eigenvalues

Function	Eigenvalue	% of Variance	Cumulative %	Canonical Correlation
1	.70[a]	54.83	54.83	.64
2	.58[a]	45.17	100.00	.60

a. First 2 canonical discriminant functions were used in the analysis.

Wilks' Lambda

Test of Function(s)	Wilks' Lambda	Chi-square	df	Sig.
1 through 2	.37	100.34	14	.00
2	.63	46.33	6	.00

With p-values < .05, both functions are significant

Output 9. Statistics of the discriminant functions

Standardised coefficients and within groups correlations with discriminants

Two tables follow in the listing, the first (not reproduced here) being the **Standardized Canonical Discriminant Function Coefficients**, and the second (Output 10) the **Structure Matrix**, which is a table of pooled within groups correlations between the independent variables and the discriminant functions.

Structure Matrix

	Function 1	Function 2
Ability to Visualise Model	-.51*	-.10
School Qualifications	.43*	-.16
Interest in Painting	-.42*	.36
Interest in Drawing a	-.22*	.12
Interest in Modelling Kits a	-.12*	.07
Interest in Computing	.01*	.00
Sex of Student	.19	.70*
Interest in Construction Kits	-.15	-.54*
Interest in Outdoor Pursuits	.19	.25*

Pooled within-groups correlations between discriminating variables and standardized canonical discriminant functions
Variables ordered by absolute size of correlation within function.

*. Largest absolute correlation between each variable and any discriminant function

a. This variable not used in the analysis.

Output 10. The **Structure Matrix**

It is clear from the information in Output 10 that the first function is contributed to positively by School Qualifications and their interest in painting, and negatively by their ability to visualise models. The second function is contributed to positively by *Sex* and negatively by *Interest in Modelling Kits* and *Interest in Outdoor pursuits*. The asterisks mark the correlations with the higher value for each variable.

The next table in the output (not reproduced), **Functions at Group Centroids**, lists the group means (for Architect, Psychologist, Engineer) for each canonical variable.

Success of predictions of group membership

The optional selection of **Summary table** from the **Classify** options in the **Discriminant Analysis** dialog box provides an indication of the success rate for predictions of group membership using the discriminant functions developed in the analysis (see Output 11). The footnote to the table indicates that the overall success rate is 72.2%.

Classification Results[a]

	Study Subject	Predicted Group Membership			Total
		Architect	Psychologist	Engineer	
Count	Architect	22	2	6	30
	Psychologist	4	25	8	37
	Engineer	5	5	31	41
%	Architect	73.3	6.7	20.0	100.0
	Psychologist	10.8	67.6	21.6	100.0
	Engineer	12.2	12.2	75.6	100.0

a. 72.2% of original grouped cases correctly classified.

Output 11. **Classification Results** table showing the predicted group membership

Output 11 also shows that the *Engineers* were the most accurately classified, with 75.6% of the cases correct. The *Architects* were next with 73.3%. The *Psychologists* were the least accurately classed, with a success rate of 67.6%. Notice also that incorrectly classified *Architects* were more likely to be classified as *Engineers* than as *Psychologists*, and that incorrectly classified *Psychologists* are more likely to be classified as *Engineers* than as *Architects*!

14.2.5   Predicting group membership

Section 14.2 posed the question of whether knowledge of pupils' scores on a number of variables could be used to predict their subjects of study at university. The analysis has demonstrated that two discriminant functions can be generated using all the variables except *Interest in Modelling Kits* and *Interest in Drawing*, and that these functions can predict 72.2% of the cases correctly. So far, however, we have not seen what the predicted subject of study was for any particular individual. Moreover, the vocational guidance officer in our example wants to make predictions of the subjects that future students will eventually take, given knowledge of their scores on the same independent variables. It is easy to do either or both of these things with the **Discriminant** procedure.

To compare the actual subject of study with the predicted subject of study, proceed as follows:
- Complete the **Discriminant Analysis** dialog box as before but, in addition, click **Save...** and then click the radio button for **Predicted group membership**. Click **Continue** and **OK**.
- The predicted group membership will appear in a new column labelled **Dis_1** in **Data View**, along with the predictions for all the other cases.
- We suggest that you actually try this and, once **Dis_1** appears in **Data View**, switch to **Variable View** and rename the variable *PredictDiscrim*. Figure 4 is a section from **Data View** showing some of the predictions of choice of subject from the discriminant analysis.

To predict the subject of study for a future student, proceed as follows:
- Enter the data for the potential students at the end of the data in **Data View**. Leave the grouping variable (*StudySubject*) blank or enter an out-of-range number so that the analysis does not include these cases when it is computing the discriminant functions.
- Then after completing the steps described above, the predicted group membership will appear in a new column labelled *PredictDiscrim* in **Data View**, along with the predictions for all the other cases.

Case	StudySubject	Sex	ConKit	ModelKit	Drawing	Painting	Outdoor	Computing	VisModel	Quals	PredictDiscrim
96	Engineer	Male	4	2	4	0	2	1	4	7	Engineer
97	Engineer	Male	3	2	2	0	0	2	4	0	Architect
98	Engineer	Male	4	1	5	1	0	2	7	7	Architect
99	Engineer	Female	1	0	0	0	6	0	2	6	Psychologist
100	Engineer	Male	6	2	2	0	4	2	4	7	Engineer
101	Engineer	Female	4	2	5	1	4	1	4	9	Psychologist

Figure 4. Section of **Data View** showing the predictions from discriminant analysis of choice of main university subject

14.3 BINARY LOGISTIC REGRESSION

14.3.1 Introduction

Logistic regression is another approach to category prediction, which carries fewer assumptions than does discriminant analysis. Moreover, with logistic regression, any number of qualitative predictors such as gender can be included in the regression; in fact, *all* the predictors may be categorical. For these reasons, it is fast overtaking discriminant analysis as the preferred technique for this kind of research problem. Returning to the example of the premorbid blood condition mentioned at the start of this Chapter, suppose that of the hundred people studied, forty-four people have the condition and fifty-six do not. Let us assign code numbers to the two categories: to those who have the condition, we assign 1; and to those who do not, we assign 0. In this section, we shall outline the use of logistic regression to predict category membership.

On the basis of the foregoing information, a prediction of category membership can be made without doing any regression at all. Since the probability that a person selected at random having the condition is 44/100 = .44 (44%) and not having the condition is 56/100 = .56

(56%), our best prediction of category membership for any particular person is to assign them to the 'condition absent' category. If we do that, we shall be right in 100% of the cases in which the condition was absent, but wrong in the 44% of cases in which the condition was present, giving us a net success rate of 56% over the hundred assignments. The purpose of logistic regression is to improve upon this success rate by exploiting any association between the dependent and independent variables to predict category membership (the dependent variable) with the greatest possible accuracy.

In what follows, it is assumed that, although the condition can only be present or absent, variables such as number of cigarettes smoked and amount of drink consumed actually increase the probability of developing the condition **continuously** throughout the range of consumption. This probability, however, cannot be expected to be a linear function of the independent variables: it is likely to rise more rapidly as scores on the independent variable increase and less rapidly at a later stage, so that the probability graph would be rather like a flattened S (See Figure 5).

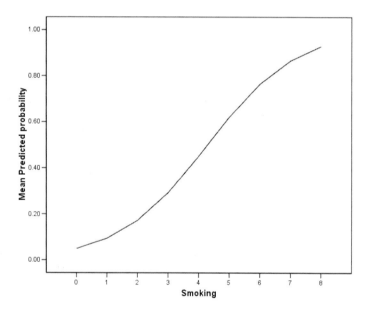

Figure 5. A logistic regression function, giving the estimated probability of a person smoking a certain number of cigarettes having the premorbid blood condition

An estimate of this curve is called the **logistic regression function**, which expresses the probability of the premorbid blood condition in terms of the number of cigarettes smoked and alcohol consumption. On the basis of the number of cigarettes that a person smokes and the amount that they drink, that person is assigned a probability by the logistic regression function.

These probability estimates can be used to assign individuals to either of the two categories of the dependent variable. First, a criterion probability (most commonly .5) is set, above which an individual will be assigned to the condition-present category. When the value of the probability estimate (from the logistic regression function) for a particular participant exceeds

.5, that participant is assigned to the group with the premorbid blood condition; if the probability is less than .5, the participant is assigned to the other category.

Recall that in **multiple regression**, the dependent variable Y is predicted from p independent variables X_1, X_2, ..., X_p by means of the regression equation

$$Y' = b_0 + b_1 X_1 + b_2 X_2 + ... + b_p X_p$$

where b_0 is the regression constant and b_1, b_2, ...,b_p are the regression coefficients.

The logistic regression function, although itself nonlinear, contains a term Z which is a linear of the independent variables:

$$Z = b_0 + b_1 X_1 + b_2 X_2 + ... + b_p X_p \quad (1) \textbf{ The logit equation}$$

The logistic regression function itself is

$$p = \frac{e^Z}{1 + e^Z} \quad (2) \textbf{ Logistic regression function}$$

where p is the probability that a person will have the premorbid blood condition and Z is the function defined in (1).

The **logit** is the log of the odds. By way of explanation of (2), note that the probability p of the occurrence of an event and the odds in favour of its occurrence are related according to $p = \text{odds}/(1 + \text{odds})$, and that (1) is known as the **logit equation**, because

$$p = \frac{odds}{1 + odds} = \frac{e^{\log_e odds}}{1 + e^{\log_e odds}} = \frac{e^{logit}}{1 + e^{logit}} = \frac{e^Z}{1 + e^Z}$$

In logistic regression, as in ordinary multiple regression, the values of the parameters b_0, b_1, ..., b_p in the logit equation (2) are chosen so that the logistic regression equation predicts the independent variable (in this case category membership) as accurately as possible.

We should note that, in contradistinction to ordinary least squares (OLS) regression, there is no mathematical solution to the problem of determining the values of the parameter estimates in the logit equation. Instead, a highly computing-intensive algorithm is used to arrive at the estimates by a series of repetitions or **iterations**. If all goes well, the estimates of the parameters from successive iterations approximate ever more closely to, or **converge** upon, stable values. It is essential, however, when running logistic regression, that the user check the iteration history to be sure that convergence has been achieved.

Binary and multinomial logistic regression

When the dependent variable consists of only two categories, the technique known as **binary logistic regression** is applicable; when there are three or more categories, **multinomial logistic regression** is the appropriate choice (see Section 14.4).

14.3.2   An example of a binary logistic regression with quantitative independent variables

For our first example, we return to the data set on the premorbid blood condition, smoking and drinking. Table 1 shows the first eight cases from some data on the incidence of the premorbid condition in 100 people, together with their average daily smoking levels and alcohol consumption. (The complete data set is given at the end of this Chapter.) The units have been selected to cover the entire range of consumption for each variable: one smoking unit is five cigarettes; one drinking unit is the equivalent of half a glass of wine or a quarter-pint of beer.

Table 1. The first eight cases in a hypothetical set of data showing the presence or absence of a blood condition along with their smoking and drinking habits

Case	Blood	Smoke	Alcohol	Case	Blood	Smoke	Alcohol
1	Yes	8	17	5	Yes	8	15
2	Yes	8	15	6	Yes	8	18
3	Yes	8	16	7	Yes	8	18
4	Yes	5	16	8	No	8	15

14.3.3   Exploring the data

As usual, we recommend a thorough exploration of the data set with familiar statistics (e.g. correlations – see Section 11.2) before embarking upon any sophisticated multivariate method. For example, the correlation procedure will show that while category membership correlates substantially and significantly with the smoking variable, it does not correlate with the level of alcohol consumption. Moreover, smoking and alcohol consumption turn out not to be significantly correlated.

See Section 11.2

Correlations

		Blood Condition	Smoking	Alcohol
Blood Condition	Pearson Correlation	1	.622**	-.188
	Sig. (2-tailed)		.000	.062
	N	100	100	100
Smoking	Pearson Correlation	.622**	1	.140
	Sig. (2-tailed)	.000		.164
	N	100	100	100
Alcohol	Pearson Correlation	-.188	.140	1
	Sig. (2-tailed)	.062	.164	
	N	100	100	100

**. Correlation is significant at the 0.01 level (2-tailed).

Output 12. Correlations among category membership (presence or absence of the premorbid blood condition), amount of smoking and level of alcohol consumption

14.3.4 Investigating interactions: centring

It has often been suggested that the effects of alcohol may be worse in heavy smokers. It would be natural, therefore, to explore the possibility of an interaction between the smoking and alcohol variables. It is standard practice, when investigating interactions between continuous variables, to subtract the mean of each variable from all its values, so that the distribution of the variable is now centred on zero. This procedure is known as **centring**. Centring does not affect the values of the correlations among the independent variables; in fact, linear transformation of the values of either variable (or both variables) in a correlation leaves the value of the correlation unaltered. When interaction terms are included in a regression model, however, the independent variables in raw form are highly correlated with their products (or their powers, if power relationships are being investigated). This potential multicollinearity problem is avoided by centring.

14.3.5 Preparing the data set

The data set for this example is large (see the Appendix to this Chapter), and it would be extremely tedious to type it into **Data View**. The set *Ch14 Blood, smoking & alcohol data* is available on WWW at:

http://www.abdn.ac.uk/psychology/materials/spss.shtml

You will find from running **Descriptives** that the means for the smoking and alcohol variables are 4.230 and 10.920, respectively, with standard deviations 2.601 and 4.153. Use **Compute** to subtract these means from the raw values of their respective variables. The new smoking and alcohol means will now be zero. Check that, although the means of the smoking and alcohol variables are now zero, the standard deviations are still 2.601 and 4.153, respectively; moreover the correlations among the three variables should be exactly as in Output 12.

14.3.6 Running binary logistic regression

In its logistic regression dialog box, SPSS uses the term **covariate** for continuous independent variables. In this example, both IVs are quantitative.

- Choose
  Analyze➜Regression➜Binary Logistic …
  to open the **Logistic Regression** dialog box (Figure 6).
- Follow the steps in Figure 6.

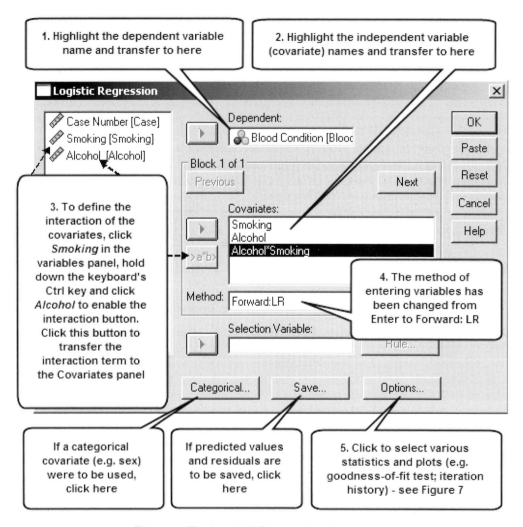

Figure 6. The **Logistic Regression** dialog box

Notice the button labelled >a*b> underneath the transfer arrow outside the **Covariates** box. This is the **interaction button**. The interaction button will come live if two variables are selected together (by keeping the Control button pressed down while selecting the second variable) and transferred to the Covariates box. The default **Method** is **Enter** (all covariates are entered in a block) but here we shall choose **Forward: LR.** In this option, the inclusion of each covariate in the model is based on the significance of the score statistic, and its possible future removal is decided on the basis of the p-value of a likelihood-ratio (LR) statistic.

• We recommend selecting some optional statistics and displays. Click **Options…** to obtain the **Options** dialog box (Figure 7). Select **Hosmer-Lemeshow goodness-of-fit** and **Iteration history**. Click **Continue** to return to the **Logistic Regression** dialog box.

• Click **OK**.

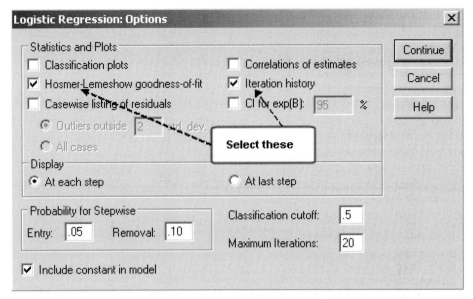

Figure 7. The **Options** dialog box with **Hosmer-Lemeshow goodness-of-fit** and **Iteration history** selected

We have seen that the logistic regression procedure maximises its predictions of category membership by a highly computer-intensive process generating successive approximations called **iterations**. If all goes well, the estimates converge (i.e. become progressively closer) to constant values, which are taken to be the best estimates. By choosing the item **Iteration history** in the **Options**, you can check that the successive iterations really have converged. It may also be necessary to increase the number in the Maximum Iterations to, say, 100 to achieve convergence.

Beware that an analysis of a data set with many variables may take some time to complete. Failure to converge may occur if some of the variables are highly correlated (the **multicollinearity** problem); the solution is to delete one or more redundant variables from the analysis.

In the **Logistic Regression** dialog box, there is another button labelled **Save...** which accesses the **Save New Variables** dialog box (not shown). Selecting items from this box will add several new variables to those already in **Data View**, including **Probabilities** and **Group membership** from the **Predicted Values** selection section, and **Standardized** and **Studentized** from the **Residuals** selection section. We suggest that, for the present, the reader should focus on the basic regression and experiment with the **Save...** button options later.

14.3.7 Output for binary logistic regression

The output for logistic regression is extensive (see Output 13), even if no options are selected. Notice that the output essentially consists of two Blocks, the first showing the opening situation, the second the steps in the **Forward Stepwise** procedure. In this section, we shall describe some of the most useful items.

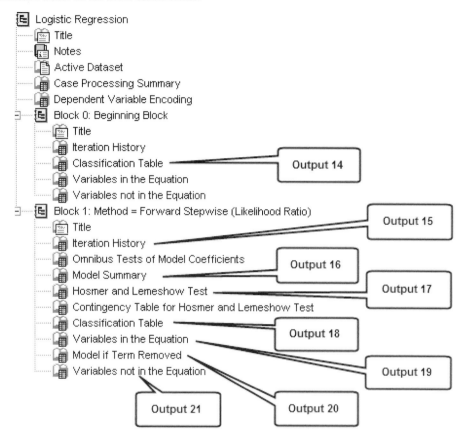

Output 13. The left-hand pane of **SPSS Viewer** showing the details of the output

First, however, some preliminary points are in order. In logistic regression, pivotal use is made of a statistic termed the **log likelihood**, which is written variously as $-2 \log(\text{likelihood})$, $-2LL$, or $-2LogL$. This statistic behaves as chi-square, and has a large value when a model fits poorly, and a small value when the model fits well. The log likelihood statistic is analogous to the error sum of squares in multiple regression: the larger its value, the more the variance that remains to be accounted for.

In the introduction, we saw that the best bet of a person's category membership was the more frequently occurring category (i.e. condition absent). The first two tables in the output (not shown here) are a **Case Processing Summary** table specifying how many cases were selected and a **Dependent Variable Encoding** table tabulating the two levels of the dependent variable (here they are *No* and *Yes*).

Next there is a block of tables called **Block 0: Beginning Block** in which the logistic regression procedure begins with a model with neither of the dependent variables present (i.e. an 'intercept only' model). This guessing stage is called **Step 0** by SPSS. Included in this block is a **Classification Table** (see Output 14) in which the Observed and Predicted values of *Blood Condition* are the same. There are no surprises here: we have already seen that the success rate without any regression is 56%. Three other tables in Block 0 (not shown here) tabulate the **Iteration history**, **Variables in the Equation** and the **Variables not in the equation**.

Classification Table [a,b]

			Predicted		
			Blood Condition		
	Observed		No	Yes	Percentage Correct
Step 0	Blood Condition	No	56	0	100.0
		Yes	44	0	.0
	Overall Percentage				56.0

a. Constant is included in the model.

b. The cut value is .500

Output 14. The 'no regression' **Classification Table**

The next block of tables of output is headed **Block 1: Method = Forward Stepwise (Likelihood Ratio)** confirming our choice of method selected in the **Logistic Regression** dialog box (Figure 6). This block contains some very interesting information. The first item is the **Iteration history** (this is provided because **Iteration history** was selected as an option in Figure 7), showing convergence of the estimates towards fixed values after five iterations for Step 1 and seven iterations for Step 2 (Output 15). Notice that at **Step 1**, *Smoking* was the first variable selected and then at **Step 2**, *Alcohol* was added (see also Output 19). The interaction *Alcohol*Smoking* was never added (see also Output 21).

Iteration History[a,b,c,d,e]

Iteration		-2 Log likelihood	Coefficients		
			Constant	Smoking	Alcohol
Step 1	1	94.933	-2.258	.477	
	2	91.805	-3.125	.646	
	3	91.662	-3.364	.691	
	4	91.662	-3.379	.694	
	5	91.662	-3.379	.694	
Step 2	1	84.827	-.915	.507	-.135
	2	75.184	-.964	.799	-.262
	3	71.727	-.812	1.079	-.400
	4	70.934	-.713	1.287	-.504
	5	70.884	-.691	1.356	-.537
	6	70.883	-.689	1.361	-.540
	7	70.883	-.689	1.361	-.540

a. Method: Forward Stepwise (Likelihood Ratio)

b. Constant is included in the model.

c. Initial -2 Log Likelihood: 137.186

d. Estimation terminated at iteration number 5 because parameter estimates changed by less than .001.

e. Estimation terminated at iteration number 7 because parameter estimates changed by less than .001.

Output 15. The **Iteration History** table showing that *Smoking* was included at Step 1 and then *Alcohol* at Step 2

The **Model Summary** table (Output 16) includes two statistics intended to be equivalent to the **coefficient of determination (R^2)** in ordinary least-squares regression. The **Cox & Snell R Square** is based on the log likelihood for the model compared with the log likelihood for a baseline model. The **Nagelkerke R Square** is an adjusted version of the Cox & Snell R^2. It adjusts the scale of the statistic to cover the full range from 0 to 1. The size of R^2 (65% after Step 2) indicates that the model contributes powerfully to the prediction of the presence or absence of the blood condition.

Model Summary

Step	-2 Log likelihood	Cox & Snell R Square	Nagelkerke R Square
1	91.662[a]	.366	.490
2	70.883[b]	.485	.649

a. Estimation terminated at iteration number 5 because parameter estimates changed by less than .001.

b. Estimation terminated at iteration number 7 because parameter estimates changed by less than .001.

Output 16. The **Model Summary** table showing various measures of R Square

Output 17 shows the **Hosmer and Lemeshow Test** of the model's goodness-of-fit. The small value of chi-square and high p-value mean that the model fits the data well. Remember that for a good fit, you want a low, insignificant value for chi-square.

Hosmer and Lemeshow Test

Step	Chi-square	df	Sig.
1	3.295	7	.856
2	7.016	8	.535

Output 17. The **Hosmer and Lemeshow Test** of the model's goodness-of-fit

This table is followed by a **Contingency Table for Hosmer and Lemeshow Test** (not shown here). Next is the Classification Table (Output 18). When the full model is applied, the success rate increases from 56% to 81%, which is an enormous improvement on the 'intercept only' predictions.

Classification Table [a]

			Predicted		
			Blood Condition		Percentage
	Observed		No	Yes	Correct
Step 1	Blood Condition	No	44	12	78.6
		Yes	10	34	77.3
	Overall Percentage				78.0
Step 2	Blood Condition	No	45	11	80.4
		Yes	8	36	81.8
	Overall Percentage				81.0

a. The cut value is .500

Output 18. The **Classification Table** showing that after Step 2, the success rate for predicting the premorbid blood is 84%

Output 19 tabulates which variables are included in the regression equation together and the order in which they were included.

Smoking is the first variable included at Step 1. Alcohol is added at Step 2

Variables in the Equation

		B	S.E.	Wald	df	Sig.	Exp(B)
Step 1a	Smoking	.694	.135	26.496	1	.000	2.001
	Constant	-3.379	.691	23.884	1	.000	.034
Step 2b	Smoking	1.361	.344	15.646	1	.000	3.899
	Alcohol	-.540	.175	9.486	1	.002	.583
	Constant	-.689	.919	.563	1	.453	.502

a. Variable(s) entered on step 1: Smoking.

b. Variable(s) entered on step 2: Alcohol.

Output 19. The table of variables added at each step

Testing the individual components of the model

Output 20 shows the increases in the **log likelihood** statistic as the variables *Smoking* and then *Alcohol* are removed from the model. It is clear that each would have a significant effect if they were to be removed. Note that the interaction *Alcohol*Smoking* is not included since this interaction was never included in the model.

Model if Term Removed

Variable		Model Log Likelihood	Change in -2 Log Likelihood	df	Sig. of the Change
Step 1	Smoking	-68.593	45.524	1	.000
Step 2	Smoking	-66.824	62.765	1	.000
	Alcohol	-45.831	20.778	1	.000

Output 20. Tests of the significance of the model's individual components

The remaining table (Output 21) shows which variables were not included in the regression equation at each Step. Notice that the interaction *Alcohol by Smoking* was never included.

Variables not in the Equation

			Score	df	Sig.
Step 1	Variables	Alcohol	14.232	1	.000
		Alcohol by Smoking	10.102	1	.001
	Overall Statistics		15.711	2	.000
Step 2	Variables	Alcohol by Smoking	.004	1	.952
	Overall Statistics		.004	1	.952

> **Alcohol** and **Alcohol*Smoking** are not entered at Step 1

> **Alcohol*Smoking** is not entered at Step 2 either

Output 21. The table of variables not included in the regression equation at each Step

On the basis of this binary logistic regression, we can conclude that smoking and alcohol consumption both independently increase the incidence of the premorbid blood condition and that 81% of the premorbid conditions (*Yes* or *No*) could have been predicted using the equation of the model.

14.3.8 Binary logistic regression with categorical independent variables

Neither binary nor multinomial regression has any problems with categorical independent variables: in fact, all the independent variables can be qualitative, as the following example will illustrate.

In Chapter 13, we described an experiment on gender and professed helpfulness, in which participants were asked by a male or female interviewer whether they would be prepared to help in a certain situation. The results are reproduced in Table 2.

Table 2. Three-way contingency table showing the results of the Gender and professed helpfulness experiment

Incidence of helping by male and female participants with male and female interviewers

Count

Sex of Interviewer			Would you help?		Total
			Yes	No	
Male	Sex of Participant	Male	4	21	25
		Female	16	9	25
	Total		20	30	50
Female	Sex of Participant	Male	11	14	25
		Female	11	14	25
	Total		22	28	50

In Chapter 13, we saw that a **loglinear analysis** of these data confirmed the presence of a three-way interaction of all three dimensions of the contingency table: *Sex of Participant*; *Sex of Interviewer* and *Would you help?* The same research question can also be approached by using binary logistic regression.   Since the purpose of the present analysis is to test the components of the model of significance, we shall not concern ourselves with the accuracy with which the final model predicts whether help will be given. For present purposes, we are only interested in the tests for the significance of the various factors.

With the file *Ch13 Helping* in the **Data Editor**, proceed as follows.

- Choose

    Analyze➜Regression➜Binary Logistic …

    to open the **Logistic Regression** dialog box (the completed box is shown in Figure 8).

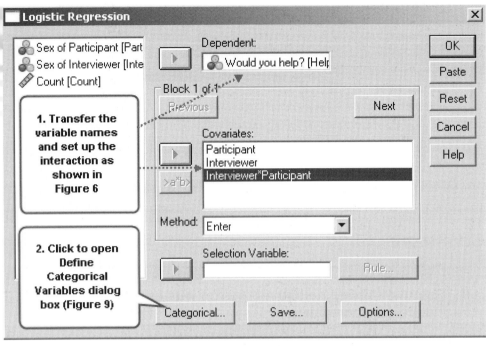

Figure 8. The **Logistic Regression** dialog box

- Transfer the dependent variable name *Would you help?* to the **Dependent** box, and the independent variables (covariates) *Sex of Participant* and *Sex of Interviewer* to the **Covariate** box. Use the **Ctrl** key to select both variables and press the interaction button >a*b> to transfer the *Interviewer×Participant* interaction to the **Covariates** box.
- Click the arrow on the right of the **Method** box and select **Forward: LR**.
- Click the **Categorical...** button to obtain the **Define Categorical Variables** dialog box (see Figure 9). Transfer the names *Participant* and *Interviewer* to the **Categorical Covariates:** box. The default type of **Contrast** is **Indicator**, which registers the presence or absence of the target category. Click **Continue** to return to the **Logistic Regression** dialog box, where you will now see the variable names marked with **(Indicator).**
- Select **Iteration history** from the options (see Figure 7 in the previous example). Click **Continue** to return to the **Logistic Regression** dialog box.
- Click **OK** to run the regression.

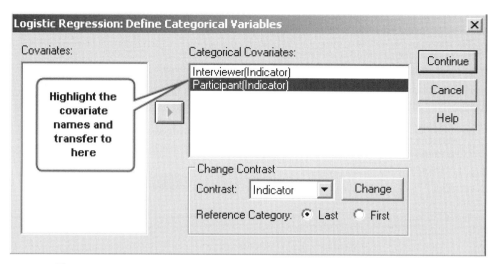

Figure 9. The completed dialog box for **Define Categorical Variables**

14.3.9   Output of binary logistic regression with categorical independent variables

The **Iteration History** table (Output 22) in **Block 1: Forward Stepwise (Likelihood Ratio)** shows that only the *Interviewer × Participant* interaction was entered in the model and that the values converged after just four iterations.

Iteration History[a,b,c,d]

Iteration		-2 Log likelihood	Coefficients	
			Constant	Interviewer(1) by Participant(1)
Step 1	1	126.262	-.027	1.387
	2	125.945	-.027	1.659
	3	125.942	-.027	1.685
	4	125.942	-.027	1.685

a. Method: Forward Stepwise (Likelihood Ratio)

b. Constant is included in the model.

c. Initial -2 Log Likelihood: 136.058

d. Estimation terminated at iteration number 4 because parameter estimates changed by less than .001.

Output 22. The **Iteration History** showing that only the *Interviewer × Participant* interaction was entered in the model

The **Classification Table** (Output 23) shows that the model predicted 59% of the results correctly using only the *Interviewer × Participant* interaction.

Classification Table [a]

			Predicted		
			Would you help?		Percentage
	Observed		Yes	No	Correct
Step 1	Would you help?	Yes	38	4	90.5
		No	37	21	36.2
	Overall Percentage				59.0

a. The cut value is .500

Output 23. The Classification Table showing a 59% success rate for predicting whether someone would help

The **Model if Term Removed** table (Output 24) shows that if the interaction were to be removed, it would have a significant effect on the model. The Table of **Variables not in the Equation** (not shown here) shows that the variables *Interviewer* and *Participant* were not entered into the model.

Model if Term Removed

Variable		Model Log Likelihood	Change in -2 Log Likelihood	df	Sig. of the Change
Step 1	Interviewer * Participant	-68.029	10.116	1	.001

Output 24. Only the Sex of Interviewer × Sex of Participant interaction is significant

This binary logistic regression, therefore, confirms the interaction that was explored in Chapter 13 with **loglinear analysis**, namely that there is a tendency for both males and females to be more helpful when the interviewer is of the opposite sex.

14.4 MULTINOMIAL LOGISTIC REGRESSION

14.4.1 Introduction

In Section 14.2, **discriminant analysis** was used to predict the university subject chosen by students on the basis of several independent variables. In Section 14.3, we introduced you to **logistic regression** which has fewer assumptions than **discriminant analysis**. SPSS's **binary logistic regression** can only be used for predicting a two-category dependent variable. If there are more than two categories, we must use **multinomial logistic regression**. The purpose of the following exercise is to see whether **multinomial logistic regression** can predict choice of Subject at University with the same level of accuracy as can **discriminant analysis**. In multinomial logistic regression, the independent variables can be either **factors** or **covariates**. In general, factors should be categorical variables (e.g. *Sex of Student*) and covariates should be continuous variables (as are all the remaining variables in our example).

14.4.2   Running multinomial logistic regression

To run the multinomial logistic regression procedure with the choice of subject data, choose:
*   **Analyze➜Regression➜Multinomial Logistic…**
    to open the **Multinomial Logistic Regression** dialog box (Figure 10).
*   Transfer *StudySubject* to the **Dependent** box, *Sex of Student* to the **Factor(s)** box and the remaining quantitative independent variables into the **Covariate(s)** box.

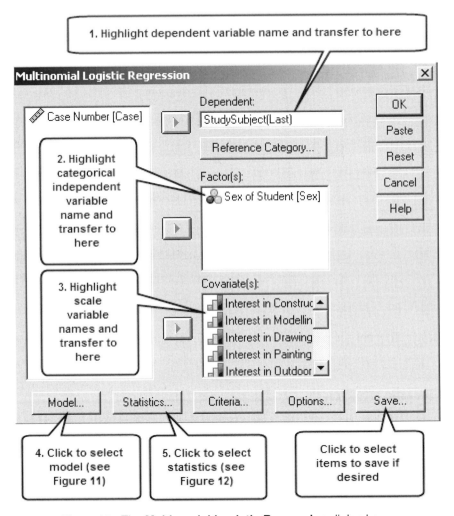

Figure 10. The **Multinomial Logistic Regression** dialog box

*   Click **Model…** at the bottom of the **Multinomial Logistic Regression** dialog box to open the **Model** dialog box (Figure 11). Activate the **Custom/Stepwise** radio button, transfer the variables to the **Stepwise Terms:** panel and choose **Forward entry** as the **Stepwise Method**. Click the downward arrow to the left of the **Stepwise Terms** box and select **Main effects** instead of **Interaction**. Click **Continue** to return to the main dialog box.

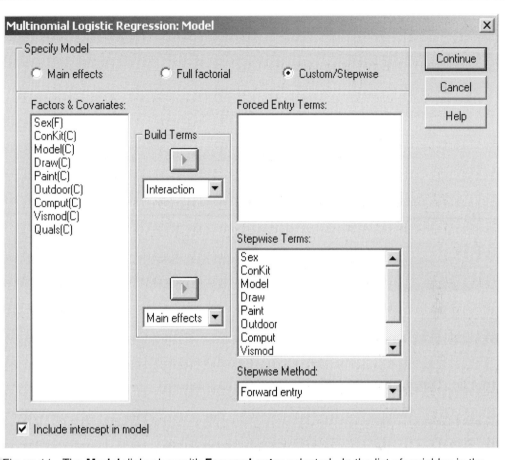

Figure 11. The **Model** dialog box with **Forward entry** selected. In the list of variables in the left panel, the letters C and F denote covariate and factor, respectively.

- Click **Statistics** to see a dialog box labelled **Multinomial Logistic Regression: Statistics**. Check the boxes as in Figure 12.
- Click **Continue** to return to the **Multinomial Logistic Regression** dialog box.
- Click **OK** to run the multinomial logistic regression.

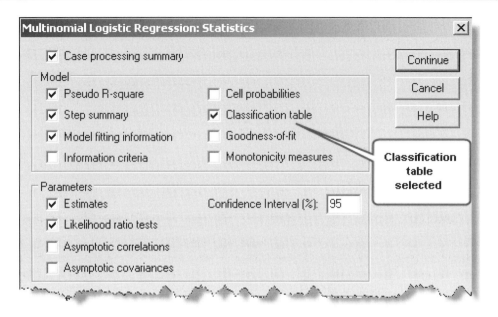

Figure 12. The upper part of the **Statistics** dialog box with **Classification table** selected in addition to those already highlighted when the dialog box is opened

14.4.3   Output of multinomial logistic regression

The output consists of several tables. First there is a **Case Summary Table** (not shown here) listing the levels of the dependent variable (*Study Subject*) and the numbers of each, and also the levels of the factor *Sex* and the numbers of males and females.

Next there is a **Step Summary** table (Output 25) showing which covariates were entered and in which order. Note that the variables *Drawing* and *Model Kit* were never entered, the same two that were omitted from the **discriminant analysis** model.

Step Summary

Model	Action	Effect(s)	-2 Log Likelihood	Chi-Square	df	Sig.
0	Entered	Intercept	235.548			
1	Entered	Sex	208.820	26.727	2	.000
2	Entered	Painting	191.144	17.677	2	.000
3	Entered	Quals	171.760	19.384	2	.000
4	Entered	VisModel	159.182	12.578	2	.002
5	Entered	Computing	146.761	12.422	2	.002
6	Entered	Outdoor	140.055	6.705	2	.035
7	Entered	ConKit	133.221	6.834	2	.033

Stepwise Method: Forward Entry

Output 25. The **Step Summary** table showing which IVs were entered in the model

Finally after several other tables not shown here, there is the **Classification** table (Output 26) showing that 72.2% of the cases were correctly predicted using the final model.

Classification

Observed	Predicted			
	Architect	Psychologist	Engineer	Percent Correct
Architect	20	2	8	66.7%
Psychologist	2	28	7	75.7%
Engineer	5	6	30	73.2%
Overall Percentage	25.0%	33.3%	41.7%	72.2%

Output 26. Predictions of category membership by multinomial logistic regression

Recall that a level of 72.2% accuracy of category assignment was also achieved by using **discriminant analysis** but the numbers correctly predicted for the three Study Subjects differed slightly. **Multinomial logistic regression** has been more successful at predicting Psychologists and slightly less successful at predicting Architects. Engineers differ by just one case.

Although the general level of accuracy of assignment is the same with the two procedures, you will find, if you use the **Save** button to obtain the assignments by both techniques in **Data View**, that there is some disagreement between the category assignments by the two procedures in individual cases.

14.5 A FINAL WORD

The use of logistic regression encounters many of the problems of interpretation that arise with multiple regression. In particular, when independent variables are correlated, there is always doubt about which makes the greatest contribution to the dependent variable. The design of any multiple regression project and the interpretation of the output require a *causal* model: a *statistical* model is insufficient.

Recommended reading

Howell (2007) and Todman & Dugard (2006) have lively and helpful chapters on logistic regression. Tabachnick & Fidell (2007) go into the technicalities in most detail. We suggest you might begin with David Howell's chapter, which sets the scene very nicely.

Howell, D. (2007). *Statistical methods for psychology (6th ed.).* Belmont, CA: Thomson/Wadsworth.

Tabachnick, B. G., & Fidell, L. S. (2007). *Using multivariate statistics (5th ed.)* Boston: Allyn & Bacon (Pearson International Edition).

Todman, J., & Dugard, P. (2006). *Approaching multivariate analysis: An introduction for psychology.* London: Psychology Press.

Appendix

The data for logistic regression

Blood	Smoke	Alcohol	Blood	Smoke	Alcohol	Blood	Smoke	Alcohol
Yes	8	17	No	5	14	No	3	13
Yes	8	15	Yes	5	9	No	2	14
Yes	8	16	No	5	12	No	2	13
Yes	8	16	Yes	5	10	No	2	12
Yes	8	15	Yes	5	10	No	2	12
Yes	8	18	Yes	5	11	No	2	9
Yes	8	15	Yes	5	12	No	2	5
No	8	15	No	5	11	Yes	2	5
Yes	8	17	Yes	5	5	No	2	14
Yes	8	17	No	5	14	No	2	13
No	8	16	No	5	10	No	2	12
Yes	8	3	Yes	5	10	No	1	14
Yes	7	15	No	4	10	No	1	13
No	7	14	Yes	4	10	No	1	4
Yes	7	3	No	4	10	No	1	3
Yes	7	15	No	4	9	No	1	14
No	7	14	Yes	4	9	No	1	13
Yes	7	3	Yes	4	9	No	1	12
Yes	7	15	Yes	4	9	No	1	12
Yes	7	3	Yes	4	9	No	1	11
No	7	14	No	4	14	No	1	12
Yes	7	1	Yes	4	8	No	1	13
No	7	14	No	4	12	No	0	13
Yes	7	13	No	4	12	No	0	12
Yes	7	13	No	4	13	No	0	2
Yes	7	18	No	4	8	No	0	14
Yes	7	15	No	4	12	No	0	12
Yes	7	2	Yes	4	7	No	0	13
Yes	6	13	No	4	13	No	0	12
Yes	6	2	Yes	4	8	No	0	10
Yes	6	10	No	4	13	No	0	12
Yes	6	2	Yes	3	6	No	0	8
Yes	6	3	No	3	12			
No	6	13	No	3	5			

EXERCISE 23

Predicting category membership: Discriminant analysis and binary logistic regression

Before you start

Before proceeding with this practical, please read Chapter 14.

Prediction of reading success at the school-leaving stage

Just before they leave school, students in the most senior class of a school are regularly tested on their comprehension of a difficult reading passage. Typically, only 50% of students can perform the task. We shall also suppose that, for a substantial number of past pupils, we have available data not only on their performance on the comprehension passage but also on the very same variables that were investigated in the exercise on multiple regression, namely, the reading-related measures that we have referred to in Table 1 below as *Logo*, *Syntax* and *Vocal*, all of which were taken in the very earliest stages of the children's education.

The full data set is given in the appendix of this Exercise. As with the multiple regression example, we hope that the data have already been stored for you in a file with a name such as **discrim**, the contents of which you can access by using the **Open** procedure. The data (*Ex23 Reading data for discriminant analysis*) are also available from WWW in the website

http://www.abdn.ac.uk/psychology/materials/spss.shtml

Table 1 shows the first and the last two lines of the data set.

<table>
<tr><td colspan="4">Table 1. Part of the data set</td></tr>
<tr><td>Logo</td><td>Syntax</td><td>Vocal</td><td>Comprehension</td></tr>
<tr><td>10</td><td>20</td><td>64</td><td>1</td></tr>
<tr><td>28</td><td>28</td><td>58</td><td>1</td></tr>
<tr><td>...</td><td>...</td><td>...</td><td>...</td></tr>
<tr><td>82</td><td>69</td><td>60</td><td>2</td></tr>
<tr><td>51</td><td>48</td><td>52</td><td>2</td></tr>
</table>

The rightmost variable is a coding variable whose values, *1* and *2*, denote, respectively, *failure* and *success* on the comprehension task.

Exploring the data set

Before moving on to the main analysis, a preliminary exploration of the data will bring out at least some of their important features. For example, if a particular variable is going to be useful in assigning individuals to categories, one might expect that, if its scores are subdivided by category membership, there should be a substantial difference between the group means. If there is no difference, the variable will probably play a minimal role in the final discriminant function. To investigate these differences, **one-way ANOVAs** can be used to compare the group means on the various independent variables. These tests, however, are requested by options in the **Discriminant** procedure. We shall therefore return to the descriptive statistics when we come to prepare the dialog box.

Since discriminant analysis assumes that the distribution of the independent variables is multivariate normal, we shall also need to look at their distributions. Here we suggest you check for extreme scores and outliers by using the **Explore** command (see Section 14.2.2) to examine the distributions of the variables.

In the **Explore** dialog box, transfer the variable names of all the predictors *Logo*, *Syntax* & *Vocal* into the **Dependent List** box. Transfer the variable name *Comprehension* into the **Factor List** box, and the variable name *Case Number* into the **Label Cases by** box. Click the **Plots** radio button in the **Display** options. Click **Plots...** and click off the check box for **Stem-and-leaf**. Click **Continue** and then **OK** to plot three sets of boxplots

- **Do the boxplots reveal any extreme cases or outliers? Are the distributions relatively normal?**

DISCRIMINANT ANALYSIS

Procedure for discriminant analysis

Run the discriminant analysis as described in Section 14.2.3. There, however, we recommended the **Stepwise** method of minimisation of **Wilks' Lambda**. In the present example, because of its simplicity, it is better to use the default method known as **Enter**, in which all the variables are entered simultaneously. Since **Enter** is the default method, there is no need to specify it. In the **Discriminant Analysis** dialog box, click **Statistics** to open the **Discriminant Analysis: Statistics** dialog box. Select **Univariate ANOVAs** and click **Continue**. In the **Discriminant Analysis** dialog box, click **Classify** to open the **Discriminant Analysis: Classification** dialog box and (in **Display**) select **Summary table**. Click **Continue**, then **OK**.

Output for discriminant analysis

The main features of the output for a discriminant analysis are explained in Section 14.2.4, which you should review. In the present example, the table labelled Group Statistics shows the number of cases in each of the categories of the variable *Comp*. The next table, headed Tests of Equality of Group Means lists **Wilks' Lambda** and **F-ratios** (with their associated p-values in the column **Sig.**) for the comparisons between the groups on each of the three independent variables.

- **Which variables have significant F ratios and which do not?**

There now follows the first of the tables labelled **Eigenvalues**, which show the output of the discriminant analysis proper. Because there are only two groups, there is only one function. The next table, **Wilks' Lambda**, tabulates the statistic **lambda**, its **chi-square value** and the associated p-value **(Sig.)**. You will notice immediately that the value of lambda is smaller than the value for any of the three IVs considered separately. That is well and good: the discriminant function *D*, which uses the information in all the IVs should do a better job than any one IV alone. Here there is an obvious parallel with multiple regression, in which the predictive ability of the multiple regression equation cannot (provided there is no multicollinearity) be less than the simple regressions of the target variable on any one predictor alone. In the case of the variable *Vocal*, however, the improvement is negligible. Since, however, two of the IVs can each discriminate reliably between the groups, the result of the chi-square test of lambda in the discriminant analysis table is a foregone conclusion. As expected, the p-value is very small. The discriminant function D can indeed discriminate reliably between the two groups on the basis of performance on the independent variables.

Ignore the table labelled Standardized Canonical Discriminant Function Coefficients. A more useful table is the next one, labelled **Structure Matrix**, which lists the pooled-within-groups correlations between discriminating variables and the standardized canonical discriminant function.

- **Are the correlations as you expected?**

Ignore the table Functions at Group Centroids.

The next set of tables relate to the classification of cases. We have shown that the discriminant function D discriminates between the two groups; but how effectively does it do this? This is shown under the heading: 'Classification Results'.

- **Write down the percentage of grouped cases correctly classified, the percentage of correct group 1 (failure) predictions and the percentage of correct group 2 (success) predictions.**

Now try out the discriminant function on some fresh data by adding them at the end of the data file (e.g. enter in the columns for *Logo, Syntax, Vocal*, the values 50, 50, 50; 10, 10, 10; 80, 80, 80 and any others you wish). Leave the column blank for *Compreh*. Then re-run the analysis after selecting **Save** in the **Discriminant Analysis** dialog box, clicking the radio button for **Predicted group membership**, and then clicking **Continue** and **OK**. The predicted memberships will appear in the variable called **dis_1** in the **Data Editor**.

- **Would someone with Logo, Syntax and Vocal scores of 50, 50, 50 respectively be expected to pass or fail the comprehension test?**

Conclusion

This Exercise is intended to be an introduction to the use of a complex and sophisticated statistical technique. Accordingly, we chose an example of the simplest possible application, in which the dependent variable comprises only two categories. The simplicity of our interpretation of a number of statistics such as **Wilks' lambda** breaks down when there are more than two categories in the dependent variable. For a treatment of such cases, see Tabachnick & Fidell (2007).

BINARY LOGISTIC REGRESSION

Procedure for binary logistic regression

We shall use the same data set for binary logistic regression as we used for discriminant analysis at the start of this Exercise. Use the procedure described in Section 14.3.6 except for **Method** that should be left at the default method **Enter**. Do not bother entering the interactions among the variables.

Output for binary logistic regression

The main features of the output for binary logistic regression are explained in Section 14.3.7, which you should review.

Examine the tables in Block 1.

- **What is the value of R^2 as calculated by the Nagelkerke formula? What is the meaning of this value?**

- **What is the value of chi-square for the Hosmer and Lemeshow test and is it significant? What do you conclude about the fit of the model?**

- **What is the overall percentage of correct predictions? How does this compare with the success rate of the discriminant analysis?**

Conclusion

In this example, the results of the **discriminant analysis** and **binary logistic regression** are similar but where there are several binary predictors, logistic regression would be the preferred analysis.

Appendix to Exercise 23 – The data

L is Logo; S is Syntax; V is Vocal; C is Comprehension

L	S	V	C	L	S	V	C	L	S	V	C	L	S	V	C
10	20	64	1	49	59	46	1	41	55	41	2	49	72	72	2
28	28	58	1	39	42	31	1	30	54	20	2	66	61	40	2
55	25	42	1	26	56	78	1	29	67	18	2	84	50	46	2
30	20	30	1	40	31	51	1	28	68	72	2	70	54	51	2
32	27	42	1	34	60	45	1	46	67	80	2	65	64	23	2
25	49	81	1	31	66	50	1	56	44	52	2	69	60	57	2
40	38	43	1	18	61	22	1	69	46	59	2	66	79	50	2
71	22	79	1	43	50	31	1	53	57	52	2	58	82	13	2
19	59	71	1	48	45	44	1	75	48	34	2	45	90	59	2
55	32	75	1	14	77	53	1	71	52	30	2	82	58	65	2
45	45	29	1	64	32	55	1	50	68	75	2	82	69	60	2
62	30	26	1	55	48	9	1	81	54	41	2	51	48	52	2
20	69	78	1					51	62	14	2				

CHAPTER 15

Latent variables: exploratory factor analysis & canonical correlation

15.1   Introduction to factor analysis

15.2   A factor analysis of data on six variables

15.3   Using SPSS syntax

15.4   Canonical correlation

15.5   A final word

15.1   INTRODUCTION TO FACTOR ANALYSIS

15.1.1   What are the 'factors' in factor analysis?

Suppose that some schoolchildren are tested on several variables, perhaps an assortment of school subjects such as foreign languages, music, mathematics, mapwork and so on. The correlations of performance on each test with every other test in the battery can be arranged in a rectangular array known as a **correlation matrix**, or **R-matrix** (Table 1).

Table 1. A correlation matrix (as output by SPSS) showing, in each row or column, the correlations of one test with each of the other tests

Correlation Matrix

		French	German	Latin	Music	Maths	Mapwork
Correlation	French	1.000	.836	.742	.032	.083	.312
	German	.836	1.000	.715	-.081	.008	.118
	Latin	.742	.715	1.000	.022	.222	.131
	Music	.032	-.081	.022	1.000	.713	.783
	Maths	.083	.008	.222	.713	1.000	.735
	Mapwork	.312	.118	.131	.783	.735	1.000

In its basic form, a correlation matrix is **square**, that is, there are as many rows as there are columns. The diagonal of cells running from top left to bottom right is known as the **principal diagonal** of the matrix. The correlations in the off-diagonal cells are the same above and below the principal diagonal (e.g. the correlation of *French* with *German* is the same as that of *German* with *French*). Each row (or column) of the R-matrix contains all the correlations involving one particular test in the battery. Since the variables are labelled in the same order in the rows and columns of the R-matrix, each of the cells along the principal diagonal contains the correlation of one of the variables with itself (i.e. 1). The R-matrix can be the starting point for a variety of multivariate statistical procedures, but in this chapter we shall consider just one technique: **factor analysis.**

The presence in the R-matrix of clusters of sizeable correlations among subsets of the tests in the battery (e.g. *Music* and *Maths*; *French* and *German*) would suggest that the tests in these clusters may be tapping the same underlying intellectual dimension or ability. If the traditional British theories of the psychology of intelligence are correct, there should be fewer (indeed, far fewer) dimensions than there are tests in the battery. The purpose of factor analysis is to identify and to quantify the dimensions supposed to underlie performance on a variety of tasks.

The **factors** produced by factor analysis are mathematical entities, which can be thought of as classificatory axes for plotting the tests as points on a graph. The greater the value of a test's co-ordinate, or **loading**, on a factor, the more important that factor is in accounting for the correlations between that test and the others in the battery. A factor, then, has a geometric interpretation as a classificatory axis in an axial reference system with respect to which the tests in the battery are represented as points in space.

The term **factor** also has an equivalent algebraic, or arithmetical interpretation as a linear function of the observed scores that people achieve on the tests in a battery. If a battery comprises eight tests, and each person tested were also to be assigned a ninth score consisting of the sum of the eight test scores, that ninth (summative) score would be a **factor score**, and it would make sense to speak of correlations between the factor scores and the real test scores. We have seen that the loading of a test on a factor is, geometrically speaking, the co-ordinate of the test point on the factor axis. But that axis also represents a 'factor' in the second, algebraic sense, and the loading is the correlation between the original test scores and those on the factor. In either interpretation, a factor is assumed to represent an underlying or latent variable, in terms of which the correlations in R are 'accounted for', both mathematically and theoretically.

In **exploratory factor analysis**, the aim is to determine the number and nature of the factors necessary to account for the correlations in the R-matrix. It is hoped that the correlations among the observed variables can be accounted for in terms of comparatively few factors. In **confirmatory factor analysis**, on the other hand, the aim is to test pre-formulated factor analytic **models** of the data. At present, SPSS offers exploratory factor analysis only.

15.1.2   Stages in an exploratory factor analysis

An exploratory factor analysis usually takes place in three stages:
1.   A **matrix of correlation coefficients** is generated for all possible pairings of the variables (i.e. the tests).
2.   From the correlation matrix, **factors** are **extracted.** The most common method of extraction is called **principal factors** or principal **components**.

3.　To make the pattern of loadings easier to interpret, the factors (axes) are **rotated** to maximise the loadings of the variables on some of the factors and reduce them on others – in other words, to achieve **simple structure**. The most commonly used method of rotation is **varimax**, which maintains independence among the mathematical factors. Geometrically, this means that during rotation, the axes remain **orthogonal** (i.e. they are kept at right angles). Other methods of rotation allow the factors to correlate, so that the axes are not kept at right angles.

Participants' scores on each of the factors emerging from the analysis can be calculated. It should be stressed that these **factor scores** are not the results of any actual test taken by the participants: they are scores on aggregates of the observed variables. Factor scores, nevertheless, can be used as representative variables for input into subsequent analyses.

Before you proceed with a factor analysis, it is advisable to obtain and inspect the **R-matrix** first. Since the purpose of factor analysis is to account for associations among the tests, the exercise is pointless if no associations exist. By convention, all variables should show at least one correlation of the order of .3 before it is worth proceeding with a full factor analysis. Should any variables show no substantial correlation with any of the others, they should be removed from R in subsequent analysis. It is also advisable to check that the correlation matrix does not possess the highly undesirable properties of **multicollinearity** and **singularity**. The former arises when variables are very highly correlated, which can arise when two tests are measuring essentially the same thing. Singularity, the extreme case of multicollinearity, arises if some of the variables are exact linear functions of others in the battery. Should the matrix show multicollinearity or singularity, some of the variables must be omitted from the analysis; otherwise a factor analysis cannot be run.

15.1.3　The extraction of factors

The factors (or axes) in a factor analysis are **extracted** (or, pursuing the geometric analogy, **constructed**) one at a time. The process is repeated with the residual data set until it is possible, from the loadings of the tests on the factors so far extracted, to generate good approximations to the correlations in the original **R matrix**. Factor analysis tells us how many factors (or axes) are necessary to achieve a reconstruction of R that is sufficiently good to account satisfactorily for the correlations that R contains.

15.1.4　The rationale of rotation

We can think of the tests in the battery and the origin of the axis (factor) set as stationary points and rotate the axes around the origin. We can do this because, although rotation will cause the values of all loadings to change, the new set of loadings on the axes, *whatever the new position of the latter*, can still be used to produce exactly the same estimates of the correlations in the R-matrix. In this sense, the position of the axes is arbitrary: the factor matrix (or **F-matrix**) only tells us *how many* axes are necessary to classify the data adequately: it does not thereby establish that the initial position of the axes is the appropriate one.

In **rotation**, the factor axes are rotated around the fixed origin until the loadings meet certain sets of criteria. The set of loadings that meets the criteria is known as the **rotated factor matrix**. The purpose of rotation is to arrive at a factor matrix with a pattern of loadings that is easier to interpret than the original factor matrix. More technically, the aim is to achieve a configuration of loadings with a rather elusive quality known as **simple structure**, which means that most tests are loaded on a minimum number of factors. The fewer the factors that are involved in accounting for the correlations among a group of tests, the easier it is to invest those factors with meaning. Simple structure is actually an ideal never achieved in practice, because the concept, in its original form, is somewhat ambiguous. Modern computing packages such as SPSS offer a selection of rotation methods, each based upon a different (but reasonable) interpretation of simple structure.

15.1.5   Confirmatory factor analysis and structural equation modelling

So far, we have considered the use of factor analysis to ascertain the minimum number of classificatory variables (or axes) we need to account for the shared variance among a battery of tests. While the researcher will almost certainly have expectations about how many factors are likely to emerge (indeed, these expectations will determine the selection of the tests in the battery), the process of factor extraction proceeds automatically until a criterion for termination is reached. In several fields, such as human abilities and intelligence, 'factor invariance' has been found: those factors accounting for the greatest amounts of variance, such as the general intelligence (*g*) factor and the major group factors, have emerged again and again in analyses with different data sets.

There are, nevertheless, some problems and issues with factor analysis. Some aspects of factor structure, such as the prevalence of a general factor as opposed to group factors, depend very much upon the composition of the test battery. Even when the same battery of tests has been used in different projects, the precise number of factors extracted has been found to vary from study to study. Moreover, the pattern shown by the loadings in the final rotated factor matrix depends upon the method of rotation used: some methods (such as **varimax**) keep the factor axes at right angles; but others (such as **quartimax**) allow **oblique** (correlated) factors. There has been much argument about which method of rotation is best, and the preferred method tends to reflect the theoretical views of the user. In the circumstances, traditional factor analytic methods seem ill-suited to the testing of specific hypotheses, and many hold the view that they are appropriate only in the early, exploratory stages of research.

The methods we have been describing are known as **exploratory factor analysis**. In **confirmatory factor analysis**, the user hypothesises that there should be a predetermined number of factors, on which the tests in the battery should show specified patterns of loadings. Such a model can then be put to the test by gathering data. Recent years have seen dramatic developments in what is known as **structural equation modelling** (for example, see Tabachnick & Fidell, 2007, Chapter 14) of which confirmatory factor analysis is just one aspect.

15.1.6   More technical terms

To understand the SPSS output, you must have at least an intuitive grasp of some factor analytic terminology.

- The **loading** of a test on a factor is the correlation between the test and the factor.
- The **communality** of a test is the total proportion of its variance that is accounted for by the extracted factors. The communality is the **squared multiple correlation R^2** between the test and the factors emerging from the factor analysis. If the factors are independent (as they will be in the example we shall consider), the communality is given by the sum of

the squares of the loadings of the test on the extracted factors. The communality of a test is a measure of its reliability.

- The **eigenvalue** (or **latent root**) of a factor is the total variance accounted for by the factor and has a theoretical upper limit of 1. If the eigenvalue of a factor is divided by the number of tests in the battery, the quotient is the **proportion of the total test variance** that is accounted for by the factor. The first factor extracted has the largest eigenvalue, the second the next largest eigenvalue, and so on. The process of extraction continues until the factors extracted account for negligible proportions of the total variance.
- If the eigenvalues of successive factors are plotted against the ordinal numbers of the factors, the curve eventually flattens out and its appearance thereafter has been likened to the rubble or scree on a mountainside. The eigenvalue plot is therefore known as a **scree plot** (see Figure 6). There is general agreement that the factorial litter begins when the eigenvalues fall below one.
- The process of **rotation** changes the eigenvalues of the factors that have been extracted, so that the common factor variance accounted for by the extraction is more evenly distributed among the rotated factors. The communalities, on the other hand, are unchanged by rotation, because they depend only upon the number of factors and the correlations among the tests.

15.2 A FACTOR ANALYSIS OF DATA ON SIX VARIABLES

Suppose a researcher has available the marks of 10 children on six tests: *French, German, Latin, Music, Mathematics* and *Mapwork* as shown in Table 2. In order to identify the psychological dimensions tapped by these six tests, it is decided to carry out a factor analysis.

Table 2. Marks of 10 children in six examinations						
Case	**French**	**German**	**Latin**	**Music**	**Maths**	**Mapwork**
1	56	66	53	47	50	48
2	46	48	43	53	69	55
3	56	51	43	40	49	45
4	29	42	39	53	56	48
5	71	67	84	66	67	60
6	56	47	58	59	67	74
7	62	69	48	59	58	66
8	46	42	38	46	38	42
9	66	73	85	34	49	42
10	36	42	48	53	59	48

15.2.1 Entering the data for a factor analysis

Enter the data using the procedures described in Section 2.3. In **Variable View**, name the six variables for the factor analysis. Include an extra variable for the case number. Ensure that there are no decimals by changing the **Decimals** column value to 0. Click the **Data View** tab at the foot of **Variable View** and enter the data in **Data View**.

Note that there are no grouping variables in this data set, because this is a purely correlational study. If a factor is, in any sense, an independent variable, it is one whose existence must be inferred from whatever patterns may exist in the correlation matrix. It is the *raison d'être* of factor analysis to make such an inference credible.

15.2.2 The SPSS factor analysis procedure

To run the factor analysis procedure:
- Choose
  Analyze➜Data Reduction➜Factor... (see Figure 1)
  to open the **Factor Analysis** dialog box (Figure 2).
- Transfer all the variable names except *Case Number* to the **Variables** box.

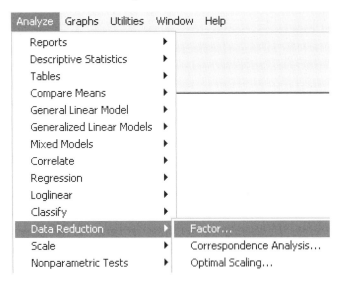

Figure 1. Finding the **Factor** dialog box

Before running the analysis, it is necessary to select some options that regulate the manner in which the analysis takes place and add some useful extra items to the output.
- Click **Descriptives...** to open the **Descriptives** dialog box (Figure 3). Click the following check boxes: **Univariate descriptives**, to tabulate descriptive statistics; **Initial solution**, to display the original communalities, eigenvalues and the percentage of variance explained; **Coefficients**, to tabulate the R-matrix; and **Reproduced**, to obtain an approximation of the R-matrix from the loadings of the factors extracted by the analysis. The **Reproduced** option will also obtain communalities and the residual differences between the observed and reproduced correlations.
- Click **Continue** to return to the **Factor Analysis** dialog box.
- Click **Extraction...** to open the **Extraction** dialog box (Figure 4). Click the **Scree plot** check box. The scree plot is a useful display showing the relative importance of the factors extracted.
- Click **Continue** to return to the **Factor Analysis** dialog box.
- To obtain the rotated F-matrix, click **Rotation...** to obtain the **Rotation** dialog box (Figure 5). In the **Method** box, click the **Varimax** radio button.
- Click **Continue** and then **OK**.

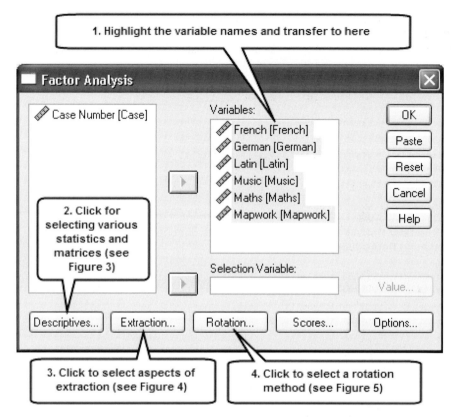

Figure 2. The **Factor Analysis** dialog box

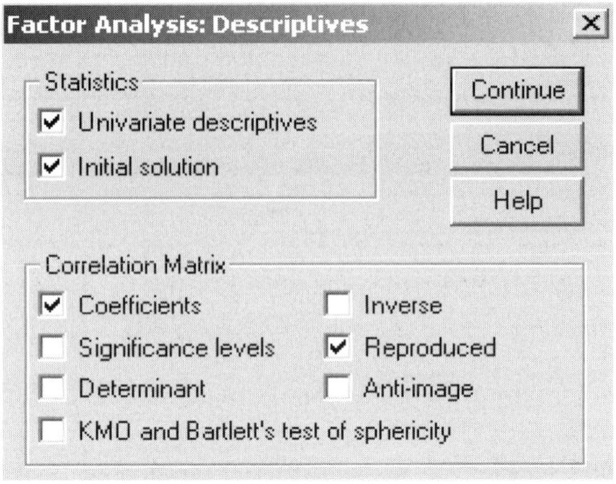

Figure 3. The **Descriptives** dialog box with **Univariate descriptives**, **Initial solution**, **Coefficients** and **Reproduced** selected

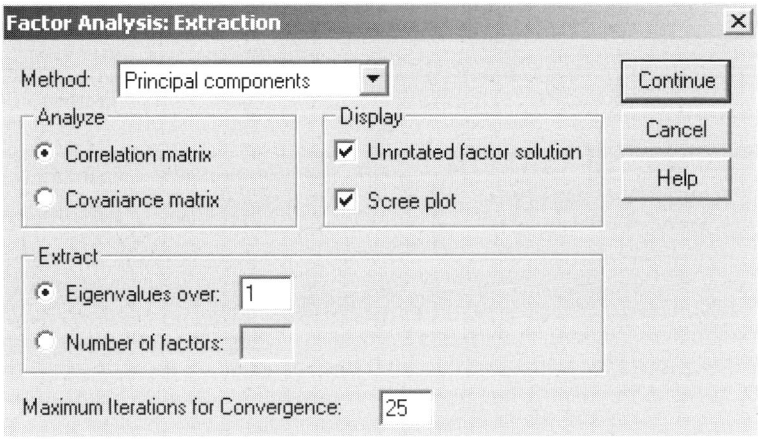

Figure 4. The **Extraction** dialog box with **Scree plot** selected

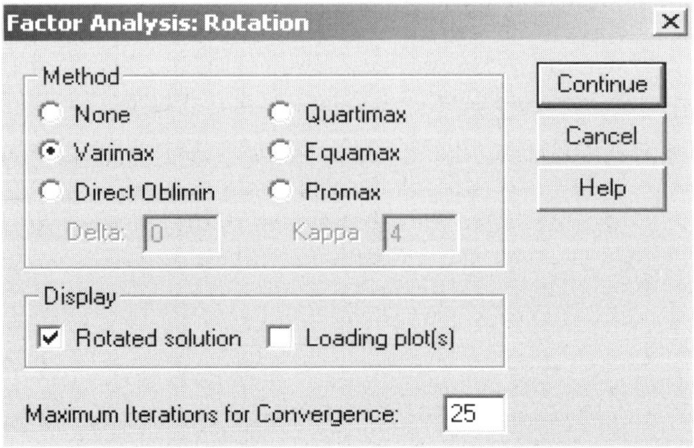

Figure 5. The **Rotation** dialog box with **Varimax** selected

15.2.3 Output for factor analysis

Descriptive statistics

Output 1 shows the specially requested descriptive statistics for the variables.

Descriptive Statistics

	Mean	Std. Deviation	Analysis N
French	52.00	13.167	10
German	55.00	12.561	10
Latin	54.00	17.233	10
Music	51.04	9.524	10
Maths	56.18	9.854	10
Mapwork	52.74	10.854	10

Output 1. Descriptive statistics for the variables

The correlation matrix (R-matrix)

The correlation matrix (edited by adding additional shading) is shown in Output 2.

		French	German	Latin	Music	Maths	Mapwork
Correlation	French	1.000	.836	.742	.032	.083	.312
	German	.836	1.000	.715	-.081	.008	.118
	Latin	.742	.715	1.000	.022	.222	.131
	Music	.032	-.081	.022	1.000	.713	.783
	Maths	.083	.008	.222	.713	1.000	.735
	Mapwork	.312	.118	.131	.783	.735	1.000

Output 2. The correlation matrix (**R-matrix**) with additional shading

Inspection of the correlation matrix in Output 2 reveals that there are two clusters of high correlations among the tests (shaded): one among *French*, *German* and *Latin*, the other among *Music*, *Maths* and *Mapwork*. Another interesting feature is that in either cluster, each test, while correlating highly with the others in the same cluster, shows small, statistically insignificant correlations with tests in the other cluster. This pattern is what we should expect if the two groups of tests are tapping different, uncorrelated abilities.

From inspection of the **R-matrix**, therefore, it would appear that we can account for the pattern of correlations in terms of two independent dimensions of ability. Presently, we shall see whether such an interpretation is confirmed by the results of a formal factor analysis. Are two factors sufficient to account for the correlations among the tests?

Communalities

Output 3 is a table of communalities assigned to the variables by the factor analysis. The communality, as we have seen, is the proportion of the variance of the test that has been accounted for by the factors extracted. For example, we see that 89% of the variance of the scores on *French* is accounted for by the factors.

Communalities

	Initial	Extraction
French	1.000	.888
German	1.000	.870
Latin	1.000	.783
Music	1.000	.852
Maths	1.000	.801
Mapwork	1.000	.862

Extraction Method: Principal Component Analysis.

Output 3. Table of variable communalities

The next table (Output 4) displays information about the factors (SPSS calls them 'components') that have been extracted. Earlier, we saw that an **eigenvalue** is the total test variance accounted for by a particular factor, the total variance for each test being unity.

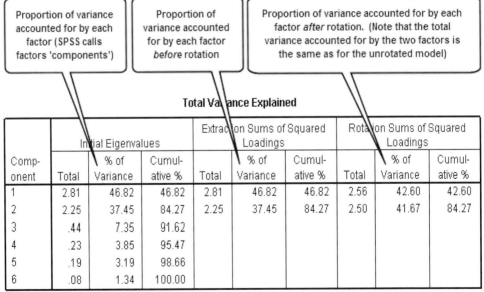

| | Proportion of variance accounted for by each factor (SPSS calls factors 'components') | | Proportion of variance accounted for by each factor *before* rotation | | Proportion of variance accounted for by each factor *after* rotation. (Note that the total variance accounted for by the two factors is the same as for the unrotated model) | |

Total Variance Explained

Comp-onent	Initial Eigenvalues			Extraction Sums of Squared Loadings			Rotation Sums of Squared Loadings		
	Total	% of Variance	Cumul-ative %	Total	% of Variance	Cumul-ative %	Total	% of Variance	Cumul-ative %
1	2.81	46.82	46.82	2.81	46.82	46.82	2.56	42.60	42.60
2	2.25	37.45	84.27	2.25	37.45	84.27	2.50	41.67	84.27
3	.44	7.35	91.62						
4	.23	3.85	95.47						
5	.19	3.19	98.66						
6	.08	1.34	100.00						

Extraction Method: Principal Component Analysis.

Output 4. Edited table of statistics relating to the two components extracted

The first block of three columns, labelled **Initial Eigenvalues**, comprises the eigenvalues and the contributions they make to the total variance. The eigenvalues determine which factors (components) remain in the analysis: following Kaiser's criterion, factors with an eigenvalue of less than 1 (i.e. factors 3-6) are excluded. From the eigenvalues, the proportions of the total test variance accounted for by the factors are readily obtained. For example, the eigenvalue of the first factor is 2.81. Since the total test variance that could possibly be accounted for by a factor is 6, the proportion of the total test variance accounted for by the first factor is 2.81 ÷ 6 = 46.82%, the figure given in the **% of Variance** column. In this analysis, the two factors that meet the Kaiser criterion account for over 84% of the variance (see column labelled **Cumulative %**).

The second block of three columns (**Extraction Sums of Squared Loadings**) repeats the output of the first block for the two factors that have met Kaiser's criterion.

The third block (**Rotation Sums of Squared Loadings**) tabulates the output for the rotated factor solution. Notice that the proportions of variance explained by the two factors are similar in the rotated solution, in contrast with the unrotated solution, in which the first factor accounts for a much greater percentage of the variance. Notice also that the accumulated proportion of variance from the two components is the same for the unrotated and rotated solutions.

Scree plot

Figure 6 shows the **scree plot**, which was specially requested in the **Factor Analysis: Extraction** dialog box. The plot provides a graphic image of the eigenvalue for each component extracted. The amount of variance accounted for (the eigenvalue) by successive components initially plunges sharply as successive factors (components) are extracted.

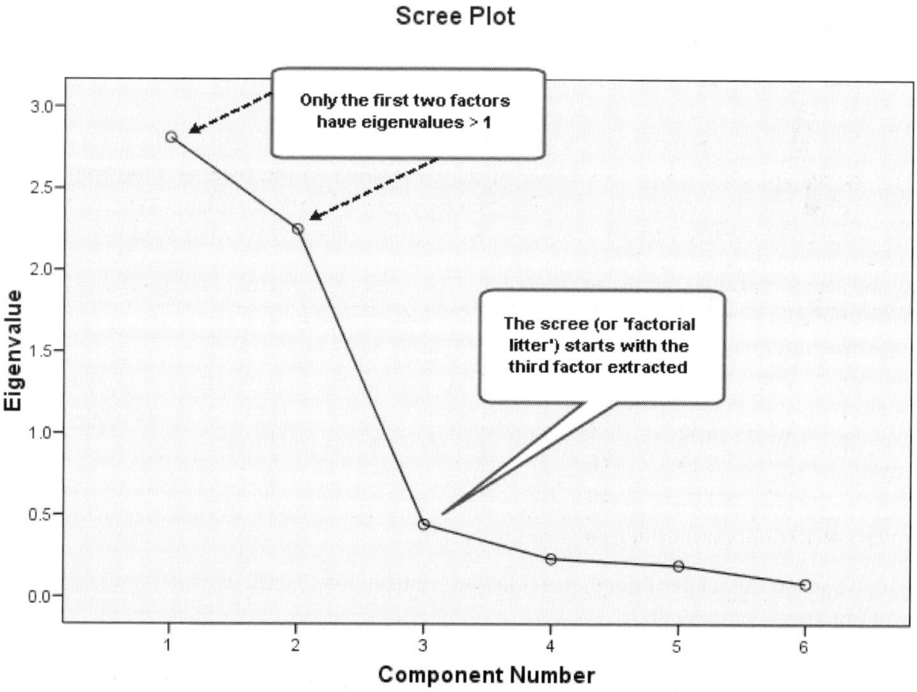

Figure 6. The scree plot

The point of interest is where the curve begins to flatten out. It can be seen that the 'scree' begins to appear between the second and third factors. Notice also that Component 3 has an eigenvalue of less than 1, so only the first two components have been retained.

The component matrix (unrotated factor matrix)

Output 5 shows the component (factor) matrix containing the loadings of the six tests on the two factors extracted.

Component Matrix[a]

	Component	
	1	2
French	.764	-.551
German	.661	-.659
Latin	.714	-.523
Music	.566	.729
Maths	.647	.618
Mapwork	.735	.568

Extraction Method: Principal Component Analysis.

a. 2 components extracted.

Output 5. The component matrix (correlations between the variables and the unrotated components)

When the factors (or 'components') are **orthogonal** (i.e. uncorrelated with each other), the factor loadings are the correlations between the variables and the factors. Thus the higher the absolute value of the loading (which can never exceed a maximum of 1), the greater the proportion of the total variance of the variable that is accounted for by the factor.

It can be seen that the factor analysis has extracted two factors, in agreement with the impression given by the correlation matrix. On the other hand, it is not particularly easy to interpret the unrotated factor matrix. Both groups of tests show substantial loadings on both factors, which is not in accord with the obvious psychological interpretation of the pattern of correlations in the original R-matrix, which seemed to arise from two independent abilities, each required for one of the two clusters of tests with high correlations.

Reproduced correlation matrix and residuals

Output 6 shows the **reproduced correlation matrix** of coefficients, computed from the extracted factors (components).

Each reproduced correlation between two tests is the sum of the products of their loadings on the factors emerging from the analysis. For example, the sum of the products of the loadings of *French* and *German* on the two factors extracted is, from the loadings in the unrotated F-matrix in Output 6, $[(0.764 \times 0.661) + (-0.551 \times -0.659)] = 0.868$, which is the value given for the reproduced correlation between *French* and *German* in Output 6. The diagonal values labelled b are the communalities listed in Output 3. Each communality is the sum of the squares of the loadings of a test on the two factors extracted: so the sum of the squares of the entries in the first row of Output 5 is 0.888, the value given as the communality for French in Output 6. Notice that they are all large – at least 78%.

The residuals are the differences between the actual and reproduced correlations. For example, the original correlation between *French* and *German* was 0.836 (Output 2) and the reproduced correlation is 0.868, so the difference is –0.032, which is the residual shown in the lower half of Output 6. Footnote *a* states the number and proportion of residuals (i.e. the differences) that are greater than 0.05. Over 8 residuals (53%) are greater than 0.05; but none is greater than 0.10.

> If the factor analytic model gives a good account of the data, the reproduced correlations should be close in magnitude to the observed values in Output 2

> The loadings labelled b are the communalities listed in Output 3 (i.e. the proportion of the variance of the test that is accounted for by the two factors extracted in the analysis)

Reproduced Correlations

		French	German	Latin	Music	Maths	Mapwork
Reproduced Correlation	French	.888b	.868	.834	.031	.154	.249
	German	.868	.870b	.816	-.107	.020	.111
	Latin	.834	.816	.783b	.022	.139	.228
	Music	.031	-.107	.022	.852b	.817	.830
	Maths	.154	.020	.139	.817	.801b	.826
	Mapwork	.249	.111	.228	.830	.826	.862b
Residuala	French		-.032	-.092	.002	-.071	.063
	German	-.032		-.101	.025	-.012	.007
	Latin	-.092	-.101		-.001	.083	-.096
	Music	.002	.025	-.001		-.104	-.046
	Maths	-.071	-.012	.083	-.104		-.091
	Mapwork	.063	.007	-.096	-.046	-.091	

Extraction Method: Principal Component Analysis.

a. Residuals are computed between observed and reproduced correlations. There are 8 (53.0%) nonredundant residuals with absolute values greater than 0.05.

b. Reproduced communalities

> The residuals show the differences between the reproduced and the original correlations: the smaller the residuals, the better the fit

Output 6. The reproduced correlation matrix and residuals

The rotated factor (component) matrix

Output 7 shows the rotated factor (component) matrix, which should be compared with the unrotated matrix in Output 5.

The purpose of rotation is not to change the number of components extracted, but to try to arrive at a new position for the axes (components) that is easier to interpret in psychological terms. In fact, the rotated component matrix is much easier to interpret than the unrotated matrix in Output 5. The three language tests now have high loadings on one factor alone (Component 1); whereas *Mapwork, Mathematics* and *Music* have high loadings on the other (Component 2). These factors are uncorrelated. This is quite consistent with what we gleaned from our inspection of the original R-matrix, namely, that the correlations among the six tests in our battery could be accounted for in terms of two independent psychological dimensions of ability.

Rotated Component Matrix [a]

	Component	
	1	2
French	.936	.105
German	.932	-.045
Latin	.880	.092
Music	-.070	.920
Maths	.065	.892
Mapwork	.163	.914

Extraction Method: Principal Component Analysis.
Rotation Method: Varimax with Kaiser Normalization.

[a.] Rotation converged in 3 iterations.

Output 7. The rotated component matrix

15.3 USING SPSS SYNTAX

So far throughout this book, the statistics provided by SPSS have been accessed by exploiting the advantages of the graphics environment that the **Windows** operating system provides. Although this is by far the most painless way of familiarising oneself with SPSS, there is an alternative approach which, for some purposes, has considerable advantages.

It is also possible to run SPSS procedures and analyses by writing instructions in **SPSS syntax**, sometimes referred to as **control language**. The commands are written in a special **syntax window**, either by typing them in from the keyboard or by pasting them in. Commands are then executed by selecting (emboldening) them and pressing the **Run** button (see below).

For many users, SPSS syntax is daunting, to say the least. It is possible to appeal to **SPSS Help** and obtain what is known as a **syntax map**, but at first sight a syntax map seems even more opaque than the written commands themselves. There are, nevertheless, great advantages in learning how to use SPSS syntax, because for some analyses there are more options available than those accessible via dialog boxes. Moreover, the syntax for a particular analysis (even one set up initially from dialog boxes) can be saved as a syntax file and re-used later with great savings in time. If an analysis has been set up from dialog boxes, pressing **Paste** (instead of **OK**) in the final dialog box will paste the hitherto hidden syntax into the **syntax window** from which it can be saved to a file in the usual way.

We believe that the most efficient way of learning SPSS syntax is by working from the dialog boxes in this way, rather than ploughing through the available texts on SPSS syntax, which are better left until one has already acquired a working knowledge of the language.

15.3.1 The use of SPSS syntax: An example

With the children's scores in **Data View**, access the **Factor Analysis** dialog box in the usual way. Make the selections as before, remembering to select the buttons at the bottom of the dialog box to specify the rotation, order a scree test, request a correlation matrix and so on. Now click **Paste**. When this is done, a window with the title **Syntax1 – SPSS Syntax Editor** will appear on the screen. This is the **syntax window**, which will contain the commands written in SPSS syntax that have just been specified by your choices from the dialog boxes (see Figure 7).

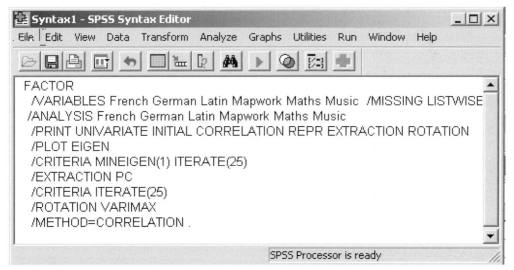

Figure 7. The syntax window and the **FACTOR** command

Some **commands** (the **data commands**) control the entry of data into SPSS. Others select and direct the statistical analysis. *In SPSS syntax, a command always ends with a full stop.* In the statement in the syntax window, there is only one full stop at the very end. This is because there is only a single command: the FACTOR command. The statement, nevertheless, is not a short one. Notice the terms /PLOT EIGEN, /ROTATION VARIMAX and so on. A phrase that begins with / is a **subcommand**. Subcommands are requests for optional extras. They are the written equivalent of pressing those special buttons at the bottom of the original dialog box.

Now select the whole of the written FACTOR command by emboldening the entire contents of the syntax window. Click the **Run** button ▶ in the toolbar above the syntax window. This has the effect of re-running the entire factor analysis. (Alternatively, select **All** from the **Run** menu.) Inspect the contents of the output window to confirm that the output is the same as before.

Saving the contents of a syntax window

To save this syntax file, select
File➔Save
and select a suitable disk drive and/or folder where the file is to be saved. The file will automatically be saved with an **.sps** extension to show that it is a syntax file (see Figure 8).

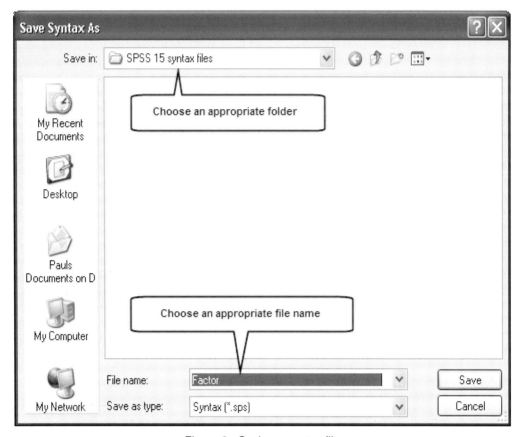

Figure 8. Saving a syntax file

Running SPSS routines from a syntax file

After opening a saved data file or entering new data into **Data View**, it is a very simple matter to run a routine from a saved syntax file.
• Select
  File➔Open➔Syntax...
  to open the **Open File** dialog box (Figure 9).
• It may be necessary to change the folder specified in **Look in** so that the required folder appears in the slot.
• Select the appropriate file name (here it is *Factor*).
• Click **Open** to open the syntax file factor in the **SPSS Syntax Editor** window.

- Now, you need only embolden the command in the window and click the **Run** button 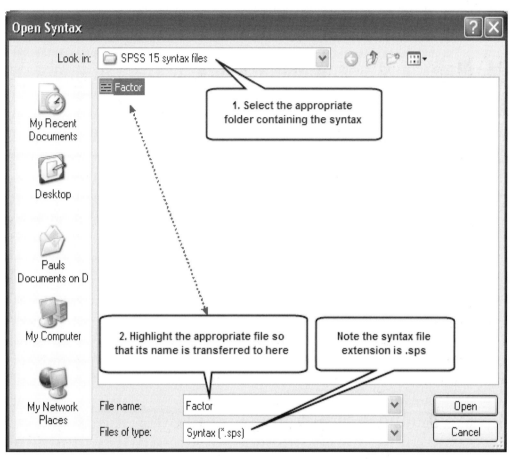 in the toolbar above the syntax window to re-run the complete factor analysis.

Figure 9. The **Open File** dialog box with the syntax file *Factor* selected

It is easy to see that with another data set comprising scores on a different battery of tests, it would be easy to edit the **FACTOR** command by changing the variable names and other specifications to match the new data in **Data View**. Inevitably, the experienced user of SPSS builds up a library of written commands, because it is quicker to carry out the analysis by editing the display in the **SPSS Syntax Editor** than to go through all the dialog and subdialog boxes again.

15.3.2   Using a correlation matrix as input for factor analysis

The graphical interface using dialog boxes is a comparatively recent development. SPSS (like several other major statistical packages) was originally designed to respond to the user's syntax commands. The translation to dialog boxes, moreover, is as yet incomplete: there are some statistical procedures that cannot yet be accessed through the graphical interface. Ultimately, to harness the full power of SPSS, you still sometimes need to use syntax commands.

Factor analysis from a correlation matrix

So far we have been considering the statistical analysis of **raw scores**, that is, data sets comprising original measurements or observations, upon which no statistical manipulations have yet been carried out. In the present factor analytic context, for example, our starting point has been a data set comprising the participants' scores on a battery of tests. Sometimes, however, it may be more convenient to use correlations (rather than raw scores) as the input for a factor analysis. The user may already have an **R-matrix** and wish to start at that point, rather than going back to the raw data. Since this cannot be done with dialog boxes, the user must turn to **SPSS syntax**. The procedure has two stages:

1.   Preparing the correlation matrix in a suitable format.
2.   Commanding SPSS to read in the matrix and run the factor analysis.

Preparation of the correlation matrix
*   Choose
    File➜New➜Syntax
    to open the **SPSS Syntax Editor** window.

The procedures must be of a specific form, but help with the matrix data command syntax is available by entering **MATRIX DATA** in the **Syntax Editor** and clicking 🔲 in the toolbar to open a window showing the structure of the syntax. Figure 10 shows the correct syntax of the commands needed for the entry of the **R-matrix** shown in Output 2. Note that it is immaterial whether upper or lower case text is used.

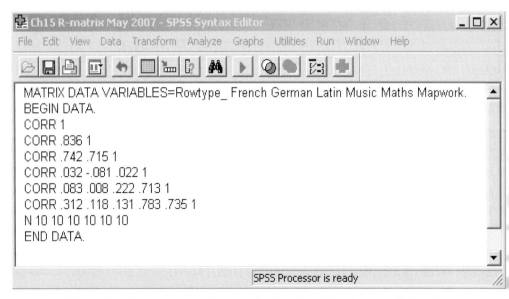

Figure 10. The commands for entering the **R-matrix** shown in Output 2

The first command is **MATRIX DATA** followed by **VARIABLES=** and a list of variable names. This command warns SPSS to prepare to receive data in the form of a matrix whose dimensions are specified by the number of variables in the list. Like all commands, it must end with a full stop. Note the compulsory variable name **Rowtype_** , which is a special string variable used to identify the type of data for each record (row).

Next come the data commands. First there is **BEGIN DATA** then the data themselves and finally the **END DATA** command. *Note the compulsory full stops after BEGIN DATA and END DATA.*

The first six rows of the data begin with the word **CORR**, which tells SPSS that the data are in the form of correlation coefficients. The final (7th) row begins with **N**, which is a count of the number of data points in each column. The terms **CORR** and **N** are instances of the generic term **Rowtype_** which appeared in the matrix data command.

The default structure of a correlation matrix is a **lower triangular matrix**. This is a square matrix with all entries above the principal diagonal omitted. If an upper triangular or square matrix were to be input, an additional **/FORMAT** subcommand would be required. The value of **N** is not needed for a basic factor analysis, but it is required for tests of significance and for assessing the sampling adequacy of the data. The correlation matrix and value of **N** are then entered (preceded in each row with **CORR** or **N**, as appropriate) between the usual **BEGIN DATA** and **END DATA** commands.

To execute the MATRIX DATA command, proceed as follows:
- Drag the cursor over all the syntax in Figure 10 to highlight the complete command.
- Click the **Run** button ▶ in the toolbar above the syntax window.
- The matrix will appear in **Data View** (Figure 11), not in **SPSS Viewer**.
- If there are any errors in the syntax, they will be flagged in the **SPSS Viewer**.

ROWTYPE_	VARNAME_	French	German	Latin	Music	Maths	Mapwork
N		10.000	10.000	10.000	10.000	10.000	10.000
CORR	French	1.000	.836	.742	.032	.083	.312
CORR	German	.836	1.000	.715	-.081	.008	.118
CORR	Latin	.742	.715	1.000	.022	.222	.131
CORR	Music	.032	-.081	.022	1.000	.713	.783
CORR	Maths	.083	.008	.222	.713	1.000	.735
CORR	Mapwork	.312	.118	.131	.783	.735	1.000

Figure 11. The data set after running the **MATRIX DATA** command

Preparation of the FACTOR command
- Return to the syntax window and type the **FACTOR** command below the previous syntax as shown in Figure 12.

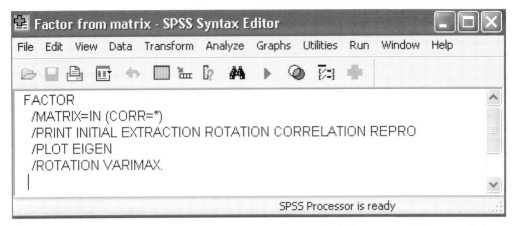

Figure 12. The **FACTOR** command for running a factor analysis from a correlation matrix in **Data View** with various options as chosen in Section 15.2.2

- Notice that the identification of the source of the matrix in the **/MATRIX =IN** subcommand is given as **(CORR=*)**. This shows that it is a correlation matrix (and not, say, a factor matrix), and that it is in the current data file (represented by *), as shown in **Data View** window. The **/PRINT** options are those selected in the **Descriptives** dialog box and the **/PLOT** option is that selected in the **Extraction** dialog box. It is not necessary to enter **/ROTATION VARIMAX** because this is the default choice if none is specified. *Again note the full stop at the end of the command: it is absolutely essential.*
- Run the **FACTOR** command by highlighting the whole command with the cursor and then clicking the ▶ icon in the toolbar at the top of the syntax window. The output for the factor analysis will be identical with that previously described in Section 15.2.3.

15.3.3   Progressing with SPSS syntax

As we said earlier, we believe that the best way of learning SPSS syntax is by pasting the minimal basic commands into the **syntax window** from the appropriate dialog boxes in the usual way, and observing how the syntax becomes more elaborate when extra options are chosen from the subdialog boxes.

The more experienced user will find it helpful, when writing a command in SPSS syntax, to access the **Syntax Help** window by writing the command in the syntax window and clicking ▦ in the toolbar to open a window showing the structure of the syntax, as mentioned in the previous Section. Optional subcommands are shown in square brackets. Relevant parts can be typed in the syntax window. Alternatively, the whole block of syntax can be copied over for editing from the **Syntax Help** window to the **Syntax** window by using **Copy** and **Paste** in the usual way. (These are in the **Options** menu of the **Syntax Help** window.) We do not recommend that you follow this procedure until you have already acquired some experience with SPSS syntax in the way we have described.

15.4 CANONICAL CORRELATION

15.4.1 Introduction

In multiple regression, the researcher is trying to predict the values of one **target, criterion** or **dependent** variable (on the left of the equation) from several **regressors** or **independent variables** (on the right of the equation). Such research is invariably motivated by a causal model: the assumption is that one or more of the variables on the right of the equation have a causal influence upon (or, at least, are indicators of) the target variable on the left.

Now suppose that instead of having just one criterion variable, we have a whole set of criterion variables, all in the same domain. It is well known, for example, that among the possible complications of diabetes is visual impairment. A researcher decides to investigate the effects of certain medical and lifestyle variables upon vision in diabetic patients. Four measures of visual functioning (DVs in this study) are investigated:
1. Colour discrimination.
2. Detection of the velocity of a moving dot.
3. The ability to see patterns in pseudo-isochromatic plates such as the Ishihara Test.
4. Visual acuity.

The independent variables (**IVs**) are a set of four medical and lifestyle variables known to be risk factors in diabetes:
1. Age.
2. Duration of the condition.
3. Control of blood-sugar level.
4. Blood pressure.

We could, of course, run several multiple regressions, one for each of the four visual variables. In doing so, however, we should run into the same problems as the researcher who runs an experiment in which there are several measures or dependent variables, among which there may be strong correlations and proceeds to run univariate analyses on each variable. The avoidance of such difficulties is the motivation for techniques such as discriminant function analysis and MANOVA. In those techniques, linear functions of the dependent variables (discriminant functions) are constructed from the observed variables and used as representatives of the set as a whole.

The purpose of the present exercise is to construct a **root pair** of representative or **canonical variates**, one from the visual set of DVs, the other from the medical set of IVs, in such a way that they correlate to the maximum possible extent. That maximum correlation between the canonical variates is known as a **canonical correlation**. After the construction of this root pair, the process can be continued to produce a second root pair with their own canonical correlation and so on.

Once we have constructed several pairs of canonical variates, we shall want to determine the visual (DV) and medical (IV) variables that make the greatest contribution to each member of every pair. The inference, of course, is that there may be a causal relationship between the key variables in the two domains. It should be noted that, although the representative canonical variates are not principal components or factors of the variables in their respective domains, they can, nevertheless, be thought of as 'latent variables' in terms of which the variance shared

among the measured variables can be explained. The correlations between the observed DVs
and IVs with their respective canonical variates are known as **loadings**.

Before embarking upon any multivariate analysis, including canonical correlation, the
researcher must ensure that the data meet certain requirements. High correlations among the
variables in either domain, for instance, can create **multicollinearity** in the key matrices
involved in the calculations. The presence of outliers must be detected and the appropriate
action taken. SPSS offers collinearity diagnostics and the identification of outliers in its
Regression procedure – see Chapter 4 of Tabachnick & Fidell (2007) for details.

15.4.2   Running canonical correlation on SPSS

Suppose twenty diabetic patients have been assessed with four tests of visual function (as
described in the previous section) and their data on the medical variables recorded (see Table
3). The visual function variables are the DVs; the medical variables are the IVs.

Table 3. Visual function and diabetic variables							
Case	ColDiscr	VelDet	Plates	Acuity	Age	Control	Duration	BloodPre
1	360	50	7	15	24	40	3	120
2	344	54	10	15	26	39	8	122
3	220	45	15	16	27	37	15	120
4	310	59	30	16	32	12	22	125
5	280	60	29	16	33	4	9	128
6	200	53	10	22	34	36	10	120
7	280	24	25	22	34	24	10	125
8	300	62	21	15	36	22	9	130
9	340	51	18	28	43	15	5	128
10	201	34	26	28	44	17	12	126
11	140	19	15	22	45	17	30	135
12	240	38	27	28	53	6	2	125
13	100	49	28	22	54	13	10	135
14	200	41	30	34	54	16	44	130
15	144	34	16	22	60	4	3	140
16	95	32	19	16	60	23	32	138
17	240	7	15	20	64	26	30	135
18	0	36	10	16	65	34	4	150
19	145	38	20	28	65	26	40	130
20	42	40	12	15	75	26	10	145

SPSS has two ways of carrying out a canonical correlation analysis, both of which require the
use of **SPSS Syntax**. One method uses a macro called **CANCORR**; the other uses an option
called **DISCRIM**, which is only available within the syntax for **MANOVA**. Here we shall use
the MANOVA procedure.

*   Prepare the data file in the usual manner in the **Data Editor**.
*   Choose **File➜New➜Syntax** to open the **Syntax Editor**.
*   Type in the following, listing the visual DVs on the left of WITH and the medical IVs on
    the right:
    MANOVA *ColDiscr VelDet Plates Acuity* WITH *Age Control Duration BloodPre*

/DISCRIM = COR
/PRINT = SIGNIF(EIGEN DIMENR).
Note especially the forward slash preceding each subcommand and the final full stop
signalling the end of the command. The names of the DVs are entered before **WITH** and
the names of the IVs after **WITH**. The **COR** option for **DISCRIM** selects the
correlations between the scores on the measured variables and the canonical variates in
each root pair. The **EIGEN** and **DIMENR** options in the **PRINT** command produce
canonical correlations, eigenvalues and a dimension reduction analysis table showing how
many of the pairs of canonical variates are significant.

- Highlight the syntax command and click the ▶ icon in the toolbar at the top of the
syntax window to run the analysis.

15.4.3 Output for canonical correlation

The output begins with a summary (not reproduced) of the number of cases processed.

As a measure of the importance of a root pair of canonical variates, SPSS uses a variance
measure it terms the **eigenvalue** λ , which is given by

$$\lambda = \frac{r^2}{1-r^2}$$

where r is the canonical correlation. (Other authors, such as Tabachnick & Fidell, 2007 (p.73),
define the eigenvalue as the square of the canonical correlation, which is technically correct.)

```
Eigenvalues and Canonical Correlations
```

Root No.	Eigenvalue	Pct.	Cum. Pct.	Canon Cor.	Sq. Cor
1	4.213	60.134	60.134	.899	.808
2	2.278	32.515	92.649	.834	.695
3	.471	6.721	99.370	.566	.320
4	.044	.630	100.000	.206	.042

Output 8. Eigenvalues, percentages of variance and canonical correlations

The first relevant table **Eigenvalues and Canonical Correlations** (Output 8) lists the
eigenvalues and canonical correlations between the first four root pairs of canonical variates.
The canonical correlations, the first two of which are .899 and .834, diminish with successive
root pairs. You can see that the value of the eigenvalue for the first root pair is $.899^2/(1 - .899^2)$
= 4.213; for the second root pair, the eigenvalue is $.834^2/(1 - .834^2)$ = 2.28. As usual in
multivariate statistics, the first move accounts for the greatest proportion of the variance we are
trying to account for and the second and subsequent 'extractions' account for progressively
less of the variance. The table shows clearly that only the first two canonical pairs have
eigenvalues > 1 and between them they account for 93% of the total variance shared by all the
root pairs (**Cum. Pct.** Column). We can therefore ignore the remaining two root pairs.

The next table, the **Dimension Reduction Analysis** (Output 9), confirms that only the first two
pairs of canonical variates are significant.

```
Dimension Reduction Analysis

Roots           Wilks L.         F Hypoth. DF    Error DF  Sig. of F
1 TO 4           .03811    4.46139      16.00       37.30      .000
2 TO 4           .19865    3.32972       9.00       31.79      .006
3 TO 4           .65115    1.67473       4.00       28.00      .184
4 TO 4           .95776     .66162       1.00       15.00      .429
```

Output 9. The dimension reduction analysis table showing how many pairs of canonical variates are significant; here only two are significant

Note that the values of **Wilks' lambda** *decrease* as we move down the table, because the *smaller* the value, the *more* important the source.

The next table **Correlations between DEPENDENT and canonical variables** (Output 10) shows the correlations or **loadings** of the DVs (i.e. the visual set) on the first two canonical variates, and the amount of variance accounted for by each root pair. Loadings of less than 0.3 are ignored. The loadings clearly show that, on the DV side, *ColDiscr* and *Plates* predominate in the first canonical variate and all the variables (*ColDiscr*, *VelDet*, *Plates* and *Acuity*) contribute to the second canonical variate. *VelDet* with a loading of .298 does not contribute significantly to the first canonical variate.

```
Correlations between DEPENDENT and canonical variables
           Function No.

Variable               1             2

ColDiscr             .686          .681
VelDet               .298          .555
Plates               .775         -.503
Acuity               .477         -.585


Variance in dependent variables explained by canonical variables

CAN. VAR.   Pct Var DE  Cum Pct DE  Pct Var CO  Cum Pct CO

      1        34.712      34.712      28.053      28.053
      2        34.176      68.887      23.749      51.802
```

Output 10. Statistics of the dependent variables

In any regression technique, a focal point of interest is the extent to which the IVs account for variance in the DVs. In canonical correlation, the **redundancy index** is the proportion of variance in either the DV or the IV set that is accounted for by the opposite canonical variate. The value of the redundancy index is given by the square of the canonical correlation multiplied by the proportion of the variance that a canonical variate extracts from the set of variables it represents.

_n some regression procedures, such as logistic regression and canonical correlation, SPSS _efers to the IVs as **covariates**. At the foot of the table in Output 10, notice the columns _eaded **Pct Var DE** and **Pct Var CO**. Here Pct Var DE stands for 'Percentage Variance of _he DEpendent variables' and Pct Var CO stands for 'Percentage Variance of the COvariates'. The value 34.712 is the proportion of the variance of the DVs accounted for by the first _epresentative canonical variate. The value 28.053 in the Pct Var CO column is the _edundancy index calculated by squaring the canonical correlation ($.899^2$) and multiplying it _y the proportion of the variance of the DVs (.34712). For the second root pair of canonical _ovariates, the variance of the DVs accounted for and the redundancy are 34.176% and 23.749%, respectively. These results show considerable overlap of explained variance _etween the canonical variates.

_utput 11 shows the same statistics for the independent variables or covariates. Here the _oadings show that blood pressure *BloodPre*, *Control* and *Age* predominate in the first _anonical variate and all the variables (*Age*, *Control*, *Duration* and *BloodPre*), contribute to _he second canonical variate. *Duration* does not contribute to the first canonical variate. In _utput 10, the columns headed **Pct Var DE** and **Pct Var CO** contained the variance of the _Vs accounted for by the representative canonical variate and the redundancy, respectively. _n Output 11, it is the other way round: the Pct Var DE column contains the redundancies and _he Pct Var CO column contains the variance of the IVs accounted for by the representative _anonical variate. Thus for the first canonical variate, the variance of the IVs accounted for is 25.967% and the redundancy is 20.985% (i.e. $.899^2$×.25967). The corresponding values for _he second canonical variate are 43.926% and 30.525%. Once again, there is considerable _verlap of explained variance between the canonical variates.

```
Correlations between COVARIATES and canonical variables
          CAN. VAR.


Covariate              1              2


Age                 -.485          -.851
Control              .577          -.599
Duration             .104          -.545
BloodPre            -.678          -.615


Variance in covariates explained by canonical variables


CAN. VAR.   Pct Var DE Cum Pct DE Pct Var CO Cum Pct CO

   1          20.985     20.985     25.967     25.967
   2          30.525     51.510     43.926     69.893
```

Output 11. Statistics of the independent variables (covariates)

_he remainder of the output can be ignored. The data are summarised in Table 4.

Table 4. Canonical correlation and correlations between variables relating to visual variables and diabetic variables

	First Canonical Variate		Second Canonical Variate	
Canonical Correlation	.90		.83	
VISUAL VARIABLES				
Colour Discrimination	.69		-.68	
Velocity Detection	.30		-.56	
Plates	.78		.50	
Visual Acuity	.48		.59	
Percentage of Variance		35%		34%
Redundancy		28%		24%
DIABETIC VARIABLES				
Age	-.49		.85	
Control of Blood-Sugar Level	.58		.60	
Duration of Diabetes	.10		.55	
Systolic Blood Pressure	-.68		.62	
Percentage of Variance		26%		44%
Redundancy		21%		31%

A pair of flow charts (Figure 13) illustrates these conclusions graphically.

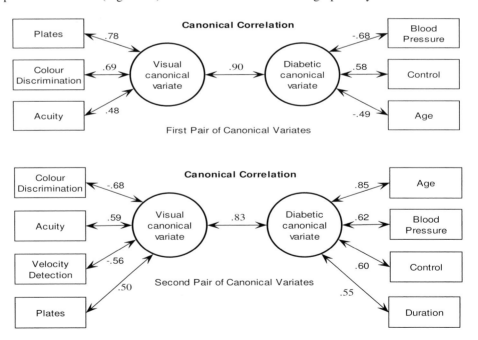

Figure 13. A pair of flow charts showing variable loadings for each canonical variate and the canonical correlation for the two pairs of canonical variates

The conclusion from this research is that there is a very high correlation between the canonical variates for both root pairs (canonical correlation coefficients = 0.90 and 0.83). The first canonical pair shows that colour discrimination, plates and to a lesser extent acuity are indexed by blood pressure, age and diabetic control. The second canonical pair shows that colour discrimination, velocity detection, acuity and plates are indexed by age, blood pressure, control and duration.

In several respects, canonical correlation resembles factor analysis. Like factor analysis, canonical correlation aims to extract latent variables and the extent to which the observed variables correlate with, or load upon, these latent variables is taken to be the extent to which the latent variables account for the observed variables. Similarly, different data sets will result in varying numbers of root pairs, just as different R-matrices yield varying numbers of common factors.

There are also, however, important differences between canonical correlation and factor analysis. The canonical variates are not principal components or factors of the variables they represent. Unlike orthogonal factors, canonical variates are not independent and account for overlapping proportions of the variance. Unlike factor analysis, moreover, there is no equivalent of rotation to facilitate the interpretation of the loadings of the variables on the canonical variates.

15.5   A FINAL WORD

In this and preceding chapters, we have described the use of SPSS to carry out a variety of statistical procedures on your data. Many of the procedures are directly accessible by completing dialog boxes. In this chapter, however, we had recourse to SPSS syntax, which can implement procedures that cannot be accessed from the dialog boxes.

SPSS syntax can also be an invaluable aid to the study of the basis principles of statistics and the properties of the most important distributions. A simple command or two can enable the user to obtain large samples from specified populations, such as F, t and other test statistics and examine their characteristics. Monte Carlo experiments are quite feasible by these means.

Einspruch (2004), in his book *Next steps with SPSS*, describes how to use looping functions and other devices to carry out operations that would be difficult or impossible to achieve without a knowledge of SPSS control language. We strongly recommend this book to anyone who wants to make progress with Syntax.

Recommended reading

The topic of factor analysis is not elementary, and the SPSS output fairly bristles with technical terms. If you are unfamiliar with factor analysis, we suggest you read the lucid texts by Kim and Mueller (1978a, 1978b), before proceeding to more difficult texts, such as Tabachnick and Fidell (2007). Tabachnick and Fidell also have a chapter on canonical correlation.

Einspruch, E. L. (2004). *Next steps with SPSS*. London: Sage.

Kim, J., & Mueller, C. W. (1978a). *Factor analysis: Statistical methods and practical issues.* Newbury Park, CA: Sage.

Kim, J., & Mueller, C. W. (1978b). *Introduction to factor analysis: What it is and how to do it*. Newbury Park, CA: Sage.

Tabachnick, B. G., & Fidell, L. S. (2007). *Using multivariate statistics (5th ed.)*. Boston: Allyn & Bacon (Pearson International Edition).

EXERCISE 24

Factor analysis

Before you start

Before proceeding with this practical, please read Chapter 15.

A personality study

Ten participants are given a battery of personality tests, comprising the following items: *Adventure*; *Agoraphobia*; *Anxiety*; *Arachnophobia*; *Extraversion*; *Sociability*. The purpose of this project is to ascertain whether the correlations among the six variables can be accounted for in terms of comparatively few latent variables, or factors.

Preparing the data set

The data are shown in Table 1. Name the variables in **Variable View** and assign longer names in the **Label** column. Ensure that the values in the **Decimals** column are 0. Click the **Data View** tab to open **Data View** and enter the data.

Table 1. The questionnaire data						
Participant	**Advent**	**Agora**	**Anxiety**	**Arachno**	**Extrav**	**Sociab**
1	44	68	71	80	54	52
2	77	30	39	41	90	80
3	50	55	46	45	46	48
4	57	33	33	39	64	62
5	45	75	74	90	55	48
6	91	47	39	48	87	91
7	54	70	66	69	44	48
8	31	40	33	36	37	36
9	45	75	85	93	50	42
10	70	35	45	44	66	78

Procedure for the factor analysis of the raw data

Follow the procedure described in Section 15.2.2, requesting the **Univariate descriptives**, **Initial solution**, **Coefficients**, **Reproduced**, **Scree plot**, and **Varimax** options.

Interpretation of the results

After a table of descriptive statistics, there is a table labelled **Correlation Matrix**. Is there any evident pattern that would suggest that the R-matrix might be accounted for in terms of relatively few factors (components)? Examine the remainder of the output in the manner outlined in Section 15.2.3, considering the **scree plot**, the table labelled **Component** (factor) **Matrix** listing the unrotated loadings for each factor, the residuals and the final rotated matrix in the table labelled **Rotated Component Matrix**.

- **How might the patterns among the correlations in the R-matrix be explained psychologically? Look at the table Rotated Component Matrix and make a list of the loadings that are greater than about 0.5 on each factor (component).**

Procedure for the factor analysis of the correlation matrix

Sometimes (e.g., after a large psychometric study) it is convenient to run a factor analysis from a table of correlation coefficients rather than from raw scores. Following the procedure described in Section 15.3.2, type the appropriate commands and the lower triangular version of the R-matrix (the correlation matrix in the **SPSS Viewer**) into the syntax window. Include the following items.

- The MATRIX DATA command with the appropriate variable names (including *rowtype_*).
- A BEGIN DATA command.
- Rows of correlation coefficients (each preceded by CORR).
- A row indicating the size of N (preceded by N and then the size of N repeated for as many variables as you have).
- An END DATA command concluding with a full stop (.).

When the data syntax is complete, run the factor analysis by dragging the cursor over all the syntax and clicking ▶ . **Data View** should now appear similar to that shown in Chapter 15, Figure 11.

If all is well, proceed to prepare the FACTOR command by studying the model shown in Chapter 15, Figure 12. Run the factor analysis by selecting the command and clicking the **Run** button, as described above. Confirm that the results of the analysis are the same as those obtained when you began with the raw scores.

Revision Exercises

The revision exercises are designed to challenge the reader as to what is the most appropriate exploratory data analysis (EDA) and/or statistical test to employ given the experimental situation presented and, where appropriate, the experimental hypothesis specified. For this reason, no help is given.

It is strongly recommended that an EDA is conducted initially in case any extreme values need to be deselected or the distribution of values makes certain statistical tests unsuitable. If necessary, deselect extreme values before conducting the appropriate statistical test.

The bullet points after each Exercise are provided in case your tutor wants to know what you have done.

Revision Exercise 1

In order to test the hypothesis that, when presented with lists of words, younger children process more information than do older children, a psychologist asked groups of older and younger children to inspect and commit to memory the same list of words and then recall the words in the list. The results were as follows:

Case	Younger	Case	Younger	Case	Older	Case	Older
\multicolumn{8}{c	}{**Number of words recalled by younger and older children**}
1	16	6	16	11	12	16	4
2	223	7	21	12	20	17	16
3	20	8	20	13	10	18	9
4	23	9	18	14	13	19	11
5	17	10	20	15	15	20	9

- **Do the data confirm the hypothesis?**
- **Describe how you reached your conclusion.**
- **Name the statistical test and express the result in the usual manner.**

Revision Exercise 2

To test the hypothesis that, in families with two female children, the second-born child is more sociable than the first-born, a researcher selected twenty two-child families. In order to ensure, in each family, the comparability of the social backgrounds of the children, only families with children of Primary School age were selected. The children were tested for sociability, each child receiving a score in the range from 0 (very unsociable) to 10 (very sociable). The scores the children obtained are shown in the table below.

Sociability scores of the first- and second-born children from twenty families					
Family	First-born	Second-born	Family	First-born	Second-born
1	4	7	11	1	5
2	1	5	12	5	8
3	8	6	13	8	9
4	2	4	14	9	9
5	0	2	15	1	4
6	8	8	16	5	7
7	9	8	17	3	4
8	2	7	18	3	6
9	4	6	19	4	5
10	6	8	20	6	7

- **Do the data confirm the hypothesis?**

- **Describe how you reached your conclusion.**

- **Name the statistical test and express the result in the usual manner.**

Revision Exercise 3

A clinician has carried out a study on the efficacy of a type of cognitive therapy, in which the aim is to reduce the number of negative, self-destructive thoughts, as recorded by the patient in a special diary. The Table shows the numbers of negative thoughts recorded by 9 patients over five days, the first two days before therapy and the remaining three days after therapy. The therapy did not begin until the third day, because the therapist wanted to establish a baseline rate with which subsequent frequencies during therapy could be compared.

Numbers of negative thoughts recorded during a course in cognitive therapy					
Patient	First day	Second day	Third day	Fourth day	Fifth day
1	22	22	9	7	6
2	20	20	10	4	4
3	18	15	6	4	5
4	25	30	13	12	16
5	31	26	13	8	6
6	19	27	8	7	4
7	25	16	5	2	5
8	17	18	8	1	5
9	25	24	14	8	10

- **Was the cognitive therapy effective?**

- **Describe how you reached your conclusion.**

- **Name the statistical test and express the result in the usual manner.**

- **A boxplot would show extreme scores for the fifth day. Would you deselect them from the data? Explain your decision.**

Revision Exercise 4

For some years there was, in social psychology in the US, much emphasis upon the advantages of a 'democratic', as opposed to an 'authoritarian' leadership style in enhancing group performance. It was suspected by some, however, that the efficacy of leadership style might depend upon the nature of the task. Perhaps, for some tasks, an authoritarian (i.e. instructional) style might actually be more effective than a democratic one (i.e. one encouraging questions and discussion)? This is the hypothesis under test.

In a project designed to test the efficacy of leadership style on group performance, groups of soldiers were trained under democratic or authoritarian leadership styles. Later, groups who had been trained under each regime were tested on one of two tasks:

1. A Structured Task, namely, the assembly of a field gun;

2. A Group Problem, in which, given equipment such as barrels and ropes, the group was required to construct a bridge across a fast-flowing river.

On the basis of their performance, each group was awarded a mark on the scale from 1 (low efficacy) to 20 (high efficacy). The results are shown in the Table:

Scores achieved on a criterion group task by twenty soldiers trained under democratic or authoritarian leadership styles		
	Leadership Style	
CriterionTask	**Authoritarian**	**Democratic**
Structured Task (Gun Assembly)	13	5
	13	5
	17	8
	15	11
	18	10
Group Problem (Bridge Construction)	9	19
	2	15
	5	18
	12	13
	7	14

- **Is the hypothesis supported?**

- **Describe how you reached your conclusion.**

- **Name the statistical test and express the result in the usual manner.**

Revision Exercise 5

There is a widespread belief (supported by actuarial evidence) that, in tests of decision-making in driving, those between the ages of fifty-five and sixty-five should outperform those in their twenties, despite the inevitable slowing of reaction speed that occurs as a person gets older. To investigate this claim, ten volunteers, five in their twenties and five in their late fifties and early sixties, were recruited to take part in a driving-simulation study.

Driving was assessed under simulated conditions of light and heavy road traffic in both daytime and in night-time illumination. Each driver received a score between 1 (poor) and 100 (excellent) for their performance in each of the four conditions.

The results are shown below:

Performance of drivers in two age groups, driving under simulated conditions of light and heavy traffic, and of daytime and night-time illumination				
	Light Traffic		**Heavy Traffic**	
Group	**Day**	**Night**	**Day**	**Night**
Older	74	55	75	15
	72	70	70	10
	70	60	60	10
	68	50	50	10
	66	65	45	5
Younger	40	15	30	30
	25	20	20	20
	30	30	10	10
	25	40	15	15
	10	45	25	25

- **Is the hypothesis supported?**
- **Describe how you reached your conclusion.**
- **Name the statistical test and express the result in the usual manner.**

Revision Exercise 6

A researcher investigated people's ratings of their state of happiness and whether they considered life to be exciting or dull in relation to whether they were white or non-white and whether they were male or female. Is there any evidence of differences among the races and sexes for their ratings of happiness and lifestyle?   Is there a relationship between happiness and lifestyle?

The data were as follows:

Number of white and non-white males and females rating themselves for happiness and lifestyle							
		Very Happy		**Fairly Happy**		**Not Very Happy**	
Race	**Sex**	**Exciting**	**Dull**	**Exciting**	**Dull**	**Exciting**	**Dull**
White	Male	84	33	92	129	5	20
White	Female	88	52	96	162	6	44
Non-White	Male	8	4	10	14	7	2
Non-White	Female	10	8	14	36	2	15
	TOTAL	190	97	212	341	20	81

- **Describe how you reached your conclusions about the researcher's questions.**

- **Name the statistical tests and express the results in the usual manner.**

Glossary

Adjusted R squared A measure of effect size in **Analysis of Variance (ANOVA)**. Other measures are **eta squared** and **omega squared**. Adjusted R squared is available in SPSS.

Alternative hypothesis (H_1) In **hypothesis-testing,** the proposition that the **null hypothesis** is false.

Analysis of covariance (ANCOVA) In the general context of **analysis of variance (ANOVA)**, an ancillary technique which corrects for the association between the dependent variable and another measured variable known as a **covariate**. A covariate is a potential nuisance variable, which may inflate the error term of the F-ratio and result in an incorrect decision about the null hypothesis.

Analysis of variance (ANOVA) A set of **univariate** statistical techniques for comparing means from experiments with three or more treatment conditions or groups. In ANOVA, the total variance is divided into components associated with treatment and error variance, which are compared by means of an **F ratio**.

Antilogarithm (antilog) Reverses the process of taking a logarithm. If $y = \log_{10} x$, $10^y = x$, where x is the antilogarithm of y. The antilogarithm of a natural logarithm is the **exponential function**. If $y = \ln(x)$, $e^y = \exp(y) = x$. (See **Logarithm**.)

Behrens-Fisher problem A problem with making an independent samples t test when the population variances are heterogeneous. Underlying the t test for independent samples is the assumption of homogeneity of variance. If that assumption is true, the t statistic is distributed as t on $n_1 + n_2 - 2$ degrees of freedom. With heterogeneity of variance, particularly when the sample sizes are unequal, the ordinary t statistic, in which there is a pooled estimate of the supposedly constant population variance, does not have this distribution. In such cases, the sample variances are no longer pooled for the calculation of the test statistic and the df is adjusted downwards by means of the Welch-Satterthwaite formula or an equivalent.

Between groups See **Between subjects**.

Between subjects designs Comparative experimental designs yielding independent samples of data, as when each participant is tested once, under only one condition and there is no basis for pairing the data. The term **between groups** is also used to describe this kind of design. (Compare with **Repeated measures**.)

Bivariate normality Two variables are said to have a bivariate normal distribution if, given a value of one variable, the distribution of the other variable at that value is normal. More technically, the conditional distributions must be normal. The correct application of the **Pearson correlation** assumes bivariate normality, which is indicated by an elliptical (or circular) scatterplot.

Bonferroni method A procedure, based on the Bonferroni inequality in probability theory, for controlling the **experimentwise** or **per family** Type I error rate by dividing the ordinary, per comparison, error rate either by the number of planned comparisons or (with unplanned or **post hoc** comparisons) by the number of pairwise comparisons possible from an array of means of specified size. Suppose an experiment is run with three conditions and that, following a significant ANOVA F ratio, we want to make pairwise comparisons among the three means. Since with three means there are three possible pairings, we divide the per comparison error rate (.05, the usual significance level) by 3, giving an adjusted per comparison significance level of .02 . An equivalent approach is to multiply the ordinary p-value by 3 and accept the null hypothesis if the adjusted p-value exceeds 0.05.

Centring In **multiple regression**, problems arise when the correlations among the independent variables of regressors are too high, in which case we have multicollinearity. The risk of multicollinearity is particularly high if interaction terms or powers are included in the regression model. The risk is reduced if the raw scores on a variable are first transformed into deviations by subtracting the mean, an operation known as centring. (It is not necessary to standardise the scores by dividing by the standard deviation as well: deviations are sufficient.)

Chi-square distribution The sum of the squares of n independent squared standard normal variables has a chi-square distribution with n degrees of freedom. A chi-square variable has a continuous distribution. The familiar chi-square statistic used in the analysis of nominal data is only an approximation to a true chi-square variable, and the approximation becomes poor when expected cell frequencies are low. The correction for continuity (Yates' correction) is an attempt to improve the approximation.

Cluster analysis A set of multivariate statistical techniques designed to account for (or classify) a multivariate data set in terms of relatively few reference groups or clusters, each cluster being interpreted as representing an underlying characteristic or property. The purpose of cluster analysis is thus similar to that of **factor analysis**, which is another set of techniques for classifying multivariate data.

Coefficient alpha (Cronbach's alpha) A measure of the reliability of a psychological test. Many psychological tests yield scores that are aggregates of the participant's responses to several items. Psychometric theory shows that the reliability of such a test increases with the number of items it contains, according to the following formula:

$$alpha = \frac{i}{i-1} \left(\frac{\sigma_Y^2 - \sum\limits_{items} \sigma_{item}^2}{\sigma_Y^2} \right)$$

where i is the number of items in the test and σ_y^2 is the variance of the complete test. The relationship between number of items and reliability obtains because the items in a test constitute a sample from the domain of possible items and, other things being equal, the statistics of large samples are less subject to variability than are those of small samples. (See **Spearman-Brown formula**.)

Coefficient of determination (CD) In simple regression, the proportion of the variance of the target, criterion or dependent variable that is accounted for by regression upon another variable (the regressor or independent variable). Its value is given by the square of the Pearson correlation: thus if $r = .60$, $r^2 = .36$, which means that 36% of the variance of the criterion variable is accounted for by regression upon the other variable. In multiple regression, the CD is the square of the multiple correlation coefficient: $CD = R^2$.

Cohen's d A measure of effect size. In the two-sample case, Cohen's d is the difference between the two treatment means divided by a pooled estimate of the standard deviation.

Cohen's kappa A measure of agreement between raters who are assigning cases to the same set of mutually exclusive categories. Cohen's statistic provides a way of measuring the reliability of psychiatric diagnosis or the use of any other standard classificatory system.

Comparison In **analysis of variance (ANOVA)**, the difference between two treatment means, either of which may itself be the mean of other treatment means. (See **Contrast**.)

Confidence interval An interval constructed around the value of a statistic such as the mean which would 'cover' or include the population value in a specified proportion of samples. A confidence interval is not a **sample space**: one cannot claim that there is a probability of .95 that the population mean lies within the limits of the 95% confidence interval obtained from a set of data. What the researcher can say is that, because the confidence interval has been constructed in such a way that it would include the population value in 95% of samples, one can be 95% 'confident' that the mean lies within the interval. Such a 'confidence', however, is not a probability.

Confirmatory factor analysis A set of techniques designed to account for an R-matrix in terms of a model in which the number of factors is pre-specified.

Contingency table A table classifying individuals with respect to two or more sets of categories (see **Qualitative variables**). The entries in the cells of a contingency table are the frequencies of individuals with the various combinations of attributes. For example, if patients are classified with respect to gender and blood group, the contingency table would show the numbers of females in group A, the numbers of males in group O and so on. A contingency table is the starting point for various statistical analyses. For example, a chi-squared test can be used to test for an association between two attributes.

Continuous variable   A quantitative variable that can have an infinite number of values within a specified interval. Height and weight are examples. In SPSS, the term **scale data** includes data on continuous variables.

Contrast   The comparison between two of an array of k treatment means can be written as a **linear contrast**, which is a weighted sum of the treatment means, such that the coefficients (weights) add up to zero. Suppose we have three treatment means and that we want to compare M_1 with M_2. The difference $M_1 - M_2$ can be expressed as the linear contrast L_1, where $L_1 = (+1)M_1 + (-1)M_2 + (0)M_3$. Similarly, if we wish to compare M_1 with the mean of M_2 and M_3, the difference $M_1 - (M_2 + M_3)/2$ can be expressed as the linear contrast L_2, where $L_2 = (+1)M_1 + (-\frac{1}{2})M_2 + (-\frac{1}{2})M_3$. In general, for a set of k treatment means M_j, the contrast L is given by $L = \Sigma c_j M_j$, where c_j is the coefficient of the treatment mean M_j. (See **Orthogonal contrasts**.)

Correction for continuity   When a continuous variable is used as an approximation to a discrete one or vice versa (as when using the normal distribution as an approximation to a binomial distribution or an approximate chi-square statistic with frequency data) the value 0.5 is first subtracted from the difference between the observed and expected values before the test statistic is calculated. The usual chi-square approximation formula, for example, becomes

$$\chi^2 = \Sigma \frac{(|O - E| - 0.5)^2}{E}$$

This is known as **Yates' correction**.

The normal approximation to the binomial becomes

$$z = \frac{X - np - 0.5}{\sqrt{npq}}$$

where p is the probability of a 'success', q is the probability of a 'failure' and n is the number of Bernoulli trials.

Correlation   A measure of a supposed linear relationship between two variables X and Y, one of the many formulae for which is

$$r_{XY} = \frac{\Sigma(X - M_X)(Y - M_Y)}{\sqrt{\Sigma(X - M_X)^2 \, \Sigma(Y - M_Y)^2}}$$

The value of r varies within the range from -1 to $+1$, inclusive.

Multiplying or dividing each raw score on a variable by a constant leaves the value of r unchanged: in fact, any linear transformation of either or both of X and Y leaves r unaltered. A nonlinear transformation, however, such as the logarithm or the square root, changes the value of the correlation.

Correlation ratio CR   A measure of effect size applicable to situations comparing two means (as in the t-test) or testing for a difference among three or more means, as in the ANOVA. Essentially, the correlation ratio is a special case of the **coefficient of determination**, which arises in the context of regression. In the two-group case, the CR is the square of the point-biserial correlation, which is the correlation between the DV and the code numbers identifying the two groups. Where there are k groups, the CR, which is known as **eta squared** (η^2), is the square of the multiple correlation coefficient from regression of the DV upon $k - 1$ grouping variables specifying group membership.

Correlational research   A strategy whereby variables are measured as they occur in the individuals studied, as opposed to being manipulated by an experimenter. Correlational research thus contrasts with **experimental** research, in which the supposedly causal variable is manipulated by the experimenter, independently of the characteristics of the participants.

Covariance   A measure of a supposed linear association between two variables. In a univariate data set, the variance is the average squared deviation of scores from their mean (though we divide by one less than the number of scores). In a bivariate data set, the covariance is the average of the cross-products of the deviations of pairs of scores on the two variables from their respective means. (We divide by one less than the number of pairs of scores.) If the scores on both variables are standardised, the covariance becomes the **Pearson correlation**.

Covariate   In the context of an experiment, a variable that may be associated with the measure or dependent variable and therefore must be taken into consideration in the analysis. In some SPSS dialog boxes, such as those for logistic regression, the term covariate denotes the predictors, regressors or independent variables, provided they are continuous.

Cross-validation   A procedure for attempting to generalise the results of a multiple regression. One approach is to divide the original data set into two sub-samples, fit a regression model to the first sub-sample and then assess the predictive value of the model when applied to the second sub-sample.   Applying a regression model to a fresh sample is likely to show a weakening of predictive power known as **shrinkage**. Shrinkage will be minimised with sufficiently large samples: Howell (2007, p506) reviews various recommendations, including the stipulation that in multiple regression we should have at least 40 or 50 more participants than there are predictors in the regression equation. The bottom line is that, with multiple regression, the more data you have, the better.

Cumulative probability The probability of a value less than or equal to a specified value. Cumulative probabilities are given by **distribution functions**.

Degrees of freedom A term borrowed from physical science, in which the degrees of freedom of a system is the number of constraints needed to determine its state completely at any point. In statistics, the degrees of freedom df is given by the number of independent observations minus the number of parameters estimated. For example, for the variance estimate based upon n observations, there are n deviations from the mean. One parameter (the mean) has been estimated, however, so $df = n - 1$. In simpler terms, once we have specified the values of $n - 1$ deviations from the sample mean, the value of the remaining deviation is fully determined, because deviations about the mean sum to zero.

Deleted residual In regression diagnostics, it is often important to determine the influence of one particular case upon the regression statistics. Two regressions are run: the first with the entire data set; the second with the case omitted. The deleted residual for the target case is $Y - \hat{Y}_{i(i)}$, where $\hat{Y}_{i(i)}$ is the estimate of the true score Y from the model calculated from the reduced data set. The difference in magnitude between the *raw residual* $Y - \hat{Y}_i$ and the deleted residual $Y - \hat{Y}_{i(i)}$ can reveal the influence of the data for one particular case upon the regression statistics.

Dependent or outcome variable In the context of a true experiment, the variable (such as performance) that is measured during the course of the study, as opposed to the variable that is manipulated by the experimenter (the independent variable or IV). The purpose of an experiment is to determine whether the IV has a causal effect upon the DV.

Discriminant analysis (DA) A **multivariate** statistical technique which is mathematically equivalent to the one-way **multivariate analysis of variance (MANOVA)**. Here, however, the purpose is to predict group membership from two or more measured variables, which are therefore regarded as independent (rather than dependent) variables. Linear discriminant functions of the independent variables which maximise inter-group differences are found and used to predict group membership.

Distribution Any table, display or formula that pairs each of the values that a variable can take with a frequency or a probability. With continuous variables, the distribution function gives the cumulative probability of specific values; the density function gives the probability density of a particular value, that is, the derivative of the distribution function at that point. (Note that with a continuous variable, the probability of any particular value is zero.)

Distribution function See **Distribution**.

Dummy variables Variables consisting of the values 0 and 1 are known as dummy variables. In SPSS, in order to compare the mean scores of three groups of participants, we can use a grouping variable with 3 different numerical values, say 1, 2 and 3, to code the conditions under which the scores were obtained. We could, however, also code group membership by means of two dummy variables, the values of each being either 1 or 0, as in the two columns of the matrix below:

$$\begin{pmatrix} 1 & 0 \\ 0 & 1 \\ 0 & 0 \end{pmatrix}$$

In general, if there are g groups, we shall need $(g - 1)$ such dummy variables to identify each group uniquely. As explained in Chapter 12, the equivalent of a one-way ANOVA can be run as a regression of the participants' scores on the dummy variables. If the number 0 is assigned to the control group on each dummy variable, the intercept will be the mean for that group and the regression coefficients will be the differences between the means of the treatment groups and the mean for the control group.

Eta squared The **correlation ratio**, a measure of effect size in **analysis of variance (ANOVA)**. Eta squared is a measure of the proportion of the total variance that is accounted for by differences among the treatment means. As an estimator, eta squared is positively biased and statistics such as **adjusted R squared** and **omega squared** are preferred as estimators.

Event An outcome of an **experiment of chance**.

Event space In an experiment of chance, the subset of the sample space containing those elementary outcomes that qualify as instances of a defined event.

Experiment A research technique in which the independent variable (IV) is manipulated to ascertain its effects upon the dependent variable (DV). Such direct manipulation is the hallmark of a true experiment, as opposed to a **correlational** study or a **quasi-experiment**.

Experiment of chance In probability theory, a procedure with an uncertain outcome, such as tossing a coin or rolling a die. The entire set of possible elementary outcomes is termed the **sample space**. An **event space** is a subset of the sample space.

Experimentwise (or per family) Type I error rate Following the analysis of variance of data from an experiment with three or more conditions, the researcher will often wish to make planned or unplanned comparisons among the means for specified groups or conditions. If the null hypothesis is true, the probability of at least one comparison showing significance is known as the experimentwise (or per family) Type I error rate. The experimentwise Type I error rate may be considerably higher than the significance level set for any one comparison and increases with the size of the array of treatment means. Conservative tests such as the

Bonferroni and Tukey methods are designed to control the experimentwise Type I error rate. The problem with basing the experimentwise Type I error rate on the entire experiment is that the criteria for the significance of comparisons can become extremely stringent. There may be grounds for defining the reference set of means as those making up only part of the experiment and thus working with a smaller 'family' of comparisons: hence the term **per family**.

Exploratory factor analysis A set of techniques designed to account for an R-matrix in terms of the minimum number of classificatory axes or dimensions, the latter being known as **factors**. (See **Confirmatory factor analysis**.)

Exponential function See **Antilogarithm**.

F distribution The distribution of the ratio of two chi-square variables, each of which has been divided by its degrees of freedom. An *F* distribution has two parameters, namely, df_1 and df_2, the degrees of freedom of the chi-square variables. The mean of the distribution is $df_1/(df_2 - 2)$, provided that $df_2 > 2$. It can be shown that the ratio of two independent estimates of the variance of a normal population is distributed as $F(df_1, df_2)$. The *F* test in **analysis of variance (ANOVA)** is an application of this result.

F ratio The ratio of two chi-square variables, each of which has been divided by its degrees of freedom. (See **F distribution**.)

Factor[1] In **Analysis of Variance (ANOVA),** a set of related categories, treatments or conditions. A factor is thus an **independent variable**.

Factor[2] See **Factor analysis**.

Factor analysis (FA) A set of techniques enabling the researcher to account for the correlations among a battery of tests in terms of a relatively small number of classificatory axes or **factors**, which are assumed to represent theoretical dimensions, latent variables or hypothetical constructs. Since a factor is also a function of the observed variables, individuals receive, in addition to scores on the tests in the battery, **factor scores** locating them on the dimension concerned. (See **R-matrix**.)

Factor score An individual's aggregate score on a combination of the scores on the tests in a battery.

Factorial experiments Experiments in which there are two or more independent variables or factors. If each level of one factor is found in combination with every level of another factor, the two factors are said to 'cross' and the factors are independent or orthogonal. In nested or hierarchical factorial designs, on the other hand, the levels of some factors are distributed among the levels of other factors, so that not every combination of conditions can be found in the experimental design.

Greenhouse-Geisser correction In **within subjects** or **repeated measures** experiments, the data may not have the property of **sphericity**, or **homogeneity of covariance**. If so, the ordinary F test may be positively biased, that is, it may give too many significant results when the null hypothesis is true. The correction adjusts the numerator and denominator degrees of freedom of the F ratio downwards by multiplying them by a constant epsilon, whose maximum value is 1. Another corrective procedure is the Huynh-Feldt method, which is less conservative than the Greenhouse-Geisser correction. SPSS offers several different corrections.

Grouping variable In SPSS, a set of code numbers indicating group membership. In Variable View, the numbers, or values, should always be assigned meaningful value labels.

Homogeneity of covariance (sphericity) A property of the **variance-covariance matrix**, which is calculated from the data obtained from an experiment with a repeated measures factor.

Hypothesis A supposition about the state of nature. In statistics, a hypothesis is a statement about a population, such as the value of a parameter or the nature of the distribution. (See **Null hypothesis; Alternative hypothesis; Hypothesis testing.**)

Hypothesis testing A statistical procedure for testing the null hypothesis (H_0) against the alternative hypothesis (H_1). On the basis of the null hypothesis, the range of possible values of the test statistic (e.g., t, F, χ^2) is divided into an acceptance region and a critical region. The critical region contains values of the test statistic that are unlikely under H_0: that is, under H_0, there is a low probability α that the value of the test statistic will fall within the critical region. The value of α is known as the significance level and is conventionally set at .05, .01 (or sometimes .001), depending on the research area. Should the value of the test statistic fall within the critical region, the statistic is said to be significant beyond (or at) the level of α. Such a significant result is regarded as evidence against the null hypothesis and therefore, indirectly, as evidence for the alternative hypothesis. The location of the critical region depends upon the alternative hypothesis. In a t test, for example, if H_1 is the two-sided assertion that the population mean is not that specified by H_0 (i.e. μ_0), the critical region is located symmetrically in both tails of the distribution, that is, above the $(1 - \alpha/2)^{th}$ percentile and below the $\alpha/2^{th}$ percentile. If, on the other hand, H_1 states that the mean is greater than μ_0, that is, H_1 is a one-sided alternative, the critical region is located entirely in the upper tail of the t distribution, above the $(1 - \alpha)^{th}$ percentile. This is known as a **one-tailed test**.

Independent samples Two samples are said to be independent if there is no basis for pairing the data they contain and the values in each have been drawn at random from the population.

Independent variable In a true experiment, a variable manipulated by the experimenter, to determine whether it has a causal effect upon the dependent variable.   In **correlational research**, the term is used to denote a predictor variable or regressor, a variable that is being investigated as possibly having a causal effect upon a target, criterion or independent variable. In that context, the 'independent variable' is not manipulated by an experimenter, but is measured as a characteristic of the participant during the course of the investigation.   The investigator attempts to neutralise the influence of possible confounds by statistical, rather than experimental means, by following a sampling strategy.

Interaction In **analysis of variance (ANOVA),** two factors are said to interact when the effects of one factor are not the same at all levels of the other factor. In other words, the **simple main effects** of one factor are not homogeneous across all levels of the other factor.

Interval data Data yielded by the measurement on a scale whose units are equally spaced on the property concerned. There has been much debate about whether data in the form of ratings (and other psychological measures) have the interval property. Arguably, therefore, not all continuous or scale data are interval data. Those who argue that ratings do not have the interval property tend to eschew the use of parametric tests and favour nonparametric or distribution-free tests. Others, however, believe that this issue is irrelevant to the choice of a statistical test.

Level In Analysis of Variance, one of the conditions or categories that make up an independent variable or **factor**[1].

Levene's test Tests for homogeneity of variance, a requirement for the independent samples t test.   A significant result on Levene's test indicates that the homogeneity assumption is untenable, a contraindication against the use of the traditional t test, which uses a pooled estimate of the supposedly uniform population variance.

Leverage In regression, the values of the statistics can be unduly influenced by atypical cases or outliers. Statistics are available for measuring the influence or leverage that such cases exert upon the regression model yielded by the analysis. If there is only one IV, the leverage exerted by the value X is measured by h, the formula for which is

$$h = \frac{1}{n} + \frac{(X - M_X)^2}{\Sigma(X - M_X)^2}$$

where n is the number of cases. The further from the mean X is, the greater the leverage it can exert, up to a maximum of 1. If there are k IVs in the regression, the average leverage exerted by the n cases is $(k + 1)/n$.

Linear Of the nature of a straight line. The straight line function $y = b_0 + b_1 x$ is the simplest in the family of linear equations $y = b_0 + b_1 x_1 + b_2 x_2 + ... + b_p x_p$. The analogues of the straight line when there are two or more IVs are, respectively, the plane (two IVs) and the hyperplane (three or more IVs). (See **Regression**.)

Loading In **factor analysis,** the loading of a test on a factor is the correlation between scores on the test and the **factor scores** of the participants in the study and is thus a measure of the extent to which performance on the test can be accounted for in terms of the factor concerned. The square of the loading is the proportion of the common factor variance of the test that is accounted for by the factor.

Logarithms or logs In a logarithmic system, numbers are expressed as powers (logarithms or logs) of a constant called the base of the system. The two most common bases are 10 and the mathematical constant e, where

$$e = \sum_0^\infty \frac{1}{x!} = 1 + 1 + 0.5 + 0.25 + ... = 2.718$$

Logarithms to the base 10 are known as common logarithms and logarithms to the base e are known as natural logarithms. If y is the common logarithm of x, we write $y = \log_{10} x$; if y is the natural logarithm of x, we write $y = \ln x$. There are three useful laws of logarithms:

$$\log(xy) = \log x + \log y$$
$$\log(x / y) = \log x - \log y$$
$$\log(x^p) = p \log x$$

The logarithm of a negative number is not defined. The logarithm of zero is minus infinity. (See **Antilogarithm**.)

Main effect In factorial analysis of variance, a factor is said to have a main effect if, in the population, the means on the dependent variable do not have the same value at all levels of the factor (ignoring all other factors in the design).

Mann-Whitney test The nonparametric equivalent of an independent samples *t-test*. It tests the null hypothesis that the two populations have the same median. Wilcoxon's rank-sum test is another nonparametric test, which produces exactly the same result as the Mann-Whitney.

MANOVA See **Multivariate analysis of variance**.

Model An interpretation of data, usually in the form of an equation or a path diagram, in which an observed score is presented as the sum of systematic and error components. The use of any standard statistical test requires that the assumptions of a specific model are applicable to the researcher's own data.

Multiple correlation coefficient R In regression, the Pearson correlation between the target or criterion variable and the estimates of its values from the regression equation. The value of R, however, unlike the Pearson correlation, cannot be negative, because the slope of the regression line, plane or hyperplane is always consistent with the orientation of the cloud of points in the scatterplot.

Multiple responses The compiler of a questionnaire may be interested in the mode of transport used by the respondents to get to their work. A single question inviting respondents to tick those modes of transport they use is likely to receive two, three or more responses, which would create problems for entry of the data into SPSS. Another approach, however, is to have a Yes/No question for each mode of transport and have the response to each question as a separate variable. SPSS offers a Multiple Response procedure which shows the frequencies with which different modes of transport are used by the respondents.

Multivariate analysis of variance (MANOVA) A generalisation of the analysis of variance (ANOVA) from the univariate to the multivariate situation, where there are two or more dependent variables.

Multivariate data A data set containing observations on three or more variables.

Multivariate normality A set of k variables is said to have a multivariate normal distribution if, given any set of values of $k - 1$ of them, the remaining variable is normally distributed. More technically, not only is the distribution of each variable considered separately (its marginal distribution) normal, but also the conditional distributions are normal. Techniques such as **Multivariate analysis of variance (MANOVA)** and **Discriminant Analysis (DA)** assume multivariate normality.

Multivariate statistics Statistical analyses in which there two or more dependent variables. Examples are **Multivariate analysis of variance (MANOVA)**, **Factor analysis (FA)** and **Principal components analysis (PCA)**. (See **Univariate statistics**.)

Nagelkerke's R^2 In logistic regression, a statistic which mimics the coefficient of determination (R^2) in ordinary least squares (OLS) regression. Nagelkerke's statistic was designed to overcome the inability of another measure, Cox and Snell's R^2, to achieve its maximum value.

Nominal data Numerical data consisting of records of category membership. Nominal data result from observations of qualitative variables.

Non-parametric or distribution-free test A test, such as the Mann-Whitney test or the Friedman test, which does not make assumptions about the population distribution such as normality or homogeneity of variance.

Normal (or Gaussian) distribution The famous 'bell curve', upon which much of classical statistical theory is based. A normal distribution has two parameters, the mean and the variance. Some naturally occurring variables, such as height and weight, have an approximately normal distribution. Since a linear function of two normal variables has itself a normal distribution, the mean of a sample of fixed size n drawn from a normal distribution is normally distributed. Moreover, the mean of a large sample of fixed size n from a non-normal distribution has an approximately normal distribution, provided n is sufficiently large. The sampling distribution of the mean can approximate a normal distribution to any degree of closeness, provided the sample is sufficiently large (central limit theorem).

Null hypothesis In statistical hypothesis-testing, the null hypothesis (H_0) is the supposition of 'no effect': in the population, there is no difference between the means; in the population, there is no association between two variables; the sample we have selected has not been drawn from a population with a different mean, and so on. The null hypothesis, therefore, is usually the negation of the scientific hypothesis. The null hypothesis cannot be proved. This truth reflects the logical fact that it is easier to falsify than to verify. If I assert that all swans are white, you can continue to question my assertion no matter how many white swans I produce; whereas the production of a single black swan would refute my claim; moreover, you do not actually have to produce a black swan to maintain your scepticism. For this reason, should a statistical test fail to show significance, the null hypothesis is not said to be true, but is 'retained' or 'accepted'. The alternative hypothesis (H_1) is the supposition that the null hypothesis is false and that, in the population, the mean, variance, correlation or whatever measure we are studying has a value other than that specified by the null hypothesis. The alternative hypothesis is usually the statistical equivalent of the scientific hypothesis.

Omega squared A measure of effect size in analysis of variance which partially corrects for the positive bias of **eta squared**.

One-tailed test In hypothesis testing, a critical region of values for the test statistic is set up such that, under the null hypothesis, the probability of a value in the region is the significance level (usually .05). Some argue that the location of the critical region should depend upon the scientific or alternative hypothesis. There are situations in which it makes sense to look for a difference in one direction only: e.g. since brain injury is unlikely to improve test performance, the critical region, arguably, should be located entirely in the lower tail of the t-distribution. Since the null and alternative hypotheses are complementary (i.e. they exhaust the possibilities), the null hypothesis becomes 'equal to or greater than', rather than 'equal to'. An unexpected result in the 'wrong' direction, therefore, cannot be declared to be significant.

Ordinal data Data containing only information about order or sequencing. Examples are sets of ranks and sequences of outcomes over a set of trials.

Ordinary least squares (OLS) regression A set of techniques designed to predict value of a target, criterion or dependent variable from values of one, two or more predictors, regressors or independent variables. The regression line, plane or hyperplane is positioned so that it minimises the sum of the squares of the residuals $Y - Y'$, where Y and Y' are the target variable and the estimate from the regression equation, respectively. This is known as the least-squares criterion.

Orthogonal contrasts Two contrasts are said to be orthogonal (independent) if the products of their corresponding coefficients sum to zero. For the set of means M_1, M_2 and M_3, for instance, the value of $(M_1 - M_2)$ does not constrain the value of $(M_1 + M_2)/2 - M_3$. We can express these two linear contrasts thus:

$$L_1 = (+1)M_1 + (-1)M_2 + (0)M_3$$
$$L_2 = (+\tfrac{1}{2})M_1 + (+\tfrac{1}{2})M_2 + (-1)M_3$$

The coefficients of the means can be arrayed in a matrix thus

$$\begin{pmatrix} +1 & -1 & 0 \\ +\tfrac{1}{2} & +\tfrac{1}{2} & -1 \end{pmatrix}$$

The sum of the products of corresponding coefficients is zero: $(+1)(\tfrac{1}{2}) + (-1)(\tfrac{1}{2}) + (0)(-1) = 0$. For an array of k means, there are $k - 1$ orthogonal contrasts, each with one degree of freedom. For each contrast L, there is an associated sum of squares SS_L. The total of the sums of squares of the contrasts in an orthogonal set is the one-way ANOVA treatment sum of squares: $\sum SS_L = SS_{between}$.

Orthogonal polynomial coefficients A matrix of orthogonal contrast coefficients, each row of which contains different values of a polynomial of the same order, the order increasing with the 2nd and subsequent rows. For example, suppose we have three treatment means summarising the results of an experiment in which the three treatment conditions were different values of a continuous variable X, where $X_1 = 1$, $X_2 = 2$ and $X_3 = 3$. Since there are 3 means, a set of two orthogonal contrasts can be constructed. We want the first row of coefficients to be different values of a linear (1st order) polynomial and the second row to be values of a quadratic (2nd order) polynomial. The two desired polynomials are of the forms $a_1 + X$ and $a_2 + b_2 X + X^2$. Substituting $X = 1, 2, 3$ into these expressions gives us

$$\begin{pmatrix} a_1 + 1 & a_1 + 2 & a_1 + 3 \\ a_2 + b_2 + 1 & a_2 + 2b_2 + 4 & a_2 + 3b_2 + 9 \end{pmatrix}$$

Using the constraints that the elements of each row must sum to zero, as must the products of the corresponding elements of each row, we solve for a_1, a_2 and b_2 to obtain the desired orthogonal set

$$\begin{pmatrix} -1 & 0 & +1 \\ +1 & -2 & +1 \end{pmatrix}$$

The upper row of contrast coefficients has an associated sum of squares whose value reflects any linear trend present in the data; the lower row reflects any quadratic trend. Each SS can be tested against the error mean square in the usual way, confirming that component of trend in the data. In practice, we need never actually solve any equations: tables of orthogonal polynomial coefficients are available in standard statistics textbooks for arrays of means of any reasonable size.

Orthogonal rotation In factor analysis, the classificatory axes (factors) can be rotated around the origin in relation to the test points in order to produce a pattern of loadings that is easier to interpret than the original pattern. If the axes are kept at right angles during rotation, the process is known as orthogonal rotation. Axes at right angles represent uncorrelated factors. In oblique rotation, however, the axes are not maintained at right angles: that is, the axes represent correlated factors.

Outcome variable See **Dependent variable**.

p-value In statistical testing, the probability, under the null hypothesis, of obtaining a value of the test statistic at least as unlikely as the value that has been calculated from the data. If the p-value is smaller than .05 or .01, the test has shown significance beyond the .05 or the .01 level, respectively. If the alternative hypothesis is one-sided, the p-value must refer to values of the test statistic in one tail only of the distribution: extreme values in the opposite direction must result in acceptance of H_0.

Part correlation See **Semipartial correlation**.

Partial correlation What remains of the correlation between two variables when their relationships with a third variable have been neutralised or 'partialled out'.

Pearson correlation A measure of the strength of a supposed linear (straight line) association between two quantitative variables, each measured on a continuous scale with units, which is so constructed that it can take values only within the range from –1 to +1, inclusive. (See **Coefficient of determination**.) The supposition of linearity must always be checked by examining the scatterplot.

Percentile A score or value below which a specified proportion of the distribution lies: the 95th percentile is the score below which 95% of the distribution lies; the 5th percentile is the value below which 5% of the distribution lies. The median (or middle score) is the 50th percentile.

Per family Type I error rate The probability, under the null hypothesis, that at least one of a set of comparisons among an array of treatment means will show significance. This term, which we owe to Tukey, has replaced the older term: **experimentwise**. With large sets of comparisons, the per family error rate greatly exceeds the significance level for each comparison, that is, the error rate per comparison, which is usually set at .05: for example, if we have a set of 5 treatment means and make all 10 possible pairwise comparisons, the probability that at least one comparison will show significance (the familywise error rate) is approximately $1 - .95^{10} = .40$. (This is an approximation, because the comparisons are not independent.)

Point-biserial correlation $r_{pt\text{-}bis}$ The Pearson correlation between a dichotomous qualitative variable (such as gender) and a continuous or scale variable. The sign of the point-biserial correlation is of no importance, because it reflects only the size relation between the arbitrary code numbers used to denote the two categories. If the t-test between the group means on the scale variable is significant, then so will be the point-biserial correlation, because the two statistics are related according to:

$$r_{pt-bis}^{2} = \frac{t^{2}}{t^{2} + df}$$

where $df = n_1 + n_2 - 2$. In this book, we stress the difference between comparing average scores on the same variable under different conditions and investigating possible associations between measured variables. The point-biserial correlation, however, expresses a comparison as an association between two variables; one of them being a set of arbitrary code numbers. The square of $r_{pt\text{-}bis}$ is a special case of the **coefficient of determination** and, as such, is a measure of effect size. In the context of comparisons among means, the coefficient of determination is known as the **correlation ratio** or eta squared η^2 and generalises from two-group designs to analysis of variance with three or more treatment means. In the multi-group case, the correlation ratio is the square of the multiple correlation coefficient R from multiple regression of the dependent variable upon sets of code numbers carrying information about group membership. (See **Dummy variables**.) The number of such coding sets is one less than the number of groups. The statistic eta squared η^2 was an early measure of effect size and other measures such as shrunken R^2 and omega squared ω^2 are now preferred.

Polynomial A sum of terms, each of which is a product of a constant and a power of the same variable thus

$$y = a_0 + a_1 x + a_2 x^2 + ... + a_n x^n$$

The highest power n is the degree or order of the polynomial. A polynomial of the nth degree has $n - 1$ turning points: a straight line (first degree) has no turning points; a quadratic (second degree) has one, a cubic (third degree) has two and so on. If a set of treatment means $M_1, M_2, ..., M_k$ can be ordered on a continuous variable X, then a $(k - 1)^{th}$ order polynomial in X can be found which fits the means perfectly.

The figures below show graphs of polynomial functions from the first degree (linear) to the third degree (cubic). Note that the number of times the curve changes direction is the degree of the polynomial minus one.

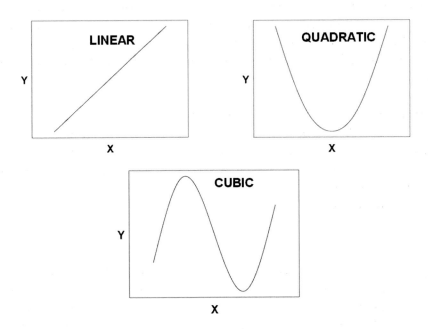

(See **Trend analysis**.)

Post hoc comparisons Unplanned comparisons of the sort one inevitably makes after the data have been gathered. Planned or a priori comparisons are decided upon before the data are gathered. Since the family of possible post hoc comparisons is usually considerably larger than a set of planned comparisons, the per family error rate associated with post hoc comparisons may also be much higher. In either case, the per family error rate can be controlled by the Bonferroni method, whereby the p-value for each comparison is multiplied by the number of comparisons in the family.

Power The probability, assuming that the null hypothesis is false, that when a statistical test is made, the null hypothesis will be rejected. The power P of a statistical test is related to the Type II error rate (β) according to $P = 1 - \beta$. Power is affected by several factors, including the significance or alpha-level, the minimum effect size that the researcher considers worth reporting, the number of participants in the experiment, the design of the experiment (between subjects or within subjects) and the reliability of the measurement.

Principal components (PC) A set of techniques enabling the researcher to account for the correlations among a battery of tests in terms of relatively few classificatory dimensions or components. In contrast with **factor analysis (FA)**, principal components is designed to account for 100% of the variance of each of the tests in the battery, rather than the variance it shares with the other tests.

Probability A measure of likelihood so constructed that it can have values only within the range from 0 (for an impossible event) to 1 (a certainty.) Probabilities arise in the context of **experiments of chance**, in which an event is viewed as a subset of the entire set of possible elementary outcomes. The results of an experiment can be viewed as an experiment of chance: the researcher's observations are usually a sample from a reference set or population of possible observations. On that basis, we can assign probabilities to ranges of values within which the sample mean might fall, assuming one of the competing hypotheses.

Probability density function (frequency function) A continuous random variable X assigns an infinite number of possible values within any specified interval in its range. The probability of any particular value of X, therefore, is zero. A probability density function, however, assigns a probability density to values of X. A probability density can be regarded as the probability of a value in the neighbourhood of a specified value. More technically, a probability density is the rate of change of the cumulative probability at that point.

Qualitative variables Characteristics or properties, such as nationality, gender and blood group, which can be possessed only in kind (not in degree) and comprise sets of categories, rather than numerical values.

Quantitative variables Characteristics or properties, such as height, weight or intelligence, that are possessed in degree, so that one individual can have more or less of the property than another. A quantitative variable consists of a set of values.

Quasi-experiment A hybrid of a true experiment and correlational research, in which sampling strategy is used in the attempt to create control groups for the purposes of comparison. In studies of the effects of smoking upon health and longevity, for example, sampling strategies are used in the attempt to equalise possible confounding variables such as education level and lifestyle. The quasi-experiment, however, has the same weakness as *correlational research*, namely, that the supposedly causal variable (e.g. smoking) is observed in the participants studied, rather than being manipulated by an experimenter. As a consequence, it can never be claimed that all possible confounds have been controlled.

Random variable (variate) In probability theory, a rule for assigning a numerical value to outcomes in the **sample space**: 'Let X be the number of spots on the upper face when a die is rolled'; 'When a coin is tossed, Let Y be 1 for a head and 0 for a tail'.

Regression The prediction of a target, criterion or dependent variable from other variables known as regressors or independent variables. The prediction is made by constructing a regression equation, the subject of which is the estimate of the criterion from the regressors.

Reliability   The extent to which a measuring instrument produces consistent results, in the sense that participants achieve scores at similar percentile levels with different testers or from occasion to occasion of testing.   The various approaches to the determination of reliability include test-retest, parallel (or equivalent) forms and split-half. (See **Validity**.)

Repeated measures (or within subjects) design   Experimental designs in which observations are made on the same participants on two or more occasions. This is an example of a randomised blocks design, a block being a set of observations that are linked in some way, as when the same person is tested on several occasions.   Such experiments yield sets of observations that can be paired or matched across samples: these four observations are John's scores; those four are Mary's.   Repeated measures designs yield correlated data, as do experiments with different groups of participants who are matched in some way. (Compare **Between subjects design**.)

R-matrix   A square array, or matrix, displaying the correlation of each of the tests in a battery with every other test. An R-matrix can be the starting point for **factor analysis**, which is a set of techniques for accounting for the correlations among the tests in terms of relatively few underlying variables or **factors**.

Rotation   In **factor analysis**, the factors can be regarded as classificatory axes with respect to which the tests in the battery can be plotted as points. The co-ordinates of each test point are the correlations between the test and the factors emerging from the analysis.   Such a correlation is known as the loading of a test on the factor concerned. Should the axes be rotated around the origin in relation to the test points, all the loadings will change. The sum of the products of the loadings of any two tests on all the axes, however, will remain constant and affords the same estimate of the observed correlation between the two tests. Rotation makes it easier to interpret the results of a factor analysis because, in relation to the original pattern of loadings, each test tends after rotation to have higher loadings on fewer factors.   (See **Orthogonal rotation**.)

Sample space   In an **experiment of chance**, the set of all elementary outcomes, each of which is assumed to be equally likely.

Scale data   A term in SPSS denoting data consisting of independent measurements on a scale with units. Examples are height, weight, intelligence, scores on questionnaires and ratings. (See **Interval data**.)

Scatterplot   A graphical display depicting a bivariate distribution, in which the axes represent the scales on the two variables and the individual is represented as a point whose coordinates are his or her scores on the variables.   An elliptical cloud of points indicates a linear association between the two variables: the narrower the ellipse, the stronger the association. A circular cloud of points indicates independence of the distributions. A Pearson correlation is a measure of a supposedly linear association between two variables and, wherever possible, the supposition of linearity should be checked by inspecting the scatterplot.

Semipartial correlation In multiple regression, what remains of the correlation between a target or **criterion** variable and one of a set of predictor variables (regressors, independent variables) when the variance shared by the predictor with the other predictors has been partialled out of the predictor (but not the DV) by regression.

Shrinkage The tendency for the predictive power of a regression model to weaken with resampling.

Simple effects In factorial analysis of variance, the effect of one factor at one particular level of another. Simple effects analysis provides a way of analysing significant interactions. A two-way interaction can be explored by testing for the simple main effects of one factor at different levels of the other. Heterogeneity of simple effects, as when they act in opposite directions, helps to explain a significant interaction. A significant three-way interaction can be further explored by testing the simple two-way interactions between two of the factors at specific levels of the third. In unplanned (post hoc) multiple pairwise comparisons, a significant simple effect is used as a justification for defining a smaller comparison family, rather than one containing all the cell means involved in the interaction.

Simple main effect See **Simple Effects**.

Spearman-Brown formula A formula, equivalent to **coefficient alpha,** which expresses the reliability of a test in terms of mean of the correlations between every possible pair of items thus:

$$reliability = \frac{i\bar{r}}{1+(i-1)\bar{r}}$$

where i is the number of items in the test and $\bar{r}$ is the mean of the correlations between pairs of items. It is clear from the formula that even if the average inter-item correlation is low, the total score on a test with many items can achieve a very high level of reliability.

Standard deviation The positive square root of the variance, often written as s, where

$$s = +\sqrt{\frac{\sum(X-M)^2}{n-1}}$$

Unlike the variance, the standard deviation measures spread or dispersion in the original units of measurement. The square root operation, however, does not negate the distorting effects of extreme scores or outliers on the value of the standard deviation. Adding a constant k to each score leaves the standard deviation unaltered. If each score is multiplied by a constant k, the standard deviation is ks. (Compare **Variance.**)

Standard normal variable See *z*.

Sum of squares (SS) The sum of the squares of the deviations of scores *X* from their mean *M*, which is given by the formula: $SS = \Sigma(X - M)^2$. The sum of squares is the numerator of the variance estimate s^2.

_t_-distribution In the one-sample case, the distribution of the statistic *t*, where

$$t = \frac{M - \mu}{s/\sqrt{n}}$$

and *M* is the mean of a sample of size *n* drawn from a normal population. The distribution of *t* has one parameter, the **degrees of freedom** *df*, the value of which is given by $df = n - 1$. A *t* distribution resembles the standard normal distribution with mean zero and standard deviation 1; but it has thicker tails and its variance is $df/(df - 2)$. As *n* increases, the *t* distribution approximates the standard normal distribution ever more closely.

Trend analysis In **analysis of variance (ANOVA)**, the independent variable, rather than merely being a set of related treatments, groups or experimental conditions, may be quantitative and continuous, as when different groups of patients ingest different quantities of a drug. If so, the question arises as to the nature of the functional relationship between the dependent variable and the independent variable. In trend analysis, the treatment sum of squares is divided into orthogonal (independent) components accounted for by linear, quadratic and more complex polynomial functions. Each component of trend can be tested for significance. (See **Orthogonal polynomial coefficients**.)

Type I error The rejection of the null hypothesis when it is actually true. The probability of a Type I error is the significance level *α* and is also known as the alpha-level, or the alpha-rate.

Type II error The acceptance of the null hypothesis when it is actually false. Its probability *β* is known as the beta-level or beta-rate. The beta-level is determined by several factors, including the sample size and the significance level. (See **Power**.)

Univariate statistics Analyses in which there is only one dependent variable. Examples are the *t tests* and **analysis of variance (ANOVA)**. (Compare **Multivariate statistics**.)

Unrelated samples See **Independent Samples**.

Validity[1] In psychological testing (psychometrics), a test is said to be valid if it measures what it is supposed to measure. This beguilingly simple definition is open to many interpretations, which is why, in Reber's Dictionary of Psychology (1985), there are more than 25 definitions of validity. In personnel selection, the predictive or criterion validity is the Pearson correlation between scores on a psychological test and a target or criterion variable (job efficiency, academic grade). In order to be valid in this sense, a psychological test must also be reliable. Reliability, however, does not ensure validity. A vocabulary test may be highly reliable; but it may be a very poor predictor of success on an IT course.

Validity[2] An experiment is said to have ecological validity when the dependent variable is a characteristic actually seen in everyday life. Is the result of a scenario study of bystander intervention generalisable to a real situation in which the protagonist is asked for (or should offer) help?

Validity[3] An experiment is said to be internally valid if the independent variable has been shown unequivocally to have had a causal effect upon the dependent variable. The internal validity of an experiment is threatened by such influences as placebo effects, extraneous variables, demand characteristics and experimenter effects.

Variable A property or characteristic consisting of a set of values or categories. (See **Qualitative variables**, **Quantitative variables**.)

Variance A measure of the extent to which scores are spread (or dispersed) around their mean. The variance estimate s^2 of a set of n scores is the sum of the squares of their deviations from the mean, divided by $n - 1$: that is, $s^2 = SS/(n - 1)$. The denominator of the variance estimate is also known as the degrees of freedom df, and the variance estimate can be expressed as SS/df. The variance is of great theoretical importance but, as a descriptive measure, its value is limited by the fact that it expresses the spread of a set of scores in squares of the original units of measurement. The positive square root of the variance estimate is known as the standard deviation s, which expresses spread in the original units of measurement. In the population, the variance is the mean squared deviation and the standard deviation is the root mean square. The df appears in the denominator of the sample variance to remove negative bias: that is, the expected value of the sample mean squared deviation is less than the value of the population variance. Adding a constant k to each score leaves the variance unaltered. Multiplying by k multiplies the variance by k^2.

Wald-Wolfowitz runs test There are situations, as when a participant makes a series of choices over a series of trials, in which the investigator is concerned with whether sequences of the same choice indicate a lack of randomness in the participant's strategy.

Welch's F test A variation of the F test which is applicable when the assumption of homogeneity of variance has been violated.

Welch-Satterthwaite formula A formula used to adjust the degrees of freedom for a variant of the t statistic in which separate variance estimates are retained. See **Behrens-Fisher problem.**

Wilks' Lambda (Λ) In the univariate one-way ANOVA, variance estimates or mean squares (MS) are made by dividing the sums of squares SS by their degrees of freedom and using the F statistic to compare the between groups and within groups estimates $MS_{between}$ and MS_{within}. In **multivariate analysis of variance (MANOVA)**, where there are several DVs, the analogue of the variance estimate is the determinant of a matrix of cross-products of deviations. There is a between groups cross-product matrix $S_{between}$ and a within groups matrix S_{within}, which are analogous to the between groups and within groups sums of squares in the one-way ANOVA. There is also a total cross-product matrix S_{total} which, in a manner similar to the univariate ANOVA total sum of squares, can be partitioned by expressing it as the sum of the between groups and within groups matrices:

$$S_{total} = S_{between} + S_{within}$$

Wilks' lambda Λ is defined as a ratio of determinants:

$$\Lambda = \frac{|S_{error}|}{|S_{between} + S_{error}|}$$

In the univariate one-way ANOVA, where there is only one DV, the formula for Λ simplifies to:

$$\Lambda = \frac{SS_{within}}{SS_{within} + SS_{between}} = \frac{SS_{within}}{SS_{total}} = 1 - \eta^2$$

where η^2 is the **correlation ratio**. It is therefore clear that while Λ, like η^2, can take values in the range from 0 to 1, inclusive, small values of Λ indicate large differences among the group means, while large values of Λ indicate small differences. An approximate F statistic can be used to test a value of Λ for significance.

Within subjects designs See **Repeated measures**.

Yates' correction A modification of the approximate chi-square formula. See **Correction for continuity**.

z The *standard normal variable*, with a mean of zero and a standard deviation of 1. Any normally distributed variable X can be transformed to z by subtracting the mean and dividing by the standard deviation. A z-score expresses a value in units of standard deviation, not the original units. A positive sign for z indicates that the value is so-many standard deviations above the mean; a negative sign indicates that the value is so-many standard deviations below the mean. Standardising a variable does NOT normalise its distribution: if the raw scores have a skewed distribution, so will the standardised scores.

References

American Psychological Association. (2001). *Publication manual of the American Psychological Association (5th ed.).* Washington, D. C.: American Psychological Association.

Anscombe, F. J. (1973). Graphs in statistical analysis. *American Statistician, 27,* 17-21.

Brown, M.B., & Forsythe, A.B. (1974). The ANOVA and multiple comparisons for data with heterogeneous variances. *Biometrics, 30,* 719-724.

Clark-Carter, D. (2004). *Quantitative psychological research: A student's handbook.* Hove and New York: Psychology Press.

Cohen, J. (1960). A coefficient of agreement for nominal scales. *Educational and Psychological Measurement, 10,* 37-46.

Cohen, J. (1962). The statistical power of abnormal-social psychological research: A review. *Journal of Abnormal and Social Psychology, 65,* 145-153.

Cohen, J. (1988). *Statistical power analysis for the behavioral sciences (2nd ed.).* Hillsdale, N.J.: Lawrence Erlbaum Associates.

Cohen, J., Cohen, P., West, S. G., & Aiken, L. S. (2003). *Applied multiple regression/correlation analysis for the behavioral sciences (3rd ed.).* Mahwah, NJ: Lawrence Erlbaum Associates.

Darlington, R. B. (1968). Multiple regression in psychological research and practice. *Psychological Bulletin, 69,* 161–182.

Darlington, R. B. (1990). *Regression and linear models.* New York: McGraw-Hill.

Einspruch, E. L. (2004). *Next steps with SPSS.* London: Sage.

Erdfelder, E., Faul, F., & Buchner, A. (1996). GPOWER: A general power analysis program. *Behavior Research Methods, Instruments, and Computers, 28,* 1-11.

Field, A. (2005). *Discovering Statistics Using SPSS (2nd ed.).* London: Sage.

Field, A., & Hole, G. (2003). *How to design and report experiments.* London: Sage.

Howell, D. C. (2007). *Statistical methods for psychology (6th ed.).* Belmont, CA: Thomson/Wadsworth.

Keppel, G., & Wickens, T. D. (2004). *Design and analysis: A researcher's handbook (4th ed.).* Upper Saddle River, NJ: Pearson Prentice Hall.

Kim, J., & Mueller, C. W. (1978a). *Factor analysis: Statistical methods and practical issues.* Newbury Park, CA: Sage.

Kim, J., & Mueller, C. W. (1978b). *Introduction to factor analysis: What it is and how to do it.* Newbury Park, CA: Sage.

Nelson, D. (2004). *The Penguin dictionary of statistics.* London: Penguin Books.

Rasbash, J., Steele, F., Browne, W., & Prosser, B. (2004). *A user's guide to MLwiN (Version 2.0).* London: Centre for Multivel Modelling, Institute of Education, University of London.

Reber, A. S. (1985). *The Penguin dictionary of psychology.* Harmondsworth, Middlesex, England: Penguin Books.

Sani, F., & Todman, J. (2006). *Experimental design and statistics for psychology: A first course.* Oxford: Blackwell.

Siegel, S., & Castellan, N. J. (1988). *Nonparametric statistics for the behavioral sciences (2nd ed.).* New York: McGraw-Hill.

Tabachnick, B. G., & Fidell, L. S. (2007). *Using multivariate statistics (5th ed.).* Boston: Allyn & Bacon (Pearson International Edition).

Todman, J., & Dugard, P. (2006). *Approaching multivariate analysis: An introduction for psychology.* London: Psychology Press.

Welch, B.L. (1951). On the comparison of several mean values: An alternative approach. *Biometrika, 38,* 330-336.

Winer, B. J. (1970). Statistical principles in experimental design - International student edition. London: McGraw-Hill.

Winer, B. J., Brown, D. R., & Michels, K. M. (1991). *Statistical principles in experimental design (3rd ed.).* New York: McGraw-Hill.

Index